ENVIRONMENTAL PSYCHOLOGY
2nd Edition

ENVIRONMENTAL PSYCHOLOGY

2nd Edition

JEFFREY D. FISHER
University of Connecticut

PAUL A. BELL
Colorado State University

ANDREW BAUM
Uniformed Services University
of the Health Sciences

HOLT, RINEHART AND WINSTON
New York   Chicago   San Francisco   Philadelphia
Montreal   Toronto   London   Sydney
Tokyo   Mexico City   Rio de Janeiro   Madrid

To my wife, Sherry L. Fisher, for her good humor and
forbearance during my academic pursuits.

J.D.F.

To Robert Allan Bell and Frances Irene Elkins Bell,
who introduced me to the environment.

P.A.B.

To my parents, Myron and Beatrice Baum, with much unstated gratitude.

A.B.

Cover Art: © M. C. Escher Heirs, % J. W. Vermeulen, Prilly CH.
Book Design: Mina Greenstein

Library of Congress Cataloging in Publication Data

Fisher, Jeffrey D.
    Environmental psychology.

  Rev. ed. of: Environmental psychology/Paul A. Bell,
Jeffrey D. Fisher, Ross J. Loomis. 1978.
  Bibliography: p. 407
  Includes index.
  1. Environmental psychology.   I. Bell, Paul A.
II. Baum, Andrew.   III. Bell, Paul A. . Environmental
psychology.   IV. Title.
BF353.F57   1984   155.9   83-12911

ISBN 0-03-059867-2

CBS COLLEGE PUBLISHING
Holt, Rinehart and Winston
The Dryden Press
Saunders College Publishing

Preface

The physical environment affects each of us in some very profound ways. It can enrich or detract from our lives. We may experience excitement and stimulation when visiting a city; relaxation from a trip to a park; or annoyance from sitting in a crowded classroom, trying to listen to the lecturer while our neighbors converse. Similarly, certain atmospheric conditions (such as temperature and humidity) make us feel good, while others make us feel bad.

Just as the physical environment plays an important role in our behavior, almost everything *we* do has environmental consequences. If we take a "Sunday drive," turn the thermostat up, throw away a can of soda, or flush the toilet—we affect our environment.

The field of environmental psychology deals with the reciprocal relationships between humans and their environment. Environmental psychologists study how, why, and in what ways this interrelationship manifests itself; and what can be done to enhance its constructive and decrease its destructive consequences. Environmental psychology is a young science, but it has come a long way in a short time. There is still much work to be done, but few would disagree that environmental psychologists have already made significant scientific and societal contributions. From the student's perspective, environmental psychology is one of those rare fields that deals with problems we constantly encounter, and often cause. Many of the most important issues facing us as individuals, and as a society, are addressed in this book.

Six years have elapsed since we wrote the first edition of *Environmental Psychology*. Although we placed a heavy emphasis on a social psychological perspective, we also drew upon other subdisciplines (and even disciplines) where relevant. We attempted to create a scholarly, comprehensive, data- and theory-based work. Instead of presenting environmental psychology as a collection of disparate areas, the text integrated the field and organized the literature with an eclectic model of environment–behavior relationships. Qualities that were popular with students, instructors, and reviewers, were retained in the second edition. An overriding goal for the second edition was to produce a major revision which was scientifically rigorous, as broad as the field, and completely up to date. We also wished to address the constructive comments and criticisms the first edition received over the years.

We had several additional goals as well. We wanted the revised text to be even more readable and student-oriented, to convey the excitement we feel for the field, and to stimulate students' thinking. We desired to produce a book that would help students to analyze environmental phenomena in a scientific manner, and which would allow them to understand the field in relation to their own lives. To these ends, we have made every effort to elaborate on empirical research with relevant examples and intriguing paradoxes. Particularly interesting material has been highlighted within boxes. To aid student involvement, each chapter begins with an enticing hypothetical example, and ends with a list of suggested projects. There are ample figures, tables, and photos to illustrate concepts discussed within the chapters.

To keep pace with the changes in the field, and to expand areas given too little coverage in the first edition, the second edition incorporates many major additions in content. Each chapter has been extensively revised and updated; the reader will encounter an exhaustive list of citations from 1979–1983, and even some from 1984. In addition, the second edition contains improved and expanded coverage of design (three chapters instead of two), a new chapter on environmental stress, and a much more complete chapter on encouraging environmentally constructive behaviors (e.g., conservation) and discouraging environmentally destructive ones (e.g., littering, vandalism). It also includes a greatly expanded section on leisure environments; new material on landscape design and assessment; and additional coverage of weather variables (sunshine, lunar phases, and air-ionization). This constitutes just a small sample of the new material which has been added.

The organization of the revision is similar to the first edition, since it has proved congenial to both students and instructors. The text begins with an introductory chapter which defines the field and presents a brief overview of environment-behavior research methods. Chapter 2 examines the ways in which the environment is perceived, how these perceptions are retained and altered by situational factors, and how they lead to favorable and unfavorable evaluations of the environment. The next five chapters discuss the ways in which the environment influences behavior. To introduce this coverage, Chapter 3 is devoted to theoretical perspectives on environment-behavior relationships. This chapter concludes with the presentation of a working model that integrates the various theoretical approaches; and we refer to this model throughout the book. Chapter 4 elaborates on the environmental stress approach, and discusses some specific stressors (e.g., natural disasters, technological catastrophe, commuting, and noise). Chapter 5 discusses weather, air pollution, and behavior; Chapter 6—personal space and territoriality; Chapter 7—crowding; and Chapter 8—cities. The next set of chapters examines design issues. The first of these, Chapter 9, focuses on the design process; Chapters 10 and 11 discuss design and behavior in defined settings such as work environments, residential environments, hospitals, learning environments, and environments of the future. Finally, Chapter 12 discusses intervention strategies for modifying our environmentally destructive behaviors and improving our relationship with the environment. The book concludes with a Methodology Appendix. This Appendix, and all chapters, are designed as independent units that will allow professors to adopt any alternative organization for their course. As a teaching aid, the text is accompanied by a complete teacher's manual which includes chapter outlines, lists of important terms, questions for discussion, suggested projects and films, and an extensive bank of essay and multiple-choice exam questions.

As was true of the first edition, the second edition was conceived as a primary text for undergraduate and graduate courses which focus on environment and behavior (e.g., environmental psychology, social ecology, architectural psychology, ecological psychology, and environmental design courses which stress human elements). It can also be used as an adjunct to other more specialized texts in both basic and more advanced courses. In addition, we view *Environmental Psychology* as a resource manual of empirical and theoretical work in the field for practitioners and researchers. Writing this book has taught us a great deal, helped to organize our thoughts, and given us an opportunity to examine our field critically and constructively. We trust that it will do the same for our audience, and as before, we invite you to send your comments on the text directly to us. After all, our own thoughts advance in large part from the collective feedback of our readership.

Jeffrey D. Fisher

Paul A. Bell

Andrew Baum

Acknowledgments

Writing or revising a text is a major undertaking in which one is bound to incur debts to many individuals. We wish to express our appreciation to the editor of the first edition of this book, Baxter Venable, for first involving us in this enterprise. Marie Schappert, our editor for the second edition, has been of immeasurable help and was truly a delight to work with. Other individuals at Holt, Rinehart and Winston who deserve special thanks for their expertise, help, and encouragement include Nedah Abbott, Ray Ashton, Barbara Heinssen, and Arlene Katz. Arlene Katz, our Project Manager at Holt, is a paragon of efficiency, organization, and wit, and her help in coordinating this enterprise has been invaluable.

One's colleagues play an important role in stimulating intellectual thinking and in reviewing its product. We would like to express our deepest appreciation to Jack Aiello, Reuben M. Baron, Robert A. Baron, Donn Byrne, Rick Crandall, Julian Edney, Gary Evans, William A. Fisher, E. Scott Geller, Carl Greenberg, Tom Greene, Carl Hummel, Eric Knowles, David Mandel, Art Patterson, Miles Patterson, Paul Paulus, James Rotton, Donald Schmidt, Eric Sundstrom, Ralph Taylor, Russell Veitch, Abe Wandersman, and Steve Worchel for providing these most valuable services to us while we were writing this book, and in some cases, throughout our academic careers. We particularly acknowledge the encouragement and forbearance of Ross Loomis, who graciously consented to our use of his contributions from the first edition, and who also provided valuable input to the second edition.

Others who played significant roles at various phases of manuscript preparation to whom we are also grateful include: Allison Fontaine and Martha Gisriel (both of whom typed, retyped, researched, xeroxed, collated, filed, and mailed multiple drafts of this manuscript, and offered helpful comments on its content as well), Kathleen Buttell, T. Kevin Blanc, Lisa Cassady, Martha Charpie, Betsy DeMulder, Jody Horn, Joanne Moran, Pamela Kerouack, Nancy Patton, Robin

Trent, and Mary Urig. Special gratitude to T. Kevin Blanc, Marjory D. Fisher, Sherry L. Fisher, Peter Oliver, John L. Rundell, Jr. and Margaret Anne Rundell for their assistance in acquiring photographs.

We especially thank our respective wives, Sherry, Patty and Carrie for their encouragement and assistance with the manuscript, and our families and friends for their patient understanding when they asked us to do something and we said— once again—that we had to work on "the book"!

J.D.F.
P.A.B.
A.B.

Contents

Preface   v

1 The Why, What, and How of Environmental Psychology   1

Introduction   1
Why Study Environmental Psychology?   1
What is Environmental Psychology?   5
Characteristics of Environmental Psychology   6
How is Research in Environmental Psychology Done?   10
Research Methods in Environmental Psychology   11
Data Collection Methods   13
Preview of the Content Areas of Environmental Psychology   15
Chapter Summary   16
Suggested Projects   16

2 Environmental Perception, Cognition, and Attitudes   18

Introduction   18
What Is Environmental Perception?   18
Conventional Approaches to Perception   19
Environmental Perception   21
Movement, Habituation, and the Perception of Change   22
Perception of Movement   22
Habituation or Adaptation   23

Perception of Change   23

Perception of Natural Hazards   26

Social and Cultural Influences on Environmental Perception   28

Environmental Cognition and Cognitive Mapping   29

Components of Cognitive Maps   30

Errors in Cognitive Maps   31

Familiarity, Gender, and Socioeconomic Class   31

Functions of Cognitive Maps   31

Memory and Cognitive Maps   32

Cognitive Organization of the Environment   32

Summary of Cognitive Mapping   32

Assessing the Scenic Environment: Landscape Assessment, Aesthetics, and
Preference   33

Descriptive Systems of Scenic Value   33

Physical-Perceptual Approaches to Scenic Value   37

The Psychological Approach to Scenic Value   39

Summary of Scenic Assessment Techniques   45

Forming Attitudes toward the Environment   45

Classical Conditioning of Attitudes   45

Instrumental Conditioning of Attitudes   48

Social Learning of Attitudes   48

Measuring Attitudes toward the Environment: The Search for the PEQI   49

Changing Attitudes toward the Environment: A Prelude   50

Do Environmental Attitudes Predict Environmental Behavior?   55

Chapter Summary   56

Suggested Projects   57

3   Theories of Environment–Behavior Relationships   58

Introduction   58

The Nature and Function of Theory in Environmental Psychology   59

Environment–Behavior Theories: Fledgling Theories in a Fledgling Field   62

The Arousal Approach   63

The Environmental Load Approach   65

The Understimulation Approach   67

Adaptation Level Theory: Optimal Stimulation   68

The Behavior Constraint Approach   70

Barker's Ecological Psychology   73

The Environmental Stress Approach   77

Integration and Summary of Theoretical Perspectives   80

Chapter Summary   81

Suggested Projects   83

4 Environmental Stress   84

Introduction   84
Stress   85
Characteristics of Stressors   85
Appraisal   87
Characteristics of the Stress Response   88
Natural Disaster   90
Characteristics of Natural Disasters   90
Effects of Natural Disasters   91
Technological Catastrophe   92
Characteristics of Technological Catastrophe   92
Noise   97
Defining, Measuring, and Perceiving Noise   97
Important Noise Variables   101
Sources of Noise   102
Physiological Effects of Noise   103
Effects of Noise on Performance   107
Noise and Social Behavior   110
Summary of Noise Effects on Behavior   115
Commuting   115
Impedance   116
Chapter Summary   117
Suggested Projects   118

5 Weather, Air Pollution, and Behavior   119

Introduction   119
Heat and Behavior   121
Perception of and Physiological Reaction to Ambient Temperatures   121
Heat and Performance   125
Heat and Social Behavior   127
Cold Temperatures and Behavior   132
Cold Temperatures and Health   132
Cold Extremes and Performance   133
Cold Extremes and Social Behavior   133
Summary of Temperature Effects on Behavior   133
Wind and Behavior   134
Perception of Wind   135
Behavioral Effects of Wind   136

Barometric Pressure and Altitude   137
   Physiological Effects   137
   Acclimatization to High Altitudes   138
   Behavioral Effects of High Altitudes   139
   High Air Pressure Effects   139
   Medical, Emotional, and Behavioral Effects of Air Pressure Changes   139
   Summary of Air Pressure Effects   140
Air Pollution and Behavior   140
   Perception of Air Pollution   142
   Air Pollution and Health   144
   Air Pollution and Performance   145
   Air Pollution and Social Behavior   146
   Summary of Air Pollution Effects on Behavior   147
Integrating Weather and Pollution Effects: A Final Note   148
Chapter Summary   148
Suggested Projects   148

6 Personal Space and Territoriality

149

Introduction   149
Personal Space   150
   Functions of Personal Space   150
   Methods for Studying Personal Space   154
   Situational Determinants of Personal Space: Research Evidence   154
   Individual Difference Determinants of Personal Space: Research Evidence   158
   Interpersonal Positioning Effects   161
   Spatial Zones That Facilitate Goal Fulfillment   162
   Consequences of Too Much or Too Little Personal Space   164
   Consequences of Personal Space Invasions   169
   Summary of Personal Space   175
Territorial Behavior: Keep Off My Turf   175
   Functions of Territoriality   178
   Research on Territoriality in Humans   179
Chapter Summary   187
Suggested Projects   190

7 Crowding

192

Introduction   192
Effects of Population Density on Animals   193
   Physiological Consequences of High Density for Animals   194

Behavioral Consequences of High Density for Animals 195
Conceptual Perspectives: Attempts to Understand High Density Effects in Animals 198
Effects of High Density on Humans 199
Methodologies Used to Study High Density in Humans 199
Feeling the Effects of Density: Its Consequences for Affect, Arousal, and Illness 202
Effects of Density on Social Behavior 204
Effects of High Density on Task Performance 210
Putting the Pieces Together: Conceptualizations of Density Effects on Humans 211
Eliminating the Causes and Effects of Crowding 218
A Look to the Future 223
Chapter Summary 224
Suggested Projects 225

The City 227

Introduction 227
Perceiving and Experiencing the City 228
Relationship Between Environmental Conditions and Imagery 232
Socioeconomic Status and Cognitive Mapping 232
Race and Cognitive Mapping 233
Gender and Cognitive Mapping 234
Relevant Experience and Cognitive Mapping 234
Summary 238
Effects of Urban Life on the City Dweller: Conceptual Efforts 238
Overload Notions 238
Environmental Stress 239
Behavioral Constraint 239
The City as an Overmanned Environment 240
Integrating the Various Formulations 240
Effects of Urban Life on the City Dweller: Research Evidence 243
Stress 243
Coping 246
Affiliative Behavior 246
Prosocial Behavior 247
Performance 248
Crime 249
Long-Term Behavioral Effects 251
Health 252
Summary 252
Environmental Solutions to Urban Problems 254
Defensible Space 254

Land Use 255
Social Factors 255
Urban Renewal 256
Summary 262
Escaping from the City 262
Chapter Summary 263
Suggested Projects 263

⑨ Architecture, Design, and Behavior 265

Introduction 265
Extent of Architectural Influence 266
An Historical Overview 266
Architectural Determinism 266
Environmental Possibilism 267
Environmental Probabilism 267
Behavior and Elements of Architectural Design 267
Lighting 267
Windows 271
Color 272
Aesthetics 272
Furnishings 273
Privacy 274
The Design Process 278
Congruence 278
Design Alternatives 278
Stages in the Design Process 278
Awareness of Design Alternatives 280
Selection of Behavioral Criteria 283
Behaviorally Based Research 283
Implementing the Design Process: Models for the Future 284
Chapter Summary 288
Suggested Projects 288

⑩ Design in Selected Environments 290

Introduction 290
The Residential Setting 291
Preferences 292
Use of Space in the Home 292
Satisfaction with the Home Environment 295

Propinquity: The Effect of Occupying Nearby Territories 296
Learning Environments 298
  Classroom Environments 298
  Libraries 300
  Museum Environments 300
Pedestrian Environments: Shopping Malls, Plazas, and Crosswalks 304
Hospital Settings 306
Residential Care Facilities for the Aged 310
  Noninstitutional Residences for the Aged 312
Chapter Summary 315
Suggested Projects 316

11 Environments for Work, Leisure, and the Future
317

Introduction 317
Work Environments 318
  Why Study the Design of the Work Environment? 318
  Designing the Office Landscape 319
  Personalization 321
  Territoriality and Status in the Work Environment 322
  Summary of Design in the Work Environment 322
Leisure and Recreation Environments 323
  Wilderness and Camping Areas 324
  Recreation Environments Affording Exercise 328
  Recreational Environments for Children 330
  Summary of Leisure and Recreation Environments 332
Future Environments 334
  Living in Space 334
  Experimental Undersea Environments 336
Chapter Summary 340
Suggested Projects 340

12 Changing Behavior To Save the Environment
343

Introduction 343
Environmental Psychology and Saving the Environment 345
Environmental Education: Teaching Us What Is Wrong
and How To Respond to It 347
Prompts: Reminders of What To Do and of What Not To Do 350

Reinforcement Techniques: What You Do Determines What You Get 352
   Positive Reinforcement: Encouraging Good Behavior 353
   Negative Reinforcement and Punishment: Alternatives to Positive
     Reinforcement 355
   Feedback: Letting Us Know How We're Doing 355
Integrating and Evaluating the Various Approaches to Eliminating
   Environmentally Destructive Behavior 355
Approaches to Specific Environmental Problems 357
   Littering 357
   Saving Energy at Home: Residential Energy Conservation 363
   Energy Conservation and Transportation 371
   Vandalism 374
Curbing Environmentally Destructive Acts: An Assessment of the Present
   and the Future 377
Chapter Summary 377
Suggested Projects 378

APPENDIX: Methodological Approaches to Environmental Psychology by David R. Mandel

379

Introduction 379
Evaluating the Adequacy of Environmental Research 380
   Internal Validity 380
   Construct Validity 381
   External Validity 381
   Experiential Realism 381
Research Design Methodologies 382
   Experimental Research: When the Researcher Creates the Conditions 383
   Correlational Studies: Capitalizing on Naturalistic "Manipulations" 386
   Descriptive Research: Telling It Like It Is 388
The Measurement Techniques 389
   Self-Report Measures 389
   Non-Self-Report Measures 399
Ethical Considerations in Environmental Research 404
   Informed Consent 405
   Invasion of Privacy 405
   Supplementary Readings 406

References 407
Name Index 448
Subject Index 461

ENVIRONMENTAL PSYCHOLOGY
2nd Edition

1 The Why, What, and How of Environmental Psychology

INTRODUCTION

WHY STUDY ENVIRONMENTAL PSYCHOLOGY?

The photographs on the next three pages depict such environmental concerns as air pollution, consequences of nuclear accidents, automobile congestion, crowding, housing design, and recycling. Do these issues interest you? Are you concerned about these problems? Would you like to see improvements in these areas? A number of psychologists have said "yes" to these and related questions, and as a result they have begun to examine the psychological consequences of environmental issues. As public and private institutions and citizens alike become more environmentally aware and more conscious of potential environmental hazards, a variety of disciplines has been called upon to help resolve some of the inevitable issues. In the past decade, many psychologists have made it known that they think psychology should be one of those disciplines. Consequently, we now have the developing field of environmental psychology.

What does psychology have to offer in relation to environmental issues? Given any particular environmental concern, a number of fields of psychology have plenty to offer. Consider air pollution, for example. Human *behavior* (the subject matter of psychology) is responsible for most urban pollution caused by automobiles and manufacturing. Therefore, human behavior will most likely provide the ultimate solution to the problem. Principles of learning, motivation, perception, attitude formation, and social interaction help explain why we ever engaged in and accepted pollution in the first place. Principles of developmental psychology, performance, social psychology, abnormal psychology, and physiological psychology help explain the deleterious effects of pollution on humans. Furthermore, principles of attitude change, behavior modification, industrial psychology, social psychology, and personality can suggest some steps that will be necessary to change behavior in order to reduce or eliminate pollution.

As another example of the application of psychology to environmental issues, consider the problem of housing design. Principles of crowding, privacy, personal space, environmental perception, and environmental design as well as effects of noise, temperature, and air circulation on behavior have much to do with whether the housing unit will provide comfort to the occupants, whether it will result in beneficial or deleterious social relations, and whether it will help the occupants be energy conscious and concerned about the physical and social quality of their neighborhood.

Figure 1–1. Among its many unpleasant effects, air pollution can interfere with our enjoyment of scenic vistas. However, visibility across a landscape scene depends not just on pollution levels, but also on such factors as the angle of the sun and the contrast between atmospheric and landscape features.

Figure 1–2. In March, 1979, an accident struck the Three Mile Island nuclear power plant, causing 400,000 gallons of radioactive water to collect in the containment building. More than a year later, unhealthy psychological reactions attributable to the accident were still apparent in some residents of the area. In some ways, these reactions resemble the responses victims have to natural disasters, but in other ways they do not. (Marc A. Schaeffer)

Figure 1–3. Approximately 52 percent of petroleum use in the US is for transportation. Of that amount, approximately 43 percent is consumed by automobile travel. Although behavioral techniques can be used to increase ridership on mass transit, both private automobile and mass transit forms of commuting are associated with various types of stress reactions. (Courtesy of John L. Rundell, Jr.)

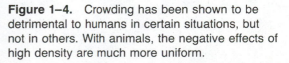

Figure 1–4. Crowding has been shown to be detrimental to humans in certain situations, but not in others. With animals, the negative effects of high density are much more uniform.

Figure 1–5A. The design of some dormitories and housing projects has been associated with withdrawal in social relationships and may encourage some forms of maladjustment.

Figure 1–5B. Other designs, however, seem to foster healthier forms of human interaction.

Figure 1–6. Recycling efforts are one means of cleaning up the environment. Besides reducing litter, recycling aluminum cans leads to far less energy use than producing new cans from ore. Given sufficient motivation, people will participate in recycling efforts. (David R. Bell)

In the process of suggesting possible solutions for environmental problems, psychologists are gaining considerable practical knowledge about relationships between behavior and environment as well as procuring invaluable information about conceptual or theoretical models of human behavior. For this reason, environmental psychology not only is practical but also provides a meaningful focus for traditional psychological disciplines. The very growth of environmental psychology is evidence that a number of psychologists (and nonpsychologists) think it is a worthwhile field of study.

WHAT IS ENVIRONMENTAL PSYCHOLOGY?

The preceding rationale for the existence of environmental psychology should convince you that the field offers present-day relevance for the discipline of psychology as well as the exciting possibility of a unique perspective on environmental problems. Yet this rationale does not really *define* the term "environmental psychology." This shortcoming is probably not surprising since the field of environmental psychology is less difficult to describe than it is to define. Perhaps it would be easier to understand this dilemma if we took a brief historical look at the field.

The scientific study of the effects of the environment on behavior can be traced at least as far back as the beginnings of scientific psychology, when 19th-century psychophysicists examined human perception of such environmental stimuli as light, pressure (touch), and sound. With the founding of behavioristic psychology in the first quarter of the 20th century, psychologists began extensive study of the effects of such "environmental" events as reinforcement schedules and early childhood surroundings on human learning, performance, and social interaction. It was not long before Lewin (1951) proposed the formula $B = f(P,E)$ to express behavior as a function of personality and environmental (extraindividual) factors. Then, by the 1940s and on into the 1980s, groups of psychologists turned to human engineering and human factors research and took a close look at the effects of certain environmental conditions, such as extremes of heat and cold, noise levels, and spatial confinement, on human performance and work efficiency. All these areas of study were concerned with the effects of the environment on humans, although practitioners in these fields did not claim to be studying environmental psychology. The subject matter of their work, however, has become incorporated into environmental psychology.

Beginning in the 1950s, architects and behavioral scientists began working together toward another objective that has become integral to environmental psychology. Specifically, these professionals became convinced that the built environment should reflect not just principles of construction and aesthetics, but also should be designed with a heavy emphasis on meeting the psychological and behavioral *needs* of those who are to occupy the buildings (Canter & Craik, 1981). Interdisciplinary cooperation in design continues today, just as the above-mentioned work in human factors and human engineering continues. Indeed, the term *architectural psychology* was and still is employed to describe much of this work (Proshansky & Altman, 1979).

The specific term "environmental psychology" actually came out of an interest in the relationship between the design of psychiatric hospital wards and evidence of therapeutic progress (see Proshansky & Altman, 1979, for a review). A number of researchers wanted to find out whether changing wall colors, rearranging furniture, or increasing or decreasing access to private spaces would help or hinder treatment (Proshansky, Ittelson, & Rivlin, 1970; Sommer & Osmond, 1961). According to Proshansky and Altman (1979), it was at a conference discussing such issues that the term "environmental psychology" was first employed to describe this focus (Ittelson, 1964).

Other lines of work have also fed into the present field of environmental psychology. Barker's work on ecological psychology (see box, p. 14) has emphasized the ways in which the entire environment influences the types of behavior that will occur within it. The work of anthropologist E. T. Hall (1959, 1966) in *proxemics,* or how we use space, and the work of researchers interested in the effects of crowding (Calhoun, 1962, 1964) have stimulated volumes of research on these areas of human-environment interaction. Other work in perception and cognition plays a significant role in environmental psychology, and with the advent of concerns over energy use and preservation of the natural environment, more and more researchers are looking into ways of changing our wasteful and destructive practices of interacting with the environment.

By the mid-1970s, these developments led a few psychology departments ("first" honors go to the City University of New York) to offer formal programs of study in environmental psychology, and many more departments began to offer courses with that title. Soon, textbooks on the subject emerged, journals devoted to the field (such as *Environment and Behavior*) were started, and organizations such as the Environmental Design Research Association and the Association for the Study of Man-Environment Relations were formed. In addition, the American Psychological Association has officially recognized environmental psychology (in conjunction with population psychology) as one of its Divisions.

Today, as with much of the early work that led up to the formation of the field, there is a definite international flavor within environmental psychology. Significant contributions, for example, have come from such areas of the world as Britain, France, Germany, Scandinavia, Turkey, Australia, and Japan (Canter & Craik, 1981), and the field is growing in the Soviet Union (Niit, 1980) as well as other countries.

Perhaps this historical perspective clarifies why it is difficult to give a specific definition of "environmental psychology." *The effects of the environment on behavior* is one obvious possibility, but this definition is inadequate for at least two reasons: (1) it is so encompassing that it implies that learning, sensation and perception, and child rearing (to name but a few possibilities) are a focal part of the field; and (2) it does not include the effects of human behavior on the environment. Thus, a definition of environmental psychology must be sufficiently restricted so as not to include tangential fields, and it must include a reciprocal relationship between humans and the environment. Limiting the definition to *the reciprocal relationships between behavior and the built environment* (Proshansky, 1976b) is somewhat more accurate, but we feel it is too narrow because it omits the non-built environment (i.e., the natural landscape). *The interrelationships between the physical environment and behavior* is more accurate, but since the field encompasses the study of crowding and personal space (which we feel involve both physical and social components), we do not believe the definition should be restricted to the "physical" environment.

Our definitional dilemma should be clear by now: How do we define environmental psychology narrowly enough so that we do not include areas that environmental psychologists would agree are not part of the field, yet broadly enough to include all the topics that environmental psychologists would insist are part of it? If given a choice, the authors of this text would opt for the following: *Environmental psychology is what environmental psychologists do* (Proshansky, Ittelson, & Rivlin, 1970). We would then proceed to describe the areas studied by environmental psychologists and the research methods they employ (which we will do in a moment). However, if forced into a corner at pencil-point by students demanding to know what answer to give to the test question, "Define environmental psychology in 25 words or less," we would hazard the following definition, with all its potential shortcomings: *Environmental psychology is the study of the interrelationship between behavior and the built and natural environment.* Since we, as authors, are entitled to an option in the matter, we pick the former (more cowardly) course of action and will now proceed to describe certain characteristics of environmental psychology that make the field unique and further delimit its scope.

CHARACTERISTICS OF ENVIRONMENTAL PSYCHOLOGY

What primarily distinguishes environmental psychology from other fields of psychology is the perspective it takes in studying its subject matter. We shall describe some characteristics of this perspective, drawing on several sources (e.g., Altman, 1976a; Ittelson *et al.,* 1974; Proshansky, 1976b; Wohlwill, 1970). This list of characteristics is by no means exhaustive but simply reflects the unique perspective of the field.

First and foremost is an emphasis on studying environment-behavior relationships as a unit, rather than separating them into supposedly distinct and self-contained components. Traditional approaches to the study of sensation and perception assume that the environmental stimuli are distinct from each other and that the perception of (or response to) the stimulus, being distinct from the stimulus itself, can be studied somewhat independently of it. Environmental psychology looks upon the stimulus and its perception as a unit that contains more than just a stimulus and a response. The stimulus–response perceptual relationship between an urban landscape and an urban inhabitant, for example, depends not just upon the individual stimuli in the landscape. It also depends upon the patterning, complexity, novelty, and movement of the contents of the landscape and upon the past experience of the perceiver (e.g., whether he or she is a long-time resident or a newcomer), his or her ability to impose structure on the landscape, his or her auditory and olfactory associations with the landscape, and his or her personality characteristics. In environmental psychology, *all* these things make up one holistic environmental–perceptual behavior unit. To use another example, to the environmental psychologist an overcrowded dining hall consists not just of separate episodes of people getting in each other's way but of a physical setting containing a high density of people who interact with each other and with the physical setting in very predictable ways, who experience certain pleasant and unpleasant emotional states, and who anticipate consequences of these conditions (Figure 1–7). Thus, the environmental setting constrains (limits, influences, and even determines) the behavior that occurs in it. Furthermore, as the occupants of this setting move about, they change some aspects of the environment and of their experience of crowding. If the behavior is studied in isolation, separate from these particular environmental conditions, the conclusions derived from the studying process will inevitably be limited. Studying environment–behavior units rather than separate components is sometimes called a *systems approach:* The psychological environment cannot be studied separately from the behavior, and the behavior cannot be studied separately from the environment, without losing valuable information. This does not mean that environmental psychologists never take a close look at a particular environment–behavior relationship in a laboratory setting, but it does mean they assume from the beginning that such dissection of an integral unit

---

HOW DO OTHERS DEFINE ENVIRONMENTAL PSYCHOLOGY?

"Environmental psychology is the discipline that is concerned with the relationships between human behavior and the physical environment." (Heimstra & McFarling, 1978)

"Environmental psychology is that area of psychology which brings into conjunction and analyzes the transactions and interrelationships of human experiences and actions with pertinent aspects of the sociophysical surroundings." (Canter & Craik, 1981)

"Is there, at present, an adequate definition of environmental psychology? We think not. . . (;) environmental psychology is what the environmental psychologists do." (Proshansky *et al.,* 1970)

"Environmental psychology is defined as the attempt to establish empirical and theoretical relationships between the behavior and experience of the person and his built environment." (Proshansky, 1976b)

Figure 1–7. To the environmental psychologist, this crowded dining hall consists not just of separate episodes of people getting in each other's way. It is a physical setting containing a high density of people who interact with each other and with the environment in very predictable ways, who experience certain pleasant and unpleasant emotional states, and who anticipate consequences of these conditions.

Another assumption made by environmental psychologists, which follows in part from the insistence on studying behavior in relation to its environmental context, is that environment–behavior relationships are really *inter*relationships: The environment does indeed influence and constrain behavior, but behavior also leads to changes in the environment. For example, if the design of a building leads people to turn a certain way upon entering it, by so turning they are experiencing a different immediate environment than the one just encountered, and this "new" environment begins to influence behavior. As another example, consider the issue of energy resources and pollution. The availability of certain energy sources in the environment determines whether certain types of energy-consuming behavior will occur, but that behavior in turn determines the type of pollution

that will result. With continued consumption, energy resources are differentially affected, and this in turn can shift consumption patterns. Note that this example also demonstrates that environment–behavior relationships need to be studied as units in order to see the whole picture.

Environmental psychology also holds a unique perspective on the distinction (or nondistinction) between applied and theoretical research. Other fields of psychology engage in theoretical or basic research ("pure" science) as the primary means of understanding behavior. The major goal of such research is to gain knowledge about the subject matter through discovering simple cause–effect relationships and building theories. If such research also leads to the solution of a practical problem (which it often does), that is well and good, but a practical application is not necessarily a goal of that research. Applied research, on the other hand, is intended from the start to solve a practical problem, and it is valued not for its theoretical relevance but for its specific utility. Whereas theoretical research more often than not is conducted in a laboratory, applied research typically occurs in a field setting. In contrast to this traditional distinction, environmental psychology usually undertakes a given piece of research for both applied and theoretical purposes at the same time. That is, almost all research in environmental psychology is problem-oriented or intended to be relevant to the solution of some practical issue, and the cause–effect relationships and theoretical material evolve from this focus. Research areas, such as the effects of pollution on behavior, changing attitudes toward the environment, and the design of environments for efficient human use, are concerned with applications, yet much of the factual content and theoretical underpinnings of environmental psychology derives directly from this type of research. The assumption of environmental psychologists that environment–behavior relationships must be studied as a unit within their natural contexts precludes in a way the dissolution of the distinction between applied and theoretical research. Once again, this does not mean that environmental psychologists cannot

will give a very incomplete picture of that unit.

take a practical problem into the laboratory for controlled study, but it does mean that the laboratory research of an environmental psychologist is oriented toward solving real-world problems (Figure 1–8).

Another characteristic of environmental psychology is that it is interdisciplinary. Environmental perception, with its emphasis on the perception of a whole scene, is relevant to the work of landscape architects, urban planners, builders, and others in related fields. The study of the effects of the physical environment (noise, heat, and space) on behavior is relevant to the interests of industrialists, lawyers, architects, and prison, hospital, and school officials. The design of environments is of concern not only to architects and designers but also to anthropologists, museum curators, traffic controllers, and office managers, to name but a few. Moreover, changing attitudes toward the environment are of concern to everyone who is aware of the dangers of pollu-

tion, urban blight, and limited natural resources. Perhaps the need for this type of interdisciplinary perspective is reflected in the growth of related fields, such as urban sociology, social biology, behavioral geography, urban anthropology, and recreation and leisure planning. Throughout this text we will draw on these and other disciplines in order to explain environmental psychological phenomena.

Another characteristic of environmental psychology is that social psychologists (or former social psychologists) account for a disproportionately large number of adherents in the field of environmental psychology. Indeed, many of the dominant names in environmental psychology have very close ties with social psychology (see box, page 10). Although some contend that this domination by social psychologists is partly due to their disaffection with the theoretical emphasis and methodological rigor of their own field, we prefer to attribute the close ties between environmental psychology and social psychology to common interests in many of the behaviors studied by both disciplines and to overlaps in methodologies. Environmental psychological concerns, such as crowding and personal space, obviously involve social behaviors and the study of environmental attitude formation and change is rooted in the social psychological study of attitudes. Furthermore, as will be evident in Chapter 5, physical environmental factors influence such social behaviors as attraction, aggression, and altruism.

The methodologies of environmental psychology and social psychology also have much in common, although environmental psychology tends to take a much more eclectic approach. This is not to say that social psychology does not use a variety of methodologies, and indeed there is considerable overlap in the research techniques of the two fields. Environmental psychology, however, tries to use all available methodologies in studying a given problem and is not afraid to use a less than rigorous approach if it promises to result in knowledge about the problem under study.

In summary, environmental psychology is char-

Figure 1–8. The laboratory research of environmental psychologists is oriented toward solving real-world problems. In this photograph, a researcher is studying the effects of noise on concentration and performance.

**THE GREAT DEBATE: HOW CLOSE ARE ENVIRONMENTAL PSYCHOLOGY
AND SOCIAL PSYCHOLOGY?**

In a famous series of articles, two established social psychologists who are now environmental psychologists, Irwin Altman (1976a, 1976b) and Harold Proshansky (1976a), debated the pros and cons of using social psychological methods and theoretical approaches to help develop the field of environmental psychology. We summarize below Altman's *pro* views and Proshansky's *con* views.

Altman (pro)	Proshansky (con)
1. The rigorous experimental methods of social psychology can add substantially to the data base of environmental psychology.	**1.** The experimental methods of social psychology are too restrictive and violate the environmental assumption of person–environment integrity.
2. Social psychological theories can give direction to the often unfocused theoretical efforts in environmental psychology.	**2.** Social psychological theories have not done an adequate job of explaining social behavior, so they should not be adopted by environmental psychologists.
3. The early promise of social psychology to solve social problems is similar to the environmental psychological promise to solve environmental problems.	**3.** Social psychology broke its promise and has not really solved the problems it set out to solve, so do not contaminate environmental psychology with these unfulfilled promises.
4. Social psychological research may lack complete applicability to environmental psychology and may be invalid in places because of violations of person–environment integrity, but it can be applied selectively to environmental problems. Its relevant portion can be exploited.	**4.** Social psychological research on attitudes, organizations, small groups, and the like does not generalize well to environmental issues and is based on violations of person–environment integrity.
5. We should draw upon the hope of social psychology "to guide the faithful, the faithless, and the uncommitted in directions we believe to be fruitful, rather than cutting them off." (Altman, 1976b, p. 369.)	**5.** What was once the great potential of social psychology has been so distorted that it will hurt rather than help environmental psychology.

acterized by the following: (1) study of environment–behavior relationships as a unit; (2) study of the interrelationships of environment and behavior; (3) a relative lack of distinction between applied and theoretical research; (4) an interdisciplinary appeal; (5) a large number of social psychologists as adherents; and (6) an eclectic methodology. Let us turn now to a more detailed description of the methodology of environmental psychology.

HOW IS RESEARCH IN ENVIRONMENTAL PSYCHOLOGY DONE?

Are environmental psychologists and other psychologists similar or different in the way they view research? As mentioned earlier, two unique qualities of environmental psychology are that it studies environment–behavior relationships as whole units and that it takes a more applied focus than other areas of psychology. These qualities affect environmental psychologists' approaches to research in several ways. Most important, environmental psychologists are more interested in conducting research in the actual setting that concerns them and in preserving the integrity of that setting than are other psychologists (Patterson, 1977; Proshansky, 1972). Thus they are more inclined to use techniques that take them to field settings rather than to abstract important aspects of reality for study in the laboratory, as is typical of many research psychologists. This stress on the "real world" has caused environmental psychologists to exhibit more methodological diversity, eclecticism, and innovation than are found in other areas of psychology. Further, owing to the more applied nature of environmental psychology, it is probably fair to say that environmental psychologists, relative to psychologists in other areas, are more concerned with directing their research toward describing and identifying relationships, giving second priority to the discovery of underlying processes and concepts.

Research Methods in Environmental Psychology

Now that we have discussed some differences in research philosophy between environmental psychologists and other psychologists, let us examine the "how" of research in environmental psychology. Basically, environmental psychologists have the same "arsenal" of research methods as other psychologists; they just use it somewhat differently. What does the arsenal include? It includes experimental methods, correlational methods, and descriptive methods. We will describe each of these techniques, first noting general strengths and weaknesses and then evaluating their appropriateness for research in environmental psychology. It will become apparent that, owing to the different research values held by environmental psychologists, their choice of methods frequently differs from that of other psychologists. The description of their methods is brief and introductory and should give you enough background to understand the methodological use in the rest of

the text. For a more thorough discussion of methods in environmental psychology, however, we recommend that you read the Appendix.

Experimental Research. Only one methodology allows researchers to identify with certainty the variable that is causing the effects they observe in an experiment. It is called the *experimental* method. In the experimental method, the researcher systematically varies an *independent variable* (e.g., heat) and measures the effect on a *dependent variable* (e.g., performance). Further, two forms of control are used in experimental research. First, only the independent variable is allowed to differ between experimental conditions, so that all other aspects of the situation are the same for all experimental conditions. Second, subjects are randomly assigned to experimental treatments. This makes it improbable (with a sufficient number of subjects) that differences between treatment conditions are caused by factors other than the independent manipulation (e.g., different personality types). Experimental methodologies may be used in both laboratory and field settings, although it is clearly more difficult to manipulate variables and establish controls in the field.

While experimental methodologies have predominated in most areas of psychology, they have not dominated research in environmental psychology to the same extent. Although the fact that they permit causal inference is an advantage, for environmental psychologists the liabilities of experimental methods frequently outweigh their benefits. One problem is that the degree of control required often creates an artificial situation, which destroys the integrity of the setting. This makes the findings less valuable to environmental psychologists and also less generalizable to the real world. Further, it frequently is possible to maintain the control necessary for an experiment only over a brief period, which makes most experimental studies short-term. Since many environmentally caused effects do not manifest themselves over the short term, this is a problem. It should be noted that both difficulties (i.e., artifi-

Figures 1–9A and 1–9B.   If we use the correlational method to study the relationship between density of shoppers and shopping behavior, we cannot be certain that density *causes* differences in behavior. To infer cause and effect, we need to use the experimental method.

ciality and temporal limitations) are less serious for field experiments than for laboratory experiments. For example, in a field setting it would be possible to study long-term high density effects in a nonartificial situation by randomly assigning students to high and low density dormitories and controlling for other differences.

Correlational Research.   As opposed to experimental research, in correlational studies the experimenter does not or cannot manipulate aspects of the situation. In this method, the relationship between *naturally occurring* situational variations and some other variable is assessed through careful observation of both. Assume that a researcher wants to compare responses to high and low density in a department store (Figure 1–9). By observing the naturally occurring variations in density and shopping behavior, he or she can make a statement about whether changes in one are *related* to changes in the other. However, since density is not manipulated and the type of control characteristic of experimental studies is not exercised, a causal inference cannot be made. Specifically, our observed relationship between

density and shopping behavior may be caused by a third variable, e.g., it might be because a different type of person shops during busy and slack hours. Further, without an experiment, we know nothing about the *direction* of a relationship between two variables (i.e., we are unsure which variable is the antecedent and which is the consequent).

Although correlational methods are clearly inferior to experimental methods in terms of ability to explain the "why" of a reaction to environmental conditions, they offer certain plus factors for the environmental psychologist. First, it is impossible or unethical to manipulate many environmental conditions that are studied, making experimental research out of the question. Second, correlational methods permit the experimenter to use the natural, everyday environment as a laboratory. In such research, artificiality is not a problem, and generalizability is greater. What types of correlational research are done by environmental psychologists? Two groups of studies can be identified. One group determines the association between naturally occurring environmental change (e.g., natural disasters) and the behavior of those in the setting. Another group assesses relationships between environmental conditions and archival data (e.g., the relationship between housing density and crime rate).

Descriptive Research. Experimental studies provide causal information, and correlational research tells us if relationships exist between variables. However, descriptive studies simply report reactions that occur in a particular situation. Since such research is not constrained by a need to infer causality or association and often need not generalize to other settings, it can be quite a flexible methodology. (For an extensive discussion of descriptive techniques that have been used, see Selltiz, Wrightsman, & Cook, 1976). The main requirement of descriptive research is that measurements be valid (i.e., they should measure what they profess to measure) and reliable (i.e., they should occur again if repeated). Under these conditions, we can assume that the results are an accurate representation of reality.

In general, descriptive techniques are used more frequently in environmental psychology than in other areas of psychology. Their use is prompted to a large extent by the developing state of the field and partly by the phenomena being studied. As Proshansky (1972, p. 455) has stated, the environmental psychologist "must be [concerned at this point] with searching out the dimensions and more specific properties of phenomena involving human behavior in relation to physical settings." Thus, we must often answer such basic questions as, "What are the patterns of space utilization?" before using more sophisticated methodologies to test for underlying causes. Descriptive research done by environmental psychologists includes studies of people's movements in physical settings, studies of the ways people perceive cities, and studies of how people spend their time in various settings. (For an example of this type of descriptive study, see the box on page 14.) Two types of descriptive research that are becoming increasingly important are environmental quality assessment and user satisfaction studies, in which environments are evaluated in terms of

their effects on users. (See the Appendix for a more thorough discussion of descriptive research.)

Data Collection Methods

Up until now, we have considered a variety of experimental methodologies used to conduct research on environmental variables. We will now change our focus and discuss the data collection techniques used with these methodologies. Basically, two types of techniques are employed: obtrusive measurement (in which the subject is aware that data are being collected) and unobtrusive measurement (in which the subject is unaware). Either technique can be used in experimental, correlational, or descriptive research. Obtrusive methods are often easier and less costly to use, but their "obtrusiveness" can affect the subjects' responses. For example, subjects may attempt to present themselves favorably to the experimenter, and this may lead to incorrect data. While unobtrusive methods raise ethical questions at times (such as invasion of privacy) and are more difficult to set up (e.g., hiding observers is not easy), they offer the important advantage of providing more realistic responses. We will discuss both these methods in the following section. (For more details on data collection methods, see the Appendix.)

Obtrusive Methods. Probably the most frequently used method of collecting data in environmental psychology is the self-report procedure. Generally, self-report dependent measures consist of interview and questionnaire responses (Figure 1–10). These can be used when the experimenter is assessing reactions to an independent variable manipulation in an experiment and in correlational and descriptive research. Other types of self-report measures also are used in descriptive research. These include cognitive mapping techniques, in which the subjects report their perception of the environment, and time budgeting techniques, in which the subjects report how they spend their time when in a particular setting. All self-report measures are necessarily obtrusive,

BARKER'S BEHAVIOR SETTINGS: ONE EXAMPLE OF DESCRIPTIVE RESEARCH

Probably the most extensive program of descriptive research ever done by an environmental psychologist was performed by Roger Barker. Barker's research centers around the concept of *behavior settings,* which he describes as public places (e.g., churches) or occasions (e.g., auctions) that evoke their own typical patterns of behavior. Barker feels the behavior setting is the basic "environmental unit" and that research that describes behavior settings in detail "identifies discriminable phenomena external to any individual's behavior" (Barker, 1968, p. 13) that have an important bearing on it.

Fourteen years of such descriptive research were summarized in the book *The Qualities of Community Life* (Barker & Schoggen, 1973). Here, the behavior settings of two towns, "Midwest" (located in the midwestern United States, with a population of 830) and "Yoredale" (located in England, with a population of 1310), were detailed. The descriptions are based on the reports of trained observers. Some of their findings are quite interesting and certainly tell us something about the character of the two towns. For example, Midwest had twice as many behavior settings involving public expression of emotions, and the structure of the settings provided children in Midwest with 14 times as much public attention as Yoredale children. Religious behavior settings also were more prominent in Midwest than in Yoredale, as were educational and government settings. However, in Yoredale, more time was spent in behavior settings related to physical health and art. We will describe Barker's behavior setting approach in more detail in Chapter 3.

since they must be administered by an experimenter.

In addition to self-report indices, observational methods of data collection are often obtrusive because a visible observer is used to record the data. One such technique used for descriptive research is behavior mapping. This entails tracking the movements of people through physical settings and observing the kinds of behavior that occur in different areas. Since observers can be taught to code just about any type of behavior an experimenter desires to study, observational techniques have also been used to record the effects of all kinds of naturalistic or manipulated variations in environmental conditions. For example, a number of researchers have used observers to record aggressive behavior as a function of changing levels of density in nursery schools. To assess the effect of space flight or undersea environments on astronauts or aquanauts, continuous observational (electronic) monitoring techniques are often employed. (Although the observer is not present in

this case, the fact that the subjects know they are being observed makes the technique obstrusive.) Finally, as discussed in the box on this page, Barker (1968) has used observers to develop descriptive accounts of behavior characteristics in different behavior settings.

Unobtrusive Methods. Since we often respond differently when we know we're being watched than when we don't, unobtrusive measures insure a greater degree of realism. While all obtrusive methods (except self-reports) can be made unobtrusive by simply hiding the means of observation, some specific types of unobtrusive methods have been developed that are quite ingenious. For example, in a clever study (described in detail in Chapter 7), Bickman *et al.* (1973) dropped stamped addressed envelopes in high and low density dormitories. They studied helping behavior as a function of density by the unobtrusive measure of how many envelopes were mailed by residents in each setting. Cialdini (1977) used lit-

JUDGMENTS OF ENVIRONMENTAL QUALITY SCALE

Think about your present perception of the environment in this experimental room. On each scale below, check the space that best describes how you would evaluate the *environment of this room.*

closed:__:__:__:__:__:__:__:	open
colorful:__:__:__:__:__:__:__:	drab
negative:__:__:__:__:__:__:__:	positive
stimulating:__:__:__:__:__:__:__:	boring
small:__:__:__:__:__:__:__:	large
attractive:__:__:__:__:__:__:__:	unattractive
tense:__:__:__:__:__:__:__:	relaxed
comfortable:__:__:__:__:__:__:__:	uncomfortable
depressing:__:__:__:__:__:__:__:	cheerful
good:__:__:__:__:__:__:__:	bad
unlively:__:__:__:__:__:__:__:	lively
bright:__:__:__:__:__:__:__:	dull
unmotivating:__:__:__:__:__:__:__:	motivating
pleasant:__:__:__:__:__:__:__:	unpleasant

Figure 1–10. An example of an environmental self-report scale (from Fisher, 1974). Each scale is scored from 1 to 7. The "negative" end (closed, drab, negative, boring, etc.) is scored as "1"; the "positive" end (open, colorful, positive, stimulating, etc.) as "7." A total score for each person is calculated by summing. Researchers can then compare scores for different people or different environments. You might try this for yourself by comparing the responses on this scale of different people to a particular room and of individuals to two different rooms.

tering to predict votes in the 1976 presidential election. To do this, he observed whether people discarded or kept a Ford or Carter communication that had been positioned on their automobile windshield and predicted that people would vote for the candidate whose communication they kept. Similarly, Webb *et al.* (1966) proposed assessing the popularity of various environmental settings in museums by measuring the number of nose and hand prints on the display case. For an extensive discussion of other clever and useful unobtrusive measures, see Webb *et al.* (1966).

PREVIEW OF THE CONTENT AREAS OF ENVIRONMENTAL PSYCHOLOGY

Thus far we have described the characteristics of environmental psychology and reviewed briefly the methodological perspective of its practition-

ers. The remainder of this book is devoted to an examination of the contents of the field, including empirical findings and theoretical perspectives. As indicated in Figure 1–11 we will begin with environmental perception, cognition, and attitudes, examining the ways in which environmental scenes are perceived, how these perceptions are retained and altered by situational factors, and how perceptions lead to favorable or unfavorable evaluations of the environment. Next we will look at ways in which the environment influences behavior, beginning with theoretical perspectives on environment–behavior relationships. We will then see how stress and other reactions to the environment are influenced by such factors as disasters, noise, temperature, air quality, personal space, and crowding. Then we will examine the behavioral relationships involved in defined settings such as cities, residential settings, hospitals, pris-

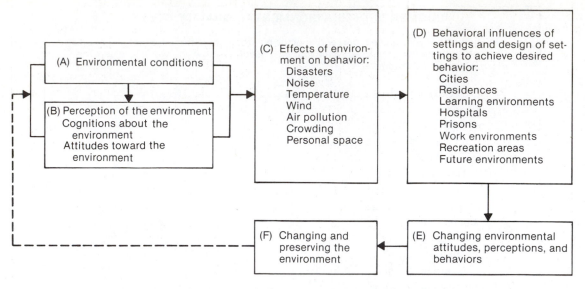

Figure 1–11.   Organization of the book.

ons, learning environments, work environments, recreation areas, and environments of the future. In doing so, we will see how knowledge of these environment–behavior relationships can be used in designing environments for maximum human utility. Finally, we will conclude with intervention strategies for modifying environmentally destructive behavior and improving our relationship with the environment.

CHAPTER SUMMARY

Environmental psychology is concerned with studying environmental issues by drawing upon the knowledge and techniques of many areas within psychology, and as such it serves as a meaningful focus for these areas. It is easier to describe environmental psychology than to define it, but one reasonable definition is that it is the study of the interrelationship between behavior and the built and natural environments. The distinguishing characteristics of environmental psychology include the following: (1) environment–behavior relationships are integral units; (2) environment–behavior relationships are reciprocal or

two-way; (3) the contents and theory of the field are derived primarily from applied research; (4) the field is interdisciplinary in nature; (5) a large number of environmental psychologists have backgrounds in social psychology; and (6) environmental psychology employs an eclectic methodology.

Methods employed by environmental psychologists include experimentation, from which cause and effect can be inferred; correlation, which is suitable for certain field settings but ambiguous in inferring cause and effect; and description, which is often a necessary first step in new areas of research. Specific research techniques are either obtrusive, in which individuals know they are being studied, or unobtrusive, in which they do not know they are a part of research.

Suggested Projects

1. How would you define environmental psychology? Would you define it at all? Is there value in defining it? Compare your answers with classmates. What do your definitions (or reasons for nondefinitions) have

in common? At the end of this course, see if you change your mind about your answers to this question.

2. Examine psychology journals (see the references at the end of the book, beginning about 1955, for articles relating to environmental psychology. During what year does the field appear to have emerged? When did it really start to grow? Is it tapering off or still growing?

3. Look up an environmental psychology research article listed in the references. What methodology was used? How could the research be done using a different methodology?

4. Make a list of environmental problems you would like to see psychology try to solve. As this course progresses, annotate your list to include the psychological principles and research you think would be applicable to solving the problems you named.

2 Environmental Perception, Cognition, and Attitudes

INTRODUCTION

Consider for a moment two imaginary individuals, one from the metropolitan area of Atlanta, Georgia, the other from the rural region around Hurley, South Dakota. What might their reactions be if we brought them together in the modest-size community of Joplin, Missouri on a March day with the temperature in the low 60s? The individual from Atlanta might think it a bit chilly compared to his accustomed warmer and more humid climate, while the individual from Hurley might consider it quite warm and pleasant compared to her accustomed cooler weather. The big city resident might consider Joplin a rather quiet town with clean air, whereas the rural resident would probably think it somewhat noisy and polluted. Further, to the city dweller Joplin might appear rather simple, lacking a central core of skyscrapers and large industrial and commercial districts, whereas the rural resident would probably evaluate Joplin as large, with a complex pattern of different styles of buildings.

Let us further suppose that our two parties go on a side trip to the Ozarks and take in some of the scenic vistas along the winding roads. One visitor might be distressed at the way abandoned farm buildings and weathered houses seem to detract from the landscape. The other visitor, however, might think the scene to be a pleasurable one, instilling feelings of a rustic back-to-nature paradise.

What are the psychological factors that result in these two individuals' different perceptions and evaluations? It is to this basic question that we turn in the present chapter. We will begin by looking at how we perceive, through experience, both individual aspects of the environment and collective or holistic aspects. We will then examine in more detail perception of movement and change and the process of habituation. Also, the factors involved in hazard perception, as well as sociocultural influences on perception, will be explored. In addition, we will see how cognitive processes are involved in our formation of cognitive maps of the environment and in assessing scenic value. Finally, in connection with these topics, we will examine how attitudes toward the environment are formed, and how they might be changed.

WHAT IS ENVIRONMENTAL PERCEPTION?

In our example above we noted that two individuals *perceived* the scenic value of the Ozarks dif- ferently. In searching for explanations for such differences, it becomes obvious that our two imaginary visitors have different backgrounds. What is curious, however, is that the actual physical scenery is identical for both of them. That is, the environment is the same, but the perceptual experience is vastly different. On the other hand, let us picture what might happen to our two fictional characters when they return "home." Even though the environments to which they return are quite different, there will be many similarities in their perceptual experiences. Clearly, then, environmental perception involves an interaction between the individual and the environment. Some of the explanations for the perceptual experience lie within the environment, and some rest within the individual. And, as we will see, a full understanding of environmental perception requires that we not separate the individual processes from the components of the environment, but rather that we examine the individual experience and the environment as a unit.

Before we elaborate on the term *environmental perception,* it will be helpful to consider the more general ideas behind what psychologists usually mean by the term perception, or what we will call *conventional perception.* Once we have discussed these conceptual roots of perception, it will be easier to understand the more encompassing processes in environmental perception.

Conventional Approaches to Perception

Our brief look at conventional approaches to perception will center on an understanding of the terminology associated with it, as some of these terms become very important in our discussion of environmental perception. First, a *stimulus* is an event in the environment *external to the organism* (cf. Neisser, 1967). The organism becomes aware of these stimuli by means of receptor nerve cells, which are sensitive to specific forms of energy, such as light, sound, or temperature. When these energy sources are sufficiently strong to stimulate the receptor cells (the organism may or may not be *aware* of the stimulus), we refer to the process as *sensation.* When a number of sensations are put together by mediational processes in the brain so that we recognize or organize a pattern out of these sensations, the process is called *perception.* According to the *constructivist* tradition, we construct these perceptions from sensations and from long-term

memory of past experience with similar sensations. That is, perceptions consist of the information processed through inferring or constructing meaning out of present sensations and memory of past sensations. Thus, we speak of the perception of a tree because we recognize a pattern of visual stimulation, including texture, color, size, and configuration, as being that of an object we are trained to know as a tree. Similarly, we perceive a beautiful symphony or an exciting rock concert through the combination and patterning of a somewhat familiar series of auditory stimulations.

In addition to the constructivist viewpoint is another tradition in the conventional approach to perception, that of the *structuralists,* who emphasize the role of physiological structures in the brain as it produces perceptions. Perception involves more than just physiological structures, however. When we say that perception involves reliance on experience and memory, we imply that *cognitive* (i.e., thinking) processes are involved in perception (cf., Neisser, 1967). When we perceive, we actively process information and rely on memory of past stimulation for comparison with newly experienced stimuli.

Still another tradition within the conventional approach to perception is that of the *functionalists,* or the *functionalism* perspective. According to this view, our perceptual processes are molded by the necessity of the organism to "get along with" the environment. For example, we compare present sensations with past ones in order to see if the present stimuli signal danger, serve as cues to food or shelter or other items vital to our survival, or are simply irrelevant (i.e., serve no *function*) for us at the moment.

The historical significance of these components in perceptual theory is beyond the scope of this chapter (for a review, see Chaplin & Krawiec, 1960). We mention them here, however, because familiarity with these terms will facilitate our description of environmental perception. We will see that there are constructions, structures, and functions associated with it. Moreover, in describing how our environmental perceptions come about, we will see that environmental perception involves more and different mechanisms as well.

PRINCIPLES OF PERCEPTUAL CONSTRUCTION

When perception theorists of the constructivist tradition say that we *construct* our perceptions, they do not mean that we "make them up," but rather that we add more to the simple sensations we experience so that these sensations are interpreted as a part of a larger whole. To illustrate, let us examine some perceptual principles, often called *Gestalt principles.* This term refers to the German word "Gestalt" (pronounced guess-TALT), which means "form" or "figure," or more literally "good form." The term is also associated with a group of Gestalt psychologists who proposed these perceptual principles (see also, Lang, 1974).

Examine the lines in Figure 2–1 (A) below. What do you see? There are six lines in the drawing, but you tend to see them not as six separate lines, but as three pairs of lines. This phenomenon illustrates the principle of *proximity,* or the tendency to group together those things that are spatially close. Now look at Figure 2–1 (B). Do you see a circle and a square? Technically you do not, and you would receive a poor grade in geometry if you drew them this way. Note that the figures are not complete (i.e., they contain gaps), yet you interpret them as complete. This phenomenon illustrates the principle of *closure,* or the tendency to join lines together to make a more perfect or complete figure.

Next, examine Figure 2–1 (C). Although the spacing is essentially the same between the Xs and Os, you tend not to see the figure as one of five rows and five columns but rather as a central cross and four groups of four Xs each, illustrating the principle of *similarity,* or the tendency to make a pattern out of similar stimuli. Finally, examine Figure 2–1 (D). You probably see it as a rectangle with a curved line across it (i.e., a geometric parabola). Or you could interpret the figure as the back of an envelope with two lines drawn off to the sides. However, because the curved line is continuous, you initially interpret the drawing as a curved line superimposed over a rectangle. This illustrates the principle of *continuity.*

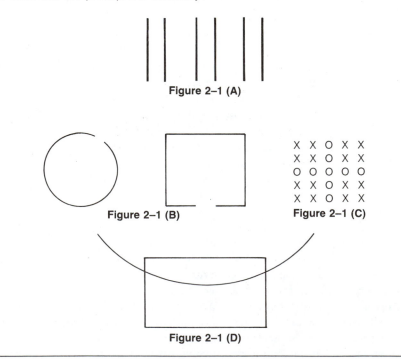

Figure 2–1 (A)

Figure 2–1 (B)   **Figure 2–1 (C)**

Figure 2–1 (D)

Figure 2–2. Environmental perception includes cognitive, affective, interpretive, and evaluative components. What thoughts and feelings do you have when viewing these two scenes?

Environmental Perception

Perhaps the most thorough discussion of the scope of environmental perception comes from the work of Ittelson (e.g., 1970, 1973, 1976, 1978) and his colleagues. For example, Ittelson (1978) notes that environmental perception includes cognitive, affective, interpretive, and evaluative components, all operating at the same time. As we perceive an environment, the cognitive processes involved might include thinking about what we can do in that environment, as well as visual, auditory, and other imagery of the scene. Moreover, we might compare this environment with alternative environments. All of these procedures, then, would involve cognitive processes in perception. In addition, our feelings (affect) about the environment influence our perception of it, and our perception of it influences our feelings. When you view the Grand Canyon, for example, you generally do so with feelings of awe and admiration. The sight of a landscape spoiled by garbage, on the other hand, is generally accompanied by anger and fear and sorrow (Figure 2–2).

In addition to cognitive and affective processes,

environmental perception encompasses the meaning we derive from an environment. Does the environment make sense to us? Does it remind us of past experiences? Does it suggest ideas? Can we interpret the events in the environment in a meaningful way? Finally, environmental perception includes valuation, or the determination of good and bad elements. We likely label the dump bad and the Grand Canyon good. The perceived quality of an environment is then part of the overall perception. Indeed, the affective and evaluative components of environmental perception are the roots of forming attitudes toward the environment.

In sum, cognitive, affective, interpretive, and valuative processes are all involved in environmental perception. Although in reviewing environmental perception we will often discuss aspects of these components separately, our conceptualization of environmental perception considers all of these processes as simultaneous events contributing to the entire experience. Whereas in conventional approaches to perception we discuss how a sensory mechanism detects a single aspect of an object in the environment, in environmental perception we are concerned with a more holistic, encompassing process. That is, we put all elements of an environment together to perceive the environment as a unit.

In addition to the cognitive, affective, interpretive, and valuative components of environmental perception, we can delineate at least three other characteristics of environmental perception, again following the lead of Ittelson. First, related to our statement that we perceive environments as a whole, we can say that the person-environment system is the ultimate unit of study in environmental perception. The person brings individual goals and values into the perceptual experience, as well as group sociocultural influences. The perceptual experience consists of many "significances," or meaningful, functional awarenesses. That is, we most likely notice those things of significance to us. These significances are experienced through the whole setting, not just through one scene of a setting. When perceiving an environment, one does not simply look from one angle at those things which can be seen without turning the head. Rather, one explores the whole environment from different angles through all sensory processes.

A second characteristic of environmental perception is that it involves taking in information about the setting, somewhat analogous to our previous references to a functional component of environmental perception. In fact, the environment contains more information than we can comprehend at once, so we must selectively process it. Part of this processing includes the meaning or interpretive component discussed before, and it is influenced by the personality, goals, and values we bring with us. As we will see in the next chapter, inability to process important information because of an information overload is one explanation for some of the detrimental effects environments have on us.

Finally, a third characteristic of environmental perception is that this perceptual process involves actions by us. We bring expectations, values, and goals to an environment and it provides us with information, but we perceive it through activity. Part of this activity is simple exploration to orient us in the environment; part of it is designed to find strategies for using the environment to meet needs and goals; and part of it is related to establishing confidence and feelings of security within the environment. The activity is always influenced by the search for meaning, our feelings, and how we evaluate the environment.

It is apparent, then, that environmental perception is a very complex and involving process. In the remainder of the chapter we will select some specific topics that elaborate on this process and reveal something of the scope of the field. First, let us examine perception of movement, habituation, and change.

MOVEMENT, HABITUATION, AND THE PERCEPTION OF CHANGE

Thus far we have talked about perception without regard to time. That is, we have noted some of the principles and properties of environmental perception as if perception is constant from one moment to the next. Once we consider time as a variable in environmental perception, three important phenomena emerge: perception of movement, habituation or adaptation, and perception of change.

Perception of Movement

At the receptor level, perception of movement is instigated by successive stimulation of neighboring receptors. That is, we feel bugs crawling on our skin because bugs trigger a series of pressure receptors as they crawl along, and we see movement because different receptors in the retina are stimulated over the time the moving object is crossing our visual field. Similarly, direction of sounds is detected by the slightly different arrival times of the sound at the ears or by the slightly different intensities of sound for the two ears. As an object that either emits or reflects sound crosses our auditory field, these different times or intensities change, so that we detect the movement.

Habituation or Adaptation

What happens if a perceptible stimulus does not change across time? The answer involves what is known as habituation or adaptation: If a stimulus is constant, the response to it becomes weaker and weaker across time. Perhaps this phenomenon can best be illustrated by an anecdote from an acquaintance of the authors. A few years ago, this individual moved into a town that had one of the world's largest cattle feedlots. If you have ever been around a feedlot, you know that the smell of tons of accumulated manure permeates the air for miles around. Our acquaintance detected this odor immediately as he neared the outskirts of the town and inquired at a local gas station about its origin. Upon asking, "What's that smell?" he was greeted by a puzzled look on the attendant's face and the reply, "What smell?" After a few days or even minutes of living around odorous substances, we become "desensitized" to the odor and do not notice it as much. The same applies to any kind of stimulation, including noise, light, taste, pressure, or temperature. Many who live near freeways, for example, at first find it difficult to sleep, but after a few nights they become habituated to the noise and have little trouble sleeping. Should they have guests some night, however, the guests are likely to be bothered by the noise (cf., Bryan & Tempest, 1973).

Explanations for adaptation or habituation tend to be either cognitive or physiological (for a brief review, see Glass & Singer, 1972). Sometimes the distinction is made that "habituation" refers to a physiological process and "adaptation" to a cognitive process. Often, however, the two terms are used interchangeably.

Physiological explanations of habituation emphasize the notion that receptors themselves fire less frequently upon repeated presentation of a stimulus. Cognitive explanations of the phenomenon emphasize a cognitive reappraisal of the stimulus as less deserving of attention after repeated presentation. The first time you hear a loud noise, you allocate considerable attention to it to find out what it is and to determine whether it is a potential source of threat. Once you know that

it is a train, a trash truck, or your neighbor's car, however, you probably evaluate it as nonthreatening to your well-being and thus attend to it less the next few times you hear it. A similar process would account for the fact that those who live near feedlots are less bothered by the smell after a short time. However, from a cognitive perspective, our feedlot example may reflect more of a response bias than a perceptual shift. That is, rather than actually perceiving the odor as less noxious, nearby residents may simply learn to respond to it less intensely or less frequently (e.g., Evans, Jacobs, & Frager, 1982).

An important factor in adaptation, which will be covered more thoroughly in Chapters 4 and 5, is the predictability or regularity of the stimulus. It is fairly easy to adapt to a constant hum in the background or to a smell that constantly permeates the immediate atmosphere. However, it is much more difficult to adapt to the irregular noise of a jackhammer or to a smell that blows in with sporadic gusts of wind. Bursts of noise or smells that come at regular or predictable intervals are easier to adapt to than unpredictable stimuli, but more difficult to adapt to than constant stimuli. Once we adapt to a stimulus and the stimulus ceases (as in the interval between bursts of noise), our adaptation to the stimulus also dissipates somewhat. When the stimulus recurs, we must adapt again. Furthermore, unpredictable stimuli require that more attention be allocated for evaluation of the stimuli as threatening or nonthreatening. Thus, predictability is an important variable in the adaptation process.

Perception of Change

If we readily adapt to environmental stimulation, how do we perceive change in such things as air pollution and urban blight? If we live in an area where air pollution is high, and we adapt to this pollution, how can we perceive changes in the level of pollution? Sommer (1972) suggests that the answer lies in the Weber-Fechner function of psychophysics. This function, derived from research in the late 19th century, is based on the amount of increment in intensity of a stimulus

ECOLOGICAL PERCEPTION OF THE ENVIRONMENT: THE WORK OF GIBSON

Our discussion of perception of the environment would not be complete without considering the perspective of Gibson's ecological perception, which in some ways is a bridge between what we have termed conventional perception and the broader concept of environmental perception. According to Gibson (1950, 1966, 1979), it is the ecological properties of environmental stimuli that are important in perception. In this case, "ecological" implies reciprocal adjustments between individual, social, and physical environments. That is, Gibson does not ask, "What is in the head?" but instead, "What setting is the head in?" Rather than perceiving individual features or cues that we organize into recognizable patterns, we respond to (detect or tune in to) meaning that already exists in an ecologically structured environment. Rather than the organism's constructing meaning, meaning is already in the environment, readily available to an appropriately attuned organism mobile enough to experience it (see also Heft, 1981).

We have noted that the conventional approach to perception considers perception of the external environment as a function of a variety of interpretive psychological processes, i.e., a stimulus activates a specific nervous system receptor, and the pattern of receptor stimulation is interpreted with the memory of past experiences to get information about the environment. From the conventional perspective, we have to interpret disconnected stimuli in order to construct something meaningful about the environment. Gibson assumes that perception of the environment is more direct and less interpretive than this. That is, perceptual patterns convey much information quite directly—without elaborate processing by higher brain centers. Furthermore, Gibson believes that perception is much more holistic, so that properties of the environment are perceived not as distinct points but rather as meaningful entities. Let us develop the Gibsonian approach to perception a bit further by exploring the concept of affordances.

Perception of Affordances

According to Gibson, we receive much valuable information *directly* through our perception of the environment. Gibson views organisms as actively exploring their environment, encountering objects in a variety of ways. Through this process, we experience the surface of an object, its texture, and angles from different perspectives. This allows us to perceive an object's *invariant functional properties* (i.e., properties of an object that do not change, such as "hardness"). The invariant functional properties of objects as they are encountered in the course of an organism's active exploration are termed *affordances*. The notion of affordances will become clearer as we look at a few examples. If an object is solid rather than liquid or gaseous, if it is inclined toward the ground at an angle other than 90 degrees, and if at least part of it is higher than the organism, then that object *affords* shelter. If an object is solid and rigid, if it is raised off the ground, if its top surface is fairly horizontal to the ground, then that object affords sitting or sittability. If an object is malleable, can be placed in the mouth whole or in pieces, and is of

that is required before a difference is detected between the new and old intensities. Stated simply, this law says that the intensity of a new stimulus required for it to be perceived as different from the present stimulus is proportionate to the present stimulus. It takes only a small increment to detect a difference in very low-intensity stimuli but a

much larger increment is needed for high-intensity stimuli. This function (though not as mathematically accurate as more modern psychophysical functions) generally applies to all forms of stimulation, including light, sound, pressure, and smell. Sommer suggests that the law should apply not just to individual stimuli in a laboratory but to

such biochemical substance as to provide nourishment, then it affords eatability.

Obviously, what affords shelter, sittability, and eatability for a fish does not necessarily do so for a human, and what affords these things for a human does not necessarily do so for an elephant. In this sense, affordances are species-specific (although there is, of course, overlap across species). Furthermore, an object affords different things to different species. Whereas a tree affords shelter to a bird and food to certain insects, it affords fuel (among other things) to humans. For this reason, affordances must be viewed from an ecological perspective.

From this perspective, we can see that affordances involve perception of the ecologically relevant functions of the environment. To perceive affordances of the environment is to perceive *how* one can interact with the environment. It is through perception of affordances that an organism can find its niche in the environment. An ecological niche, according to Gibson, is simply a set of affordances that are utilized. In this regard, humans possess a remarkable talent: We can alter an environment so that it affords anything we want, e.g., more expensive shelters, more beautiful scenery, and so on. In doing so, we may change the affordances of that environment with respect to other humans and other organisms. When we dam a river to create a lake, which affords us water and recreation, we may also change the immediate environment so that it affords life support for fish and waterfowl but does not afford life support for groundhogs and bats or for the farmer who lost his or her land to the lake. Perception of this changed environment, then, depends on the gain and loss of affordances for each organism (Figure 2–3).

Figure 2–3. When we change an environment, as in building a residential subdivision on farmland to afford us shelter, the immediate environment no longer readily affords life support for wild animals or for the farmer. Perception of this environment, according to Gibson, depends on the gain and loss of affordances for each organism.

urban pollution as well. That is, a community with little pollution should become alarmed when massive clouds of brown smog suddenly appear, but large urban areas with heavy smog should require extremely high levels of additional pollution before becoming alarmed. Similarly, we might expect strip zoning in small communities where careful neighborhood planning exists to be noticeable enough to spur the community to action against such blight. Larger communities where strip zoning is commonplace, however, would probably not care as much when one more fast-food chain appears on the strip. One oil derrick on an undisturbed seashore is noticed immedi-

A PROBABILISTIC MODEL OF PERCEPTION

We have noted several theoretical perspectives of the ways our perceptual system works, including structuralism, constructivism, functionalism, and Gibson's ecological perception. Although the mathematics are too complex for a broad discussion here, we should note one other perspective, that of Brunswik (1956, 1969). Brunswik's approach is known as a *lens model* or as *probabilistic functionalism.* He envisions the perceptual process as analogous to a lens, wherein stimuli from the environment become focused through our perceptual efforts. We know, however, that not all stimuli are what they seem to be. Recall the Gestalt figures from page 20. How do we decide which way to interpret or focus this stimulus information? Brunswik answers that we do so by assigning a probability to each possible interpretation, relying in part on our past experience with the environment. Through this experience we know which interpretations are more trustworthy or ecologically valid than others. We then choose the interpretation that appears most valid, and test it out against reality. If it does not correspond to reality, we modify it against another set of probabilities (see also, Craik & Appleyard, 1980).

ately, but one derrick added to a field of 50 probably goes unnoticed.

Sommer proposes that we take advantage of the Weber-Fechner phenomenon in changing detrimental environmental behaviors. Any time we are asked to change our life styles to preserve the environment, there is resistance. But what if the change in life style is so small as to go unnoticed? We might be able to make subtle changes that have a great impact on the environment. Requiring that beverages be sold in returnable containers, for example, is not as drastic a measure as banning beverages in all containers. Requiring that recyclable containers be separated from other trash is an even smaller step than banning nonreturnable containers, and so on. In other words, if the perceptible change is small, we will be less resistant to it than if it is large.

Furthermore, change that is rapid (such as rotation or burning) is more easily detected than change that is slow (such as growth). There is ecological and survival value in knowing that one's environment is changing rapidly, as when one's forest homeland is burning. Unfortunately, comparable damage that occurs slowly (as when pollution from nearby cities kills trees), is less noticeable. This fast–slow distinction becomes critical with hazard perception, as we will see in the next section.

PERCEPTION OF NATURAL HAZARDS

Up to this point, we have generally discussed environmental perception in terms of the perceptual organization of specifiable stimuli in the environment. We now turn to a broader conceptualization of the term ''perception,'' in which we talk about ''mental concepts'' of the environment and its potential impact upon us. In a sense, we now concentrate more on the cognitive organization of complex perceptions and less on the components of individual perceptions.

A special area of interest for environmental perception is the phenomenon of hazard perception: What factors influence whether or not individuals are aware of hazards and aware of the potential consequences of being hazard victims? We present here several factors that research has found to be important in hazard perception. Factors involved in the perception of hazards have been reviewed elsewhere (Burton & Kates, 1964; Burton, Kates, & White, 1968; Kates, 1976; Saarinen, 1969). Among these factors are the crisis effect, the levee effect, and adaptation.

The *crisis effect* refers to the fact that perception of a disaster is greatest during and immediately following its occurrence, but greatly dissipates between disasters. Flood potentials, for example, are largely ignored until there is a flood. Once the flood occurs, there is a rush to study the problem together with some implementation of public works programs. Efforts to prevent the next disaster, however, almost disappear after this initial rush of activity. The same principle holds for droughts: We take strong water conservation measures only when drought arrives. We do not practice stringent measures between droughts, and we do not limit population in areas that are drought-prone so that there is more water available in time of drought.

The *levee effect* pertains to the fact that once measures are taken to prevent a disaster, people tend to settle in around the protective mechanism. Levees are built to keep floodwaters in rivers and out of populated areas. After a levee is built, however, houses and factories are constructed on what was once considered to be a dangerous floodplain. Apparently, people are lulled into thinking the levee will protect them from all future floods. Unfortunately, levees are built with projected figures for floodwaters in mind, and

projections often go wrong. Most communities lining the Mississippi River are testimony to this fact. The levee effect also applies to such preventive measures as breakwaters along coasts and reservoirs in drought-prone areas: Once built, people flock to settle nearby (Figure 2–4).

A third factor involved in hazard perception is *adaptation*. Just as we adapt or habituate to a noise or odor, so, too, do we adapt to threats of disaster. Apparently, we can hear so much about a hazard that it no longer frightens us. Large populations in earthquake-prone regions of the world, such as California, Iran, Japan, and parts of China, attest to this adaptation phenomenon. Floods, mine disasters, and hurricanes follow the same principle: People in the area "learn to live with it." In learning to live with it, they generally discount the possibility that they themselves might become victims (e.g., Kates, 1976).

Several variables appear to influence adaptation to potential hazards. For one thing, when the hazard is closely related to the well-being or resource use of a community, the inhabitants are more aware of the danger. Individuals whose busi-

Figure 2–4. The crisis effect, the levee effect, adaptation, and other factors involved in hazard perception help explain why people build on flood-plains.

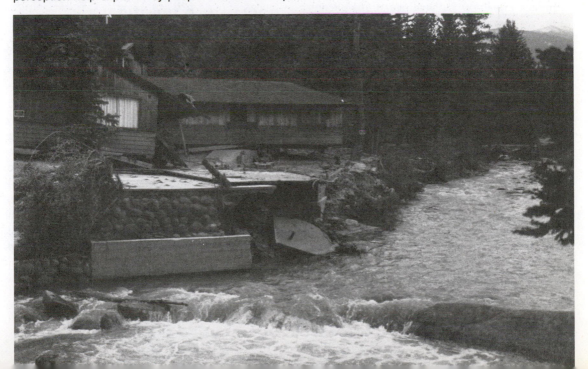

nesses depend on coastal tourist industries, for example, may take more precautions against hurricane damage than residents whose well-being does not depend on the tourist industry. Farmers are much more aware of drought hazards than are nonfarmers in the same area. Ski resort operators are probably also more likely to be aware of drought hazards, and individuals with lung diseases are more sensitive to air pollution than those with healthy lungs. Thus, if one's well-being is closely related to the resource that poses a hazard, one is less likely to adapt in perceiving the hazard.

In addition, frequency of disasters influences cognitive judgments of potential harm, as does personal experience with similar disasters. Those who have lived through floods or hurricanes or droughts are more aware of the risks than those who have not had firsthand experiences. Probably because each repetition of a disaster serves to remind us of the dangers, the more times we experience a disaster the more conscious we are of potential risks.

Another phenomenon involved in hazard perception appears to be personality. Sims and Baumann (1972) noted that although the heaviest concentration of tornadoes is in the Midwest, most tornado-related deaths occur in the South. After eliminating natural explanations of this phenomenon, such as stronger storms or higher concentrations of population in the South, the researchers suggested that there might be regional differences in subjective perception of danger and thus less preparation for disaster by southerners. The researchers found such differences related to the personality dimension of internal–external locus of control. ''Internals'' believe they are in control of their own fate, whereas ''externals'' believe outside forces, such as powerful persons, government, God, or fate, control their destinies (Rotter, 1966). In interviewing residents of Illinois and Alabama, Sims and Baumann found that the Illinois residents felt luck had far less to do with their fate than Alabama residents did. Furthermore, Illinois residents appeared to take more precautions when storms approached, such as listening for weather bulletins and warning neighbors, whereas Alabama residents paid less attention to the need to listen for radio or TV bulletins. Apparently, then, personality plays some role in determining humans' perceptions of their control over hazards.

In another study of flood victims in Carman, Manitoba, Canada, it was found that another personality characteristic was associated with efforts to minimize flood damage, such as through elevating houses, installing sump pumps, and purchasing insurance (Simpson-Housley *et al.,* 1982). Individuals of this personality type are known as repressers (Bell & Byrne, 1978), and tend to deal with threat by denying the existence of the threat and not verbalizing uneasy feelings about a potential danger. Although intuitively it seems odd that such individuals would be the ones to take more precautions against disaster, perhaps by doing so they feel they are in a better position to deny or avoid damage if a disaster did occur in the area. Whatever the case, it does appear that personality plays a role in determining humans' perceptions of their control over hazards (see also, Hanson, Vitek, & Hanson, 1979; Jackson, 1981; Payne & Pigram, 1981; Shippee, Burroughs, & Wakefield, 1980).

SOCIAL AND CULTURAL INFLUENCES ON ENVIRONMENTAL PERCEPTION

We have emphasized in our discussion of conventional environmental perception that experience and learning play a role in organizing perceptions. In order to have an accurate perception of a geographical location, we must learn something about the local geography. Since social and cultural factors, such as sex roles, socioeconomic status, and exposure to modern architecture, influence what one learns or what one has the opportunity to experience, it stands to reason that such factors influence how one learns to perceive the environment. Research suggests that this is indeed the case.

A classic example is the fact that certain cultures emphasize rectangular construction, and others emphasize curvilinear construction or at least less rigor in erecting vertical and rectilinear walls (Allport, 1955; Allport & Pettigrew, 1957; Gregory, 1966; Segall, Campbell, & Herskovits, 1966). As a result, members of cultures with "carpentered environments" see lines on two-dimensional surfaces in a different way than do members of cultures with less carpentered environments. Take the Müller-Lyer illusion depicted in Figure 2–5 as an example. To most of us, the horizontal line at the top appears longer than the one on the bottom, even though both lines are actually the same length. Apparently, because we live in an environment in which construction is rectangular, we see the two-dimensional lines as representing corners in three-dimensional space. We therefore infer that the horizontal line at the top is farther from us than the diagonal lines and thus must represent the crossing of quite a distance of space. The horizontal line at the bottom, however, appears to be closer than the diagonal lines and thus appears to span less space than the line at the top. Members of African cultures that use rounded construction and pay less attention to rectilinear (straight line) corners tend not be deceived by this illusion: Their culture and ecology have taught them that intersecting diagonal lines do not imply depth (see also Bartley, 1958).

Another example of social influences on environmental perception involves perception of air pollution. Barker (1976) reviewed several studies that show socioeconomic levels are related to perception or tolerance of air pollution. In general, high socioeconomic level residents who live in relatively unpolluted suburban areas are less concerned about pollution than are lower socioeconomic level citizens who are more likely to live near sources of pollution. Those most aware of and concerned about air pollution, however, are higher socioeconomic level individuals who live in areas with high levels of pollution. Barker offers an explanation for this perceptual difference by noting that when high pollution levels exist, lower socioeconomic groups either are primarily concerned with more immediate problems of day-to-day living or believe they are helpless to fight the problem of air pollution. (In Chapter 3 we will see how the phenomenon of "learned helplessness" sometimes explains the lack of response to environmental threat.)

ENVIRONMENTAL COGNITION AND COGNITIVE MAPPING

We have discussed some of the ways in which our sensory-perceptual system operates. Even when we are not actively viewing, hearing, or smelling an environment, we can still experience it mentally and determine something about our location in it from this mental experience. To illustrate this concept, think about the layout of your campus. Better still, take a few moments to draw a sketch of the campus. Your mental representation or *cognition* about the layout is termed a *cognitive map,* and the general way of thinking about, recognizing, and organizing this layout is termed *environmental cognition.* These cognitive maps are, again, present for us whether we are in the mapped environment or somewhere else. Moreover, there are a number of factors which influence our cognitive maps, and there are several aspects of the environment which go into their makeup. The concept of cognitive mapping has its roots in the work of E. C. Tolman (1948), who described the way rats learn to "map" the envi-

Figure 2–5. The Müller-Lyer illusion. To those of us raised in built environments, the line at the top appears longer than the one on the bottom.

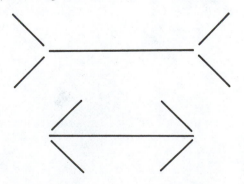

ronment of an experimental maze. Work by Lynch (1960) gave the impetus to studies of humans' cognitive maps of cities, and more recent work has expanded our knowledge of mapping techniques in many environments. Because cognitive mapping has very close ties with environmental psychologists' interest in cities, we will reserve most of our discussion of the topic for Chapter 8 on city environments, and we will encounter cognitive maps again when we discuss environmental design. For now, let us consider some of the components of cognitive maps and the factors that influence them.

Components of Cognitive Maps

Return to your sketch of your campus. Are there obvious streets designated on it? Are there broad areas you could designate as ''Fraternity Row'' or ''dormitory area'' or ''athletic complex''? Lynch (1960) found that five categories of features could be used to describe and analyze cognitive maps: paths, edges, districts, nodes, and landmarks. *Paths* are traffic arteries such as streets, walkways, or riverways. *Edges* are limits of the maps that tend to follow a line but are not functioning as paths, such as a seashore or wall. *Districts* are larger spaces of the cognitive map that have some common character, such as ''Fraternity Row,'' the ''Chinatown'' of many cities, or the central business district of a town. *Nodes* are major points of focus, typically associated with intersections of major paths or breaks in them, such as a downtown square, a traffic circle, or the interchange of two freeways. Finally, *landmarks* are specific structures that people use for reference points and which are usually visible from some distance, such as the Washington Monument or a tall building in a city. Can you identify examples of these five categories on your campus map (see also Figure 2–6)?

Figure 2–6. Diamond Head can be seen from almost all parts of Honolulu. Such a visible landmark is part of the cognitive maps of most residents. In fact, orientation in Honolulu is not based on traditional north-east-south-west directions, but rather on the more identifiable Diamond Head-ward, Ewa (a community in the opposite direction from Diamond Head), mauka (toward the mountains), and makai (toward the sea).

Errors in Cognitive Maps

Cognitive maps are, of course, rarely perfect representations of the physical environment, but rather are rough conceptualizations. In fact, we can identify several sources of error that frequently occur in them (Downs & Stea, 1973; Evans, 1980; Lee, 1970; Milgram, 1977). First, cognitive maps tend to be incomplete. We often leave out minor paths and details, but we can also omit districts and major landmarks. Second, we often distort our representation of the environment by placing things too close together, too far apart, or aligning them improperly. For example, we tend to represent nonparallel paths as being parallel, nonperpendicular paths as being perpendicular, and curved paths as being straight (Appleyard, 1969, 1970; Byrne, 1979; Evans, 1980; Lynch, 1960). Moreover, we tend to distort spatial relationships based on our ideas of larger categories within which we place smaller concepts (Stevens & Coupe, 1978). To illustrate, draw a map of the western United States and indicate the location of San Diego and Reno. Do not read further until you have done so. Finished? Except for some of you on the west coast, most people place San Diego west of Reno because they think of California being west of Nevada. As you will see upon consulting a US map, San Diego is actually east of Reno! While you are at it, check your map of the western US again. Most of you probably have a distorted cognitive map based on two omissions—Alaska and Hawaii are the two western-most states, but probably do not appear on your map! A third type of error involves augmentation, or the addition of features to a map that are not there, such as adding a peninsula that does not exist. Altogether, then, our cognitive maps are clearly *not* always very accurate representations of the physical environment.

Familiarity, Gender, and Socioeconomic Class

The types of errors in our cognitive maps, as well as the degree of detail in them, vary according to several factors. The major factor influencing cognitive maps is familiarity. As you might expect, a number of studies have shown that the more familiar we are with an environment, the more accurate and detailed are our cognitive maps of it (e.g., Appleyard, 1970, 1976; Evans, 1980; Hart & Moore, 1973; Moore, 1974). Other research has shown that males sometimes draw more thorough sketches in cognitive mapping studies (Appleyard, 1976), although a number of investigators find no such sex differences (e.g., Francescato & Mebane, 1973; Maurer & Baxter, 1972). To the extent that sex differences are present, they are most likely due to differences in familiarity with an area. Moreover, familiarity probably also explains why higher socioeconomic status groups draw more thorough maps than less well-off groups (e.g., Orleans, 1973). That is, upper-class individuals probably have more experience with a broader area of a city than lower-class individuals whose mobility is restricted. In sum, the longer we have experience with an area and the more mobile we are within it, the more thorough our cognitive maps of it are likely to be.

Functions of Cognitive Maps

Now that we have seen what cognitive maps are and some of the dynamics of the mapping process, we might ask, "What do they do for us?" The answer seems to be that they serve the adaptive functions of letting us get around in our environment efficiently and of helping us locate valuable items (food, shelter, meeting places) within the environment (Downs & Stea, 1973, 1977; Evans, 1980; Kaplan, 1973). Without a cognitive map, we would have to search for locations in our environment in a haphazard manner, hitting or missing the desired location in a very inefficient way. The organization of the layout of the environment in our memory solves this inefficiency problem, and helps us find new as well as old locations. Moreover, we can use cognitive maps to communicate locations to others and to understand others' communications about location to us. Being able to "visualize" the directions someone gives us, and associating the directions with familiar landmarks, paths, and districts enhances our ability to follow directions.

Memory and Cognitive Maps

Exactly how is a cognitive map represented in the brain? Environmental psychologists have differing opinions on the matter (Evans, 1980). One view is that we have somewhat of a mental "picture" or replica of the environment in our memory. This view, termed *analogical* (meaning the mental map is an analogy of the real world) or *imaginal* (meaning we have an image of the environment in the mind), says that the cognitive map roughly corresponds point for point to the physical environment, almost as if we have a "picture" of the environment stored in the brain (Kosslyn, 1975; Shepard, 1975). Another view, the *propositional* approach, advocates more of a meaning-based storage of material. That is, the environment is represented as a number of concepts or ideas, each of which is connected and has a number of associations, such as color, name, associated sounds, and height. When we call on this propositional map, we search our memory for these various associations, which may be represented through a sketch we draw (Pylyshyn, 1973). Current thinking combines these two approaches and says that cognitive maps contain both propositional and analogical elements (e.g., Evans, 1980; Kosslyn & Pomerantz, 1977). For example, most information about the environment may be stored in memory through propositions, but we can use the propositional network to construct an analogical image. More and more research is being conducted in this area, and before too many years we will likely have definitive answers as to how the process of storage and retrieval of cognitive maps occurs.

Cognitive Organization of the Environment

In addition to specific work on cognitive maps, recent research on environmental cognition gives us some ideas about the ways our spatial cognitions of the environment are organized. For example, when people are asked to judge whether a pair of states (e.g., Georgia and Mississippi) are closer together than another pair (e.g., Michigan and Iowa), the more similar the distances within

the two pairs, the longer it takes to make a decision (Evans & Pezdek, 1980). Moreover, recall of distance between two points on a map is longer the greater the distance on the map (Kosslyn, Ball, & Reiser, 1978). From such evidence we can conclude that cognitive representations of the environment require scanning for judgments to be made about them, and the more information we must scan, the longer it takes to make judgments about spatial relationships.

Other interesting studies also show that cognitive organization influences judgments we make from cognitive maps. For example, judgments of traversed distance, that is, distance we have travelled over a given period of time, is in part dependent on the number of right turns we make (Sadalla & Magel, 1980). Students walking a path designated by a line of tape placed on a floor judge a path to be longer the more right turns it contains. In addition, the more intersections a path crosses, the longer the path is judged to be (Sadalla & Staplin, 1980b). Finally, consider a third study (Sadalla & Staplin, 1980a) involving paths marked with tape. One path has intersections marked with proper names that occur frequently in the English language (e.g., Lewis), and another path has intersections marked with relatively unfamiliar names (e.g., Talbot). You are more likely to recognize and remember the familiar names. In addition, these researchers found that you are likely to judge the familiar-name path as being longer, presumably because you have more information about it stored from associations with the familiar names. Thus, when traversing the path mentally to estimate its distance, you must scan more information, so you assume it is longer. In general, then, the more information we must scan in our memory while making a "mental journey" through an environment, the farther the distance we assume we have traversed.

Summary of Cognitive Mapping

In sum, cognitive maps are mental representations of spatial relationships in the environment. Landmarks, paths, districts, edges, and nodes are the

major components of cognitive maps, and the more familiar we are with an area the more accurate and thorough our cognitive maps are likely to be. Cognitive maps serve the adaptive function of helping us locate things of importance in the environment, and may be thought of as propositional networks in memory which can be visualized. The more information in our cognitive maps, the longer it takes to make judgments about distance in them.

ASSESSING THE SCENIC ENVIRONMENT: LANDSCAPE ASSESSMENT, AESTHETICS, AND PREFERENCE

Suppose we are building a new condominium project in a resort area. Current residents of the area do not want us to detract from any scenic view they might have. On the other hand, prospective occupants of the new project will want as scenic a view as possible. Furthermore, when our new condos are seen from a distance, we do not want them to detract from the entire setting. How, then, do we maximize the scenic qualities for all involved? Much of the work in environmental perception concerns this type of question. At the core of such a question is the problem of determining the components of scenic quality. That is, just exactly what makes a scene attractive? Is a scene more valued if it contains a forest? If so, should the trees be large, small, or mixed in size and species to maximize scenic value? Should the forest cover the whole scene or be broken up by a clearing? Does a rustic barn enhance the scene or detract from it? What if the electric utility needs to run a high voltage power line through our scene? Is there a way to make the poles and wires blend with the scene, or is a contrast with the other elements of the scene desirable?

Historically, our opinions of such scenes have varied with time. As indicated by a number of writers (Greene, 1983; Jackson, 1975; Nash, 1974; Turner, 1920), Americans once thought of the ''wilderness'' as the environment to be conquered as settlers moved west. Most of the east-

ern US was actually vast forest land before European settlers and later Americans began clearing it for farming. The prairies of the central US were fenced for ranching and cultivated for farming, and so on. Today, the trend is toward a ''back to nature'' philosophy in which we preserve rather than conquer the natural environment. We now ask, ''Are there ways of manipulating the natural and human-built components of a scene to make it more valued?'' As we will see in this section, there are several approaches to finding which arrangements of a scene make it desirable. Although much of the research involves assessment of ''natural'' landscapes, we will see that attempts have been made to apply these principles to the built environment as well. Interestingly, perhaps due to our current ''back-to-nature'' tendencies, principles of scenic quality for more natural environments do not apply very well to scenes of the built environment. Indeed, on the average, scenes of the built environment are valued less than scenes of more natural environments.

Greene (1983) describes three broad approaches to assessing scenic environments: a descriptive approach, based on procedures used by landscape architects; a physical-perceptual approach, in which efforts are made to identify concrete physical objects in the scene which contribute to perceived value; and a psychological approach wherein conceptual ideas (e.g., complexity), based on subjective judgment, are believed to contribute to value. Although there is considerable overlap in these approaches, use of this classification system helps organize the various efforts of researchers in determining scenic values. Let us now turn to these approaches in more detail.

Descriptive Systems of Scenic Value

Greene (1983) points out that landscape architects rely on a number of elements and principles in describing a scene, especially those derived from work by Litton (1968). Although these elements and principles are not scientifically derived, they

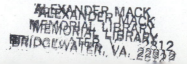

HOW THE BRAIN INTERPRETS DISTANCE

Historically, depth perception has been an important issue in perception, since there is controversy over how we translate a two-dimensional image on the retina into three dimensions. In general, perception theorists believe that, given the information we take in, the three-dimensional world we experience is a construction. Since depth perception is the basis for knowing space, and since what we do in the environment influences our interpretation of space, we think that perception of distance or depth is a crucial element in environmental perception.

How do the different sense modalities tell us the distance to an object? For sighted humans, vision is probably the most important sense modality for perceiving distance. Some visual distance cues require the use of both eyes and are called *binocular*. Others require only one eye and are called *monocular*. An important binocular cue within 15 or 20 feet is *convergence* or the extent to which the eyes move toward the inside or outside of the head to focus on an object. The farther away an object, the more parallel the lines of regard for the two eyes. Assuming that tiny nerves can detect differences in muscular tension for the eyes, the cues from these nerves should communicate distance to environmental objects that are within 15 to 20 feet of the viewer. Another binocular depth or distance cue is *retinal disparity* or the extent to which the image on each retina is different. In general, the greater the disparity (up to a point), the more one perceives depth in a scene. It is through retinal disparity that a stereoscope enables us to see depth: each eye sees a slightly different picture.

Monocular cues for distance include accommodation, size, texture, linear perspective, shadowing, aerial perspective, overlap, movement perspective, and height in the visual field. *Accommodation* refers to the adjustment of the lens to focus on objects. Since the lens must thicken to focus on near objects and lengthen to focus on more distant objects, *if* nerves can detect this accommodation process (there is some question about this detection capability), then the brain can use this information to interpret distances up to about 15 or 20 feet.

Size as a depth cue pertains to the fact that close objects appear large, whereas distant objects appear smaller. If we know that a typical adult human is five to six feet tall, someone whose image takes up a very small portion of the retina is assumed to be at a greater distance from us than someone who takes up a much larger portion.

Texture means the smoothness or roughness of a *surface.* If we know that a surface is rough (as with most brick walls), but we cannot see the roughness of the texture, then we have a pretty good idea that the surface is in the distance. The more texture we can see, the closer we can assume an object is to us.

Linear perspective refers to the fact that parallel lines tend to converge in the distance. If you look down a railroad track, the rails near you are far apart but come together at a point on the horizon. Also, lines coming together to form a corner appear to be diagonal with respect to the

do provide a convenient way of describing a scene, and thus the term ''descriptive'' is appropriate. The basic elements of a scene in this system are line, form, color, and texture, which are components long recognized by artists in their creative efforts. The line of a road might meet the line of a mountaintop, for example, and the smooth texture of a pasture might contrast with the rough texture of a rocky coastline. These elements are organized according to *dominance principles,* such as enframement, convergence, and contrast. *Enframement* can be thought of as a scene containing its own ''picture frame.'' A classic example would be tall trees in the fore-

horizontal and vertical dimensions. By manipulating these angles, we can make a two-dimensional drawing appear to be three-dimensional.

When we use *shadowing* to imply depth or distance, we take advantage of the fact that light usually comes from above. If we see a dark spot on an object and think the dark spot is a shadow, we assume one of two things: Either a small object closer to the light source than the big object is casting a shadow, or a dent or hole in the large object is shielded from the light source. Thus, if we can readily see an object that can cast a shadow on another object, and if we know the position of the light source, we know which object is closer.

Aerial perspective refers to the fact that light from a distance is diffused (scattered) more than light from a nearby source. As a result, colors of distant objects are less distinct.

Overlap describes the phenomenon whereby a close object can partially block our vision of a distant object. If a pillar in an arena blocks your view of the performance below, you know that the pillar is closer than the objects on the stage.

Movement perspective refers to the fact that close objects appear to go by faster than distant objects, whether it is you or the objects themselves that are moving. A bee and a distant jet airliner may take up the same amount of space on the retina, but the slower-moving jet is assumed to be at a greater distance.

Finally, *height in the visual field* as a distance cue pertains to the fact that near objects usually appear at the bottom of our visual field, whereas far objects appear at the top. If you look at the horizon, this phenomenon becomes obvious: The distant horizon is at the center or upper part of the visual field, the nearby ground is at the bottom, and the infinity of outer space is at the top, obscured of course by the atmosphere (Figure 2–7, A to D).

Other sense modalities can also be used for perception of distance. Consider hearing, for example. Loud sounds usually come from nearby sources. Freeway traffic sounds louder at 50 feet than at 200 feet. Furthermore, as with diffusion of light across great distances, sounds become less distinct the farther away their source. Although you can hear an outdoor rock concert a mile or more away, at such distances it is difficult to make out much in the way of tonal differences or words. Still another sound cue for distance is the use of echoes. We rarely hear sounds that bounce off distant objects, but we can hear sounds bouncing off the walls of a hallway or theater. Blind persons are particularly adept at picking up echoes. A blind friend of one of the authors has the ability to stand in an area of a college campus, snap his fingers, and tell you the direction of all trees and buildings within 200 feet.

Smell also can be used to detect distance. For example, chemical odors tend to become less concentrated the farther you get from their source. How often have you entered a new town or neighborhood, smelled freshly baked dough, and said, "We must be *near* a bakery"? Temperature receptors in the skin can likewise be used to detect proximal distances to very hot or cold objects. You know you are "too close" to a furnace or air conditioning outlet by the temperature of the surrounding air and of your skin.

ground "framing" the distant scene of a pasture, with mountains in the background. In general, enframement adds value to a scene. *Convergence* refers to two or more lines coming together in a scene. The line of a row of trees in an orchard, for example, might converge with the line of a stream. Items placed at a point of convergence are likely to receive more visual attention, and thus "dominate" the scene. Finally, *contrast* refers to marked differences in line, form, color, or texture. High contrast emphasizes components of a scene, whereas low contrast tends to make elements blend. In general, more valued scenes have human elements which "blend" with natural ele-

Figure 2–7. Selected monocular depth cues. Size constancy *(A)*, linear perspective *(B)*, height in the visual field *(C)*, texture *(D)*.

Figure 2–8. Enframement, contrast, and convergence are three dominance principles used in the descriptive approach to assessing scenic quality. Can you identify these principles in this photograph?

ments (i.e., have low contrast). Natural components with high contrast, such as the Grand Tetons, or certain human constructions with high contrast, such as the Golden Gate Bridge, also add to scenic value (Figure 2–8).

As Greene (1983) points out, such descriptive approaches to evaluating scenes are widespread in practice and are generally useful. However, they have the disadvantage of being based on the opinions of "experts," whose views may not match the opinions of the untrained general population (see also, S. Kaplan, 1979a, 1979b). Someone familiar with a local scene may think it to be quite valuable and pleasing, regardless of the fact that its dominance principles violate the wisdom of professional designers (e.g., R. Kaplan, 1977). Returning to our initial example of a condominium developer who wants to put in a new building at a resort, the descriptive approach would indicate that the design of the building should blend with the natural environment and should provide enframed views of the area. Or should it? Perhaps

it would be better if the condominium contrasted with the natural environment, especially if the architecture contained some stunning new concepts. As you can see, there is plenty of room for subjective judgment when employing these descriptive approaches to assessing scenic value.

Physical-Perceptual Approaches to Scenic Value

An alternative and more scientific method of determining scenic value is through what Greene (1983) terms the physical-perceptual approach. Here, one quantifies actual physical objects in a scene and, through sophisticated mathematical techniques, determines how much or how little of an object yields the greatest scenic value according to a panel of judges. For example, Shafer, Hamilton, and Schmidt (1969) assessed the preferences of individuals for landscapes in New York state and found that preferences were associated with such factors as the area of immediate vegetation multiplied by the area of distant vege-

Table 2–1. **RELATIONSHIP OF SEVERAL VARIABLES TO EVALUATIONS OF SCENIC BEAUTY IN AN ARIZONA FOREST***

Amount of Downed Wood − .87	*Average Tree Diameter* .73	*Stumps* − .60
.89 Distribution of Downed Wood	.93 Modal Diameter of Trees	− .76 Density of Trees
.87 Evidence of Manipulation of Downed Wood	.82 Variability of Density	− .74 Proportion of Ponderosa Pine
.84 Variability of Downed Wood	− .78 Amount of Rocks	.72 Variability of Downed Wood
− .80 Density of Trees	.76 Variability of Diameter of Trees	− .72 Tree Cover (Crown Canopy)
− .74 Tree Cover (Crown Canopy)	.74 Proportion of Ponderosa Pine	.72 Amount of Rocks
− .71 Proportion of Ponderosa Pine	− .68 Stumps	.70 Dominant Visual Depth
.71 Average Size of Downed Wood	− .64 Brightness	.70 Evidence of Manipulation of Downed Wood
.67 Amount of Sky in Frame	− .62 Variability of Downed Wood	− .68 Average Diameter of Trees
.63 Stumps	− .62 Amount of Downed Wood	.64 Distribution of Downed Wood
− .62 Average Diameter of Trees	.60 Density of Trees	.63 Amount of Downed Wood

*Boldface headings refer to main variables. The numbers to the right of these headings are correlations between the main variable and estimates of scenic beauty (the closer the correlation is to 1.00 or − 1.00, the stronger the relationship; negative correlations mean that the lower the magnitude of the variable, the higher the scenic beauty). Factors under the main variable heading make up that variable. Numbers to the left are correlations between each factor and the main variable. (From Daniel & Boster, 1976.)

tation, vegetation multiplied by area of water, and so on. In another study, Zube, Pitt, and Anderson (1974) studied scenes of the Connecticut River Valley and found that scenic quality was related to such components as land-use compatibility, absolute relative relief (i.e., how much height appeared in a scene, such as from hills), height contrast, and density of edges of bodies of water. Other features that have been found to be important include debris in stream beds, width and height of stream valley, and stream velocity (Pitt, 1976), as well as natural water area, ruggedness, and naturalism (Palmer & Zube, 1976). The results of a study by Daniel and Boster (1976) using a similar Scenic Beauty Estimation (SBE) technique are depicted in Table 2–1 for scenes from the Apache-Sitgreaves National Forest in Arizona.

This physical-perceptual approach does have scientific merit. Whereas the descriptive approach may result in disagreement on the value of a scene, physical-perceptual approaches show cross-cultural agreement (Zube & Mills, 1976) and consistency within a culture (Anderson, Zube, & MacConnell, 1976). Part of the consistency may involve the nature of the judgments about a scene. In general, judgments of preference for a scene show more variability and individual differences, whereas judgments of quality or value seem to be more consistent and have less

Table 2–1. Continued

Tree Density .74	Distribution of Downed Wood −.78	Crown-Cover Canopy .61
.95 Tree Cover	.98 Evidence of Manipulation of Downed Wood	.95 Density of Trees
−.94 Evidence of Manipulation of Downed Wood	−.92 Density of Trees	−.87 Evidence of Manipulation of Downed Wood
−.92 Distribution of Downed Wood	.90 Amount of Downed Wood	−.87 Variability of Downed Wood
−.91 Variability of Downed Wood	.87 Variability of Downed Wood	−.86 Distribution of Downed Wood
.89 Proportion of Ponderosa Pine	−.86 Tree Cover	−.85 Amount of Sky in Frame
−.87 Dominant Visual Depth	−.78 Proportion of Ponderosa Pine	−.84 Dominant Visual Depth
−.82 Amount of Sky in Frame	.76 Amount of Sky in Frame	.84 Proportion of Ponderosa Pine
−.80 Amount of Rocks	.74 Dominant Visual Depth	−.74 Amount of Downed Wood
−.80 Amount of Downed Wood	.71 Average Size of Downed Wood	.74 Amount of Shadow
−.76 Stumps	.67 Amount of Rocks	−.72 Stumps
.71 Amount of Shadow	.65 General Slope of Terrain	−.69 Amount of Rocks
−.65 Average Size of Downed Wood	.64 Stumps	−.68 Brightness
−.62 Brightness		−.65 Average Size of Downed Wood
−.60 Average Diameter of Trees		

individual variation (Coughlin & Goldstein, 1970; Craik, 1970a, 1970b; Fines, 1968; Pitt, 1976; Zube, 1973). Moreover, physical-perceptual approaches do a very respectable job of predicting assessments of scenes (Pitt & Zube, 1979). However, the models derived from such efforts do not always make intuitive and theoretical sense (S. Kaplan, 1975; Weinstein, 1976), and can be cumbersome to work with. What good does it do one, for example, to know that diameter of trees times area of water to the third power predicts scenic value? Returning to our example of the condominium developer, we would need to measure all of the physical components of a scene, discover which of those predict scenic value, and modify the scene to get the maximum value. Such an approach can be and is useful as long as the predictors are simple ones to work with and are relatively few in number. However, the elements that make one scene desirable may make another scene undesirable, so we need to go through the procedure any time we want to modify a different area.

The Psychological Approach to Scenic Value

In addition to the descriptive and physical-perceptual approaches, another method of assessing sce-

PERCEPTION OF AIR POLLUTION IN NATIONAL PARKS

The National Park Service and others are becoming concerned about the impact of air pollution on the scenic vistas of our national parks. Currently, a research program is underway to determine the effects of visual pollution on the enjoyment of a park visit (Malm *et al.,* 1982). Work on this project distinguishes between layered haze and uniform haze. The layered variety is seen as a distinct band, such as a plume of smoke or a band of discolored air across the horizon. Uniform haze, on the other hand, is an overall reduction in air quality (Figure 2–9). In this research, subjects view slides depicting scenic vistas, such as Navajo Mountain in Bryce Canyon National Park in Utah, or a scenic area of the Grand Canyon, and evaluate Perceived Visual Air Quality (PVAQ). So far, researchers have discovered a number of relationships between PVAQ and the type of pollution present. For example:

1. The more contrast between layered haze and a mountain, the worse the PVAQ.
2. The more contrast between layered haze and sky color, the worse the PVAQ.
3. When seen against a background of sky, dark plumes result in a worse PVAQ than light plumes; there is no difference in PVAQ for light vs. dark plumes seen against a background of a scenic feature (such as a mountain).
4. Haze layers or plumes that do not obstruct scenic features have little effect on PVAQ.
5. The more scenic features are obscured by haze, the worse the PVAQ.

Ultimately, this project should result in a better understanding of the effects visual air pollution has on scenic assessment, and will lead to ways of minimizing the deterioration of scenic quality.

Figure 2–9.   This is a scene of Navajo Mountain from Bryce Canyon National Park, similar to the type used in the research program described above. Note the band of pollution across the mountain, which is an example of layered haze. (Although the layer is less obvious in a black and white photo than in color, it can be seen as a lighter streak running the width of the picture just above the mountain.)

nic value is through what Greene (1983) terms the *psychological* approach. Although similar to the physical-perceptual approach, the psychological approach uses not physical components of the scene to predict its value, but rather uses the psychological organization of the elements in the scene. Predictors such as complexity, ambiguity, and coherence, for example, are typically found in models derived from this approach. Moreover, objective, physical measures of complexity or similar psychological predictors in a scene are difficult to obtain, so measures of these factors must be obtained from subjective judgments. In a typical procedure, a panel of judges evaluates scenes on dimensions such as complexity, ambiguity, spaciousness, or uniqueness, and then the same or another panel judges the quality or beauty of the scenes. We present below two such schemes, the aesthetics conceptualization of Berlyne, and another approach to environmental preference developed by Kaplan and Kaplan.

Environmental Aesthetics: The Search for Beauty in Environments. When we examine the multiplicity of factors that influence the perception and evaluation of the environment, the question inevitably arises as to how we make judgments of beauty. Why do we consider a strip mine ugly and a tree-lined boulevard beautiful? Why is the Eiffel Tower thought (by some) to be an attractive landmark but an oil derrick thought (by some) to be an eyesore? The work of Berlyne (1960a, 1972, 1974) on aesthetic judgments in general has been applied to such questions of environmental aesthetics (e.g., Mehrabian & Russell, 1974; Wohlwill, 1976).

Two concepts are central to Berlyne's notions of aesthetics: collative stimulus properties and specific versus diversive exploration. Collative properties of stimuli elicit comparative or investigatory responses. That is, they involve some sort of perceptual conflict that causes us to compare the collative stimulus with other present or past stimuli in order to resolve the conflict. Included among Berlyne's collative properties are *complexity,* or the extent to which a variety of compo-

nents make up an environment; *novelty,* or the extent to which an environment contains new or previously unnoticed characteristics; *incongruity,* or the extent to which there is a mismatch between an environmental factor and its context; and *surprisingness,* or the extent to which our expectations about an environment are disconfirmed. Wohlwill (1976) advocates dividing complexity into diversity (variety of elements) and structural or organizational complexity (variety of structure rather than of components) and adding ambiguity (defined as a conflict between potential interpretations of an environment).

Berlyne also distinguishes between two types of exploration. *Diversive exploration* occurs when one is understimulated and seeks arousing stimuli in the environment, as when one is "trying to find something to do." *Specific exploration* occurs when one is aroused by a particular stimulus and investigates it to reduce the uncertainty or satisfy the curiosity associated with the arousal. Originally, Berlyne formulated his notions of collative properties as adjuncts to his notions of exploration and showed through considerable research that exploration of a stimulus was a function of its complexity, novelty, incongruity, and surprisingness.

Later work by Berlyne (1974) suggested that aesthetic judgments are related to collative properties and exploration along two dimensions. The first dimension is called "uncertainty-arousal." Research suggests that as uncertainty or conflict increases, arousal associated with specific exploration increases. The second factor is called "hedonic tone." This factor is related in an inverted-U fashion to uncertainty: As uncertainty increases, hedonic tone (degree of pleasantness) first increases, then decreases. The latter dimension is closely related to diversive exploration: Apparently we are happiest with intermediate levels of stimulation or uncertainty and do not care for excessive stimulation or excessive arousal. Berlyne contends that aesthetic judgments are related to a combination of these two factors, uncertainty-arousal and hedonic tone. Consequently, those environments that are intermediate on the scale of collative properties and thus intermediate in terms of uncertainty, conflict, or arousal should be the environments judged most beautiful. That is, environments that are intermediate in complexity and novelty and surprisingness should be judged the most beautiful, whereas environments that are extremely high or low in terms of these collative properties should be judged less beautiful or even ugly.

Although Berlyne's suggestion of a curvilinear relationship between uncertainty and beauty is supported somewhat by research on nonenvironmental stimuli (e.g., paintings, music), Wohlwill (1976) points out that data on environmental aesthetics are mixed with respect to corroboration of Berlyne's ideas. The property of complexity appears to offer the strongest support for the validity of Berlyne's ideas as applied to environmental aesthetics. Schwarz and Werbik (1971), for example, made films of simulated trips along a scale-model street in which complexity was varied by manipulating distance of the houses from the street and angle of the houses to the street. Aesthetic judgments were highest at intermediate levels of complexity. Wohlwill (1976) reported similar results by exposing subjects to slides of human-built environments that varied in terms of complexity: Scenes with intermediate complexity were the most liked (Figure 2-10). Interestingly, it is difficult to test this hypothesis with natural scenes because natural scenes do not have as high a level of complexity as scenes of human-built environments (Kaplan, Kaplan, & Wendt, 1972; Wohlwill, 1976).

With respect to novelty, incongruity, and surprisingness, Wohlwill (1976) reports that an inverted-U relationship between aesthetic judgments and these collative properties in environments is difficult to find. Indeed, current research suggests that a rectilinear (direct or straight line) relationship is more correct: The greater the novelty and the surprisingness and the less the incongruity, the more liked the environment. Incongruity in this respect has important implications for site location of human-built structures in natural environments. Generally, the mix of human-built and natural elements is seen as incongruous, but if

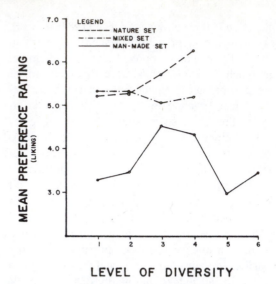

Figure 2-10.   Relationship of complexity (diversity) and preference ratings for natural scenes, human-built scenes, and natural–human-built mixed scenes. Note that natural scenes are preferred over built scenes, and that the highest levels of diversity can be found only in human-built scenes. Adapted from Wohlwill, J. F., Environmental aesthetics: The environment as a source of affect. In I. Altman and J. F. Wohlwill (eds.), *Human Behavior and Environment: Advances in Theory and Research* (Vol. 1). New York: Plenum, 1976.

there is a predominance of natural elements, such a scene can still be viewed as aesthetically pleasing. For example, a number of buildings dotting a wooded hillside tends to be less pleasing aesthetically than a single dwelling on the hillside. A final note on Berlyne's aesthetics: Just as we noted that extreme complexity cannot be found in natural environments, current research has not found aesthetic judgments curvilinearly related to the collative properties of novelty, incongruity, and surprisingness possibly because it has not employed high enough levels of these properties in the environmental scenes that were used.

The Kaplan and Kaplan Preference Model.
Berlyne's work on general aesthetics has important implications for environmental aesthetics. It

does not, however, answer all the questions concerning environmental evaluation. For one thing, Berlyne assumes that identifiable properties in stimuli lead to uniform judgments of beauty or ugliness. Our examination of environmental perception, though, suggested that there are considerable individual differences in perceptions of environments. Presumably, such individual differences should be reflected in evaluations of environments. Moreover, Berlyne assumes that the beautiful is also the preferred. On this basis, once we can identify that which is beautiful, we should be able to predict preferences (i.e., people should prefer what they consider to be beautiful). But how do we explain the fact that some people, if given a choice, would live in upstate New York, others in tropical Florida, others in the near-desert regions of Arizona, and still others along the coast near San Francisco? And why would some people not care for the swamps of Louisiana and others not care for the plains of Kansas? To answer these questions, we need to turn to research on environmental preference. Specifically, we will examine the research of Stephen and Rachel Kaplan and of Joachim Wohlwill.

S. Kaplan (1975) and R. Kaplan (1975) describe the procedures they use in constructing a model of environmental preference. Basically, these researchers collect a large number of slides of various landscapes and ask respondents to classify them according to certain schemes (similar–dissimilar, like–dislike, and so on). Next, using sophisticated mathematical techniques, the experimenters try to identify the elements in the scenes that led to this classification and evaluation. In this way, they derive several factors that can be used to predict preferences for various types of environments. S. Kaplan (1979a, 1979b) describes four factors that appear most important:

1. *Coherence,* or the degree to which a scene "hangs together" or has organization—the more coherence, the greater the liking.
2. *Legibility,* or the degree of distinctiveness that enables the viewer to categorize the contents of a scene—the greater the legibility, the greater the preference.

Figure 2–11. The Kaplans have identified mystery as one factor leading to increased preference. A roadway bending out of sight in the distance generates mystery and seems to require a lot of inference about what lies beyond, while promising information in the future.

3. *Complexity,* or the number and variety of elements in a scene—the greater the complexity, the greater the liking.
4. *Mystery,* or the degree to which a scene contains hidden information so that one is drawn into the scene to try to find this information (e.g., a roadway bending out of sight on the horizon)—the more mystery, the greater the preference (Figure 2–11).

The similarity of some of these dimensions (e.g., complexity, coherence) to Berlyne's collative properties is obvious. A distinction between the Kaplan model and the Berlyne perspective, however, is that the Kaplan model emphasizes the informational content (in a functional or ecological sense) of a scene as one basis for preference judgments. For example, coherence and legibility relate to "making sense" out of the environment, or being able to comprehend it and what is going on in it, and being able to orient oneself within it. On the other hand, complexity and mystery can be considered aspects of "involvement" with the environment, or the degree to which one is

Table 2–2. ORGANIZATION OF THE KAPLAN AND KAPLAN MODEL OF ENVIRONMENTAL PREFERENCE

Complexity of Dimensions Required for Gaining Information	Result of Information Processed	
	Making Sense	Involvement
Two-Dimensional	Coherence	Complexity
Three-Dimensional	Legibility	Mystery

Source: S. Kaplan, 1979a.

stimulated or motivated to want to comprehend it. Table 2–2 represents these components of the Kaplan and Kaplan model as a 2-by-2 matrix. As can be seen, one dimension of this matrix is the ''making sense'' vs. involvement distinction. The other dimension of this matrix revolves around the degree of effort required to analyze the components of the environment or, as indicated in Table 2–2, the complexity of dimensions required in the strategy of analyzing the scene. That is, coherence and complexity are thought to require less inference or analysis, whereas legibility and mystery require a more entailed strategy. In addition to these four factors, Kaplan and Kaplan emphasize the role of familiarity, naturalness, and spaciousness in assessing scenic value. In general, the familiar, tried-and-true, old and genuine aspects of a scene make it desirable; the more green and ''natural'' it is the higher its assessed value; and the more defined the spaciousness the better. With regard to the latter, a broad expanse (such as a desert that never seems to end) is not as desirable as one with some suggested boundaries and definite objects that can be explored (Kaplan & Kaplan, 1978, 1982).

The Kaplan model has been derived from scenes of such diverse environments as roadsides and drainage areas. It has considerable utility in specifying the dimensions that should be considered in designing landscapes, especially when there is a wide range of choice in obtaining just the right combinations of locations on the evaluative dimensions. In other words, the more variety one has to work with, the easier it is to create the preferred landscape.

Evaluation of the Psychological Approach.
The Berlyne conceptualization of aesthetics and the Kaplan and Kaplan preference model are but two specific examples of what we have termed the psychological approach to scenic assessment. Greene (1983) reviews the work of others along these lines. It is encouraging to note that in most cases dimensions such as complexity, coherence, and ambiguity or mystery are found by most researchers to predict scenic value. Unfortunately, there is as yet insufficient agreement on how many of these dimensions we need to assess a scene adequately, and the way we combine the dimensions in judging one scene is not always the way we combine them to judge other scenes. That is, complexity may best predict quality in one scene and mystery may best predict quality in another. For a given scene, however, the psychological approach is useful. Once again returning to the example of our condominium developer, we would expect that judgments of complexity, coherence, and so on in our landscape would help predict changes in scenic quality as we make suggested changes in the design and location of the building.

Before concluding, we should ask how we might account for the fact that in using the same psychological dimensions for evaluating identical environments, individuals often differ in their preferences. One answer lies in Wohlwill's

(1974, 1976) concept of *adaptation level*. Individuals may have different levels of preference for complexity, causing the objectively measurable level of complexity in one scene to be too low for one individual but too high for another. In other words, experience may lead different individuals to prefer different levels of complexity. Wohlwill refers to an individual's optimum level on any one dimension as his or her adaptation level, meaning that deviation from that optimum requires adaptive measures (e.g., arousal reduction or sensation-seeking). In Chapter 3 we will see how adaptation level can be used to explain not only individual differences in environmental evaluation but also individual differences in responses to environmental stimulation.

Summary of Scenic Assessment Techniques

Following the lead of Greene (1983), we have classified scenic assessment approaches as either descriptive, physical-perceptual, or psychological. Although there is overlap among these categories, they are useful for organizing the research that has been conducted to date. Descriptive approaches make use of such elements as line, form, color, and texture, and organize them according to such dominance principles as convergence, enframement, and contrast. Physical-perceptual approaches are scientifically derived and predict how specific physical components of a scene contribute to its perceived value. The mathematical variations of these physical components often make little conceptual sense, however. Psychological approaches obtain judgments of such perceived dimensions as complexity, mystery, coherence, and legibility, and relate these to aesthetic value or preference. These dimensions often vary from scene to scene and from individual to individual, however. Nevertheless, all three approaches are valuable steps in the direction of determining ways of maximizing scenic value, and continued research promises to provide more consistency among the techniques. In the meantime, each approach has advantages in evaluating individual environments for practical purposes.

FORMING ATTITUDES TOWARD THE ENVIRONMENT

Once we perceive air pollution, water pollution, an unusual landscape, or any other aspect of the environment, how do we decide whether to admire it, abhor it, ignore it, eliminate it, or reproduce it? If we decide we do not like it, does that mean we will try to do anything about it? These are the central issues in the study of attitude formation. Generally, an attitude can be defined as a tendency to evaluate an object or an idea in a positive or negative way. That is, attitudes involve affect or emotion—feelings of pleasantness or unpleasantness, like or dislike, for something. Some theorists would add that attitudes also involve cognitions or a set of beliefs that support, justify, or derive from the affective feelings, and still other theorists would include in the definition of attitude a set of behaviors or behavioral dispositions consistent with affect and cognitions. Since environmental perception includes affective and cognitive components, it is easy to see that environmental perception and environmental attitudes are closely related.

For more than two decades, social psychologists have studied and theorized about the factors involved in attitude formation. For a much more thorough discussion of the area than we can give here, we refer you to any basic textbook in social psychology. Although some would question the validity of applying social psychological knowledge of attitudes to environmental psychology (e.g., Proshansky, 1976a), we think that what social psychologists have learned about attitude formation is quite applicable to environmental attitudes. Basically, attitude formation involves principles of learning: Most attitudes appear to be formed through classical or instrumental conditioning, or through social learning.

Classical Conditioning of Attitudes

Suppose that when you first started attending junior high school the school building was typical of other such buildings in your locale. Assume the faculty and curriculum were of average quality and the student body was also typical for your immediate geographic surroundings. Would you not expect that the attitudes of the student body and faculty toward the school environment, curriculum, and education in general also would be "average"? Now suppose we introduce an unpleasant environmental factor, such as the pungent odors of a slaughterhouse and fertilizer plant on the property next to the school. We might certainly expect the attitudes of the student body toward the environment of the school building to be quite negative. Moreover, since the students would not like the smell of the air in the school, they very likely would begin to dislike the curriculum and the faculty and perhaps even show a disdain for education in general.

This example is based on a true situation. The junior high school and slaughterhouse are depicted in Figure 2–12. How were these students' attitudes toward their school environment formed? One theory of attitudes suggests that the basic attitude formation process follows the principles of classical conditioning (Byrne & Clore, 1970; Doob, 1947; Lott & Lott, 1968; Staats, 1968). In classical conditioning (also known as Pavlovian, respondent, or Type I conditioning), we start with an automatic or unconditioned response to an unconditioned stimulus, such as the negative emotional or affective response to pungent odors. Next, we pair a neutral or "conditioned" stimulus, such as a school building, with the unconditioned stimulus for several trials (see Figure 2–13). That is, we present the conditioned stimulus

Figure 2–12. Students in the junior high school to the left experience strong odors from the slaughterhouse in the background. What sort of attitudes toward education might we expect from these students?

followed by the unconditioned stimulus and observe the unconditioned response. After enough trials we can omit the unconditioned stimulus and observe the same affective response (now called a "conditioned response") to the previously neutral (but now conditioned) stimulus. In other words, from an attitudinal standpoint, we learn an unfavorable attitude toward something (an environment, a person, an object, an idea) because it is associated with something we did not like in the first place. Favorable attitudes are learned in the

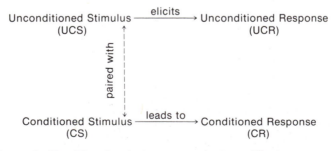

Figure 2–13. The classical or respondent conditioning process.

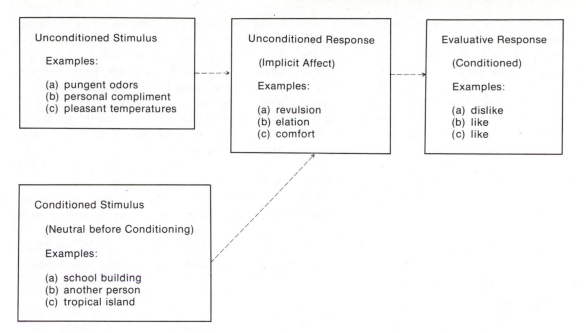

Figure 2–14. The Byrne-Clore Reinforcement–Affect Model of Evaluative Responses.

same way—through association with a liked stimulus. Thus, whether we like or dislike a campground, a neighborhood, a factory, a school, or a city depends to a large extent on the positive and negative experiences we associate with it. Even passing or failing a test can have much to do with how well we like the room in which the class meets.

What sort of attitude do we form toward an environment if we associate it with several pleasant and several unpleasant experiences? From the classical conditioning perspective, the reinforcement–affect model of evaluative responses proposed by Byrne and Clore (1970) is highly applicable. This model, depicted in Figure 2–14, posits that rewarding and punishing reinforcing stimuli (such as pleasant or unpleasant odors, personal compliments or insults) from the physical and social environment elicit covert affective responses in the recipient. That is, rewarding stimuli make us "feel good," and aversive stimuli make us "feel bad." This part of the model is identical to the unconditioned stimulus–uncondi-

tioned response portion of the classical conditioning paradigm, except that the response is an implicit affective reaction rather than an overt behavior. The model further states that any neutral stimulus (such as an environment or a person) associated with the rewarding or punishing stimuli will come to elicit the same degree of positive or negative affect. That is, neutral stimuli are conditioned to elicit unpleasant or pleasant feelings. The overt evaluational response toward either the reinforcing stimuli or the conditioned stimulus is then a function of the degree of pleasantness or unpleasantness of the affective state associated with that stimulus. Thus, when it comes to evaluating the environment, pleasant and unpleasant associations with an environment are *averaged*. Of course, such evaluations are, in the strictest sense of the term, attitudes if they involve assessments of attraction, comfort, beauty, and the like. In the Byrne-Clore model, as in classical conditioning, *any* neutral stimulus associated with pleasant or unpleasant environmental events (i.e., with the unconditioned stimulus) will come to elicit positive or negative affect and will be evaluated accordingly. In our example of the school, unpleasant odors are first associated with the building, then with the faculty and curriculum, then with education per se. This phenomenon is known as *stimulus generalization,* meaning that a variety of related stimuli eventually evoke the same response. Through stimulus generalization, attitudes toward a particular eyesore may generalize first to a neighborhood, then to a community, and then to the residents of the area. Indeed, as we will discuss in Chapter 5, bad odors do lead to negative evaluations of both social stimuli and one's surroundings (Rotton, 1983; Rotton *et al.,* 1978).

Instrumental Conditioning of Attitudes

In addition to classical conditioning, attitudes can be learned through instrumental conditioning, also known as operant, Skinnerian, or Type II conditioning (see also Hildum & Brown, 1956; Insko, 1965). What sort of attitudes would you expect from workers who were told their wages would be increased if they reported their factory environment to be pleasant? What sort of attitudes toward strip mining would you expect from miners whose jobs depend on the mine? What sort of attitudes toward the Environmental Protection Agency would you expect from industry executives who are repeatedly punished for violating pollution laws?

These questions can best be answered by assuming that the attitudes involved are instrumental. That is, expression of an attitude leads to positive or negative consequences, and the attitude that is rewarded will be maintained and strengthened. If your first experience with a slot machine is a lucrative jackpot, you are likely to try the machine several more times. If, however, the machine malfunctions and you receive an electric shock, you are unlikely to keep trying it. Environmental attitudes are often formed in a similar manner. If saving aluminum cans is rewarded by cash payments for the cans, then attitudes (and behavior) toward such cans are likely to be positive. If car pooling to save energy, cut down on freeway traffic volume, and reduce exhaust pollution is punished by members' being forced to ride with a particularly obnoxious person, then attitudes (and behavior) toward car pooling are likely to be negative. Thus, rewards and punishments frequently instrumentally condition our attitudes toward the environment.

As a broader example, labor and management in industries that practice strip mining find pro-strip mining attitudes to be instrumental to their well-being. If it is not practical to mine a particular region in any other way, banning strip mining would probably mean the loss of jobs. Holding pro-strip mining attitudes and supporting pro-strip mining legislation should result in keeping the strip mine open and thus in saving jobs. Merchants who depend on the buying habits of the mine workers would find it "rewarding" or instrumental to hold pro-strip mining attitudes. Local politicians who want to stay in office would also find it instrumental to hold pro-strip mining attitudes. Because of the immediate economic consequences of holding pro-environmental or anti-strip mining attitudes (i.e., anti-strip mining attitudes would be punishing), few residents of a strip mining community could be expected to hold anti-strip mining attitudes. From the instrumental conditioning perspective of attitude formation then, the polarity (pro or con) of an attitude is a function of the positive and negative consequences of holding that attitude.

Social Learning of Attitudes

Another way in which attitudes are formed is through *social* learning. According to social learning theory (e.g., Bandura, 1974), if we observe another person (model) behave in a certain way, we may imitate that behavior. If we see the model rewarded for the behavior, or if we as observers are rewarded for imitating, we are more likely to reproduce the behavior. If, on the other hand, we see the model punished or are punished ourselves, we are less likely to imitate. For example, if a child sees his or her parents constantly litter along highways, the child is likely to imitate the parents, especially if the parents inadvertently reward the child for littering. If we are asked to adjust our thermostats to save fuel, and we see our neighbors comply with this request, we are much more likely to adjust our own thermostats than if our neighbors refuse to comply. As a result, our attitudes toward this form of energy conservation are likely to follow the examples set by others.

These processes of attitude formation are not necessarily independent of each other in any given situation. What if, for example, in our childhood we saw our parents regularly use pesticides, we spilled a pesticide on ourselves one year and became violently ill, and we lost our own garden crop to insects in a later year when we did not use pesticides? In this example, social learning, classical conditioning, and instrumental conditioning are all playing a part in the formation of our attitudes toward the use of pesticides.

MEASURING ATTITUDES TOWARD THE ENVIRONMENT: THE SEARCH FOR THE PEQI

Measuring attitudes toward the environment is much like measuring attitudes toward anything else. Generally, a variety of self-report type scales are used, on which respondents express their opinions about particular environments. The scale depicted on page 15 in Chapter 1 is an example of this type of an environmental attitude measurement technique.

A special effort has been made in recent years to develop measures of environmental quality. Using sophisticated technology, it is possible to assess pollution levels, noise levels, property deterioration, and other directly measurable aspects of the environment. Such measures can be incorporated into an objective indicator, a physical Environmental Quality Index (EQI). However, since the word ''quality'' implies a subjective evalua-

tion, there must be subjective agreement about the composition of an EQI.

An alternative method of assessing environmental quality, which does not require sophisticated technology (although it does require complex psychological measurement techniques) and which allows for individual differences in environmental perception, is the Perceived Environmental Quality Index, or PEQI (pronounced ''Pee-kwee''). The PEQI is designed to serve a number of assessment purposes. It incorporates a support function for the preparation of environmental impact statements and provides baseline data for evaluating environmental intervention programs. It also facilitates comparison of trends in the same environment over time, comparison of different environments at the same time, and detection of aspects of the environment that observers use in assessing quality (which in turn can be used for establishing standards for design and management). Currently, PEQI's exist for assessing air, water, and noise pollution, residential quality, landscapes, scenic resources, outdoor recreation facilities, transportation systems, and institutional or work environments (Craik & Zube, 1976). Some of the dimensions that have been found useful in various PEQI's are depicted in Table 2–3. For examples of specific PEQI's the reader is referred to McKechnie (1974) and Mehrabian and Russell (1974).

The dream of early advocates of the PEQI was to develop a universal standard index or PEQI that could be used to assess all environments. To date, however, only very specifically focused PEQI's have been developed. Bechtel (1976) suggests that the universal PEQI may be an impossible dream. He points out that there are far too many individual and situational determinants of environmental perception for any one instrument to do the job adequately or accurately. Our earlier discussion of such differences in perception bears testimony to Bechtel's reservations. Nevertheless, the PEQI can be quite useful even in very limited situations, and it is the hope of some environmental psychologists that given enough years of PEQI

Table 2–3. SOME DIMENSIONS USED FOR PERCEIVED ENVIRONMENTAL QUALITY INDICES*

Land Dimensions	Residential Quality Dimensions
Topographical texture	Feelings about living in the area
Ruggedness number	Traffic safety
Mean evaluation	Noise that disturbs outdoor activities
Mean slope distribution	Safety of self and property
Naturalism contrast	Solicitors
Height contrast	Maintenance by residents
Area of view	Animal nuisance
Length of view	Alienation among residents
Percentage of tree cover	Nonautomobile mobility
Land use compatibility	Characteristics of people in the area

*Items measuring one or more of these dimensions are included in a PEQI. One's reported satisfaction–dissatisfaction or like–dislike of these elements is a measure of perceived environmental quality. For a *composite* PEQI, a score is reported for each dimension. For a *global* PEQI, one score is reported as a summary index of all dimensions. (Compiled from Carp *et al.,* 1973; Craik & Zube, 1976; Zube, Pitt, & Anderson, 1974.)

development and testing, the impossible dream can be achieved.

CHANGING ATTITUDES TOWARD THE ENVIRONMENT: A PRELUDE

We have seen how attitudes toward the environment are formed and how evaluations are made. What if someone holds environmentally destructive attitudes and is not bothered by scenes of environmental degradation? What can we do to change these attitudes? We will reserve more thorough considerations of these questions for Chapter 12, but for the present we will examine some of the ways social psychologists have found to change attitudes. In addition, we will consider an obviously important issue: If we change attitudes, do we necessarily change behavior?

We frequently hear environmentally oriented messages stated in such a way that they seem to be arousing fear, as in such messages as "Save energy before we run out!" or "Pollution kills!" or "The pollutants from the smokestack cause cancer!" Do such fear appeals change attitudes,

or would the message be just as effective without the fear components? According to the drive reduction theory of attitude change, fear appeals do indeed foster attitude change (Higbee, 1969). This approach is diagrammed in Figure 2–15, in which it can be seen that fear appeal messages increase emotional arousal. The drive reduction theory then makes the assumption that most humans, when aroused by an unpleasant emotion such as fear, will behave in such a way as to reduce this arousal; thus the term "drive reduction" is useful in describing this process. If the fear appeal message also contains recommendations for avoiding the dangerous consequences of not heeding the message, together with assurances that accepting these recommendations will avoid those consequences, then individuals are likely to change their attitudes in the direction of the message in order to reduce their level of arousal. Once the attitude moves in the direction of the message, the reduction in arousal becomes reinforcing (as in instrumental conditioning described earlier), so that the changed attitude becomes strengthened.

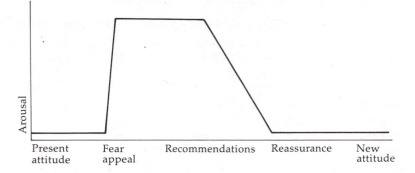

Figure 2–15. The drive-reduction model of the effect of fear appeals on attitude change. Fear appeals increase arousal. Recommendations for avoiding disastrous consequences provide reassurance that one will not be the victim of an ill fate, so arousal returns to a low level. This reduction in arousal reinforces acceptance of the recommendations so a new attitude is formed.

As an example of this drive reduction process, consider an experiment conducted by Harris and Jellison (1971). In this study, subjects heard a message concerning the evils of overuse of pesticides together with suggestions for avoiding the deadly consequences. While they were listening to the message, subjects received faked feedback from a physiograph (they did not realize it was faked) about their degree of fear arousal. Some subjects received no indication of arousal, others received indications of arousal but no indications of arousal reduction, while another group received indications of low arousal during the fear appeal but high arousal during the recommendation part of the message. A fourth group of subjects received feedback suggesting high arousal during the fear appeal but reduced arousal following the recommendations for avoiding the dangers. As predicted by the drive reduction theory, when subjects' attitudes about the use of pesticides were checked, the greatest change toward reduced use of pesticides occurred in the fourth group, which received arousal feedback during the fear appeal but reduced arousal feedback following the recommendation part of the message. According to the drive reduction theory, then, fear appeals may be a successful way of changing attitudes about the environment, provided the fear

appeal is followed by specific suggestions for avoiding the fear-arousing consequences. For more information on the conditions under which fear appeals may lead to attitude change, the reader is referred to Leventhal (1970).

Why are some individuals so resistant to changing their abusive attitudes toward the environment? According to theorist Jack Brehm (1972), part of the answer may be a phenomenon he terms *psychological reactance*. The concept of psychological reactance is based on the notion that humans desire freedom of thought and action, and that they resist any attempt to restrict this freedom. When a particularly forceful individual tries to persuade us to think his or her way about an issue, we sometimes feel that our freedom of choice in deciding about the issue is being threatened. We may resist this threat by rejecting the persuader's arguments and strengthening our own convictions. For example, suppose we wish to convince an audience that buying beverages in recyclable containers is better than buying drinks in nonreturnable, nonbiodegradable containers. If we become very abusive and overly forceful in our persuasive attempts, we may so threaten our audience's freedom of thought that they completely reject our message and continue their environmentally destructive behavior. According to

AN ECOLOGICAL ATTITUDE SURVEY—HOW DO YOU STAND?

Maloney, Ward, and Braucht (1975) constructed an inventory of ecological attitudes and knowledge. Answer the following true–false and multiple-choice questions, then check the answer key and discussion following to see how you did.

1. I'd be willing to ride a bicycle or take the bus to work in order to reduce air pollution.
2. I guess I've never actually bought a product because it had a lower polluting effect.
3. I feel people worry too much about pesticides on food products.
4. I would probably never join a group or club which is concerned solely with ecological issues.
5. I keep track of my congressman's and senator's voting records on environmental issues.
6. It frightens me to think that much of the food I eat is contaminated with pesticides.
7. I would be willing to use a rapid transit system to help reduce air pollution.
8. I have never written a congressman concerning pollution problems.
9. It genuinely infuriates me to think that the government doesn't do more to help control pollution of the environment.
10. I'm not willing to give up driving on a weekend due to a smog alert.
11. I have contacted a community agency to find out what I can do about pollution.
12. I feel fairly indifferent to the statement: "The world will be dead in 40 years if we don't remake the environment."
13. I'm really not willing to go out of my way to do much about ecology since that's the government's job.
14. I don't make a special effort to buy products in recyclable containers.
15. I become incensed when I think about the harm being done to plant and animal life by pollution.
16. I would donate a day's pay to a foundation to help improve the environment.
17. I have attended a meeting of an organization specifically concerned with bettering the environment.
18. I'm usually not bothered by so-called "noise pollution."
19. I would be willing to stop buying products from companies guilty of polluting the environment, even though it might be inconvenient.
20. I have switched products for ecological reasons.
21. I get depressed on smoggy days.
22. I'd be willing to write my congressman weekly concerning ecological problems.
23. I have never joined a cleanup drive.
24. When I think of the ways industries are polluting, I get frustrated and angry.
25. I probably wouldn't go from house to house to distribute literature on the environment.
26. I have never attended a meeting related to ecology.
27. The whole pollution issue has never upset me too much since I feel it's somewhat overrated.
28. I would not be willing to pay a pollution tax even if it would considerably decrease the smog problem.
29. I subscribe to ecological publications.
30. I rarely ever worry about the effects of smog on myself and family.
31. Soil pollution is generally due to: (a) sparse rains; (b) improper farming methods; (c) poisonous metals; (d) overfertilization; (e) poor crop rotation.

32. Most smog in our big cities comes from: (a) automobiles; (b) supersonic jets; (c) industrial plants; (d) large trucks; (e) refuse disposal.
33. High concentrates of chlorinated hydrocarbon residues: (a) cause sheep to die; (b) are found in large amounts in our atmosphere; (c) accumulate in flesh-eating birds and upset breeding behavior; (d) are no longer legal in pesticides; (e) are readily biodegradable.
34. Mercury has been found at unacceptable levels in: (a) fruit; (b) vegetables; (c) seafood; (d) beef; (e) soft drinks.
35. Which of the following does not appreciably reduce pollution by automobiles? (a) properly tuned engine; (b) high octane gas; (c) low lead gas; (d) smog control devices; (e) propane engines.
36. The most common pollutants of water are: (a) arsenic, silver nitrates; (b) hydrocarbons; (c) carbon monoxide; (d) sulfur, calcium; (e) nitrates, phosphates.
37. Ecology is best described as the study of: (a) the relationship between man and the environment; (b) the relationship between organisms and the environment; (c) pollution and its control; (d) the environment; (e) recycling of products.
38. Which of the following materials usually takes longest to decompose? (a) tin; (b) iron; (c) copper; (d) aluminum; (e) steel.
39. Birds and fish are being poisoned by: (a) iron; (b) mercury; (c) silver; (d) lead; (e) magnesium.
40. All but one of the following decompose in ocean water: (a) sewage; (b) garbage; (c) tin cans; (d) plastic bags; (e) chemical fertilizer.
41. What is the harmful effect of phosphates on marine life? (a) causes cancer; (b) renders fish sterile; (c) induces nervous reactions in fish; (d) makes H_2O cloudy; (e) feeds algae, thereby suffocating fish.
42. Which of the following well-known groups is primarily interested in conservation issues? (a) Boy Scouts of America; (b) The Sierra Club; (c) Kiwanis; (d) 4-H Club; (e) The Ecology Association.
43. Practically all of the lead in our atmosphere is caused by: (a) cars; (b) industrial plants; (c) airplanes; (d) burning refuse; (e) cigarettes.
44. DDT takes how long to deteriorate into harmless chemicals? (a) it never does; (b) 10 to 20 months depending on the weather; (c) about 200 years; (d) about 400 years; (e) anywhere from several days to several years.
45. Ecology assumes that man is a (an) _____ part of nature. (a) differential; (b) integral; (c) inconsequential; (d) superior; (e) original.

Analyzing Your Score

This ecological attitudes and knowledge inventory consists of four subscales: Affect (A), or the degree of emotionality an individual associates with environmental issues; Verbal Commitment (VC), or the tendency of an individual to state things he or she is willing to do with regard to environmental issues; Actual Commitment (AC), or what a person states he or she actually does with regard to environmental issues; and Knowledge (K), or how much an individual actually knows about ecological issues. These researchers have found that higher (ecologically supportive) scores on all four subscales are obtained by Sierra Club members than by college students, and that college students score higher than noncollege citizens. Furthermore, the Affect subscale is positively correlated (i.e., a high score on one subscale tends to indicate a high score on the other subscale) with the Verbal Commitment subscale and the Actual Commitment subscale. The

(continued)

Actual Commitment and Verbal Commitment subscales are somewhat correlated with each other, but the Knowledge subscale is not correlated with any of the other subscales.

The scoring key and means for three groups are given below. How do you compare?

Key

Score one point for each answer indicated below. Score each subscale separately. The numbers below refer to the questions that go with each scale. The letters refer to proecological answers.

Affect: 3-F, 6-T, 9-T, 12-F, 15-T, 18-F, 21-T, 24-T, 27-F, 30-F

Verbal Commitment: 1-T, 4-F, 7-T, 10-F, 13-F, 16-T, 19-T, 22-T, 25-F, 28-F

Actual Commitment: 2-F, 5-T, 8-F, 11-T, 14-F, 17-T, 20-T, 23-F, 26-F, 29-T

Knowledge: 31-c, 32-a, 33-c, 34-c, 35-b, 36-e, 37-b, 38-d, 39-b, 40-d, 41-e, 42-b, 43-a, 44-c, 45-b

Means reported by Maloney *et al.* (1975) for three groups:

	Affect	*Verbal Commitment*	*Actual Commitment*	*Knowledge*
Sierra Club	9.00	8.68	8.61	11.35
College Students	7.77	6.37	3.61	8.64
Noncollege	6.12	5.02	1.97	6.75

Scale, key, and means from Maloney, M. P., Ward, M. O., and Braucht, C. N. A revised scale for the measurement of ecological attitudes and knowledge. *American Psychologist*, 1975, *30*, 787–790. Copyright 1975 by the American Psychological Association. Reprinted by permission.

the theory of psychological reactance, a better strategy would be to use a less forceful communication that lets those in the audience make up their own minds.

Once our audience has developed a pro-environmental attitude, how do we prevent it from being changed by less environmentally conscious individuals? According to theorist William McGuire (1961), one way is to *inoculate* our audience against future antagonistic arguments. Such future appeals are likely to include many of the persuasive techniques that we have found effective in swaying the audience to our side. What happens when we present numerous arguments supporting our position, and then the opposing side presents arguments supporting their position? Our audience may find one set of arguments more compelling than another, but which side they accept is anybody's guess and probably depends on many factors. According to McGuire, a better strategy is not just to argue *for* our position but

also to argue *against* the opposite view. By so inoculating the audience, that is, by giving them reason to discount the content of the opponent's arguments, we may so reduce the strength of the opposing view (at least in the minds of our audience) that our position is overwhelmingly persuasive. According to the inoculation approach, when trying to persuade an audience to recycle products, reduce pollution, or adopt conservation-oriented land use policies, the most effective technique is not only to state our view in a persuasive manner but also to state the opposing view ourselves and then offer arguments that refute the opposing position. Alternatively, we could structure the situation so that the audience would develop their own arguments against the opposing view.

It should be obvious that the theories and techniques employed by social psychologists to explain the formation and change of attitudes about social issues can also be used to explain the formation and change of environmentally sound or environmentally destructive attitudes. We should note that other attitude change techniques that we have not covered do exist. We have selected these examples simply because they seem particularly appropriate to the issue presented.

Do Environmental Attitudes Predict Environmental Behavior?

The reason we want to change environmentally destructive attitudes is that we assume attitudes influence behavior. For example, we assume that if someone thinks recycling is a good idea, that person will actively engage in recycling efforts. Similarly, Hummel (1977) has demonstrated a weak link between awareness of pollution and inquiries about pro-environmental groups. But how strong is the attitude–behavior link? For years, social psycholgists have been convinced that on the surface, at least, attitudes often are not consistent with behaviors (cf., Wicker, 1969a). O'Riordan (1976) has reviewed the literature on the relationship between environmental attitudes and behavior and arrives at essentially the same conclusion.

For example, one study noted that during the Arab oil embargo, conservation attitudes went hand-in-hand with conservation behaviors, but after a few weeks conservation behaviors greatly dissipated (Murray *et al.*, 1974). We would think that most people would be concerned about air pollution when official agencies issue smog alerts. Yet Pirages and Ehrlich (1974) noted that following appeals to reduce automobile use during such hazardous periods, San Franciscans did not do so.

If specific attitudes do not reliably predict specific behaviors, is there really an attitude–behavior link? Several alternatives have been offered that promise hope (see also O'Riordan, 1976). For one thing, it may be that attitudes sometimes *follow from* behavior (Bem, 1971; Festinger, 1957; Heberlein, 1972, 1976). That is, it may be that if we first change behaviors, attitudes consistent with those behaviors will develop (see especially Festinger, 1957, on cognitive dissonance theory). Although there is some support for this position in the social psychological literature, it certainly does not always hold true. Just because we are paying for pollution control devices on our cars does not mean that our attitudes toward air

---

ENVIRONMENTAL CONCERN AND ENVIRONMENTAL BEHAVIOR

An interesting study of the relationship between attitudes toward the environment and behavior reflecting these attitudes comes from work by Russell Weigel and his associates (e.g., Weigel & Newman, 1976; Weigel & Weigel, 1978). To assess attitudes, these researchers developed an Environmental Concern Scale, somewhat similar to the one on pages 52–54. Scores from this scale reflect general beliefs about such issues as stronger antipollution laws, conservation of natural resources, protection of wildlife, and reducing energy use. Several weeks after residents of a New England community completed the scale, assistants of the researchers approached the respondents and asked them to sign petitions opposing such issues as oil drilling off the New England coast and construction of nuclear power plants. Later, the respondents were asked to participate in a litter clean-up project and to assist in a recycling effort.

Did scores on the Environmental Concern Scale predict behavior? In general, they did indeed! The more concerned respondents were about environmental issues, the more likely they were to assist with the later behavioral requests. Interestingly, specific behaviors (e.g., signing one petition) did not relate to Environmental Concern Scale scores as well as more general classes of behaviors (e.g., number of petitions signed). Such results would be expected according to our current understanding of the ways attitudes relate to behavior, though there are, of course, exceptions (cf., Heberlein & Black, 1976, 1981; Tucker, 1978).

pollution are changing (O'Riordan, 1976). It could be, of course, that attitudes both precede behaviors and follow from them.

Another alternative to the direct attitude–behavior link has been proposed by Fishbein (1967). According to this view, expressed attitudes are influenced by social norms. These norms, together with attitudes, predict behavioral intentions, which in turn predict overt behaviors. For example, it is normative today to express concern over environmental problems, although actual feelings about air or water pollution may not be as strong as the social norm. As a result, we may say that we *intend* to be environmentally conscious, even though we may not behave in environmentally sound ways. According to Fishbein and Ajzen (1975), a general attitude may not predict a specific behavior; but a multiple-item scale measuring components of an attitude is more likely to predict a *class* of behaviors. A pro-environmentalist may not keep the thermostat at 65°F in the winter, but someone who adheres to several pro-environmental concepts probably *does* engage in more pro-environmental behaviors (recycling, car pooling, water conservation) than someone who is not concerned about the environment.

Another approach to the attitude–behavior problem is that although specific attitudes may also predict specific behaviors, sets of attitudes predict specific behaviors. For example, O'Riordan (1976) found that after all attitudes of consumers toward particular detergents were examined, it became possible to predict whether they would use phosphate or nonphosphate detergents. Just because someone is aware of the environmental dangers of phosphate detergents does not mean he or she will use nonphosphate detergents. Beliefs about which detergent does a better job of cleaning and attitudes about cost may be so important that the individual will not buy the nonphosphate alternative. Even though someone holds an attitude that there is an energy problem, the belief that there is a conspiracy by the oil companies may be so strong that conservation behaviors do not follow (Hummel, Levitt, & Loomis, 1978).

Bruvold (1973) suggests that clusters of attitudes or cognitions are interwoven with behaviors and behavior alternatives, so that in order to change environmental behaviors we must change attitudes and behaviors at the same time. For example, we could encourage energy conservation by imposing monetary penalties for waste (e.g., high taxes on gas-guzzling cars) and monetary rewards for conservation (e.g., rebates on small cars and house insulation), while at the same time starting a massive advertising campaign on the evils of waste and the value of conservation.

The nature (if any) and strength of the relationship between environmental attitudes and environmental behaviors are obviously very complex issues. Resolving these issues must certainly await years of research. In the meantime, is it really worth the effort to try to change environmental attitudes in the direction of greater environmental consciousness? Given the consequences of continued environmentally destructive ways, we think the answer is obviously ''Yes!'' In Chapter 12, we will suggest some of the directions these efforts should take.

CHAPTER SUMMARY

Whereas the conventional approach to perception examines the ways the brain interprets messages from sensory organs about specific elements in the environment, environmental perception views the perceptual experience as more encompassing. Ittelson suggests that environmental perception contains cognitive, affective, interpretive, and evaluative properties. Moreover, environmental perception examines the person–environment system as the unit of study and considers information processing as central to the perceptual process. In addition, environmental perception involves activity on our part, especially in the realm of exploring the environment to see what needs it meets.

Adaptation or habituation refers to the weakening of a response following repeated exposure to a stimulus. Adaptation becomes critical in hazard perception, in which such phenomena as the crisis effect and the levee effect are noted. Cultural and social factors can also influence perception, especially when individuals are raised in either mostly built or mostly natural environments.

Environmental cognition encompasses the general ways of thinking about, recognizing, and organizing the layout of an environment. Cognitive maps are our mental representations of this layout, and can be analyzed through examining their major components: paths, edges, districts, nodes, and landmarks. Cognitive maps are not perfectly accurate representations of the environment; they do contain errors. Familiarity with an area helps explain sex differences and socioeconomic differences in the details of cognitive maps. Current thinking includes the idea that cognitive maps are stored in the brain through a propositional, meaning-based network, and the idea that organization may also be analogical or imaginal.

Methods of assessing scenic quality of an environment can be classified as descriptive, physical–perceptual, or psychological. The descriptive approach employs such dominance principles as convergence, enframement, and contrast. The physical–perceptual approach quantifies physical components of the scene and derives a mathematical formula for predicting scenic value from these physical elements. The psychological approach, on the other hand, uses psychological rather than physical properties of the scene to predict value. Berlyne proposes that aesthetic judgments are a function of collative properties (complexity, novelty, incongruity, and surprisingness) and of diversive and specific exploration. Although Berlyne indicates that environments with intermediate levels of the collative properties should be evaluated as most beautiful, research suggests that at least for natural environments, high concentrations of a collative property lead to the highest judgments of beauty. The Kaplan and Kaplan model of preference has identified the dimensions of coherence, legibility, complexity, and mystery as most important in scenic assessment. Familiarity and naturalness are also positively associated with preference for a scene.

Environmental attitudes can be formed through classical conditioning, in which environments are associated with positive and negative events; through instrumental conditioning, in which we are rewarded or punished for holding certain attitudes; or through social learning, in which attitudes are formed by observing the attitudes and behaviors of others. One device for measuring our feelings about environments is the Perceived Environmental Quality Index, or PEQI.

Changing attitudes toward the environment involves such techniques as fear appeals, avoidance of psychological reactance, and use of inoculation procedures to counter opposing arguments. An important related item is whether attitudes really predict behavior. Apparently, if enough specific attitudes are measured and enough behavioral criteria pooled, environmental attitudes can to some extent predict environmental behaviors.

Suggested Projects

1. Ask several friends to draw cognitive maps of your campus. Are the major components and errors similar, or do they differ according to the academic majors of your friends? Are cognitive maps of the campus more detailed and accurate than maps of the community?

2. Look in magazines for various kinds of natural and human-built scenes. What dominance principles are present? What would you do to the human-built scenes to make them more attractive?

3. Use the same scenes from Number 2 above. Try to rank them in terms of collative properties. Do these properties relate to your judgments of beauty in the pictures? Are there differences between natural and built environments? Do classmates agree with your rankings?

4. Administer an environmental attitude survey (use the one on page 52 or construct your own) to a large number of students. Do attitudes differ as a function of students' majors, sex, or size of hometown?

3 Theories of Environment–Behavior Relationships

INTRODUCTION

Let us travel back for a moment to a mythical kingdom where there lived an intelligent people ruled by a benevolent royalty. For reasons no one could understand, the kingdom was plagued by periodic winds that could ruin crops, topple peasant homes, and even blow the royal knights off their royal horses. One day a particularly strong wind hit the kingdom, and the royal family decreed that the damage associated with the winds had to stop. They promptly summoned the royal scientist and informed her (forward-looking, nonsexist mythical kingdoms did exist at that mythical time, you know!) that if she wished to remain on the royal payroll she would have to find a way to keep the wind from wreaking havoc on the kingdom. She began by recording everything that happened when a wind struck. Her most enlightening discovery was that the more the wind bent the chains of the royal drawbridge, the greater the damage observed across the kingdom. "Eureka!" shouted the scientist, "I can stay on the royal payroll!"

She then went to the royal chainmaker and procured 10 three-foot lengths of chain, each made out of a different weight of links. Outside the royal castle she erected a horizontal bar and suspended the chains over it in order of their weight. She now had a way to measure the force of any wind coming through the kingdom. Keeping careful notes, she observed that a wind capable of moving the eight lightest chains would destroy the peasants' huts, any wind that moved the nine lightest chains would knock the royal knights off their royal horses, and any wind that moved all 10 chains would tear the shutters off the royal dining room. The scientist then arranged for the royal family to hire a royal chainwatcher, who observed the chains and sounded a warning to the royal family and to the peasants whenever the chains indicated a wind strong enough to disrupt their lives was about to hit.

Having thus saved her own royal job, the scientist went on to make more and more scientific observations of the effects of winds of varying forces on the daily lives of the kingdom's inhabitants. Soon she was able to predict from the "chain strength" of the wind not only crop losses but also the disruptive effects of the wind on family life, children walking to school, milk production of the royal dairy herd, and even the pleasantness of the mood of the royal family. Priding herself on the scientific merit of her discoveries, she published her work in the royal scientific journals. When the royal family saw the journal article, "Effects of Wind Chain Force on the Royal Kingdom: A Psychological Stress Theory," they were puzzled as to why psychological stress had anything to do with wind. Summoning the royal scientist, they queried her about the matter. She replied that although *physical effects* of the wind could be easily observed, in her opinion the *psychological* reaction to loss of property, inconvenience, and being knocked off one's horse was another important influence of the wind in the kingdom.

The idea of stress in her model was based more on inference than on direct observation, but using the concept of psychological stress had some distinct advantages. Specifically, it helped explain why wind had some of the same effects on people as marital stress, battle fatigue, and the loss of crops through drought. Moreover, incorporating the idea of psychological stress into her model of wind effects helped predict such things as loss of work efficiency and the mood of the royal family when making important decisions for the kingdom. Finally, the scientist explained, since much is known about controlling psychological stress, using this knowledge to train the kindgom's inhabitants in more healthy ways of reacting to the wind should help reduce many of the undesirable consequences of exposure to it.

The above tale is intended to illustrate the scientific approach to studying environment–behavior relationships as well as the role of theory in such scientific endeavors. As typically happens in environmental psychology, our mythical scientist first made observations about the effects of wind on behavior, then made theoretical inferences about these effects, and finally used the theoretical notions to explain even more behavioral phenomena. In this chapter we will examine the use and development of those theories in environmental psychology that attempt to explain the influence of environment on behavior. We will begin with a general discussion of the concept and function of theory, then examine some specific psychological theories that have evolved on the nature of environment–behavior relationships, and conclude with our own synthesis of these various orientations.

THE NATURE AND FUNCTION OF THEORY IN ENVIRONMENTAL PSYCHOLOGY

The scientific method is really little more than a specific way of gaining knowledge. Scientists, whether devotees of environmental psychology or any other field, assume there is a great deal of order in the universe that can be discovered with appropriate methodology. Before the application of scientific inquiry, however, this universal order is perceived more as chaos or uncertainty than as something systematic. Science (or more specifically the scientific method) is simply a set of procedures for reducing this uncertainty, thereby gaining knowledge of the universal order. It is to these procedures that we owe our progress thus far in environmental psychology. Other approaches to gaining knowledge do exist of course, such as the methods of religion. In religion, the basis of reducing uncertainty is tradition, faith, revelation, and, in many cases, experience. The basis of reducing uncertainty in the scientific approach, on the other hand, is mathematical prediction of *observable* events. Once we can predict

with near perfection what will happen to phenomenon "A" (e.g., crime or violence) when a change occurs in phenomenon "B" (e.g., population density), we have taken a giant step toward a scientific understanding of these phenomena.

For example, before the application of scientific methods, we do not know the principles involved in getting people to reduce air pollution. We assume that such principles exist, however (e.g., appealing to conscience, fear appeals, government regulations, administering punishment), and that through scientific inquiry we can not only discover them, but we can also predict how much air pollution will be reduced by applying the principles in varying amounts and combinations. Moreover, the principles should also predict the positive and negative consequences of their application (e.g., cleaner air, better health, potentially reduced profits and productivity of an industry, higher utility bills). Such predictions, however, are rarely perfect. To the extent that our prediction of the phenomena is not perfect, uncertainty remains about the portion of the ordered universe under study. Like the royal scientist, we continue our quest for knowledge.

Given this perspective of scientific inquiry, it becomes apparent that, at least in its basic form, environmental psychology accepts the notion of *determinism.* That is, scientists assume that events in the universe are *caused* by other events in the universe, and that through scientific inquiry these causes can be discovered and their effects predicted. Using scientific methods, environmental psychologists observe fluctuations in these causes (e.g., climate changes, inadequate space in an office) and predict the subsequent effects (e.g., violence, reduced productivity, efforts to change interior design of space). In psychology, the basic assumption is that behavior is determined by the environment, genetics, or intrapsychic (cognitively or emotionally generated) events. Research in psychology, then, is the search for the antecedents of our various behaviors. From the perspective of a purist, once we decide that a phenomenon, psychological or otherwise, is indeterminate or is unpredictable, we are really saying that this phenomenon is not within the realm of scientific inquiry and that we cannot gain knowledge about it through scientific methods.

If we make the assumption of determinism in environmental psychology and proceed with scientific research, what happens next? Like the royal scientist, we probably start with simple observations. We might observe, for example, that as population density increases in urban areas, crime rates go up. We have observed two phenomena, population density and crime rates, and we have noted a relationship between the two: as one increases, the other increases (i.e., they are positively correlated). We might then *hypothesize,* or formulate a hunch, that high population density leads to increased aggression and violence. The critical step in scientific methodology is the next one—that of testing the hypothesis. All methods of gaining knowledge generate hypotheses. What makes science unique is the method of verifying the hypotheses. Whereas religion may rely on faith, tradition, or individual experience to verify hypotheses, science insists that hypotheses be verified by publicly observable

(empirical) data. Recall that we described in Chapter 1 several means of acquiring such data. When these observable data do not support the hypothesis, the scientist must either modify the hypothesis or generate an entirely new hypothesis and test it again. If we were to find, for example, that putting several groups of people into crowded rooms did not increase their level of aggressiveness, we would have to reject our simple hypothesis that crowding leads to increased aggression. We might then modify the hypothesis to state that in conditions of poverty, crowding leads to increased aggression and then test this hypothesis by comparing poor and rich individuals under uncrowded and crowded conditions. We then would accept or reject this hypothesis on the basis of the publicly observable data.

This level of scientific research is generally referred to as *empirical,* meaning observable. Once we have gathered a number of empirical facts, we might then proceed to a more abstract and theoretical level. Historically, environmental psychology has followed this course: Once enough empirical facts are known, theories begin to be constructed to explain these facts. Before discussing the general nature of theory, however, perhaps a word on the distinction between empirical laws, theories, and models is in order. Empirical laws are statements of simple observable relationships between phenomena (often expressed in mathematical terms) that can be demonstrated time and time again. Such things as the law of gravity, the law that magnetic opposites attract, and the law of effect in psychology (e.g., behaviors that lead to pleasurable consequences are likely to be repeated) are easy to demonstrate at an empirical level. Theories usually involve more abstract concepts and relationships than empirical laws and consequently are broader in scope. Theories are not as a rule demonstrable in one empirical setting but are inferred from many empirical relationships. Finally, a model is usually more abstract than an empirical law but is often not as complex as a theory, and it is thus an intermediate step between the demonstration of an empirical law and the formulation of a theory. The distinction can be made that a model is the application of a previously accepted theoretical notion to a new area, but in practice the terms ''model'' and ''theory'' are often used interchangeably.

Basically, a *theory* consists of a set of concepts plus a set of statements relating the concepts to each other. At the theoretical level, we might say that the undesirable effects of high population density are *mediated* by the stress associated with high density. That is, high population density leads to stress, and stress in turn may lead to a variety of undesirable consequences, such as increased violence or mental illness. The concept of stress in this example is relatively abstract, in that it is not directly observable but rather is inferred from events that are observable. Such inferred phenomena are often termed *intervening constructs* or *mediating variables*. Empirically, we might infer stress from autonomic arousal (e.g., increased blood pressure, heart rate, or galvanic skin response), from verbal and nonverbal signs of anxiety, or from a disintegrated quality of behavior. The distinction between direct observation and abstract inference is one of the main differences between the empirical and theoretical levels of scientific inquiry.

We can identify at least three basic functions of theories. First, theories help us to predict relationships between variables, which implies that we can control what happens to one variable by regulating another variable. For example, if we know that certain conditions of crowding lead to violence (i.e., cause violence), we can control the violence to some extent by changing the crowded conditions. If our crowding theory says that stress mediates a relationship between crowding and violence, we might also control violence by controlling stress.

A second function of theories is to summarize large amounts of data. Instead of having to know thousands of pieces of data about the levels of stress and violence under thousands of levels of crowding, if we have a good theory we can summarize all this information in a few theoretical statements. Such summaries in turn help us predict events that we may not yet have observed at the empirical level.

A third function of theories is the generalization of concepts and relationships to many phenomena, which helps to summarize the knowledge in a particular area. For example, if our theory states that high levels of stress lead to increased levels of violence, this implies that we can generalize the theoretical notion to *any* factor that increases stress, including crowding, noise, poverty, marital discord, and (as our royal scientist suggested) wind. Furthermore, if we can establish that a particular environmental event, such as wild fluctuations in temperature, is stressful, then we can infer from our stress theory that this environmental event will lead to more violence. If empirical evidence does not suggest that a theory generalizes very well, the theory should be modified or rejected in favor of theories that do offer good generalizability (Figure 3–1).

In addition to these three basic functions, theories are useful in other ways. For one thing, they help to generate additional research by suggesting new relationships between variables. Many scientists assert that the best research is that generated by theories. Another use for theories is in the application of research to practical problems. Solutions to problems are often needed quickly, with little time available for basic research. If theories already exist, they can suggest solutions or at least directions for testing solutions. In a broader sense, theories can help guide policy decisions. Nuclear theory, for example, gives us an idea of the feasibility of widespread use of nuclear generators for electricity as well as an idea of the environmental hazards involved and thus is useful in establishing public and private policies on nuclear power.

Theories in environmental psychology, as in any scientific field, must be constantly evaluated, just as hypotheses must be verified. The basic functions of theories suggest the criteria by which theories should be evaluated. First, a theory is valuable to the extent that it predicts. Given two

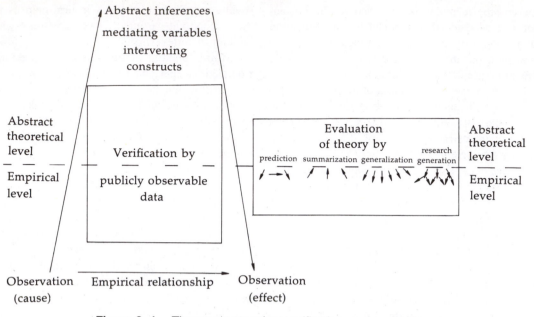

Figure 3–1.   Theory construction, verification, and evaluation.

theories about the same environment–behavior relationship, the one that predicts most accurately most of the time is considered more valuable. Second, good theories do a superior job of summarizing many empirical relationships. Third, a valid theory must be very generalizable. Again, given two theories about the effects of noise on performance, the one that applies to more situations is the more valuable. Fourth, the most useful theories suggest new hypotheses to be tested empirically. In most scientific endeavors, much of the significant research is generated from theories rather than used to construct new theories. Since this research is crucial to our understanding of the phenomena under study, theories that suggest new areas of investigation are highly valued. Because one of the problems often mentioned with environmental psychology is the lack of direction in its research, many environmental psychologists await the appearance of theories that will suggest more unifying approaches. We turn now to some of the theories already in use in environmental psychology.

ENVIRONMENT–BEHAVIOR THEORIES: FLEDGLING THEORIES IN A FLEDGLING FIELD

As we have just stated, one of the difficulties facing environmental psychology is the lack of a unifying direction in the research of the field. Since one of the functions of good theories is to provide a focus for research, a number of environmental psychologists have made efforts to build models and theories about environment–behavior relationships. Elaborate theories that meet the criteria of good prediction, summarization, generalization, and research generation are not feasible at this time for at least two reasons. First, the field of environmental psychology is so young that in many cases not enough observations have been made and not enough data have been collected for researchers to be confident about the concepts and relationships (the building blocks of a theory) involved. Second, where sufficiently proven concepts and relationships do exist they are so diverse (i.e., they tend to differ from one piece of research to another) that they are difficult to define with the degree of specificity required for a theory (see also Proshansky, 1973).

Since elaborate theoretical systems are not very feasible in environmental psychology at this time, less elaborate theories, each restricted to its own predictive domain, have been developed within the field. Theories or models restricted to environmental perception (e.g., the Kaplan and Kaplan model) have been covered in the previous chapter. In this chapter, we will present a set of theories whose predictive domains are restricted to the effects of environmental conditions on behavior. The empirical data to which these theories are most applicable will be described in subsequent chapters on such topics as noise, weather, air pollution, the city, personal space, and crowding. Specifically, we will examine for now the following six theoretical perspectives, which are probably the most dominant ones in environmental psychology: (1) the arousal approach; (2) the stimulus load approach (overload and underload); (3) the adaptation level approach; (4) the behavior constraint approach; (5) the ecological psychology approach; and (6) the stress approach. Because much of the contribution of these first five approaches (especially the first four) can be incorporated into various aspects of the stress approach, and because stress formulations have been relied upon heavily in environmental psychology, we will elaborate upon environmental stress even more in the next chapter.

Before elaborating on these various approaches, it will be helpful to keep several points in mind. First, theoretical concepts are not always easy to grasp, and the reader may feel overwhelmed with just one reading of this chapter. Full development and application of the material will become clearer in subsequent chapters. Second, we often rely on more than one theory to explain a given phenomenon. As we will see in the discussion of stress, the mediators of these various conceptual approaches often occur together, and it is sometimes useful to appeal to more than one approach to explain the data.

Finally, different theories are useful at different levels of analysis. As we will see, ecological psychology is especially applicable to group behavior, whereas the other approaches are often more useful at the individual level of analysis.

The Arousal Approach

One effect of exposure to environmental stimulation is increased arousal, as measured physiologically by heightened autonomic activity (increased heart rate, blood pressure, respiration rate, adrenaline secretion, etc.) or behaviorally by increased motor activity, or simply as self-reported arousal. From a neurophysiological perspective, arousal is a heightening of brain activity by the arousal center of the brain, known as the *reticular formation* (Hebb, 1972). Berlyne (1960a) has characterized arousal as lying on a continuum anchored at one end by sleep and at the other by excitement or heightened wakeful activity. Since arousal is hypothesized to be a mediator or intervening variable in many types of behavior, a number of environmental psychologists have turned to this concept to explain many of the influences of the environment on behavior.

In fact, Mehrabian and Russell (1974) have identified arousal as one of three dimensions (the others are pleasure and dominance) along which *any* environment can be described. The arousal model makes distinct predictions about the effects on behavior of *lowered* arousal (i.e., toward the "sleep" end of the continuum) as well as *heightened* arousal, and is quite useful in explaining some behavioral effects of such environmental factors as temperature (Bell, 1981), crowding (Evans, 1978; Seta, Paulus, & Schkade, 1976), and noise (Broadbent, 1971). We should emphasize that pleasant as well as unpleasant stimuli heighten arousal. An attractive member of the opposite sex or a thrilling ride at an amusement park can be just as arousing as noxious noise or a crowded elevator.

What happens to behavior when the arousal level of the organism moves from one end of the continuum to the other? As you might expect,

DETECTING LEVELS OF AROUSAL: MEASURE FOR MEASURE

Measuring arousal is one of the greatest problems for research that uses this concept to explain behavior. Since arousal is a relatively abstract concept, it must be inferred from empirical evidence. Listed below are some of the indicators that researchers have used as empirical evidence of arousal:

Heart rate
Blood pressure
Respiration rate
Blood vessel constriction
Galvanic skin response, or GSR (electrical conductance of skin due to sweat)
Palmar sweat index (reaction of palm sweat with a chemical)
Urine secretion
Brain wave activity
Physical activity level
Muscle tension
Skin temperature
Self-report scales

Unfortunately, these measures do not always indicate the same level of arousal. In fact, at the same time one measure indicates increased arousal, other measures may indicate decreased arousal. Such a predicament certainly arouses consternation on the part of the researcher! (See the Appendix for additional discussion of these methods.)

several things occur. For one, arousal leads people to seek information about their internal states. That is, we try to interpret the nature of the arousal and the reasons for it. Is the arousal pleasant or unpleasant? Is it due to people around us, to perceived threat, or to some physical aspect of the environment? In part, we interpret the arousal according to the emotions displayed by others around us (Schachter & Singer, 1962; Scheier, Carver, & Gibbons, 1979). In addition, the causes to which we attribute the arousal have significant consequences for our behavior. For example, if we attribute the arousal to our own anger, even though it may be due to a factor in the environment, we may become more hostile and aggressive toward others (e.g., Zillmann, 1979). However, attributing the arousal to anger may not be the only reason for increased aggression. According to several theories of aggression (Berkowitz, 1970; Zillmann, Katcher, & Milavsky,

1972), if aggression is the response most likely to occur in a particular situation, then heightened arousal will facilitate aggression. We find, for example, that when noise increases arousal, it may also increase aggression (Geen & O'Neal, 1969). (See also Chapter 4.)

Another reaction we have when we become aroused is to seek the opinions of others. We in part compare our reactions to those of others to see if we are acting appropriately and to see if we are better off or worse off than others (Festinger, 1954; Wills, 1981). This process is known as *social comparison*. Victims of a natural disaster, for example, become very aroused by the circumstances and seek to compare their fate with the fate of others.

Arousal also has important consequences for performance, especially as formulated through the *Yerkes-Dodson Law*. According to this law, performance is maximal at intermediate levels of

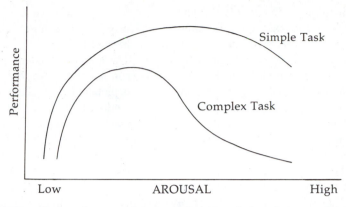

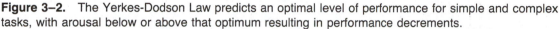

Figure 3–2. The Yerkes-Dodson Law predicts an optimal level of performance for simple and complex tasks, with arousal below or above that optimum resulting in performance decrements.

arousal and gets progressively worse as arousal either falls below or rises above this optimum point. Moreover, the inverted-U relationship between arousal and performance varies as a function of task complexity. For complex tasks, the optimum level of performance occurs at a slightly lower level of arousal than for simple tasks, as depicted in Figure 3–2. This curvilinear relationship appears consistent with other findings (see page 41) that humans seek an intermediate level of stimulation—too much or too little is undesirable (Berlyne, 1960a, 1974). From an environment–behavior perspective, we would expect that as environmental stimulation from crowding, noise, air pollution, or any other source increases arousal, performance will either improve or deteriorate, depending on whether the affected person's response is below, at, or above the optimum arousal level for a particular task (see also Broadbent, 1971; Hebb, 1972; Kahneman, 1973). Apparently, low arousal is not conducive to maximum performance, and extremely high arousal prevents us from concentrating on the task at hand.

The arousal approach fares reasonably well as a theoretical base in environmental psychology, although it does have shortcomings. Performance and aggression can be predicted from the effects of the environment on arousal, and the arousal notion does generalize to several environmental

factors, most notably noise, heat, and crowding. Unfortunately, arousal is very difficult to measure (see box, page 64). Physiological indices of arousal are not always consistent with each other and are often not consistent with self-report paper-and-pencil measures of arousal (cf., Cervone, 1977; Lacey, 1967). Whereas one measure may indicate increased arousal in a given situation, other measures may show decreased or unchanged arousal. Which measure to choose in predicting behavior thus becomes a serious problem. Nevertheless, the arousal notion is a useful one and will probably continue to be incorporated into those environment–behavior relationships to which it is applicable.

The Environmental Load Approach

Imagine you are trying to study for three exams you have the following day but your roommate wants to watch television, there is a loud party next door, and two friends come by to entice you to go out for a drink. How can you possibly study for your exams with all this going on? The situation is similar to the circumstances under which the environmental load approach explains environment–behavior relationships. One consequence of exposure to many types of environmental stimuli is that attention becomes focused on them, often to the detriment of other stimuli relevant to the organism's functioning. Cohen (1978) and Milgram (1970) have developed this attention-narrowing process into models that handle much of the data collected about exposure to novel or unwanted environmental stimuli. Rather than explaining the effects of complex environmental stimulation by using strictly the concept of arousal, Cohen and Milgram suggest that the limited capacity of humans to process information accounts for the effects of exposure to these stimuli. Specifically, when the amount of information from the environment exceeds the individual's capacity to process all that is relevant, *information overload* occurs. In response to this overload, the primary coping strategy is to ignore some of the stimulus inputs. It is this ignoring of inputs, according to the environmental load theorists, that accounts for the positive or negative behavioral effects of excessive environmental stimulation (Broadbent, 1958, 1963; Cohen, 1978; Easterbrook, 1959).

A more detailed explanation of the environmental load approach can be found in Cohen's (1978) model, which contains the following four basic assumptions:

1. Humans have a limited capacity to process incoming stimuli and can invest only a limited effort in attending to inputs at any one time.
2. When environmental inputs exceed capacity to attend to them, the normal strategy is to ignore those inputs that are less relevant to the task at hand and to devote more attention to those that are relevant.
3. When a stimulus occurs that may require some sort of adaptive response (or when an individual thinks such a stimulus will occur), the significance of the stimulus is evaluated by a monitoring process, and a decision is made about which coping responses, if any, to employ. Thus, the more intense or unpredictable or uncontrollable an input, the greater its adaptive significance and the more attention paid to it. Furthermore, the more uncertainty generated

by an input about the need for an adaptive response, the more attentional capacity allocated to it.
4. The amount of attention available to a person is not constant and may be temporarily depleted after prolonged demands. After attending to prolonged demands, the total capacity for attention may suffer from an overload. For example, after studying hard for several hours, it is difficult to do anything that demands much attention.

What happens to behavior when an overload occurs? The answer depends on which stimuli are given adequate attention and which are ignored. Generally, stimuli most important to the task at hand are allocated as much attention as needed, and less important stimuli are ignored. If these less important stimuli tend to interfere with the central task, ignoring them will enhance performance. If, however, a task requires a wide range of attention, as when we must do two things at once, performance on less important tasks will deteriorate. In an interesting demonstration of this process, Brown and Poulton (1961) required subjects driving a car either in a residential area (relatively small number of important inputs) or in a crowded shopping center (relatively large number of important inputs) to listen to a series of taped numbers and determine which numbers changed from one sequence to the next. More errors were made on this secondary numbers task when subjects drove in the shopping center, presumably because in the shopping center more attention had to be allocated to important stimuli connected with driving, to the detriment of the less important stimuli of the numbers task.

According to the overload model, once capacity for attention has been depleted owing to prolonged demands, even small demands for attention may cause overloading. Interestingly, once exposure to unpleasant or excessive stimulation has ceased, behavioral aftereffects, such as decreased tolerance for frustration, errors in mental functioning, and less frequent altruistic behavior, may occur (see Chapters 4 and 5 for research examples). The overload model attributes these aftereffects to a reduced capacity to attend to relevant cues. Milgram (1970) suggests that the deterioration of social life in large urban areas is caused by the ignoring of peripheral social cues and a reduced capacity to attend to them because of the increased demands of everyday functioning. Thus, urban ills, such as bystanders ignoring others in distress, may be due in part to an environmental overload in which the hustle and bustle of everyday life in the city requires so much attention that there is very little left over for "peripheral" social concerns. Some city dwellers may be forced to develop an aloof attitude toward others in order to allocate enough time to everyday functioning (see Chapter 8).

The environmental load model stands up to theoretical scrutiny about as well as the arousal model. It does predict some of the behavioral consequences of excessive environmental stimulation. However, there are many difficult-to-determine "if's" incorporated into the model, including whether or not in a given situation an overload occurs, whether a specific task is important, whether ignoring less important stimuli facilitates or impairs performance on a particular task, and whether demand has been sufficiently prolonged to deplete attentional capacity. In terms of generality, the model applies to mental and motor performance and to at least some social behaviors. As far as generating research is concerned, the environmental load model does suggest many possibilities, including evaluating whether or not a given environment is likely to produce an overload, and assessing the extent to which attentional depletion contributes to social and environmental problems.

The Understimulation Approach

The environmental overload approach suggests that many environment–behavior relationships, especially those leading to undesirable behavioral and affective (emotional) consequences, are a function of too much stimulation from too many sources. A number of theorists have suggested, however, that many environment–behavior prob-

lems result from *too little* stimulation. Sensory deprivation studies (e.g., Zubek, 1969) suggest that depriving individuals of all sensory stimulation leads to severe anxiety and other psychological anomalies, and other research has documented the deleterious effects of understimulation on the maturational development of the young (e.g., Schultz, 1965). Drawing on these sources, some theorists suggest that the environment should sometimes be made *more* complex and stimulating in order to restore excitement and a sense of belonging to individuals' perceptions of their environment.

Although cities may have an overstimulating social environment, they may subject inhabitants to an understimulating physical environment. Urbanologist A. E. Parr (1966) contends that fields, forests, and mountains contain an unending variety of changing patterns of visual stimulation, but that urban areas contain the same patterns repeated on every street. In many tract housing developments in particular, the structures all resemble each other. According to Parr, the giant skyscrapers lining city streets and the interiors of modern windowless structures instill a sense of enclosure rather than a sense of being drawn to the next horizon. Parr and others assert that this lack of stimulation leads to boredom and is in some way responsible for such urban ills as juvenile delinquency and vandalism, and poor education (cf., Heft, 1979b).

To better study some of these problems of understimulation, Wohlwill (1966) advocates scaling environments along a number of dimensions of stimulation, including intensity, novelty, complexity, temporal change or variation, surprisingness, and incongruity. As we will see in Chapter 8, the desire for these types of stimulation may explain why people leave cities in great numbers to live in more "natural" environments.

As a theoretical approach by itself, the understimulation angle does help predict some environment–behavior relationships, but it stands in marked contrast to arousal and overload theories that examine the same environments and find too much stimulation. Moreover, some researchers claim there are benefits to be derived from deprivation of sensory stimulation (e.g., Suedfeld, 1975). We will reserve further judgment on the understimulation theory until we have examined a theoretical approach that attempts to consolidate the understimulation and overstimulation approaches.

Adaptation Level Theory: Optimal Stimulation

If the research evidence supporting the arousal and overload theories suggests that too much environmental stimulation has deleterious effects on behavior and emotions, and if the evidence supporting the understimulation approach suggests that too little stimulation similarly has undesirable effects, it stands to reason that some intermediate level of stimulation would be ideal. This is the approach taken by Wohlwill (1974) in his *adaptation level* theory of environmental stimulation. Borrowing from Helson's (1964) adaptation level theory of sensation and perception, Wohlwill begins with the assumption, for example, that humans dislike crowds, at least on certain occasions, as when trying to make last-minute Christmas purchases or trying to leave a packed football stadium at the end of the game. On the other hand, most of us do not like total social isolation all day either. Wohlwill believes that the same applies for all types of stimulation, including temperature, noise, and even the complexity of roadway scenery. What we usually prefer is an optimal level of stimulation.

Categories and Dimensions of Stimulation.

At least three categories of environment–behavior relationships should conform to this optimal level hypothesis, according to Wohlwill. These categories are sensory stimulation, social stimulation, and movement. Too much or too little sensory stimulation is undesirable, too much or too little social contact is undesirable, and too much or too little movement is undesirable. (Do you see the similarity between this notion and the Yerkes-Dodson Law described under arousal theory?) These categories in turn vary along at least three

dimensions that have optimal levels. The first dimension is *intensity*. As we have noted, too many or too few people around us can be psychologically disturbing. Too little or too much auditory stimulation has the same unwanted effect. We have all experienced the irritation of neighbors making distracting noise while we were trying to listen to a lecture or concert, of loud stereos playing when we are trying to study, and of children screaming when adults are trying to carry on a conversation. On the other hand, if you have ever been in a soundproofed chamber for very long, you know that the absence of external sound becomes very unnerving after only five or ten minutes.

Another dimension of environmental stimulation is *diversity,* both across time and at any given moment. Too little diversity in our surroundings produces boredom and the desire to seek arousal and excitement. Too much diversity, as in the typical ''strip'' of fast-food franchises, gas stations, and glaring neon signs common in many towns and cities, is considered an eyesore. Considerable research (see Wohlwill, 1974) indicates that the perceived attractiveness and the degree of pleasant feelings associated with a human-built scene are maximized at an intermediate level of diversity (see the section on aesthetics in Chapter 2).

The third dimension of stimulation is *patterning* or the degree to which a perception contains both structure and uncertainty. The total absence of structure that can be coded by our information processing mechanisms, such as diffuse light of a constant intensity or a single tone at a constant volume, is disturbing. By the same token, a very complex pattern that contains no predictable structure is also disturbing. To the extent that a modern built environment is so diverse and complex that we have difficulty imposing a perceptual structure on it, we probably experience that environment as stressful. Urban street patterns are a good example of this dimension. Parallel streets in intersecting grid patterns can be monotonous. On the other hand, complex layouts with no predictable numbering or no easy access to major arteries can cause a headache. An intermediate level of patterning, with gently winding streets and cul-de-sacs, is usually comfortable, yet pleasantly stimulating.

Optimizing Stimulation. After assuming the general rule that there are optimal levels of environmental stimulation, Wohlwill introduces a modifier to this rule by further assuming that each person has an optimal level of stimulation, which is based on past experience. Thus, Tibetan tribesmen, who live comfortably at altitudes with so little oxygen that most of us would have difficulty maintaining consciousness, have *adapted* to a level of oxygen concentration quite different from what most of us would consider ideal. Similarly, those of us who live in cities probably have a higher level of tolerance for crowds and less tolerance for isolation than do most residents of rural areas. After a rurally raised person has lived in a city for a few months or years, he or she probably acquires a greater tolerance for crowds than the rural resident who never moves to a city. Wohlwill refers to this shift in optimal stimulation level as *adaptation,* defined as "a quantitative shift in the distribution of judgmental or affective responses along a stimulus continuum, as a function of continued exposure to a stimulus" (1974, p. 134). Adaptation levels not only differ from person to person as a function of experience but may also change with time following exposure to a different level of stimulation. Thus, how one

evaluates and reacts to a given environment along a particular dimension is in part determined by how much that environment deviates from one's adaptation level (AL) on that dimension. The more an environment deviates from the adaptation level, the more intense the reaction to that environment should be.

Adaptation versus Adjustment. Adaptation level theory postulates an interesting environment–behavior relationship in the distinction between adaptation and what Sonnenfeld (1966) calls *adjustment.* Adaptation refers to changing the response to the stimulus, whereas adjustment refers to changing the stimulus itself. For example, adaptation to hot temperatures would involve gradually getting used to the heat so that we do not sweat as profusely on exposure to it. Adjustment would involve either wearing lighter clothes or installing an air conditioning system so that the temperature stimulus striking our skin is much cooler. For most organisms and for early human societies, adaptation was probably a more realistic option than adjustment. For modern societies with advanced technology, however, adjustment is so clearly a realistic option that we prefer it over adaptation. Witness, for example, the response to government appeals to adjust thermostats so that heating and air conditioning the indoor environment will use less energy (Figure 3–3). Rather than adapt to temperatures that are only slightly above or below what we perceive as optimal, we

---

OPTIMAL LEVELS OF PRIVACY

Adaptation level theory predicts that individuals prefer an optimal level of stimulation. Environmental psychologist Irwin Altman (1975) suggests that the same holds for privacy. That is, there are times when the demands of privacy require isolation (e.g., when bathing), and there are other times when we do not want isolation (e.g., when performing on stage). For any given situation, we each have our own level of desired (optimal) privacy. When others impinge on our privacy, we try to restore our desired level by backing off, avoiding eye contact, or erecting barriers. When we have too much privacy, we try to increase social interaction, maintain eye contact, and remove barriers. The chapters on personal space and crowding will elaborate on this pattern of social interaction.

Figure 3–3. If we humans were as willing to adapt to the environment as we are to adjust to it, we would be less reluctant to lower our thermostats to meet energy crises.

prefer to await the development of new technologies that will let us maintain the old adaptation level. In general, adaptation level theory suggests that when given a choice between adapting and adjusting, people will take the course that causes the least discomfort.

Breadth versus Specificity. It should be obvious that adaptation level theory incorporates some of the best features of stress, overload, and understimulation theories. As such, it has rather broad generality, applying to physical and social environments as well as to all forms of sensation and perception. AL theory also suggests that future research might well concentrate on the adaptation process in order to solve many environmental problems. One problem that arises with this theory, however, is that since it allows for so much individual variation in adaptation level, it becomes very difficult to make more general predictions about environmental preference and environment–behavior relationships. This problem typically arises in behavioral science theories. The more specific the elements from which predictions are made, the less general the predictions; the more general the predictors, the less specific the predictions.

Another problem with AL theory is that it is often difficult to identify an "optimal" level of

stimulation before we make a prediction. Recall, for example, our discussion of environmental aesthetics in the previous chapter, in which it was proposed that an intermediate level of complexity would lead to optimal judgments of beauty. This prediction often proves incorrect, in part because we have difficulty defining what we mean by an intermediate level of complexity. In order for AL theory to work, we would need to see what conditions maximize judgments of beauty, then define that level of complexity as intermediate. What is really needed is more research which quantifies levels of environmental stimulation. Only then can we know how well AL theory predicts environment–behavior relationships.

The Behavior Constraint Approach

According to the theoretical perspectives we have examined thus far, excessive or undesirable environmental stimulation leads to arousal or a strain on the information-processing capacity. Another potential consequence of such stimulation is loss of perceived control over the situation. Have you ever been caught in a severe winter storm or summer heat wave and felt there was nothing you could do about it? Or have you ever been forced to live or work in extremely crowded conditions and felt the situation was so out of hand there was nothing you could do to overcome it? This loss of perceived control over the situation is the first step in what is known as the *behavior constraint* model of environmental stimulation (Proshansky, Ittleson, & Rivlin, 1970; Rodin & Baum, 1978; Stokols, 1978; Zlutnick & Altman, 1972).

The term "constraint" here means that something about the environment is limiting or interfering with things we wish to do. According to the behavior constraint model, the constraint can be an actual impairment from the environment or simply our belief that the environment is placing a constraint upon us. What is most important is the cognitive interpretation of the situation as being beyond our control.

Once you perceive that you are losing control over the environment, what happens next? When you perceive that environmental events are constraining or restricting your behavior, you first experience discomfort or negative affect. You also probably try to reassert your control over the situation. This phenomenon is known as *psychological reactance* (Brehm, 1966; Brehm & Brehm, 1981). Any time we feel that our freedom of action is being constrained, psychological reactance leads us to try to regain that freedom. If crowding is a threat to our freedom, we react by erecting physical or social barriers to "shut others out." If the weather restricts our freedom, we might stay indoors or else use technological devices (e.g., snow plows, air-conditioned cars) to regain control. According to the behavior constraint model, we do not actually have to experience loss of control for reactance to set in; all we need do is *anticipate* that some environmental factor is about to restrict our freedom. Mere anticipation of crowding, for example, is enough to make us start erecting physical or psychological barriers against others.

What happens if our efforts to reassert control are unsuccessful in regaining freedom of action? The ultimate consequence of loss of control, according to the behavior constraint model, is *learned helplessness* (Garber & Seligman, 1981; Seligman, 1975). That is, if repeated efforts at regaining control result in failure, we might begin to think that our actions have no effect on the situation, so we stop trying to gain control even when, from an objective point of view, our control has been restored. In other words, we "learn" that we are helpless. Students who try to change a class schedule but are rebuffed by the registration office numerous times soon "learn" that they are helpless against bureaucracy. Similarly, if efforts to overcome crowding are unsuccessful, we may abandon our efforts to gain privacy and change our life styles accordingly. During the severe winter of 1977 in the eastern United States, there were many reports of individuals "giving up" trying to keep warm when their fuel supplies were depleted, and a number died as a result. While less severe than death, learned helplessness often leads to depression.

The behavior constraint model, then, posits three basic steps: perceived loss of control, reac-

tance, and learned helplessness. The use of this model thus far in environmental psychology has been relatively limited, although components are often discussed within the context of the stress or load models. Whether treated within the behavior constraint model or within some other model, it is clear that perceived loss of control has unfortunate consequences for behavior, and that restoring control enhances performance and mental outlook. For example, Glass and Singer (1972) found that telling subjects they could reduce the amount of noxious noise in an experiment by pressing a button reduced or eliminated many of the negative effects of the noise, even though subjects did not actually press the button. That is, simply perceiving that they could control the noise reduced the adaptive costs of that stressor. Perceived control over noise has also been found to reduce its negative effects on aggression (Donnerstein & Wilson, 1976) and helping behavior (Sherrod & Downs, 1974). Moreover, perceived loss of control over air pollution seems to reduce efforts to do anything about the problem (Evans & Jacobs, 1981). Similarly, perceived control over crowding reduces its unpleasant effects (e.g., Langer & Saegert, 1977; Rodin, 1976) and perceived control over crime may motivate us to employ more prevention measures (Miransky & Langer, 1978; Tyler, 1981). Perceived control also has implications for institutional environments. Langer and Rodin (1976), for example, manipulated the amount of control residents of a nursing home had over their daily affairs. For instance, one group was told the staff would take care of them while another group was told they were responsible for themselves. One group was given plants to raise themselves, while the other group was given plants to be cared for by the staff. After three weeks, residents in the high control group showed greater well-being and enhanced mood and more activity than the low control group (see also, Moos, 1980; Rothbaum, Weisz, & Snyder, 1982; Schulz, 1976).

Several attempts have been made to elaborate on the types of control we can have over our environment. Averill (1973), for example, distinguishes between categories of: (1) behavioral control, in which our behavior can change the environment (e.g., turning off a loud noise); (2) cognitive control, in which we appraise a situation as less threatening (e.g., deciding there is no danger in working outdoors during a heatwave); and (3) decisional control, in which we choose one or more of several options (e.g., choosing to live in a quiet rather than a noisy neighborhood). Apparently, the amount of control we have is important: Being able to control both onset and termination of a noise results in better adaptation than control over just onset or just termination of the noise (Sherrod, *et al.,* 1977). In sum, the greater the control we perceive over our environment, the better we are able to adapt to it successfully.

Just as research has progressed on the perceived control component of the behavior constraint model, so has research on the reactance and learned helplessness components. For our present discussion, the work on learned helplessness seems especially important. For example,

Hiroto (1974) found that when subjects were given a chance to terminate an aversive noise, those who had previously been able to control it learned to terminate it. Those who had previously been unable to control the noise, however, responded as if they learned to be helpless, and failed to learn the termination procedure. Similarly, a field study with school children found that those who attended noisy schools near Los Angeles International Airport showed more signs of learned helplessness than those from quieter schools (Cohen *et al.,* 1980, 1981).

Recently, learned helplessness effects have been interpreted in terms of attribution theory (e.g., Abramson, Seligman, & Teasdale, 1978; Hanusa & Schulz, 1977; Miller & Norman, 1979; Tennen & Eller, 1977). Attributions are inferences about causes for events or about characteristics of people or events. Although the details of the attribution interpretations of learned helplessness are too extensive for in-depth coverage here, we can make a few general statements. In gen-

---

PERCEIVED CONTROL AND RESEARCH ETHICS: A DILEMMA

We have noted that perceived control over unpleasant environmental stimulation such as noise reduces the negative consequences of exposure to the stimuli. An interesting problem in this regard has arisen in the area of laboratory research on environmental stressors. Gardner (1978) notes that for years it was possible to demonstrate such effects as reduced proofreading speed and accuracy when laboratory subjects were exposed to uncontrollable noise. Subsequent research, however, has failed to find these detrimental effects. What went wrong? Gardner provides evidence that the "culprit" is a set of research ethics guidelines established by the Federal government and implemented by universities and other research institutions. Among these guidelines is a requirement that subjects be informed of potential risks when participating in experiments, even though the risks are minimal. Moreover, subjects must be told that they are free to terminate the experiment at any time, and must sign an "informed consent" statement disclosing the risks and the termination provision. Gardner provides evidence that such informed consent procedures amount to giving subjects perceived control over the stressor, and thus stress effects are reduced! The situation is then an ethical dilemma: How can one ethically do research on stressful environmental conditions if the ethical procedures in effect eliminate the negative reactions to those conditions? Gardner proposes that where risks are minimal, the need to know about these effects justifies modification of the informed consent procedures. Such a decision would rest with an institutional review board to ensure the safety of subjects. Alternatively, more emphasis may have to be placed on field research involving natural observation. Ultimately, we suspect the ethical dilemma can never be fully resolved.

eral, helplessness effects are more likely to occur if we attribute our lack of control over the environment to: (1) stable rather than unstable factors (e.g., to our physical or mental inability to do anything about it rather than to our temporary lack of time to act on it); (2) general rather than specific factors (e.g., attributing pollution to all industry rather than to a specific factory); and (3) internal rather than external locus of control (e.g., attributing our discomfort in a crowd to our own preference for open spaces rather than to the behavior of others in the crowd).

Research on reactance, perceived loss of control, and learned helplessness is certain to continue, whether interpreted from the perspective of the behavior constraint model or from some other perspective. The model itself has considerable, though limited, utility. In instances of perceived loss of control, the model is quite useful in predicting some of the consequences. In cases in which there is no reason to infer perceived loss of control, however, other mediators such as stress, arousal, and overload, are probably necessary to explain environment–behavior relationships.

Barker's Ecological Psychology

The theoretical perspectives reviewed up to this point have been concerned primarily with the specific effects of the environment on behavior, but, with the exception of the behavior constraint model, they have not been concerned with the effects of behavior on the environment. Yet, as we have noted many times, behavior inevitably influences the environment. The ecological psychology approach views environment–behavior relationships as two-way streets or, in other words, as ecological interdependencies.

Barker (1968, 1979) and his colleagues are the principal advocates of the ecological approach. The focus of Barker's model is the influence of the *behavior setting* on the behavior of large numbers of people, which he has termed the *extra-individual* behavior pattern. The unique aspect of Barker's approach is that the behavior setting is an entity in itself. It is not an arbitrarily defined social scientific concept but actually exists and

has a physical structure. In order to understand just how this behavior setting functions, we will first look at some characteristics of the behavior setting, then see how the setting fits into Barker's theory of undermanning.

The Nature of the Behavior Setting. A number of behaviors can occur inside a structure with four walls, a ceiling, and a floor; but if we know that the cultural purpose of this structure is to be a classroom, then we know that the behavior of the people in the structure will be quite different than if its purpose is to be a church, a factory, or a hockey arena. The fact that this behavior setting is in a built environment also tells us that the extraindividual behavior will be different from that in the natural environment of a forested wilderness or a desert. This cultural purpose exists because the behavior setting consists of the interdependency between *standing patterns of behavior* and a *physical milieu*. Standing patterns of behavior represent the collective behaviors of the group, rather than just individual behaviors. These behaviors are not unique to the individuals present, but they may be unique to the setting. If the behavior setting is a classroom in a lecture-oriented course, then the standing patterns of behavior would include lecturing, listening, observing, sitting, taking notes, raising hands, and exchanging questions and answers. Since this *en masse* behavior pattern occurs only in an educational behavior setting, ecological psychologists would infer that knowing about the setting helps us predict the behavior that will occur in it. The physical milieu of this behavior setting would include a room, a lectern, chairs, and perhaps a chalkboard and microphone. Once the individuals leave the classroom, the physical milieu still stands, so the standing behavior patterns are independent of the milieu. Yet they are similar in structure *(synomorphic)* and together create the behavior setting (Figure 3–4). A change in either the standing behavior patterns (as when a club holds a meeting in the classroom) or the physical milieu (such as when the class is held outdoors on the first warm day of spring) changes the behavior setting.

Figure 3–4. According to Barker's ecological psychology, knowing about the physical setting tells us much about the behaviors that occur there. In the behavior setting shown, what behaviors can you always expect to see?

factors as efficiency of operation, handling of responsibility, and indications of status. In addition, as Bechtel (1977) notes, ecological psychology can be useful in assessing environmental design. By carefully examining the behavior setting, one can analyze such design features as pathways, or links between settings, and focal points, or places where behavior tends to concentrate. In the lobby of a building, for example, it is important to separate pathways to various elevators, offices, and shops in order to avoid congestion and confusion. An information center in the lobby, though, would be most useful if placed at a focal point. As another example, open-plan (i.e., no internal walls) designs in schools and offices, although having advantages, often lead to inadequate boundaries between behavior settings, thereby causing interference with the intended functions (e.g., Oldham & Brass, 1979). We will discuss more of these kinds of design implications in Chapters 10 and 11.

How can one use the behavior setting conceptualization to understand environment–behavior relationships? Perhaps a few examples can best illustrate the utility of this approach (see also, Wicker & Kirmeyer, 1976). One very famous application of ecological psychology is depicted in the box on page 14. In this study Barker and his colleagues (Barker & Wright, 1955; Barker & Schoggen, 1973) compared a small town in Kansas with one in England. Among the findings were that behavior settings under the control of businesses were more common, and the behavior in them lasted longer, in the British setting rather than the American setting. In settings involving voluntary participation, however, Americans spent more time and held more positions of responsibility than did Britons. (The significance of such findings will be more apparent below in the discussion of manning.) Wicker (1979) notes that ecological psychology methods are very useful for such diverse goals as documenting community life, assessing the social impact of change, and analyzing the structure of organizations for such

How Many Peas Fill a Pod: The Theory of Manning. What happens if a behavior setting such as a classroom or theater has too few or too many inhabitants for maximum functioning efficiency? Do students at small schools, for example, take on more roles of responsibility than students at larger schools? Studies of these questions from the ecological psychology perspective have led to the theory of manning (Barker, 1960; Barker & Gump, 1964; Wicker & Kirmeyer, 1976; Wicker, McGrath, & Armstrong, 1972). We should note that efforts have been made to substitute a less sex-linked word, such as "staffing," for the word "manning;" however, since the theory is still best known as the theory of manning, we will, with hesitation and caution, use the more traditional terminology.

In order to understand the undermanning concept, let us first define some terms proposed by Wicker and his colleagues that are related to the concept. The minimum number of inhabitants needed to maintain a behavior setting is defined as the *maintenance minimum*. The maximum number of inhabitants the setting can hold is the *capacity*. The people who meet the membership requirements of the setting and who are trying to become a part of it are called *applicants*. *Performers* in a setting carry out the primary tasks, such as the teacher in a classroom, the workers in a factory, or the cast and supporting staff in a play. *Nonperformers,* such as the pupils in a classroom or the audience in a theater, are involved in secondary roles. Maintenance minimum, capacity, and applicants are different entities for performers and nonperformers. For example, maintenance minimum for performers in a classroom would be the smallest staff (teachers, custodians, secretaries, deans) required to carry out the program. For nonperformers, maintenance minimum would be the smallest number of pupils required to keep the class going. Capacity for performers in a classroom might be determined by social factors (e.g., how many teachers are most effective in one setting) and by physical factors, such as the size of the room, number of lecterns, and so on. For nonperformers, room size is the primary determinant of capacity. Whether your classes contain 10 or 1,000 students depends in most cases as much on classroom size as on educational policy. For performers, applicants are the individuals who meet the requirements of the performer role and who seek to perform, as in the number of teachers available to teach a given class. Applicants for nonperformers are those who seek nonperforming roles, as in the number of students trying to get into the class. If students are available but do not seek to get into the class, or if teachers do not want to teach a given class, then they are not considered applicants.

If the number of applicants to a setting (either performers or nonperformers) falls below the maintenance minimum, then some or all of the inhabitants must take on more than their share of roles if the behavior setting is to be maintained. This condition is termed *undermanning*. If the number of applicants exceeds the capacity, the setting is *overmanned,* and if the number of applicants is between maintenance minimum and capacity, the setting is *adequately manned*.

When conditions of undermanning exist, the consequences for the inhabitants of the setting are many. As stated earlier, inhabitants must take on more specific tasks and roles than would otherwise be the case. As a result, inhabitants would have to work harder and at more difficult tasks than they would otherwise, and peak performance on any one task would not be as great as in an adequately manned setting. Furthermore, admissions standards to undermanned settings would have to be lowered, and superficial differences among inhabitants would be largely ignored, whereas in adequately manned settings these differences would be highlighted to fit each person into his or her most appropriate role. Each inhabitant in an undermanned setting is more valued, has more responsibility, and interacts more meaningfully with the setting. Since undermanned settings have more opportunities for the experience of failure as well as success (owing to the increase in number of experiences per inhabitant), these settings are likely to result in more feelings of insecurity than adequately manned settings. The consequences of undermanning are summarized in Table 3–1.

Overmanning, on the other hand, results in adaptive mechanisms being brought into play to deal with the huge number of applicants. One obvious solution would be to increase the capacity, probably through enlarging the present physical milieu or moving to a larger one. Another adaptive mechanism would be to control the entrance of clients into the setting, either through stricter entrance requirements or through some sort of funneling process (Figure 3–5). For example, Wicker (1979) describes how ecological psychologists implemented and evaluated a queuing (waiting line) arrangement at Yosemite National Park to alleviate overcrowding and associated disruptive behavior at bus stops. Still another regulatory mechanism would be to limit the amount of time inhabitants can spend in the setting. These three mechanisms are elaborated in Table 3–1.

Table 3–1. CONSEQUENCES OF UNDERMANNING AND MECHANISMS FOR REGULATING THE POPULATION*

Consequences of Undermanning

1. Lowering of admissions standards for applicants.
2. Individual participation in more tasks and roles.
3. Individual involvement in more difficult tasks.
4. Lowering of performance in each task.
5. More frequent experience of success and failure.
6. More feelings of insecurity.
7. Greater valuing of each individual.
8. Less attention paid to differences between individuals.
9. Greater assumed responsibility by each individual.

Mechanisms for Regulating the Population of a Behavior Setting

1. Regulating access of applicants into the setting:
    by altering admissions standards for applicants;
    by forcing applicants to wait in holding areas.
2. Regulating the setting's capacity:
    by changing the arrangement or contents of the physical milieu;
    by increasing or decreasing staff (performers) to handle applicants;
    by assigning staff (performers) to different tasks as demands of applicants increase or decrease.
3. Regulating the time applicants or inhabitants can occupy the setting:
    by admitting applicants at different rates;
    by determining the priorities for admitting different classes of applicants;
    by changing the standing patterns of behavior to facilitate the flow of applicants.

*Adapted from Wicker and Kirmeyer (1976). Courtesy of Plenum Publishing.

In general, predictions from the theory of manning have been supported by research. For example, in a laboratory study involving too many, too few, or an intermediate number of participants to run a complex racing game, those in undermanned conditions reported more feelings of involvement in the group and having an important role within the group (e.g., Wicker *et al.,* 1976). Studies of large versus small high schools (Baird, 1969; Barker & Gump, 1964) suggest that students in small schools (which are less likely to be overmanned) are indeed involved in a wider range of activities than students from large schools, and are more likely to report feelings of satisfaction and of being challenged. Similar results have been reported for colleges as well (Baird, 1969). Studies of large versus small churches (e.g., Wicker & Kauma, 1974; Wicker, McGrath, & Armstrong, 1972; Wicker & Mehler, 1971; Wicker, 1969b) also indicate that members of small churches are likely to be involved in more behavior settings within the church (e.g., choir, committees) and to be involved in more leadership positions; such predictions are based on the assumption that smaller churches are more likely to be undermanned and larger churches overmanned. Altogether, then, these and other studies suggest that the theory of manning is very useful in assessing involvement and satisfaction within a number of environments, from businesses (e.g.,

Greenberg, 1979) to mental institutions (e.g., Srivastava, 1974) to schools and churches.

Barker's approach has its advantages and disadvantages. It necessitates a field observation methodology (described in the Appendix), which gives the theory the advantage of using real-world behavior. However, it includes the disadvantage of not being able to study as many detailed cause-and-effect relationships in the laboratory (though certainly some laboratory research on ecological psychology principles has been and will continue to be conducted). We again have a theory that is so broad in its scope that specific predictions become difficult to make and troublesome to confirm. Since this approach is designed to study group behavior, it does a respectable job of handling group data, but it does not handle individual behavior as well as other theories. Finally, ecological theory does generate many research questions, such as what common properties of certain behavior settings result in the same group behavior, what happens when the structure of a behavior setting changes, and what effects one behavior setting has on behavior in another setting.

The Environmental Stress Approach

One theoretical approach, which is widely used in environmental psychology, is to view many elements of the environment, such as noise and heat, as stressors. Stressors, such as job pressures, marital discord, natural disasters, the stress of moving to a new location, and urban crowding and noise, are considered to be aversive stimuli that threaten the well-being of the organism. Stress is an intervening or mediating variable, defined as the reaction to these stimuli. This "reaction" is assumed to include emotional, behavioral, and physiological components. The physiological component was initially proposed by Selye (1956), and is often called *systemic stress*. The behavioral and emotional components were proposed by Lazarus (1966), and are often called *psychological stress*. Today, environmental psychologists usually combine all of these components into one theory or model (e.g., Baum,

Figure 3–5. Funneling is one way to regulate entrance into a potentially overmanned behavior setting.

Singer, & Baum, 1981; Lazarus & Cohen, 1977). As we discuss specific stressors (heat, noise, crowding) in subsequent chapters, we will, accordingly, indicate specific physiological and psychological consequences of exposure to these stressors. We should emphasize that physiological and psychological stress reactions are interrelated, and do not occur alone. We will see this point as we elaborate upon the environmental stress conceptualization in this chapter and the next. Before proceeding further, we should note that sometimes the term "stress" is restricted to environmental events, and an additional term, "strain," is used to describe the organismic (i.e., within the organism) component. However, we will use "stress" to refer to the entire stimulus-response situation and "stressor" to refer to the environmental component alone.

Part of the response to an aversive or stressful stimulus is automatic. Selye's (1956) *general adaptation syndrome* or *GAS* consists of three stages: the alarm reaction; the stage of resistance;

and the stage of exhaustion. Initially there is an alarm reaction to a stressor, whereby autonomic processes (heart rate, adrenaline secretion, and so on) are speeded up. The second stage in the stress process, the stage of resistance, also begins with some automatic processes for coping with the stressor. If heat is the stressor, sweating occurs; if extreme cold is the stressor, shivering might begin.

The concept of stress, however, involves not just a simple automatic stimulus-response relationship, but contains a number of important cognitive components (i.e., involving thought processes) as well. To begin with, not all stressful stimuli are aversive enough in themselves to evoke the automatic alarm and resistance responses. In order for the stress process to begin, there must be cognitive appraisal of a stimulus as threatening. To use an environmental example, 90° F (32° C) to a native southerner is not likely to be very stressful in midsummer. To someone living in Barrow, Alaska, however, the mere thought of experiencing 90° F for a few hours a day may well be evaluated as threatening. In other words, the same stimulus that may not be stressful in one situation may be stressful in another—the stimulus has not changed, but the individual's appraisal of it as threatening or nonthreatening has changed. Moreover, cognitive appraisal that an aversive event, such as crowding, is pending is often sufficient to elicit a stress response, even though the physical event itself does not happen (e.g., Baum & Greenberg, 1975).

Lazarus (1966) suggested that this cognitive appraisal is a function of individual psychological factors (intellectual resources, knowledge or past experience, and motivation) and cognitive aspects of the specific stimulus situation (control over the stimulus, predictability of the stimulus, and immediacy or "time until impact" of the stimulus). The more knowledge one has about the beneficial aspects of a source of noise, or the more control one has over the noise (in terms of terminating or avoiding it), the less one is likely to evaluate that stimulus as threatening, and the less stressful the

situation is likely to be. Cognitive appraisal of a situation is more complex than merely assessing its potential threat (see Baum, *et al.*, 1982 for a review). Some appraisals may be oriented toward *harm-loss,* or "damage already done." That is, once a disaster has struck, the appraisal is usually not that a threat is pending, but that a blow has already occurred. In addition, one might appraise some situations, such as climbing a mountain, as stressfully *challenging*.

Once a stimulus has been evaluated as threatening, other cognitive factors come into play. Recall Selye's notions of the alarm reaction (stage 1) and the automatic coping mechanisms of resistance (stage 2). In the stage of resistance many coping processes are also cognitive, so that the individual must decide on a behavioral coping strategy. According to Lazarus (1966), the coping strategy is a function of individual and situational factors, and may consist of flight, physical or verbal attack, or some sort of compromise. A distinction is usually made between *primary appraisal,* which involves assessment of threat, and *secondary appraisal,* which involves assessment of coping strategies. Lack of success in the coping process may increase the tendency to evaluate the situation as threatening. Associated with this cognitive coping process are any number of emotions, including anger and fear. To use another example, the stress reaction to a large crowd in a city might consist of evaluation of the crowd as threatening, physiological arousal, fear, and flight to a less crowded area.

Coping strategies may be classified as (1) *direct action,* such as information seeking, flight, or attempts to remove or stop the stressor; or (2) *palliative,* such as employing psychological defense mechanisms (denial, intellectualization, etc.), using drugs, meditating, or reassessing the situation as nonthreatening. To the extent that direct action is not available or practical, palliative strategies become more likely. For example, for residents near the Three Mile Island nuclear disaster, direct action was limited in effectiveness, so palliative measures would be more probable (Baum *et al.,* 1980; Houts *et al.,* 1980).

If the coping responses are not adequate for dealing with the stressor, and all coping energies have been expended, the organism will enter the third stage of the GAS, the stage of exhaustion (Figure 3–6). Fortunately, something else usually happens before exhaustion occurs. In most situations, when an aversive stimulus is presented many times, the stress reaction to it becomes weaker and weaker. Psychologically, this process is called *adaptation*. Adaptation to a stressor may occur because neurophysiological sensitivity to the stimulus becomes weaker, because uncertainty about the stressor is reduced, or because the stressor is cognitively appraised as less and less threatening. Visitors to a polluted city, for example, initially may suffer overt physiological symptoms (such as shortness of breath) and may express a great deal of fear about the potential health consequences of exposure to atmospheric pollutants. On successive days in the city, however, these visitors, realizing that they have not died yet, may "lose" the fear of breathing the air (see also Chapter 5).

Adaptation to stress is both beneficial and costly. Almost all events in life, from birth to attending school to driving on freeways at rush hour, involve some degree of stress. Obviously, the individual who has been exposed to stress and has learned to handle it is better able to deal with the next stressful event in life. In this sense, the "teaching" function of stress is beneficial to the organism, as long as the stress can be handled. We will see in Chapter 4 that environmental stress sometimes improves performance, probably because the arousal associated with stress (if it is not too severe) facilitates performance. Exposure and adaptation to stressful events may also be costly, however. If the total of all stresses at any one time exceeds the capacity of the individual to cope with them, some sort of breakdown, physical or mental, is almost inevitable. Psychosomatic disorders, performance decrements, and lowering of resistance to other stressors are often the costs of adapting to prolonged or excessive stress. Still another cost, one that we have treated previously as a separate theoretical approach, is the resulting

Figure 3–6. The stress model. Adapted from Selye (1956) and Lazarus (1966).

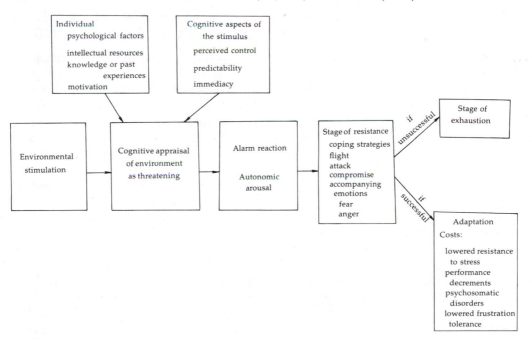

cognitive overload: Our information-processing capacity becomes so overloaded by the stressor that we ignore other important stimuli, including other human beings and stimuli relevant to job performance, safety, and health. Some costs of adaptation may occur during exposure to the stressor, including performance decrements and physiological wear and tear. Other costs may occur after the stressor is no longer around. For example, as we will see in Chapter 4, even after an aversive noise has stopped, tolerance for frustration, accuracy of mental functioning, and even altruistic behavior may continue to be impaired (see also Cohen, 1980).

When we evaluate the effectiveness of using stress as a mediator for a theoretical approach in environmental psychology, we find that it does an admirable job with the data in its predictive domain. The stress approach does help predict many of the consequences of environmental deterioration as well as the presence or absence of observable effects of such specific stressors as crowding and extremes of heat and cold. In this respect, the stress approach has a great deal of generality: It applies to many situations and accounts for the combined effects of many environmental and social stressors that are present at the same time. Perhaps for this reason the stress approach suggests many directions for new research. If we treat a given environmental event as a stressor, then we should be able to predict its effects, with or without the presence of other stressors, from our knowledge of the effects of other stressors. Furthermore, we should be able to use present knowledge about coping with stress to help control reactions to unwanted environmental stressors. On the other hand, one problem with using only the stress approach as a theoretical inroad in environmental psychology is that the identification of stressors is somewhat ambiguous. For example, suppose we expose individuals to a particular stimulus and get no stress reaction. Should that stimulus be regarded as something other than a stressor, or did those particular individuals just not evaluate it as threatening under the experimental circumstances?

We have stated earlier that some components of the arousal, environmental load, adaptation level, behavior constraint, and ecological approaches fit very well into an environmental stress framework. We have seen, for example, that overload can be viewed as one consequence of coping with stress, and that heightened arousal is a component of stress. Similarly, an optimal level of stimulation (i.e., stimulation at the adaptation level) should result in little evidence of a stress reaction, and multiple constraints on behavior as well as severe overmanning or undermanning might be expected to lead to considerable signs of stress. In sum, all these theoretical approaches are interrelated and seem in many ways compatible with the stress formulation. We will elaborate upon these compatibilities in the next chapter when we discuss environmental stress in more detail, and in subsequent chapters where we concentrate on specific environmental stressors. Before doing so, it might be instructive to see how we can integrate the major features of all but the ecological psychology approach into one large model.

INTEGRATION AND SUMMARY OF THEORETICAL PERSPECTIVES

It is worth repeating the earlier caution that the above discussion has by no means covered all theories employed by environmental psychologists. Rather, they are simply the most common approaches presently in use, and they are not at all mutually exclusive. Each theory selects one or two mediators inferred from empirical data and attempts to explain a large portion of the data using that mediator. Just because one mediator explains a particular set of data, however, does not mean that other mediators are not operating in the same set of data. It is entirely conceivable, for example, that loud noises produce information overload, stress, arousal, and psychological reactance all at the same time in the same individual. Furthermore, regardless of which of these mediators is involved (either alone or in combination), any number of coping responses are likely to result, such as flight, erecting barriers or other protective devices, ignoring other humans in need, and directly attempting to stop or reduce the stimulus input at the source. Although one particular mediator may best predict or explain which coping responses will occur in a given situation, other mediators are not necessarily excluded from that or similar situations. It is our position that all of the mediating processes discussed thus far probably occur at some time, given all the possible situations in which environmental stimulation influences behavior. Therefore, we now present an eclectic scheme of environment–behavior relationships as a summary and integration of the theoretical concepts discussed up to this point.

This scheme of theoretical concepts is presented in the flow chart in Figure 3–7. Objective environmental conditions, such as population density, temperature, noise levels, and pollution levels, exist independently of the individual, although individuals can act to change these objective conditions. The scheme includes such individual difference factors as adaptation level, length of exposure, perceived control, and personality, as well as such social factors as liking or hostility for others in the situation. Perception of the objective physical conditions depends on the objective conditions themselves as well as on the individual difference factors and the perceptual processes discussed in the previous chapter. If this subjective perception determines that the environment is within an optimal range of stimulation, the result is homeostasis, or an equalization of desired and actual input. On the other hand, if the environment is experienced as outside the optimal range of stimulation (e.g., understimulating, overstimulating, or stimulating in a behavior-constraining manner), then one or more of the following psychological states results: arousal, stress, information overload, or reactance. The presence of one or more of these states leads to coping strategies. If the attempted coping strategies are successful, adaptation or adjustment occurs, possibly followed by such aftereffects as lowered frustration tolerance, fatigue, and reduced ability to cope with the next immediate stressor. Cumulative aftereffects might include any of these but would also include a degree of learning about coping with future occurrences of undesirable environmental stimulation. Should the coping strategies not be successful, however, arousal and stress will continue, possibly heightened by the individual's awareness that the strategies are failing. Potential aftereffects of such inability to cope include exhaustion, learned helplessness, severe performance decrements, and mental disorders. Finally, as indicated by the feedback loops, experiences with the environment influence perception of the environment for future encounters and also contribute to individual differences for future experiences.

We present this model not as a completely developed environmental theory, but merely as an attempt to integrate the various mediating concepts that have been applied to environment–behavior relationships. There undoubtedly exist data that do not support one aspect or another of this integration. However, we think this eclectic approach will help explain many of the environment–behavior relationships to be covered in the next four chapters. In these chapters, we will discuss how the physical environment (noise, heat, cold, wind, air pollution), personal space, and crowding influence specific behaviors. When appropriate, we will point out how the various theoretical notions in this chapter help explain those specific influences.

CHAPTER SUMMARY

The scientific method assumes determinism, the belief that events in the universe are caused by other events. Environmental psychology, as a science, seeks to understand these cause-and-effect relationships through prediction and uses publicly observable data to verify these predictions. Once enough predictions are verified, theories are constructed, which consist of a set of concepts and a set of statements relating the concepts to each other. Usually, theories infer that a more or less abstract variable mediates the relationship be-

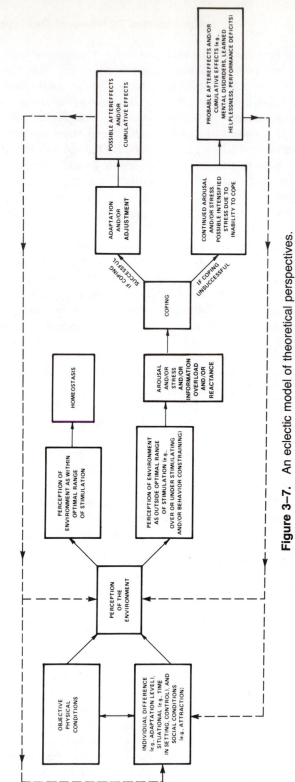

Figure 3–7. An eclectic model of theoretical perspectives.

tween one observable variable and another. Good environmental theories should predict and summarize empirical data, should generalize to many situations, and should suggest ideas for research.

The arousal approach to environment–behavior relationships suggests that environmental stimulation leads to increased arousal. According to the Yerkes-Dodson Law, this increased arousal will improve or impair performance, depending on whether the individual's arousal is below or above an optimal level. Other behaviors, such as aggression, also tend to follow this curvilinear relationship with arousal.

The information overload theory proposes that there is a limited capacity to process information and that when excessive stimulation occurs, peripheral inputs are ignored in order to give adequate attention to primary tasks. The result is that responses to these peripheral nonsocial or social stimuli are minimal or nonexistent. The understimulation theory notes that monotonous environmental stimulation leads to boredom and thus to behavioral deficiencies. Wohlwill's approach posits an individual difference variable, or adaptation level (AL), such that stimulation levels above or below this AL will bring discomfort and efforts to reduce or increase the stimulation. The behavior constraint model proposes that perceived loss of control over the environment leads to reactance or efforts to regain freedom of action. If these efforts at reassertion are unsuccessful, learned helplessness may be the result. Barker's ecological psychology model examines environment–behavior interdependencies and focuses on the behavior setting as the unit of study. If the number of applicants to a setting falls below maintenance minimum, performers and nonperformers in that undermanned setting must take on additional roles in order to maintain the setting.

The stress model of environment–behavior relationships posits that once stimuli have been evaluated as threatening, coping strategies are brought into play. These strategies can be beneficial, as when their use results in learning more efficient ways of coping with stress. However, prolonged exposure to stress can lead to serious aftereffects, including mental disorders, performance decrements, and lowered resistance to stress.

Finally, there is no reason to assume that only one mediator operates in any given environment–behavior situation. An eclectic model is offered that attempts to integrate a number of different theoretical concepts.

Suggested Projects

1. Construct your own model of environment–behavior relationships. How well can you integrate the various theoretical perspectives discussed in this chapter and the previous one?

2. Observe a behavior setting for a week. What behavior patterns are always present? Is the setting undermanned, overmanned, or adequately manned?

3. Keep a diary for a week or more of all the events that constrain your behavior. Do you respond with reactance, learned helplessness, or some other behavior?

4. Keep a log of your performance levels in classroom, study, and leisure situations, noting your arousal level and amount of environmental stimulation. Does your performance vary as a function of arousal level, overload, or underload?

4 Environmental Stress

INTRODUCTION

In the last chapter we considered a number of different theoretical approaches to the study of environmental psychology. One of these approaches was environmental stress, and we reviewed several aspects of stress and how it affects us. This chapter will consider environmental stress in more detail, and examine four important examples of stress: natural disaster, technological disaster, noise, and commuting to work.

One important question that should be answered before we go any further is "Why focus an entire chapter on stress?" A possible answer is that stress is a popular concept at the moment; it has been adopted by a number of fields and has spilled over into the popular press. Stress is used to explain bad moods or unusual behavior, and the growth of stress management techniques such as meditation, relaxation, and biofeedback speak to this popularity. Indeed, one can hardly pick up a magazine without finding an ad for a "Do it yourself biofeedback system" or a book on "learning to live with stress."

One of the reasons for this popularity (and for focusing on stress in this chapter) is that stress theory allows us to draw connections among a number of different kinds of situations. Historically, research in environmental psychology has been problem-oriented. Separate literature, or groups of studies, has tended to form around each problem. There were people who studied disasters, people who studied noise, people who studied the effects of commuting, and so on. When these groups got together at professional meetings, they were very interested in what the others were doing, but because each topic had been studied separately, researchers did not immediately see the relationships among the different issues. While this did not stop us from learning about single problems, it did slow the progress of research because studies of one form of environmental problem were not being used to help understand others.

This has changed somewhat, and one of the reasons has been the use of an environmental stress notion to integrate research on a number of different issues. During the 1970s, studies began to demonstrate that some of the effects of natural and technological disasters, exposure to noise, and commuting (as well as other phenomena) were similar, that they were influenced by some of the same variables, and that the processes and effects of these seemingly disparate events were in some ways comparable. Once it became clear that these events were related and they were cast together in a stress framework, it became easier to verify their similarities.

This is not to say that all of these events are exactly the same. Rather, they are similar in some respects. Using stress as an organizing model provides a convenient way of seeing these similarities and predicting effects from one event to another. Recall from Chapter 3 the basic purposes of a theory. By viewing these different environmental events as stressors, *predicting* their effects and the relationships among them has been made easier. The stress approach has also proven to be a good way of *summarizing* and *integrating* many studies and findings on a number of different environmental problems. Finally, this perspective has helped researchers *generalize* their findings to new phenomena and situations, and thus is important in studying and explaining events such as disaster, noise, and commuting.

This does not reduce the importance of the other theories discussed in Chapter 3, which are also useful in understanding responses to disaster, noise, and commuting. However, they are somewhat less global in their approach, and may apply more readily to some problems than to others. In the following chapters, it will become clear that while the stress model does a good job in the present context, other models may be more appropriate for understanding the effects of certain other environmental conditions. It will also become apparent that the general environment–behavior model which we proposed at the end of Chapter 3 can be quite useful in exploring the effects of many environmental conditions.

STRESS

Before beginning our coverage of several different sources of stress—disasters, noise, and commuting—we will elaborate in some detail on the concept of stress. (This should prove useful in our later coverage of specific stressors.) In Chapter 3, we discussed *stress* as a process by which environmental events that threaten or challenge an organism's well-being evoke various responses from the organism, as well as coping behavior directed toward the threat. Environmental events that initiate this process (i.e., which threaten an organism's well-being and elicit coping) are called *stressors*. The reaction they cause is called the *stress response,* characterized by emotional changes, behavior directed toward reduction of stress, and physiological changes such as increased arousal. The process, then, involves all parts of the situation—the threat itself, perceptions of the threat, coping with the threat, and, ultimately, adapting to it.

We will organize our discussion of stress into three basic parts. First, we will consider the *characteristics of stressors* (such as how long they last or how often they occur). Since the degree to which these events actually cause stress is dependent upon how they are interpreted (i.e., whether people notice them and decide that they might be harmful or aversive), we should also discuss the *appraisal of stressors*. Finally, the kinds of *stress responses* that occur (including anxiety, depression, illness, withdrawal, and aggression) will be considered.

Characteristics of Stressors

While some environmental events are threatening to almost everyone, and others are threatening to very few, many events can cause a range of problems. In all cases these are *potential* problems—they may or may not occur in a given situation. Nothing is automatic, and no stressor should always be considered threatening. Rather, some events are more likely to be viewed as threats or challenges than others. The probability of an event becoming stressful is determined by a number of factors, including characteristics of the specific event and the way people appraise it. We will discuss the characteristics of various stressors here, and reserve our discussion of the appraisal process for later.

Lazarus and Cohen (1977) have described three general categories of environmental stressors. At first they appear to vary along a single dimension—*severity of impact*. However, we shall see that they actually vary along a number of additional dimensions as well.

Cataclysmic events are overwhelming stressors that have several basic characteristics. They are usually sudden, and give little or no warning of their occurrence. They have a powerful impact, elicit a more or less universal response, and usually require a great deal of effort for effective coping. Natural disaster, war, or nuclear accident are all unpredictable and powerful threats that generally affect all of those touched by them. The accident at Three Mile Island, the heat waves in the American southwest, as well as the more common tornadoes, hurricanes, and other natural disasters (Baker & Chapman, 1962; Baum *et al.,* 1980; Pennebaker & Newtson, 1983; Sims & Baumann, 1972) can all be considered in this category of stressor.

Because cataclysmic events are usually sudden, the powerful onset of such occurrences may initially evoke a freezing or dazed response by victims (Miller, 1982; Moore, 1958). Coping is difficult and may bring no immediate relief. However, the severely threatening period of such an event usually (but not always) ends quickly, and recovery begins. A tornado may strike for only a brief time and other cataclysmic events may be over in a few days (Baum, Fleming, & Davidson, 1983). When the process is allowed to proceed without a return of the stressor, rebuilding progresses and more or less complete recovery is generally achieved. In the case of Three Mile Island or Love Canal, where rebuilding is not what is needed (nothing was actually destroyed), and the damage already done is less important than the damage that may yet come, recovery may be more difficult.

One important feature of cataclysmic events, which is in some ways beneficial for the coping process, is that they impact on a large number of people. Affiliation with others and comparing feelings and opinions with them have been identified as important styles of coping with such threats (e.g., McGrath, 1970; Schachter, 1959), for social support can moderate the effects of stressful conditions (e.g., Cobb, 1976). In other words, having people around to provide support, a source of comparison for one's emotional and behavioral responses, and other forms of assistance can reduce the negative impact of a stressor.

Because people are able to share their distress with others undergoing the same difficulties, some studies have suggested that cohesion results among these individuals (Quarantelli, 1978). Of course, this does not always happen, and residents cannot "band together" to fight a stressor indefinitely. When a stressor persists in an apparently unresolvable manner, problems of a different kind can arise.

A second group of stressors may be termed *"personal stressors."* These include such events as illness, death of a loved one (e.g., Greene, 1966; Parkes, 1972; Hackett & Weisman, 1964), or loss of one's job (Kasl & Cobb, 1970)—events that are powerful enough to challenge adaptive abilities in the same way as cataclysmic events. Personal stressors generally affect fewer people at any one time than cataclysmic events, and may or may not be expected. Frequently with personal stressors the point of severest impact occurs early and coping can progress once the worst is over, although this is not always the case. Often the magnitude, duration, and point of severest impact of cataclysmic events and personal stressors such as death and loss of a job are similar. However, the relatively smaller number of people who experience a particular personal stressor at any one time may be significant, because there are fewer others to serve as sources of social support. As we mentioned earlier, this can moderate the effects of negative events.

Background stressors are persistent, repetitive, and almost routine. They are considerably less powerful than the stressors discussed above, their effects are more gradual, and they usually are much more chronic. They may be *daily hassles*— stable, low-intensity problems encountered as part of one's routine. For example, consider the following description of a typical morning, provided by a student who lived off-campus and commuted to an urban university:

I get up and go downstairs for breakfast. There's always a mess down there—my roommates don't clean up and I've got to do it. Anyway I clean up and eat, get dressed and ready for school. Then I've got to go out and coax my car to start. I usually have to kick it a few times, but sometimes it won't start and I've got to take a bus—which is always late, crowded, and too hot.

While many background stressors are mundane and of relatively low intensity, some may not even be noticeable, like certain instances of air pollution (e.g., Evans & Jacobs, 1981). Any one or two background stressors may not be sufficient to cause great adaptive difficulty, but when a number occur together they can exact a cost over time, and may be as serious as cataclysmic events or personal stressors. Regular and prolonged exposure to certain low-level background stressors may even require more adaptive responses in the long run than more intense stressors. For example, long-term exposure to noise (Cohen, Glass, & Singer, 1973), neighborhood problems (Harburg *et al.,* 1973), and long-term commuting stress (Singer, Lundberg, & Frankenhaeuser, 1978) can be quite problematic.

With background stressors, it is often difficult to identify a point at which the "worst is over," and it may not be at all clear that things will get better. In fact, things may go from bad to worse. In addition, the benefits for coping of having others who "share in the experience" may not be as great as for other types of stressors. This may be because the intensity of background stressors is frequently so low as to never raise the need for affiliation; or, alternatively, social support may not be appropriate in these situations.

Appraisal

The degree to which people will view an event as stressful is determined by *appraisal*. During appraisal, a great deal of information is considered and decisions are made about danger, threat, and the like. Several different types of appraisal are possible. *Harm or loss assessments* focus on damage that has already been done (Lazarus & Launier, 1978). For example, victims of a natural or technological disaster could be expected to make harm/loss evaluations. In contrast, *threat appraisals* are concerned with future dangers. Environ-

mental toxins such as pesticides may evoke perceived threats to one's health, and threat appraisals may precede exposure to them. The ability to anticipate potential difficulties allows us to prevent their occurrence, but may cause us to experience anticipatory stress. *Challenge appraisals* are different from the others because they focus not on the harm or potential harm of an event, but on the possibility of overcoming the stressor. Some stressors may be beyond our coping ability, but we all have a range of events for which we are confident of our ability to cope successfully. Stressors that are evaluated as challenges fall within this hypothetical range (Lazarus & Launier, 1978).

A number of factors have been identified that affect our appraisals of environmental stressors. These include the characteristics of the condition in question (e.g., how loud a particular noise is), situational conditions (e.g., whether what we're doing is compatible with or inhibited by the potential stressor), individual differences, and environmental, social, and psychological variables. To cite but one example, the upper-middle class resident of a large city may be less likely to experience difficulty as a result of urban conditions than a poorer resident of the same city. Or, he or she may be better able to avoid the seamy side of the city, and thus less likely ever to be exposed to aversive urban conditions. Attitudes toward the source of stress will also mediate responses; if we believe that a condition will cause no permanent harm, our response will probably be less extreme than if it carries the threat of lasting harm. If our attitudes are strongly in favor of something that may also harm us, we may reappraise threats and make them seem less dangerous. Overall, then, the appraisal of stressors is based on properties of the situation, attitudes toward the stressor or its source, individual differences, and many other factors.

Another moderator of stress appraisals may be social support, the feeling that one is cared about and valued by other people—that he or she belongs to a group (Cobb, 1976). Many have long believed that interpersonal relationships can somehow protect us from many ills. However, the effects of having or not having social and emotional support have not always been clearly demonstrated.

Coping styles or behavior patterns also appear to affect the ways in which events are appraised, as well as which types of coping are invoked. Work on a number of these dimensions, such as repression–sensitization (the degree to which people think about a stressor), screening (a person's ability to ignore extraneous stimuli or to prioritize demands), and denial (the degree to which people ignore or suppress awareness of problems), has indicated that people differing along these dimensions may interpret situations differently (e.g., Byrne, 1964; Collins, Baum, & Singer, 1983; Janis, 1958; Mehrabian, 1976). A study by Baum *et al.* (1982), for example, suggests that individuals who cope with overload by screening and prioritizing demands are less susceptible to the effects of crowding than people who do not cope in this way.

Glass (1977) has described a stress-relevant coping style. Individuals who manifest a Type A behavior pattern are those who respond to stress as if it were control-threatening, and who interpret most threats as stressful. Their greater likelihood of experiencing stress and its physiological concomitants, as well as the time urgency, competitiveness, and hostility that accompany this response, cause Type A's to be at higher risk for coronary heart disease (Glass, 1977). It is tempting to speculate that their behavior pattern might make Type A's more susceptible to many stressors for which loss of control is a direct antecedent or cause (e.g., noise, crowding) (Baron & Rodin, 1978; Baum & Valins, 1979; Cohen, 1980).

Perceived control is generally an important mediator of stress, providing a sense of being able to cope effectively, to predict events, and to determine what will happen. Most researchers define perceived control as the belief that one can affect what happens to him or her (Glass & Singer, 1972). Whether the ability to determine outcomes is real or merely perceived, the belief that one has

control seems to reduce the negative effects of stress. Much of the evidence for this comes from studies of noise, which we will deal with in a later section.

Another example of how control may affect appraisal comes from the growing literature on cognitive control. Providing subjects with information about a stressor prior to subjects' exposure to it helps them to plan and predict what will happen. Such information increases perceived control and reduces the threat appraisal made when the stressor is experienced. For example, the stress associated with surgery or aversive medical procedures can be reduced by providing patients with accurate expectations of what they will feel (e.g., Johnson, 1973; Johnson & Leventhal, 1974). Other studies have found that accurate expectations reduce crowding stress (Baum, Fisher, & Solomon, 1981; Langer & Saegert, 1977).

Characteristics of the Stress Response

When appraisals are made, responses are determined as well. If an event is interpreted as threatening or harmful, stress responses are more likely. In other words, if an appraisal is "negative" and an event is seen as being dangerous, responses that prepare us to cope will ensue. These stress responses involve the whole body. Physiological changes are part of this response, most reflecting increased arousal. At the same time, emotional, psychological, and behavioral changes may also occur as part of the stress response.

Some responses to environmental stress are virtually indistinguishable from those evoked by direct assault on body tissue by pathogens. Recalling Selye's three-stage process, it appears that stress results in heightened secretion of corticosteroids during the alarm reaction, followed by a decline in reactivity through resistance and exhaustion. Subsequent work has also identified the catecholamines—epinephrine and norepinephrine—as active in stress. Research has associated emotional distress with these same patterns of arousal (e.g., Konzett, 1975; Schachter & Singer, 1962). Further, challenge, loss of control or predictability, and psychosocial stressors have been linked to increased adrenal activity (Frankenhaeuser, 1978; Glass, 1977; Konzett *et al.*, 1971).

Increased catecholamine and corticosteroid secretion is associated with a wide range of other physiological responses, such as changes in heart rate, blood pressure, breathing, muscle potential, inflammation, and other functions. Prolonged or sudden elevation of circulating catecholamines may damage body tissue, and is suggested as a cause of the development of hardening of the arteries and other diseases of the blood vessels (Schneiderman, 1983). Catecholamines also appear to affect cognitive and emotional functioning, and elevated levels of epinephrine or norepinephrine in the blood may affect our mood and behavior.

These findings may also be viewed as consistent with pioneering work by Cannon (1929, 1931) who suggested that epinephrine has a positive effect on adaptation. Epinephrine provides a biological advantage by arousing the organism, thus enabling it to respond more rapidly to danger. When extremely frightened or enraged, we experience an arousal that may be uncomfortable, but which readies us to act against the thing that scares or angers us. Thus, stress-related increases in catecholamines may facilitate adaptive behavior.

Some studies have shown superior performance on certain tasks following epinephrine infusion (Frankenhaeuser, Jarpe, & Mattell, 1961) and among people with higher catecholamine output in the face of challenge (e.g., Frankenhaeuser, 1971). On the other hand, arousal has been associated with impaired performance on complex tasks (cf. Evans, 1978). Decreases in problem-solving abilities, increases in general negativity, impatience, irritability, feelings of worthlessness, and emotionality may all accompany a stress response, and emotional disturbances such as anxiety or depression may occur.

Cognitive deficits associated with stress may be caused by behavioral strategies that are used for coping with stress—"tuning out" or narrowing one's field of attention (e.g., Cohen, 1978). When under stress, we may be unable to concentrate or unwilling to put effort into a task (e.g., Glass & Singer, 1972). In other ways, our coping response may be specific to the stressor being experienced, reflecting the specific causes of our discomfort. People may respond to crowding caused by too many people by withdrawing and avoiding social contact, whereas their response to crowding caused by limited space might be aggression (e.g., Baum & Koman, 1976). A person might respond to job loss actively if the loss was caused by a lack of effort rather than ability, or may become helpless under certain conditions.

Aftereffects are not specific to certain stressors, but appear to reflect more general effects (Cohen, 1980). Defined as consequences experienced after exposure to a stressor has terminated, these fit in with Selye's (1976) notion of limited adaptive energy. As exposure to stress increases, adaptive reserves are depleted, causing aftereffects and reductions of subsequent coping ability. Evidence for the existence of poststressor effects comes from a number of sources, including research on the effects of noise (e.g., Glass & Singer, 1972; Rotton *et al.*, 1978; Sherrod & Downs, 1974; Sherrod *et al.*, 1977), crowding (Sherrod, 1974; Evans, 1979), and electrical shock (Glass *et al.*, 1973).

Psychological effects that linger or persist may also reflect consequences of adaptation. Calhoun (1967, 1970) has referred to *refractory periods,* which are periods of time during which an organism recovers from a bout with a stressor. If the refractory period is interrupted by another encounter, increased stress-relevant problems are likely.

Thus far we have considered stress from a conceptual perspective. We now turn to some specific instances of environmental stress. We will discuss natural disasters, technological catastrophes, noise, and commuting. Other environmental stressors will be discussed in later chapters.

NATURAL DISASTER

Earlier in the chapter, when we described cataclysmic events, we frequently made reference to natural disasters. Natural disasters are an extremely good example of this kind of event; they can be very destructive, sudden, terminate quickly, and require a great deal of effort in order to cope. Natural disasters include almost any threatening event that occurs in the natural environment. They are not caused by people's actions, but their effects can be increased or decreased by certain actions.

Our definition of natural disasters thus includes extreme weather of any kind (heat, cold, hurricanes, tornadoes, blizzards, ice storms, wind storms, monsoons, etc.). Earthquakes and volcanic eruptions, mudslides and avalanches are also natural disasters, but may be affected by human alteration of the earth. Underground bomb testing, for example, could cause many of these events under certain conditions.

We also include floods in our definition, even though these are often caused by a combination of natural events (e.g., rain) and actions taken by people (e.g., improper use of riverbanks). Some floods are almost entirely caused by humans, as in the case of dam failure. These would be more appropriately considered as technological mishaps or catastrophes. Other cataclysmic events that are human-made, including mine disasters, air crashes, nuclear accidents, toxic waste contamination, and the like, may also be considered technological mishaps.

Research on natural disaster is difficult to conduct for a number of reasons. To start with, these events are almost always studied *after they have already occurred*. As a result, we cannot get information about people before they were exposed to the disaster and, therefore, cannot demonstrate changes in mood and behavior. A second problem is the choice of an appropriate control group. With whom shall we compare our findings from victims of a storm or earthquake? Finally, choice of measures is difficult, since research must often be conducted in recently devastated, often chaotic conditions far from the researchers' laboratory. Obtaining samples is also problematic, since recruitment for a study often must be done quickly. Many times, one cannot sample randomly and must resort to quasirandom sampling (e.g., selecting every third person seen on a given street). This may cause the sample to be nonrepresentative of the entire area affected by the mishap and can limit the degree to which we can make general statements about our findings.

Characteristics of Natural Disasters

Partly because of these measurement problems, our understanding of natural disasters is not complete. However, a great many studies of these events have been done, and we have learned a great deal about them. We are now familiar with the basic properties of cataclysmic events such as natural disasters. Because they are sudden, they are usually unpredictable. Depending upon the event, we may have more or less warning—living near a fault tells you that there may be an earthquake, but it does not tell you when it will occur, and living in a "tornado belt" tells you much the same about tornadoes. Weather alerts often provide warning of imminent tornadoes, but do not specify exactly where the funnel will touch down. These reports can provide adequate warning of some storms and floods, but often do not. Natural disasters are generally not well predicted and are typically viewed as uncontrollable.

The destructive power of a natural disaster is sometimes enormous and usually substantial. In other words, they usually do damage and sometimes wreak havoc. The sheer magnitude of the impact of some disasters makes them unique among stressors. Natural disasters often last only seconds or minutes and rarely persist for more than a few days. Heat waves and cold spells may persist longer, but most storms, quakes, and other mishaps are over quickly. Once the crisis has passed, coping can proceed and rebuilding and recovery can be achieved. Usually, this coping requires a great deal of effort.

Effects of Natural Disasters

More than any other symptom, researchers report a stunned, numb response to the immediate impact of disaster (Boman, 1979; Crashaw, 1963; Erikson, 1976; Lifton & Olson, 1976; Rangell, 1976). Quarantelli and Dynes (1972) noted that panic was a rare response among survivors, that many acted calmly and rationally. This may seem surprising, but with a few exceptions, such as response to fires in crowded nightclubs, panic does not occur very often.

Most studies of the effects of disasters have used psychiatric interviews of selected groups of survivors. As a result, most findings are expressed as frequency of psychiatric problems, and, for the most part, anxiety, depression, and other stress-related emotional disturbances have been found among victims of floods, tornadoes, hurricanes, and other natural disasters (Logue, Hansen, & Struening, 1979; Milne, 1977; Moore, 1958; Penick, Powel, & Sieck, 1976; Taylor & Quarantelli, 1976). Generally, these effects have been found to last up to a year, but they are not nearly as widespread among victims as one might expect. Studies rarely show more than 25–30 percent of victims suffering psychological effects months after a disaster, and it appears that people who lost more in the disaster are those who continue to suffer (e.g., Parker, 1977). In other words, it is more accurate to conclude that the loss of a home or a loved one in a disaster leads to psychological problems than that natural disasters invariably cause lasting problems.

This is consistent with research by Erikson (1976) who suggested that many of the symptoms of disaster survivors arise from the destruction of the community. Disorientation and "lack of connection" are common symptoms among disaster survivors when the community has been torn. Older people may emphasize the loss of items that symbolize their lifetimes; a tree or a garden, for example. Children take their cues from their parents (Crashaw, 1963) and respond to their parents' fear or lack of it. When they are exposed more directly to environmental disruption, they react strongly to scenes of death and mutilation

(Newman, 1976). They may also regress to earlier stages of behavior.

As we noted earlier, stress formulations as well as other theories or approaches to the study of environmental events can be used to understand the phenomena we will describe in this chapter. Destruction of a community can involve *behavioral constraint,* as options for activity are reduced and behavioral freedom is limited. People may be forced to leave their homes and move to large shelters where behavior must conform to emergency rules. Water and power service may be disrupted, further limiting what people can do, and plans are unavoidably changed by the sudden impact of the event. When our behavior is constrained, we may react negatively to the loss of freedom, feel badly, and act in ways to reestablish our freedom. Continuous constraints on our behavior that cannot be removed may eventually cause us to experience helplessness. Fortunately, once the emergency is past, constraints are reduced—people may return to their homes and normal services are restored. However, for those who are made homeless or who have lost a family member or close friend, constraints and their negative effects may continue. Rebuilding or relocating are necessitated and choices of activities are further limited by losses and the need to cope with them.

In communities that have lost many people in a disaster, *ecological* perspectives may help to explain the effects of the event. You will recall that *manning* refers to the number of people in a setting. Over- and undermanning, in which too many or too few people are present in the setting, are viewed as negative states that cause problems. Communities are settings, and there are roles that must be played in them. When a large number of the members of the community suddenly die, the community may become *undermanned,* and those remaining are forced to assume multiple roles. This can cause strain and, coupled with problems caused directly by specific losses, can help to explain the effects of disaster.

Natural disasters, then, can affect people in a number of ways. They are clearly stressful, limit freedom and behavioral options, and may cause a shortage of people, leading to the breakdown or disruption of a community. In many ways, these events are similar to disasters caused by human-made parts of the environment. Disasters involving failure of the things we have built, such as dams, bridges, power plants, and mines, also appear to be stressful.

TECHNOLOGICAL CATASTROPHE

To a large extent our dominance of the natural environment and our adaptation to its hazards has been achieved through advances in technology. Improvements in the quality of life, prolongation of life, mastery over disease, and the like are based on a broad technological network we have created. These machines, structures, and other human-created additions to our environment share unparalleled responsibility for supporting our way of life. For the most part, they accomplish this goal and work well under human control. However, this network occasionally fails, and something goes wrong. Hence we have blackouts of major cities, leakage of toxic chemicals from waste dumps, dam failures, and bridge collapses.

Characteristics of Technological Catastrophe

To a certain extent, technological catastrophes share the same characteristics as natural disasters. They may be acute and very sudden, as in the case of a dam failure or blackout. These technological mishaps are usually brief and the worst is soon over. However, other technological catastrophes are more chronic. The discovery of contamination at Love Canal began a chronic period of distress for area residents, as did the nuclear accident at Three Mile Island. For people affected by these events, the worst was not over quickly, nor was it easily identified. A great deal of uncertainty can accompany such events.

The effort required in coping also varies with the technological catastrophe in question. Some

such events are more like natural disasters, and require a great deal of effort to cope. Others, like a blackout, for example, probably require less overall effort than a sudden, massive flood following a dam break.

Interestingly, technological catastrophes may be more apt to threaten our feelings of control than natural disasters. This is somewhat paradoxical since natural disasters are inherently uncontrollable and we never really expect to be able to control their occurrence. Technological catastrophes, on the other hand, are the effects of an occasional loss of control over something we normally control quite well. If this loss of control is intermittent, temporary, and not indicative of an entire collapse, why is it so disquieting?

It is possible that because technological catastrophes are losses of control we are supposed to have, they shake our confidence in our ability to control events in the future. These events are never *supposed* to happen—technological devices are designed never to fail unpredictably, and to warn us when they are worn out. Thus, nuclear power plants are not supposed to have accidents *ever* and toxic waste dumps are not supposed to leak. But these things do happen, and often appear to strike at random. Instead of saying "No accidents will happen," we may often find ourselves wondering "Where will the next explosion occur?" "Which plane will crash?" "Which waste dump will leak?" and so on. While the above analysis is somewhat speculative, it provides some feel for the complexities of people's responses to technological catastrophes. These kinds of events can reduce general perceptions of control and lead to stress (Davidson, Baum, & Collins, 1982).

The Buffalo Creek Flood.   One disaster with a human-made cause has been studied rather intensively. In February 1976, a dam built of coal slag by the Buffalo Mining Company collapsed. The dam prevented thousands of tons of water and coal slag from flooding the town of Saunders and a string of small towns in the Buffalo Creek

SCAPEGOATS AND DISASTERS

Rumors during and after disasters can develop around who or what was to blame. One pattern is to project blame for disasters onto targets that are not really responsible, rather than to blame those directly involved (Drabek & Quarantelli, 1967). For example, there is a tendency to *generalize* blame to "big shots" who are in charge of large organizations or who are known to be wealthy and influential. A construction failure in a city is more likely to be blamed on city hall than on the inspector who worked on that particular project. There is also reluctance to blame the dead following a disaster. A race driver who lost control of his car and died along with several spectators is later regarded as a hero for keeping his car from colliding with other cars on the track.

Drabek and Quarantelli report that one counterproductive outcome of scapegoating is to focus attention on personalities rather than causes. Another is to delay or completely halt changes in municipal codes, disaster planning, and other direct actions designed to prevent or at least control future disasters.

Valley of southern West Virginia. When the dam broke, everything was destroyed.

The town of Saunders disappeared and several other settlements were also obliterated by the flash flood careening back and forth between the walls of the valley. The flood lasted only about 15 minutes, but the devastation was nearly complete. One hundred and twenty-five people were dead and more than 5,000 were left homeless. The valley had been physically altered; few remnants of valley life remained.

The Buffalo Creek flood was clearly due to failure of a human-made device—the dam holding back the creek. As with other technological mishaps, the flood was never supposed to happen. As a result, it was even less predictable than the storms that had swollen the creek behind the dam. And, as we have suggested, this disaster, partly because of its human origins, appears to have had more chronic effects on the victims than ordinary floods or natural disasters. While many of the specific effects are similar to those observed in studies of natural disaster, they seem to have had more lasting consequences.

Research at Buffalo Creek has identified a number of problems occurring as late as two years after the flood. Among these are:

1. *Anxiety*—Fears about the disaster and about the changes in life style that came in its aftermath were common (Gleser, Green, & Winget, 1978; Lifton & Olson, 1976; Titchener & Kapp, 1976).
2. *Withdrawal or numbness*—Almost all researchers at Buffalo Creek noted apathy and blunted emotion after the flood (Lifton & Olson, 1976; Erikson, 1976; Rangell, 1976).
3. *Depression*—Many survivors lost everything they had worked a lifetime for and became sad and subdued (Titchener & Kapp, 1976; Killijanek & Drabek, 1979).
4. *Stress-related physical symptoms*—Almost all somatic or bodily symptoms, including gastrointestinal distress, aches and pains, and so on, were increased (Titchener & Kapp, 1976).
5. *Unfocused anger*—Survivors found themselves angry and upset. When disasters are human-made, the rage tends to be worse. This is due, in part, to the fact that although there was a culpable agent, identification of a specific person to blame was difficult (Lifton & Olson, 1976; Gleser,

Green, & Winget, 1978; Hargreaves, 1980).

6. *Regression*—Children often regressed to earlier stages of behavior (Newman, 1976; Titchener & Kapp, 1976).

7. *Nightmares*—Dreams about dying in the disaster and about dead relatives occurred frequently. Sleep disturbances were common as well (Gleser, Green, & Winget, 1981; Newman, 1976).

Titchener and Kapp (1976) noted that traumatic neurosis was evident in more than 80 percent of the sample they studied. Anxiety, depression, character and life style changes, and maladjustments and developmental problems in children occurred in more than 90 percent of the cases. Anxiety, grief, despair, sleep disturbances, disorganization, problems with temper control, obsessions and phobias about survival guilt, a sense of loss, and rage were some of the symptoms. Lifton and Olson (1976) listed several characteristics of the flood at Buffalo Creek that intensified the reactions to it: the suddenness, the human-cause factor, the isolation of the area, and the destruction of the community. Survivors were aware of the symptoms. They were surprised at how long they had survived and afraid that recovery was impossible (Lifton & Olson, 1976).

The Three Mile Island Accident.   Research at Three Mile Island (TMI) also illustrates the kinds of effects that can occur over a long period of time following a technological catastrophe. In March 1979, an accident occurred in Unit 2 at the TMI nuclear power station. Through a number of equipment failures and human errors, the core of the reactor was exposed, generating tremendous temperatures. The fuel and equipment inside the reactor was damaged and by the time the reactor was brought back under control, some 400,000 gallons of radioactive water had collected on the floor of the reactor building. In addition, radioactive gases were released and remained trapped in the concrete containment surrounding the reactor.

During the crisis, which lasted several days, there were a number of scares. Some people feared a nuclear explosion, others a meltdown, and still others feared massive radiation releases. Information intended to reduce fears often increased them because it was contradictory or inconsistent with other information that had been released. An evacuation was advised, and this probably contributed to the chaos and fear of the moment.

There is little doubt that the accident at TMI caused stress. During the crisis period there was a good probability that threats would be appraised; research suggests that most people living near the plant were threatened and concerned about it (Flynn, 1979; Houts *et al.*, 1980). Immediately after the accident, studies found greater psychological and emotional distress among nearby residents than among people living elsewhere (Bromet, 1980; Dohrenwend *et al.*, 1979; Flynn, 1979; Houts *et al.*, 1980).

Despite the fact that the severe threats associated with the accident disappeared relatively quickly, it does not appear that the kind of recovery that characterizes the aftermath of many natural disasters followed at TMI. First, the potential danger of radiation release remained long after the reactor was brought under control. The radioactive gas remained trapped in the containment building for more than a year after the accident. For some area residents the potential for exposure from this source remained a threat, due to occasional leaks of small amounts of the gas. Approximately 15 months after the accident, this gas was released in controlled bursts into the atmosphere around the plant. The radioactive water remained in the reactor building and decontamination had not advanced significantly some four years after the accident.

Research on the chronic effects of living near TMI is still ongoing, but there is evidence that stress effects persisted among some area residents up to two years after the accident. Bromet (1980), for example, has reported evidence of emotional distress among young mothers living near TMI. A series of studies has also identified stress effects among some TMI area residents 15 to 22 months after the accident (Baum *et al.*, 1983; Baum, Gatchel, & Schaeffer, 1982; Schaeffer & Baum, 1982).

These studies were conducted with few subjects, but they examined behavioral and physiological aspects of stress as well as self-reported measures. Symptom reporting, task performance, and physiological arousal were measured, the latter by obtaining urine samples from subjects. In general, these studies found that some residents of an area within five miles of the TMI plant reported more emotional and psychological distress, more somatic distress, showed greater stress-related task performance problems, and exhibited higher levels of physiological arousal than did control subjects. Though levels of these variables did not indicate severe stress, they did suggest chronic moderate magnitude difficulties. Control subjects lived near an undamaged nuclear plant, a coal power plant, or near no plant at all, and all of them lived more than 80 miles from TMI.

These studies also reported effects of several variables that we have considered as influencing stress. Not all TMI residents seemed to be stressed. Fleming *et al.* (1982) found that TMI area residents who reported having little or no social support exhibited greater evidence of stress than did those who had a great deal of support. Differences along coping style dimensions were also found. TMI area residents who were more concerned with palliative coping (managing their emotional response) showed fewer stress symptoms than did TMI subjects who were more concerned with taking direct action and manipulating the problem (Collins, Baum, & Singer, 1983). Finally, the continued uncertainty at TMI appears to have suppressed feelings of personal control among TMI area residents, and those who reported the least confidence in their ability to control their surroundings exhibited more symptoms of stress than did residents who were more confident (Davidson *et al.*, 1982).

Clearly, not all technological catastrophes are like these. For a number of reasons, each accident

Figure 4–1. Like other technological mishaps, the accident of Three Mile Island has had long-lasting effects. (Marc A. Schaeffer)

or failure has unique aspects to it. These studies illustrate the potential for acute and chronic consequences of technological catastrophe. In many other instances (e.g., power blackouts) the problem is far less serious, and the effects are much more transient.

In addition to causing stress, technological catastrophes also involve processes related to the other theoretical orientations discussed in Chapter 3. With few exceptions, technological mishaps lead to behavioral constraint, loss of control, and the problems associated with these states. Evacuation, whether temporary (as at TMI) or more permanent (as at Love Canal), disrupts and limits what we can do. At TMI, people may find it more difficult to sell their homes if they live near the reactor, and thus may be limited in their freedom to move. At Buffalo Creek, the destruction of almost everything in the valley also severely limited what people could do, and required almost complete attention to a circumscribed set of recovery options. People could, for example, rebuild their homes and places of business, move to a "safer" nearby area, or "call it quits" and leave altogether. Very few realistic options may be available following such an event.

Manning levels may become important when a community loses many members, but for some technological catastrophes this is not the case. At TMI, the number of people living in the community has not been drastically reduced, while in the Buffalo Creek flood, many people died. Manning theory will prove useful when losses have occurred in much the same way as for natural disasters.

Figure 4–2. Examples of sound waves. Frequency increases from top to bottom; amplitude increases from left to right.

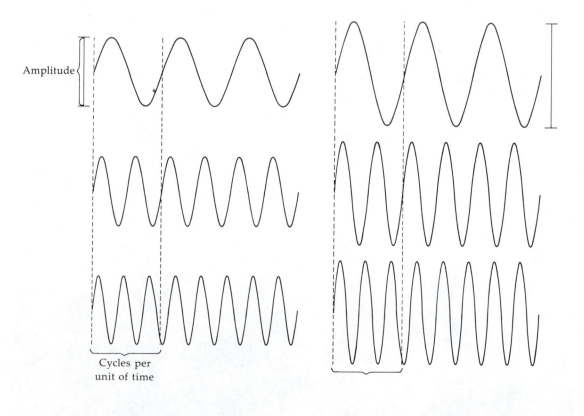

NOISE

Having covered several stressors classified as cataclysmic events, we turn now to a discussion of two *background stressors*—noise and commuting. Noise is a different kind of environmental stressor from the ones we have discussed thus far. It is considerably less powerful or overwhelming than disaster, and is usually encountered repetitively in separate episodes. In addition, the noise that influences human behavior is usually a human-made by-product of civilization. Like technological catastrophes, noise does not typically occur in the natural environment. We will discuss this stressor in great detail, because noise has been very thoroughly researched. It will be helpful first to define noise and to discuss its measurement before examining its effects on physiology, performance, and social behavior.

Defining, Measuring, and Perceiving Noise

The simplest and most common definition of noise is that it is "unwanted sound." You may enjoy listening to your favorite rock group on your stereo, but if the music disturbs your roommate's studying or sleep, then as far as your roommate is concerned the moving sound of the talented musicians is noise. The sound of a garbage truck making pick-ups early in the morning may be necessary in order to maintain healthy sanitation, and for the early riser this sound may provide a wake-up cue signaling a bright new day. But if you do not wish to be roused so early in the morning, then the motorized contraption is making noise. Loud industrial machinery, jet aircraft, keypunch machines, and pneumatic hammers also generate noise, but only if someone finds the sound undesirable. Thus, the concept of noise implies both a significant psychological component ("unwanted") as well as a physical component (it must be perceived by the ear and higher brain).

The measurement of sound involves primarily its physical component, although the brain's interpretation of the sound is also crucial to the structure of the measuring scale. Physically, sound is created by the rapidly changing pressure of air molecules at the eardrum. As these molecules are forced together, positive pressure is created relative to the negative pressure when the molecules pull apart. This alternating pressure can be represented graphically by waves, the peaks of the waves representing positive pressure and the valleys negative pressure (Figure 4–2). These alternating pressures cause the eardrum to vibrate. The eardrum then transmits these vibrations through the structures of the middle and inner ear to the basilar membrane in the cochlea (Figure 4–3A and B.) Tiny hair cells in this membrane, which are activated by the noise vibrations, pass along the noise stimulation through the auditory nerve to the temporal lobe of the brain. In the conventional sense, auditory *sensation* consists of the activation of the nervous system by the sound stimulus. *Perception* begins somewhere between the basilar membrane and the temporal lobe of the brain, where a code we have yet to unravel allows the organism to interpret the sound stimulus as high or low in pitch and volume.

Examine the waves depicted in Figure 4–2 once again. Physically, the more times per second the wave motion completes a cycle (from peak to valley), the greater the *frequency* of the sound. Psychologically, frequency is perceived as pitch, i.e., highness or lowness. The normal human ear can hear frequencies between 20 and 20,000 cycles per second, or hertz (Hz). However, most sounds we hear are not one frequency but a mixture of frequencies. Psychologically, purity of frequency is known as *timbre* or *tonal quality*. Sound stimuli that consist of a very few frequencies are often called "narrow band," whereas stimuli with a wide range of frequencies are called "wide band." A very wide range of unpatterned frequencies is called "white noise."

Besides varying in frequency characteristics, sound waves vary according to height or amplitude, experienced psychologically as loudness: The greater the amplitude, the louder the sound. The loudness of a sound is related to the amount of energy or pressure in the sound wave. The

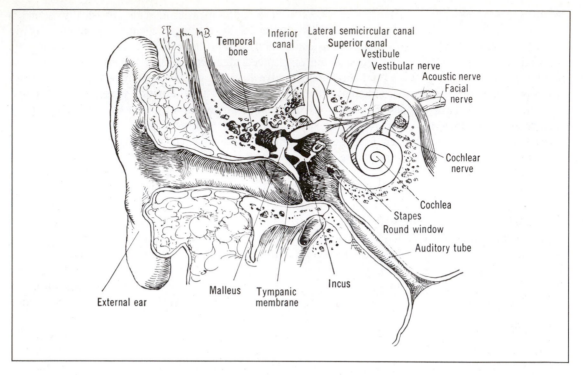

Figure 4–3A. Schematic diagram of human ear, showing important structures associated with perception of sound. (From Gardner, E. *Fundamentals of Neurology,* 6th ed. Philadelphia: Saunders, 1975.)

smallest pressure or *threshold* distinguishable by the human ear is about 0.0002 microbars, or dynes per square centimeter, where a dyne is a measure of pressure. At 1000 microbars, the pressure is experienced more as pain than as sound. Since a scale of sound ranging from 0.0002 microbars to 1000 or more microbars would be cumbersome to work with, a scale of sound pressure

Table 4–1. DECIBEL EQUIVALENTS OF MICROBARS

Sound Pressure in Microbars	Equivalent Decibels
0.0002	0
0.002	20
0.02	40
0.2	60
2.0	80
20.0	100
200.0	120
2000.0	140

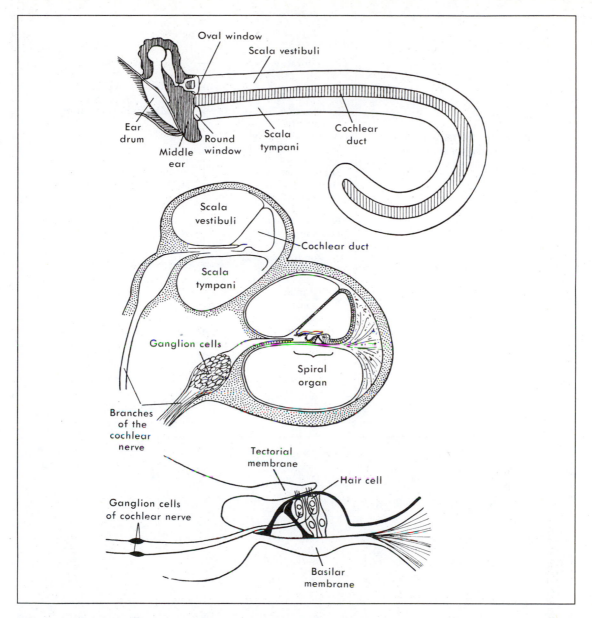

Figure 4–3B. Internal structure of human auditory system, (From Gardner, 1975.)

has been developed that uses decibels (dB) as the basic units of sound, where decibels are a logarithmic function of microbars. Table 4–1 gives the corresponding decibel equivalents of the audible range of microbars. Note that an increase of 20 decibels represents a tenfold increase in pressure. Figure 4–4 presents some common sounds

associated with various points on the decibel scale.

The decibel scale measures the *physical* component of sound or noise amplitude. However, this scale does not accurately reflect the *perception* of loudness. That is, an increase of 20 dB does mean that one sound has 10 times more pres-

Figure 4–4. Some common sounds associated with the decibel scale.

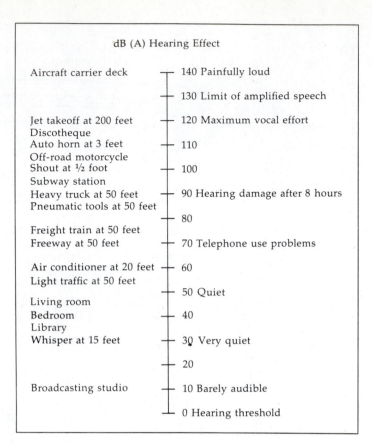

dB (A) Hearing Effect

Sound	dB (A)	Hearing Effect
Aircraft carrier deck	140	Painfully loud
	130	Limit of amplified speech
Jet takeoff at 200 feet	120	Maximum vocal effort
Discotheque		
Auto horn at 3 feet	110	
Off-road motorcycle		
Shout at ½ foot	100	
Subway station		
Heavy truck at 50 feet	90	Hearing damage after 8 hours
Pneumatic tools at 50 feet		
	80	
Freight train at 50 feet		
Freeway at 50 feet	70	Telephone use problems
Air conditioner at 20 feet	60	
Light traffic at 50 feet		
	50	Quiet
Living room		
Bedroom	40	
Library		
Whisper at 15 feet	30	Very quiet
	20	
Broadcasting studio	10	Barely audible
	0	Hearing threshold

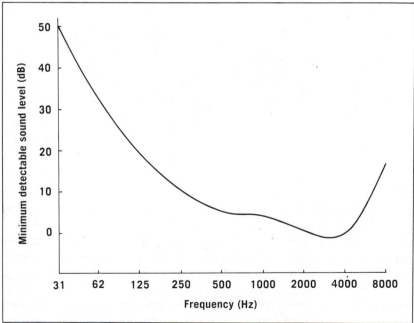

Figure 4–5. Sensitivity of the human ear to different frequencies of sound. (From Turk, A., Turk, J., Wittes, J. T., and Wittes, R. *Environmental Science,* Philadelphia: Saunders, 1974.)

sure than another, but it does not mean that the more intense sound will be perceived as 10 times louder. The main reason for this lack of physical-perceptual correspondence is that the human ear is differentially sensitive to sounds at different frequencies, as indicated in Figure 4–5. That is, below about 500 Hz and above about 4000 Hz, it takes a more intense sound even to be detected than it does between 500 Hz and 4000 Hz. To find a loudness scale that reflects human perception, we have to turn to *phons* or *sones*.

A phon is defined as the level in dB of a 1000 Hz tone when it is judged to be of the same loudness as the sound being tested. That is, to determine the phon level of a given sound, we ask a subject to adjust a 1000 Hz tone until the two sounds appear to be of equal loudness. The dB level of the 1000 Hz tone at the point of apparently equal loudness is then considered the phon level of the sound being tested. A sone, on the other hand (Stevens, 1955), is determined by starting with a 1000 Hz tone at 40 dB. The perceived loudness of this tone is defined as one sone. A sound perceived to be twice as loud as this standard tone is defined as two sones, a sound three times as loud is three sones, and so on. Obviously, the relationship between decibels, phons, and sones will depend on the frequencies as well as the intensities of the sounds measured. Figure 4–6 depicts equivalent dB, phon, and sone levels for three frequencies. Note that for these frequency and dB levels, an increase of 20 dB (representing a tenfold increase in pressure) represents a two-to-fourfold increase in perceived loudness. (For a more detailed discussion of sound, see Kryter, 1970.)

Important Noise Variables

Noise is a disturbing environmental phenomenon because it is, by definition, unwanted. It is this irritating and distracting psychological component that causes noise to be a problem. Kryter (1970) and Glass and Singer (1972) point out that some types of noise are more annoying than others. Three major dimensions influencing the annoyance characteristics of noise are: (1) volume; (2) predictability; and (3) perceived control.

How are we affected by noise at different volumes? Above 90 dB, which is the level of noise produced by a heavy truck 50 feet away, noise becomes not only psychologically disturbing but also, after repeated periods of exposure for eight hours or more, physiologically damaging to hearing. Moreover, the louder the noise, the more likely it will interfere with verbal communication, the greater the arousal and stress associated with it, and the more attention one allocates to it.

Unpredictable, irregular noise is also more annoying than predictable, constant noise. A constant unbroken noise (especially if it is not loud) is not disturbing. Once we break it up into periodic ''bursts,'' however, the noise becomes more disturbing; if we then make the bursts of noise aperiodic (i.e., coming at unpredictable or irregular intervals), the disturbing quality becomes even more pronounced. The more unpredictable the noise, the more arousing it is, and the more likely it is to lead to stress (unpredictable noises may be evaluated as more novel or threatening than predictable ones). In addition, more unpredictable noises require greater attention to understand and evaluate them, leaving less total atten-

Figure 4–6. Equivalent decibel, phon, and sone levels for selected frequencies. *(Interpolated from Kryter, 1970, after Zwicker, 1960.)*

Frequency	63 Hz			1000 Hz			10,000 Hz		
dB	50	80	90	50	80	90	50	80	90
phon	70	106	115	80	106	114	76	103	111
sone	8	97	180	16	95	172	14	78	140

tion available for other activities (e.g., Easterbrook, 1959). Finally, it is easier to adapt to a predictable noise, since the same stimulus is presented over and over again; with unpredictable noise, adaptation is more difficult.

Noise over which we have no control is also more disturbing than noise we can control readily. If you have the means to stop or muffle a noise, you are less annoyed by it than if you cannot control it. For example, if you are using a noisy power saw, you can control the noise by stopping the saw. If your neighbor uses the saw next door, however, you have less immediate control over the noise, and so it is more disturbing. From the theoretical perspectives discussed previously, uncontrollable noise is more arousing and stressful, requires more attention allocation, and is more difficult to adapt to than controllable noise. From the behavior constraint approach, lack of control over noise can lead to psychological reactance and attempts to regain freedom of action by trying to assert control. If such efforts are unsuccessful, learned helplessness can result (see Chapter 3), in which a person simply accepts the noise and never tries to control it, even though control may become possible at a later time.

These three noise variables can, of course, occur in any combination. That is, we can have loud, predictable, uncontrollable noise, or quiet, unpredictable, uncontrollable noise, and so on. As we will see in a while, loud, unpredictable, uncontrollable noise has the most deleterious effects on behavior. Although these three factors are probably the most important in determining the effects of noise on behavior, research (Borsky, 1969) suggests that other factors also influence how annoying noise is. Annoyance increases if: (1) one perceives the noise as unnecessary; (2) those who generate the noise are perceived as unconcerned about the welfare of those who are exposed to it; (3) the person hearing the noise believes it is hazardous to health; (4) the person hearing the noise associates it with fear; and (5) the person hearing the noise is dissatisfied with other aspects of his or her environment.

Sources of Noise

As you might guess, noise can come from almost anywhere. Because it has a subjective component (it must be judged as unwanted), noise can come from anything that makes a sound. And, as you would also expect, the same sound may be unwanted at some times but not unwanted at other times. A dripping faucet passes as a faint whisper against the background sound of a busy afternoon, but at night, when we are trying to sleep, it can be noisy indeed.

In spite of this, there are contexts in which most people complain about noise. These settings are ones in which sound is either so loud that it is considered to be noise, or is a little softer but more interfering, irregular, or disruptive. We will briefly discuss two of the common settings where noise can be a problem.

Transportation Noise. Noise caused by cars, trucks, trains, planes, and other modes of transportation is of great interest for a number of reasons. First, it is very widespread. Surveys have indicated that automobile noise is the most often mentioned source of urban noise and that opening of new highways is associated with increases in annoyance among nearby residents (Lawson & Walters, 1974). Reports estimate that up to 11 million Americans are exposed to vehicular noise at or above levels that risk hearing loss (Bolt, Beranek, & Newman, Incorporated, 1976; Galloway *et al.*, 1974). Increases in air traffic have increased noise levels around airports, and studies have shown that about 2/3 of those people living near airports where aircraft noise is a problem report annoyance and unhappiness about the noise (e.g., Burrows & Zamarin, 1972; McLean & Tarnopolsky, 1977). Rail traffic also continues to be a problem. Estimates in New York City alone suggest that a half million residents are exposed to loud (85–100 dB) noise from rapid transit trains (Raloff, 1982). Thus, the pervasiveness of noise generated by transportation systems makes it important to study.

A second characteristic of transportation noise is that it is usually loud. This is clear from the sound levels noted above, as well as from estimates of sound levels near airports (ranging from 75–95 dB). A quick glance at Figure 4–4 also provides evidence of this, as do recent EPA measurements of noise levels in third floor apartments next to freeways in Los Angeles (90 dB) (Raloff, 1982).

Occupational Noise. Noise exposure in the workplace is a second major problem and has also received a great deal of research interest. It is also very pervasive and the sound levels in many occupational settings are loud. More than half of the nation's production workers are exposed to regular noise levels above the point at which hearing loss is likely, and more than 5 million are exposed to levels above the legally permissible ceiling of 90 dB (OSHA, 1981). Construction workers may be exposed to equipment noises of 100 dB, aircraft mechanics to levels ranging from 88–120 dB, and coal miners to continuous levels between 95 and 104 dB (Raloff, 1982).

Physiological Effects of Noise

Hearing Loss. Although very loud sounds (e.g., 150 dB) can rupture the eardrum or destroy other parts of the ear, damage to hearing from excessive noise usually occurs at lower noise levels (90 to 120 dB) because of temporary or permanent damage to the tiny hair cells in the cochlea of the inner ear (Figure 4–3). Such hearing loss is measured in terms of a baseline of "normal" amplitude thresholds at given frequencies. When a hearing loss occurs at a given frequency, it requires more than the normal amplitude (in dB) for a person to hear that frequency, i.e., the amplitude threshold is greater. The usual index of hearing loss for a given frequency, then, is the number of decibels above the normal threshold required to reach the new threshold. Such hearing losses are generally identified as one of two types: (1) temporary threshold shifts (TTS), in which the normal threshold returns within 16 hours after exposure to the damaging noise; and (2) noise-induced permanent threshold shifts (NIPTS), which

are typically measured a month or more after the cessation of exposure to the damaging noise (Kryter, 1970).

Hearing loss, which affects millions of people, is a serious problem in this country. A 1972 Environmental Protection Agency (EPA) survey estimated that close to three million Americans suffer *noise-induced* hearing loss. A report by Rosen *et al.* (1962) compared the extent of the problem in the United States with a much quieter Sudanese culture, and found that 70-year-old Sudanese tribesmen have hearing abilities comparable to those of 20-year-old Americans! To avoid serious hearing loss among industrial workers, the Occupational Safety and Health Administration (OSHA) has established guidelines that allow only eight hours a day of exposure to 90 dB noise, four hours for 95 dB, two hours for 100 dB, and so on. Yet a diesel truck at 50 feet emits noise of 95 dB. Thus individuals living near heavy traffic routes are undoubtedly exposed to noise levels for periods of time exceeding government industrial standards. The potential consequences of such exposure are reflected in the box on page 104.

Absolute levels of noise alone do not determine hearing loss. Recent research, for example, suggests that certain drugs may increase the damaging effects of noise (Miller, 1982). Studies with animals have indicated that administration of an antibiotic in conjunction with exposure to noise can increase the effects of the noise and cause greater hearing loss than would the drug or noise levels alone (Raloff, 1982). Other drugs, including aspirin, may also interact with noise and increase effects on hearing, but evidence remains mixed. At this point it appears that a few drugs can, in combination with noise, cause increased hearing loss, but the magnitude of effect of most is small.

College students and teenagers are frequently exposed to another damaging source of noise—loud rock music. Several studies (e.g., Lebo & Oliphant, 1968) have found that rock groups playing in discotheques are exposed to from 110 to 120 dB music for nonstop periods of up to one

BEYOND THE LABORATORY: COSTS IN THE CLASSROOM

Cohen, Glass, and Singer (1973) theorized that urban noise may impair the educational development of children if it is severe enough. Studying a large high-rise apartment complex situated over a noisy highway in New York City (see Figure 4–7), the investigators found that noise exposure on the lower floors of the complex was more severe than on the upper floors. While carefully controlling for such factors as social class and air pollution, which might also vary with the floors of the building, the researchers found that children on the noisier lower floors had poorer hearing discrimination than children on the upper floors. Moreover, the hearing problems of children on the lower floors may have influenced their reading ability, for it was found that they had poorer reading performance than children on the upper floors!

In another study, Bronzaft and McCarthy (1975) compared the reading skills of children from two sides of a school building. One side of the building was adjacent to elevated railroad tracks, but the other side was much quieter. It was found that 11 percent of teaching time was lost in classrooms facing the noisy tracks. Not surprisingly, the reading skills of children on the quieter side of the building were superior to those of children on the noisy side (see also Crook & Langdon, 1974).

Research also suggests that aircraft noise has effects on children's performance. Cohen *et al.* (1980), studied children attending school near the Los Angeles International Airport. Some were in schools in which aircraft noise was very loud (up to 95 dB), while others were in schools where there was considerably less noise. After controlling for the effects of socioeconomic variables and accounting for differences in hearing loss, results of a multimeasure assessment indicated that children attending noisier schools had more difficulty solving com-

Sheldon Cohen

Figure 4–7. This is the high-rise apartment building used in the study described here. Note the traffic passing underneath.

plex problems. In addition, Damon (1977) found that children living in housing where traffic noise was high were more likely to miss school.

Can such problems be prevented? The report by Ward and Suedfeld (1973) suggests that they can. In response to a plan for routing a major highway next to a classroom building, the researchers played tape recordings of traffic at noise levels that simulated those of a real highway. Interference with learning was discovered before construction began, suggesting that we can plan ahead to avoid problems of this kind.

and one-half hours. Serious hearing loss can result (the federal industrial limit for 110 dB sound is 30 minutes a day). Other research (EPA, 1972) has studied hearing loss across samples of several age groups, and found a typical rate of failure on a hearing test of high frequencies to be 3.8 percent of sixth graders, 10 percent of ninth and tenth graders, and a whopping 61 percent of the 1969 college freshman class!

Physical Health. We have suggested that exposure to high levels of noise leads to increased arousal and stress. We might expect, then, that the incidence of diseases related to stress (hypertension, ulcers, etc.) would increase as one is exposed to' higher levels of noise. Research evidence on this relationship is not conclusive. On the one hand, Cohen, Glass, and Phillips (1977) reviewed studies done in this area and concluded that, in general, the evidence for noise as a pathogenic agent is weak. On the other hand, noise has been linked to spontaneous outbreaks of illness related to stress (e.g., Colligan & Murphy, 1982) and to incidence of neurological and gastrointestinal problems (National Academy of Science, 1981). Ulcers in particular appear more likely among workers exposed to occupational noise. Doring *et al.* (1980) have suggested that sound can affect intestinal tissue directly, so it does not even have to be heard to predispose a worker to digestive problems. In addition, at least one study (Ando & Hattori, 1973) has found an association between exposure of expectant mothers to aircraft noise and infant mortality. Finally, survey or correlational studies (see Chapter 1) have found that frequent exposure to noise is associated with reports of acute and chronic illness (Cameron, Robertson, & Zaks, 1972) and with increased consumption of sleeping pills and need to see a physician (Grandjean *et al.,* 1973). The latter studies, however, are weak, since they do not control for related factors such as housing conditions, income, or education.

It can also be readily demonstrated that exposure to high concentrations of noise (e.g., living near an airport, working in a noisy setting) leads

to heightened electrodermal activity, constriction of peripheral blood vessels, higher diastolic and systolic blood pressure, and increased catecholamine secretions (e.g., Cohen *et al.,* 1980; Frankenhaeuser & Lundberg, 1977; Glass & Singer, 1972; Knipschild, 1980). In addition, workers exhibit lower blood pressures and lower levels of epinephrine in their urine when they wear hearing protectors that reduce the intensity of noise (Ising & Melchert, 1980). The physiological changes accompanying exposure to noise are also associated with stress reactions and cardiovascular disorders, but few controlled *experimental* studies have been conducted that indicate a direct link between noise and heart disease.

Correlational studies have examined health problems of industrial workers as a function of exposure to noise. These studies (e.g., Cohen, 1973; Jansen, 1973) typically find that exposure to high noise levels is associated with cardiovascular disorders, allergic reactions, sore throat, and digestive disorders. Interestingly, younger and less experienced workers appear to suffer more from noise exposure, suggesting that more experienced workers have adapted to the noise. Unfortunately, such industrial studies rarely control for other factors that may account for adverse health effects, such as factory conditions, exposure to pollutants, and stressful work activity, so that conclusions about effects of noise on health must be guarded. Furthermore, some studies (e.g., Finkle & Poppen, 1948; Glorig, 1971) report no association between industrial noise exposure and many of the disorders we have noted.

Overall, it is difficult to relate noise *directly* to adverse effects on physical health. More likely, adverse effects of noise exposure on health occur primarily in conjunction with other stressors (such as industrial pollutants, on-the-job tensions, economic pressures, and so on), or are limited to those who are particularly susceptible to certain physiological disorders (Cohen *et al.,* 1977).

Noise and Mental Health. We have noted that exposure to high levels of noise leads to the heightened physiological activity typical of stress.

Figure 4–8. Some research has tried to associate airport noise with mental health problems of residents in the area. Although the findings are controversial, there is limited evidence that psychiatric hospital admissions are unusually heavy for areas surrounding airports.

Since stress is a causal factor in mental illness, we might expect noise exposure to be associated with mental disorders (for a review, see Cohen *et al.*, 1977; Kryter, 1970). Indeed, industrial surveys typically report that exposure to high-intensity noise is associated with headaches, nausea, instability, argumentativeness, anxiety, sexual impotence, and changes in affect or mood (Cohen, 1969; Cohen *et al.*, 1977; Miller, 1974; Strakhov, 1966). As with surveys on physical health and noise, however, the results of these studies must be interpreted with caution, since other stresses related to home and work are not fully taken into account. In a relevant experimental study, Ward and Suedfeld (1973) found that exposure to ''piped in'' traffic noise caused people to experience more tension and uncertainty and led people to talk faster than a group exposed to ambient sound conditions.

An interesting and controversial series of studies has attempted to examine the relationship between airport noise and mental health. In one study (Abey-Wickrama *et al.*, 1969), researchers compared psychiatric admission rates for high and low noise areas around London's Heathrow Airport. Higher admission rates occurred in the noisy area. Chowns (1970) challenged these results because the populations of the two areas may have differed in important ways, although Herridge (1974) and Herridge and Low-Beer (1973) found similar though weaker results with improved survey techniques (Figure 4–8).

As with physical health, we must tentatively conclude that to the extent noise contributes to mental illness, it does so in combination with many other factors that precipitate mental disorders. However, in addition to influencing stress, noise exposure may lead to loss of perceived control and learned helplessness (see Chapter 3), which in turn increase susceptibility to psychological disorders. Cohen *et al.* (1977) noted that residents of high-noise areas tend to ''give up'' and not complain about the noise because they perceive their voices will not carry weight with authorities. Together with the social and economic burdens typical of high-noise areas of cities, a sense of hopelessness and helplessness may develop, which can lead to psychological disorders.

Effects of Noise on Performance

Laboratory research on the influence of noise on performance has shown mixed results. For a detailed review, the reader is referred to Kryter (1970) and to Glass and Singer (1972). Briefly, whether noise affects performance adversely, favorably, or not at all depends on the type (e.g., predictable or unpredictable) and intensity of noise, the type of task performed, and the stress tolerance and other personality characteristics of the individual (e.g., Finkelman, 1975; Finkelman & Glass, 1970; Glass & Singer, 1972; Hamilton & Copeman, 1970; Hockey, 1970). In general, data from laboratory research suggest that, under most circumstances, noise in the range of 90 to 110 dB does not adversely affect performance of simple motor or mental tasks. However, noises in this amplitude range that are unpredictable (intermittent at irregular intervals) will interfere with performance on vigilance tasks, memory tasks, and complex tasks in which an individual must perform two activities simultaneously. On the other hand, Glass and Singer (1972) found that even these performance problems were minimal for individuals who perceived that they had control over the noise (i.e., could stop it if they wished). Other research (Broadbent, 1954) suggests that sudden, loud, unpredictable noises may momentarily distract an individual from a task and thereby cause errors if the task requires much vigilance or concentration. Woodhead (1964) noted that recorded sonic booms cause momentary errors in a task requiring intense concentration. Still other research has indicated that noise effects on performance may depend in part on personality, as in Auble and Britton's (1958) finding that only subjects who are high in anxiety are adversely affected by noise on certain types of tasks. Finally, limited research (e.g., Corcoran, 1962) suggests that the arousal properties of noise may actually facilitate performance for individuals who have been deprived of sleep for a day or more.

How can we explain why noise affects performance only under certain circumstances? To answer this question, we can turn to the theoretical approaches discussed in Chapter 3. For example, adaptation level theory predicts variation in performance for different levels of skill, experience, and stimulation for each individual. Furthermore, the Yerkes-Dodson Law and the arousal approach suggest that noise that is arousing will facilitate performance on simple tasks, up to a point. High levels of arousal interfere with performance on complex tasks, and extremely high levels of arousal interfere with performance on simple tasks. Data from research on noise and performance are consistent with this explanation.

The environmental load approach also explains much about the relationship between noise and performance. Unpredictable noise requires more allocation of attention than predictable noise, so it should interfere more with performance. For complex tasks, very much attention is required for optimal performance, and any noise that distracts attention will hurt performance. Finally, the behavior constraint approach explains why lack of perceived control over noise hurts performance: When control is apparently lost, more effort may be given to restoring control than to attending to the task at hand.

Noise has more than just immediate effects on performance. Glass, Singer, and Friedman (1969) had subjects perform tasks after a 25-minute exposure to 108 dB noise. One task involved attempts to solve puzzles that were actually unsolvable (Figure 4–9). The number of attempts to solve such puzzles served as an index of tolerance for frustration, or persistence. The second task involved proofreading a manuscript, which required considerable vigilance and concentration. Compared to a no-noise control group and groups exposed before the task to either predictable *or* controllable noise, subjects exposed before the task to 108 dB of unpredictable *and* uncontrollable noise showed one-half to one-third as much tolerance of frustration and also made considerably more proofreading errors. Apparently, the aftereffects of noise can be as severe as the effects during perception of the noise. In a similar experiment, it was found that aftereffects depend on the amount of perceived control (Sherrod *et al.*, 1977). These researchers gave some subjects con-

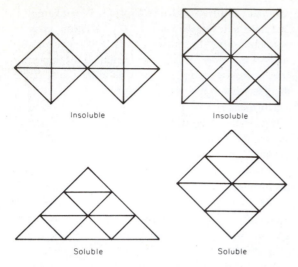

Insoluble   Insoluble

Soluble   Soluble

Figure 4–9. Examples of puzzles used by Glass and Singer (1972). Figures must be drawn without crossing a line or lifting the pencil. (Adapted by Glass & Singer from Feather, 1961.)

trol over starting the noise, others control over stopping the noise, and still others control over both starting and stopping it. Another group had no control over the noise. Results showed that the greater the perceived control, the more persistent subjects were in working unsolvable puzzles once the noise had stopped.

Such aftereffects can also be explained by the theoretical approaches discussed previously. For example, arousal remains elevated for a time after an arousing stimulus (such as noise) has ceased. Thus, this "carried over" arousal can account for some aftereffects. The environmental load approach also suggests that once an attention-getting noise has stopped, a fatigue effect ensues, and it takes time to reallocate enough attention to perform a mental task. If the noise is presented with perceived control, less attention is allocated to it to begin with, so recovery time is less, and the potential for learned helplessness is decreased.

Research in Office and Industrial Settings.
One of the most serious problems of background noise in commercial and industrial settings is its

interference with communication (Mackenzie, 1975; Nemecek & Grandjean, 1973). When a number of distinct auditory signals are presented simultaneously, it is often difficult for the human ear to distinguish or discriminate among them. This phenomenon is known as *masking,* and it accounts for our difficulty in hearing others talk in the presence of loud background noise. The background noise in the Glass and Singer (1972) research was created by combining simultaneously the sounds of a mimeograph machine, a calculator, a typewriter, two people speaking Spanish, and another person speaking Armenian, with the final effect being little discriminability among the various sounds due to masking. Interestingly, it has been found that loud background conversation interferes with performance more than noise that is not distinguishable as conversation (Olszewski, Rotton, & Soler, 1976). Apparently, we try to hear background conversation as communication, so we pay a lot of attention to it. Nonconversational noise, however, requires less attention but does interfere with efforts to communicate.

Difficulty in hearing a communication varies not only according to amplitude and frequency of background noise (the more similar the frequency of the noise and of the communication, the worse the interference), but also according to the distance between communicator and listener. Figure 4–10 demonstrates the combined effects of ambient noise amplitude and interpersonal distance on communication. These "acceptable" levels of background noise are sometimes referred to as "speech interference levels" or SIL's (Beranek, 1957). Limited research (e.g., Acton, 1970) indicates that some communicative adaptation to background noise does occur, so that we can learn to communicate effectively in the presence of many types of background noises. Thus, industrial workers accustomed to a noisy environment were found to be more effective in communicating against a loud background noise than were university employees accustomed to a quieter environment. Beranek (1956, 1957) examined self-reports of employees in offices and factories to determine what noise levels they considered ac-

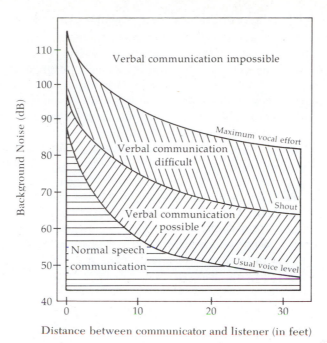

Figure 4–10. Relationship between communication effort, noise level, and interpersonal distance. (Adapted from Miller, 1974.)

ceptable in their work environments. Results correlated quite well with what might be predicted from SIL data, suggesting that 55 to 70 dB is acceptable for executive offices. Many designers and builders use these standards today (Mackenzie, 1975).

Research on the effects of noise on productivity in industrial settings generally finds no direct effect of noise on nonauditory performance (Kryter, 1970). However, several studies have purported to show that noise reduction can boost productivity. Broadbent and Little (1960) found that in a film-producing factory, reduction of ambient noise from 99 dB to 89 dB resulted in fewer errors by workers. Kovrigin and Mikheyev (1965) reported that increasing background noise from 78–80 dB to either 85, 90, or 95 dB reduced the number of letters sorted per hour by postal employees. Kryter (1970) suggests that because such studies are conducted in field settings not subject to strict laboratory control of extraneous vari-

ables, the results are inconclusive at best. Reduction of noise, for instance, may boost employee morale, which in turn boosts productivity. In other words, mediating variables, such as morale, fatigue, or communication difficulty, may be more significant than direct effects of noise on performance. Nevertheless, if noise influences productivity even indirectly, industry would certainly want to take such influences into account by designing equipment and working space with noise levels in mind.

Concern over productivity, morale, and detrimental health effects of noise has led many industry and government officials to emphasize noise abatement factors in office and industrial settings (see also Mackenzie, 1975). Among the more common abatement procedures are: use of thick carpeting, suspended and acoustical tile ceilings, sound-absorbing wall materials, heavy draperies, and even plants. Other approaches involve making machines quieter in the first place, such as putting a layer of felt between typewriters and desks, enclosing computer printout equipment with felt or foam-lined covers, and producing equipment with less noisy components. Still another approach is to mask noise with constant-humming ventilating equipment or piped-in music. Whatever the technique, we suspect that an increasing emphasis by labor and management will be placed on reducing noise in working environments.

Noise and Social Behavior

If noise has stressful, arousing, attention-narrowing, or behavior-constraining properties, exposure to it will be likely to influence interpersonal relationships. We will now look at three specific social relationships—attraction, altruism, and aggression—to determine just what noise can do to social interaction.

Noise and Attraction. One might expect loud, disturbing noise to have a deleterious effect on feelings of liking toward others, as predicted by the reinforcement-affect model of evaluative responses (pages 46 to 47). That is, noxious stimuli associated with others may lead to less pleasant evaluation of those others. One way to measure attraction, as suggested by research on personal space (see Chapter 6), is to examine physical distances between ourselves and others; we stand or sit closer to those people we like than to those we dislike. Thus, if interpersonal distance is an indicator of attraction and if noise decreases attraction, we would expect noise to increase interpersonal distancing. In support of this hypothesis, Mathews, Canon, and Alexander (1974) found that even a noise of 80 dB increased the distance at which individuals felt comfortable with each other. Also, in a correlational study, Appleyard and Lintell (1972) found less informal interaction among neighbors when traffic noise was greater. While this could suggest that noise lowers attraction toward others, additional interpretations are possible.

Other researchers (Bull *et al.,* 1972) have found equivocal results on the relationship be-

tween noise and attraction. These researchers found that although exposure to 84 dB of background noise led to less liking in most cases, females actually reported more liking for similar others when exposed to noise. Research by Bell and Barnard (1977) suggests a partial explanation for this unexpected finding. Apparently, males exposed to noxious environmental stimulation momentarily prefer more distant, less affiliative social interaction. Females, on the other hand, may well prefer closer, affiliative social interaction in order to share their uneasiness with others who are experiencing discomfort. Thus, in some circumstances noise may decrease attraction, and in other cases it may increase attraction. Kenrick and Johnson (1979), for example, have shown that among females, exposure to aversive noise may increase attraction toward one who shares the aversive experience with the subject, but decrease attraction toward someone not actually experiencing the noise.

One explanation for some effects of noise on attraction is that noise affects the amount of information that people gather about another person. Theories that suggest that noise causes people to narrow their attention and focus on a smaller part of their environment also suggest that noise causes people to pay attention to fewer characteristics of other people. Thus, noise could cause a distortion in perceptions of other people. Research by Siegel and Steele (1980) suggests that this may be the case, finding that noise led to more extreme and premature judgments about other people but did not cause these judgments to be more negative.

Noise and Human Aggression. Research on the effects of noise on aggression has been much more conclusive than research on noise and attraction. Several theories of aggression (Bandura, 1973; Berkowitz, 1970), predict that under circumstances in which aggression is a dominant response in the behavior hierarchy, increasing an individual's arousal level will also increase the intensity of aggressive behavior. Thus, to the extent that noise increases arousal, it should also in-

THE SST: WHY SO LOUD?

One of the marvels of space-age technology is supersonic flight and the arrival of the supersonic transport (SST) for commercial passengers. The American version of the SST was scuttled for economic and environmental reasons. The British–French Concorde, however, went into production and has been controversial ever since. Among its problems is noise. Engines on an SST must be slim and trim for better flight. As engine diameter decreases and speed increases, jet exhaust noise becomes greater. Typical Concorde noise on a runway is 100 to 120 dB, depending on one's distance from the jet. This is 10 to 20 dB greater than subsonic jets. Research suggests that a single flight of an aircraft 10 dB louder than another produces the same annoyance level as 10 flights of the less noisy aircraft.

Another noise problem with the SST is sonic booms. These thunderclap sounds are produced by any supersonic aircraft. Sound travels at a speed of 334 meters per second (747 miles per hour). The SST moves faster than the noise it produces (since passengers are ahead of the sound, they do not hear it as someone on the ground does). Consequently, the sound waves crowd together, increasing their pressure and causing a sonic boom. The tail of the aircraft leaves a partial vacuum, lowering the pressure as it passes. The result is an increase in pressure followed by a decrease. These pressure changes move away from the jet in

the pattern of cones (Figure 4–11), so that anyone on the ground between the two cones hears the boom. If the aircraft is long enough, the positive and negative pressure changes may be heard as two distinct sounds. The boom itself continues from the time the aircraft breaks the sound barrier until it resumes subsonic speeds, but a person on the ground hears it for only 0.1 to 0.5 second. Thus, the entire area over which the SST flies at supersonic speeds will experience the sonic boom. For this reason, the SST is currently forbidden to fly over the United States at supersonic speeds. (From Turk *et al.*, 1974.)

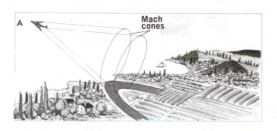

Figure 4–11. Cones representing increased and decreased pressure in a sonic boom. The area where the cones intersect the ground (shaded gray) experiences the sonic boom. (From Turk, A., Turk, J., Wittes, J. T., and Wittes, R. *Environmental Science*. Philadelphia: Saunders, 1974.)

crease aggression in individuals already predisposed to aggress.

Geen and O'Neal (1969) sought to test this hypothesis by first showing subjects either a nonviolent sports film or a more violent prizefight film, with the expectation that the violent film would predispose subjects to aggress. Next, subjects were provided with an opportunity to aggress against a confederate "victim" by ostensibly delivering electric shocks to that person. In many

studies of aggression, subjects are given the chance to shock a confederate or stooge victim and the shock level (intensity, duration, or number) they choose is the index of aggression. No shocks are actually administered, although the subject, until the end of the experiment, is led to believe that he or she is actually delivering shocks. During the shock phase of the experiment, Geen and O'Neal exposed half the subjects to the normal noise level of the laboratory and the

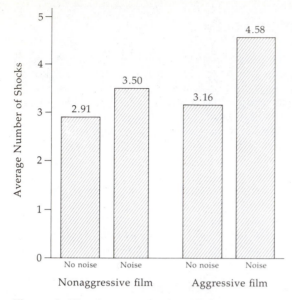

Figure 4–12. Average number of shocks delivered to the victim as a function of noise level and type of film. (Adapted from Geen and O'Neal, 1969.)

other half to a two-minute burst of continuous 60 dB white noise (i.e., a broad band of frequencies). It was predicted that the 60 dB noise would increase the level of aggression of subjects exposed to the violent film. Results, as depicted in Figure 4–12, suggested that both the violent film and the added noise increased the number of shocks delivered to the victim. Furthermore, the greatest aggression occurred under the condition that combined the violent film with the arousing noise, as originally predicted.

Additional laboratory research on noise and aggression has been conducted by Donnerstein and Wilson (1976). It will be recalled that Glass and Singer (1972) found unpredictable noise to be more aversive than predictable noise. One would thus expect unpredictable noise to be highly arousing and consequently to lead to heightened aggression, in accordance with the dominant response hypothesis noted above. Donnerstein and Wilson therefore exposed subjects to either 55 dB or 95 dB of unpredictable, one-second noise

bursts while they were ostensibly administering electric shocks to a confederate of the experimenter. In addition, half the subjects previously had been either angered or not angered by this victim. As expected, angered subjects delivered more intense shocks than nonangered ones. Furthermore, the 95 dB unpredictable noise increased aggression relative to the 55 dB unpredictable noise only for angered subjects. Apparently, noise made no difference in the intensity of shocks delivered by nonangry subjects.

Following Glass and Singer's findings that controllable noise is less aversive and arousing than uncontrollable noise, we would expect that if subjects were given perceived control over noise, the noise would be less aversive and less likely to facilitate aggression. Donnerstein and Wilson tested this hypothesis by conducting a second experiment to determine the effects of additional noise variables on aggression. As subjects worked on a set of math problems, they were exposed either to no artificial noise, to 95 dB of unpredictable and uncontrollable noise, or to 95 dB of unpredictable noise that they believed they could terminate at any time (i.e., over which they perceived they had control). All noise was terminated when subjects began the shock phase of the experiment, so that only the aftereffects of noise could influence aggression. As in the previous experiment, subjects were either angered or not angered by the victim, in this case immediately after the math task. The results, depicted in Figure 4–13, suggest that more intense shocks were delivered by angry than by nonangry subjects, and that unpredictable and uncontrollable noise increased aggression for angry subjects. The 95 dB noise had no effect on aggression, however, when subjects perceived they had control over it.

The finding that noise only increased aggressiveness when people were angry suggests again that the noise served to facilitate aggression caused by anger rather than creating or causing the aggression directly. Konecni *et al.* (1975) also found this to be the case—noise only increased aggressiveness when subjects had been provoked and made angry.

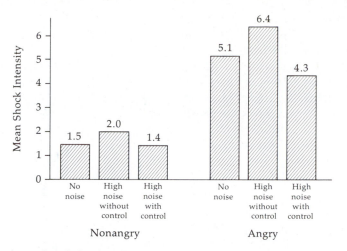

Figure 4–13. Mean intensity of shock delivered by subjects as a function of noise condition and anger arousal. (Adapted from Donnerstein and Wilson, 1976.)

These experiments suggest, then, that under circumstances in which noise would be expected to increase arousal or a predisposition to aggress (i.e., when subjects were already angry), aggression is increased. However, when the noise does not appreciably increase arousal (as when an individual has control over it) or when the individual is not already predisposed to aggress, noise appears to have little, if any, effect on aggression.

Noise and Helping. Research suggests that noise influences at least one more social phenomenon—whether or not people help each other. It seems reasonable to assume that aversive noise that makes us irritable or uncomfortable will make us less likely to offer assistance to someone who needs help. Research in social psychology has indicated that people are more likely to help others when they are in a good mood than when they are more negative (e.g., Isen, 1970), and since noise can result in the latter condition, it is likely that helping would also be affected. Another reason for this expected decrease in helping is offered by the environmental load approach discussed in Chapter 3. Since noise reduces the attention paid to less important stimuli, if social cues that someone needs help are less important

than cues associated with a more important task, then noise should make us less aware of signs of distress. Cohen and Lezak (1977) demonstrated that the content of slides depicting social situations was less well remembered under noisy than under quiet conditions when subjects were asked to concentrate initially on material other than the slides. Under such conditions, social cues in the slides were relatively unimportant, so noise interfered with attending to these cues.

Consistent with this, two experiments, one conducted in the laboratory and the other in the field, suggest that noise does indeed decrease frequency of helping (Mathews & Canon, 1975). In the laboratory experiment, subjects were exposed to 48 dB of "normal" noise, to 65 dB of white noise piped into the laboratory through a hidden speaker, or to 85 dB of white noise from the same speaker. As subjects arrived for the experiment, they were asked in turn to wait in the laboratory for a few minutes with another individual (actually a confederate of the experimenter) who was seated and reading a journal. On the confederate's lap were additional journals, books, and papers. After a few minutes the experimenter called for the confederate who, upon getting up, "accidentally" dropped the materials right in front of the subject. The dependent measure of helping was whether or not the subject helped the confederate to pick up the spilled materials. Results suggested a definite decrement in helping in the loud noise conditions: 72 percent of the subjects helped in the normal noise condition, 67 percent in the 65 dB condition, and only 37 percent in the 85 dB condition.

The Mathews and Canon field experiment revealed even more interesting results. In this study, a confederate dropped a box of books while getting out of a car. To emphasize his apparent need for aid he wore a cast on his arm in half of the experimental situations. Noise was varied by having another confederate operate a lawnmower nearby. In the low-noise condition, the lawnmower was not running, and background noise from normal sources was measured at 50 dB. In the high-noise condition, the lawnmower was running without a muffler, putting out an 87 dB din. Once again, the dependent measure of helping was how many passing subjects stopped to assist the confederate to pick up the dropped books. As can be seen in Figure 4–14, noise had little effect on helping when the confederate was not wearing a cast. But when the confederate wore a cast (high-need condition) the loud noise reduced the frequency of helping from 80 percent to 15 percent! Apparently, noise led subjects to attend less to cues (i.e., the cast) that indicated that the person needed help.

A series of studies by Page (1977) also provide evidence that noise can reduce the likelihood that people will help each other. In one study, subjects encountered a confederate who, with an armful of books, had dropped a pack of index cards. They were exposed to one of three levels of noise (100 dB, 80 dB, or 50 dB) at the time they saw the confederate drop the cards. Results of this study suggested that people helped most under low levels of noise. However, these results were not strong (see also Bell & Doyle, 1983).

A second study reported by Page (1977) found stronger results. In this one, subjects saw a confederate drop a package while walking past a construction site. When the jackhammers were being

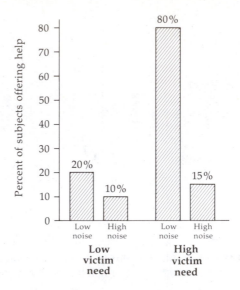

Figure 4–14. Percentages of subjects offering help as a function of noise level and need of victim. (Adapted from Mathews and Canon, 1975.)

used on the site, noise levels were 92 dB; when they were not being used, levels were 72 dB. Thus, depending on the jackhammers, subjects saw a confederate drop a package during one or another level of noise. People were less likely to help the confederate when noise levels reached 92 dB than they were when it was a relatively quiet 72 dB.

These results suggest that people who experience noise simply may not notice that someone needs help. Page (1977) conducted one more study in which people were approached and directly asked whether or not they could provide change for a quarter. In this context, "narrowing of attention" could not explain any negative effects of noise on helping. However, noise once again decreased the likelihood that people would respond to the request.

The reasons for the suppressing effects of noise on helping behavior are not yet known for sure, but the most likely explanations still appear to be the "narrowing of attention" notion and the "mood" explanation. Nevertheless, each of these has been disconfirmed by at least one study. A study that argues against the idea that noise reduces helping by putting people in bad or irritable moods was reported by Yinon and Bizman (1980). They exposed subjects to one of two noise levels (high or low) while they worked on a task, and then gave them positive or negative feed back on their performance. After this, subjects encountered someone who asked them for help. One might expect the combination of the negative feedback and loud noise to dampen subjects' moods and cause them to refuse to help. This is not, however, what was found. Under the high-noise condition, there were no differences in helping between the positive and negative feedback groups. Only under low noise did the feedback make a difference. Apparently, the loud noise distracted people from focusing on the feedback or provided a reason for the negative feedback. Although it is still possible that mood states were involved, their role in this study does not appear to be crucial.

We have seen thus far that perceived control over noxious noise reduces its impairment of performance and its facilitation of aggression. A study by Sherrod and Downs (1974) similarly demonstrated that perceived control reduces the negative influence of noise on helping behavior. In that study, subjects participated in a proofreading task while simultaneously monitoring a series of random numbers presented on audio tape. Three conditions were established: (1) a control condition in which the numbers were superimposed on the pleasing sounds of a seashore (e.g., waves striking the beach); (2) a complex noise condition in which the numbers were superimposed over a round of Dixieland jazz and another voice reading prose; and (3) a perceived control condition using the same tape as the complex noise condition but with the subjects told they could terminate the distracting noise if they so desired. After 20 minutes in one of these situations, subjects left the laboratory and were approached by an individual asking their assistance in filling out forms for another study. The most help was volunteered by subjects in the seashore sound condition, for whom noise was least noxious. Subjects in the perceived control condition offered more help than subjects in the uncontrollable complex noise condition. Thus, the effects of noise on helping behavior depend on several factors, among which are perceived control of the noise, volume of the noise, and stimulus characteristics of the person needing assistance.

Summary of Noise Effects on Behavior

Noise can lead to increased arousal, stress, narrowing of attention, and constraints on behavior. The aversiveness of noise depends on volume, predictability, and perceived control. In combination with other stressors, noise may have adverse effects on physical and mental health. Whether noise hurts or helps performance depends on the type of noise, the complexity of the task, and individual factors such as personality and adaptation level. Noise interferes with verbal communication and may affect productivity. Depending on the situation and the type of noise, noise may increase or decrease attraction, facilitate aggression, or interfere with helping behavior.

COMMUTING

The final background stressor we will consider is commuting. Like noise, commuting may be stressful in a single exposure, but is usually experienced repetitively in milder episodes. Stokols and Novaco (1981) have noted a number of costs of commuting, with emphasis on automobile commuting. Among the problems caused by our dependence on individual vehicles for commuting are energy overconsumption and safety issues. Another problem appears to be the stress of commuting and its effects on psychological and physical health.

Commuting stress has a number of sources. Research has found that traffic volume (the number of cars on the road) is associated with arousal. Higher traffic volume is related to increases in reports of chest pains and measures of heart rate, blood pressure, heartbeat irregularities, and skin conductance (Aronow *et al.*, 1972; Michaels, 1962; Stokols *et al.*, 1978; Taggart, Gibbons, & Somerville, 1969).

Michaels (1962) also found that limited access to the commuting route (i.e., fewer intersections, less entering traffic) led to less tension (measured by skin conductance) than did unlimited access. Research suggests that more complicated routes, such as those requiring one to pass other cars or to negotiate dangerous curves and intersections, are associated with higher blood pressure and faster heart rate (Littler, Honour, & Sleight, 1973).

Commuting stress is also affected by conditions such as temperature, noise, humidity, and air pollution (Stokols & Novaco, 1981). When all of these characteristics of commuting are considered together, a range of stressful commutes can be conceptualized, from the brief, simple commute on empty roads to the hot, sweaty, complex commute through rush hour.

Impedance

In order to better account for these contributing factors, Stokols, Novaco, and their associates have used a construct called *impedance* (Stokols & Novaco, 1981; Stokols *et al.*, 1978). Defined as any circumstances or conditions that interfere with one's transit between two points, impedance includes almost all of the factors noted above. Some, such as heat, which may seem to interfere, are not as applicable as others, such as traffic volume and road design. The greater the number of turns required, other cars to be negotiated, intersections to be crossed, curves to be cornered, stop lights to deal with, construction barriers encountered, or other such disruptions, the greater the impedance.

In a sense, then, impedance indexes the ease of a commute. High impedance commutes are more difficult and, therefore, may be more stressful. Novaco, Stokols, Campbell, and Stokols (1979) and Stokols *et al.* (1978) report evidence of this. Subjects were paid volunteers from two industrial firms. Of the 100 participants, 61 were men and

39 were women. During initial testing, all had been driving the same route to work for at least eight months.

On the basis of subjects' descriptions of their commutes, they were divided into low, medium, and high impedance groups. The first consisted of 27 subjects whose commutes fell in the lowest 25 percent of total time and distance. The medium impedance group consisted of 22 commuters who fell in the middle 30 percent of distributions for time and distance. The third group consisted of 36 people falling in the upper 25 percent of time and distance distributions. Table 4–2 clearly shows that higher impedance reflected longer distances and commuting time.

The table also shows something else. A range of measures was collected from participants immediately after five different trips to work in a single week. On three of these days, blood pressure and heart rate were measured, and on the other two days, measures of tolerance for frustration and other aftereffects of stress were collected. Subjects also reported their impressions of each trip.

As is shown in the table, impedance influenced a number of these measures. However, the effects are not as great as one would have expected. What was more clearly indicated by these results was that personal variables such as how one copes with commuting are just as important as characteristics of the commute in determining stress. The researchers found consistent effects of coping style indicating that high impedance commutes caused fewer problems for Type A drivers than for Type B drivers, while medium impedance commutes were somewhat *more* stressful for Type A than for Type B drivers.

The evidence suggests that commuting can be stressful, but that the extent to which stress is experienced will depend on a number of factors. As with other stressors, characteristics of the source (the actual commute) are important. Road design, traffic volume, trip complexity, and weather conditions are all aspects of the commuting environment that affect stress. In addition, personal factors such as coping style are important in

Table 4–2. EFFECTS OF IMPEDANCE ON COMMUTING STRESS.

Group:	Low Impedance	Medium Impedance	High Impedance
Distance (miles) of commute	less than 7.5	10–14	18–50
Time (minutes) in commuting	less than 12.5	17–20	30–75
Systolic blood pressure (mmHg)	123	130	132
Diastolic blood pressure (mmHg)	76	77	79
Satisfaction with commute (7 pt. scale)	5.9	5.6	4.5
Traffic congestion and inconvenience (7 pt. scale)	3.2	4.1	4.8

From Stokols, D., Novaco, R. W., Stokols, J., and Campbell, J. Traffic congestion, Type A behavior, and stress. *Journal of Applied Psychology,* 1978, *63,* 467–480.

determining appraisal and response to different commuting conditions. Further research is clearly called for to provide a better understanding of when and for whom commuting stress will occur and what its long-term consequences might be.

CHAPTER SUMMARY

In discussing stress, we considered three different aspects of it—*stressors* (events that provoke stress); *appraisal* (interpretation of the situation); and *response*. Lazarus and Cohen (1977) have considered three general classes of stressors: (1) cataclysmic phenomena; (2) powerful personal events that challenge adaptive abilities in the same way as cataclysmic events, but affect fewer people; and (3) "daily hassles."

The appraisal or interpretation of stressors has also been considered. The key issue at this level is whether or not the stressor will be perceived as threatening. Responses to stressors are determined by the extent to which the stressors are perceived as harmful, rather than the objective danger (Laz-

arus, 1966). Lazarus and Launier (1978) have specified the following types of interpretations:

1. Harm or loss assessments involving analysis of damage that has already occurred
2. Threat appraisals concerned with future dangers
3. Challenge appraisals focused on the possibility of overcoming the stressor

The final determination of the degree of harm or threat presented by a stressor will be affected by several mediating variables, such as attitudes toward the stressor, availability and extent of social support systems, and certain dispositional variables such as perceived control and coping styles.

The physiological response to stress is accompanied by behavioral and psychological responses as well. As noted by Lazarus, individuals may respond to stress with action directed toward the source of stress, or may respond by palliative coping methods. Behavioral and psychological responses will be affected by factors such as the accuracy of expectations and individual susceptibility to stress and can be accompanied by consequences such as anxiety, depression, increased symptom reporting, decreases in problem-solving abilities, and heightened aggressiveness.

Each of the stressors that we considered conforms in many ways to this description of stress. Each has unique aspects as well. Natural disasters and technological catastrophes are more threatening than are noise and commuting, and occur in different ways. Each appears to be affected by different appraisals and means of coping, and they all appear to have a wide range of effects.

Natural disasters are sudden and powerful, but are usually acute—they are of relatively brief duration. Once the disaster has passed, various means of coping may be directed at recovery and a number of psychological problems may occur. Though there is some concern for long-range effects of these events, research evidence of this is equivocal and most studies report acute reactions.

Technological catastrophes are similar to natural disasters, though they may be more chronic and seem more uncontrollable. These events are also powerful, but are caused by failure of the human-made environment rather than a natural event. Research indicates that technological catastrophes can have psychological, emotional, behavioral, and physiological effects, and that these effects may become chronic.

Noise and commuting are less powerful and usually less sudden than either form of cataclysmic event, but may have cumulative effects, especially when experienced episodically or repetitively. Noise may have a number of effects, including aftereffects, which occur after termination of the noise. Both may cause behavioral, psychological, and physiological changes.

Suggested Projects

1. Keep a log of the things that happen to you for a few days. Make sure you include hassles, such as a fight with your boy/girl friend, as well as good things, like making up. Also keep track of how you feel during those days. Do you feel differently when you've had a lot of problems or changes? How does your experience fit with our discussion of stress?

2. Disasters are difficult to study. One problem is that all of the people affected by them are not equally influenced. Some people may be strongly affected—a flood can wash away their homes and loved ones, while others may escape threat or harm completely. Can you figure out a way of making a scale measuring how much stress may ensue? *(Hint: just thinking about how much money was lost will not be sufficient.)*

3. If you can, obtain a sound level meter from the psychology, physics, or speech and audiology department. Observe sound levels in places you go every day. Are there different behaviors associated with different levels? Now list the places, sound levels, and behaviors you observed and add a note on what the primary source (e.g., traffic, people talking) of the sound was. Do you see any patterns in these three sets of data?

5 Weather, Air Pollution, and Behavior

INTRODUCTION

Consider for a moment the following facts:

Heat wave conditions have been shown to be associated with riots.
Extremely hot or cold temperatures may be a causal factor in automobile accidents.
Skyscrapers can increase wind speeds at ground level, causing serious injury to pedestrians.
Low air pressure environments, as well as concentrations of carbon monoxide, deprive the body of needed oxygen.
Researchers who found traces of cancer-causing hexachlorobenzene in the air on Eniwetok Atoll in the Pacific feel there is no place on earth free of this pollutant.
Some researchers claim that pollution, including air pollution, accounts for 50 to 90 percent of all cases of cancer in humans.

These examples illustrate a few of the reasons environmental psychologists are interested in the effects of temperature, humidity, wind, air pressure, and air pollution on behavior. We are all familiar with certain consequences of exposure to these environmental factors. When "it gets cold" outdoors, we behave in ways that minimize discomfort, such as putting on heavy coats. When the wind blows down the street at 50 miles per hour, we behave in ways that will minimize our discomfort from wind exposure, such as not riding a bicycle and walking at an angle to the ground to maintain our balance. When air pollution alerts are broadcast, we may restrict our outdoor activity.

Research in the past decade has told us much more about what behavior to expect when people are exposed to abnormal levels of heat, cold, air pollution, and wind. Such research lets us answer rather detailed questions about specific environment–behavior problems. For example, *how* do high outdoor temperatures affect the level of aggressive and violent behavior in society, as suggested by the popular notion of the "long, hot summer effect"? Or *how* do weather changes affect mental health and interpersonal relations? Such questions about the influence of the physical environment on personal and interpersonal behavior are becoming more and more important for at least two reasons. First, humans are constantly exposed to natural changes in the physical environment. Parts of this country typically undergo temperature changes from −20°F to 100°F (−29°C to 38°C) in different seasons. Some cultures exist in hot tropical climates, whereas others thrive in arctic conditions. Do such temperature differences influence behavior? What if climatological changes, which according to many climatologists are becoming more and more extreme, should result in exaggerated cold or hot temperatures? If a "long, hot summer effect" really does exist, and if climatological changes result in average daily summer temperatures of 110°F in urban centers, are we likely to see disastrous rioting and violence? Whatever the case, it becomes important for us to know the influence of extreme or even very mild natural changes in the physical environment.

The second major reason we need to know more about the effects of the physical environment on behavior is that we ourselves are making drastic changes in the natural environment, changes that we may be able to correct if they can be shown to have deleterious effects on behavior. For example, if high winds have negative effects on mental health, physical well-being, and behavior, we may want to reevaluate building designs that actually increase wind speeds in pedestrian areas. Another example is the case of modern technology actually heating up our cities. Waste heat from the compressors of air conditioners, heat-absorbing concrete, and air pollutants that trap heat close to the surface (the "greenhouse effect") are actually heating up cities to levels 10°F or more above the temperature of the surrounding countryside. Can we possibly be adding to a "long, hot summer effect" by the way our daily living habits alter the physical environment?

Whether the source of environmental stimulation is from natural or human causes, the concern of environmental psychologists is the same: What differences in behavior can be expected under different conditions in the physical environment? In the previous three chapters we have seen how we perceive the general environment and how we can view environment–behavior relationships from several theoretical perspectives. In the present chapter we will examine two types of important physical environmental factors in detail, concentrating on how we perceive and measure these factors, how they affect

---

SOME EARLY VIEWS OF CLIMATIC DETERMINISM

Although we mention many effects of weather variables in this chapter, their overall effect on behavior, relative to other factors such as social environment, economics, and motivation, is not as overwhelming as some would have us believe. It is instructive, however, to examine some earlier views of the significance weather and climate have for us.

Huntington (1915, 1945), for example, suggested that an ideal climate was necessary for the development and growth of advanced civilization. Should this ideal climate resemble the warmth and carefree image of the tropics? No, according to Huntington, it should not. Rather, it should have contrasting seasons and frequent fronts to provide stimulation and challenge to the inhabitants. Such a climate exists, of course, in the industrialized European and North American regions.

Markham (1947) suggested that the most important climatic factor for the development of a civilization was living in a cool enough region that technology became necessary in order to keep warm. He noted, for example, that the Romans developed a central heating system, using pipes to distribute warmth through buildings. How important is this factor? Markham noted that this heating system deteriorated shortly before the decline of Roman civilization.

Although these and other scholars (e.g., Durkheim, 1897; Mills, 1934) believed climate is one of the most, if not *the* most, influential determinants of individual and cultural development, current research suggests that its impact is not as important as other factors. Moreover, it is overstepping the cause-and-effect boundaries of methodology to assume that just because a civilization occurs in a given climate, the climate is a prerequisite for that civilization. However, we will see in this chapter that weather and climate do have *some* direct impact on us.

us, and how these effects can be explained from various theoretical perspectives. Specifically, we will look at the behavioral effects of weather variables—heat, cold, wind, and barometric pressure—as well as at the effects of air pollution. As we do so, perhaps it would be helpful to keep Figure 3–7 (page 82) in mind as an overall framework. That is, the objective physical environment (e.g., heat, pollution), situational factors, and our perception of the environment as outside an optimal range lead to mediational states (e.g., arousal) and to coping strategies. In the process, health, performance, and social behavior may be affected.

We should mention one caveat before proceeding: Although we will primarily discuss each of the following factors separately (e.g., cold, wind, and low air pressure), in actuality they often occur together so it is often difficult to attribute a given behavior change to any one of the factors. We will have more to say on combinations of factors later in the chapter.

HEAT AND BEHAVIOR

Ambient temperature is a term used to describe the surrounding or atmospheric temperature conditions. In the natural environment, humans experience a range from arctic cold to debilitating tropical heat. As stated previously, temperature is one factor in the physical environment that humans are changing through urbanization and industrialization. Hurt (1975) notes that air conditioners in the downtown area of Houston put out enough waste heat (i.e., heat blown out the window off the ''hot'' end of the compressor) in eight hours to boil 10 kettles of water the size of the Astrodome! Unfortunately for those who must go outdoors, this heat and heat from additional sources stays in the general area of the city, so that urban centers are typically 10 to 20°F hotter than surrounding agricultural areas. As will be seen in this section and the next, extremes of heat and cold, regardless of the source, can have dramatic effects on people. We will first treat the perception of high and low temperatures together; then we will examine separately the effects of heat and cold on behavior.

Perception of and Physiological Reaction to Ambient Temperatures

Perception of temperature involves physical as well as psychological components. The primary *physical* component is simply the amount of heat in the surrounding environment, typically measured on the Fahrenheit or Celsius scale. One *psychological* component of temperature perception is centered on the internal temperature of the body, known as *core* temperature or deep body temperature. Another psychological component involves receptors in the skin (thermoreceptors), which apparently are sensitive to changes in ambient temperature. (For a reference on the existence of thermoreceptors in the skin, see Gardner, 1975.) These skin receptors do not transmit nerve impulses based on actual temperatures but on differences in temperature between the skin and the environment. If the surrounding environment is much hotter than the body, warmth will be perceived. If the environment is much cooler than the body, cold will be perceived. This is why you may perceive even mildly warm water as very hot when your hands are extremely cold from being exposed to winter air.

Since perception of ambient temperature is largely dependent on differences between body and ambient temperatures, the mechanisms controlling body temperature have much to do with the perception of ambient temperature. Body temperature is regulated by the need to keep core temperature close to 98.6°F (37°C). Since death occurs when core temperature rises above 113°F (45°C) or drops below 77°F (25°C), there is definite survival value in maintaining it at a normal level. Without a defensive or adaptive mechanism, the body would overheat when exposed to high ambient temperatures and would ''freeze'' when exposed to cold ambient temperatures. Fortunately, a number of such adaptive mechanisms, under the general control of a brain center known as the *hypothalamus*, are available for use whenever core temperature is threatened by adversely hot or cold ambient conditions. When core temperature becomes too hot, the body responds by activating mechanisms designed to lose heat, such as sweating, panting, and peripheral vasodilation. The latter process refers to dilation of blood vessels in the extremities, especially those near the surface of the skin, which allows more blood to flow from core areas to surface regions. This blood carries with it the excess core heat, which is removed through air convection or sweating (note that peripheral vasodilation allows more sweat to reach the surface of the skin). In "heat wave" emergencies, the body may increase the supply of water available for evaporation by suppressing urine formation and extracting water from body tissues. Such dehydration causes us to become thirsty and to replenish our body's supply of water, which is another process mediated by the hypothalamus. When these adaptive mechanisms fail, a number of physiological disorders can result, including heat exhaustion, heat stroke, heat asthenia, and heart attack (see box, page 124). Interestingly, blood pressure may increase upon initial sensation of ambient heat, owing to a "startle" response or alarm reaction (see page 78). Once vasodilation begins, blood pressure drops. With heat stroke, blood pressure may rise again, then fall off as coma and death approach. Clearly, blood pressure is not a good measure of arousal when someone is exposed to heat (see page 65).

Prolonged exposure to moderately high ambient temperatures need not have disastrous consequences. Individuals who move from cool climates into very warm climates can adapt to the hot environment without too much difficulty. This adaptation process is known as *acclimatization*, and it primarily involves changes in physiological adaptive mechanisms. For instance, the body may "learn" to start sweating much sooner after the onset of high ambient temperatures (Lee, 1964).

Sometimes the distinction is made between *acclimatization*, meaning adaptation to multiple stresses in an environment (e.g., temperature, wind, humidity) and *acclimation*, meaning adaptation to one specific stressor in an experimental context (see Frisancho, 1979). In our discussion, we will use the term acclimatization, since in most environments we must adapt to more than one element. Frisancho (1979) indicates that acclimatization may occur through developmental changes, through genetic adaptation, or through physiological and behavioral changes following prolonged exposure to heat. The Saharan Touareg, for example, have tall, slender bodies that maximize surface cooling area in proportion to the amount of body tissue that produces heat. Behaviorally, the Touareg avoid heavy exercise during the highest temperatures of the day, and wear loose, porous clothing (Beighton, 1971; Frisancho, 1979; Sloan, 1979). Non-native visitors to hot regions, moreover, can usually acclimatize in a few days. Leithead and Lind (1964) suggest that maximum efficiency in acclimatization occurs with exposure of 100 minutes per day (Figure 5–1).

Physiology of Cold Stress. In contrast to overheating, when core temperature becomes too cold, the body reacts by activating mechanisms that generate and retain heat, resulting in increased metabolism, shivering, peripheral vasoconstriction, and piloerection. Peripheral vasoconstriction serves just the opposite function of peripheral vasodilation; it keeps core heat inside the body and away from the surface where it is easily lost through convection. This constriction process also makes more blood available to internal organs, which are generating more heat through increased metabolism. *Piloerection* refers to the stiffening of hairs on the skin, usually accompanied by "goose bumps." This skin reaction increases the thickness of a thin layer of insulating air close to the skin, which again helps to minimize heat loss by convection.

Acclimitization to cold environments may take several forms (see also Bell & Greene, 1982). For example, the Alacaluf Indians of Tierra Del Fuego have an elevated metabolism that seems to keep body temperature elevated in the cold envi-

Figure 5–1. Acclimatization may occur through genetic changes, developmental changes, physiological changes, or behavioral changes. This desert is normally very hot and dry, but can be cool and wet at times. What would you do to acclimatize to this environment?

ronment (Hammel *et al.*, 1960). Bushmen of the Kalahari Desert and Australian Aborigines have another adaptive mechanism for tolerating very low nighttime temperatures. In these populations, shivering does not occur as it would in unacclimatized individuals, but rather core temperature actually drops at night (LeBlanc, 1975). Moreover, LeBlanc (1956) reported reduced shivering in a group of Canadian soldiers who had been moved to a cold climate, and Budd (1973) found a similar pattern for Australians of European heritage on an Antarctic expedition. Exposure to cold increases circulation in the hands for Eskimos (Le Blanc, 1975) and for fishermen on the Gaspé Peninsula of Quebec (LeBlanc, 1962). In sum, several mechanisms are available for acclimatization to cold environments.

Complicating Factors. Since perception of ambient temperature depends to some extent on the functioning of the body's thermoregulatory adaptive mechanisms, any environmental factor that interferes with these mechanisms will influ-

ence perception of ambient temperature. The primary environmental factors in this regard are humidity and wind. The higher the humidity in a hot environment (i.e., the more saturated the air with water vapor), the lower the capacity of the air to absorb water vapor from sweat. This is the reason, for example, that conditions of 100°F and 60 percent humidity are perceived as more uncomfortable than those of 100°F and 25 percent humidity. Thus, perception of ambient temperature is not a function of temperature alone. Psychologically, the problem of perceptual measurement can be partially solved by taking into account a comfort level that is influenced by both temperature and humidity, thus creating a new ambient environment index known as *effective temperature*. A chart showing some effective temperatures is presented in Table 5–1.

Since the amount of air flowing over the skin determines how much sweat is evaporated as well as how much body heat is carried off by convection, wind speed must also be taken into account in perceiving ambient temperature. The ''chill

Table 5–1. EFFECTIVE TEMPERATURE (°F) AT 0 PERCENT HUMIDITY AS A FUNCTION OF ACTUAL TEMPERATURE AND HUMIDITY

Relative Humidity (%)	Thermometer Reading (°F)					
	41°	*50°*	*59°*	*68°*	*77°*	*86°*
	Effective Temperature					
0	41	50	59	68	77	86
20	41	50	60	70	81	91
40	40	51	61	72	83	96
60	40	51	62	73	86	102
80	39	52	63	75	90	111
100	39	52	64	79	96	120

factor'' index does just that. For example, an ambient temperature of 23°F with a wind speed of 15 mph has the same psychological effect as an ambient temperature of −1°F with no wind. Table 5–2 depicts the broad range of the chill factor index. In very cold ambient temperatures, it becomes extremely important for thermoregulatory survival to take wind-chill into account. Just how critical this factor can be is illustrated by the fact that exposed human skin will freeze in less than one minute at −40°F with a 6 mph wind, at −20°F with a 20 mph wind, and at 0°F with a 30

PHYSIOLOGICAL DISORDERS ASSOCIATED WITH PROLONGED HEAT STRESS

When the body's adaptive mechanisms to heat stress fail to keep core body temperatures close to 98.6°F, a number of physiological disorders can occur. Among the more common are:

1. Heat exhaustion, characterized by faintness and nausea, vomiting, headache, and restlessness. This disorder results from excessive demands on the circulatory system for blood. Water needed for sweating, blood needed near the skin surface for heat loss through convection, and blood needed for normal or increased metabolic functioning place too much strain on the body's capacity to supply blood. Continued loss of salt and water through sweating compounds the problem. Replacement of lost water and salt, together with rest, will both prevent and cure heat exhaustion.

2. Heat stroke, characterized by confusion, staggering, headache, delirium, coma, and death. This disorder results from the complete breakdown of the sweating mechanism. Because body heat cannot be lost, the brain overheats. Survival or prevention of brain damage depends on quick action—the most effective being immersion in ice water. When a victim collapses from heat, the continuation of sweating implies heat exhaustion; the absence of sweating implies heat stroke.

3. Heat asthenia, characterized by fatigue, headache, mental and physical impairment, irritability, restlessness, insomnia, loss of appetite, and lethargy. Its specific causes are unknown, although one theory implicates the clogging of sweat glands by excessive perspiration. The cure for heat asthenia includes intake of water and change of climate.

4. Heart attack, resulting from excessive demands on the cardiovascular system due to increased need for blood by the body's cooling mechanisms. During urban heat wave conditions, most deaths beyond what would normally be expected are caused by heart attacks.

For more information on heat and cold disorders, the reader is referred to Folk (1974).

Table 5–2. WIND-CHILL INDEX*

Actual Temperature (°F) at 0 mph	Wind Speed			
	5 mph	15 mph	25 mph	35 mph
	Equivalent Temperature (°F)			
32	29	13	3	−1
23	20	−1	−10	−15
14	10	−13	−24	−29
5	1	−25	−38	−43
−4	−9	−37	−50	−52

*Equivalent temperatures (°F) at 0 mph as a function of actual temperature and wind speed.

mph wind! Finally, we should note that thermal comfort may also vary somewhat with personality (Carlton-Foss & Rohles, 1982).

Heat and Performance

Laboratory Settings. Laboratory studies of the influence of high ambient temperatures on performance have examined such varied behaviors as reaction time, tracking, and vigilance, as well as memory and mathematical calculations (Bell, Provins, & Hiorns, 1964; Griffiths & Boyce, 1971; Pepler, 1963; Poulton & Kerslake, 1965; Provins, 1966; Provins & Bell, 1970; Wilkinson *et al.*, 1964). In general, temperatures above 90°F (32°C) will impair mental performance after two hours of exposure for unacclimatized subjects. Above this same temperature,

PHYSIOLOGICAL DISORDERS ASSOCIATED WITH PROLONGED COLD STRESS

If cold exposure persists for long periods of time, two serious consequences can result. One danger is frostbite, characterized by the formation of ice crystals in the skin cells. Since the initial reaction of the body to cold stress is constriction of surface blood vessels, freezing of the skin is not uncommon. Another danger of cold exposure arises when the adaptive mechanisms fail to maintain core body temperature. A decline in core temperature is known as *hypothermia*. In the initial stages of hypothermia, cardiovascular activity, including heart rate and blood pressure, is dramatically increased. As core temperature falls between 86°F and 77°F (30 to 25°C), cardiovascular activity falls off and becomes irregular. Below a core temperature of 77°F, death due to heart attack is likely to result. At an intermediate stage of hypothermia, clouding of consciousness and coma may well occur. If the victim has not found shelter by this time, the loss of mental functioning may preclude an effort to seek warmth or assistance. Since inadequate clothing in extremes of cold is most likely to precipitate hypothermia, it is those individuals caught unprepared for cold stress, such as mountain climbers faced with sudden cold winds or shipwreck victims in arctic waters, who are most likely to suffer the disorder. Removal of wet clothing and provision of warmth are necessary to save the lives of hypothermia victims.

moderate physical work will suffer after one hour of exposure. As temperatures increase, shorter exposure times are necessary to show performance decrements (e.g., Poulton, 1970). Interestingly enough, some researchers find that heat has no influence on performance, others find that heat is detrimental to performance, and still others find that heat improves performance. Moreover, some studies suggest that as temperatures rise, performance first improves and then deteriorates, whereas other studies show this pattern for one task but the reverse pattern (i.e., initial decrements followed by improvements) for other tasks (see Bell, 1981 for a review). Before examining possible explanations for these complex findings, let us first examine heat research from applied settings.

Industrial Settings. Industrialists, such as steel manufacturers, are naturally concerned about the effects of blast furnaces and other hot industrial environments on workers who are in these surroundings for eight or more hours a day. Generally, exposure to such industrial heat can cause dehydration, loss of salt, and muscle fatigue, which taken together can reduce endurance and hence impair performance. For example, one study found that productivity of women apparel workers declined as temperatures increased (Link & Pepler, 1970). In order to overcome or avoid such problems, care is generally taken to insure that workers have an adequate intake of water and salt, are not exposed to intolerably hot conditions for long periods of time, wear protective clothing, and, when new on the job, have adequate time to adapt to working conditions (see Crockford, 1967; Hill, 1967).

The consequences of not taking such precautions are illustrated in an interesting study by Wyndham (1969), conducted in a gold mine. In this study, randomly selected workers shoveled rocks into a mining car during a five-hour work period. Workers were either unsupervised, supervised by an inefficient foreman, or supervised by an efficient foreman with a high performance record. Under temperature conditions of 86°F (30°C) or below, workers shoveled more rocks when su-

pervised by the superior foreman than by the poor foreman or when unsupervised. At temperatures above 92°F (33°C), however, supervision had no effect on productivity: All workers showed equally poor performance.

Classroom Settings. Temperature appears to have some effects on classroom performance. Pepler (1972) studied climate-controlled (air-conditioned) and nonclimate-controlled schools near Portland, Oregon. In nonclimate-controlled schools, academic performance showed more variance (i.e., wider distribution of test scores) as temperatures rose. However, at climate-controlled schools, such variability did not occur on the warmest days. Apparently, some students suffer more than others when heat waves hit the classroom! Support for this finding has been reported by Benson and Zieman (1981), who found that heat hurt the classroom performance of some children but actually helped the performance of others (see also Griffiths, 1975) (Figure 5–2).

Military Settings. If ambient heat has any deleterious effect on performance, the consequences of moving unacclimatized troops into a tropical area (e.g., from New England to Vietnam) could be disastrous. Adam (1967) has reviewed a number of British military studies that generally found that 20–25 percent of troops flown into tropical regions from more moderate climates suffered serious deterioration in combat effectiveness within three days and became in effect "heat casualties." Solutions to this problem include allowing several days for acclimatization or expanding the number of troops available to allow for heat casualties.

Interpreting the Data. How can we account for the complexity of the above research findings? Why does heat sometimes hurt performance and sometimes help it? Bell (1981, 1982) offers several suggestions, which require an integration of several theoretical perspectives presented in Chapter 3. First, *arousal* explains some heat effects. Initally, exposure to heat may cause a brief

Figure 5–2. Research suggests that many weather variables, including heat and barometric pressure, may influence disruptive behavior and academic performance of children in the classroom. Interestingly, for some children heat has beneficial effects, whereas for others it has detrimental effects.

ample, found that as heat increased, performance on a secondary task suffered, but performance on a primary task did not. A fourth mediator of heat effects is probably *perceived control,* as advocated by the behavior constraint model. According to this interpretation, as heat stress increases, individuals feel less and less in control of the environment, and thus performance deteriorates. Greene and Bell (1980), for example, found that subjects in a 95°F (35°C) environment felt more dominated by it than did subjects in more comfortable temperatures (see also Cervone, 1977). Finally, each individual almost certainly has an *adaptation level* or maximum level of tolerance for heat. Wyndham (1970), for example, has reported considerable variation in acclimatization to heat, with individuals having lower body temperatures being most tolerant of high ambient temperatures (see also Rohles, 1974; Wilkinson, 1974). In sum, arousal, core temperature, attention, perceived control, and adaptation level all probably operate as explanatory mechanisms in understanding the effects of heat stress on task performance.

"startle" response that heightens arousal and hence improves performance (e.g., Poulton, 1976; Poulton & Kerslake, 1965; Provins, 1966). Moreover, Provins (1966) suggests that heat may eventually lead to overarousal, causing performance decrements (cf., Bell, Loomis, & Cervone, 1982), as would be predicted by the Yerkes-Dodson Law (see pp. 64–65). Eventually, high temperatures would result in physical exhaustion (see box p. 124) as the body can no longer keep core temperature at a safely functioning level, so performance would completely deteriorate. A second mediator of performance, then, is *core temperature* (see Provins, 1966). A third mediator of performance is *attention,* as examined in the overload interpretation of environmental stress. As heat stress increases, attention is narrowed toward stimuli central to the task at hand, so that performance on noncentral activities deteriorates (e.g., Bursill, 1958; Pepler, 1963). Bell (1978), for ex-

Heat and Social Behavior

Heat and Attraction. Most individuals exposed to high ambient temperatures will report that subjectively they feel uncomfortable and perhaps irritable. We might expect that such negative feelings also will give us an unpleasant disposition toward others. According to one model of attraction (Byrne, 1971), we should expect a decrease in interpersonal attraction when we are experiencing the unpleasant effects of debilitating heat (see page 47). Griffitt (1970) demonstrated precisely this effect by asking subjects to evaluate anonymous strangers who seemed to agree with subjects on either 25 percent or 75 percent of a set of attitudes. Subjects performed this evaluation task under an effective temperature of either 67.5°F (74° dry-bulb, 30 percent humidity) or 90.6°F (100° dry-bulb, 60 percent humidity). The results, depicted in Figure 5–3, indicate that high

AMBIENT TEMPERATURE AND DRIVING: CAN TEMPERATURE CAUSE ACCIDENTS?

In a review article, Provins (1958) noted that efficiency of driving an automobile may well be affected by ambient temperature. Obviously, cold temperatures that contribute to icy road conditions in turn contribute to accidents. But cold or hot temperatures may also directly affect driving performance in at least four ways:

1. Temperatures below 50°F or above 90°F reduce grip strength and impair muscle dexterity, which could diminish control over steering, braking, and shifting gears.

2. Temperatures below 50°F or above 90°F also reduce tactile discrimination (sensitivity of touch), which could reduce a driver's "feel" for the road.

3. Temperatures below 55°F or above 90°F impair vigilance and tracking performance, possibly making a driver less cognizant of potential hazards and traffic directional or signaling devices.

4. If high or low temperatures produce irritation, drivers may become more aggressive and take more dangerous risks.

When high wind speeds (such as would be experienced by drivers of convertibles or motorcycles) are added, these temperature effects probably become more severe. Perhaps still more frightening is the possibility that increased levels of carbon monoxide and oxidants in the blood of drivers further reduce mental responsiveness (cf., Ury, Perkins, & Goldsmith, 1972). Data are scarce and somewhat inconclusive on the influence of these environmental variables on driving efficiency, but there will certainly be more research in the future exploring this potentially tragic influence.

ambient temperatures decreased attraction, regardless of the degree of attitude similarity.

However, research by Bell and Baron (1974, 1976) suggests that heat may have a relatively minor influence on attraction under other circumstances. In two experiments, these researchers found that heat did not influence attraction toward another person in the room if that person had recently complimented or insulted a subject. In this situation, the compliment or insult appears to be so overwhelming as to "wipe out" any possible influence of heat (see also Bell & Garnand, in press).

Heat and Aggression. During the urban and campus riots of the 1960s, a popular belief arose that riotous acts of violence were in some way precipitated by the unrelenting heat of the summer months. Indeed, this supposed influence of heat on aggression was popularly known as "the long, hot summer effect." It became common for television commentators and newspaper editorial writers to mention fears that "It's going to be another long, hot summer!" High ambient temperatures became even more suspect when the United States Riot Commission (1968) noted that, of the riots in 1967 on which records were available, all but one began on days when the temperature was at least in the 80s. A more formal study by Goranson and King (1970) strongly suggested, as evidenced in the graph in Figure 5–4, that heat wave or near heat wave conditions were associated with the outbreak of the riots.

Such correlational evidence is not sufficient for inferring a cause-and-effect relationship between high ambient temperatures and aggression. In order to explore the possible existence of such a relationship more closely, Baron and his colleagues initiated a series of laboratory experiments, using as a measure of aggression the willingness of subjects to administer electric shocks to a confederate of the experimenter (Baron, 1972; Baron & Lawton, 1972; Bell & Baron, 1976).

In one experiment, Baron and Bell (1975) ar-

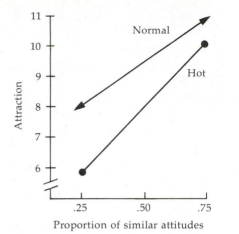

Figure 5–3. Heat decreases attraction between two strangers, regardless of the degree of attitude similarity between the individuals. (From Griffitt, W. Environmental effects on interpersonal affective behavior: Ambient effective temperature and attraction. *Journal of Personality and Social Psychology,* 1970, *15*, 240–244. Copyright 1970 by the American Psychological Association. Reprinted by permission.)

ranged for subjects to be either provoked or complimented by a confederate before being given an opportunity to aggress against this individual by means of ostensible electric shock. It was found, as might be anticipated, that subjects in comfortable ambient temperature conditions (73 to 74°F) were more aggressive toward an anger-provoking confederate than toward a complimentary confederate. However, subjects in uncomfortably hot conditions (92 to 95°F) showed just the opposite behavior: These individuals showed reduced aggression toward the insulting confederate but increased their level of attack against the friendlier one. Why should high ambient temperatures produce a pattern of results opposite to that produced by comfortable ambient temperatures? Further research suggested a possible explanation (Baron & Bell, 1976a; Bell & Baron, 1976).

According to this explanation, negative affective feelings may be a mediator in the relationship between heat and aggression. This mediating relationship takes the curvilinear form of an inverted U. Up to a critical inflection point, negative affect increases aggressive behavior, but beyond this point, stronger negative feelings actually reduce aggression, since flight behavior or other attempts to minimize discomfort become

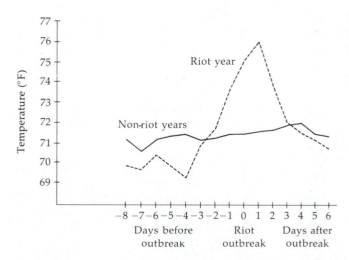

Figure 5–4. Average daily mean temperatures before, during, and after riot outbreak. (From Goranson & King, 1970. Reproduced with permission of the authors.)

more important to the individual than aggressive activity (see Figures 5–5; 5–6).

Tests of the proposition of a curvilinear relationship between negative affect and aggression, using heat as one factor influencing affect, have been quite affirmative (Bell & Baron, 1981; Palamarek & Rule, 1979). What these findings suggest with regard to the relationship between high ambient temperatures and aggression is that there is a critical range of uncomfortably high ambient temperatures in which aggression may well be facilitated. On the other hand, extremely high ambient temperatures, especially when combined with other sources of irritation or discomfort, may become so debilitating that aggression is no longer facilitated and may well be reduced when individuals prefer to concentrate on escaping the heat. But do the field data support the existence of this curvilinear relationship? Three pieces of field evidence provide suggestive support. First, examination of the United States Riot Commission (1968) report of the 1967 urban riots indicates that, although the temperatures on the days the riots broke out were high for the cities involved, they rarely exceeded 100°F, which is a common high temperature for many cities where riots did not occur. Second, Schwartz (1968) reported evidence that political violence (coups, assassinations, terrorism, guerrilla warfare, and revolts) occurs most often when the climate of a country is moderately warm and less often when the climate is very hot or cool. Such evidence is certainly not sufficient proof of the curvilinear hypothesis, but it does provide tentative field support for laboratory findings. More recently, Baron and Ransberger (1978) examined 102 cases of collective violence between 1967 and 1972. Consistent with the curvilinear hypothesis, they found that the incidence of violence peaked in the mid 80s (°F), but fell off above or below this point. In other research, Bell (1980) found that subjects who were angry at an experimenter evaluated that experimenter more negatively in a hot than in a cool environment. In still another experiment, Baron (1976) found that automobile drivers honked their horns (which can serve as a measure of irritation or hostility) more when temperatures were above 85°F (29°C) than below. For drivers in air-conditioned cars, however, heat did not increase horn-honking.

What can one conclude from the above research? First, there is considerable laboratory and archival support for the inverted-U relationship between the discomfort produced by heat and sub-

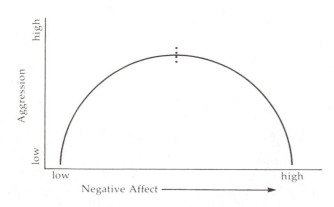

Figure 5–5. Theoretical relationship between negative affect and aggression. Up to a point, uncomfortable conditions facilitate aggression; past that point, more severe conditions decrease aggression. (From Baron, R. A., & Bell, P. A. Aggression and heat: The influence of ambient temperature, negative affect, and a cooling drink on physical aggression. *Journal of Personality and Social Psychology*, 1976, *33*, 245–255. Copyright 1976 by the American Psychological Association. Used by permission.)

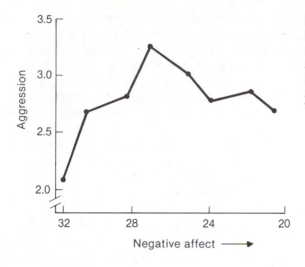

Figure 5–6. Obtained laboratory relationship between negative affect and aggression. (Adapted from Bell, P.A. & Baron, R.A. Aggression and heat: The mediating role of negative affect. *Journal of Applied Social Psychology* 1976,6, 18–30. Copyright 1976 by V.H. Winston & Sons. Used by permission.)

sequent aggressive behavior. However, some evidence seems at first glance to be inconsistent with this interpretation (e.g., Carlsmith & Anderson, 1979), and there must certainly be exceptions to the rule. Rotton and Frey (1981), for example, report that the curvilinear relationship does hold, but only for some forms of violence (see also Cotton, 1982). Moreover, studies which find simply that violence increases with heat and does not fall off at higher temperatures may not have examined high enough temperatures. Clearly, at extremely high temperatures, near the point of physical exhaustion, aggression should be inhibited. At what point this decline in violence occurs is up to debate. The extensive laboratory evidence cited above, together with much of the evidence on the history of riots, coups, assassinations, and other violence, lends strong support to the inverted-U relationship between heat-induced discomfort and aggression. As will be seen, there is additional evidence from research on cold temperatures and discomfort from unpleasant odors to support this relationship (see also Baron, 1978; Bell & Baron, 1981).

We should add that an alternative explanation of the relationship between heat and aggression, which is not inconsistent with the negative affect interpretation, involves the role of the hypothalamus (see page 122) in both thermoregulation and aggression (Boyanowsky *et al.*, 1981–82). According to this interpretation, the hypothalamus works to increase sympathetic nervous system arousal (heart rate, blood pressure, respiration rate) in the presence of some anger-provoking situations, but works to decrease these processes during some phases of heat exposure. The resultant conflict in signals, it is thought, increases irritation and physiological distress, which leads to an increase in aggression. Should this process occur at the intermediate level of negative affect (see Figure 5–5), it would be entirely compatible with the negative affect explanation discussed above. Interestingly, Boyanowsky *et al.* report that the presence of a thermometer within easy view of research subjects reduces their level of aggression in hot conditions, presumably because it provides an explanation to them for their discomfort that is separate from aggression-provoking anger.

Heat and Helping Behavior. A third type of social behavior that may be affected by high ambient temperatures is that of offering assistance to someone in need of help. Some social psychological research has indicated that when people feel unpleasant, they are not inclined to help others, whereas other research suggests that when people feel bad they do indeed help others in order to feel better (e.g., Cialdini & Kenrick, 1976; Weyant, 1978). Since heat obviously produces discomfort, what might it do to helping behavior?

One study found that after leaving an uncomfortably hot experimental room, subjects were less likely to volunteer their assistance in another experiment than subjects who had been in a more comfortable environment (Page, 1978). Another study (Cunningham, 1979) similarly found that when asked to help in an interview, willingness to help declined as temperatures rose in summer months, but willingness to help increased with temperature increases during winter months. Other research, however, has failed to find a relationship between heat and helping. For example, outdoor temperature was found to have no effect on the amount of tips left at an indoor restaurant (Cunningham, 1979). Moreover, neither high nor low temperatures reduced helping when a person: (1) using crutches dropped a book; (2) lost a contact lens; (3) dropped a sack of groceries; or (4) asked for help in a survey (Schneider, Lesko, & Garrett, 1980). Data from Bell and Doyle (1983) also failed to show that heat has any effect on helping, either during or after exposure to the high temperatures. With so little data available, it is difficult (and unwise) to draw firm conclusions about the relationship of heat to helping behavior. It is possible, though, that discomfort increases helping in some cases and decreases it in others, so that these two tendencies may "cancel out" each other in many instances (e.g., Cunningham, Steinberg, & Grev, 1980).

COLD TEMPERATURES AND BEHAVIOR

If the physiological reaction to cold ambient temperatures (i.e., below 68°F or 20°C) is in many ways the opposite of the reaction to heat, what effects does such exposure have on behavior? The answer is somewhat complex, for several reasons.

First, humans rarely have to work or interact in unprotected cold climates. We usually wear protective clothing in uncomfortably cold situations. If we do not, disease or death is not unlikely. Because of the clothing factor, conclusions on performance in the cold are somewhat difficult to interpret. If workers on the Alaskan pipeline wore heavy clothing, their efficiency was not dramatically affected. This does not, however, mean that cold temperatures do not affect performance. A second reason the relationship between cold temperatures and behavior is complex is that different parts of the body are often cold, while others are not. Whether only the hands are cold, or whether core temperature is lowered, may make a difference. Finally, in the section on heat we noted that increases of 10° to 15°F above comfort levels (i.e., 70°F) often facilitate performance and other behavior. Comparable temperatures below comfort levels (e.g., 55 to 65°F, 13 to 18°C) are rarely studied. Instead, research on cold tends to concentrate on behavioral effects of temperatures below 55°F (13°C). With these facts in mind, let us now examine some of the research on cold temperatures and behavior.

Cold Temperatures and Health

We have already mentioned that prolonged exposure to cold can lead to hypothermia and frostbite. Do people living for long periods of time in cold climates experience health effects due to the cold temperatures? The answer appears to be "probably not directly." Eskimos in North America and Lapps in northern Scandinavia do not seem to suffer prolonged disorders associated with cold temperatures. Any noticeable differences from other societies are probably the result of culture. If adequate clothing and shelter are available, cold temperatures are not all that hazardous to health.

Mental health also appears not to be directly related to cold temperatures. A study on health at Antarctic stations (Gunderson, 1968) found that, although residents experience insomnia, anxiety, depression, and irritability, these effects appear more attributable to isolation and work requirements than to climate. To the extent that climate is a factor, concern about it and perceived threat from it are probably more important than temperature itself.

Cold Extremes and Performance

Humans on Arctic expeditions, military maneuvers, and in underwater diving occupations often experience extremes of cold. Research on cold stress and performance (see Fox, 1967; Poulton, 1970; Provins & Clarke, 1960 for reviews) suggests that even temperatures of 55°F (13°C) can reduce efficiency in reaction time, tracking proficiency, muscular dexterity, and tactile discrimination (sensitivity of touch). As temperatures fall below this level, performance usually deteriorates further. Some evidence (cf. Fox, 1967) suggests that this deterioration is at least partly due to overload and heightened arousal. That is, the body's mechanisms are heavily allocated to maintaining adequate core temperature, so there is not enough energy or attention left for optimum performance on manual and mental tasks. If the hands are exposed, loss of tactile discrimination and stiffening reduce manual dexterity. If the hands do not become cold, lowered core temperature may still hurt performance, though probably not as much. Interestingly, if the hands are kept warm, considerable cooling of the rest of the body can be tolerated without severe performance decrements (e.g., Gaydos, 1958; Gaydos & Dusek, 1958).

Whether less chilling temperatures (55 to 65°F, 13 to 18°C) actually enhance performance cannot be stated with confidence. However, we might speculate that if the physiological reactions to slightly cooler temperatures increase arousal without overburdening the body's adaptive mechanisms, performance might be slightly enhanced (e.g., Clark & Flaherty, 1963).

Some people appear to be more bothered by cold than others, and performance is less severely affected by cold for some individuals (cf. Fox, 1967). Furthermore, practice on tasks in cold temperatures can improve performance, so adaptive mechanisms are effective, and adaptation level almost certainly plays a role in temperature-performance relationships in conditions of cold.

Cold Extremes and Social Behavior

Surprisingly little research has been done on the effects of cold ambient temperatures and social behavior. One interesting bit of evidence does suggest that "low" temperatures around 62°F (16°C) make subjects feel more affectively negative (Bell & Baron, 1977). Consequently, one might expect low ambient temperatures to influence aggression in the same curvilinear fashion as high ambient temperatures. Bell and Baron (1977) found exactly this result: Moderately negative feelings associated with cold temperatures tended to increase aggression, but more extreme negative feelings associated with cold actually decreased aggression. Although such results are far from conclusive, they are supported by other research (Bennet *et al.*, 1983) and do suggest that more studies would be valuable in this area (see also Boyanowsky *et al.*, 1981–82).

As cited above for heat effects, Cunningham (1979) reported a slight decrease in helping with an interview as temperatures declined in the winter, although Schneider *et al.* (1980) found no effects of cold temperatures on helping. Informal observation has shown that cold, harsh winters tend to increase helping behavior and to reduce crime rates. Bennet *et al.* (1983) report supportive evidence for these observations and suggest a cold weather helping norm as one explanation. Others have noted that the severe winter of 1977 resulted in many acts of kindness, such as people rescuing others and sharing food and shelter. In addition, criminal activity during that winter was relatively mild. Attributing such behavior to temperature is speculative, and, as is the case for evidence on heat and helping, there is too little research available to draw any firm conclusions on the relationship of cold temperatures to helping behavior.

Summary of Temperature Effects on Behavior

The body reacts to high and low ambient temperatures by losing or preserving body heat, respectively. Associated physiological activity tends to increase arousal, leading to improved performance at low levels of arousal and deteriorated performance at higher levels. Attention, perceived control, and adaptation level also play a role in the relationship of temperature to behavior. Heat has been shown to affect attraction, aggression, and helping behavior in complex ways, depending on other factors. Cold ambient temperatures appear to influence aggression in much the same way as hot temperatures, and may increase helping behavior under some circumstances.

WIND AND BEHAVIOR

Anyone familiar with the "Windy City" of Chicago knows how discomforting wind can be when all you want to do is walk along a sidewalk. Few areas of the country can escape this natural phenomenon, although winds tend to be more severe in certain regions. Winds formed in tornadoes and hurricanes can easily reach speeds in excess of 80 mph. Parts of the Rocky Mountain states, espe-

---

SUNLIGHT: ITS MANY EFFECTS

One weather variable that has significant impact on humans is sunlight. As indicated by Frisancho (1979), thermonuclear reactions within the sun convert millions of tons of hydrogen into millions of tons of helium every second, releasing radiant energy in the process. Approximately eight seconds after it leaves the sun, some of this energy reaches the earth in various wavelengths. Ranging from short to long wavelengths, the energy takes the form of x-rays, ultraviolet rays, visible light, infrared rays, and radiowaves. The wavelengths shorter than visible light are hazardous to life. Fortunately, most of these wavelengths are either absorbed by ozone, blocked by ozone, or "consumed" in the process of making ozone high in the atmosphere. Ozone is a form of oxygen in which three atoms are molecularly combined (O_3). As you are probably aware, there has been concern in recent years that several human-generated substances, most notably fluorocarbons in aeorsol propellants, destroy the layer of ozone that protects us from harmful solar radiation. When it hits certain atmospheric pollutants, sunlight leads to photochemical smog (see p. 141). The solar energy that does reach the surface of the earth can also harm us through sunburn and as a factor in skin cancer. To protect us from some of this danger, the skin produces melanin and other dark pigments to act as a partial shield, a process we know as tanning (see Frisancho, 1979).

Sunlight is not just potentially harmful, of course, but provides us with light, heat, and, through photosynthesis, food. Moreover, sunlight induces the skin to produce Vitamin D.

Behaviorally, increased hours of sunlight have been associated with increased suicide rates and crime rates (see Moos, 1976). These effects most probably are not caused directly by sunlight, but rather by increased opportunities to encounter social stress (which may lead to depression and suicide) and increased opportunities to engage in criminal activity.

Interestingly, two recent experiments by Cunningham (1979) suggest that sunlight not only leads to good moods in people, but is also associated with increased altruistic behavior! In one of these experiments, people in Minneapolis were greeted by an experimenter as they walked outdoors, and were asked to answer a few brief questions. Subjects were more willing to answer the questions the more sunshine was present, regardless of any other weather conditions in both summer and winter. In the second experiment, waitresses in a restaurant were found to receive more tips as a function of the amount of sun shining. This relationship was found even though customers were indoors and were not experiencing direct sunlight at the time of leaving the tip. Moreover, the more sunlight, the more positive the mood of the waitresses. Cunningham interpreted these results in terms of mood: The more pleasant we feel, the more willing we are to be kind to and to help others (cf., Cialdini & Kenrick, 1976; Weyant, 1978). Apparently, sunlight really does have prosocial benefits!

cially those regions where the mountains meet the plains, experience wind speeds of over 100 mph several times a year. Fortunately, because of the altitude and climate, such Chinook winds are so thin and dry they do little physical damage, but they do cause discomfort and inconvenience (try riding a bicycle in one!). Such natural winds are not all that humans are exposed to. As indicated in more detail in Chapter 10, tall buildings create uncomfortable and even dangerous winds in the hearts of our major cities (see box page 305). Because of the influence of buildings on natural wind patterns, these human-made (or human-altered) winds can far exceed natural winds in both *speed* and *turbulence* (gustiness and shifting directions). As urban structures are built taller, we can expect even more exposure to these unnatural winds. Thus, we suspect that potential effects of wind on behavior will become a more important topic for future research within environmental psychology.

Perception of Wind

Although the body has specialized receptors for detecting light, sound, odors, and so forth, there are no receptors designed specifically for wind detection. Thus, to detect wind we have to rely on several perception systems. If you are actually in a wind, pressure receptors in the skin probably tell you the most about its presence: the stronger the wind, the more pressure on exposed skin. If the wind is particularly cold or hot, moist or dry, temperature receptors in the skin also signal its presence. Muscular effort in resisting the wind is still another clue you can use to detect the force of a wind. The sight of others being blown over or of flags whipping tells you about the force of the wind even if you happen to be in a shelter. Finally, wind makes noise as it brushes past the ears or as it moves around obstacles, and the intensity and frequency of these sounds give you a clue to the wind's presence and force.

One of the earliest and most widely known indexes for evaluating wind is a scale developed by Admiral Sir Francis Beaufort in 1806. This scale, depicted in Table 5–3, was originally devised for activities at sea, but it has been adapted to land use over the years. As can be seen from this scale, wind effects range from problems of keeping hair combed to having difficulty walking and

Table 5–3. BEAUFORT WIND SCALE AND RELATED EFFECTS

Beaufort Number	Wind Speed (mph)	Atmospheric and Behavioral Effects
0,1	0–3	Calm, no noticeable wind.
2	4–7	Wind felt on face.
3	8–12	Wind extends light flag; hair is disturbed; clothing flaps.
4	13–18	Dust, dry soil, loose paper raised; hair disarranged.
5	19–24	Force of wind felt on body; drifting snow becomes airborne; limit of agreeable wind on land.
6	25–31	Umbrellas used with difficulty; hair blown straight; walking becomes unsteady; wind noise on ears unpleasant; windborne snow above head height (blizzard).
7	32–38	Inconvenience felt when walking.
8	39–46	Generally impedes progress; great difficulty with balance in gusts.
9	47–54	People blown over by gusts.

Adapted From Penwarden, A. D. Acceptable wind speeds in towns. *Building Science*, 1973, *8*, 259–267. Copyright 1973 by Pergamon Press and A. Penwarden, Building Research Establishment, U.K., 1974. Used by permission.

even to being knocked off one's feet by gusts of 45 mph or more. Cases have actually been reported of individuals (especially elderly persons whose agility is less than ideal) being killed by winds that blew them over.

More scientific and precise scales of wind effects on humans have been proposed by Penwarden (1973). Some of these proposed indexes include force of wind on the body (which takes body surface area into account), angle at which one can lean into a wind without falling over, degree of increased metabolic rate from walking into a wind, and body heat loss due to various types of winds. This body heat loss index would of course be influenced by moisture content and temperature of the wind, as indicated in the previous discussion of "wind-chill."

Behavioral Effects of Wind

Very little systematic research has been conducted to date on the specific behavioral effects of wind. A very intriguing series of wind studies, however, has been reported by Poulton *et al.* (1975). These researchers exposed female subjects to winds of either 9 mph or 20 mph, with varying degrees of turbulence, in a wind tunnel. Basically, these wind conditions were intended either to be just strong enough to be noticeable and cause slight discomfort or to be extremely uncomfortable and detrimental to performance. Air temperature varied between 65°F and 70°F, with humidity at 70 to 85 percent. Among the findings were that high wind and gustiness (1) significantly deflected subjects from walking a straight path; (2) increased the time required to put on a raincoat from 20 to 26 seconds; (3) increased the time required to tie a headscarf by 30 percent; (4) increased subjects' blinking by 12 to 18 blinks per minute; (5) increased the time required to pick selected words from a list and to find a circled word in a newspaper; (6) caused more water to be spilled when poured into a wine glass; and (7) increased feelings of discomfort and perceived windiness (see also Cohen, Moss, & Zube, 1979).

Taken altogether, these results generally suggest that winds influence affective feelings and at least some types of performance. Since some of these effects can be quite disturbing subjectively, we anticipate that many cities will adopt codes to regulate the extent to which new buildings will be allowed to produce annoying winds.

Correlational research has examined interesting behavior patterns associated with winds around the world, such as the Foehn, Bora, Mistral, and Sirocco in Europe, the Sharav and Chamsin in the Near East, the Chinook in Colorado and Santa Ana in California, and the pomponio in Argentina (Sommers & Moos, 1976). The Foehn and Chinook are warm, dry winds that descend from mountains. It is not uncommon for residents in these regions to attribute depression, nervousness, pain, irritation, and traffic accidents to wind (Sommers & Moos, 1976). In the Near East, some governments even forgive criminal acts that are committed during the periods of disturbing winds. In an empirical study, two researchers (Muecher & Ungeheuer, 1961) measured performance on several tasks. As expected, performance was worse on days of Foehnlike weather than on less stormy days. In addition, they and other researchers (e.g., Moos, 1964) report that accident rates increase just before or during the approach of the winds. Rim (1975) examined performance of individuals on psychological tests during hot, desert wind (Sharav) periods in Israel, and compared their scores with subjects taking the tests on less turbulent days. The windy days led to higher scores on neuroticism and extraversion, and to lower scores on IQ tests and other measures. Although results are often inconsistent, research in the United States has shown some relationship between windy days and poor classroom behavior (e.g., Dexter, 1904) and between wind speed and mortality rates, felonies, and delinquency (Banzinger & Owens, 1978) (for a review of these studies, the reader is referred to Campbell & Beets, 1981). Whether these effects are directly attributable to wind, to air pressure changes (see below), or even to atmospheric ion changes, is subject to debate (see box, page 141). Also, temperature and other weather changes usually accompany winds, so more than one factor may account for wind effects. Quite probably, these weather conditions increase the stress one experiences, and the heightened stress leads to many of the psychological effects discussed in Chapter 4. Moreover, attention, arousal, and loss of perceived control are likely to mediate many wind effects. Further discussion along these lines is presented in the following section on altitude and barometric pressure.

BAROMETRIC PRESSURE AND ALTITUDE

Many people live at rather high altitudes, such as in the Rocky Mountain region of the United States, the Tibetan Plateau of southern China, the Andes, and the high plains of Ethiopia. Others of us travel to these high places. Still others experience high altitudes in aircraft or experience below sea-level conditions during underwater dives. At high altitudes we are exposed to a variety of stresses, most notably *hypoxia* or reduced oxygen intake resulting from low air pressure. Other high altitude stresses include increased solar radiation, cold temperatures, humidity, high velocity winds, reduced nutrition, and strain from negotiating rough terrain (Frisancho, 1979). In underwater environments we also experience problems from high pressures, cold temperatures, and physical exertion. Thus, it is appropriate to examine the physiological and behavioral changes associated with altitude and air pressure differences. (For more detailed reviews, the reader is referred to Frisancho, 1979; Heath & Williams, 1977; Miles, 1967; Pawson & Corneille, 1978; and Walder, 1967.)

Physiological Effects

Normal atmospheric or barometric pressure at sea level is 14.7 pounds per square inch. Lower than normal pressures occur as one rises higher and higher above sea level. Under normal air pressure conditions, oxygen is taken into the body through the alveolar walls of the lungs, with the pressure difference between the atmosphere and sides of the walls being just enough to "force" oxygen into the body. In low pressure environments, however, it becomes more difficult for the oxygen to pass through the alveolar walls, resulting in reduced oxygen available, or the hypoxia noted above (see also Ernsting, 1963, 1967). Hypoxia has a number of physiological and behavioral consequences; and, it should be mentioned, hypoxia is not limited to high altitude environments, but is also a major problem in carbon monoxide pollution, as discussed in the section of this chapter on air pollution. Most habitable environments are located below 15,000 feet, though at much higher altitudes, two special air pressure problems occur. First, above 30,000 feet, the pressure on the interior (body) side of the lung walls becomes so much greater than the pressure on the atmospheric side that oxygen actually passes from the blood into the atmosphere. Second, above 63,000 feet, air pressure is so low that water in the body at a core temperature of 98.6° will actually vaporize!

As stated above, the hypoxia at high altitudes has a number of physiological ramifications (see Frisancho, 1979, for a detailed discussion). Visitors to high altitude areas are likely to experience deeper, and perhaps more rapid, breathing to help compensate for hypoxia. As a result, more carbon dioxide is removed from the lungs, leading to increased alkalinity of the blood. In addition, resting heart rate increases, though maximum heart rate during exercise decreases. Consequently, total cardiac output is reduced, and enlargement of the heart may occur (Frisancho, 1979). Red blood cell count increases, hemoglobin concentration increases, but plasma volume decreases, so total blood volume is largely unaffected. Moreover, retinal blood vessel diameter increases and light sensitivity of the retina decreases. Also, an increased desire for sugar will likely be experienced, although hunger is suppressed and weight loss is likely. Hormone production is also affected by high altitudes: Adrenal activity increases and thyroid activity decreases. Testosterone production and sperm production decrease, and menstrual complaints may increase. In sum, initial exposure to high altitudes leads to many physiological changes.

Acclimatization to High Altitudes

Fortunately, most of the physiological changes noted above are short-term responses to high altitudes, and acclimatization to the environment at these elevations does occur (Frisancho, 1979). For example, hemoglobin concentration levels off after six months and testosterone production returns to normal after a week of high altitude exposure. Acclimatization is not without long-term consequences, however. Frisancho (1979) points out that populations native to high altitude areas do show physiological differences from low-land natives, probably as a result of developmental adaptations. For example, high-altitude natives show larger lung capacity, higher blood pressure in the pulmonary (leading to the lung) arteries,

---

A RECYCLED CYCLE: MOON PHASES AND BEHAVIOR

Folklore and commonly held beliefs maintain that many aspects of our behavior are related to phases of the moon. Sexual prowess, menstrual cycles, birth rates, death rates, suicide rates, homicide rates, and hospital admission rates are among the phenomena various people claim to be affected by the moon. Often, it is maintained that a full moon increases strange behavior. Other beliefs are that the tidal pulls of full and new moons influence human physiology or psychic functioning, or that the moon's perigee (closest distance to the earth) and apogee (farthest distance from the earth) influence us in strange ways. Indeed, the word *lunacy* is derived from a belief in a relationship between the moon and mental illness.

From time to time, research appears that actually gives credence to such beliefs. For example, Blackman and Catalina (1973) found that full moons were associated with an increase in the number of patients visiting a psychiatric emergency room. In another study, Lieber and Sherin (1972) reported a relationship between moon phase and homicide. Rape, robbery and assault, burglary, larceny and theft, auto theft, drunkenness, disorderly conduct, and attacks on family and children have also been linked to a full moon (Tasso & Miller, 1976). At first glance, then, it would appear that science has confirmed the folklore of the ancients (see also Garzino, 1982).

Not so fast! Closer examination of the data indicates that the mysticism of the lunar cycle may be more myth than reality. Campbell and Beets (1978), Campbell (1982), and Frey, Rotton, and Barry (1979) review the available research on the topic and conclude that no firm relationship exists between any lunar variable and human behavior, although lunar tides do affect some marine organisms (see also Jorgenson, 1981; Lester, 1979; Lester, Brockopp, & Priebe, 1969). For example, studies conducted over a period of three to five years may report a relationship between the full moon and suicide or homicide for only one of the years studied. Researchers who conclude that such a relationship exists are ignoring the fact that it does not exist for the other years, or that these behaviors are actually lower during full moons for another year. Moreover, it is consistently found that crimes increase on weekends. For some periods of the year, lunar phases may coincide with weekends. Data based on only these periods will obviously show a relationship between the moon and crime, but data based on other periods will show the opposite relationship or no relationship at all. In addition, a self-fulfilling prophecy may operate: If police believe crime increases during a full moon, they may become more vigilant at these times and thus arrest more people. Altogether, the evidence reviewed by Campbell and Beets (1978) and by Frey, Rotton, and Barry (1979) suggests that positive links between moon phases and behavior are spurious and are attributable to mere chance probabilities in the data or to variables not considered by individual investigators. Nevertheless, given the tenacity of beliefs in moon phases causing disruptive behavior, we suspect the lunacy of it all will continue for some time!

lower blood pressure for the rest of the body, enlarged areas of the heart, larger chest size, lower weight at birth, slower growth rates, and slower sexual maturation (Frisancho, 1979). Although some of these differences may be attributable to nutrition, genetics, and culture, many of them are almost certainly tied to the hypoxic environment of high elevations.

Behavioral Effects of High Altitudes

Obviously, extreme hypoxia will lead to loss of consciousness and death. Performance impairment, however, occurs well before this extreme stage. To the extent the body can compensate for hypoxia, high altitudes will not show substantial performance decrements. During strenuous work, however, the capacity of the body to compensate for hypoxia is taxed, and performance decrements are likely to be observed. Task performance can be impaired by altitudes as low as 8,000 feet. Learning of a new task can be impaired by rapid decompression to altitudes as low as 5,000 feet. In general, learning of new things is more affected by high altitudes than is recall of previously learned material (Cahoon, 1972; Denison, Ledwith, & Poulton, 1966; McFarland, 1972). We should note that such learning impairments are generally of small magnitude, and people living at high altitudes are certainly capable of learning!

High Air Pressure Effects

Extremely high pressure is experienced primarily under the sea. For each 33 feet of depth, the pressure increases by 14.7 pounds per square inch (psi), or by "one atmosphere." Thus, at 33 feet, the pressure is 29.4 psi (two atmospheres), at 99 feet the pressure is 58.8 psi (four atmospheres), and so on. Hazards encountered at such pressure extremes (see also Miles, 1967; Walder, 1967) include:

1. Increased breathing difficulty caused by reduction of maximum breathing capacity (reduced by 50 percent at a depth of 100 feet);
2. Oxygen poisoning caused by breathing excess oxygen or oxygen under pressure;
3. Nitrogen poisoning caused by the narcotic effects of breathing nitrogen under extreme pressure. Symptoms include light-headedness and mental instability;
4. Decompression sickness caused by nitrogen bubbles forming in body tissues (especially in the circulatory system) when one rapidly changes from a high pressure to a lower pressure environment. The "bends" is one relatively acute form of decompression sickness. Permanent damage to the bones may also result from rapid decompression.

Most of these high pressure problems can be corrected or prevented by breathing the proper mixture of air for the diving depth and by surfacing slowly to permit the gradual release of nitrogen from tissues.

Medical, Emotional, and Behavioral Effects of Air Pressure Changes

Low and high barometric or atmospheric pressures are not only associated with altitude. All of us, in fact, are subjected to often dramatic swings in barometric pressure associated with weather changes. Hurricanes, cyclones, and other "tropical storms," for example, are special types of low pressure weather systems. Clear, sunny skies on the other hand, are generally associated with high pressure. Do these changes in barometric pressure affect our feelings and behavior? According to a number of researchers, the answer is "yes," although the picture is a bit cloudy (pun intended) in that: (1) the data are not always consistent from study to study; and (2) humidity, temperature, and wind variations accompanying pressure changes may account for the observed psychological changes (see also Campbell & Beets, 1977; Moos, 1976).

In general, researchers have observed three types of effects that air pressure changes have on people: increased medical complaints, increased suicide rates, and increased disruptive behavior. With respect to medical complaints, many arthritis victims claim that their condition worsens with changes in weather. Indeed, Hollander and Yeostros (1963) have reported scientific evidence of both increased complaints and medical indications of increased arthritic impairment associated with a combination of falling barometric pressure and rising humidity. Moreover, Meucher and Ungeheuer (1961) report an association between general medical complaints and changing weather, especially low pressure or stormy weather.

A number of studies have been conducted over the years to examine the relationship of mental hospital admissions and suicide rates to weather changes. Both of these clinical occurrences show fluctuations with seasons, with the highest rates coinciding with the increased temperatures and daylight hours of spring and summer months (see Campbell & Beets, 1977; Moos, 1976). Suicide rates, however, show some specific variation with barometric pressure. In general, suicides increase as barometric pressure falls, and decrease as pressure rises (Digon & Block, 1966; Mills, 1934; Sanborn, Casey, & Niswander, 1970), although not all researchers agree that such a relationship exists (e.g., Digon & Block, 1966; Pokorny, Davis, & Harberson, 1963).

Finally, several studies have shown that disruptive school behavior and police dispatch calls fluctuate with weather, especially air pressure changes. Even at the turn of the century, one researcher found that low barometric pressure, as well as wind and humidity fluctuations, were associated with poor behavior in the classroom (Dexter, 1904). Similar findings have been reported more recently (e.g., Auliciems, 1972; Brown, 1964; Russell & Bernal, 1977). Also, it has been found that complaints to police and investigative activity increase with low pressure and high temperature, and that accident reports and related investigations increase with stormy weather (Sells & Will, 1971; Will & Sells, 1969).

What do the above findings mean? Are our mental health and behavior helpless victims of barometric and other weather changes? Fortunately, the answer seems to be "probably not." First, the effects of weather changes on most psychological and behavioral indices are small relative to the influence of other factors, such as so-

cial conflict. Second, to the extent that weather does affect behavior, it probably does so indirectly, as an added stressor (i.e., as "the straw that broke the camel's back"). For example, increased suicide rates associated with pleasant weather probably reflect increased time available to interact in stressful social situations, and increased opportunities to worry about these social stresses (see Moos, 1976). Similarly, weather changes may simply provide something else to worry about and cope with, adding to the strain on adaptational capacity that has been built up by other stressors. Nevertheless, the additional stresses brought about by the weather must be dealt with, and may have important consequences, especially under times of other duress. (For another viewpoint, see the box on p. 141.)

Summary of Air Pressure Effects

Low air pressure is associated with high altitudes and stormy weather conditions. High pressure is found in underwater environments and in fair weather circumstances. At high altitudes, the major stress is hypoxia, or low oxygen intake. Adaptation to hypoxia may have short-term and long-term consequences, including respiratory, cardiovascular, and hormonal changes, as well as performance impairment. High pressure in underwater environments may lead to breathing difficulty, oxygen poisoning, nitrogen poisoning, and decompression sickness, although steps may be taken to avoid these problems. Low pressure associated with weather changes may coincide with increased medical complaints, high suicide rates, and increased disruptive behavior. These observations associated with weather may be due to weather variables other than air pressure, and are likely attributable to additional stress to go along with social stresses and other sources of duress.

AIR POLLUTION AND BEHAVIOR

All of us are aware that air pollution has become one of the primary environmental problems of the past two decades. We now know that exhaust gases from automobiles, gaseous and solid air-

AIR IONIZATION AND ELECTROMAGNETIC FIELDS: MEDIATORS OF WEATHER–BEHAVIOR RELATIONSHIPS?

Lightning and other factors may ionize the air; that is, the molecules in the air partially "split" into positively and negatively charged particles. Moreover, extremely low frequency electromagnetic fields (ELF-EMF) are associated with some low altitude weather disturbances. Could it be that these factors play a role in the influence of the weather on behavior? Some researchers think so, at least to some extent. For example, there is evidence that *negative* ions slow brain waves (Assael, Pfeifer, & Sulman, 1974), speed up reaction time (Hawkins & Barker, 1978; Slote, 1961; Wofford, 1966), facilitate other performance tasks, and enhance positive moods (DeSanctis, Halcomb, & Fedoravicius, 1981). *Positive* ions, on the other hand, are associated with worsening performance and mental outlook. Interestingly, one interpretation of the disruptive effects of the Sharav wind in Israel (see pp. 136–137) is that this wind generates an excess of positive ions (Sulman *et al.*, 1970).

Research on low frequency electromagnetic fields suggests that such fields may slow reaction time, impair estimation of time (constricting time), and lead to complaints of headaches and lethargy (for reviews, see Beal, 1974; Persinger, Ludwig, & Ossenkopf, 1973).

Whether or not ions and ELF-EMF account for the effects of weather on behavior is unknown. As with all individual weather variables, more than one factor is operating at a time, so it is difficult to conclude that any one mechanism "causes" the observed behavior or feeling state. It is intriguing to consider the possibility, however, and we are sure that experimentation and speculation will continue in the area (cf., Charry & Hawkinshire, 1981).

borne particles from industrial wastes, and even the smoke from forest fires and cozy fireplaces in the home can have seriously adverse effects on health. Among the common pollutants are carbon monoxide, sulfur dioxide, nitrogen dioxide, particulate matter, hydrocarbons, and photochemical pollutants formed from the reaction of other pollutants with light and heat. Fortunately, with increased social consciousness and passage of such legislation as the Clean Air Act, we are well on our way to reducing many types of air pollution. Nevertheless, the air is still being contaminated

AIR POLLUTION: THEN AND NOW*

Air pollution is not just a modern problem caused by automobiles or factories. Recent evidence uncovered by anthropologists and medical specialists suggests that hundreds of years ago humans may have suffered the side effects of air pollution. The body of an Eskimo woman who apparently died in an earthquake or landslide some 1600 years ago was discovered on Saint Lawrence Island in the Bering Sea in 1972. Because the body must have been frozen shortly after death, medical specialists were able to perform a detailed autopsy; they found that the woman had black lung disease, which resulted from breathing some form of highly polluted air. Experts speculate that years of inhaling fumes from lamps that burned seal oil or whale blubber could cause black lung, a disease frequently found in coal miners. Human beings have been capable of modifying their environments, including the air they breathe, for centuries, and air pollution (caused by people changing the environment around them) may have a long history.

*From Associated Press story in *Rocky Mountain News*, February 12, 1977.

and will continue to be for many years to come (see box p. 141). In this section we will examine some of the available research on air pollution and behavior. We will start with how we perceive air pollution and then examine the health effects, performance effects, and social effects of air pollution (for a more thorough review of air pollution and its behavioral effects, the reader is referred to Evans & Jacobs, 1981).

Perception of Air Pollution

We have seen that perception of heat and cold depends on physical and psychological factors. Perception of air pollution follows a similar pattern. What do you think of when you hear the term "air pollution"? Probably, you think of two bad things—bad odors and smog-like conditions. Unfortunately, we do indeed depend primarily on our sense of smell and on atmospheric visibility in perceiving air pollution. We say *un*fortunately because many of the most harmful types of air pollution are not detectable in these ways. Carbon monoxide, for example, is both odorless and col-

orless. Moreover, airtight homes designed to restrict heat loss may be two or three times more polluted than outside air (Guenther, 1982; see also Sterling, 1979).

To detect particulate pollution, we may of course observe dust on our belongings; for some pollutants, eye and respiratory irritation are cues (cf., Barker, 1976). For our purposes, however, we will first examine perception of air pollution through smell and vision, and then look at an alternative means of perception.

Perception of Air Pollution Through Smell.
When pollution *is* detectable through smell, how do we perceive the smell? The answer appears to be chemically, through the *olfactory membrane*. The olfactory membrane lies at the top of the nasal passages, just behind the nose. This membrane, which is similar to the basilar membrane in the cochlea, is lined with hair cells. By a mechanism we still do not understand, gaseous chemicals stimulate these cells as they pass by, sending signals to the brain, which interpets the

---

BODY ODOR: PRIMITIVE AIR POLLUTION

One of the most offensive odors in American culture is body odor. Many cultures, such as a number of Middle Eastern societies, consider body odor inoffensive. Americans, however, have been conditioned to think of body odors as embarrassingly repulsive, so we bathe frequently and change clothes almost every day (note implications for water conservation).

A clever study by McBurney, Levine, and Cavanaugh (1977) attempted to scale body odors and determine whether humans can detect their own odors. Eleven male graduate students were paid 10 dollars to wear a T-shirt for 48 hours without using deodorants or bathing. Subjects had to exercise vigorously for at least one hour during the 48-hour period. At the end of this period, each subject sealed the T-shirt in a plastic bag and returned it to the experimenters. Each subject then smelled all the shirts in a random order and rated the anonymous owner on a series of scales. In addition, 14 undergraduates also smelled and rated the shirts.

Subjects generally agreed on which shirts smelled best and which worst. Persons associated with the most unpleasant odors were also rated, relative to less unpleasant-smelling persons, as unsociable, dirty, unfriendly, unintelligent, nervous, unsophisticated, unpopular, unattractive, unhealthy, fat, poor, unappealing to the opposite sex, active, strong, industrious, athletic, and masculine. Finally, the graduate students rated their own shirts as smelling less unpleasant than the other shirts.

Can you think of implications for how manufacturers might evaluate their own foul industrial odors?

signals as various odors. Several factors determine whether the olfactory membrane detects a specific odor. For one thing, the chemical stimulating the membrane usually has to be heavier than air. Also, sufficient quantities of the chemical have to be present. This is one reason "sniffing" the air helps you detect odors. To the extent that pollutants are capable of stimulating the olfactory membrane, humans can detect air pollution through smell (for reviews of odor detection, see Berglund, Berglund, & Lindvall, 1976; Turk, Johnston, & Moulton, 1974).

Perception of Air Pollution Through Vision. In addition to noticing smells, most of us infer air pollution from smog-like conditions. That is, we use visual perception to determine the presence or absence of pollution. If a scene looks hazy, especially if the haze is brown, we perceive that there is considerable pollution present. At least two research studies have suggested that visibility is the primary cue that average citizens use in detecting air pollution (Crowe, 1968; Hummel, Levitt, & Loomis, 1973). These researchers asked the open-ended question, "What do you think of when you hear the term 'air pollution'?" There was a strong tendency for respondents to specify effects of pollution, such as smoke or smog, rather than to specify causes, such as factories or automobiles (see Table 5–4).

Other Means of Detection. As stated at the beginning of this section, really harmful pollution is often not detectable by its smell or visibility.

What, then, can be used to perceive the presence of pollution? Although sophisticated chemical detection equipment is one possibility, much simpler means are available to everyone. We might turn to pollution experts to find out what to use. According to Hummel, Loomis, and Hebert (1975), experts use automobile concentration as the primary cue in detecting pollution. Since automobiles account for about 50 percent of urban pollution, this certainly makes sense. Hummel *et al.* (1975) found that experts base their judgments of pollution far more on the concentration of automobiles than do nonexperts, and nonexperts tend to use visibility as a cue more than experts do. Other cues useful in detecting air pollution include the absence of rain (rain cleanses the air), the presence of tall buildings (which block winds), and the presence of stop-and-go traffic as opposed to freeway traffic (idling and accelerating automobiles produce more pollution than automobiles moving at a constant speed). Why not instruct the public in the use of such cues as a means of detecting pollution that otherwise would go unnoticed? Hummel (1977) presents evidence that such instruction is indeed possible.

Other Factors Affecting Judgments of Air Pollution. In concluding our discussion of perception of air pollution, we should note that our perceptual awareness of pollution may change with our exposure to it, and may also depend on other factors (see also Evans & Jacobs, 1981). For example, lower socioeconomic status individ-

Table 5–4. CLASSIFICATION OF TYPICAL DEFINITIONS OF AIR POLLUTION*

Component of Definition	Percentage of Respondents Using Each Component	
	Urban Sample	Student Sample
Specific manifestation (smoke, haze)	43	14
Causative source (cars, industry)	22	43
Effects (health or property damage)	18	9
Combination (two or more of above)	17	34

*Note that causes are specified less than half the time. (From Hummel, Levitt, and Loomis, 1973.)

uals tend to be less aware of air pollution than other groups (Swan, 1970). Moreover, time of day and the particular season also make a difference (Barker, 1976). Interestingly, we tend to think "the other guy" has more pollution than we do. That is, we think our own immediate geographic area is less polluted than adjacent areas (DeGroot, 1967; Rankin, 1969).

Does prior exposure to air pollution decrease or increase our awareness of it? Unfortunately, the evidence is mixed on this question. For example, Wohlwill (1974) compared two groups of people in one location: those who had moved there from a highly polluted region, and those who had moved there from a relatively unpolluted area. The current location was considered more polluted by those from the unpolluted area than by those from the highly polluted area; this suggests that the two groups were using different adaptation levels in making their assessments. In essence, these findings suggest that the more people were familiar with pollution, the less they were bothered by it (see also Evans, Jacobs, & Frager, 1979). Data from Lipsey (1977) and Medalia (1964) support the opposite position: The more people encounter pollution, the more concerned they become about it. For example, Medalia (1964) found that the longer people had lived near a malodorous paper mill, the more aware they were of its pollution. Whether we actually adapt perceptually to the presence of air pollution or become more sensitive to it with exposure, then, is unclear. As we will discuss in the next two sections, however, there is some evidence that we adapt physiologically and behaviorally to air pollution.

Air Pollution and Health

A story by David Brand in the July 24, 1981 *Wall Street Journal* noted the activities of the Polish Ecology Club in trying to get the Polish government to clean up that country's environment. As an example of the magnitude of the problem, the story reported that the Skawina aluminum smelter was designed in the early 1950s to produce 15,000 tons per year, but that by 1980 it was turning out 53,000 tons of aluminum per year. Manufacturing aluminum requires large quantities of electricity to keep furnaces hot. However, in 1978, when the Skawina plant's generators broke down, aluminum fluoride was added as a flux so the managers could keep the process going at a lower temperature. Tragically, however, a side result was an increase in the release of hydrogen fluoride gas. The plant had no filters and belched out pollutants in quantities 40 times greater than legal limits. The Solidarity union movement eventually convinced the government to close the plant, but the damage had been done. Immediate health problems included sore throats and breathing difficulties. In the long run, though, most of the plant's 2,400 workers planned to take early retirement because they were too sick to get jobs anywhere else.

The hazardous effects of air pollution on health are becoming well known. From time to time, very high concentrations of pollutants have been known to increase the death rate for urban areas, as exemplified by the December, 1952 disaster in London, in which 3,500 deaths were attributed to excessive levels of sulfur dioxide (Goldsmith, 1968). Such disasters, however, are relatively rare. More worrisome are adverse health effects of high concentrations of pollutants that occur more frequently (Coffin & Stokinger, 1977; Evans & Jacobs, 1981; Garland & Pearce, 1967; Goldsmith & Friberg, 1977; National Academy of Sciences, 1977; Rose & Rose, 1971; Schulte, 1963). In the US, for example, 140,000 deaths are attributable to pollution each year (Mendelsohn & Orcutt, 1979), and the annual cost of air pollution in the US has been estimated at 16.1 billion dollars (and dollars for the year 1973, at that) (Lave & Seskin, 1973).

Carbon monoxide (CO), the most common pollutant, prevents body tissues (including those of the brain and heart) from receiving adequate oxygen, a condition known as hypoxia (see p. 137). Prolonged exposure to heavy concentrations of CO can lead to very serious health problems, including visual and hearing impairment, Parkinsonism, epilepsy, headache, fatigue, memory dis-

Figure 5–7. Exposure to air pollutants such as carbon monoxide, oxides of nitrogen, oxides of sulfur, particulates, and photochemical smog, can lead to many adverse health effects, including cardiovascular problems, visual and hearing impairment, epilepsy, memory disturbances, and even retardation and psychotic symptoms. Pollution also affects performance and social behavior.

turbances, and even retardation and psychotic symptoms. Particulates, such as those containing mercury, lead, or asbestos can cause respiratory problems, cancer, anemia, and neural problems, among other things. Photochemical smog can cause eye irritation, respiratory problems, cardiovascular distress, and possibly cancer. Oxides of nitrogen also impair respiratory function and may lower resistance to disease. Finally, oxides of sulfur are primarily associated with, once again, respiratory impairment. For most pollutants, the elderly and the ill are the most likely victims. Physicians have identified an air pollution syndrome (APS) caused by combinations of pollutants and characterized by headache, fatigue, insomnia, irritability, depression, burning of the eyes, back pain, impaired judgment, and gastrointestinal problems (cf. Hart, 1970; LaVerne, 1970). Indeed, the list of ailments aggravated, if not caused, by air pollution seems endless. Some experts believe that 50 to 90 percent of human cancer is related to some form of pollution, including air and water pollution and food contam-

ination (*Time*, June 13, 1977). Even psychiatric admissions are higher when air pollution levels are high (Rotton & Frey, 1982; Strahilevitz, Strahilevitz, & Miller, 1979) (see Figure 5–7).

Interestingly, there is some evidence that we can adapt physiologically to some pollutants, including photochemical smog (Hackney *et al.*, 1977) and sulfur dioxide (Dubos, 1965). However, the extent of such reduced physiological reactivity is unknown (see also Evans & Jacobs, 1981), and there are certainly limits to which any organism can adapt to changes in the chemical environment.

Air Pollution and Performance

Most available research on pollution and performance involves studies of carbon monoxide (CO), which results from the incomplete burning of substances containing carbon (see Evans & Jacobs, 1981; National Academy of Sciences, 1977, for reviews). It has been found that concentrations of CO at 25 to 125 parts per million (ppm) are typical on freeways at rush hour. In one study, Beard and Wertheim (1967) exposed volunteers to concentrations of CO ranging from 50 ppm to 250 ppm for various periods of time and asked them to make discrimination judgments about time intervals. It was found that 90 minutes of exposure to CO at 50 ppm significantly impaired performance on the time judgment task. As CO concentration increased, shorter periods of exposure were required for similar levels of impairment. Using rats, these researchers also found that 11 minutes of exposure to 100 ppm adversely affected learning in an operant conditioning situation.

Breisacher (1971) has reviewed research indicating that air pollutants, including CO, also adversely affect human reaction time, manual dexterity, and attention (see also Beard & Grandstaff, 1970; Gliner *et al.*, 1975; O'Donnel *et al.*, 1971; Putz, 1979; Ramsey, 1970; Rummo & Sarlanis, 1974). Such research suggests that air pollution on major traffic arteries may impair driving ability enough to increase the frequency of automobile accidents. This possibility is supported by results of a study by Lewis *et al.* (1970), in which subjects were exposed to "clean" air or to air drawn 15 inches above ground at a traffic site handling 830 vehicles per hour. Performance decrements occurred in three out of four information-processing tasks for subjects breathing the polluted air (see also Horvath, Dahms, & O'Hanlon, 1971). In sum, carbon monoxide appears to be quite deleterious to performance.

Research on other pollutants shows similarly deleterious effects. Nitrogen dioxide and sulfur dioxide, for example, impair sensory processes (Izmerov, 1971). Photochemical smog components, on the other hand, may or may not affect performance adversely (Holland *et al.*, 1968; Hore & Gibson, 1968; Lagerwerff, 1963; Ury, 1968; Wayne, Wehrle, & Carroll, 1967). Taken altogether, though, it is clear that most pollutants adversely affect human performance.

Interestingly, there is at least some evidence that we adapt to air pollution behaviorally. That is, after prolonged exposure, our behavior differs from that of those who have experienced only brief exposure. Evans, Jacobs, and Frager (1979),

for example, found that long-term residents of the Los Angeles area tended to deny the threat of pollution, felt they were less vulnerable to its effects, and felt they knew more than they actually did about pollution hazards. Those who were newcomers to the area, however, felt more positively about the value of mass transit to reduce pollution and more readily looked for information about pollution. Moreover, those newcomers who were internal in locus of control (i.e., felt they controlled their own destiny) were more likely to avoid outdoor activity on high smog days. Feeling that one is in control of the situation has also been shown to reduce the effects of malodorous pollution on frustration (Rotton, Yoshikawa, & Kaplan, 1979). In sum, pollution not only affects performance negatively, but we also develop ways of coping with some of these negative effects.

Air Pollution and Social Behavior

Research has shown that malodorous air pollution influences at least three types of social behavior. First, recreation behavior in particular, and outdoor activity in general, are restricted by pollution (Chapko & Solomon, 1976; Peterson, 1975). Second, Rotton *et al,* (1978) examined the effects of ammonium sulfide and butyric acid on interpersonal attraction. In one experiment, it was found that ammonium sulfide increased attraction for similar others with whom subjects thought they were interacting. Apparently, a "shared stress" phenomenon occurred, as in the research on noise and attraction described in Chapter 4. That is, if subjects thought they were sharing the experience of exposure to the unpleasant odor, attraction toward similar others increased. In a second experiment, however, the same researchers found that subjects who did not expect to interact with others evaluated those others less favorably if exposed to ammonium sulfide or butyric acid than if not exposed. It seems that the unpleasant affective states associated with pollution lead to decreased attraction if not shared with others, but to increased attraction if shared. Malodorous air pollution affects more than just attraction to people. Interestingly, foul odors also reduce liking for

DOES CIGARETTE SMOKE POLLUTE THE AIR?

For a number of years we have known that tars and nicotine can have disastrous effects on the health of smokers. There is now a growing body of evidence that nonsmokers breathing the air in a room where others are smoking may also suffer ill effects. For example, cigarette smoke has been shown to contain significant quantities of carbon monoxide and probably some degree of DDT and formaldehyde as well. A nonsmoker inhaling the air around a person who is smoking will often experience an increase in heart rate, blood pressure, and breathing rate (Luquette, Landiss, & Merki, 1970; Russell, Cole, & Brown, 1973).

Opposition to smoking in public places is growing. Many states have adopted laws prohibiting smoking in elevators, stores, and some restaurants. A number of antismoking groups, including ASH (Action on Smoking and Health), GASP (Group Against Smokers' Pollution), and SHAME! (Society to Humiliate, Aggravate, Mortify, and Embarrass Smokers) have adopted tactics ranging from mildly to overtly hostile in efforts to discourage smokers from "lighting up" in front of them. THANK YOU FOR NOT SMOKING signs are becoming more common, as are such signs as YES, I MIND IF YOU SMOKE, SMOKERS STINK, and KISSING A SMOKER IS LIKE LICKING A DIRTY ASHTRAY. Newly discovered hostile tactics include plucking cigarettes from smokers' mouths and dunking one's hand in a smoker's water glass with the explanation, "You don't pollute my air, I won't pollute your water!" We need not comment on the behavior that is likely to follow such action except to say that it is likely to be consistent with theories of aggression.

Recent research has confirmed that nonsmokers are indeed disturbed by cigarette smoke. In one study (Bleda & Sandman, 1977), smokers were evaluated negatively by nonsmokers if they smoked in the presence of the nonsmokers. Other research indicates that nonsmokers have increased feelings of irritation, fatigue, and anxiety when exposed to cigarette smoke (Jones, 1978). In another study (Bleda & Bleda, 1978), it was found that persons sitting on a bench in a shopping mall fled faster if a stranger next to them smoked than if he or she refrained from smoking. Interestingly, smoke-induced irritation in nonsmokers may occur primarily when individuals are less involved in tasks at hand, rather than when they are intensely motivated by their activities (Stone, Breidenbach, & Heimstra, 1979). Finally, cigarette smoke may not just lead to feelings of irritation and dislike, but to overt hostility as well. Both feelings of aggression (Jones & Bogat, 1978) and hostile behavior (Zillmann, Baron, & Tamborini, 1981) increase in the presence of others' cigarette smoke.

paintings and photography (Rotton, Yoshikawa *et al.*, 1978).

In another experiment, Rotton *et al.* (1979) investigated the effects of exposure to ethyl mercaptan and ammonium sulfide on aggression. Using the shock methodology common in aggression research (see the section on heat and aggression), the researchers ostensibly allowed subjects to shock a confederate. In accordance with the research on heat and aggression, it was anticipated that exposure to a moderately unpleasant odor (ethyl mercaptan) would increase aggression, but that exposure to a more unpleasant odor (ammonium sulfide) would decrease aggression. Consis-

tent with these predictions, it was found that relative to a no-odor control group, the moderate odor increased aggression. In addition, there was suggestive evidence (though not satistically reliable) that the stronger odor decreased aggression.

Summary of Air Pollution Effects on Behavior

Air pollution consists mainly of carbon monoxide, photochemical smog, particulates, and oxides of nitrogen and sulfur. We primarily detect pollution through reduced horizon visibility, smell, and eye and respiratory irritation. Unfortunately, some deadly forms of pollution cannot be detected readily using these means. Respiratory and cardiovascular problems are the most notable effects of various pollutants, although a number of other adverse health effects are associated with pollution. Performance deteriorates upon exposure to pollutants in sufficient quantities, especially carbon monoxide. In addition, malodorous pollutants may either decrease or increase attraction and aggression. Physiological and psychological stress, arousal, perceived control, and adaptation level all seem to have some mediational influence in pollution effects.

INTEGRATING WEATHER AND POLLUTION EFFECTS: A FINAL NOTE

For the most part, we have treated individual weather and pollution variables as if their effects on health, mental outlook, and behavior are separate from other factors. We wish to conclude by noting that such singular effects rarely occur in our lives. That is, as noted previously, hot days are often associated with high barometric pressure and calm winds. Stormy days usually involve changes in temperature, wind, humidity, and air pressure. High altitudes not only result in reduced oxygen supply, but in increased exposure to solar radiation. Moreover, low winds and temperature inversions increase the concentration of air pollutants, and high humidity can intensify the effects of photochemical smog. Thus, all of the weather and pollution variables we have considered in this chapter are interrelated, and one can rarely conclude with certainty that a given behavior or health effect is attributable to any one of these factors (cf. Rotton & Frey, 1982).

CHAPTER SUMMARY

Weather and air pollution have definite influences on human behavior. Exposure to heat or cold results in a number of physiological adaptive steps aimed at maintaining a stable core body temperature. Heat impairs performance only when it is

extremely uncomfortable and may actually facilitate performance if it is only moderately uncomfortable. Heat tends to reduce interpersonal attraction and to increase aggression at moderately uncomfortable levels but decrease it at extreme levels of discomfort. Extremes of cold (below 55°F) impair performance and may also influence aggression in the same manner as extremes of heat. Winds can be quite disturbing and interfere with many types of performance. Health complaints and accident rates also appear to be associated with high-wind conditions. Low barometric pressure at high altitudes leads to hypoxia and other forms of physiological distress, but we can adapt to low and high pressure environments. Changes in air pressure associated with weather patterns can have deleterious effects on us. Air pollutants cause or aggravate a variety of ailments, most notably respiratory and cardiovascular problems. Carbon monoxide in sufficient quantity impairs performance. Malodorous pollutants can increase or decrease attraction and aggression, depending on other factors. In general, weather and pollution effects occur in combination with other weather and pollution variables.

Suggested Projects

1. Keep a daily record of temperature and humidity readings. Obtain crime reports from the local newspaper or from the police department. Is there a relationship between weather and crime?
2. Keep daily records of temperature, humidity, and wind conditions. Using a stopwatch, check walking and bicycle riding speeds of students as they make their way across campus. Do these speeds vary with weather conditions?
3. Using a sound-level meter, check the noise levels of winds on a breezy day. Is the noise level higher around buildings?
4. Time the length of lectures in your various classes. Are weather conditions related to length of lectures?

6 Personal Space and Territoriality

INTRODUCTION

Imagine you are on a planet quite different from ours in some ways. While the people look just like we do, their behavior is certainly distinct. It is common for them to walk right up to others, even strangers, and to stand right against them. People seem to have no concept of the need to maintain a "buffer" of space around one's body. They don't mind if total strangers touch their most private parts. When waiting for a bus, instead of distributing themselves evenly and maintaining space between each person, individuals simply form a mass of bodies, each touching the other. And on the beach, people who are together lie on top of each other, rather than spacing themselves evenly on a blanket.

In addition to these affectations, you find there is no such thing as territorial behavior. People move randomly from one dwelling to another, and have no place to call "home." They do not knock before entering a new place, but simply walk in and use what is there. The next day they move somewhere else, taking some of the things that were in the place they had been with them. Nobody seems to mind that they have nowhere to call their own, or that at any moment a complete stranger might walk in on whatever they are doing.

What would life be like on such a planet? How would you feel, and what would you be able to accomplish in life, if you had to live there? While this "fantasy" may seem rather extreme, it should make you aware of your need to maintain a portable personal space "bubble" between yourself and others, and of your territorial needs. In this chapter we will discuss personal space and territoriality, two ways in which people interact with their environment. *Personal space* is defined as an invisible boundary surrounding us, into which others may not trespass. It moves with us, expanding and contracting according to the situation in which we find ourselves. For earthlings, invasion of one's personal space often leads to withdrawal and to other compensatory reactions (Sommer, 1966). In contrast to personal space, *territory* is a relatively stationary, visibly bounded area that is home-centered. We'll provide a more comprehensive definition of territorial behavior later in this chapter, and will describe the important role it plays in our lives. For now, it is important to note only the differences between personal space and territory. Specifically, personal space is invisible and body-centered, regulating *how closely* individuals will interact; territory is visible, stationary, and home-centered, regulating *who* will interact (Sommer, 1969).

PERSONAL SPACE

The term "personal space" was coined by Katz (1937). The concept is not unique to psychology, since it also has roots in biology (Hediger, 1950), anthropology (Hall, 1968), and architecture (Sommer, 1959). Both popular and scientific interest in personal space have intensified greatly during the last two decades. In fact, over 300 published experiments have been done in this area since 1959 (Aiello & Thompson, 1980b; Altman & Chemers, 1980).

Functions of Personal Space

What is the function of the personal space bubble we maintain around ourselves? A number of conceptual explanations have been suggested, which correspond to some of the theoretical formulations we reviewed in Chapter 3. An *overload* interpretation of why we maintain an interpersonal distance between ourselves and others is that such spacing is necessary to avoid overstimulation (cf. Evans, 1974). According to this notion, too close a proximity to others causes us to be bombarded with excessive social or physical stimuli (e.g., facial details, olfactory cues). An alternative formulation, the *stress* interpretation, assumes that we maintain personal space to avoid a variety of stressors associated with too close a proximity. Further, the *arousal* conceptualization posits that when personal space is inadequate, individuals experience too much arousal. A fourth conceptual perspective is the *behavior constraint* approach, which suggests that personal space is maintained to prevent our behavioral freedom from being impinged upon. For example, Altman (1975) views personal space as a means of maintaining adequate privacy and an appropriate level of intimacy. (Some of the functions of personal space are apparent in Figure 6–1.)

Two other explanations of why we maintain personal space have been suggested. One, proposed by anthropologist E. T. Hall (1963, 1966), and discussed in more detail on page 165, conceptualizes personal space primarily *as a form of nonverbal communication*. In this context, the distance between individuals determines the quality and quantity of stimulation that is exchanged (e.g., tactile communication occurs only at close proximity). Distance also communicates information about the type of relationship between individuals (e.g., whether it is intimate or nonintimate), and about the type of activities that can be engaged in (e.g., lovemaking can't occur between individuals who are far apart). A final perspective is afforded by *ethological* models (cf. Evans & Howard, 1973). These formulations assume that personal space functions at a cognitive level and has been selected out by an evolutionary process to control intraspecies aggression, to protect against threats to autonomy, and thereby to reduce stress. We should note, however, that in contrast to the contention of ethological models that personal space evolved naturally, most researchers (e.g., Altman, 1975; Duke & Nowicki, 1972) would probably argue that it is more a product of learning. However, once learned, our spatial behavior seems to be governed unconsciously (i.e., we do not have to "think" about how to position ourselves in different situations).

If the conceptual perspectives are integrated, personal space may be seen to have two primary sets of purposes. First, it has a *protective* function and serves as a buffer against potential emotional and physical threats (e.g., too much stimulation, overarousal leading to stress, insufficient privacy, too much intimacy, physical attacks by others). Its second function involves *communication*. The distance we maintain from others determines which sensory communication channels (e.g., smell, touch, visual input, verbal input) will be most salient in our interaction. To the extent that we choose distances that transmit intimate or nonintimate sensory cues and that suggest high or low concern with self-protection, we are communicating information about the quality of our relationship with another person (i.e., the level of intimacy we desire to have with them).

What determines the size of the personal space we prefer to maintain between ourselves and others? The distance we maintain must be appropriate to fulfill the two functions of personal space—

Figure 6–1. In relatively large areas, groups arrange themselves so that they are surrounded by a more or less constant amount of space in each direction. In addition to constant spacing *between* various groups, members of individual groups maintain relatively constant personal space from each other. (Sherry Fisher)

protection and communication. One determinant of the amount of space necessary to accomplish these functions is the situation (i.e., who we're with and what we're doing). Some relationships and activities demand more distance than others for appropriate communication and adequate protection. Situational conditions aren't the only determinants of the size of our personal space, however. Some individuals habitually preserve minimal personal space zones, while others maintain relatively large personal space zones. Individual differences in spatial behavior probably reflect different learning experiences concerning the amount of space necessary to fulfill the protective and communicative functions (cf. Montagu, 1971). Some individual differences that affect

IS PERSONAL SPACE REALLY A BUBBLE?

Researchers, including the authors of this text, have a tendency to liken personal space to a bubble of sorts that surrounds us and fulfills a number of functions. For example, Hayduk (1978) believes that personal space corresponds to the three-dimensional representation in Figure 6–2. It is generally cylindrical, and of a consistent shape above our waist, but seems to taper off below it. Also, our definition of personal space on page 149 as an "invisible boundary surrounding us, into which others may not trespass" clearly connotes the idea of some type of bubble. While this concept is attractive because it gives us a concrete image to visualize and may thereby aid our understanding, it has some drawbacks that may lead to misunderstanding if it is taken too literally.

First, one might begin to think that if personal space is analogous to a bubble, it is the same size for all individuals and in all situations. Clearly, this is not the case. As we'll see in this chapter, people have varying spatial zones, and the amount of space we desire between ourselves and others expands and contracts depending on the situation. Second, one could easily get the idea that since it is "personal," personal space is somehow attached to an individual in all situations. This is also not true: The concept has meaning only with respect to another individual and doesn't apply to distance between people and desks, for instance. Finally, the label "personal space" may emphasize the idea of *space* and thus suggest that researchers are concerned only with distance. As we will see in this chapter, researchers studying personal space also must focus on other behaviors, such as body orientation and eye contact, in order to get a complete understanding of our spatial behavior (Knowles, 1978; Patterson, 1975).

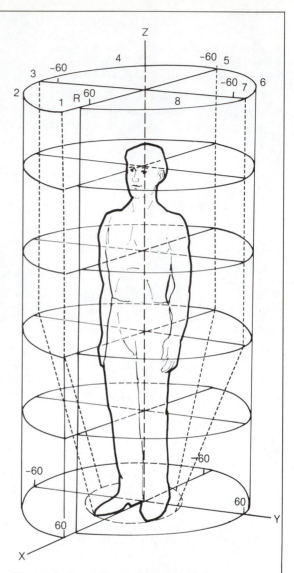

Figure 6–2. A three-dimensional view of the shape of personal space. (From Hayduk, L. The vertical profile of personal space, Edmonton, Alberta, Canada T6G 2H4: University of Alberta, unpublished).

spatial behavior are sex, race, culture, and personality.

One of the first observational studies of the effect of *situational conditions* and *individual difference* variables on spatial behavior was conducted by E. T. Hall. Concerning the effect of situational conditions, Hall (1963, 1966) suggested that Americans use four ranges of personal space in their interactions with others, depending upon their relationship to them and the activity. Hall's assertions were corroborated in an extensive review of the personal space literature by Altman and Vinsel (1977). The zones (labeled *intimate, personal, social,* and *public*) vary in terms

of the quality and quantity of stimulation that is exchanged (see Table 6–1). With respect to the effect of individual differences on spatial behavior, Hall observed in cross-cultural investigations that cultures vary widely in terms of spatial behavior, an observation which has been corroborated in a review of a large number of studies done in recent years (Aiello & Thompson, 1980b). Cultural differences were attributed by Hall to different norms regarding the sensory modalities seen as appropriate for communication between interactants. A quotation from Hall (1968, p. 84) nicely summarizes this finding and suggests how individual differences in spatial behav-

Table 6–1. TYPES OF INTERPERSONAL RELATIONSHIPS AND ACTIVITIES, AND SENSORY QUALITIES CHARACTERISTIC OF HALL'S SPATIAL ZONES*

	Appropriate Relationships and Activities	*Sensory Qualities*
Intimate distance (0 to 1½ feet)	Intimate contacts (e.g., making love, comforting) and physical sports (e.g., wrestling)	Intense awareness of sensory inputs (e.g., smell, radiant heat) from other person; touch overtakes vocalization as primary mode of communication.
Personal distance (1½ to 4 feet)	Contacts between close friends, as well as everyday interactions with acquaintances	Less awareness of sensory inputs than intimate distance; vision is normal and provides detailed feedback; verbal channels account for more communication than touch.
Social distance (4 to 12 feet)	Impersonal and businesslike contacts	Sensory inputs minimal; information provided by visual channels less detailed than in personal distance; normal voice level (audible at 20 feet) maintained; touch not possible.
Public distance (more than 12 feet)	Formal contacts between an individual (e.g., actor, politician) and the public	No sensory inputs; no detailed visual input; exaggerated nonverbal behaviors employed to supplement verbal communication, since subtle shades of meaning are lost at this distance.

*Based on Hall, 1963. (Reproduced by permission of American Anthropological Association. *American Anthropologist*, 65,5:1003–1026, 1963.)

ior may be the source of considerable miscommunication:

Americans overseas were confronted with a variety of difficulties because of cultural differences in the handling of space. People stood ''too close'' during conversations, and when the Americans backed away to a comfortable conversational distance, this was taken to mean that Americans were cold, aloof, withdrawn, and disinterested in people of the country. It was quite obvious that these apparently inconsequential differences in spatial behavior resulted in significant misunderstanding and intensified culture shock, often to the point of illness, for some members of the American overseas colonies.

Methods for Studying Personal Space

While Hall's studies were primarily observational and qualitative in nature, many experimentally based investigations have considered the effect of situational and individual difference variables on personal space. In this research, three different experimental methodologies have been employed. Most of the studies exploring factors that affect personal space have used *simulation methods,* in which subjects manipulate the personal space between dolls or symbolic figures under various experimental conditions. *Laboratory methods* are also employed. In this approach the personal space between subjects (who generally know they are being observed) is measured as a function of experimental conditions. Finally, a third series of studies has used *field methods*. These involve observing and experimenting with interpersonal positioning in naturally occurring situations, as a function of individual difference or situational variables. Note that while laboratory and field methods involve actual spatial behavior between individuals, simulation methods do not. (For a more detailed discussion of these methods, see the Methodological Appendix).

Fortunately, many of the important relationships between situational and individual difference variables and the size of personal space have been corroborated using several different experimental approaches. While this has occurred with some regularity (Duke & Nowicki, 1972; Knowles, 1980; Little, 1965), in other cases there have been dissimilar findings for studies that used different methods to assess the same spatial relationship. Knowles and Johnsen (1974) suggested that although there is sometimes a general association between the various methods used to measure personal space (i.e., they can be considered to be indicators of the same dimension), the level of convergence is only moderate. Others (e.g., Jones & Aiello, 1979) have suggested that different measures of personal space are *not* measuring the same thing. In general, since it appears that laboratory and field methods are consistently better measures of our spatial behavior than simulation techniques (Aiello & Thompson, 1980b; Hayduk, 1978; Jones & Aiello, 1979; Love & Aiello, 1980), they should receive preference from investigators both when planning research, and in interpreting discrepant results.

Having discussed the methodologies used to study interpersonal distancing behavior, we now shift our focus to some of the more representative findings that have accumulated. Our review will deal first with relationships observed between situational conditions and personal space. Next, we'll discuss findings on the effects of individual difference variables on spatial behavior.

Situational Determinants of Personal Space: Research Evidence

Experimentally based studies have explored the effects on spatial behavior of attraction between individuals, interpersonal similarity on various dimensions (e.g., age, race), and context of interaction (e.g., positive versus negative). Such studies have identified a number of rather consistent relationships.

Attraction and Interpersonal Distance. How does attraction between people who are interacting affect the size of the personal space between them? Love songs often lament one lover's longing for physical closeness with a distant other and suggest that the greater the attraction between individuals, the more physically close they wish to be. There is some truth to this popular notion, but the relationship between affection and personal space is somewhat more complex and depends on the sex of the interactants.

Studies (Allgeier & Byrne, 1973; Byrne, Ervin, & Lamberth, 1970; Edwards 1972) indicate that when males and females interact, increased attraction is associated with closer physical distance. In one study, Byrne and his colleagues (1970) manipulated attraction by sending male-female pairs, who were similar or dissimilar on a variety of personality traits, on a "coke date." From research in social psychology we know that similar individuals tend to be more attracted to each other than dissimilar individuals (Byrne, 1971). When the "matched" or "mismatched" couples returned from the date, the experimenter measured their degree of mutual liking, as well as the distance between them as they stood in front of his desk. The "matched" couples liked each other more and stood closer together than the "mismatched" couples. Additional studies have examined whether the attraction-proximity relationship for opposite sex dyads occurs because the male moves closer to the female, because the female moves closer to the male, or because both the male and the female move closer to each other. These studies (e.g., Edwards, 1972) suggested that the smaller distances between close friends of the opposite sex were primarily attributable to females moving closer to males they were attracted to (i.e., females respond more to attraction by their spatial positioning than do males).

If the spatial behavior of females is primarily responsible for the attraction-proximity relationship, then the distance between female-female pairs should be determined by their degree of mutual attraction, while the distance between male-male pairs should not. In line with this assumption, it has been shown that while female-female pairs position themselves closer together with increased liking, positioning does not vary with liking for male-male pairs. In one experiment (Heshka & Nelson, 1972), pairs of adults were

unobtrusively photographed by researchers as they walked down the street. The use of a standard in each of the pictures permitted a fairly accurate estimate of the distance between interactants. After taking the photograph, the experimenter approached the unknowing "subjects" and asked them what type of relationship they had. It was observed that female-female pairs interacted at closer distances as their relationship became more intimate, while distance between male-male pairs did not change as a function of friendship.

Why is it that the attraction-proximity relationship holds for females but not for males? One explanation derives from socialization differences between the sexes, which may be reflected in spatial behavior with liked others. For males, who are socialized to be fearful of homosexual involvement and to be independent and self-reliant overall (Maccoby, 1966), and who have less experience with intimate forms of nonverbal communication (Jourard & Rubin, 1968), spatially immediate situations with liked males or females are ambivalent. Close distances with liked males may trigger concerns about homosexuality, close distances with liked females may evoke concerns about dependency, and for males physical closeness and its attendant high degree of sensory stimulation is generally somewhat foreign. On the other hand, females are socialized to be more dependent, to be less afraid of intimacy with others of the same sex, and generally to be more comfortable in affiliative situations (Maccoby, 1966). They also have more experience as senders and receivers of intimate nonverbal messages (Jourard & Rubin, 1968). Thus, it isn't surprising that they have less difficulty responding spatially to liked others.

The research demonstrating that in some cases people in dyads interact at closer distances with increasing friendship suggests that closer personal space is an outcome of increased attraction. Do individuals viewing people interacting at close range infer higher degrees of attraction (see Figure 6–3)? The available research evidence suggests that closer distances do serve as indicators of attraction to observers. Mehrabian (1968) found that photographs of people interacting at four feet were judged to show a more positive interpersonal relationship than photographs of individuals seated 12 feet apart. Other studies (Haase & Pepper, 1972; Wellens & Goldberg, 1978) have reported similar findings.

Effect of Other Types of Similarity on Interpersonal Distance. We mentioned earlier that one type of similarity (personality similarity) leads to attraction, which elicits closer interpersonal positioning (Byrne *et al.,* 1970). Since other types of similarity have been shown to affect attraction in the same manner as personality similarity (Byrne, 1971), similarity on these other dimensions should also lead to closer interpersonal positioning. This has been found to be true in a number of studies. For example, closer distances are maintained between individuals of similar rather than dissimilar age (Latta, 1978; Willis, 1966), race (Campbell, Kruskal, & Wallace, 1966; Willis, 1966), sexual preference (e.g., heterosexual vs. bisexual) (Barrios *et al.,* 1976), and status (Lott & Sommer, 1967). One setting where status is highly salient is in the military. When initiating an interaction with a superior, the greater the dissimilarity between the initiator and the other in terms of rank, the greater the interpersonal distance maintained (Dean, Willis, & Hewitt, 1975). Finally, it is at once interesting and unfortunate that "normals" prefer to interact at closer interpersonal distances with other "normals" (i.e., similar others) than with people who are stigmatized or have handicaps (dissimilar others) (Dabbs & Stokes 1975; Kleck *et al.,* 1968).

Why should similarity and attraction lead to closer interpersonal distances than dissimilarity and dislike? People generally anticipate more favorable interactions with similar (liked) than with dissimilar (disliked) others (Byrne, 1971). Since one of the functions of personal space is protection against perceived threats, we *should* be willing to interact at closer distances with similar others than with dissimilar others because we anticipate fewer threats from them. Maintaining

FIGURE 6–3. Interpersonal distance, as well as such nonverbal behaviors as body angle, eye contact, and facial expression, tell us quite a bit about the quality of the relationship among individuals. (Peter Oliver)

close interpersonal distances with liked others is also a means of fulfilling the communicative function of personal space. By choosing close distances, we convey information to liked others that we are attracted to them and that we expect to communicate intimate sensory cues to them.

Type of Interaction and Interpersonal Distance. If qualities such as degree of friendship and similarity create expectations of pleasant interactions which in turn affect interpersonal positioning, then situational qualities (e.g., type of interaction, discussion topics) which can be placed on a pleasant-unpleasant dimension should also affect the size of our personal space. This line of reasoning is supported by studies that have varied the affective quality of the interaction situation and observed that negatively toned situations precipitate larger spatial zones (Dosey & Meisels, 1969; Karabenick & Meisels, 1972; Rosenfeld, 1965) (see Figure 6–4, A–E). In their study, Karabenick and Meisels found that subjects who were

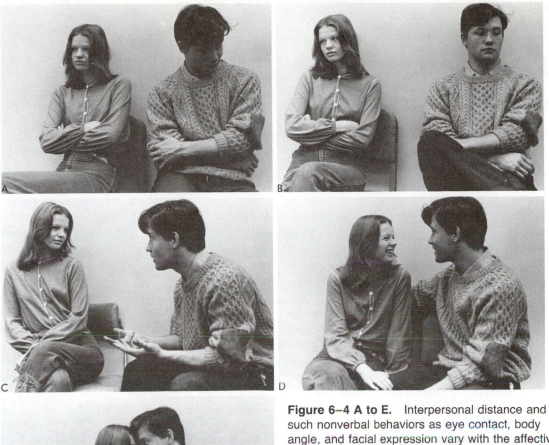

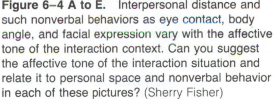

Figure 6–4 A to E. Interpersonal distance and such nonverbal behaviors as eye contact, body angle, and facial expression vary with the affective tone of the interaction context. Can you suggest the affective tone of the interaction situation and relate it to personal space and nonverbal behavior in each of these pictures? (Sherry Fisher)

given negative feedback about their performance stayed farther away from a confederate than subjects who were given positive feedback. While it appears that affectively negative situations generally lead to more distant interactions, there is a special case in which contrasting results are sometimes found. When subjects are angered as a re-

sult of personal insults, they may show closer interaction distances than nonangered subjects (Meisels & Dosey, 1971). This may be seen as a retaliatory stance that facilitates communication of anger. However, some recent studies (O'Neal *et al.*, 1979; O'Neal *et al.*, 1980), suggest that anger, like the other negative affects, may also produce farther distances. It is unclear what is responsible for these discrepant results.

Individual Difference Determinants of Personal Space: Research Evidence

In addition to situational conditions, differences between individuals or groups that reflect diverse learning experiences also determine the size of personal space. For example, cultural or subcultural norms may dictate whether individuals believe it is appropriate to communicate by means of touch, and thus govern the distance chosen to fulfill the communicative function. In terms of the protective function, learned values relevant to the amount of space needed for protection against perceived threats, and experiences which determine the amount of sensory stimulation one is accustomed to, will affect spatial behavior. We will find that while there *are* consistent relations between individual difference variables and personal space preferences, some findings are inconsistent. In part, this may be due to the use of different methods in different studies (e.g., simulation vs. field and lab techniques). Generally, we have tried to "weight" results from studies using laboratory and field methods more than the results of studies employing simulation techniques in arriving at our conclusions.

Racial and Cultural Determinants of Personal Space.

Assuming that individuals raised in different cultures and subcultures have diverse learning experiences (Edwards, 1972, 1973), we might expect cross-cultural differences in interpersonal distancing as well as dissimilarities among subcultural groups within a single culture.

There is evidence relating to *cross-cultural* variations in spatial behavior, although the patterns revealed in the research are sometimes inconsistent (Aiello & Thompson, 1980b; Altman & Vinsel, 1977). Hall (1966) proposed that in highly sensory "contact" cultures (e.g., the Mediterranean, Arabic, and Latin American peoples), where individuals use smell and touch as well as

other sensory modalities more, people should interact at closer distances. In contrast, more reserved "noncontact" cultures (e.g., northern European and Caucasian American peoples) should exhibit larger interaction distances. This assertion has received support. Hall (1966), Watson and Graves (1966), and Little (1968) have found that Latin Americans, French, Greeks, and Arabs maintain smaller interaction distances than Americans. Further, Sommer (1969) and Little (1968) reported that the English, Swedish, and Swiss are similar to Americans in the size of their spatial zones. Thus, although the research is not entirely consistent and many cultures have yet to be studied (Aiello & Thompson, 1980b), various cultural groups may need different distances to fulfill the protective and communicative functions of personal space.

The research on *subcultural differences* in spatial behavior within our culture is more confusing. As was indicated earlier, there is evidence that subcultural groups tend to interact at closer distances with members of their own subculture than with nonmembers (Willis, 1966). Also, it seems as if Hispanic-American groups interact more closely than Anglo-Americans (e.g., Aiello & Jones, 1971; Ford & Graves, 1977). Black Americans interact more closely than white Americans while young, but at greater distances in adolescence (Aiello & Thompson, 1980b).

Unfortunately, findings on subcultural differences in the range of distances at which members interact have sometimes been inconsistent. It has been suggested (Hayduk, 1978; Patterson, 1974) that socioeconomic status may be a better predictor than subculture of learning experiences related to spatial behavior. Although members of a particular subculture may vary greatly in their living conditions, members of a socioeconomic group tend to live under relatively similar conditions. In support of this reasoning, Scherer (1974) found that black and white children of low socioeconomic status interact at a common distance, while black and white middle-class children also interact at a common, but greater, distance.

Sex Differences in Personal Space. We mentioned earlier that males and females display different spatial behavior with *liked* than *disliked* others. Females interact at closer distances with liked others, while males do not differentiate spatially as a function of attraction. Another interesting question centers around the relative distances at which females and males interact with others, regardless of degree of attraction. Do males generally maintain closer interpersonal distances than females when interacting with people, or is the reverse true?

In terms of interpersonal distance from others of the same sex, it is typically found that in same-sex dyads, female-female pairs maintain closer distances than male-male pairs. This has been shown in a wide variety of situations, ranging from playground interactions among children (Aiello & Jones, 1971) to structured interviews (Pellegrini & Empey, 1970). Again, these findings may be seen as reflecting a stronger female socialization to be affiliative, more experience by females with intimate nonverbal modalities (Jourard & Rubin, 1968), and a greater male concern about not being intimate with others of the same sex (Maccoby, 1966). Further, it should be noted that when dyads are of mixed sex, they generally maintain closer distances than same-sex male or female dyads (Hartnett, Bailey, & Gibson, 1970).

Interestingly, some recent research suggests that a woman's point in the menstrual cycle affects the personal space she chooses to maintain with opposite sex others. Females' personal space zones tend to be larger during the menstrual flow than during the middle of the cycle (Sanders, 1978). This has been interpreted as reflecting the midcycle peak in sexual desire (e.g., Benedak, 1952). In effect, hormonally determined sexual receptivity affects the personal space in opposite sex interactions.

Age Differences in Personal Space. Research focusing on personal space from a developmental perspective has been directed at answering two questions: the age at which personal space is first established; and the extent to which children's spatial behavior changes as they become older. There are many estimates concerning when children begin to exhibit personal space preferences. Duke and Wilson (1973) and Eberts and Lepper (1975) found behavioral evidence of personal space in children between 45 and 63 months of age, but other studies (Meisels & Guardo, 1969) have found that exhibition of personal space begins at a later age. Unfortunately, none of this research sheds much light on the way in which spacing mechanisms evolve. The second question concerns whether personal space changes with age. Overall, studies addressing this issue suggest that the younger the child, the less spatial distance is preferred across a variety of interaction contexts (Aiello & Aiello, 1974; Price & Dabbs, 1974; Pederson, 1973; Willis, Carlson, & Reeves, 1979) (Figure 6–5 and 6–6). This pattern has held up across cultures (e.g., Lerner *et al.* 1976; Lomranz *et al.*, 1975). It appears that adult-like spatial norms are first exhibited around the time of puberty (Aiello & Aiello, 1974; Aiello & Cooper, 1979; Altman, 1975). In

Figure 6–5. Children don't display totally adult-like spatial behavior until puberty.

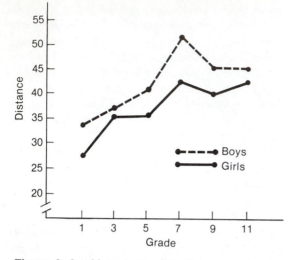

Figure 6–6. Mean interaction distances of male and female dyads at six grade levels. (From Aiello, J. R., and Aiello, T. The development of personal space: Proxemic behavior of children 6 through 16. *Human Ecology*, 1974, 2, 177–189. Reprinted by permission.)

addition, there is evidence that interpersonal distances are less among the elderly (Heshka & Nelson, 1972).

Personality Determinants of Spatial Behavior. A major attempt has been made by researchers to identify personality traits associated with differential concern about maintaining personal space. Since personality represents one's way of looking at the world and reflects learning and experience, it seems reasonable that personality orientations should be reflected in spatial behavior.

One personality variable that has been explored in terms of its implications for interpersonal distancing is internality-externality. A study by Duke and Nowicki (1972) demonstrated differences in personal space between internals and externals and provided an excellent example of how spatial behavior may reflect learning experiences. The theory of internality-externality views an individual's orientation (internal or external) as a reflection of past learning about internal or external causation of events. *Internals* view reinforcements as under the control of the self; *externals* view reinforcements as controlled by external sources. Consistent with this theoretical framework (and with the assumption that learning is reflected in spatial behavior), Duke and Nowicki found that externals desired more distance from strangers than internals. It appears that if past learning leads to the belief that one is in control of a situation, one feels more secure at close distances with strangers than if past learning leads to the belief that events are controlled externally.

Several other studies have found that spatial behavior differs as a function of personality. In this context, Horowitz, Duff, and Stratton (1964) and Sommer (1959) compared the spatial needs of schizophrenics and ''normals'' and found that schizophrenics require more space. Using simulation techniques, Weinstein (1965) and Fisher (1967) found that emotionally disturbed children placed toy figures farther apart than normal children. It has been observed in several studies that anxious individuals maintain more personal space than nonanxious people (Karabenick & Meisels, 1972; Patterson, 1977), and that extroverts maintain less space than introverts (Cook, 1970; Patterson & Holmes, 1966). Also, those with high self-esteem have smaller personal space than those with low self-esteem (Frankel & Barrett, 1971), and people high in need for affiliation prefer closer distances than those low in need for affiliation (Mehrabian & Diamond, 1971). Finally, Kinzel (1970) compared the body buffer zone of violent and nonviolent prisoners. He found that violent prisoners required nearly three times as much space around themselves as nonviolent prisoners to feel comfortable. Similar patterns of results are reported by Roger and Schalekamp (1976). Again, it is reasonable to assume that such patterns of spatial differences are the reflection of different learning and experience. One experiential factor which could be expected to lead to different spatial behavior, but which doesn't, is being blind. Hayduk and Mainprize (1980) found no differences in the spatial behavior of blind and sighted individuals.

Unfortunately, many of the studies that have attempted to relate *individual personality traits* to spatial behavior have been less enlightening and have resulted in conflicting findings (cf. Hayduk, 1978; Patterson, in press). Patterson (1974) has proposed a procedure that promises to be more fruitful than the *individual* personality trait approach. Rather than studying single personality traits and their relationship to spatial behavior, Patterson conceptualized personality dimensions in more general terms. He looked at *clusters* of personality variables related to a general approach tendency for social situations. His research demonstrated that such a strategy may yield better, more stable predictors of interpersonal distancing than focusing on individual traits. Another way to maximize the possibility of observing relationships between personality variables and personal space has been suggested by Karabenick and Meisels (1972). Specifically, it may be necessary to study such relationships in situations in which the personality trait in question is salient (e.g., studying the relationship between aggressiveness and personal space in an anger-provoking situation), as opposed to the neutral contexts generally employed.

Physical Determinants of Personal Space.

Although we've focused primarily on situational and individual difference determinants of personal space (as has past research), studies also suggest some interesting *physical* determinants of interpersonal spacing. First, a number of architectural features affect personal space (see Figure 6–7). For example, Savinar (1975) found that males had more need for space when approached by an experimenter if ceiling height was low than if it was high. White (1975) reported that personal space increased with reductions in room size and decreased with increases in room size, and Daves and Swaffer (1971) found that individuals desire more space in a narrow than a square room. Also, Baum, Reiss, and O'Hara (1974) suggested that installing partitions in a room can reduce feelings of spatial invasion. Do we maintain closer distances with others when "in the dark" than when

there is light? Gergen, Gergen, and Barton (1973) report that we're more likely to touch others (the ultimate in closeness) when it is dark than under more typical lighting conditions.

In addition to architectural features, one's position in a room, whether sitting or standing, and whether indoors or out also affect personal space. Concerning position in a room, several studies (cf. Dabbs, Fuller, & Carr, 1973; Tennis & Dabbs, 1975) found that over a variety of subject populations, people exhibit greater personal space when in the corner of a room than when in the center. Also, it seems that we maintain closer distances when standing than while seated (Altman & Vinsel, 1977). With respect to spatial differences as a function of being indoors or outdoors, Little (1965) and Pempus, Sawaya, and Cooper (1975) found that subjects kept more distance between themselves and others when indoors than when outdoors. The "corner-center," "sitting-standing," and "indoor-outdoor" relationships may all reflect differential physical availability of escape; when we know we can get away, we're content with less space.

Interpersonal Positioning Effects

Do the same variables that determine the size of our spatial zones affect other aspects of spatial positioning? Studies have shown that besides determining the distance between interactants, individual difference and situational variables affect the body orientation that we maintain between ourselves and others.

One individual difference variable that has been found to affect spatial positioning is sex. While males prefer to interact with liked others in an across (i.e., face to face) orientation, females prefer to have liked others adjacent to them. In two related studies, Byrne, Baskett, and Hodges (1971) manipulated the attraction between a subject and two confederates so that the subject liked one of the confederates but disliked the other. The subject was then asked to join the confederates in another room where his or her choice of seats with respect to the liked and disliked confederates

Figure 6–7. One clever *physical* means of coaxing us to position ourselves in close proximity to others, employed by some "fast food" restaurants, is to paint a line down the center of the table. Do you think that you would be less anxious having someone sit down beside you at this table than at a table without the line?

was recorded. In the first experiment, which involved side-by-side seating, females sat closer to the liked confederate than to the disliked one, while males showed no preference. In the second experiment, which involved face-to-face seating, males sat across from the liked confederate, while females showed no preference.

The cooperativeness or competitiveness of the interaction situation also affects spatial positioning. In an initial study, Sommer (1965) observed the spatial arrangement of individuals who were cooperating or competing and found that cooperating pairs sat side by side, while competing pairs sat across from each other. A second study found corroborative results. Subjects anticipated either a cooperative or a competitive interaction and sat opposite a decoy in competitive conditions and adjacent to him or her in cooperative conditions.

Spatial Zones That Facilitate Goal Fulfillment

What distances are most "appropriate," and thus lead to the best results in a dyadic learning situation? What seating position in a classroom will promote the most teacher-student interaction? And where should a therapist position him- or herself to elicit the most self-disclosure on the part of a client, or a doctor sit when giving a patient important health recommendations? These are obviously important questions, and show the applied significance of research on personal space. Unfortunately, at present there are no completely satisfactory answers, though there is some research that makes an attempt to provide some preliminary ones.

Optimal Spacing in Learning Environments. We do know that the distance between a teacher and a student affects learning, at least when the two are in a dyadic interaction. Although the results are slightly contradictory, they suggest, in general, that interactions at Hall's personal distance zone (Skeen, 1976), and even at his intimate zone (Miller, 1978), may lead to better performance by the student than the other spatial zones. For example, in the study by Skeen (1976), a subject performed a serial learning task either six inches (intimate distance) or three-and-one-half feet (personal distance) from the experimenter. For tasks of varying levels of difficulty, the learner's performance was better at the personal distance than at the intimate one. In the study by Miller (1978), subjects received instruction at a distance from the instructor corresponding to one of Hall's four zones. Here, the students did better when taught at the intimate distance zone than at the other three. While the results of these studies are somewhat inconsistent, taken together they suggest that Hall's closer zones, rather than his farther ones, may lead to the best learning by students in teacher-student dyads.

What about typical classroom situations, where there are many students present? Although there is currently no research which definitively identifies how far from the instructor you should sit in order to get the best grade, a study by Kinarthy (1975) may at least provide a hint. In this experiment, trained observers recorded the amount of communication between the students and the instructor. It was reported that seating position does affect communication in the college classroom, even after statistical procedures were used to control for the fact that in many cases students chose their own seats. (Without such controls, it could be the type of person who chose a particular position, rather than the position itself, which caused the effects.) Where is the best place to sit? It seems as if the middle, front section of the classroom is a relatively high communication zone. Sitting there promotes verbalization (except for those who are very low verbalizers), and facilitates attention (Koneya, 1976; Schwebel & Cherlin, 1972; Sommer, 1969) (see Figure 6–8). It has been found that people who choose middle-front seats also get the best grades in the class (Becker *et al.*, 1973; Sommer, 1972). While the relationship between seating position and grades is just correlational, there is also some *experimental* evidence which partially supports it (Stires, 1980).

Optimal Spacing in Professional Interactions. An interesting question concerns the distance at which people feel most comfortable disclosing personal information about themselves to clinical psychologists. Again, this topic hasn't been thoroughly researched, although there are some preliminary results. Generally, studies suggest that an intermediate distance is preferred for a counseling situation (Brokemann & Moller, 1973), and that psychiatric patients talk most about their fears and anxieties at that distance (Lassen, 1973). This pattern of effects also holds for college students. When Stone and Morden (1976) had students discuss personal topics with a therapist at a distance of two feet, five feet, and nine feet, they found that students volunteered the most personal information at the five foot distance. Since this distance is culturally appropriate for such communications and is expected for them (Brokemann & Moller, 1973), these data support Hall's (1968) prediction that deviation from the appropriate distance elicits negative effects. It should be noted, however, that these data do not generalize to self-disclosures in nonclinical interactions between two strangers (cf. Skotko & Langmeyer, 1977).

How far should a medical doctor position him- or herself from a patient so that the patient's compliance with medical regimen will be highest? Ac-

Figure 6–8. Students' participation in class activities as a function of seating positions. (From Sommer, R. Classroom ecology, *Journal of Applied Behavioral Science*, 1967, 3, 500. Copyright 1967 by NTL Institute Publications.)

Instructor		
57%	61%	57%
37%	54%	37%
41%	51%	41%
31%	48%	31%

cording to available evidence, the answer depends on whether the doctor is delivering basically "accepting" or "neutral" evaluative feedback for the patient's self-disclosures. In that study (Greene, 1977) close physical proximity strengthened adherence to dieting recommendations when "accepting" feedback was offered, but lowered compliance when "neutral" feedback was given. It may be that the feedback suggested to the patient the type of relationship she had with the practitioner. When feedback was accepting, the closer distance was appropriate and led to more positive effects than the less appropriate, farther distance. On the other hand, when feedback was neutral a farther distance was viewed as appropriate and led to more positive effects than a close distance. Another way of saying this is that when the intimacy of both the verbal and environmental "channels" was equivalent, more positive effects occurred than when there were inconsistencies.

Optimal Spacing to Facilitate Group Processes. Can the spacing between people be manipulated to affect group processes in order to accomplish some desired end? A number of studies suggest an affirmative answer. Suppose one wants to promote interaction within a group. This calls for *sociopetal* spacing (spacing which brings people together, such as the conversational groupings found in most homes), rather than *sociofugal* space (space which separates people like the straight-line arrangement of chairs found in airports or bus terminals) (Osmond, 1957). In an early study, Sommer and Ross (1958) were called in to examine conditions at a Saskatchewan hospital, where a newly opened ward with a lovely, cheerful decor seemed to be having a depressing and isolating effect on patients. They observed that chairs were lined up against the walls, side by side. All the chairs were facing the same way, and rather than seeing each other, people just gazed off into the distance. When Sommer and Ross rearranged the chairs into small, circular groups, the frequency of interactions among patients almost doubled. Other studies have similarly found that arranging space so that people

face each other more directly results in greater interaction between group members (Mehrabian & Diamond, 1971). A nonfacing orientation may elicit longer pauses, more self-manipulative behaviors and postural adjustments, and perhaps even more negative ratings of group interaction (Patterson *et al.,* 1979).

How could one manipulate his or her spatial positioning in a group in order to become its leader? It seems that in small group settings, people direct most of their conversation to the person sitting across from them (i.e., the one who is the most highly visible) (Michelini, Passalacqua, & Cusimano, 1976; Steinzor, 1950). Also, people who occupy a central position in a group initiate the most communications (Michelini *et al.,* 1976). This suggests that one could become highly influential merely by choosing a central spatial orientation where others eye them directly. This assumption has received some support. Those who choose the end of a rectangular table are more likely to be elected foreman in simulated jury studies (Strodtbeck & Hook, 1961) or to otherwise dominate overall group interaction. Of course, this could be due to the fact that dominant individuals *choose* to sit at the "head" of the table, or it could be a reciprocal relationship. Experimental work needs to be done to identify the cause of this effect.

Consequences of Too Much or Too Little Personal Space

We have seen that situational, individual difference, and physical-environmental variables determine our preferred personal space zone. And we've also seen that some spaces facilitate goal fulfillment more than others. At this point, it is interesting to consider what happens when we interact with another person under conditions of "inappropriate" (i.e., too much or too little) personal space. For example, imagine an interaction with a vacuum cleaner salesperson who insists on extolling the virtues of his or her product at an inappropriately close distance (e.g., three inches) or an inappropriately far distance (e.g., 10 feet). Would you be likely to buy a vacuum cleaner from this person? Since personal space serves some important functions, we can assume that inappropriate distancing often has negative consequences for the interactants.

Predicting the Effects of Inappropriate Distances. The effects of inappropriate positioning can be described in the context of the general environmental stressor model introduced in Chapter 3 and presented in Figure 6–9. Before we discuss the model, however, recall that we've observed throughout our coverage of research on personal space that situational conditions and individual differences determine optimal interpersonal distances. It is evident in Phase I of the model that whether we perceive our personal space as optimal or nonoptimal at a particular objective distance from another person depends on situational conditions (e.g., attraction) and individual differences (e.g., personality). If we perceive our personal space as within an optimal range, homeostasis is maintained. If we perceive it as outside this range, a variety of responses may occur.

What is the nature of our response to nonoptimal personal space? The same conceptual formulations used earlier to explain *why* we maintain personal space (e.g., overload, arousal, and behavior constraint) predict the effects of inappropriate interpersonal distancing. For example, *overload* notions predict that stimulus overload occasioned by an inappropriate personal space should cause performance decrements and elicit coping responses directed at lowering stimulation to a more reasonable level. Coping responses may include giving different priorities to inputs so that only important stimuli are attended to (e.g., ignoring some of the incoming information) and erecting interpersonal barriers (e.g., acting coldly toward others). In terms of the *stress* approach, inappropriate positioning leads to a stress reaction, which may have emotional, behavioral, and physiological components. Coping responses are directed at reducing stress to a more acceptable level. The *arousal* conceptualization assumes that being too close leads to overarousal and suggests coping mechanisms designed to lower arousal.

Finally, the *behavior constraint* approach suggests that inadequate personal space should lead to an aversive feeling state and to coping responses that attempt to reassert freedom.

We noted earlier that Hall (1966) proposed a model based on communication properties to explain personal space and that ethological models have also been applied (cf. Evans & Howard, 1973). In terms of Hall's formulation, it might be predicted that inappropriate distance constitutes a negative communication and leads to negative attributions and inferences. The ethological approach makes still another set of predictions. It assumes that when personal space is inadequate, fear and discomfort are experienced due to feelings of aggression or threat (cf. Evans, 1978).

How can we integrate all these formulations? Although each of the approaches proposes a somewhat different reaction to inappropriate positioning, we should not view them as competing with each other. Rather, it is probable that inappropriate personal space may at times lead to each of the responses we have described. Further, the predictions of all of the conceptual schemes may be integrated into the sequence of events shown in Phase II of Figure 6–9. When personal space is inadequate, various coping responses are employed, which may or may not be successful. When coping is successful, it leads to adaptation or habituation, and aftereffects are less likely. If coping is unsuccessful, inappropriate positioning can lead to aftereffects such as dislike for the other, poor performance, and so on.

The Consequences of Inappropriate Spacing. What type of research evidence exists concerning the consequences of inadequate personal space? Several studies have shown that when two people interact in an inappropriate spatial zone, unfavorable feelings and inferences are elicited. In an experiment on the effects of distance between a subject and a communicator on persuasion, Albert and Dabbs (1970) hypothesized that negative feelings and attributions would be elicited if a communicator and a subject were positioned more or less than five feet apart, an appro-

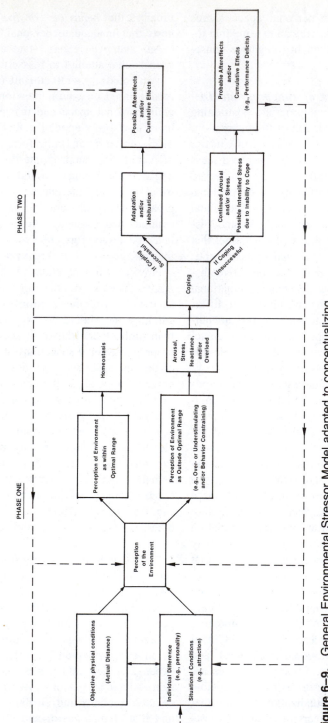

Figure 6–9. General Environmental Stressor Model adapted to conceptualizing reactions to inappropriate personal space.

priate distance for such interpersonal contacts. Accordingly, the communicator (actually an experimenter) and the subject were constrained to interact at the ''appropriate'' distance of five feet, or at one of two inappropriate distances (i.e., 2 feet or 15 feet). Several effects were measured, and the findings basically supported the prediction. It was observed that subjects paid more attention to the communicator and rated him or her as more of an ''expert'' at the five-foot distance than at either of the other distances.

Boucher (1972) found parallel results using schizophrenics as subjects. First, interviewers sat down with patients at a distance that was inappropriately close, appropriate, or inappropriately distant. The distance manipulation was accomplished by fastening both chairs to the floor at one of the three ranges so that people in ''inappropriate'' positions could not adjust their proximity to a more comfortable zone. Following a 10-minute interview under these conditions, the subject's attraction to the interviewer was assessed. It was found that more attraction was expressed for the interviewer at the appropriate distance than at the distances that were inappropriately close or far.

Several studies suggest that maintaining inap-propriate interpersonal distance is associated with considerable anxiety. For example, Dabbs (1971) found that a persuasive communicator who was positioned too close caused subjects to feel more pressured, unfriendly, and irritated than they did when a more appropriate distance was maintained. And when Aiello and Thompson (1980a) had subjects converse at either a comfortable distance or an uncomfortably far one, subjects who sat too far apart not only felt ill at ease, but blamed the other for their discomfort, even though the other was clearly not responsible! Patterson and Sechrest (1970) reported that subjects evidenced more positive feelings when interacting with a confederate at a moderate distance (4 feet) than at either a close distance (2 feet) or a far distance (8 feet). Similarly, Bergman (1971) found that subjects in discussion groups with chairs separated by two inches on each side showed more palmar sweat (a measure of arousal) than subjects in discussion groups with chairs separated by three feet. In a recent study, Hayduk (1981) found a linear relationship between the *degree* to which a spatial arrangement was inappropriate and the degree of people's discomfort. Also, he reported that subjects with smaller per-

---

TURNING OTHERS OFF WITHOUT TRYING: A SOURCE OF MISCOMMUNICATION BETWEEN CULTURES

Due to differences between cultures in personal space zones, it is easy for people who are trying to be courteous in their interactions with those from other cultures to be perceived as discourteously inappropriate. Such individuals might be labeled ''obnoxious'' and the entire interaction could become strained and unprofitable. One way to deal with this would be to train people to interact spatially with members of other cultures in the way those people typically act. So if an American positions him- or herself with an Arab like Arabs do when interacting with each other, they should elicit more favorable reactions. Instead of seeming aloof and ''cold,'' they might be viewed as warm and caring. A study by Collett (1971) tried this strategy and it worked! Some English students were trained in Arab nonverbal behaviors (including closer personal space zones), while others were not. Subjects then spoke about love with an Arab for five minutes, and were later rated on a variety of dimensions. The Arab subjects preferred Englishmen with ''training'' to those without it. This suggests that both knowledge about spatial behaviors and ability to exhibit them may be very helpful in making interactions with people from other cultures profitable. Perhaps such training should be ''standard fare'' for diplomats and international businessmen.

sonal space zones responded more positively to inappropriately close distance than subjects with larger ones. Interestingly, a study by Fisher (1974) suggests that inappropriate distances with a similar (liked) other lead to less negative reactions than the same distances with a dissimilar other.

In addition to lowering attraction and persuasibility and causing negative affect, what other effects can inappropriate spatial positioning have? According to Argyle and Dean (1965), nonverbal compensatory reactions should occur to restore a comfortable equilibrium when the physical distance between two individuals is too close or too far. Specifically, they posit that interactants attempt to maintain an optimal level of *immediacy,* which is a function of physical distance and such

nonverbal behaviors as eye contact and body orientation. If immediacy is too great on one dimension, adjustments will be made on others. Thus, when individuals are physically too far or too close, equilibrium will be achieved by adjustments in such nonverbal behaviors as the rate of eye contact and the body orientation of the interactants.

Although all the implications of this proposition have yet to be tested, a number of studies have provided support for Argyle and Dean's formulation. In one study (Patterson, 1974), subjects interacted with an interviewer at both an appropriate and an inappropriate distance, and changes in eye contact and body orientation were recorded. The results of the distance manipulations on eye contact and body orientation were in line

---

COMPENSATION VERSUS RECIPROCATION: TOO CLOSE ISN'T ALWAYS TOO BAD

Up until now, we've suggested that inappropriate interpersonal distancing leads primarily to negative consequences (e.g., dislike) and to compensatory reactions (e.g., indirect body orientation). However, we have also noted that there is some conflicting evidence. A recent conceptual formulation (Patterson, 1976, 1978) suggests a way of integrating both sets of data. Patterson hypothesizes that when two individuals are interacting, a sufficient change in the intimacy of one of them (e.g., moving too close) produces a changed state of arousal in the other. Depending on cognitions about the situation, this arousal may be labeled as either a positive or a negative emotional state by the other person. If the arousal is negatively labeled, a compensatory response (such as moving farther away) will occur. On the other hand, if the arousal is positively labeled, a reciprocal response (moving still closer to the other) will occur. This model makes an important point: The situation should determine whether the effects of interacting at a very close range will be negative (i.e., eliciting compensatory reactions and dislike) or positive (i.e., eliciting reciprocal reactions and liking). For example, reciprocity may occur when two people like each other, while compensation may occur when they are unsure about the relationship or dislike one another (Firestone, 1977; Ickes *et al.,* in press).

A study by Storms and Thomas (1977) supports the notion that the situation determines whether interacting at close range is positive or negative. In this study subjects interacted with another who was either friendly or similar, or unfriendly or dissimilar at a very close or normal distance. The other was liked more when he sat close than at a normal distance in the friendly or similar conditions. In effect, when the situation is positive, closeness may facilitate a desire for reciprocal intimacy. On the other hand, the subject was liked less when he sat close than farther away in the unfriendly or dissimilar conditions. Closeness in this situation promoted disliking, and a desire for a compensatory response.

with the equilibrium hypothesis. It was found that with too much proximity, body orientation became less direct and percentage of eye contact decreased. Other studies consistent with the equilibrium hypothesis have shown that decreased directness of body orientation leads to greater proximity among individuals in the situation (Aiello & Jones, 1971; Felipe & Sommer, 1966). In addition, the longer subjects interact under inappropriate conditions the greater the degree of compensation which is observed (Sundstrom & Sundstrom, 1977). However, it should be noted that research has not always supported the predictions of the equilibrium notion (cf. Altman, 1973), and that some studies find opposite results (i.e., closeness begets closeness). One way of resolving this apparent conflict is suggested in the box. Others have suggested modified equilibrium theories which better correspond to certain experimental findings (e.g., Aiello, 1977; Aiello & Thompson, 1980a).

Consequences of Personal Space Invasions

Research on the consequences of too much or too little personal space suggests that when *ongoing interactions* take place at inappropriate distances, they may lead to lower attraction, negative inferences, and compensatory behaviors. However, what happens when a person is sitting alone minding his or her own business, with no intention of interacting with anyone, and a stranger sits down at an uncomfortably close proximity?

The Effects of Being Invaded on Flight Behavior. An early study of the effects of personal space invasions was conducted by Felipe and Sommer (1966). At a 1500-bed mental institution where patients spent a great deal of time outdoors, a stranger (actually an experimental confederate) approached lone patients at a distance of six inches. If the subject attempted to move away, the confederate moved so as to maintain a close positioning. The flight behaviors of the "invaded" group were compared with those of patients who were not invaded but who were

watched from a distance. As can be seen in Figure 6–10, after one minute 20 percent of the experimental subjects and none of the control subjects had fled. After 20 minutes, 65 percent of the experimental subjects had left their places, and only 35 percent of the control subjects displayed such a reaction.

Similar results for flight behavior after personal space invasion were reported by Konecni, *et al.* (1975). In this study (see Table 6–2), it was observed that both male and female pedestrians crossed the street more quickly as personal space invasions became more severe. Smith and Knowles (1978) reported the same thing, and also observed that invaded pedestrians formed more negative impressions of the invader, and experienced more negative moods, than those in control conditions. In addition, Patterson, Mullens, and Romano (1971) reported that "invaded" subjects turned away, avoided eye contact, erected barriers, fidgeted, mumbled, and displayed other compensatory and coping reactions more than "noninvaded" control subjects. Such reactions are common in individuals who choose not to es-

Figure 6–10. Cumulative percentage of patients departing at various intervals. (Based on data from Felipe & Sommer, 1966.)

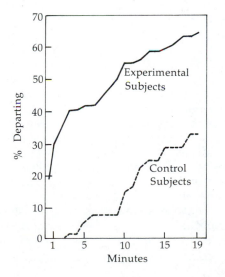

Table 6–2. TIME IN SECONDS TAKEN TO CROSS THE STREET BY EXPERIMENTAL CONDITION*

Sex of Subjects	Experimenters' Lateral Distance from Subjects (in feet)			
	1	2	5	10
Male	7.65	8.45	9.09	9.08
Female	8.94	8.95	9.41	9.79

*Based on data from Konecni *et al.*, 1975.

cape altogether, or who don't have the option of escape. In a study by Terry and Lower (1979), it was found that in the latter group the more severe the invasion, the more intense the attempts at perceptual withdrawal. Finally, in research with children, it was found that personal space invasions caused behavior to become more primitive, and to be characterized by increasing movements (e.g., fidgeting) (Bonio, Fonzi, & Sanglione, 1978).

TOO CLOSE FOR COMFORT: SEX DIFFERENCES IN RESPONSE TO INVASIONS OF PERSONAL SPACE

A study by Fisher and Byrne (1975) found sex differences in victim's responses to personal space invasions and demonstrated that invasions affect victims on a broad array of dimensions.

As you recall from earlier in the chapter, it has been found that males prefer to position themselves *across from* liked others, while females prefer to position themselves *adjacent to* liked others (Byrne *et al.*, 1971). On the basis of these findings, Fisher and Byrne reasoned that for each sex the spatial position most favored for "liked" others should be the one least favored for an invading stranger. Specifically, it was hypothesized that females should respond more negatively than males to side-by-side invasions of personal space, while males should respond more negatively than females to face-to-face invasions.

The subjects were males and females who were sitting alone at tables in a library. As they attended to their business, they were "invaded" by a male or female "invader" from either a face-to-face or an adjacent position. After five minutes, the invader appeared to have concluded his or her work and left the area. Three minutes later, an experimenter arrived, claiming to be a student who was conducting a study of people's impressions of various stimuli for an introductory psychology class. The experimenter also claimed to have noticed that someone had been sitting at the subject's table and wondered if the subject could indicate his or her impressions of that person as well as impressions of the library environment on questionnaires. The questionnaires specifically tapped the subject's affective state, attraction toward the invader, perception of the aesthetic quality and crowdedness of the environment, and the positiveness of motivation attributed to the invader.

How did invasion victims respond to the questionnaires? Regardless of the invader's sex, males responded negatively on all measures when the invader sat across from them but were not affected by an adjacent invasion. Females responded negatively when the invader sat adjacent to

Effects of Being Invaded on Arousal. If "invasions" are uncomfortable experiences for the target, invasion victims might be expected to evidence higher levels of physiological arousal than noninvaded controls. Only a few studies (Evans & Howard, 1972; McBride, King, & James, 1965) have systematically considered the effects of invasion on physiological arousal. A very ingenious study by Middlemist, Knowles, and Matter (1976) bears directly on this question. The setting for the study was, of all places, a three-urinal men's lavatory! The unknowning subjects were lavatory users who were "invaded" by a confederate at either a close or a moderate distance. In the control condition, the confederate was not present. How was arousal measured under these three levels of personal space invasion? Since research indicates that stress delays the onset of urination and shortens its duration, it was reasoned that if closer invasions cause stress, greater delay of onset and shorter duration of urination should result. Accordingly, an experimenter stationed in a nearby toilet stall with a periscope and two stopwatches recorded the delay of onset and persistence of urination. As can be seen in Figure 6–11 A & B, and 6–12, results confirmed the assumption that personal space invasions are stressful. Close interpersonal distances increased the delay and decreased the persistence of urination. Perhaps installing partitions could add to people's comfort in lavatories.

One implication of the arousal elicited by personal space invasions is its effect on task performance. In line with the Yerkes-Dodson Law (page

them but were not affected by one who sat across from them. It is as if special significance is associated with opposite positioning for males and adjacent positioning for females, and invading these "special" zones leads to particularly negative reactions.

The results of the study led Fisher and Byrne to make a simple prediction that, if confirmed, would lend additional support to their findings. It was assumed that if males dislike invasions from across, they should place their books and personal effects between themselves and facing seats in a library, and if females dislike adjacent invasions, they should place their possessions between themselves and adjacent seats. To test these hypotheses, an observer was sent into the library to record where males and females placed their possessions. The hypotheses were confirmed: Males erect barriers primarily between themselves and facing positions, while females erect barriers between themselves and adjacent positions.

Why is it that the sexes seem to attribute special significance to different spatial positioning arrangements? One possible explanation lies in the socialization process, with males taught to be relatively competitive and hence more sensitive to competitive cues, and females taught to be relatively affiliative and more sensitive to affiliative cues (Maccoby, 1966). Adjacent seating (which occurs in affiliative situations) may signal affiliative demands to females. Females like to have someone they "feel safe with" in this relatively intimate affiliative position and react negatively when it is occupied by a stranger. On the other hand, facing seats (which occur in competitive situations) may signal competitive demands to males. Males like to have a trusted (and nonthreatening) friend in this competitive position.

It's rather humorous, but the sex differences observed in the Fisher and Byrne research may be the source of considerable miscommunication between the sexes. A female who wants to befriend an unknown male may be surprised to find that a nonthreatening (to her) eyeball-to-eyeball approach causes consternation and alarm. In the same way, a male who attempts to ingratiate himself with an unknown female by sitting down beside her in a nonthreatening (to him) position may be surprised to find he elicits a "Miss Muffet" reaction.

Figure 6–11A and 6–11B. Observation apparatus which was used to study the effects of arousal from personal space invasions in a men's room. As you can see, the periscope is quite unobtrusive when hidden by the stall. (Eric Knowles)

64), available evidence suggests that the consequences of invasion-induced arousal for performance depend on the complexity of the task. With simple tasks, performance doesn't seem to be negatively affected by having another too close. With more complex tasks, invasions take a toll. For example, Evans and Howard (1972) and Barefoot and Kleck (1970) found decrements in performance on information-processing tasks as a function of personal space invasion. Thus, it may

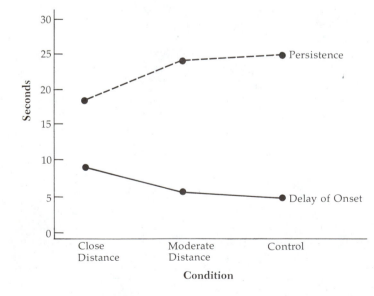

Figure 6–12. Mean persistence and delay of onset for urination at three levels of personal space invasion. (From Middlemist, Knowles, and Matter, 1976. Copyright 1976 by The American Psychological Association. Reprinted by permission.)

be that if somebody invades your space when you are in the library studying, the quality of your work will suffer.

Other Effects of Being Invaded. If personal space invasions are aversive for the target, they should elicit a host of additional behavioral reactions. For example, it would seem reasonable to assume that if your personal space were invaded by someone, you'd be less likely to help him or her if given the opportunity. Two sets of studies have looked at the effect of personal space invasions on helping and have reached conflicting conclusions. In one group of studies (Konecni *et al.*, 1975; Smith & Knowles, 1979), a confederate first violated the subject's personal space and then dropped one of several objects. It was found that when the personal space violation was severe, victims failed to retrieve even objects that seemed to be important. In addition to failing to help the *invader*, Smith and Knowles (1979) reported that the reluctance to help on the part of those who had experienced "severe" invasions also generalized to an unwillingness to assist others in need of aid. A second set of studies (e.g., Baron & Bell, 1976) found the opposite: Personal space invasions facilitated helping. However, in these studies confederates asked the subject for help when at either an "invaded" or an appropriate distance. These conflicting findings can be readily resolved. In the first set of studies, the victim may have attributed the invasion to negative intent, dismissed the invader as a "nasty" person, and refused to help him or her. In the second, the invader's violation may have been attributed to the importance of the request rather than to negative personal qualities and therefore resulted in greater helping.

Thus far, we have seen that personal space invasions can occasion physiological arousal, and cognitive and behavioral responses. Although there are many possible ways to view the relation between these, Smith and Knowles (1979) suggest an interesting possibility, which supports Patterson's theory of compensation vs. reciprocation (see the box on page 168). Based on some studies

they did, Smith and Knowles imply that our initial response to a personal space invasion involves *arousal*. As we know, arousal can have many behavioral consequences, in and of itself. However, they argue that arousal is also followed by a secondary, cognitive response. In effect, our arousal response draws our attention to the target, and causes us to try to understand why we are aroused, and why the invader behaved as he or she did. Characteristics of the invader and the situation affect the explanations which we arrive at. These, in turn, determine our attributions to the invader, our liking for him or her, whether we will help them if they are in need, etc.

After exploring the effects of personal space invasion on a wide array of behaviors, an interesting question remains: Do all personal space invaders elicit the same reactions in their victims, or is it more aversive to be "victimized" by some people than by others? The model proposed by Smith and Knowles (1979) would suggest that it is more aversive to be invaded by some people than others. While relatively few studies have looked at this question, there are some suggestive findings. First, some evidence indicates that it may be more upsetting to be invaded by a male than by a female. Murphy-Berman and Berman (1978) and Bleda and Bleda (1978) observed that male intruders were evaluated more negatively, and elicited more movement in their victims than female intruders. Perhaps this is because we attribute more negative motives to male than female invaders. It is also interesting to note that males generally react more negatively to invaders than females (Garfinkel, 1964; Patterson, Mullens, & Romano, 1971). Additional studies suggest that the degree of choice invaders have in their action affects how negatively they are evaluated (Murphy-Berman & Berman, 1978) and it seems that invaders who smoke elicit more flight reactions in their victims than those who don't (Bleda & Bleda, 1978). What about the effect of invaders of different ages? Fry and Willis (1971) had children who were 5, 8, and 10 years old stand 6 inches behind adults in theater lines. It was found that 5-year-olds were given a positive response,

HOW DO GROUPS RESPOND TO PERSONAL SPACE INVASIONS?

In general, we've restricted our attention to the effects of personal space invasions on lone individuals. In a very interesting study, Knowles (1972) extended this line of research to an exploration of how *groups* of people respond to personal space invasions. His findings suggest that *groups,* like individuals, engage in compensatory responses when their space is invaded, constituting evidence for a group analogue to personal space.

What did Knowles do to establish that groups, like individuals, engage in compensatory responses when invaded? On a city street he had a confederate approach a pair of pedestrians (subjects) walking in the opposite direction. The invader walked so that it appeared he or she intended to walk right between the two pedestrians. It was found that over half the pairs moved together to avoid an intrusion and that some reprimanded the invader; this suggests that groups try to maintain their personal space—even in the face of invasion. Further, avoidance of intrusion was more frequent when the pedestrians consisted of a male and a female rather than individuals of the same sex. In a more recent study, Knowles and Brickner (1981) found that the more cohesive the dyad, the more it resisted intrusion, i.e., protected its "group space." (Further evidence of personal space at the group level will be provided later in this chapter, when we discuss research by Knowles on the other side of this question: how we respond when we have to invade the space of interacting groups.)

8-year-olds were ignored, and 10-year-olds were given a cold reaction. Thus, as children get older, they are treated more as adult invaders. Finally, in a study that examined whether the status of the invader affects reactions to him or her, Barash (1973) varied the clothing confederate invaders wore and found that those who wore "faculty-like" attire evoked faster flight than those who wore casual clothing.

How could one ameliorate some of the negative effects in the victim, when forced to invade someone's personal space? Research by Quick and Crano (1973) found that just saying "Hello" lowered the number of victims who fled, while Sundstrom and Sundstrom (1977) suggest that asking permission can make a difference. And Schavio (1975) reported that invaders who were reading newspapers elicited more favorable responses in victims than a "no newspaper" control. But perhaps the best way to avoid torturing those you invade comes from research by Smith and Knowles (1979), who suggest that "negative reactions occur only when there is no immediately apparent and appropriate reason for the invader to be standing close." So, as long as you behave so

that your victim believes you have a good reason for your invasion, you may be able to avoid inflicting pain on others.

The Effects of Invading Another's Personal Space. We have spoken about how it feels to be the victim of a personal space invasion but have said nothing about how it feels to be the invader. Investigators have been looking at what happens when people are placed in dilemmas that require them to become personal space "invaders." Several studies have found that people do not even like to *approach* the personal space of others. In one study (Barefoot, Hoople, & McClay, 1972), a lone confederate was stationed 1, 5, or 10 feet from a water fountain. Fewer passersby approached the fountain when doing so would violate the confederate's personal space (i.e., at the 1-foot distance) than when it would not (i.e., at the 5- or 10-foot distances). While people will avoid the water fountain when the setting is uncrowded, it becomes easier to invade someone's personal space (and take a drink) under crowded conditions (Thalhofer, 1980). This may be because we become "overloaded" when it is crowded, and are less attentive to social cues (e.g., that we may cause another person discomfort). Another study demonstrated that it may be aversive to approach the personal space of a group, as well as a lone individual. Knowles *et al.* (1976) positioned groups of varying size on a hallway bench and observed "deflection" in the walking patterns of passersby as they walked past the seated confederates. As the number of confederates on the bench increased, passersby were "deflected" farther away. Thus, it appears that approaching the personal space of either lone individuals or groups is a threatening experience, to be avoided if possible.

Several other experiments have looked at the invader's reactions to physically penetrating, rather than merely approaching, the personal space of interacting dyads. Some studies suggest that it is easier to invade the personal space of someone who is smiling at you, than someone displaying a neutral face (e.g., Lockhard, McVittie, & Isaac, 1977). And, at least for males, it may be still easier to violate the space of one who has his or her back toward you (Hughes & Goldman, 1978). Efran and Cheyne (1973) found that passersby are less likely to "invade" if the individuals in the dyad are conversing, if they are occupying Hall's personal space zone rather than social distance, and if they are of the opposite sex. Similar results were reported by other studies (e.g., Bouska & Beatty, 1978), which also found that an "invasion" was less likely if the interactants appeared to be high status (e.g., a businessman, a priest). When it is necessary to invade, the status of the victims also determines how the invader treats them. High-status individuals receive "positive deferential" behaviors (e.g., signals of appreciation), while those with low status receive signs of negative deference (e.g., derogation) from the invader (Fortenberry *et al.*, 1978).

But it is aversive to violate the personal space of others under any conditions. In a finding that shows how taxing it is to invade interacting dyads, it was observed that subjects forced to invade tended to look at the floor rather than ahead and to close their eyes (Cheyne & Efran, 1972;

Efran & Cheyne, 1973). Further, Efran and Cheyne (1974) reported that the act of invading interacting dyads has affective consequences: Subjects in "invasion" conditions displayed more negative moods and more hostile facial responses than noninvading control subjects.

How does the invader react to penetrating a group larger than a dyad? Knowles (1973) created "targets," groups of two or four persons who were interacting in a hallway so that passersby had two choices: to violate the group space or to go around the interactants. Fewer people penetrated the four-person than the two-person group, and low-status individuals were invaded more often than high-status individuals. Thus, not only individuals and dyads but larger groups appear to be aversive to invade. For the invaders, the permeability of interacting targets depends on such factors as status, group size, and sexual composition. Further, it is apparent that groups, like individuals, are recognized as having a sort of personal space. (Note that the study reviewed in the box on page 174, in which groups responded as a unit to a confederate invader, also supported the idea of personal space at the group level.)

Summary of Personal Space

Personal space regulates how closely we interact; its purposes are protection and communication. The amount of personal space we maintain with others varies as a function of individual differences, situational conditions, and even physical variables. Individuals find it unpleasant when constrained to interact with others at inappropriate distances, or when forced to invade the personal space of others. With this in mind, we move on to discuss territorial behavior.

TERRITORIAL BEHAVIOR: KEEP OFF MY TURF

We mentioned at the beginning of this chapter that personal space tends to be invisible, movable, body-centered, and regulates how closely individuals will interact. Territory is visible, stationary, and tends to be home-centered, regulating who will interact (Sommer, 1969). Also, territories are generally much larger than personal space; and whether or not we are on our own territory, we still maintain a personal space zone (see Figure 6–13).

One way of viewing *territories* is as places which are owned or controlled by one or more individuals. Anyone who has ever been on the sending or receiving end of a statement like "Don't ever set foot on my property again" has confronted the concept of *territoriality* head on. Although most of us have an instinctive feeling of what territoriality is, it is difficult to define, and there is considerable controversy among researchers about what constitutes the best definition. Our definition of territoriality in humans is representative of "mainstream" views in the field (for commentaries on the definitions used by diverse groups of researchers, see Altman & Chemers, 1980; and Taylor & Brooks, 1980). For us, *human territoriality can be viewed as a set of behaviors and cognitions an organism or group exhibits, based on perceived ownership of physical space.* Perceived ownership as used here may refer either to actual ownership (e.g., as with your home) or to control over space (e.g., you may control but not own your office, if it is part of a building owned by another). Territorial behaviors serve important motives and needs for the organism and include occupying an area, establishing control over it, personalizing it, thoughts or beliefs about it, and in some cases defending it. Note that the concepts of "territory" and "territoriality" illustrate the interdependent nature of human-environment transactions. Without a territory there would be no territoriality, and vice versa (Carpenter, 1958).

According to Altman and his colleagues (Altman, 1975; Altman & Chemers, 1980), there are three types of territories used by humans, and this distinction has been supported in research by others (Taylor & Stough, 1978). These differ in their importance to the individual's or group's life—primary territories are most important, followed by secondary and public territories. They also differ in the duration of occupancy, the cognitions they foster in the occupant and others (e.g., the extent of perceived ownership), the amount of personalization, and the likelihood of defense if violated. (These differences are highlighted in Table 6–3.) As we will discuss later, different types of territories provide different benefits for individuals (e.g., primary territories such as a bedroom promote privacy and allow for the expression of one's identity, functions *not* promoted in a public territory). Therefore, based on the type of activity we want to engage in and the needs it poses, we choose a particular type of territory (Taylor & Ferguson, 1978).

Territorial behavior is practiced by humans and animals. Some researchers consider human territoriality to be *instinctive,* some consider it to be *learned,* and some consider it an *interaction* of the two (cf. Alland, 1972; Ardrey, 1966; Klopfer, 1968). According to the instinct view, territorial behavior in humans is instinctively determined, as it is in animals. Both species have a drive to claim and defend territory (Ardrey, 1966; Lorenz,

Figure 6–13. Fences and signs are among the many ways people demarcate and defend their territories. (Sherry Fisher)

Table 6–3. TERRITORIAL BEHAVIORS ASSOCIATED WITH PRIMARY, SECONDARY, AND PUBLIC TERRITORY*

	Extent to Which Territory Is Occupied/Extent of Perceived Ownership by Self and Others	Amount of Personalization/Likelihood of Defense If Violated
Primary Territory (e.g, home, office)	*High.* Perceived to be owned in a relatively permanent manner by occupant and others.	*Extensively personalized;* owner has complete control and intrusion is a serious matter.
Secondary Territory (e.g., classroom)	*Moderate.* Not owned; occupant perceived by others as one of a number of qualified users.	*May be personalized to some extent during period of legitimate occupancy;* some regulatory power when individual is legitimate occupant.
Public Territory (e.g., area of beach)	*Low.* Not owned; control is very difficult to assert, and occupant is perceived by others as one of a large number of possible users.	*Sometimes personalized in a temporary way;* little likelihood of defense.

*Based on Altman (1975)

1966) (e.g., humans and animals mark off their turf to keep others out, and respond with vocal warnings and bodily threats to invaders). Since the earth has a limited amount of space, and we are all driven to make and defend territorial claims, conflict is inevitable. Needless to say, this set of beliefs makes some fairly pessimistic predictions regarding the future of humankind. However, few investigators hold that human territorial behavior is entirely instinctive.

The position that territoriality is learned suggests that, unlike animals, in humans territoriality results from learning and culture. For example, people learn through socialization that certain places are associated with particular roles. And the patterns of learning that occur depend on culture (e.g., some cultures are nomadic and relatively aterritorial, while others are highly territorial). Because human territoriality is learned, even

when humans and animals exhibit similar behaviors, such as aggression against an intruder, the same mechanisms may not be responsible. For humans aggression is learned (Baron, 1977), and it is but one of many possible responses to a territorial violation, rather than a predominant one.

Finally, there is the perspective that human territorial behavior results from an interaction of instinct and learning. This view holds that both processes contribute to our territorial actions. The exact way in which this may occur is yet to be specified (Altman & Chemers, 1980). However, it is quite possible that we are predisposed toward territorial behaviors through instinct, but that learning determines the intensity and form of our territorial actions. Alternatively, it has been proposed that instinct guides some types of elementary territorial behaviors, while learning is responsible for more complex ones (Esser, 1976).

Functions of Territoriality

Just as there are differences between humans and animals in the mechanisms responsible for territorial behavior, there are differences in the functions it plays for each. While it should not be forgotten that there are variations between species (e.g., Carpenter, 1958), animals maintain territory for such important functions as mating, dispersing the population more evenly, food gathering and protecting food supplies, shelter, rearing of young, and controlling intraspecies aggression. Thus, territories are often quite essential to survival for them (Sundstrom, 1977). Also, animals tend to defend territories vigorously when violations occur (Edney, 1976).

Humans are more flexible with respect to use of territories for functions such as those mentioned above. For us, many of the purposes territories serve are not as closely related to survival, and they may be seen primarily as "organizers" on a variety of dimensions (e.g., they promote predictability, order, and stability in life) (Edney, 1975). For example, territories allow us to "map" the types of behavior we can anticipate in particular places, who we will encounter there, what someone's status is, etc. In this way they help us plan and order our daily lives. Territories also contribute to order due to their relationship to social roles (e.g., the boss controls his office, the company lounge, lunchroom, etc.). Precisely how territories function to "organize things" depends on the particular space in question (for some examples, see Table 6–4). In addition to their organizing function, territories may lead to feelings of distinctiveness, and a sense of personal identity. People may experience higher self-concept due to the territories they possess, and the ways they have personalized them. They may even proudly refer to themselves as "the man who lives in the red house on Oak Street."

A broader concept of the functions of territory for humans may be achieved through an analysis

---

Table 6–4. THE ORGANIZING FUNCTIONS OF HUMAN TERRITORIES IN SOME EVERYDAY SETTINGS*

For People in	*Organizing Function of Territory*
Public places (e.g., a library, the beach)	Organizes space; provides an interpersonal distancing mechanism.
Primary territories (e.g., a bedroom)	Organizes space by providing a place which promotes solitude; allows intimacy; expresses personal identity.
Small face-to-face groups (e.g., the family)	Clarifies the social ecology of the group and facilitates group functioning; may provide home court advantage.
Neighborhoods and communities	Promotes an "ingroup" who "belong" and can be trusted; differentiates them from an "outgroup" who don't belong and can't be trusted. In some urban areas, territorial control makes a space safe to use.

*After Taylor (1978).

in terms of the environment-behavior theoretical formulations (e.g., arousal, overload) discussed in detail in Chapter 3, and earlier in this chpater in the context of personal space. For example, in terms of the *overload* approach, clearly defined territories lend a sense of order that reduces the amount and complexity of incoming stimulation, and makes life easier to cope with. In effect, they afford role organization (e.g., the host has one role and the visitor another); allow us to assume continuity in the future (e.g., we'll always be able to sleep in our house); and afford us control over inputs from the outside world (e.g., ''No Trespassing'' signs keep out extraneous inputs). *Stress* formulations view territories as functioning to reduce stress by controlling the amount of stressful stimuli we must contend with. From the *arousal* perspective, territories hold down arousal (e.g., by moderating the amount of stimulation we are exposed to). In the context of the *ethological* conceptualization, territories may be seen as preventing aggression and affording identity. Finally, in line with the predictions of *control* models, the fact that some territories may promote privacy and thereby facilitate unhindered performance of chosen behaviors should be quite beneficial. They should also have favorable effects since the ''owner'' of a territory controls access to it and what goes on there.

Before concluding, we should address the dissimilarities between humans and animals with regard to territorial defense. In general, humans very rarely resort to actively defending their territories, while animals actively defend their turf. This is not to suggest that relatively dramatic forms of territorial defense never occur in humans; indeed many international conflicts (e.g., the Arab-Israeli wars), as well as interpersonal difficulties (e.g., fights with a roommate over use of the stereo) involve territorial defense and associated aggression. However, one reason for the generally lower degree of territorial defense in humans than animals is that people generally recognize and avoid each other's territory. This varies, of course, with the type of territory (as depicted in Table 6–3 on page 177). In addition, humans

routinely entertain others on their turf without aggression, while this is not the case for animals. When human territorial aggression does occur, it often takes a different form than that of animals. While human territory-related fighting tends to occur more often at the group level (e.g., one nation versus another), animal fighting is more frequently at the individual level. Unfortunately, humans now have the capacity to destroy one another's territory without physically invading, through the use of long-range weapons (Edney, 1976).

Research on Territoriality in Humans

Past research on territorial behavior has focused mostly on animal populations, and relatively little has dealt with territoriality in humans. Those studies which have been done have looked at territorial behavior in both groups and individuals, employing methodologies that ranged from controlled laboratory and field experimentation to naturalistic observation. In some cases these methodological approaches have inherent problems when applied to human territorial behavior, which may account for the overall lack of research.

Laboratory experiments are difficult to perform because territoriality implies a strong attachment between an individual and a place, which is not easy to approximate under artificial laboratory conditions. Introducing experimental manipulations (e.g., territorial invasions) into real world settings (e.g., libraries) where people do perceive a degree of territorial ''ownership'' avoids this problem, and has provided some rich data in recent years. In addition, many researchers have relied on nonmanipulative (and nonexperimental) field observation of behavior in naturally occurring territories.

Unfortunately, nonmanipulative observation is often fraught with interpretive problems. For example, Hansen and Altman (1976) report an interesting relationship between not personalizing one's dorm room (or primary territory) with posters and personal effects, and later dropping out of school during the semester. Students who decorated their turf were more likely to "survive" the rigors of college than those who did not. However, what these data mean is very unclear. It could be that personalizing one's territory leads to feelings of security, which promote success in school. On the other hand, personalizing one's dorm room may reflect commitment to it, and lack of personalization may indicate a sense of alienation from that setting. Or, those people who plan to stay could simply invest more time decorating—an interpretation which is considerably less interesting! Some other studies employing nonmanipulative observation of territorial behaviors are similarly difficult to interpret.

In the remainder of this chapter, we will review research using various methods to study territoriality in humans. It will become clear that territorial behavior occurs in many settings, and that it has some important consequences.

Evidence for Territorial Behavior Between Groups. Suttles (1968) observed the territorial actions between various ethnic groups on Chicago's South Side (public territory). Each group claimed and defended a separate territory, and there were some "shared territories" in which certain community resources were used separately by each ethnic group in a prescribed fashion. Different groups could use them but never at the same time, or in the same area. Another interesting example of group territoriality stems from an analysis of street gang behavior in Philadelphia (Ley & Cybriwsky, 1974a). It was found that street gangs are highly territorial, taking their names from a street intersection at the center of their territory. Each gang demarcates its territory, and territorial domains are recognized by gang and nongang youth. Outsiders usually avoided the in-group's turf, but were greeted with hostility when they entered.

What functions does territoriality between groups serve? Such actions tend to facilitate trust *within* the group. Just sharing a territory can lead to feelings of group identity and security, perhaps because people in the same territory share common experiences (Taylor, 1978). And the security

afforded by a territory is important: In some areas of a city (e.g., those with gangs), territorial control of a space makes it safe to use (Taylor, 1978). However, the in-group cohesion resulting from territories can have negative effects (e.g., the formation of gangs). It may also cause "outsiders" to be viewed with suspicion. Both of these consequences are likely to elicit aggression.

Evidence for Territorial Behavior Within Groups. Just as Archie Bunker defends his prized chair from family, friends, and enemies, group members often adopt certain areas as "theirs." In primary territories, families have territorial rules that facilitate the functioning of the household (McMillan, 1974). These support the social organization of the family by allowing certain behaviors by some members, in particular areas (e.g., the parents can engage in intimacy in the bedroom undisturbed) (Taylor & Stough, 1978). In one study of territoriality in family life, it was found that people who share bedrooms display territorial behavior, as do individuals at the dining table (e.g., through seating patterns). Family members generally respect each other's territorial markers, such as closed doors (Altman, Nelson, & Lett, 1972), and a violation of territorial rules often leads to punishment of the one at fault (Sheflen, 1976).

Territorial behavior within groups is not limited to primary territories. Lipman (1967) found that residents of a retirement home made almost exclusive claims to certain chairs in the day rooms. They defended their "territory" despite considerable psychological costs and physical inconvenience. Even students stumbling into the 8:00 A.M. class display territorial behavior. Haber (1976) found that in formal-style (e.g., traditional lecture) classes, about 75 percent of the students claimed a particular seat, and occupied it more than half of the time. In informally run classes this occurred for only 30 percent of the students. Also, of those students who claimed a seat to be their territory, 83 percent chose the one that they occupied during the first, second, or third class period. In addition to choosing a seat as their territory, many students used markers to delineate their turf. "Marking" (e.g., placing books and possessions to defend one's turf) is also frequent in libraries and cafeterias, among other places (e.g., Fisher & Byrne, 1975; Taylor & Brooks, 1980).

A number of researchers have investigated whether some members of intact groups are more territorial than others. Studies with animals show a strong relationship between dominance within a group and territoriality, generally finding that more dominant animals are more territorial. Although research with humans has sometimes demonstrated mild support for the dominance-territoriality relationship found in animals, in some studies opposite results have been observed. Whether this inconsistency is the result of methodological difficulties (e.g., problems in defining dominance and territoriality operationally, use of unusual subject populations) or the absence of reliable relationships between dominance and territoriality in humans, is at present somewhat uncertain (cf. Edney, 1975). In any event, it seems that the relationship between dominance and territoriality is quite complex.

One attempt to interpret these conflicting findings is an analysis made by Sundstrom (1976). Sundstrom suggested that whether more dominant individuals will display higher or lower territorial behavior depends heavily on the situational context. He posited that in environments where there are only a few desirable places (e.g., private rooms in a boys' home), dominant individuals should end up with them and hence appear to be highly territorial. In contrast, when a setting has no areas that are more desirable than others, dominant individuals should roam over large amounts of space and appear to be very low in territoriality. This hypothesis has been supported, at least in a suggestive sense, by a series of studies. In the stark and rather uniform confines of a mental hospital, Esser *et al.* (1965) obtained suggestive evidence of an inverse relationship between dominance and territoriality (i.e., more dominant individuals displayed less territoriality). In a home for juvenile delinquents, which presumably had

more environmental variation, a direct relationship was found between dominance and territoriality. In addition to its dependence on the level of environmental variation in a setting, the dominance-territoriality relationship also depends on group composition and social organization. It has been shown that adding and removing group members or changing the social organization of the group can significantly affect the nature of dominance-territoriality relationships (DeLong, 1973; Sundstrom & Altman, 1976).

Researchers (e.g., Esser, 1973; Taylor, 1978) suggest that where a dominance-territoriality relationship does exist, it should *facilitate* group functioning. This has yet to be tested experimentally—but why do *you* feel this represents a viable hypothesis? Investigators propose that if those with high dominance are recognized as having access to the best spaces, this helps clarify the ecology of the group and thus reduces conflicts within it (e.g., Taylor, 1978).

Evidence for Territorial Behaviors When Alone. Territoriality also exists for individuals who are alone. In fact, research suggests that people may feel a stronger ownership of a setting when alone than when part of a group (Edney & Uhlig, 1977). Thus, members of a family or roommates may feel lower responsibility to maintain their turf, and may individually exert less surveillance over it, than single occupants. This effect would be similar to the finding of a "diffusion of responsibility" in groups (cf. Latané & Darley, 1970), which is reported in social psychology. It also suggests that there may be more vandalism, theft, etc. in group than individual residences.

Signals of Territoriality: Communicating Territorial Claims. What do a backyard fence, a chair with a coat on its back, a nameplate on an office door, and a blanket at the beach have in common? All are ways of communicating territorial ownership to others as well as, perhaps, reassuring oneself regarding our ownership or propriety over something (Truscott, Parmalee, &

Werner, 1977) (see Figure 6–14). We engage in these behaviors in primary, secondary, and in public territories. How effective are our various defense strategies in warding off territorial invaders? While it might be speculated that they would be increasingly effective as one moves from public to primary territories, this has yet to be demonstrated. Research has focused primarily on assessing the relative effectiveness of various types of territorial signals in a given setting.

Sommer and his associates (1969) conducted studies that looked at the relative effectiveness of various strategies for warding off territorial invaders in libraries. At low levels of overall density, people were less likely to sit down at tables with any kind of marker (e.g., a sandwich, a sweater, books) than at tables without such personal effects. However, under conditions of high density, it appears that potential invaders take an attribu-

tional approach to interpreting whether or not particular markers really represent someone who intends to return. To the extent that markers are personal and valuable (a sports coat, a notebook with a name on it), territorial ''ownership'' tends to be respected. However, when attributions of intent are not clear, as when the marker is a library book or a newspaper, the resulting uncertainty coupled with the fact that there are few available seats tends to lead to invasions. It should be noted that although we and others (e.g., Taylor, 1978) consider such markers as books and coats to be territorial indicators, there is debate as to whether they function mainly as territorial markers or an interpersonal distance maintainers (cf. Becker & Mayo, 1971). Resolution of this subtle point is left to future researchers.

Ley and Cybriwski (1974a) suggested another interesting means of indicating turf ownership.

Figure 6–14. Note the various forms of territorial defense which people employ.

They found that in Philadelphia, wall graffiti offer an accurate indication of gang territorial ownership. As a general rule, gang graffiti (i.e., graffiti that include a gang's name) become denser with increasing proximity to the core of the gang's territory. These graffiti are readily accepted by neighborhood youth as an accurate portrayal of each gang's area of control. It was also found that often, when street gangs invaded each other's territory, they spray-painted their name in the rival gang's turf. The "invaded" gang generally responded by adding an obscene word after the rival gang's name! Gangs that were not respected (or feared) generally had turf covered with a large amount of graffiti put there by neighboring gangs.

Territory and Aggression. One of the most interesting aspects of territoriality is the relationship between territory and aggression. Although it is not always realized, territory may serve either as an instigator to aggression *or* as a stabilizer to prevent aggression. The function it serves depends upon a number of situational conditions.

One factor that affects the relationship between territoriality and aggression is the status of a particular territory (i.e., whether it is unestablished, disputed, or well-established). When territory is unestablished or disputed, aggression is more common. Observational evidence to this effect is provided by Ley and Cybriwsky (1974a), who found that street gangs engaged in more intergang violence when territorial boundaries were ambiguous or unsettled than when they were well-established. The volatile situations involving the Arab countries and Israel and the Russian and Chinese border conflicts also serve as potent indicators that territorial disputes lead to violence. Parallel evidence is available for animals: It has been found that animals fight more when territories are being established or are under dispute than after territorial boundaries have been well drawn (Eibl-Eibesfeldt, 1970; Lorenz, 1966).

While unestablished or disputed territory promotes aggression, established territorial boundaries often lend stability and lead to reduced hostility in humans as well as in animals (O'Neal &

McDonald, 1976). For example, Altman and his associates (1975) observed that confined groups which established territories early in their confinement evidenced smoother interpersonal relationships and were more stable socially than groups that failed to establish territories early. O'Neill and Paluck (1973) reported a drop in the level of aggression in groups of retarded boys after the introduction of identifiable territories. What are the dynamics of the process by which territorial boundaries decrease aggression? We mentioned earlier that territorial behavior serves an organizing function, indicating what is "ours" and what is "theirs." Thus, well-established territories should be less subject to intrusion, which tends to elicit aggression. In line with this analysis, several investigators (e.g., Mack, 1954; Marine, 1966) have found that the separation of neighborhood ethnic groups by clearly defined boundaries led to decreased territorial intrusion, and less intergroup conflict.

When territorial invasions do occur, what are the consequences? As we mentioned earlier, there is a strong relationship between territorial invasion and aggression in animals (cf. Carpenter, 1958; Wallis, 1964), but in humans it is more complex and appears to depend more on situational conditions. For example, Altman (1975) proposed that the attributions we make for a violation will mediate our response, and that we will only consider aggression when we feel the other's behavior was malicious. And generally, we try other verbal adjustive responses (e.g., warning the individual to leave, threatening them), as well as physical ones (e.g., putting up a fence, or a "No Trespassing" sign) first, resorting to aggression only when these are unavailable or unheeded. In addition, Edney (1974) suggested that for humans many forms of "appropriate" territorial invasion (e.g., when guests are present) exist that do not elicit aggression.

One additional factor that may determine whether invasion leads to aggression in humans is the location of the territory "under seige" along a primary territory–public territory dimension. Invaders of primary territories are likely to elicit the most intense aggression (see Figure 6–15). By definition, primary territories are more central to the owner's life and are associated with more legitimate feelings of control than public territories, so invaders are seen as more threatening and hence are dealt with more harshly. The intensity of the territorial invasion–aggression relationship for primary territories is reflected in the ambiguity of many local laws dealing with the prosecution of a homeowner accused of killing an intruder (Geen & O'Neal, 1976). One possibility for preventing invasion of primary territories is for homeowners to erect markers of territorial defense (e.g., "No Trespassing" signs). Edney (1972) compared homeowners who displayed such markers with those who didn't. He found that individuals who erected forms of territorial defense had lived in their houses longer and intended to stay longer than people without territorial markers. Further, residents who displayed markers answered their door bells faster, which may be interpreted as a sign of defensive vigilance.

In contrast to the defensive posture assumed by holders of primary territory, a study by O'Neal, Caldwell, and Gallop (1975) found weaker evidence for territorial defense in public territory. This study was conducted with children who were exposed to a manipulation designed to induce possessiveness toward a carpeted play area. Children were led to another room, where they could press a button to electrically shock a clown who was advancing toward their turf. Invasions under these conditions did not lead to a convincing demonstration of aggression. However, some studies suggest that even in public territories we may exhibit defensive behaviors toward intruders. Haber (1976) found that when a participant-observer intruded onto a seat in a class that a person had sat in consistently, about one-quarter of the victims demanded return of their seat while three-quarters retreated. If the class was characterized by low density, or if the "owner" had "marked" the seat, the probability of demanding its return was much higher. Also, research by Taylor and Brooks (1980) indicates that as the *value* of the invaded public territory increases (e.g., a library

carrel vs. a seat at a table), the likelihood of its defense rises. On the other hand, even under some of the conditions identified above as maximizing the likelihood of defense (e.g., marking), several studies (e.g., Becker, 1973; Becker & Mayo, 1971) suggest a strong reluctance on the part of subjects to defend public territories.

Also relevant to the "primary"–"public" territory distinction, it has been found that whether a territory is perceived as temporary or permanent affects our level of aggression in defending it. Schmidt (1976) reported that occupants of permanent territories challenged invaders more quickly, and gave them more hostile treatment than occupants of temporary territories. For example, they were more punitive to invaders, and also more aggressive to strangers following an invasion, than those in temporary territories. So invasions of permanent territories may promote more aggression toward the instigator, as well as more generalized aggression, than violations of temporary territories.

Territory as a Security Blanket: Home Sweet Home. If individuals are willing to defend territories from invasion by resorting to aggression, it would seem that such areas must be associated with a number of important benefits. The assertion that territories have beneficial aspects is supported by the conceptual analysis we put forward earlier, which suggested that many properties of territories are associated with positive effects. The truth of the saying "Home Sweet Home" has been assessed in a number of experiments. In a study which also supported the assumptions of Altman's (1975) conceptual distinction between primary, secondary, and public territory, Taylor and Stough (1978) found that subjects reported the greatest feelings of control in primary territories (e.g., dormitory rooms), followed by secondary territories (e.g., a fraternity house) and public territories (e.g., a bar). In a great deal of research, feelings of control are related to a sense of well-being, as well as other positive effects (e.g., beneficial implications for health). And a study by Edney (1975) using Yale undergraduates

Figure 6–15. Owners of primary territory can show a great deal of defensive vigilance if their territories are violated. (Sherry Fisher)

highlights additional benefits of being on one's turf. The experiment took place in the dormitory room (primary territory) of one member of the pair, where the other member was a "visitor." Subjects who were in their own territory were rated by visitors as more relaxed than residents rated visitors, and residents rated the rooms as more pleasant and private than visitors did. Residents also expressed greater feelings of passive control. In a related study, Edney and Uhlig (1977) reported that subjects induced to think of a room as their territory felt less aroused, attributed their behavior more to the room, and found the setting to be more pleasant than others in a control group.

An additional advantage of being "at home" is that under conditions that do not promote liking (e.g., competition, disagreement, or unequal roles), the resident has a "home court" advantage which allows him or her to dominate the visitor. Martindale (1971) reported that dormitory residents were more successful at a competitive negotiation task on "their own turf" than were visitors. Similarly, Conroy and Sundstrom (1977) found that when resident-visitor dyads held dissimilar opinions (conditions which cause dislik-

ing), residents talked more and exerted more dominance over the conversation than visitors. When the two had similar opinions (conditions which promote liking) visitors talked more and dominated the conversation. The authors interpreted residents' allowing this as a sort of "hospitality effect." Taylor and Lanni (1981) have shown that residents have an advantage under conditions which do not facilitate liking, in triads as well as dyads, for both low and high dominance individuals. The effect is even true of larger groups and in settings other than primary territory. In a comparison of the "home" and "away" records of the University of Utah football team over a three-year period, Altman (1975) found that the team won two-thirds of its home games and only one-fourth of its away games (see the box).

Given that territories may be quite beneficial, it is unfortunate that the design of many settings, especially institutions, does not foster them. Most mental hospitals, old age homes, residential rehabilitation settings, prisons, etc. do not contain architectural features, or permit behavior (e.g., bringing personal possessions; personalizing an area) which promote feelings of personal terri-

AN ANALYSIS OF THE "HOME COURT ADVANTAGE"

Just how pervasive is the "home court" advantage in professional and college sports? A study by Schwartz and Barsky (1977) looked at the outcomes of 1880 major league baseball games, 182 professional football games, 542 professional hockey games, and 1485 college basketball games which took place in a recent year. They assumed that in the absence of a home court advantage, about half of a team's total wins for the season should occur at home and "on the road." What did they find? The results are shown below in Table 6–5. For all sports, there is a decisive home court advantage. This varies somewhat according to the sport in question, ranging from professional baseball where 53 percent of the total wins occur at home, to professional hockey, where 64 percent of the wins during the season occurred at home. The analysis of basketball records, which employs slightly different techniques and which is therefore not incorporated into the table, suggests still a higher proportion of college basketball contests are won in the home court. This implies that the advantage of the home team becomes more pronounced for indoor than for outdoor sports.

Table 6–5. PERCENTAGE OF GAMES WON BY HOME TEAM IN BASEBALL, FOOTBALL, AND HOCKEY IN A GIVEN YEAR. (TIES ARE EXCLUDED)*

	Sport			
	Professional Baseball	Football		Professional Hockey
Home Team Outcome		Professional	College	
Win	53	58	60	64
Lose	47	42	40	36
Total	100	100	100	100

After Schwartz and Barsky. Reprinted from, *Social Forces (55,* March 1977) "The Home Court Advantage" by B. Schwartz and Stephan Barsky. Copyright © The University of North Carolina Press.

Exactly what types of differences in team play occur when "at home" and "away"? The researchers found that the underlying factor in the home court advantage is that superior offensive play occurs at home compared to "on the road"; there are no differences for defensive play. How strongly should the home court advantage be "weighed," as compared with factors like team quality? Strikingly, analyses of the data suggested that the advantage from just being on one's own turf can actually be as significant in determining the outcome of a game as the quality of the team!

Are the same factors responsible here as were responsible for the dominance of the individual who is "at home" in the dormitory studies described earlier (e.g., control)? While these undoubtedly play a role, there is one element in a sports context which is not present when two people are interacting in a dormitory room—home audience support. And Schwartz and Barsky (1977) feel that this factor—the applause for the home team and jeers for the visitors—is an important determinant in the home court advantage in sports.

tory. The contention that these would benefit patients (Barton, 1966) has been demonstrated in research. When areas were redesigned to increase territoriality, or residents were allowed to personalize the environment, the social atmosphere of the ward improved and there were more positive feelings toward the environment (Holahan & Saegert, 1973; Holahan, 1976a).

Designing space so that it appears to be someone's turf has other advantages as well. When spaces have clear boundaries that signal they "belong" to somebody, there is evidence that less crime and vandalism occur. In a study of low-cost urban housing developments, Newman (1972) found that public areas having no clear symbols of ownership were more likely to be vandalized than those with well-marked boundaries. (See also the discussion of this in Chapter 8.) Although these findings have been subjected to methodological criticism (cf. Adams, 1973), supportive evidence is provided in a study that observed locations where cars were vandalized in inner-city Philadelphia (Ley & Cybriwsky, 1974b). It was suggested that more vandalism took place near "public" places such as factories, schools, and vacant lots than in areas that signaled territorial ownership, such as private dwellings and small businesses. While the nature of the research precludes a definitive statement, it seems that people tend to respect properties that can be identified as someone's territory more than properties that cannot be easily identified.

An interesting study by Brown (1979) identified a number of specific characteristics of residential areas in general, and homes in particular, which are associated with burglary. Before we tell you what she found, take a look at the houses in Figures 6–16A and B. Which do *you* think you would rob if you were a burglar? Brown found that signs of defensibility, occupancy, and territorial concern were different in a sample of homes that were not burglarized, than in a corresponding sample which were. Specifically, burglarized homes differed in that the *symbolic barriers* they possessed were public, as opposed to private. For example, burglarized homes had fewer assertions of the owner's private identity (e.g., name and address signs), more signs of public use (e.g., public street signs in front of them), and fewer attempts at property demarcation from the street (e.g., hedges, rock borders). They also had fewer *actual barriers* (e.g., fewer locks or fences to communicate a desire for privacy, and deter public access). Also, on streets where burglaries occurred, there were fewer *traces* (e.g., signs of occupancy) which showed the presence of local residents. Burglarized houses had fewer parked cars and sprinklers operating, and residents were less apt to be seen in their yards by the researchers. In this regard a garage was significant, since it often makes it ambiguous whether or not people are home (e.g., a garage without windows can disguise the absence of the car). More burglaries occurred in homes without garages, perhaps because for them the absence of cars makes it likely that the house is empty. Finally, in houses where burglaries occurred, *detectability* (the potential for exercising surveillance) was lower, and neighboring houses were less visually accessible.

Designers should consider the above findings. Too often areas do not communicate the types of territorial messages they should, or are ambiguous with regard to their territorial status, due to designed-in characteristics. In addition, some territories don't promote the sorts of activities people need to use them for (e.g., the value of primary territory may be hampered due to a lack of adequate soundproofing, or too much visual access). This often leads to lack of use, to use by the wrong parties, or to various types of misuse. Care during the design process could prevent this.

CHAPTER SUMMARY

Personal space is invisible, mobile, and body-centered, regulating how closely individuals interact. It has two purposes—protection and communication. The size of the spatial zone necessary to fulfill the protective and communicative functions

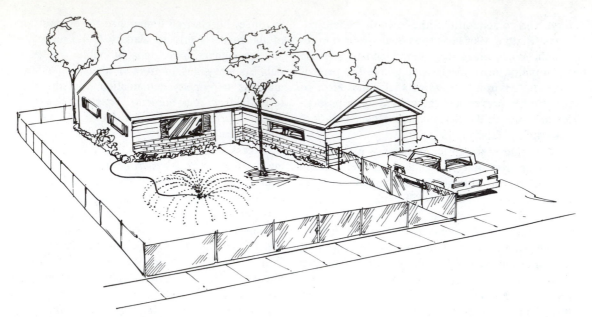

Figure 6–16A.　A nonburglarized house on a nonburglarized block. (From Brown, 1979; reprinted by permission.)

Figure 6–16B.　A burglarized house. (From Brown, 1979; reprinted by permission.)

TERRITORIAL BEHAVIOR AND FEAR OF CRIME IN THE ELDERLY

We have seen that when symbols of ownership are present, less crime and vandalism may occur. Are people who display more territorial markers (e.g., "No Trespassing" signs, fences, external surveillance devices) less fearful of being victims of crime than people who don't display such markers? In an interesting study, Patterson (1978) explored this problem with an elderly population in central Pennsylvania. Since fear of crime is a major source of anxiety for older citizens (some studies have shown it to be greater than fear of illness), determining the effectiveness of territorial markers in ameliorating such fears is important from both an applied and a conceptual perspective.

Patterson had interviewers approach the homes of elderly citizens to record unobtrusively any territorial markers. After gathering these data, the interviewer approached the homeowner and conducted an interview. The interview consisted of several sets of questions, including fear of property loss (e.g., "When I am away, I worry about my property") and fear of personal assault (e.g., "There are times during the night when I am afraid to go outside"). What were the results of the study? It was found that displaying territorial markers was associated with less fear of both property loss and assault, especially for males (see Figure 6–17).

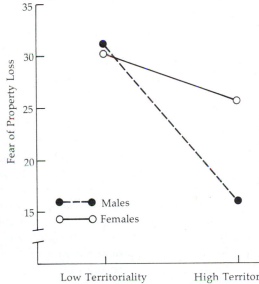

Figure 6–17. Fear of property loss by males and females high and low in territoriality. (From Patterson, A. H. Territorial behavior and fear of crime in the elderly. *Environmental Psychology and Nonverbal Behavior*, 1978, *3*, 131–144.)

What do these data mean? It is clear that there is an important relationship between reduced fear of crime in the elderly and territorial behavior. However, since this study is correlational, the mechanism by which territoriality is associated with reduced fear is not clear. One possibility is that erecting territorial markers gives one perceived and perhaps actual control and thus leads to feelings of safety. A more recent study by Pollack and Patterson (1980) tentatively supports this interpretation. If this is the case, there is a clear design implication: Encourage people to display territorial markers to enhance their feelings of security. But there is another explanation that cannot entirely be ruled out: Those elderly homeowners who feel sufficient mastery of the environment to erect territorial boundaries are also those who would feel secure from victimization in any event. If this is the case, the implications of the research would seem less clear.

changes according to situational variables (e.g., attraction, activity being engaged in) and individual difference variables (e.g., race, personality). Individuals find it aversive (1) when they are constrained to interact with another person under conditions of inappropriate (too much or too little) personal space; and (2) when their personal space is "invaded" by others. Interacting at inappropriate distances leads to negative affect and negative inferences; personal space invasions precipitate withdrawal and compensatory reactions.

Territory is visible, stationary, and home-centered, regulating who will interact. It serves somewhat different functions in humans and animals; in humans it serves a variety of organizational functions. Human groups and individuals exhibit territorial behavior and have adopted a variety of territorial defense strategies that vary in effectiveness. Territorial invasion by others may or may not lead to aggressive responses by the target, depending on the situation. Further, being on one's own turf has been shown to have a number of advantages and elicits feelings of security and improved performance. Finally, areas that appear to be someone's territory are less likely to be vandalized.

Suggested Projects

1. A scale called the C.I.D.S. or Comfortable Interpersonal Distance Scale (Duke & Nowicki, 1972) permits us to diagram the shape of our personal space without even getting out of our seat! It works like this.

   Imagine that Figure 6–18 represents an imaginary round room, for which each radius is associated with an entrance. You are positioned at dead center, facing position number 8. For each of the 8 radii, respond to an imaginary person approaching you by marking a mark on the radius indicating where you would prefer the stimulus person to halt (i.e., the point at which you think you'd begin to feel uncomfortable by the individual's closeness). After you've marked all 8 radii, connect the points

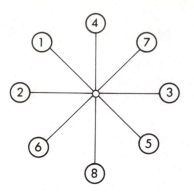

Figure 6–18.   Diagramming the shape of personal space. (From Duke, M. P. Nowicki, S. "Diagramming the Shape of Personal Space: A New Measure and Social Learning Model for Interpersonal Distance." *Journal of Experimental Social Psychology,* 1972, 6:119–132.)

you've marked and you'll know the shape of your personal space.

The C.I.D.S. may also permit you to verify some of the relationships that we've described between situational and individual difference conditions and personal space without leaving your chair. For example, imagine that the approaching individual is a friend and mark the radius; then do the same imagining that he or she is a stranger. Does your experiment confirm the results of Byrne and his coworkers (1970), who found that people maintain smaller personal space zones for friends than for strangers? Do the same for an approaching individual who is racially similar or dissimilar to yourself or for any of the other relationships we've discussed. You'll see how the C.I.D.S. is a useful means of assessing the effects of many factors on spatial behavior. But before you begin, we have one note of caution. Be sure to remember that because the various measures of personal space are not perfectly related (see discussion on page 154), failure to replicate studies with the C.I.D.S., which originally used different methods, does not necessarily mean that the original measures are invalid. Thus, while a replication on the C.I.D.S. of earlier findings that employed other methods is valuable supportive evidence, failure to replicate should not be seen as terribly damaging.

2. Your nearby library offers an opportunity for you to study the fine art of territorial defense. Before you go, make some hypotheses about the relative effectiveness of various types of territorial markers for repelling potential invaders. Consider the possible effects of a wide range of markers, including some you expect to be highly effective and some you expect to be less effective. Collect the necessary materials and report to the library for your experiment.

When you arrive at the library, make a mental note of the overall level of population density, and place each of the artifacts you've brought at a separate empty table, trying not to use too many of the study tables in any one room for your experiment. After you've distributed them all, "make the rounds" of all your experimental tables at 15-minute intervals, noting which markers are more effective and which are less so in preventing territorial invasion. Repeat the procedure using different levels of population density.

3. Position yourself and a same-sex other on either side of a busy doorway through which many people must pass. Face each other and engage in a lively conversation for 15 minutes. Watch the reactions of the passersby, whom you have placed in the role of personal space "invaders." What do they do? Do they force their way through, wait for you to invite them to pass, or look for an alternative exit? Next, remain in your positions but stop conversing for 15 minutes, and note whether the reactions of passersby change. Is your personal space more or less difficult to invade when you are talking? Finally, follow the same procedures with an opposite-sex other positioned across the arch from you. Do you find that passersby find it more difficult to violate the personal space of same-sex or opposite-sex dyads?

7 Crowding

INTRODUCTION

Suppose you are put in charge of a large experimental device called a "mouse universe." You begin with eight "colonizer" mice (four males and four females) in the apparatus and are told female mice can bear a litter of four to eight pups once a month. You are instructed that your job as keeper of the mice is to create a veritable paradise for them, in which they can live and bear young in complete harmony and protection from their natural enemies. As an incentive for you to do your job well, your employer offers you a bonus if the population of the "universe" increases dramatically under your guidance. To insure that you obtain the bonus, you study what can be done to provide a utopian setting for the residents. You decide to supply unlimited food, water, and nest-building materials and to provide an ideal air temperature. Furthermore, although you don't enjoy it, you vow to clean the feces that accumulate on the floor of the "universe" frequently so as to minimize disease and further assure collecting your reward.

After creating your "ideal" environment, you sit back and watch, thinking of how you'll spend your new riches. At first, things run smoothly; the males are establishing territories and mating with the females in their areas. The females are constructing nests, bearing young (very quickly, to your satisfaction), and successfully raising them to weaning. However, when the population begins to get very large, you observe that the inhabitants start behaving quite differently than before. Their odd behavior increases with expanding population size. Although some animals are still able to maintain their normal life style, most males no longer function effectively as territorial defenders and procreators of the species, and most females no longer function well as bearers and rearers of young. The birthrate declines rapidly. In addition, the mortality rate of the young becomes extremely high, and some animals become hyperactive, homosexual, and cannibalistic. You envision your bonus disappearing and wonder why these ungrateful creatures are doing this to you. You gave them everything they could possibly need—or did you?

While the strange behavior of the mice as the population increased may have been unexpected and seemingly bizarre, it really isn't. Experiments have shown that if animal populations are allowed to multiply unchecked, the resulting high density conditions lead to considerable disease and behavioral disorders, even when other aspects of the environment (food, water) are seemingly ideal (Calhoun, 1962; Christian, 1963; Marsden, 1972; Ng, Marsden, Colburn, & Thoa, 1973). In fact, this description of high density behavior is based on the results of actual experiments. Such research with animals provided a major impetus for studying the effects of high density on humans, which is the focus of this chapter.

Another impetus to research on how high density affects humans was the environmental movement (e.g., the writings of Barry Commoner, 1963; Paul Ehrlich, 1968) and the awareness of impending over-population problems that these writers generated. It seems as if we are going to live in a world characterized by higher and higher population densities, which makes the importance of studying the effects of high density on humans paramount. For example, the present population of the world is four billion (Frejka, 1973), and it is increasing by approximately 78 million annually. If current growth patterns continue for the next 50 years, world population will more than double (*Population and the American Future,* 1972), and most of this growth will occur in impoverished, underdeveloped countries (Frejka, 1973). Further compounding this growth is the continuing trend toward urbanization in many countries (*Population and the American Future,* 1972; Keyfitz, 1966), which will intensify the crowding caused by an expanding population.

Will the expected high density on "Spaceship Earth" lead to negative behavior in humans as it did with the mice in our imaginary universe? A final impetus for studies on human crowding was correlational work done by sociologists, which examined the association between human population density and behavior and health abnormalities. As you may remember from Chapter 1, correlational research does not allow us to infer causality. However, these studies did suggest that increases in human population density may sometimes be associated with pathology.

In this chapter, we will discuss research and theory on the effects of high density. Our discussion will begin with a brief overview of experimental and conceptual work on the reactions of animals to this condition. We will then proceed to the primary focus of the chapter—the effects of high density on humans. After a review of this area, some conceptualizations that attempt to explain human responses to high density will be discussed. The last section of the chapter will focus on several means of alleviating the causes and the effects of high density.

EFFECTS OF POPULATION DENSITY ON ANIMALS

Two basic forms of research methods have been used to explore the effects of density on animals. These include *laboratory methods* (which tend to be experimental) and *naturalistic observation* (which tends to be descriptive). For a discussion of how density is manipulated in the laboratory, see the box, p. 194. An example of laboratory research with animals was provided in our introduction. In contrast, studies employing naturalistic observation assess behavior in "real world" settings, as it is affected by naturally occurring density variations. An example of naturalistic observation is provided by Dubos (1965). Dubos found that when Norwegian lemmings become overpopulated, they migrate to the sea, where many drown. He attributed this to density-induced malfunctions of the brain. Similarly, Christian (1963) observed the rising and falling population patterns of a herd of deer isolated on an island in the Chesapeake Bay. In both of these instances, density occurred independently of the attempt to study it.

Figure 7–1. Crowding refers to the way we feel when there are too many people and/or not enough space. (Kevin Blanc)

THE COMPONENTS OF POPULATION DENSITY IN LABORATORY AND NATURALISTIC RESEARCH

At first thought, it probably seems to you that density is simply a people-to-space ratio. However, population density can be measured (and manipulated by experimenters) in a number of ways. For example, if you were planning to study the effects of population density on sexual behavior in animals, how would you create high and low density conditions? Two predominant approaches have been used in past research with animals and humans. These approaches focus on one or another component of the density ratio (number of people to amount of space available). One is to vary group size while keeping area constant, which is a manipulation of *social density*. This might entail putting 15 rats in an apparatus in the low density condition and 75 in the same device for high density. Or, it might entail starting out with 15 rats and observing behavioral change as they reproduce, and density increases. The second approach is to vary area while keeping group size constant, a manipulation of *spatial density*. To manipulate spatial density you might place 15 rats in a 4 ft. × 5 ft. apparatus in the low density condition, and 15 rats in a 3 ft. × 4 ft. device in the high density condition.

As we will see later in this chapter, there is quite a bit more to the distinction between social and spatial density. They are not simply ways of manipulating density and *are not interchangeable.* Rather, they reflect different conditions with different problems and consequences.

Is it better to manipulate social density than spatial density, or vice versa? The answer to both is "no" and "it depends on what you are studying." Both manipulations are somewhat imperfect. Social density variations include the confounding of group size and space supply (i.e., group size and space per individual are changed at the same time). In contrast, spatial density manipulations confound room size and space per individual (i.e., room size and space per occupant are changed at the same time). One thing we will find in our literature review is that the way in which density is manipulated sometimes affects the results obtained (i.e., social and spatial density manipulations don't *always* yield the same results).

Given these brief examples of how research with animals is done, let us turn to what has been found in past studies. Our discussion will first highlight some of the more consistent physiological and behavioral responses to being "densely packed" and will then attempt to place these findings in a conceptual perspective.

Physiological Consequences of High Density for Animals

Past research has shown that when animals interact under high population densities, negative physiological effects occur. Interestingly, many of these effects parallel the characteristic reactions of Selye's General Adaptation Syndrome, discussed in Chapter 3. For example, high density is associated with changes in a number of body organs, such as the kidneys, liver, and brain (Myers *et al.,* 1971). Such changes are hardly indicative of good health. Another consistent finding is that high social and spatial density lead to abnormalities in endocrine functioning, which may be seen as an indicator of stress (Christian, 1955).

One important effect of high density on endocrine functioning is that it leads to decreased fertility in both males and females (Christian, 1955; Snyder, 1966, 1968). For example, it has been found that males living under high density conditions produce fewer sperm than males living under low density (Snyder, 1966). With females, estrus cycles of "low density" animals have been found to begin at an earlier age, occur more frequently, and last longer than those of "high density" animals (Snyder, 1966). Given such differences, it is not surprising to find both smaller litter sizes and less frequent births in crowded populations (Crew & Mirskowa, 1931; Snyder, 1966).

Behavioral Consequences of High Density for Animals

Some extremely interesting and provocative studies have found that various high density manipulations can cause significant disturbance to normal social organization in animals (Calhoun, 1962; Christian, 1963; Snyder, 1966; Southwick, 1955). The pioneering work of John B. Calhoun in this area serves as an excellent example of how high density affects populations of animals. Calhoun has studied both rats and mice, but his most startling study was based on rat colonies. Calhoun placed a small number of male and female rats in the apparatus pictured in Figure 7–2 and allowed them to bear young and eventually overpopulate. (Note the similarity to the situation described in

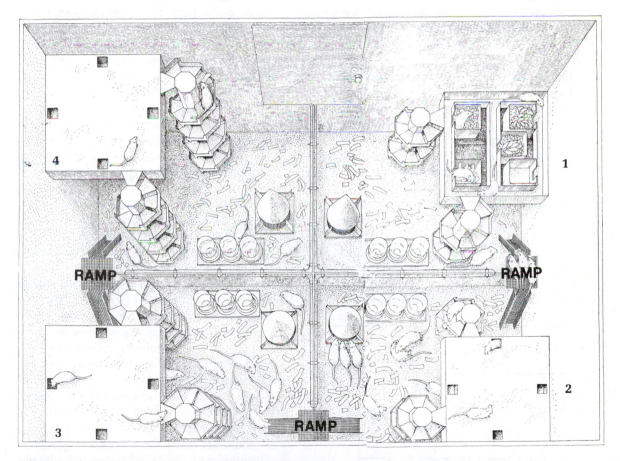

Figure 7–2. The "universe" used by Calhoun (1962) to study the effects of high density on rodent behavior. There are no ramps between pens 1 and 4, which means that they are essentially "end" pens. This eventually precipitates a behavioral sink in pens 2 and 3. (From Calhoun, J. Population density and social pathology, *Scientific American,* February 1962, 140–141. Copyright 1962 by Scientific American, Inc. All rights reserved.)

our introduction.) The "universe," which can comfortably handle 48 animals, consists of a 10 ft. × 14 ft. platform divided into four cells, each with a capacity of 12 animals. One important feature of the universe is that ramps connect all the pens except the two "end" pens, which eventually causes many animals to crowd into the central pens. Pens labeled "1" and "4" take on the role of end pens, while the other two become more central (see Figure 7–3)

Before they become extremely crowded, "average" male rats busy themselves accumulating a harem, mating with members of the harem, and defending territory. They roam freely around the environment, don't fight much, and don't mate with females in other harems. Females occupy themselves with building nests and raising the young. They don't fight, and they resist advances from males outside their harems. How do rats behave under conditions of high density? As we shall see, Calhoun observed that under high density the normal social order disintegrated, and a new one emerged.

Allowing the animals to overpopulate had adverse effects on the social behavior of all the occupants of the universe, and these effects were particularly negative in cells 2 and 3, where

Figure 7–3. If the arrangement of pens 1, 2, 3, and 4 is changed from the one in the top diagram to the one depicted below it, pens 1 and 4 remain "end" pens with only one entrance/exit.

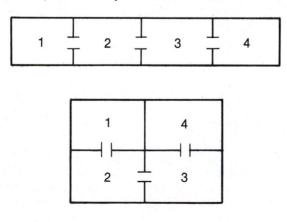

crowding was acute. (Calhoun calls this extremely crowded area, which is described in the box on page 197 a *behavioral sink.*) In the two end pens, males and females still attempted to enact their normal social roles as dominant males guarded the sole entrance and maintained a semblance of normal territorial behavior. But, in the behavioral sink, neither males nor females carried out their roles effectively. For example, although females in the less crowded pens tried to nurse their young, to build nests for them, and to transfer them in the event of harm, none of these behaviors was effectively engaged in by mothers in the behavioral sink. This accounts, at least in part, for the fact that the infant mortality rate in the behavioral sink was extremely high, with 80 to 96 percent of all pups dying before being weaned. In contrast (but nothing to be pleased about), only about 50 percent of the pups in the less crowded "end" pens suffered this fate. While dominant males protected estrous females in the less crowded pens, packs of socially deviant males in the crowded inner pens relentlessly pursued estrous females, who were unable to resist their advances. This led to a high rate of mortality from diseases in pregnancy (almost half of the females in these pens died by the 16th month), which was not experienced by female residents in the less crowded pens.

Within the bizarre setting of Calhoun's "universe," several social classes emerged, varying in the extent and type of their pathological behavior. There were four groups of males. First, there was a group of dominant males which generally lived in the less crowded pens. As noted earlier, these were the most normal animals in Calhoun's "universe." They were also the most secure, since the majority of the other animals were victims of almost continuous aggressive attacks. The second group, which Calhoun called the "beautiful ones," consisted of pansexual males. These animals could not discriminate between appropriate and inappropriate sex partners and made advances to females who were not in estrus as well as to males. The third class of males was completely passive and ignored other rats of both sexes. The

WHAT IS A BEHAVIORAL SINK?

At this point, you probably have the general (and correct) impression that a "behavioral sink," such as existed in pens 2 and 3, is an area in which the negative effects of high density are intensified. However, up to now we haven't discussed the dynamics by which behavioral sinks are formed. According to Calhoun (1967), a behavioral sink develops when a population that is uniformly distributed becomes nonuniformly distributed in groups far exceeding optimal size. Two processes are involved in "behavioral sink" formation. First, some aspect of the environment or the behavior of the animals makes population density greater in some places than in others (the absence of ramps connecting pens 1 and 4 did this in Calhoun's study). Second, animals come to associate the presence of others with some originally unrelated activity. For example, in Calhoun's studies, animals came to associate food (a reinforcer) with the presence of others, which caused them to be attracted to areas where there were many animals. As we have seen, the intense crowding and the attendant need to make accommodations to so many others was clearly detrimental to the social order. Can you think of any areas in the human environment that would qualify as "behavioral sinks"?

Given an understanding of the dynamics of the behavioral sink, how can this condition and its associated pathology be remedied? One approach taken by Calhoun was to substitute granular food (which can be eaten very quickly) for the hard food pellets (which were very time-consuming to eat) used in his earlier studies. Consequently, it took much less time for animals to eat, decreasing the probability that two or more animals would be eating simultaneously and that the conditioning process previously described would occur. In these studies, behavioral sinks failed to develop, and the pathological behavior associated with high density was less intense, although by no means low. Can you think of a similar means of eliminating the human behavioral sinks you thought of earlier?

fourth and most unusual group of males Calhoun termed "probers." These animals lived in the behavioral sink and were hyperactive, hypersexual, homosexual, and cannibalistic. Classifying the female rats was relatively simple. One group (which lived in the behavioral sink) was completely abnormal, could fulfill no sexual and maternal functions, and "huddled" with the male rats. The second group (which lived in the less crowded pens) behaved much more like "normal" rats.

Calhoun's work has been central to the continued study of high density animal populations. For example, Southwick (1967) found increases in aggression with increasing density in a group of monkeys. However, other studies (e.g., Anderson *et al.*, 1977) have found density-related increases in withdrawal rather than aggression among monkeys. Still other studies have found

that crowding affects the sexual behavior of rats born in high density settings (e.g., Chapman, Masterpasqua, & Love, 1976; Dahlof, Hard, & Larsson, 1977).

Having discussed the effects of high density on social behavior and physiological responses, we might ask what other consequences high density has for animals. While a complete discussion is beyond our scope, a final effect worthy of mention is that high density is associated with decrements in learning and task performance. Goeckner, Greenough, and Maier (1974) raised rats in groups of 1, 4, and 32. It was found that animals raised in crowded conditions showed poorer performance on complex tasks, though no performance deficits were found for simple tasks. Further, Bell *et al.* (1971) reported decreased maze exploration and activity levels in settings with high social density.

Conceptual Perspectives: Attempts to Understand High Density Effects in Animals

Given that animals respond negatively to crowding, what is responsible for these reactions? A number of attempts have been made to explain the negative effects of high density on animals. In a sense, these perspectives view the negative responses of animals to high density as adaptive mechanisms that act to prevent extinction due to overpopulation. Although none of the conceptual schemes has received the unqualified support of the scientific community, they are useful in adding to our understanding of the effects of density on animals. At this point, we should consider the various viewpoints as "possibilities" and expect the eventual explanation to be an integration of several approaches.

One conceptualization of the effects of high density on animals has been proposed by Calhoun (1971). This formulation can be used to explain both the extremely negative consequences that occurred in the behavioral sink and the relatively negative effects that occurred elsewhere. First, Calhoun assumes that species of mammals are predisposed by evolution to interact with a particular number of others (Figure 7–4). This is termed their "optimal group size." It leads to a tolerable number of contacts with others each day, some of which are gratifying and some of which are frustrating. Calhoun suggests that as the group increases beyond the optimal size, the ratio of frustrating to gratifying interactions becomes more unfavorable. Further, interruptions in necessary periods of solitude increase, and these are experienced as aversive. This state of affairs becomes extremely debilitating when the number in the group approaches twice the optimal number, and a sustained period under such conditions produces the sort of effects observed in Calhoun's "rat universe."

Another conceptualization of the negative effects of high density on animals is social stress theory (Christian, 1955; Wynne-Edwards, 1962). From this perspective, it is assumed that social consequences of high density (e.g., increased so-

Figure 7–4. Calhoun suggests that animals are evolutionarily predisposed to interact with a particular number of others. When more than the "optimal group size" are present, interactions become aversive, and at twice the optimal size conditions may become debilitating. (Sherry Fisher)

cial competition, effects on social hierarchies) are stressful and that stress produces an increase in the activity of the adrenal glands as part of a stress-like syndrome. (Recall the evidence described earlier that high density is associated with changes in endocrine functioning.) It is believed that increased adrenal activity is responsible for many of the negative physiological and behavioral effects associated with high density. Interestingly, social stress theory predicts that glandular activity may also moderate a population *increase* when populations are very small. Since its social consequences are not stressful, low density does not elicit stress, and thus it facilitates higher birth rate, longer life span, and so on. Social stress theory involves a type of endocrine feedback system that keeps density at an acceptable level.

An explanatory framework based on territorial behavior has been proposed in the works of Ardrey (1966) and Lorenz (1966). It assumes that the negative effects of density on animals are caused primarily by aggression induced by territorial invasions. These writers suggest that as population density increases beyond an optimal level, violations of territorial "rights" increase, precipitating high levels of aggression. (The relationships between territorial invasion and aggression in animals is discussed in Chapter 6.) Such aggression results in the negative physiological and behavioral effects described earlier as associated with high density. Under conditions of low density, territories are not violated, aggression is low, and the species can increase toward the optimal level. This formulation, however, cannot explain the effects of density on those animals that are relatively nonterritorial and more socially oriented.

Another way to integrate these formulations as well as others (cf. Frank, 1957; Krebs, 1972; Pearson, 1966, 1971; Pitelka, 1957) has been proposed by Wilson (1975). First, it is assumed that there is a tendency for populations to return to an optimal level of density. How does this occur? It is accomplished by "density-dependent controls" (e.g., by varying levels of aggression, stress, fertility, emigration, predation, and disease). According to Wilson, such controls operate through natural selection. For example, at high density, selection may favor an aggressive organism, which will bring the population into decline. At low density, aggressive organisms would be at a disadvantage, and the population would evolve back toward more gentle behavior, permitting it to enlarge. In effect, such a process protects the species from extinction caused by under- or overpopulation.

Summary. Animals experience various severe negative physiological and behavioral reactions to high density conditions. These include changes in body organs, glandular malfunctions, and extreme disruption of social and maternal behavior. Calhoun's research with rodents powerfully demonstrates many of these effects and shows that they are intensified when behavioral sinks develop. Before we conclude, however, we should add one caveat. Although the findings we discussed in this section are quite consistent, it is important to note

that there are some variations among species in the reactions that occur (Figure 7–5). Finally, several different conceptual schemes have been proposed to explain animal reactions to high density.

EFFECTS OF HIGH DENSITY ON HUMANS

After reviewing a series of studies on the physiological and behavioral effects of high density on animals, as well as some conceptual frameworks in which to view them, it is tempting to speculate about whether this same pattern of effects can generalize to humans. Scientists and philosophers have puzzled over the differences between humans and animals for centuries, and endless arguments have emerged. (See the box on page 201 for a discussion of what we can assume about humans from our study of the literature on animal behavior.)

Differences between humans and animals notwithstanding, most early research on human crowding assumed that for us, like animals, high density would lead to uniformly negative effects (Figure 7–6). To the surprise of everyone, and in line with our admonitions, this has not been the case. While for animals high density is generally aversive, for humans it depends more on the situation. For the most part, the effects of high densities on people are neither severe nor uniform. Our discussion of human response to density will first highlight research findings and then integrate them in terms of the general environment-behavior model presented in Chapter 3. Before proceeding, however, we will pause to consider the methodologies used to study human reactions to density.

Methodologies Used to Study High Density in Humans

The method most often used to study high density in humans is *laboratory experimentation*. Laboratory studies have a number of advantages over other techniques, as discussed in Chapter 1 and in the methodology Appendix. However, for explor-

Figure 7–5. While it is generally the case that animals respond negatively to high density, for some it constitutes "standard operating conditions" and does not lead to negative consequences. Optimal population densities for some species may appear quite crowded to us. (James O. Whittaker)

Figure 7–6. In general, humans evidence more variable reactions to high density than animals do. Sometimes we like it; sometimes we don't. (James O. Whittaker)

WHAT DOES ANIMAL RESEARCH TELL US ABOUT HUMANS?

As a rule, it is difficult to assume that generalization from animals to humans will occur (although in reading this chapter you will find that both sometimes respond similarly). Why shouldn't we expect findings that hold for animals to be true for humans? First, animal behavior appears to be determined largely by biological factors, whereas humans depend much more on learning and cultural inputs (Swanson, 1973). Humans also have more means at their disposal to adapt to high density. For example, naturalistic high density for animals is almost always accompanied by a lack of food, yet humans who live in such conditions are often adequately fed. Finally, the fact that most animal data are based on organisms that exist only in crowded settings limits their generalizability to humans, who often have at least brief opportunities to escape (Evans, 1978).

If there are difficulties in generalizing from animal research to humans, what value does animal research have? We should view animal studies as important in their own right for what they say about the impact of density on animals and as a rich source of hypotheses concerning how humans *may* respond to high density. For example, the notion of unwanted interaction and social regulation that forms the basis of Baum and Valins' (1977) studies of college dormitories (page 206) was directly derived from Calhoun's notion of balancing frustrating and gratifying interactions. The value of animal work as a source of hypotheses about human reactions to high density is enhanced by several methodological strengths of animal research over human research:

1. There are ethical problems in studying *long-term* high density in humans: These make it difficult to do the type of well-controlled studies commonly done with animals.
2. Since animals bear young more quickly than humans, it is possible to observe the cycle in which they reproduce and overpopulate in a much shorter period of time.
3. It is easier to study physiological and behavioral responses of animals without disturbing the process being monitored than it is with humans.

ing high density in humans, they have two disadvantages worthy of mention. First, creating high density conditions in the laboratory is somewhat artificial, which may affect generalizability to the "real world." Second, laboratory studies can explore only very short-term high density effects, which is a serious problem. In attempts to remedy these deficiencies, researchers have increasingly turned to *field research* techniques (i.e., field experiments and field studies). These offer greater realism than laboratory experiments and permit us to study longer-term density effects. However, while *field experiments* permit us to make causal inferences, *field studies* do not. *Quasi-experimentation,* a field study technique that is discussed in the methodology Appendix, allows us both the realism of field settings (e.g., prisons, dormitories) and the ability to attempt a causal inference.

A final research technique for studying high density in humans is *sociological-correlational* research. This is used primarily by sociologists and involves correlating census-tract types of indices of population density with frequency of abnormal behaviors. These studies have generally looked at correlations between pathology findings and two indices of density: *inside density* (e.g., number of persons per residence or per room) and *outside density* (e.g., number of persons, dwellings, or structures per acre). Unfortunately, early sociological-correlational research failed to control for a number of variables that may vary along with density (e.g., income, education), and the results are of questionable value. A "second generation" of studies has statistically controlled for these confounding variables. Although they represent an improvement over earlier sociological-correlational research, several important weaknesses remain. First, so many different indices of inside and outside density are used that meaningful comparison among studies is difficult. Second, while they tell us whether disorders are associated with density, these studies still give us very little information about the specific causes of pathology. Variations in density from home to home or tract to tract cannot be accounted for and, of course, causality cannot be inferred.

Having reviewed the methodologies used in human research on high density, we now turn to the research itself. Our review will be organized into conceptually related areas: how density makes us feel (i.e., its consequences for affect, arousal, and illness), how density affects our social behavior (i.e., its effects on interpersonal attraction, aggression, and prosocial behavior), and how density affects task performance.

Feeling the Effects of Density: Its Consequences for Affect, Arousal, and Illness

Affect. One of the most common assumptions that people make about crowding is that it makes people "feel bad." In line with this observation, several studies report that high social density may cause negative affective states (Evans, 1975; Sundstrom, 1975). One field study (Saegert, MacIntosh, & West, 1975) had subjects perform a series of tasks in either crowded or uncrowded settings. It was observed that subjects reported more anxiety in the dense than in the nondense conditions, although this probably doesn't surprise anyone who has ever had to perform a task with hordes of others "breathing down one's neck." Also, a study by Baum and Greenberg (1975) found that the mere anticipation of being in a crowd elicits a negative mood.

Before concluding that crowding invariably leads to negative mood, however, we should consider some evidence that suggests the negative feelings caused by high density may be stronger in males than in females. Several studies (Freedman *et al.*, 1972; Ross *et al.*, 1973) found that

while males experience more negative moods in high than in low spatial density conditions, the reverse is true for females (Figure 7–7). One way to explain these effects is the finding in the personal space literature (see Chapter 6) that males have greater personal space needs than do females. Alternatively, these findings may reflect the female socialization to be more affiliative (and therefore to have more of an affinity for crowds), and the male socialization to be more competitive (and to see crowds as a source of threat) (Maccoby, 1966). Research indicates that women may approach crowded settings in more cooperative ways than do men (Karlin, Epstein, & Aiello, 1978; Taylor, 1978). Or, it is possible that density does not cause any kind of mood, but rather serves to intensify whatever the prevailing mood in the situation might be—a density-intensity effect (Freedman, 1975). We will discuss this notion later in this chapter.

It is important to note that the studies discussed above that found uniformly negative moods were primarily studies of high social density. The studies that report sex differences in these feelings were studies of high spatial density. Recall that we said that spatial and social density referred to more than just methodological differences—they may reflect very different kinds of problems. It is possible that high social density is equally aversive to men and women, but that high spatial density is only bothersome for males. We will elaborate more on this later.

Physiological Arousal. If high density affects our feelings, can it also lead to physiological effects, such as increased heart rate? As we have seen, stress has an arousal component, and several studies have examined this arousal as it applies to crowding. In one experiment, Evans (1979) had mixed-sex groups of five males and five females participate in a three and one-half-hour study in either a large or a small room. Participants' heart rate and blood pressure were recorded both before the experiment began and after three hours. Results indicated that in high density conditions, subjects showed higher pulse rate and

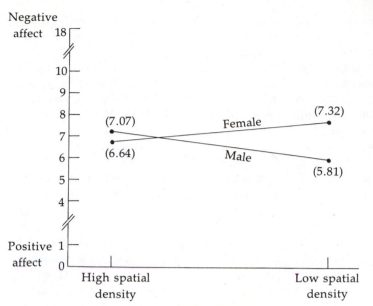

Figure 7–7. Ratings of affective states for males and females in high and low spatial density conditions. Higher scores = more negative affect. (After Ross *et al.*, 1973.)

blood pressure readings than in more spacious conditions. Several other physiological indices of arousal are also affected by high density. For example, skin conductance (a measure of arousal) has been found to increase significantly over time for subjects in high but not in low spatial density (Aiello, Epstein, & Karlin, 1975). Saegert (1974) found that exposure to a large number of others leads to arousal as measured by palmar sweat. Finally, Heshka and Pylypuk (1975) compared cortisol levels (indicative of stress) of students who spent the day in a crowded shopping area and students who stayed on a relatively uncrowded college campus. When compared with the control group, males who had been in crowded conditions had elevated levels, but females did not.

Field studies in Sweden have also investigated stress-related arousal in crowded settings (e.g., Lundberg, 1976; Singer, Lundberg & Frankenhaeuser, 1978). Lundberg studied male passengers of a commuter train, comparing their response to trips made under crowded and uncrowded conditions. Despite the fact that even under the most crowded conditions there were seats available for everyone, reported crowding increased as more people rode the train. Further, Lundberg collected urine samples from his subjects and found higher levels of epinephrine among subjects after crowded trips than after less crowded ones (epinephrine is an endocrinological marker of stress-related arousal).

Other results of both studies, however, qualified the nature of these findings. Regardless of how crowded the train was, riders who boarded at the first stop experienced less crowding and had lower levels of epinephrine in their urine than did passengers boarding halfway to the city. Despite the fact that their ride was considerably longer (72 minutes vs. 38 minutes), those boarding at the first stop entered an empty train and were able to choose where to sit and with whom they traveled. Groups of commuters, for example, could be assured of finding seats together. In this way, they could buffer themselves from the crowding that would soon occur by structuring the setting before it became crowded. Apparently, the control afforded initial passengers reduced the effects of increasing numbers of riders along the way, while the lack of control associated with boarding an already crowded car resulted in increased arousal (Lundberg, 1976; Singer *et al.*, 1978).

Illness. It would seem reasonable that if high density leads to negative feeling states and to physiological overarousal, residing under such conditions would have negative consequences for health. There is evidence that this assertion is at least partly correct. Corroborative evidence is provided by McCain, Cox, and Paulus (1976), who report that in a prison setting inmates who lived in conditions of low spatial and social density were sick less often than those who lived in high densities. Subsequent studies indicated that crowding was related to blood pressure increases and to death rates (Paulus, McCain, & Cox, 1978) (see Figure 7–8). D'Atri (1975) and D'Atri and Ostfeld (1975) also found that social density increases were associated with rising blood pressure. Further evidence is provided in studies done with college dormitory residents. For example, Stokols and Ohlig (1975) observed an association between reports of crowding and visits to the student health center. Baron *et al.* (1976) found evidence of more visits to the infirmary by residents in high than low social density dormitories. Dean, Pugh, and Gunderson (1975, 1978) have also reported associations between crowding and illness complaints aboard naval vessels.

Additional support for a relationship between high density and illness is provided by *sociological-correlational* studies. Specifically, evidence exists for a link between inside density and illness but not between outside density and illness. For example, Marsella, Escudero, and Gordon (1970) found an association between inside density and physiological symptoms, and Galle, Gove, and McPherson (1972) reported that inside density was significantly correlated with mortality. For outside density, several investigators (Freedman *et al.,* 1975; Galle *et al.,* 1972; Schmitt, 1966) found no relationship with ill health, and two studies (Levy & Herzog, 1974; Winsborough, 1965) reported an inverse relationship between hospital admissions and household density. The reason for this pattern of effects is unclear.

Figure 7–8. As population size increased in prison settings, the death rate in the prison also increased. Decreased population size was associated with lower mortality. These findings controlled for a number of factors, including violent deaths. The correlation between death rates and population size was .81. (Based on data in Paulus, McCain, & Cox, 1978.)

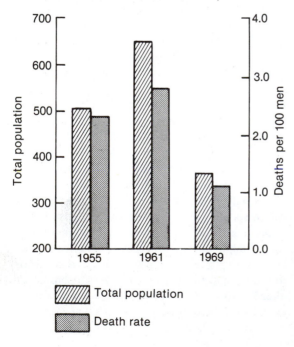

Summary. Having considered the effects of high density on affect, arousal, and illness, we can draw several tentative conclusions. First, it appears that high density leads to more negative affective states (especially in males) and to higher levels of physiological arousal, as measured on a wide variety of indices. Further, there is evidence (although somewhat inconsistent) that high density is associated with illness. With this capsule summary in mind, we now turn our focus to the effects of high density on such social behaviors as interpersonal attraction, withdrawal, altruistic behavior, and aggression.

Effects of Density on Social Behavior

Attraction. Will we tend to like a stranger more if we meet him or her in a crowded subway car or in a more spacious setting? Generally, it

Table 7–1. SATISFACTION WITH ROOMMATE UNDER CROWDED AND UNCROWDED CONDITIONS*

	Uncrowded	Crowded
Satisfaction with roommate	4.9	3.7
Perceived cooperativeness of roommate	4.7	3.9

*Higher numbers indicate more positive responses. (Based on data from Baron *et al.*, 1976.)

seems as though high density leads to decrements in attraction, whether we are merely anticipating confinement, are confined for a relatively short period, or are confined for a long time. For example, Baum and Greenberg (1975) found that merely expecting high density elicited dislike: Students who were told 10 people would eventually occupy a room liked those they waited with less than did subjects who were told only four would be present. In a study of short-term high density confinement, groups of eight males who were together for an hour attributed more friendliness to other group members under low than under high spatial density (Worchel & Teddlie, 1976). Looking at long-term density effects, Baron and his colleagues (1976) reported that dormitory residents living in "triples" (three students in a room built for two) were less satisfied with their roommates and perceived them to be less cooperative than students living in "doubles" (Table 7–1).

Although it appears that high density leads to lower attraction, there is evidence (as noted earlier for affective state) that under conditions of high spatial density, this response is more char-

acteristic of males than of females (cf. Epstein & Karlin, 1975; Freedman, Klevansky, & Ehrlich, 1971; Ross *et al.*, 1973; Stokols *et al.*, 1973). For example, in an experiment by Epstein and Karlin (1975), male and female subjects participated in same-sex groups of six. Consistent findings on a variety of measures indicated that while males responded more negatively to group members in high than in low spatial density conditions, females liked group members more under high density conditions (Table 7–2). We speculated earlier that sex differences in response to high density may be due to different size personal space zones or to differential cooperative and competitive socializations.

Epstein and Karlin (1975) suggest another possibility. They state that while both males and females experience arousal from high density, social norms permit females to share their distress with others in their group, which leads to liking and cohesion. The same norms prohibit males from sharing stress, which causes a more negative response. In a follow-up experiment (Karlin *et al.*, 1976), it was found that when females were not permitted to interact with each other, their

Table 7–2. RATINGS OF PERCEIVED SIMILARITY UNDER CROWDED AND UNCROWDED CONDITIONS*

Sex	Crowded	Uncrowded
Male	5.7	4.4
Female	4.2	5.7

*Lower numbers indicate greater perceived similarity. (Based on data from Epstein & Karlin, 1975.)

HIGH DENSITY IN THE DORM:
WHERE WOULD YOU LIKE TO LIVE NEXT YEAR?

One of the most often studied residential environments is the college dormitory. The effects of high residential density in this setting were reported by Baum and Valins (1977). The investigators performed a number of studies comparing the responses to high density of students assigned to suite-style dormitories and students assigned to corridor-style dormitories. Corridor residents shared a bathroom and a lounge with 34 residents on the floor; suite residents shared a bathroom and a lounge with only four to six others (see Figures 7–9A and B). All students shared a bedroom with one other student. While the suite and corridor designs were identical in terms of space per person and number of residents per floor, as you might guess, they led to dramatic differences in the number of others that residents encountered constantly.

What were the behavioral effects of the greater number of interpersonal contacts in corridor-style dormitories? Corridor residents responded differently than suite residents in a number of ways. They perceived their floors to be more crowded, felt they were more often forced into inconvenient and unwanted interactions with others, and indicated a greater desire to avoid others. Corridor residents were also far less sociable, perceived less attitude similarity between themselves and their neighbors, and were less sure of what their neighbors thought of them as people. Not surprisingly, a significantly lower number of corridor residents reported that the majority of their friends lived on the same floor.

It was also found that living in a suite or a corridor-style dormitory led to different behaviors in other places and with other people. For example, Baum and Valins reported that corridor residents looked less at confederates and sat farther away from them while waiting for an experiment. Corridor residents also performed significantly worse than suite residents on tasks under cooperative conditions, although they performed better under conditions that inhibited personal involvement with the opponent.

What do these data mean? It may be that corridor residents find themselves "overloaded" by their high level of interaction with others, or that they experience frequent *unwanted interactions,* and their withdrawal responses may be interpreted as coping strategies that prevent such involvement. Baum and Valins suggest that high density living in suites and corridors may be considered as a type of social conditioning process. Obviously, this process results in a more positive orientation to others in suite-style than in corridor-style dormitories. Subsequent studies linked this

---

positive reactions to high density were attenuated. Support for this interpretation has been limited, with one study reporting the opposite kind of effect (Keating & Snowball, 1977). However, this way of viewing sex differences in crowding response is an important and useful one.

Withdrawal. In support of Baum and Valins' observation that withdrawal may be associated with high levels of social contact (box, above), studies have found that withdrawal may function as an anticipatory response to high density, as a means of coping with ongoing high density, and

as an aftereffect. For example, the mere expectation of high social density elicits withdrawal responses, including lower levels of eye contact, head movements away from others (Baum & Greenberg, 1975; Baum & Koman, 1976), and maintenance of greater interpersonal distances (Baum & Greenberg, 1975). Withdrawal also occurs during ongoing high density interactions: Subjects are more willing to discuss intimate topics under low density conditions (Sundstrom, 1975), and both children (Hutt & Vaizey, 1966; Loo, 1972) and psychiatric patients (Ittelson, Proshansky, & Rivlin, 1972) interact less frequently

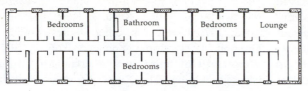

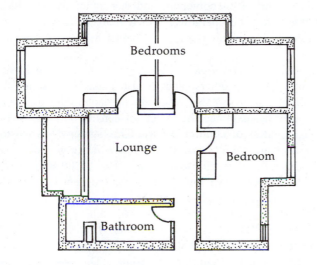

Figure 7–9 A and B. Floor plan of corridor-style dormitory (above) and suite-style dormitory (below). (From Baum & Valins, 1977, Published with permission of Lawrence Erlbaum Associates.)

difference to prosocial behavior, interpersonal bargaining, and response to violations of social norms (e.g., Davis, 1977; Reichner, 1979; Sell, 1976).

Is there any way to make life in corridor-style dormitories more tolerable? Baum and Valins found that membership in small local groups, when it occurred, tended to reduce many of the negative effects of corridor living. How does your own experience as a dormitory resident correspond to Baum and Valins' observations and conclusions?

as room density increases. Finally, it appears that withdrawal can constitute an aftereffect of exposure to density. Males were less likely to volunteer for another experimental session after high social density (Dooley, 1974), and groups of males preferred larger personal space and recalled fewer names after exposure to high density (Joy & Lehmann, 1975).

Prosocial Behavior. If high density leads to lower attraction and to withdrawal responses, how might it affect helping? For example, suppose you lost a contact lens or something else of value.

Where would you be most confident of finding someone who would help you look for it: in a high-rise or a low-rise building? In a large city or in a small town? Interestingly, most research on how density affects prosocial behavior has been done in field settings like these. In fact, one set of studies has compared helping in buildings characterized by high and low density, and a second has compared prosocial acts in large cities and small towns.

In studies that explored helping as a function of building density, it was found consistently that greater density leads to less helping. For example,

Bickman *et al.* (1973) compared prosocial acts in high, medium, and low density dormitories. Envelopes, which were stamped and addressed, were dropped in the dormitories, and helpfulness was measured by the number that were picked up and placed in the mail. The results showed that 58 percent were mailed in the high density condition, 79 percent in the medium density condition, and 88 percent in the low density condition. In an interesting corroborative study, Jorgenson and Dukes (1976) observed the effect of social density on compliance with a prosocial request (printed on signs) for cafeteria users to return their trays to designated areas. It was found that fewer users complied during high density periods (Figure 7–10).

The second line of research, which compared urban and rural helping, provides more equivocal evidence concerning a density-prosocial behavior relationship. In one group of studies, it was found that city dwellers were less helpful and less informative to strangers than rural dwellers. Urbanites were less likely to admit a stranger who needed to use a telephone, less likely to assist a caller who had mistakenly called a wrong number, less likely to correct overpayments in making change,

and less likely to report a theft than rural dwellers (Gelfand *et al.,* 1973; Korte & Kerr, 1975; Milgram, 1970). However, other studies (Forbes & Gromoll, 1971; Korte, Ypma, & Toppen, 1975; Weiner, 1976) failed to find urban–rural differences in helping. Thus, it seems safe to say that unwillingness to help others isn't necessarily an urban phenomenon, and that additional variables may be operating. (For a more thorough discussion of this issue, see Chapter 8.)

Aggression. If density can make us less likely to help others, does it also make us more apt to hurt them? One research approach to this question has explored the effects of density on aggressiveness of children's play. This strategy has led to inconsistent results. Some studies (e.g., Aiello *et al.,* 1979; Ginsburg *et al.,* 1977; Hutt & Vaizey, 1966) have found that increased density leads to more aggression; others have found the reverse (e.g., Loo, 1972); and still others (e.g., Price, 1971) have found no effect. Loo suggested the possibility that density affects children's aggression in a curvilinear fashion. This assertion was supported by a study that observed that moderately high density led to increased aggression in males, while very low and very high density led to decreased aggressiveness (Loo, 1978). Subsequent study, however, has shown increases in aggression under conditions of high social density among boys (Loo & Kennelly, 1979). In another attempt to resolve these findings, Rohe and Patterson (1974) suggested that competition over scarce resources is a major determinant of children's aggression in high density situations. If there are more kids than toys and each child wants a toy, aggression is more likely than if there are enough toys to go around. Rohe and Patterson hypothesized and found that increases in spatial density led to more aggression only if resources were limited. This relationship was also reported by Smith and Connolly (1977), who found that increased aggression during play occurred if playground equipment was made more scarce.

Since children are presumably less restrained

Figure 7–10. A number of interesting field studies have shown that residents of low-rise buildings are more willing to help others than residents of high-rise buildings. (Sherry Fisher)

and more outwardly aggressive than adults, it may be that high density has less overt effects on adult aggressiveness. These effects may be more subtle. Studies have suggested that children's responses to high density change with continuing development (Aiello *et al.*, 1979; Loo & Smetana, 1978). Several studies have addressed the aggression-enhancing effects of high density among adults.

Overall, it appears that increased density leads to aggression in adult males but not in females, a familiar pattern in the high density research. For example, Stokols and his associates (1973) studied same-sex groups of eight in either a large or a small room and found that males rated themselves as more aggressive in the small room, while the reverse was true of females. Freedman *et al.* (1972) also found that increasing spatial density was associated with increasingly aggressive behavior among men but not among women. Schettino and Borden (1976) used the ratio of people in a classroom to the total number of seats as an index of density and found that density was significantly correlated with self-reported aggressiveness for males but not for females.

Baum and Koman (1976) found sex differences in aggressive response to anticipated crowding as well, but *only* when spatial density increased. Men in small rooms expecting to be crowded behaved more aggressively than did women in the same situation. Further, they were more aggressive in the small room than when a larger room was used. However, increases in *social* density did not produce increased aggression. In fact, in conditions where subjects expected large numbers of people rather than limited space, subjects tended to withdraw rather than act aggressively. This is consistent with the findings discussed above, which were produced primarily by manipulation of spatial density. Once again, social and spatial density appear to have somewhat different effects on people. Apparently, the aggression-enhancing effects of density are related to spatial resource problems and not to problems created by the presence of too many people.

Regardless of whether spatial or social factors induce aggressiveness during crowding, it is clear that the magnitude of these effects is less than overwhelming. Those studies that have found increases in aggressiveness during crowding have reported them primarily among men and the effects have been mild at worst. Also, the measures of aggression in these studies have been very artificial. Subjects sentencing a hypothetical criminal to a longer prison term or taking more central seats in a small room—the types of measures used in the studies—are not the kinds of aggression many expect to find in crowded environments.

One reason for this artificiality may be the kinds of settings that have been studied. Most investigations of adults and aggressive response during high density have been conducted in the laboratory. Obviously, the kinds of indices one can use to measure aggression in such a situation are limited. It is not possible to examine aggression leading to real harm (such as in criminal acts), and instead, laboratory studies have focused on response to bargaining games, jury simulations, and other approximations of real-world aggression. This is a serious limitation to our understanding of density and aggression.

These problems are only partly resolved by the field studies that have been attempted. Such research shows a tenuous relationship between high density and various indicators of crime (e.g., Galle, Gove, & McPherson, 1972), and one study reported evidence that high density is more strongly associated with fear of crime than with actual victimization (Gifford & Peacock, 1979).

Summary. Our discussion of the effects of density on social behavior (i.e., attraction, withdrawal, altruism, and aggression) allows us to draw several tentative conclusions. First, it appears that high density leads to less liking of both people and places, and that this relationship is stronger for males than for females. High density also causes withdrawal in a wide variety of situations. Concerning altruism and aggressive behavior, the findings are somewhat inconsistent, but there seems to be at least a weak relationship between high density and these behaviors. The differences between social and spatial density also appear to be important. With these ideas in mind, we turn our focus to the effects of high density on a final and extremely important dimension—task performance.

Effects of High Density on Task Performance

One of the most critical questions that can be asked about high density is whether it affects task performance. The answer has important implications for the design of all types of living and working spaces (e.g., schools, factories). Most early studies used simple tasks and were consistent in finding no decrements under high social or spatial density (Bergman, 1971; Rawls *et al.*, 1972; Stokols *et al.*, 1973). For example, Freedman and his associates (1971) found that density variations did not affect performance for any of a series of tasks. Later work, generally using more complex tasks, supports a somewhat different conclusion (Dooley, 1974; McClelland, 1974; Saegert, 1974; Saegert, MacIntosh, & West, 1975). As shown in Table 7–3, Paulus *et al.* (1976) found that both high social and high spatial density led to decrements in complex maze task performance, but these decrements were more pronounced under conditions of high social density. In a field setting, Aiello and his coworkers (1975) found decrements in complex task performance over time in overcrowded dormitory rooms (three persons in a room built for two), as compared with less crowded rooms (two persons in a room built for two). Evans (1979) also found

poorer complex task performance under crowded conditions, but did not find any impairment of simple task performance. Klein and Harris (1979) found evidence of poorer complex task performance while anticipating crowding.

How can we reconcile our finding of high density decrements on some tasks but not on others? One explanation centers around the fact that high density leads to arousal (cf. Evans, 1975a), and is consistent with our discussion of arousal in Chapter 3. The Yerkes-Dodson Law, a formulation that relates arousal to task performance, states that arousal *should* interfere only with complex task performance. In terms of this law, our observation that high density causes decrements only in complex task performance would be expected, rather than discrepant. Since the Yerkes-Dodson Law has been supported in numerous research contexts in the psychological literature, it seems quite tenable as an explanation here. In addition, Paulus (1977) offers some alternative suggestions for why density hasn't consistently affected task performance. He concludes that such factors as the psychological salience of the others present, the feelings of being evaluated, and the number of tasks subjects must perform may be important as well.

An alternative explanation for inconsistent findings has been offered by Heller, Groff, and Solomon (1977). They propose that many studies of crowding have focused only on the physical aspects of a setting at the expense of the kinds of interactions that are typical of high density settings. Thus, some studies occupy subjects with

Table 7–3. ERRORS IN MAZE PERFORMANCE AS A FUNCTION OF SPATIAL DENSITY AND SOCIAL DENSITY*

Low spatial density	34.20
High spatial density	37.44
Low social density	32.13
High social density	39.50

*Based on data from Paulus *et al.*, 1976.

tasks so that interaction is minimized. Heller *et al.* suggest that this kind of a design reduces the likelihood of finding effects on task performance. In support of this, they showed that decrements in task performance occurred only under conditions characterized by high density *and* interaction among subjects. High density settings in which subjects did not interact very much did not produce task performance decrements (see Figure 7–11).

Another potential explanation is provided by a study reported by Schkade (1977). She manipulated spatial density and expectancy (how well subjects thought they would do on the task). Results of this study showed that the poorest task performance occurred when density was high and expectations were low—that is, subjects did not expect to do well on the task. Problems with task performance under crowded conditions may be evident primarily when negative outcomes are anticipated.

A final and very important question is whether high density can cause *aftereffects,* as well as immediate effects, on performance. As you will recall, noise is a stressor that has been linked to

Figure 7–11. Interaction is necessary for density-related task performance deficits to occur. (Adapted from Heller, Groff, & Solomon, 1977.)

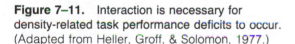

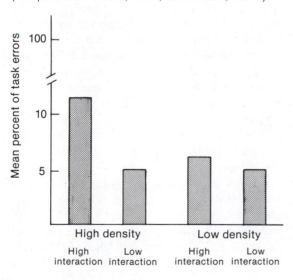

consequences occurring *after* exposure, and some studies suggest that crowding has lingering effects as well. For example, it was found that subjects exposed to high density later showed less persistence at working on unsolvable puzzles than subjects exposed to low density (Dooley, 1974; Evans, 1979; Sherrod, 1974). In an attempt to determine whether perceived control would lessen aftereffects, Sherrod (1974) gave some subjects the option of leaving a crowded room to complete the study in a spacious setting (i.e., perceived control). Although no one took advantage of the option, this group showed fewer aftereffects than the group that wasn't offered an opportunity to leave. The similarity of these findings to those observed by Glass and Singer with noise (reviewed in Chapter 4) further suggests that noise and high density may affect people in similar ways.

Putting the Pieces Together: Conceptualizations of Density Effects on Humans

Up to this point, we've explored a number of density-behavior relationships, finding that high density may lead to various negative effects. As suggested in the general environment–behavior model from Chapter 3, we have seen that high density, like other potential stressors, may lead to (1) immediate effects such as physiological arousal and negative affect; (2) coping responses (e.g., withdrawal); and (3) aftereffects and cumulative effects (e.g., illness). However, high density doesn't always have negative consequences. For example, it inhibits altruistic behavior in some situations but not in others. Hence, the most appropriate conclusion might be that density negatively affects some of the people some of the time in some ways.

Basic Models. What is it about high density that causes those negative effects that do occur? Stokols (1976) identified three conceptual perspectives (overload, behavior constraint, and ecological approaches) used by different researchers to answer this question. All the approaches have been covered in detail in Chapter 3. Briefly, the *overload concept* posits that high density can be aversive because it may cause us to become overwhelmed by sensory inputs. When the amount and rate of stimulation occasioned by high density exceed our ability to deal with it, negative consequences occur. In contrast to the overload approach, the *behavior constraint approach* views high density as aversive because it may lead to reduced behavioral freedom (e.g., fewer behavioral choices, more interference). Thus, whether or not we'll experience negative effects depends on what we want to do and whether high density constrains us. Finally, the *ecological model* assumes that high density can have negative consequences since it may result in insufficient resources for people in the setting. Resources are broadly defined and include anything from materials to roles. When density causes them to become insufficient, negative effects occur (Figures 7–12 and 7–13).

Not surprisingly, additional explanations have been offered to account for density and its negative effects. Baum and Valins (1977), for exam-

Figure 7–13. Overload models predict that when the amount and rate of stimulation occasioned by high density exceeds our ability to deal with it, negative effects occur. The situation pictured above (entering a circus) lasted only for a short time, but imagine being confined under such conditions for a week! (Sherry Fisher)

Figure 7–12. An unfortunate situation—the necessity to wait in line to use bathroom facilities because of crowds. Both behavior constraint models and ecological models would predict that this would be aversive. (Sherry Fisher)

ple, built upon an overload framework in proposing that negative consequences are caused by *unwanted interaction*. While too many contacts (overload) may be distressing, it is not always the case—under some circumstances, a large number of social interactions may be bearable or even fun. However, when these interactions are unwanted, or when one cannot predict whether they will be wanted or not, problems may be more likely. Thus, difficulties in regulating when, where, and with whom one may interact can lead to a surfeit of unwanted interactions and, eventually, to stress. In support of this, Baum and Valins (1977) consistently found crowded dormitory residents complaining about unwanted or unregulable contacts with neighbors.

Another explanation, the *behavioral interference formulation*, asserts that when inadequate space or large numbers of people interfere with goal-directed behavior, negative effects are experienced (e.g., Schopler & Stockdale, 1977). This explanation is loosely derived from the behavior constraint model discussed earlier, and has been supported by studies showing that interference does increase reported crowding and negative effects (Heller *et al.*, 1977; Sundstrom, 1975). Unwanted interaction can be included here as well, as Schopler and Stockdale point out that it can disrupt or prevent goal achievement. Further, the presence of social structure, or rules governing conduct (which reduce interference) has been found to reduce negative consequences (Baum & Koman, 1976; Schopler & Walton, 1974) and studies have directly linked aspects of interference or the importance of blocked goals to the intensity of stress (McCallum *et al.*, 1979; Morasch, Groner, & Keating, 1979; Schopler, McCallum, & Rusbult, 1978).

So, we now have five different potential critical determinants of density leading to negative effects (see Table 7–4). There is no doubt that all of them are relevant and that there are also other ways of looking at high density. How can we resolve these competing explanations? Or, must we resolve them so much as combine them into a more unified perspective? Bear in mind that some are more theoretically sophisticated, such as the overload or ecological models, but that these are far more speculative and untested than the constraint, interference, or unwanted interaction models. However, despite the fact that the different formulations were presented as competing with one another, it is probably true that too much stimulation, too many constraints on our behavior, excessive unwanted social contact, interference, and resource inappropriateness *each* account for some negative effects of high density (Baum & Fisher, 1977).

More recent conceptual efforts have focused on more parsimonious explanations for why high

Table 7–4. SUMMARY OF THEORETICAL PERSPECTIVES ON CROWDING*

Conceptual Approach	Critical Cause(s) of Crowding	Primary Coping Mechanisms	Reference
Social overload	Excessive social contact; too much social stimulation	Escape stimulation; prioritize input and disregard low priorities; withdrawal	Milgram, 1970; Saegert, 1978
Behavior constraint	Reduced behavioral freedom	Aggressive behavior; leave situation; coordinate actions with others	Stokols, 1972; Sundstrom, 1978
Unwanted interaction	Excessive unregulable or unwanted contact with others	Withdrawal; organization of small primary groups	Baum & Valins, 1977; Calhoun, 1970
Interference	Disruption or blocking of goal-directed behavior	Create structure; aggression; escape	Schopler & Stockdale, 1977; Sundstrom, 1978
Ecological	Scarcity of resources	Defense of group boundaries; exclusion of outsiders	Barker, 1968; Wicker, 1980

*Adapted from Stokols (1976).

density has the effects that it does. Two related notions, control and privacy, have been used in this light because they cross the lines of the models in Table 7–4 and unify several theoretical currents. We will discuss the control perspective in some detail here; we discuss privacy elsewhere.

As you will recall from Chapter 4, *perceived control* is a potent mediator of stress. When we believe that we can control a stressor or other aspects of a situation, the aversiveness of stress appears to be reduced. It follows that even if no other problems are apparent, losing or not having control can also be stressful. Several researchers have proposed that high density can cause a loss of control (or prevent someone from ever having control) and that this loss of control is the primary mechanism by which density causes stress (Baron & Rodin, 1978; Baum & Valins, 1979; Schmidt & Keating, 1979; Sherrod & Cohen, 1979).

Can we really explain the negative effects of high density as a loss of control? The answer is "yes," even though at times the explanation seems a little strained. Some explanations fit well—Baum and Valins' notion of *unwanted interaction* is a control-based perspective. Negative effects are the result of contact that is too frequent, which makes control over when, where, and with whom people interact difficult to maintain. As a result, interactions become unpredictable and frequently unwanted. The *behavior constraint* notion is also control-based, describing high density as eliminating behavioral options and reducing freedom to behave as one might like. For example, having inadequate space can constrain our behavior by making it impossible to control the nature of interaction with others. We can generally control the degree of intimacy in one-on-one interactions by adjusting the distance we stand from people, but in a very crowded room, we may find ourselves with no choice—we must stand close to people whether we know them well or not. In this manner, we can lose control over intimacy regulation.

Interference can also be viewed as a threat to control as our attempts to achieve one or another goal are repeatedly blocked or disrupted. And re-source problems, the focus of *ecological* models, can limit our choices and restrict our ability to exercise control. To some extent, all of these "consequences" of high density that have been related to negative effects do cause a reduction in control. But, is there any direct research evidence for the relation between density and control?

Research examining the links between high density and loss of control has taken two different tacks. The first has been to manipulate personal control (provide some subjects, and not others, with perceived control) and see if it has any effect on experience in high density settings. For example, Rodin, Solomon, and Metcalf (1978) observed subjects' response to riding in an elevator crowded with confederates of the experimenter. They observed a tendency for people to gravitate toward the elevator floor selection panel (a control panel, if you will), so they manipulated whether subjects were able to stand near it (high control condition) or not (low control condition). The results indicated that subjects standing near the panel felt better than those in a different corner. They also thought that the elevator was larger than subjects not near the panel.

A somewhat different approach was taken by Sherrod (1974). As we have seen, Glass and Singer (1972) found that noise was associated with negative aftereffects that were reduced if subjects had control over the noise. Sherrod conducted a similar study with density instead of noise. Once again, negative aftereffects were associated with stress when control was not available. Subjects who had more perceived control, on the other hand, did not exhibit negative aftereffects following exposure to high density.

Rodin *et al.* (1978) also examined high density in a laboratory, providing subjects with varying degrees of control over the setting. Those with control felt better than those without. These studies all demonstrate that control can reduce the effects of high density relative to no-control, high density experiences. They do not, however, demonstrate that high density itself has consequences similar to those associated with loss or lack of control.

However, that bit of evidence has also been reported by researchers. Rodin (1976) conducted two studies in field settings and found that chronically high residential density was associated with helplessness-like behavior. Learned helplessness is a syndrome in which people who are exposed to uncontrollable settings learn that they cannot control the setting, and hence stop trying to do so (Seligman, 1975). This manifests itself in reduced motivation and cognitive activity. Rodin's subjects, who were children and adolescents, showed symptoms of helplessness that were associated with density in their homes (see the box below).

Baum and Valins (1977) also found symptoms of helplessness among people exposed to high density in their residential environment over prolonged periods. More recently, this has been directly linked to perceptions of control in residential settings (Baum, Aiello, & Calesnick, 1978; Baum & Gatchel, 1981). As people relinquished their beliefs that they could control these settings, their behavior became increasingly like that associated with helplessness.

All of these studies taken together suggest that control is involved in negative high density effects. When control is available, high density has less impact on people than when it is not available. Further, chronic exposure to high density appears to be associated with learned helplessness. Additional evidence of these links is

---

CROWDING IN THE HOME AND IN THE SCHOOLS

Imagine yourself growing up in a small apartment with five other people who are continuously interacting with each other and with you. With so many people in so little space, you may grow up to feel the world is a complex place in which you have little power to influence events (cf. Altman, 1975; Baron & Rodin, 1978). What consequences does this have? Seligman (1975) has demonstrated that when we come to believe we cannot control our outcomes by responding appropriately (as may result from living in high density conditions), we no longer perform effectively in a number of situations. This syndrome is called "learned helplessness."

Two interesting and provocative studies by Rodin (1976) demonstrated the relationship between residential density and susceptibility to "learned helplessness." In her first experiment, Rodin hypothesized and found that children who lived in high density conditions were less likely than those in low density to try to control the administration of rewards they were to receive. In a second experiment, she exposed subjects from both groups to an initial frustrating task on which responses and outcomes were noncontingent. Rodin found that children from high density homes did significantly worse on a subsequent task for which outcomes were contingent. Thus, it appears that home density is an important determinant of both the use of control and performance after frustrating noncontingent reward situations.

Besides the home environment, what other settings may be sources of "learned helplessness" training? One important culprit may be the schools. Baron and Rodin (1978) suggest that as classroom size increases, learned helplessness training begins to occur. They argue that larger classroom sizes lead to lower student expectations for control of reinforcement, because teacher feedback concerning student work becomes less discriminative. For example, as class size goes up, individualized student-teacher interactions decrease, and generalized (rather than individualized) praise and criticism increase. Clearly, such conditions could lead to a state of learned helplessness and its negative consequences for performance. If Baron and Rodin's hypothesis proves to be correct, it could have a profound impact on our educational system. What have your experiences been in small and large classes?

needed, but it is fairly clear that the effect of density is at least partly determined by people's perceptions of control.

A Summary Perspective on High Density Effects.

Given that high density involves an array of potentially disturbing elements (e.g., loss of control, overstimulation), how can we explain the fact that it only sometimes influences our behavior? Many researchers (Desor, 1972; Loo, 1973; Rapoport, 1975; Stokols, 1972) have addressed themselves to this issue. A conceptualization of the effects of density on humans is presented in Figure 7–14. As you will notice, the conceptual scheme is a special case of the general environment–behavior model presented in Chapter 3.

In Phase I of our conceptualization, an important distinction is made that explains why high density is sometimes stressful (leading to negative effects) and other times is not. In terms of this distinction (first proposed by Stokols, 1972), *high density* is viewed as a physical state involving potential inconveniences (e.g., loss of control, stimulus overload, lack of behavioral freedom, lack of resources), which may or may not be salient to a person in the situation. Whether or not these conditions are salient depends on: (1) individual differences between people (sex, personality, age); (2) situational conditions (time in the setting, presence of other stressors); and (3) social conditions (relationships between people, intensity of interaction). If the negative aspects of high density are not salient, the environment is perceived as being within an optimal range, homeostasis is maintained, and no negative effects occur. If the constraints of high density are salient, *crowding* occurs. Crowding is conceptualized as a psychological state characterized by stress and having motivational properties (e.g., it elicits attempts to reduce discomfort).

Having incorporated the density-crowding distinction into our model, we turn now to Phase II, which specifies the consequences of the psychological state of crowding. As in other stressful situations (see Chapter 4), it is assumed that the stress associated with crowding involves coping responses that are directed toward reducing stress (e.g., withdrawal). Interestingly, the overload, behavior constraint, and ecological approaches, as well as the others, each predict qualitatively different types of coping responses (see Table 7–4 for a description of these varying responses). However, the sequential links specified in our model between stress, coping, adaptation, and aftereffects conform to the general environment–behavior model found in Chapter 3. It is assumed that when coping is successful in handling stress, adaptation or adjustment occurs, and the individual is less likely to experience aftereffects or cumulative effects. If coping is unsuccessful, the stress continues, and the individual is extremely likely to experience aftereffects and cumulative effects (e.g., illness).

Coping is an important part of any model of crowding for two reasons. First, it is usually directed at reducing the causes or effects of crowding, and second, it is a continuous process. From the moment that crowding is first experienced or anticipated, people attempt to deal with it. These attempts are dynamic, continuously unfolding until adaptation is achieved, the crowding dissipates, or fatigue makes further coping impossible (e.g., Altman, 1975). This notion of dynamic coping underlying crowding suggests that responses to crowding change as the situation changes.

This kind of coping process has been addressed by research examining adjustments in high spatial and social density settings (Greenberg & Baum, 1979; Greenberg & Firestone, 1977). Greenberg and Firestone observed adjustments of verbal and visual behavior in settings where other forms of coping were blocked by the nature of the situation. Greenberg and Baum reported continuing adjustment and readjustment of these social behaviors among subjects who anticipated changing degrees of crowding in the session in which they were participating.

How well is our application of the general environment–behavior model to high density situations supported by relevant data? Unfortunately, most of the studies done on high density to date

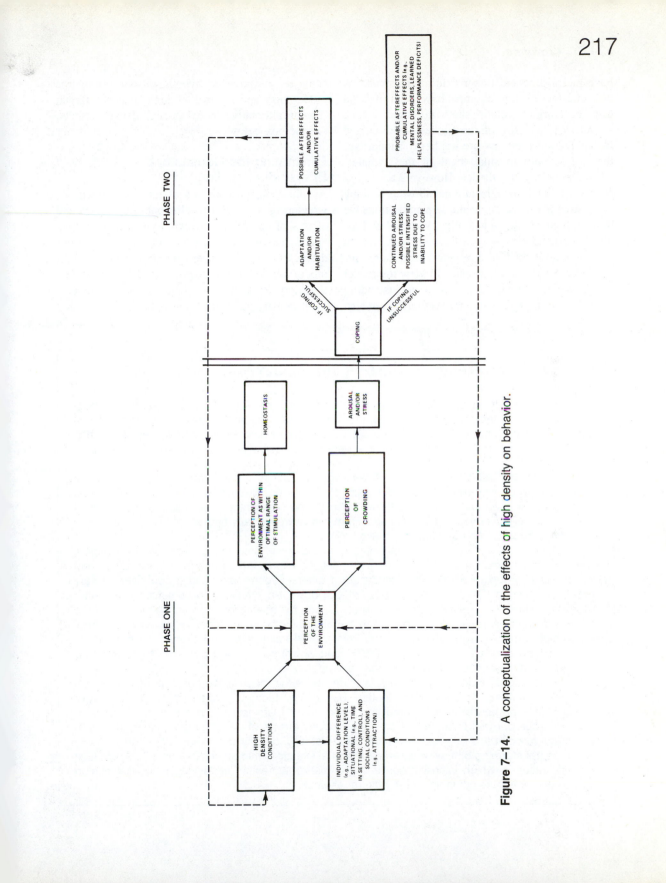

Figure 7–14. A conceptualization of the effects of high density on behavior.

have had a practical rather than a conceptual focus, and few *explicit* attempts have been made to test the various relationships proposed in the model. While many of the studies we discussed in our literature review are implicitly supportive, they apply only to small parts of the "whole" encompassed by the model. However, a few experiments which have been done allow us to draw suggestive evidence about the sequential links we have posited. Such studies (e.g., Worchel & Teddlie, 1976) support many of the assertions, but we will have to await future research for a more precise test. At this point, we should view the model as a tentative but viable means of understanding the effects of high density on behavior. It can also serve as a source of hypotheses concerning the moderation and control of high density effects. (For an alternative model of high density effects, see the box below.)

Eliminating the Causes and Effects of Crowding

At this point in our discussion, you might be wondering how we can eliminate the causes and effects of crowding. We will explore two distinct approaches to this question: (1) using predictions derived from our general environment–behavior model applied to high density; and (2) employing a variety of alternative strategies (e.g., government density guidelines, birth control).

AN ALTERNATIVE APPROACH: THE DENSITY-INTENSITY MODEL

We have summarized a model that distinguishes between density and crowding and that specifies a number of factors that may cause crowding and its attendant effects. Freedman (1975) takes another position, which has been a source of great debate among environmental psychologists. In general, he does not support the density-crowding distinction accepted by most researchers.

He also argues that density intensifies reactions that would occur in any case in a particular situation. High density heightens the importance of other people and magnifies our reactions to them. Thus, for Freedman, high density will intensify the pleasantness of positive situations and intensify the negativeness of aversive ones. From this viewpoint, any number of factors can cause a negative reaction in a high density situation.

In his intensification notion, Freedman has provided a link between crowding and *contagion*, which is said to occur when the behaviors or emotions expressed by one person rapidly spread throughout a group of people. In a study using different room sizes and group sizes to vary density, Freedman, Birsky, and Cavoukian (1980) observed reactions to humorous films. After viewing the films, a confederate began to applaud, and the spread of this reaction throughout the group was noted. As one would expect from the intensification notion, contagion was more extensive in high density groups. Freedman and Perlick (1979) similarly found intensification of contagion with high density; and Freedman (1975) and Schiffenbauer and Schiavo (1975) reported additional evidence consistent with the general model.

There is no doubt that among the effects of density is the magnification of response to various situational variables. At baseball or football games, excitement is often intensified by larger crowds, while negativity may be amplified if the home team loses and the drive home is in bumper-to-bumper traffic. Yet, this is only one of many effects of density. Freedman *et al.* (1980) are careful to point this out, and it remains clear that high density can exert independent effects as well as transforming otherwise pleasant or neutral situations into unpleasant ones. Identification of those cases in which intensification is the primary mechanism underlying response to high density and when it is not is an area for future research.

Predictions from the General Environment–Behavior Model Applied to High Density. One extremely valuable feature of this model is that it provides a framework for speculation and research about how to moderate the causes and effects of crowding. This can be of great conceptual and applied significance. As you recall, the model specifies that individual differences among people, situational conditions, and social conditions determine whether or not high density is perceived as ''crowding.'' Research has supported this assertion. We will briefly discuss representative individual differences, situational conditions, and social conditions found to affect our reactions to high density.

Identifying *individual difference* variables that determine whether high density is experienced as crowding is of practical value, since it allows us to select those individuals who will be least sensitive to the constraints of limited space. For example, we know that in a variety of situations, males are more apt to experience crowding than females, and we have suggested several explanations for this. Preferences for the amount of personal space one desires also vary and appear to affect the degree to which crowding is experienced. For example, Aiello *et al*. (1977) found that subjects with preferences for large interpersonal distances were more adversely affected in a high density setting than were subjects with smaller distance preferences. Those who liked to sit far away from people showed greater physiological arousal, discomfort, and poorer task performance than did people who preferred to sit closer. Dooley (1974) also found evidence of personal space-based differences. However, Staff (1976) did not find evidence that ''appropriateness'' of interpersonal distances influenced mood under high spatial density conditions.

Personality characteristics also moderate our reactions to high density. It has been found that internals (who feel they control their fate) display a higher threshold of crowding than externals (who feel events are controlled by outside forces) (Schopler & Walton, 1974; Schopler *et al*., 1978). The primary problems encountered in high

density settings may also affect the ways in which individual differences are important. For example, Baum *et al*. (1982) found that people who screen themselves from interaction and organize their surroundings were better able to cope with social density than were people who did not screen themselves. One would expect that this variable would be less important when spatial problems were paramount.

Of course, these differences were found for American subjects and may not hold across other cultures. In Japan, neuroticism, introversion, and self-esteem have been related to crowding (Iwata, 1979). There may be important cross-cultural differences in reactions to high density. The personal space literature (see Chapter 6), sociological-correlational studies (Sundstrom, 1978), and work on privacy (Altman, 1975) suggest that future research will reveal such cultural differences.

A final individual difference variable that has been linked to reactions to high density is one's adaptation level (from past experience under high density conditions). A number of investigators have hypothesized that people with a history of high density living are less likely to experience crowding in a novel situation than are people with a history of isolation. For example, it has been found that the Japanese, residents of Hong Kong, and the Logoli (all of whom live under extremely high density) have developed social mechanisms that may be viewed as adaptive for high density living. While several studies (Eoyang, 1974; Wohlwill & Kohn, 1973) support this hypothesis, Paulus and his colleagues (1975) found that the longer an inmate was imprisoned, the lower was his or her tolerance for crowding. Thus, the relationship between adaptation level and the experience of crowding may be seen as suggestive only. The next box describes another individual difference variable affecting reactions to high density.

In addition to being moderated by individual difference variables, our reactions to high density are also affected by *situational conditions*. An important situational condition is the degree of control we have. Complementing those we discussed earlier, several additional studies have found that

TELEVISION VS. OUTDOOR LEISURE: IMPACT ON CROWDING

As we have seen, a number of variables can influence the ways in which crowding affects us. In a field study of residents of public housing in Edmonton, Canada, Gillis (1979) found evidence of life style influence on crowding. People who enjoyed outdoor leisure activities—people who liked to cook out on a grill, go on picnics, sunbathe, and so on—were more likely to experience crowding in dense buildings than were residents who preferred other activities. Individuals who spent much of their leisure time away from home or watching television, on the other hand, appeared to be less susceptible to crowding stress. Life styles that increase contacts (or likely contacts) between neighbors are more likely to engender feelings of crowding in dense settings than are life styles that decrease the likelihood of social contact.

allowing people increased control over a situation leads to less perceived crowding (Langer & Saegert, 1977) and to fewer negative effects (Baum & Fisher, 1977; Langer & Saegert, 1977; Sherrod, 1974). The applied potential for introducing control in high density situations is great. For example, providing individuals who live in conditions of high density with training that enhances control (e.g., giving pointers about how to share space and insure privacy) may help alleviate crowding and its negative effects.

Other situational conditions may also affect our reactions to high density. The relationship between time under high density and crowding is somewhat unclear, but it is probably fair to suggest that the longer the period of confinement, the more aversive the response (Aiello *et al.*, 1975; Ross *et al.*, 1973). Of course, it is recognized that very prolonged confinement may affect one's adaptation level, and thus may become less problematical. Such situational factors as whether we are in a primary environment (like a home) or a secondary environment (like a restaurant), and the extent to which other stressors, such as noise, are involved also affect crowding. When we are in a primary environment (Stokols, 1976, 1978; Stokols, Ohlig, & Resnick, 1979) and when other stressors are operating (Sundstrom, 1978), we may be more likely to experience crowding. Finally, in terms of activities, there is suggestive evidence that we are more likely to experience

crowding when engaged in work than when engaged in recreation (Cohen, Sladen, & Bennett, 1975).

In addition to individual differences and situational conditions, *social conditions* can be manipulated to affect whether or not we are crowded. These are variables that make up the social "climate" of a high density situation, such as the degree of friendship and the level of social interference and interaction. For example, our relationship with the people we're with may determine how crowded we feel: Less crowding is experienced with liked rather than disliked others (Fisher, 1974) and with acquaintances than with strangers (Cohen *et al.*, 1975). To the extent that we experience social interference (interruptions) by others or excessive proximity or immediacy (too direct eye contact or body orientation) (Sundstrom, 1975), crowding is more likely. Finally, crowding is more often experienced in unstructured task situations than in structured ones (Baum & Koman, 1976).

High density within primary groups (e.g., families) has repeatedly shown fewer effects than it has in other groups—when density *within* apartment units is examined, for example, it appears to be negligible as a factor associated with illness or behavioral difficulties (e.g., Giel & Ormel, 1977). Degree of acquaintance and relative position of an individual in a group's dominance hierarchy also affect crowding: the presence of friends or the possession of high status tends to reduce the aversiveness of large numbers of people or cramped spaces (Arkkelin, 1978).

The importance of social conditions in determining crowding can be illustrated by considering the effects of overassignment of student residents in dormitory rooms. We have referred to these studies several times in this chapter—studies of the consequences of having three students live in a room designed for only two. Initial study of this phenomenon (Aiello *et al.*, 1975; Baron *et al.*, 1975) revealed that "tripling" of roommates was associated with negative mood, increased health complaints, and suppressed task performance. Subsequent study revealed similar evidence of stress in tripled rooms (Karlin, Epstein, & Aiello, 1978).

These kinds of findings made sense, given the increased difficulties in sharing resources, coordinating activities, and achieving privacy that were created by the addition of a third roommate. Yet the question remained—was this a problem of too many people or too little space? Baum *et al.* (1979) reasoned that it was neither. Going back to the social psychological literature on groups, they found confirmation of a notion that many of you already know—three-person groups are very unstable and susceptible to coalition formation such that two people get together and exclude the third (e.g., Kelley & Arrowood, 1960). Given this, it seemed possible that the primary problem was not that there were too many roommates or not enough space. Instead, it was that there were three roommates, one of whom was likely to feel left out and, as a result, have less control over the shared bedroom. This "isolate," when compared with the other two roommates, would have less input into how the room was arranged and used, have greater difficulty achieving privacy, and would feel more crowded.

Research examining the formation of coalitions in these situations has provided support for this interpretation (Aiello, Baum, & Gormley, 1981; Baum *et al.*, 1979; Reddy *et al.*, 1982). These studies indicated that students living in tripled rooms were likely to feel left out by roommates,

and that those who felt like isolates also reported more problems related to using the room, and felt more crowded. Tripled residents who did not feel left out reported experiences and moods more like those students living in doubled rooms.

An extension of this logic examined the effects of tripled and quadrupled rooms (Reddy *et al.*, 1982). If the instability of three-person groups was responsible for these effects, one would expect the residents of four-person rooms to feel less crowded than residents of three-person rooms. If, on the other hand, the primary problem is the absolute number of roommates, the quadrupled rooms would be associated with greater crowding. Results indicated that isolates were more likely in the tripled rooms and that nonisolate residents of tripled rooms reported experiences similar to those reported by quadrupled residents. Isolates, on the other hand, reported more problems with crowding than either of the other groups. From this kind of research, we can see the importance of considering social processes in attempting to understand crowding.

Architectural Mediators of Crowding. Now that we have tried to provide you with a feeling for some of the conditions that moderate the experience of crowding, it should be interesting to consider how we can modify existing environments or plan new ones so that crowding is less of a problem. (For a complete discussion of the design process, see Chapter 9.) What would you do if you were a planner charged with evaluating (and possibly modifying) some of the plans for a building in terms of the level of crowding that residents are likely to experience? First, you'd probably assess objective physical conditions (i.e., space allotted to each resident) in terms of adequacy for the type of functions to be performed in that space. Next, you'd estimate how spatial needs would be affected by anticipated situational conditions (e.g., how well they could be expected to get along), and individual differences (e.g., adaptation level). From your evaluation of objective physical space plus situational, social, and individual difference conditions, you'd have an idea of how much of a crowding problem there would be. If you anticipated insufficient space, you could institute some of the architectural modifications we'll describe below.

How can environments be designed or modified to alleviate crowding and its consequences? A number of studies suggest alternatives that can be incorporated into existing structures or planned into new ones. For example, greater ceiling height is associated with less crowding (Savinar, 1975). Rectangular rooms seem to elicit less crowding than square rooms of the same area (Desor, 1972), and rooms that contain visual escapes (e.g., windows and doors) are rated as less crowded than areas without such escapes. Clearly, such features would be fairly difficult to change in a structure that has already been built. In terms of more feasible modifications, placement of activities in the center rather than in a corner or along a wall elicits less crowding (Dabbs, Fuller, & Carr, 1973), and a number of studies (Baum, Reiss, & O'Hara, 1974; Desor, 1972) provide suggestive evidence that adding flexible partitions in rooms lessens feelings of crowding. It has been found that brightness (provided by wall and accent colors or appropriate light sources) leads to less perceived crowding, and that the presence of visual distractors (e.g., pictures on walls, advertisements on transportation vehicles) leads to more perceived space (Baum & Davis, 1976; Worchel & Teddlie, 1976). For a discussion of whether it is worse to design a room having high social or high spatial density, see the box on p. 223.

Interventions in High Density Settings.

While many intervention strategies can be derived from models of crowding, only a few have actually been implemented. Some focus on dealing directly with the negative mood created by high density—treating the consequences of crowding. Others have attempted to provide skills or information, or to modify high density environments in ways that would help people to cope, thereby preventing or reducing crowding.

Karlin *et al.* (1979) reported a study which

sought to reduce the anxiety and arousal associated with crowded transportation settings. Three therapeutic interventions were used to treat subjects in a laboratory analogue of transportation settings. Subjects were given training in *muscle relaxation, cognitive reappraisal* (subjects were told that they could improve their mood by focusing on the positive aspects of the situation), or *imagery* (subjects were instructed to concentrate on a pleasant, distracting pastoral image). A fourth group received initial instructions to relax, but were given no other training.

Responses to crowding among subjects in these four groups provided mixed support for the value of therapeutic intervention. Subjects given cognitive reappraisal instructions showed more positive responses to the setting than did subjects in the other groups. The effectiveness of muscle relaxation and imagery treatments in reducing the impact of high density was less marked.

A second form of intervention has involved what is often referred to as providing heightened *cognitive control*. Cognitive control refers to the increased sense of predictability or controllability that we gain when we are given prior warning or information about a situation. In medical settings, for example, providing patients with information about how they will feel, what will happen, or what they can do about their feelings *before* surgery or aversive medical examinations can reduce distress and complications later on (e.g., Johnson & Leventhal, 1974). When behavioral control is limited, providing such information increases a person's sense of control, and, as we noted in Chapter 4, perceived control can reduce the aversiveness of stress.

Langer and Saegert (1977) reported an experiment in which information about crowding was given to some subjects before they entered grocery stores varying in actual density. This information focused on how they would feel if the store was crowded. Some subjects did not receive any information, and all subjects were given a task to perform that required them to move around the store and find a number of items. The results suggested that when density was higher,

SOCIAL VS. SPATIAL DENSITY: WHICH IS MORE AVERSIVE?

Should a designer faced with the unenviable choice worry more about creating a design with high social density or high spatial density? Research on high density suggests some subtle differences in the effects of high social and high spatial density. Based on a careful analysis, researchers have tentatively concluded that manipulations of social density are more aversive than manipulations of spatial density (cf. Baum & Valins, 1979; Paulus, 1977). Specifically, they found that high social density will produce negative effects more consistently than high spatial density and that while social density manipulations are *generally* aversive, spatial density manipulations are often problematical only to males in same-sex groups (Paulus, 1977). (Go back and see how many of the sex differences we discussed are the result of spatial density manipulations.)

Why might an overabundance of others be more distressing than too little space? The answer is unclear, but there are some hypotheses. One explanation put forth by Baum and Valins suggests that people are more immediately aware of problems created by large numbers of others than by spatial limitations. For example, the loss of control that results when too many people are in a room is frequently more serious than that caused by being in too small a room. What are the theoretical consequences of the assertion that social and spatial density may affect us differently? While we should not draw the conclusion that the effects of spatial limitations are inconsequential, we should develop predictive frameworks that account for the differences in the two manipulations. Several investigators (Baron & Rodin, 1978; Baum & Koman, 1976) have begun to evolve such a set of predictions.

performance on the task was poorer. In addition, Langer and Saegert found that subjects who had been given prior information about crowding performed better on the task and reported a more positive emotional experience in the store than did subjects who did not receive information. Having information about how they might feel allowed subjects to better select appropriate coping strategies and to behave more confidently (Langer & Saegert, 1977).

This finding has been replicated in both laboratory and field settings (Baum, Fisher, & Solomon, 1981; Fisher & Baum, 1980; Paulus & Matthews, 1980). These studies have suggested other mechanisms by which providing information may heighten one's sense of control, but the basic finding remains the same: Increasing one's sense of control in a high density setting reduces the aversive impact of crowding.

Additional strategies for dealing with high density have been examined. One is preventive in nature, seeking to eliminate the causes of crowding before they are experienced. Baum and Davis (1980), for example, reported a successful architectural intervention in high density dormitories (see box on page 277). By altering the arrangement of interior dormitory space, they were able to prevent residents from experiencing crowding stress. Other strategies are sure to arise. What is important, then, is to understand that interventions into high density settings can be effective if they consider the specific dynamics of the situation they are addressing.

A LOOK TO THE FUTURE

Given a constant level of density, we know we can moderate crowding by selecting for individual differences and by varying situational, social, and architectural conditions. An alternative way to alleviate crowding, which should be an important future goal, is to control the level of population density itself. One means of accomplishing this would be strict government "density guidelines" and "space standards." These are particularly important in areas in which the government has direct authority, such as the construction of prisons, low-income housing, and schools. However, standards might also apply to private dwellings and working places. At present, most federal and local regulations concerning acceptable levels of density are not stringent enough, and even these are not rigidly enforced. Since it has been shown that the public often wants to improve environmental conditions, but government fails to respond (cf. Wall, 1973), it will probably take intense public pressure to bring about necessary improvements.

A second way to insure lower population density is through attitude and behavior change on an individual level. Considering the destructive potential of overpopulation, perhaps it is time to rethink many of our beliefs concerning proper family size. Changes in population growth in the United States suggest that many of us are doing this. However, in other nations there are still tremendous annual increases in population. In terms of behavior change, it is important to seek ways of decreasing the rate of unwanted and illegitimate births. One means of accomplishing this is through the appropriate use of birth control. The importance of birth control is underscored by data showing that most unmarried American couples initially having intercourse use no contraceptive devices (Eastman, 1972) and the finding that over three-quarters of young, sexually active females have "almost never" used any birth control method (Zelnick & Kanter, 1974). Other social psychological research has focused on how to make purchasing and using birth control devices less psychologically stigmatizing (Fisher, Fisher, & Byrne, 1977).

CHAPTER SUMMARY

Considerations of global overpopulation make the study of high density effects particularly important. This area of investigation has become increasingly popular and has included research with both human and animal populations. Two types of density manipulations are commonly used:

varying *spatial density* (in which space is manipulated and group size held constant), and varying *social density* (in which group size is manipulated and space is constant). With animals, it appears that the physiological and behavioral effects of high density are almost uniformly negative. It has been found that animals experience changes in body organs and glandular malfunctions that affect birth rate and also experience severe disruptions of social and maternal behaviors. A number of conceptual schemes have been developed to account for animal reactions to density.

Human reactions to high density depend more on the particular situation. While density doesn't have a totally consistent negative effect on humans, it leads to aversive consequences on a wide variety of dimensions. Concerning its effect on feeling states, high density leads to negative affect (especially in males) and to higher physiological arousal. There is also some evidence that it is associated with illness. In terms of its effects on social behavior, high density has been found to result in less liking for others (especially in males), and it is associated with withdrawal from interaction. Also, there is suggestive evidence that high density leads to aggression and to lower incidence of prosocial behavior. Finally, for task performance, it leads to decrements for complex but not for simple tasks, and it may also be associated with aftereffects.

Overall, high density causes (1) immediate effects on behavior; (2) coping responses; and (3) aftereffects. A number of explanatory schemes (e.g., overload, behavior constraint, and ecological models) attempt to explain why high density is aversive, and each stresses a different element of density as critical. Why doesn't high density always lead to negative consequences? A model that differentiates between high density and crowding accounts for this finding. It is suggested that while high density contains negative aspects, it is individual difference and situational and social conditions that determine whether these are salient and whether "crowding" occurs. The model specifies a progression of effects that follow when crowding is experienced and also offers ways to eliminate the causes and effects of crowding.

Suggested Projects

1. In our discussion about eliminating the causes and effects of high density, we stated that varying situational and social conditions moderate perceived crowding. A simple procedure used by Desor (1972) allows us to verify this relationship and many more that have been highlighted throughout the chapter. The procedure is the "model room technique." First, get a shoe box, or a somewhat larger size carton. Modify it a bit so that it looks something like a room. (You may be creative and make elaborate windows, draperies, and so on if you like, but be sure to leave the top off.) Next, take a large number of clothespins, small blocks, pieces of styrofoam, or the like, which can be modified to stand up and to look something like people. Now you are ready to start doing "model room" experiments.

   How do you begin? First, decide what relationship you want to test. Let's assume you want to test the assertion that people will feel more crowded in primary environments than secondary ones. Have a willing subject imagine that the box is his or her living room (a primary environment). Tell the subject to place figures in the box up to the point at which he or she feels the room is crowded. Count the number of figures in the box, and then remove the figures. Next, tell the subject the box is a restaurant (a secondary environment) and ask him or her to place figures in the box until the space seems crowded. Determine how the number of figures placed in the box varies, depending on whether it is described as a primary or a secondary setting. You now have data concerning the "threshold" of crowding in primary and secondary environments. If you find a lower threshold of crowding in primary than in secondary environments, you may have supportive evidence for Stokols' (1976) assertion that we experience crowding more readily in a primary than in a secondary setting. Some other hypotheses to test using this procedure are listed below:

   a. Test Baum and Valins' (1977) assertion that people who live in corridor dormitories avoid social contact situations more than people who live in suite-style dormitories. (To do this, you'll need two groups of subjects, one living in corridor dormitories, the other living in suite dormitories.)
   b. Test whether different personality types have different thresholds of crowding by first administering personality tests and then relating the test results to the number of figures the subjects place in the box.

2. By comparing other people's reaction in crowded and uncrowded natural settings, you can get a feeling for how high density affects you. Select a "real world" setting that varies over time in the number of people who are present. For example, a bus or train that becomes more crowded as it approaches the end of the line would be ideal. Your school cafeteria or library, which vary in terms of density over time, would also work. Then, pick a number of dimensions (e.g, friendliness of people toward one another, eye contact, defensive postures, object play) to observe for behavioral changes as population density increases. Compare how people respond on these dimensions in high and low density situations. By employing this procedure in a variety of settings, you can gain firsthand experience about how people react to high density.

3. We cited some evidence showing that people who like each other respond more favorably to high density than people who dislike each other. One reaction to high

density confinement with a disliked other should be a variety of coping strategies. Check whether high density with a disliked other leads to coping by making an informal study of residents on your domitory floor. First, list five residents who like their roommates, and five who don't. Look into the rooms of both groups, and note the arrangement of furniture. If confinement with a disliked other leads to coping, furniture should be arranged so as to block interaction and insure privacy.

4. Make several comparisons concerning environmentally destructive behavior between high-rise and low-rise (i.e., high and low density) dormitories on your campus. Compare grafitti, damage to furniture and public telephones, and so on to assess whether more aggressive behavior accompanies higher levels of density.

8 The City

INTRODUCTION

Imagine yourself watching television coverage of a monumental press conference taking place in New York City. It seems that after more than 350 years New Yorkers have decided that Peter Minuit's agreement to buy New York from a tribe of Indians may not have been fair and equitable. In an attempt to remedy the situation, they have located the present chief of the tribe, who is working as a riveter on a new skyscraper in midtown Manhattan. The cameras zoom in on the following conversation between the chief and three officials of New York City, who have climbed up the girders and are speaking to the Indian while he eats his lunch.

"Chief, we're here on behalf of the City of New York and we understand that your ancestors sold the island of Manhattan for 24 dollars."

The chief said, "That's true. The Dutch drove a hard bargain in those days. We were robbed."

"Well," said the second official, "we New Yorkers have always felt very bad about it, and we want to make it up to you. How would your people like to buy the place back?"

"For how much?" the chief asked suspiciously.

"Twenty-four dollars."

"That's a lot of money," the chief said.

"We're willing to throw the Bronx, Brooklyn, Queens, and Staten Island in the package."

The chief stared down at the traffic jam below him.

"I don't think my people would be interested," he said.

"If it's a question of financing," the third official said, "you could give us four dollars down and four dollars a month."

Smoke and smog kept drifting up, and the chief wiped his eyes with a red bandanna. "It isn't a question of the money. We just don't want it."

The first official said, "Chief, this is a golden opportunity for your people. Not only would you get all the land, but you'd have Lincoln Center, the Metropolitan Museum of Art, the Verrazano Bridge, and Shea Stadium."

The chief said, "White man speaks with forked tongue. Who gets the subway?"

"Why you do, of course."

"The deal's off," the chief said.

While they were talking, police sirens sounded and three men down below came running out of a bank, guns blazing. . . .

The first official said, "It's obvious you don't know a good thing when you see it. We're sorry we even brought it up."

The three officials started their long climb down. Waiting nervously at the bottom was the mayor.

"What did he say?" the mayor wanted to know.

"No dice."

"I was afraid of that," he said. "Well, I'll have to think of something else."*

Obviously, this story by humorist Art Buchwald doesn't portray cities very favorably, and we should note that urban areas have many positive aspects. As we will see in this chapter, urban life can offer very satisfying interpersonal and social relationships with others. And nowhere is there such diversity, novelty, intensity, and choice as in the city. Cities provide an immense variety of cultural and recreational facilities, such as concert halls, museums, sports stadiums, educational facilities, and all types of restaurants. Further, there is a much wider variety of services available to the average city dweller than to the resident of a small town. A quotation from the *Wall Street Journal,* which describes a unique *official* service offered by the city of New York makes this point in style. The paper asked, "How do you get rid of a dead elephant?" It answered its question as follows: "Bring it to New York: City's offal truck will take expired rhinoceroses, yaks, and mules off your hands" (October 3, 1972).

One way to think of the city is as a place characterized by *multiple and contrasting realities.* Within the city both ends of almost any continuum (e.g., excitement and boredom; safety and danger) can and do exist simultaneously. Cities can potentially pull people apart and bring them together, yield opportunities for us and in other ways constrain our behavior. There are good and bad, rich and poor, isolation and integration within the city's limits. Urban life is good for some people and bad for others, optimal for some activities but not for others (Krupat, 1982).

However *you* choose to view cities, they are an environmental feature that you will probably have to contend with throughout your life. In fact, cities and their suburban outgrowths are where most of us live. Today more than 70 percent of the population of the United States lives in small or large metropolitan areas (US Department of Commerce, 1981), compared with 6 percent in 1800 (Gottman, 1966). In 1850, only 2 percent of the world's population lived in metropolitan areas with over 100,000 population. Today, 24 percent do, and by the end of the century, 40 percent will live in such areas (Davis, 1972). Further, there were only seven metropolitan areas in the world with over 500,000 population in 1800, 42 in 1900, and there are more than 200 today (Gottman, 1966). All of this has caused Davis (1973, p. 5) to conclude, "In all industrial nations it is the rural population which is abnormal, not the cities."

In this chapter, we'll discuss cities in some detail. Our working definition of cities is a slightly modified version of that proposed by Proshansky (1976c). Specifically, cities are considered to be a large number of people and activities concentrated in a given geographical area for the purpose of providing the dimensions of human life we call organized society. The chapter will begin with a look at the ways in which we perceive and experience the city. Next, we'll consider some conceptual perspectives that have been proposed for understanding and predicting the effects of urban life. We will then move on to a discussion of studies on how city life affects us. Finally, we'll discuss various solutions that have been proposed to cure the ills of urban existence.

PERCEIVING AND EXPERIENCING THE CITY

Cities are masses of streets, buildings, and other structures that we all perceive differently. Some

*From Buchwald, *Son of the Great Society.* Copyright 1965, 1966 by Art Buchwald. Reprinted by permission of G. P. Putnam's Sons.

of us attend more to the longer avenues of skyscrapers, some of us more to the smaller side streets (Figure 8–1 A, B, and C). How can we explain our perception of cities? In Chapter 2 we discussed some *general* processes involved in perception, as well as a more specific type of analysis, called *cognitive mapping,* which can be applied to the question of urban perception.

Figure 8–1 A, B, and C. While the city can be quite unattractive, it can also be quite pleasant, even with the mixture of the old and the new. (Sherry Fisher)

Cognitive mapping analyzes the way in which spatial information is acquired, stored, decoded, and applied to the comprehension of the everyday physical environment (Stea, 1974). While cognitive mapping is applicable to other areas, our attention will be restricted to the perception of cities. What is a cognitive map of a city? Cognitive maps are ''cities of the mind'' that we carry around in our heads, representing the city *as we know it*. While the map-in-the-head metaphor has been criticized as being overly simplistic (cf. Kuipers, 1982), for introductory purposes it will suffice. A typical cognitive map is juxtaposed with an aerial map of the same area of Jersey City in Figure 8–2 A and B. As you will note, compared to ''reality'' the cognitive map is sketchy, incomplete, and distorted. In a sense, it is highly impressionistic, almost like a projective test reflect-

ing our views of the city. What do we use such cognitive maps for? Basically, we use them to ''find our way around'' (i.e., to identify objects and to see their spatial relationships), and as a way to code practical or emotional meaning (Lynch, 1960). In other words, cognitive maps tell us the location (distance and direction) of objects that are important to us. (For a description of how researchers elicit and ''read'' our cognitive maps, see the box on page 231.)

To the extent that our cognitive image of a city is adequate in terms of clarity and completeness, we experience a number of important benefits. First, such a map permits us the mobility we need to obtain important goods and services from a variety of sources. The more complete our map, the wider our range of behavioral options. Second, when our cognitive map is adequate, our experi-

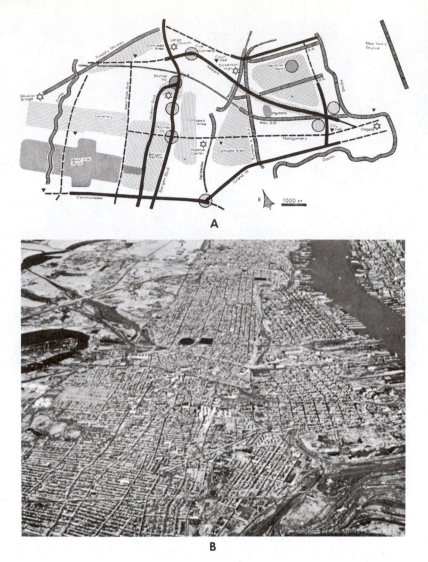

Figure 8–2 A and B.   Cognitive and aerial map of Jersey City (Lynch, K. *The image of the city:* Cambridge: M. I. T. Press, 1960.)

ences in the city will be less confusing and more meaningful, affording us a degree of emotional security.

At this point, you may be wondering how we acquire our cognitive maps. Basically, they result from a two-way process: The environment provides the basic relationships (e.g., buildings, roads, distances), and we organize them and give them meaning. Since our images are a joint prod-

uct of ourselves and our environment, there is no simple one-to-one relationship between cognitive maps and reality. Thus, if a city dweller's background makes certain aspects of the environment more important to him or her than other aspects, these will be "featured" in the cognitive map. For example, Appleyard (1976) found that city planners, who are trained to view cities in a specialized way, had cognitive maps that differed

HOW DO RESEARCHERS READ OUR COGNITIVE MAPS?

How are mental maps, which are generally "tucked away" in the depths of our minds, brought to a level of awareness by researchers who want to study them? Many techniques have been used (cf. Evans, 1980); the first of these was employed by Lynch (1960). How did Lynch manage to get inside people's heads? First, he asked city dwellers to draw a quick map of their city, as if they were making a rapid description of it to a stranger. Next, he asked them to list distinctive elements of the central district and to describe several trips through it in terms of the physical areas they passed through and their emotional reactions. Combining the data, Lynch fashioned a graphic display that he called a "cognitive map."

How can cognitive maps be analyzed? Lynch analyzed his data in terms of the presence or absence of five key elements: paths, districts, edges, nodes, and landmarks (see Chapter 2 for a description of each of these terms). Lynch derived these five features from the sketch maps drawn by subjects, and his conceptualization has been verified by Magaña (1978), using very different techniques. In addition to evaluating the presence or absence of certain features, Lynch compared the responses of subjects with those compiled by trained observers sent out into the field to record "reality." This allowed him to determine discrepancies between the real and the "imaged" environment.

How good is the methodology Lynch used? A review by Evans (1980) suggests the technique has adequate reliability. However, a number of important criticisms have been leveled against the "draw-a-map" technique. For example, it has been noted that a map drawn for a stranger might not coincide with one's own image. Further, maps may be more of a reflection of drawing ability than of one's real image (for a complete discussion of relevant problems, see Evans, 1980). To offset various limitations, additional techniques, such as identifying slides and creating models of a city, have been developed. Many of these are described in Blaut and Stea (1971), Mark (1972), Milgram *et al.* (1972), and Stea (1974), although it is beyond our scope to review them here. Some are improved versions of Lynch's technique, and others are radically different approaches.

markedly from those of local residents. The contribution of individuals and their values also accounts for why cognitive maps are composed not only of visually prominent objects but also of elements important for emotional, political, or other reasons. However, although cognitive maps are imperfect representations that vary for each person, a predominant image of a particular city generally emerges. This dominant impression consists of the "overlaps" in the images constructed by groups of individuals. Thus, while individual New Yorkers probably see their city differently, their perceptions overlap in many areas, such as Central Park, Yankee Stadium, and Harlem, and form an overall cognitive map of New York. Such an image would be quite different from a map drawn by Bostonians of their city.

Since cognitive maps are beneficial, it becomes important to understand what objective physical qualities of the urban landscape lead to maps that are relatively clear and complete. If we know which aspects of the city make it more easily mapped, this information can be used for planning and design purposes. For example, knowing which physical components afford clear imagery allows us to make "corrections" and modifications in objective physical conditions, so that the environment can be experienced in a more complete fashion. Finally, since there should be a relationship between image and activity (e.g., it is unlikely that we'll use a service in a part of town not included in our cognitive map), knowledge of which physical settings are imaged clearly could give us some ability to predict behavior.

Relationship Between Environmental Conditions and Imagery

Milgram and his associates (1972) proposed a general formula that allows us to estimate a recognition or "image" factor for any scene in the city. This formula reflects the influence of both physical factors (e.g., closeness of a building to areas frequented by the public, architectural distinctiveness of a building) and social factors (e.g., social or psychological significance of a building to the public). The formula is RECOGNITION = f (centrality to population flow × architectural and/or social distinctiveness). The general validity of this formula has been supported in a study by Appleyard (1976). However, Milgram *et al.* fail to take into account physical characteristics other than centrality and distinctiveness. De Jonge (1962) found that the formation of urban images was easiest when the street plan had a regular pattern and a dominant path. A study by Porteus (1977) revealed that when urban areas had accessible hilltop viewpoints people were more likely to form cohesive images of them (Figure 8–3 A and B). Recognition is further enhanced when the layout of an area corresponds to the activity for which it is used (Steinitz, 1968). (For a discussion of an urban area which seems to be especially difficult to image, see the box on page 234.)

The concept of *legibility* refers to how easily the parts of a city can be recognized and organized in a coherent pattern (Lynch, 1960). This concept has had an important influence on the fields of planning and architecture. Some of the research we described above suggests ways of increasing legibility. In addition, Lynch believes that easily visible landmarks and clearly bounded city districts enhance legibility. While good legibility is an asset (e.g., it can facilitate mobility, give a heightened sense of security), if urban environments are *too* legible they could become so uninteresting and boring that we wouldn't even want to explore them (Kaplan, 1973). An urban environment needs to contain sufficient novelty, challenge, and uncertainty to keep it interesting to people.

While work relating physical aspects of the city to cognitive images is important, it is also interesting to consider individual difference variables as a source of more and less adequate images. Past research has found that a variety of individual differences affect the quality of our cognitive maps. Knowledge of the influence of such factors as socioeconomic level and race on mapping is useful for design and for behavior predictions.

Socioeconomic Status and Cognitive Mapping

A number of studies have found differences in urban imagery as a function of socioeconomic status. In terms of this variable, it has been found that individuals at higher socioeconomic levels tend to include more area in their cognitive maps. In fact, a study done in Los Angeles showed that the wealthy may be familiar with up to 1000 times as much of the city as individuals of low socioeconomic status (Los Angeles Department of City Planning, 1971). Further, the cognitive maps of high socioeconomic status individuals were more accurate and more objective. Several explanations for these effects come to mind. First, there may be fewer opportunities or reasons to travel locally, or different modes of transportation (e.g., bus or subway as opposed to automobile) available to lower socioeconomic classes. In fact, it has been shown that when lower-class individuals have greater opportunity for locomotion than upper-class ones, this pattern is reversed (cf. Appleyard, 1976). Second, individuals of low socioeconomic status may have had less practice in drawing and/or using maps than those of high socioeconomic status, which might account in part for the findings. Third, they may reflect different cognitive styles (e.g., class differences in viewing the environment) (Evans, 1980). In addition to differences in the expansiveness and accuracy of cognitive maps as a function of socioeconomic status, another important distinction has been observed. High socioeconomic status city residents tend to be more involved with historical settings and areas of scenic beauty; low socioeconomic status individuals prefer settings with lots of job

Figure 8–3 A and B. Buildings that are architecturally distinctive are especially likely to be included in our cognitive images. Especially cohesive cognitive images are formed of areas that have accessible hilltop viewpoints.

opportunities and shopping. Thus, it can be seen that people's cognitive maps reflect what is most important to them (Appleyard, 1970, 1976; Goodchild, 1974).

Race and Cognitive Mapping

Unfortunately, studies relating race to perception of cities do not permit us to disentangle race from socioeconomic status, so we can't be certain which is the critical variable. One study done of Anglo, black, and Mexican-American children in Houston found that the images drawn by Anglo children were more extensive than those drawn by either of the other groups (Maurer & Baxter, 1972). Also, Anglo children were more facile at drawing maps of the city, and their neighborhood maps referred to more play spaces. These differences are difficult to interpret, since they may re-

COGNITIVE MAPS, REAL MAPS, AND SUBWAYS

Although the 4.5 million New Yorkers who ride the subway each day eventually acquire an adequate cognitive map of it, this is no easy task. The 17 million people who visit New York each year and ride the subway have an even harder time. This is because subways have many features that prevent good cognitive map formation. They are underground (allowing little visibility), lack details that allow us to distinguish one place from another, and follow quite irregular and extensive routes. With 240 miles of track, 500 stations, 27 train routes, and dozens of transfer points (Bronzaft, Dobrow, & O'Hanlon, 1976), the New York subway system presents a difficult image for a cognitive map.

Since it is reasonable to assume that subway riders have to rely on publicly observable forms of information (e.g., maps posted in stations) more than they would in other places, visual displays are quite important in guiding them on their way. In the past decade, the basic design of the official New York Subway Map has been changed six times. (The latest version of the map is presented in Figure 8–4.) To test how helpful a subway map is in assisting passengers, Bronzaft and her colleagues (1976) attempted to determine whether the information it provides can be utilized efficiently by subway riders. They asked 20 individuals to use the map to take four trips each through unfamiliar parts of the system. Their trips were rated either "acceptable" (reasonably direct) or "unacceptable" (too indirect). What were the results of the study? It was found that none of the subjects followed "acceptable" patterns for all four trips, only three followed "acceptable" patterns for three of the trips, and overall only 46 percent of the trips were "acceptable." These findings suggest a need for systematic research on how to design maps and other visual aids in areas where cognitive map formation is especially difficult.

flect socioeconomic status. It should be noted that some studies (Ladd, 1970) find no differences in cognitive mapping between blacks and Anglos. Before a definitive statement can be made about how race affects urban imagery, studies that separate out the effects of confounding variables are needed.

Gender and Cognitive Mapping

The issue of sex differences, so prominent in recent years, is reflected even in research on cognitive mapping. Most cognitive mapping studies have found no sex differences in knowledge of the environment (Evans, 1980), and when sex differences do occur, they seem to reflect differences in neighborhood exposure. For example, it has been observed that wives' maps of their local neighborhoods covered approximately twice the area as those of their husbands, but that, overall, husbands had more comprehensive schema of the neighborhood, including its environs (Orleans &

Schmidt, 1972). These findings may result from wives' spending more time and having more interactions close to home, while husbands may travel from a suburban location to work in an entirely different area. It will be interesting to see if current changes in the status of women are reflected in future cognitive mapping studies.

Relevant Experience and Cognitive Mapping

We have suggested above that our cognitive maps may be clearer and more detailed for areas we are familiar with than for those we have visited infrequently. In fact, amount of relevant experience in the environment could even be the key variable in explaining differences in urban imagery found for socioeconomic status, race, and sex (Evans, 1980). What is the *evidence* for the familiarity-imagery relationship? Saarinen (1964) explored perceptions of the Chicago Loop, as affected by individuals' familiarity with the area. He found

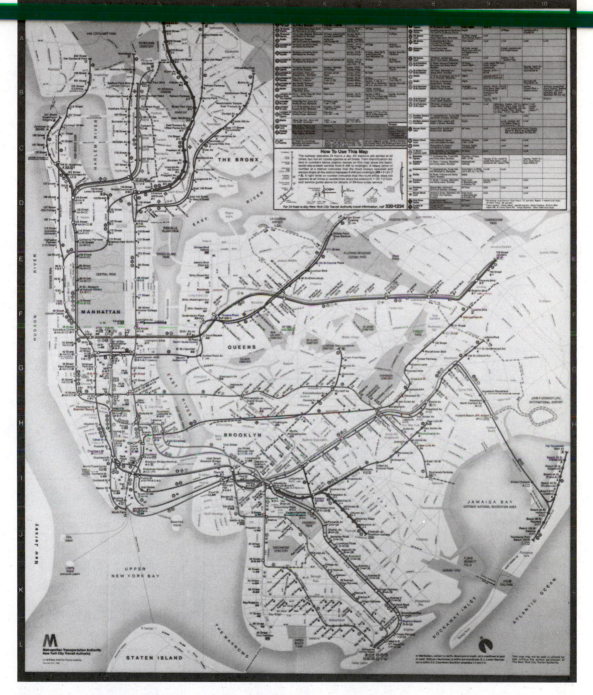

Figure 8–4. Replica of the revised Fall 1980 New York Subway Guide's map and legend. (Courtesy of the New York Transit Authority.)

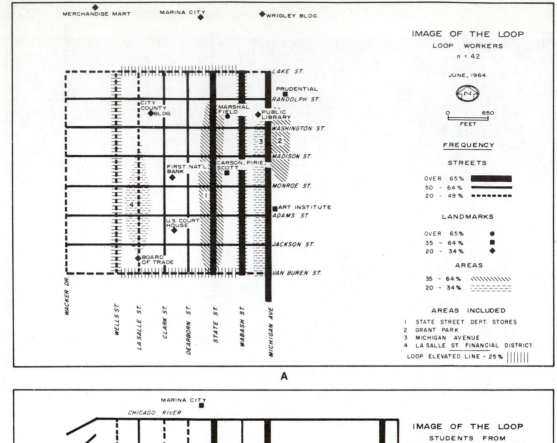

A

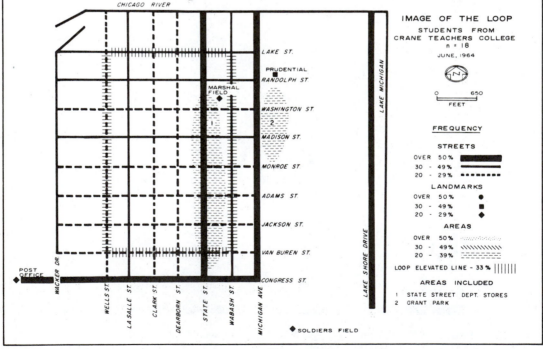

B

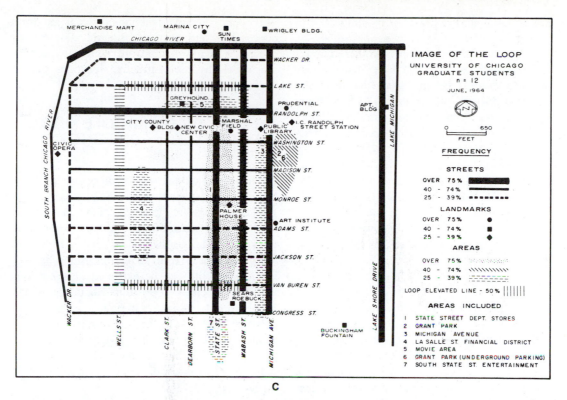

Figure 8–5 A, B, and C. Cognitive maps of the Chicago Loop, as affected by different degrees of familiarity with the area. (T. F. Saarinen, *Perception of the Environment* (Washington, D. C. : Association of American Geographers, Resource Papers for College Geography No. 5, 1969, pp. 16–17, figures 2, 3, and 4. Reprinted by permission.)

that people displayed different cognitive images as a function of their degree of experience with the Loop. Those who worked within it tended to make a more tightly defined area with more internal detail; groups from outside tended to include a broader area, with more emphasis on external landmarks, such as Lake Michigan and Lake Shore Drive (Figure 8–5 A, B, and C). In corroborative studies, Saarinen (1967) found that cognitive maps of the University of Arizona campus differed as a function of students' majors, and Holahan (1978) reported that students drew more complete and detailed maps of campus areas they used more frequently.

Up to this point, our discussion has centered on the determinants of our perception of the physical aspects of the city. We've described many of the

factors responsible for the coherence and completeness of an urban image, and we have speculated about how images affect behavior. Another aspect of urban perception deals less with physical dimensions and more with the evaluative impressions we form about the "character" of a city. If we can eventually isolate the specific aspects of the city that determine people's judgments of its character, perhaps we can plan urban areas so as to elicit desired effects.

What "atmospheres" are associated with different cities? Milgram (1970) compared London, Paris, and New York. He found that New York is distinguished by its physical qualities (e.g., architecture), its pace, and its effect on the emotions more than Paris or London. The impression of London involved its social quality and characteristics of Londoners more than its physical surroundings, and Paris impressed people equally on physical and social dimensions. Do these impressions mesh with yours, if you have visited or read about these places? Another study that compared the "atmospheres" of Columbus, Ohio, Cambridge, Massachusetts, Boston, and New York showed that many subtle characteristics are readily picked up by residents and visitors (Lowenthal & Riel, 1972). For example, New York was described as high-class, fashionable, lively, and exciting, but also as vulgar, foreign, and dangerous. Boston was seen as old, quaint, and "different," while Columbus and Cambridge were both described as green, parklike, and neat (see also the box on Capsule Images).

Summary

Cognitive maps are cities of the mind that reflect the way spatial information is acquired, stored, decoded, and applied to comprehension of the everyday physical environment. They are formed by an interaction of objective physical conditions, and characteristics of an individual (e.g., a person's experiences and values). When our cognitive maps of a city are complete, we experience many important benefits. The extent to which a city affords adequate cognitive mapping depends on a number of factors. Certain aspects of cities

also elicit evaluative reactions, such as judgments concerning "atmosphere." Identification of those aspects of cities that afford complete cognitive maps and favorable affective reactions may be useful for design purposes.

EFFECTS OF URBAN LIFE ON THE CITY DWELLER: CONCEPTUAL EFFORTS

Having discussed the way urban environments are perceived, let us shift our focus to conceptual efforts concerned with understanding and predicting the effects of urban life. As you read the descriptions of the various theoretical perspectives, try to make predictions from them concerning how and when urban life can be expected to affect those who live in cities. Also think about the suggestions offered by each theory for preventing the negative aspects of city life and preserving the positive ones. If you find you need more background information on the various models, or more sense of what distinguishes each from the others, see Chapter 3.

Overload Notions

How do overload notions (cf. Milgram, 1970) apply to understanding and predicting urban behavior? Overload theorists view city existence as a

---

CAPSULE IMAGES

What is the first thing you think of when you imagine the city of Pittsburgh? Although Pittsburgh has been relatively free of smog for years, many of us probably think of the single image, "smog." In an attempt to dispel its unfavorable image, Pittsburgh now publicizes itself as the "Renaissance City." Both "Smoggy City" and "Renaissance City" are examples of what might be called "capsule images," or brief, undifferentiated designations (Porteus, 1977).

Capsule images mask the complexity of the city by presenting a single, unified view. They may be flattering or extremely unflattering to the city in question and may change over time. As with any stereotype, capsule images are often somewhat inaccurate but may contain a kernel of truth. Although some are created or promoted by the cities themselves in an attempt to elicit a favorable opinion, others cause great dismay. Consider the set of images associated with Chicago (Kane & Alexander, 1965; Tuan, 1974). It was once known as Garden City and Gem of the Prairies and later as Hogopolis, Cornopolis, the Country's Greatest Rail Center, and the Hub of American Merchandising.

Figure 8–6. One effect of overstimulation in urban settings is that there are a lot of things we do not notice. (Wide World Photos.)

profusion of stimulation, including too much exposure to the actions and demands of others, confrontation with endless choices, and exposure to excessive visual and auditory stimulation. For example, in a city the size of San Francisco one can encounter as many as 300,000 people within a 15-minute walk (Sadalla & Stea, 1978). This plethora of stimuli is frequently more than we can deal with and requires us to employ coping strategies in order to lower stimulation to a more reasonable level. Coping strategies are many and varied and include setting priorities on inputs so that only important stimuli are attended to (which may result in ignoring those in need of help), erecting interpersonal barriers (e.g., behaving in an unfriendly fashion), establishing specialized institutions (e.g., welfare agencies) to absorb inputs, and shifting burdens to others (e.g., requiring exact change on buses) (see Figure 8–6). But even successful coping may be costly, leading to such aftereffects as exhaustion, fatigue, or disease. When successful coping does *not* occur, the individual will be subject to continued overload and is extremely likely to suffer serious physical or emotional damage.

Environmental Stress

A number of researchers (cf. Glass & Singer, 1972) have applied the environmental stress approach to understanding and predicting reactions to urban life. In general, this approach views the presence of *particular* negative stimuli (e.g., noise, crowding) as critical for the negative effects of city life, as opposed to the overload assumption that too much stimulation per se is the critical element. The negative elements of city life may be experienced as threatening and may elicit stress reactions, which have emotional, behavioral, and physiological components. Stress reactions lead to a variety of coping strategies, which may be either constructive (e.g., using reasonable means to control the stressor) or destructive (e.g., aggression). If coping is successful in eliminating threat, adaptation occurs, and long-term consequences of the stressor are often prevented. If coping is unsuccessful, long-term costs are likely to result.

Behavioral Constraint

Besides overload and environmental stress notions, the behavioral constraint formulation can be applied to the analysis of urban behavior. This formulation assumes that city dwellers experience constraints on their behavior (such as those caused by fear of crime, or getting "stuck" in traffic jams), that aren't generally shared by those people who live in rural areas. What kinds of consequences result from the feeling that one's behavior is constrained? Initially, behavioral constraint notions predict that individuals experiencing this situation will evidence a negative feeling state and will make strong attempts to reassert their freedom. However, predictions of the consequences of long-term adaptation may be more pessimistic. If our efforts at reasserting control are repeatedly unsuccessful, or if we are overwhelmed by too many uncontrollable events, we may be less likely to attempt control of urban settings even when it actually is possible to control them. While city life does impose many constraints on behavior, it should be noted that in some ways it is *less* constraining than small town life. For example, urbanites probably have more control over the information others obtain about their activities than those living in "small towns."

The City as an Overmanned Environment

A final approach to understanding urban behavior makes use of overmanning theory (Gump & Adelberg, 1978; Wicker, McGrath, & Armstrong, 1972). As you recall from Chapter 3, overmanning occurs when the number of participants exceeds the capacity of the system. How does this concept apply to understanding behavior in urban settings? A brief look at any city is sufficient to convince us that we are looking at an overmanned environment. In terms of overmanning theory, city dwellers should respond to such conditions by experiencing feelings of competition and marginality, by establishing priorities for interaction, and by attempting to exclude others from their lives. If overmanning is habitual, these behaviors may come to characterize everyday existence. On the other hand, it should be kept in mind that cities offer more diverse behavior settings and

more behavior settings to choose from, and this could have *positive* effects.

Integrating the Various Formulations

Each of the views we've presented posits a different element of urban life as the critical factor in potential negative effects. Moreover, each suggests somewhat different reactions to urban life. How can we resolve the discrepancies in the various conceptual perspectives? We should bear in mind that these formulations are relatively speculative and untested and therefore should be viewed in a tentative light. Although the approaches are presented as competing with one another, it is probably the case that too much stimulation, too much stress, too many behavioral constraints, and overmanning *each* accounts for some of the negative effects that may result from an urban existence. Eventually, a "compromise" model may emerge, which subsumes the valid predictions of each approach by using a more parsimonious construct.

Overall, it should be noted that on a general level all the views can be integrated into the sequence of events presented in Figure 8–7. As indicated in the figure (which you will recognize as a special case of the general environment–behavior model presented in Chapter 3), objective urban conditions interact with differences among individuals, situational conditions, and social conditions to determine one's experience of the environment. If the environment is outside the individual's optimal range (i.e., if it is overstimulating, contains too many stressors, constrains behavior, or is overmanned) stress is experienced, which elicits coping. It is assumed that when coping is successful in handling stress, adaptation or adjustment occurs, and the individual is less likely to experience aftereffects or cumulative effects (e.g., illness). If coping is unsuccessful, the stress continues, and the individual is likely to experience aftereffects or cumulative effects (e.g., illness).

How well is our model supported by existing data? In the next section, in which we summarize

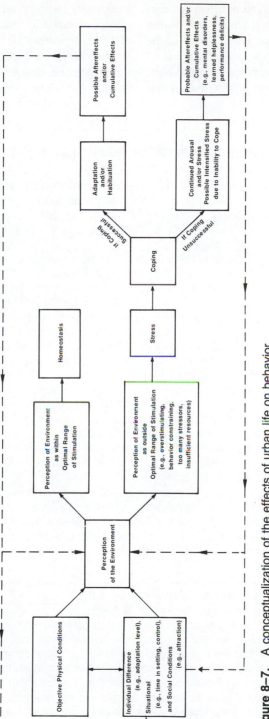

Figure 8–7. A conceptualization of the effects of urban life on behavior.

results of research on the effects of urban environments, we will see that: (1) relatively few studies have been done in this area; and (2) none of the studies can be considered an explicit attempt to test all the relationships proposed in the model. One problem with the model is that it does not sufficiently take into account the potential *positive* effects of city life (box below). However, many of the experiments we will discuss are implicitly supportive, even though they apply to only a small part of the whole encompassed by the model.

PREDICTING THE POSITIVE EFFECTS OF CITY LIFE

The traditional conceptual frameworks that have been designed by researchers to understand and predict the effects of urban life (e.g., overload theory), focus primarily on the negative aspects of urban existence (cf. Proshansky, 1976c). Are there any perspectives that enable us to specify the conditions under which positive effects of city life will occur? A few notions that predict such effects are now emerging.

Contrasting with overload theory, which suggests that the high level of stimulation characteristic of the city will have negative effects, an adaptation level approach (cf. Geller, 1980) implies that this is not necessarily the case. Drawing on the concepts of optimal level of stimulation and adaptation level, which we've discussed in Chapter 3, Geller argues that stimuli (such as the urban setting) which are intense, complex and/or novel may lead to positive *or* negative effects. The effects will vary across persons (e.g., depending on their past experiences). For certain people the city may offer an optimal level of stimulation: Many people cannot live anywhere else but a city. For others, urban settings are horribly aversive. However, it could also be argued that the city offers so much diversity (e.g., quiet parks, busy streets) that somewhere within its environs it could harbor an optimal level of stimulation for everyone. The effects of urban life will also vary over time. Those not used to the city often find it to be too noisy, too crowded, etc., but after they adapt more complex stimuli are tolerated and may even be preferred. Also, we may find the city to be a perfect setting for some activities, but awful for others.

Proshansky (1976c) assumes that the complex physical properties of cities impose behavioral and experiential requirements on the individual, which in turn affect the way he or she deals with the environment in the future. To Proshansky, the elements of city life may render the urban dweller a relatively versatile person, who can approach new situations in a particularly adaptive fashion. There is research evidence to support this claim (e.g., Weiner, 1976). Further, Freedman's (1975) density-intensity theory, reviewed in Chapter 7, suggests that urban density may sometimes intensify positive experiences. This would predict that urbanites respond to certain positive events (e.g., a festive Thanksgiving Day parade) more heartily than their rural counterparts because of high density.

A final viewpoint that implies positive consequences of city life has been proposed by Fischer (1976), who suggests that cities may sometimes serve to strengthen interrelationships within a subcultural group (such as Chinese-Americans). Strengthened relationships can lead to positive effects that could not otherwise happen (e.g., bringing people with common values together).

While the above assertions are interesting and may prove to be important, it should be noted that they have not yet entered the mainstream of environmental psychology. One reason for this may be the *problem-oriented* focus of the field. Because environmental psychologists are interested in solving problems, they have not formulated theories for conceptualizing what is *good* about city life. Since the most popular theories tend to dictate research questions, it is not surprising that past research on the effects of cities has tended to place a greater emphasis on the negative rather than on the positive views.

EFFECTS OF URBAN LIFE ON THE CITY DWELLER: RESEARCH EVIDENCE

Having reviewed conceptual efforts that deal with the effects of the city, we now turn to past research focusing on how urban life affects city dwellers. This research has relied on two methodological approaches. One (the "single variable" approach) attempts to synthesize a picture of urban life from studies of how various *individual* stressors present in the city (e.g., noise, pollution) affect urbanites' behavior. These studies have often been done in "real world" settings, where the stressor under study varies naturally, rather than at the will of an experimenter. To explore the effect of urban noise on psychiatric disorders, one might compare the mental health of the residents on two streets that differ only in their closeness to a noisy factory. This strategy may allow us to approximate a cause-and-effect relationship between a potential urban stressor and behavior, although the nonrandom assignment of subjects to conditions may lead to problems in causal inference. (See the Appendix for a thorough discussion of this issue.)

While the "single variable" approach allows us to synthesize a picture of urban life (after considering the separate effects of various stressors), it forces us to piece the picture together from a multitude of individual elements. The city represents the *simultaneous* presence of a great many stressors, and the effects of cities on human behavior are multiply determined in a very complex manner. A realistic view of the consequences of urban stressors may come from considering how they affect us collectively. Research using this approach generally compares cities (which obviously contain a full range of urban stressors) with nonurban areas on various dependent variable dimensions. One might attempt to assess how urban life affects willingness to help others by comparing prosocial behavior in urban and rural settings. Such studies give us a feeling for how urban conditions collectively affect aspects of human behavior but sacrifice the ability to identify a specific cause. Since cities and nonurban areas vary in many ways besides the presence or absence of environmental stressors, we must be aware that differences between urban and rural behaviors could be caused by differences in populations, social conditions, physical conditions, or a combination of these (cf. Korte, 1980). It should be noted, however, that urban versus rural comparisons are still one of our best opportunities to determine how city life affects behavior.

In the sections that follow, we will discuss the effects of urban life on a variety of dimensions (e.g., stress, coping strategies, affiliative behavior). Whenever possible, our coverage will include the findings of relevant studies that use both the "single variable" and the "urban versus rural" methodological approaches. This should yield a balanced coverage in which the two methods complement each other.

Stress

Although urban areas differ from each other—some are obviously much better places to live than others—comparisons of urban and rural areas generally suggest that cities contain more stressful environmental features. A number of stimuli identified as potential stressors are more prevalent in cities than in small towns. For example, noise levels have been found to increase with the size of a community (Dillman & Tremblay, 1977). One study by the EPA showed that the quietest times in inner-city apartments were noisier than the noisiest moments in small town living areas (EPA, 1972). Pollution is also greater with increasing city size (Hoch, 1972), and serious pollution is almost unique to cities. In fact, one breath of city air contains 70,000 dust and dirt particles, and just living in New York City is equivalent to smoking 38 cigarettes a day (Rotton, 1978). In addition, both crowding and crime are much more frequent in urban than in rural areas (Fischer, 1976).

Cities also tend to be warmer than surrounding areas, since large numbers of people, automobiles, and industries produce heat, and large buildings and pollution trap it (Fischer, 1976). The pace of life is faster in the city. For example, it has been found that residents' walking speed

Table 8–1.　WALKING SPEED IN CITIES OF VARIOUS SIZES*

Country	Town/city	Population	Observed velocity (m/sec)
Ireland	Galway	29,375	1.25
	Limerick	57,161	1.27
	Dublin	679,748	1.56
Scotland	Inverness	53,179	1.43
	Edinburgh	470,085	1.51
United States	Seattle	503,000	1.46

*After Bornstein, M. H. The pace of life: revisited. *International Journal of Psychology*, 1979, *14*, 84.

varies as a linear function of the size of the local population (Bornstein, 1979) (see Table 8–1). In addition, urban areas have less sunshine, more rain and more wind due to air pollution, the high density of city buildings, and the greater heat in urban areas (e.g., Elgin *et al.*, 1974). Also there is greater exposure to a class of events we will call ''extra demand and inconvenience'' (see Figure 8–8 A and B). An example of ''extra demand and inconvenience'' is spending time commuting on crowded highways, an experience which can be quite stressful (Stokols *et al.*, 1978). Urbanites are also exposed to more bureaucratic hassles, which we all know can induce stress (Glass & Singer, 1972).

It is sad to note that, in some ways, urbanites most intensely exposed to urban stressors are those with other problems as well. It seems that people who are poor, poorly educated, and generally discriminated against by society live in

Figure 8–8 A and B.　When trying to "get around" in urban areas, crowds can be a source of extra demand and inconvenience. (Peter Oliver)

those areas of the city with the greatest pollution (McCaull, 1977). The poor probably are exposed to more urban crowding, noise, and crime as well. Given the fact that these people are already vulnerable to stress, adding the environmental stressors characteristic of urban life can be especially problematic.

With all the evidence indicating that living in the city should be experienced as more stressful, do urban and rural dwellers really *perceive* different levels of stress? Although there are few data bearing on this point, a study by Franck, Unseld, and Wentworth (1974) provides suggestive evidence that this may be the case. Investigators interviewed a sample of students who were newcomers to either a small town or a large city. It was observed that the urban newcomers reported experiencing significantly more tension when living in the city than in their previous residence; the reverse was observed for rural newcomers. When sources of stress were broken down into those associated with the physical environment and those associated with the social environment, some additional differences emerged. For physical stressors (e.g., pollution, noise, crowding), urbanites reported being affected far more adversely than rural dwellers. For social stressors, results depended on the particular stressor. *Public* social stressors (e.g., slums, aversive individuals one must deal with) were experienced more strongly by urban newcomers (see Figure 8–9). However, some rural newcomers complained about the lack of cultural diversity in their environment. *Personal* social stressors (stressful personal relationships) did not differ significantly for the two groups. These findings are suggestive but should be interpreted with caution, as should all studies involving urban and rural comparisons.

A study by Wohlwill and Kohn (1973) suggested that perception of stressors in urban and rural areas depends on one's adaptation level (measured by the size of the town one resided in previously). In their study, people from small, middle-sized, and large communities who had migrated to Harrisburg, Pennsylvania were asked to make judgments concerning extent of crowding,

frequency of crime, and feelings of safety. Although the results weren't totally consistent, it was found that individuals coming from relatively large communities assessed Harrisburg as safer, less crime-ridden, and less crowded than those coming from smaller communities. (These findings support Geller's conceptualization of the effects of city life, portrayed in the box on page 242). It is important to note that in addition to adaptation level, many other types of individual differences may affect the perception of stressors in cities. For example, variables such as one's length of residence, one's need for stimulation, and one's socioeconomic status might influence the way urban stressors are experienced. Unfortunately, little research has been done in this area, and what exists has been inconclusive. Further, although future research is clearly needed before we can draw such a conclusion, in addition to affecting experience of environmental stressors, individual difference variables will probably also be found to affect other responses to urban settings (such as coping).

Figure 8–9. Public social stressors, including aversive individuals one must encounter, are more frequent in the city. Such people may also be viewed as victims of urban life. (Peter Oliver)

Coping

If urban life is more stressful than rural life, our general stressor model would assume that active coping strategies would be more characteristic of urban populations. Again, there is evidence that this is the case. In their study, Franck and her coworkers (1974) found that urban newcomers seemed to adopt a cognitive mode involving more planning and deliberation than rural newcomers do. For example, 67 percent of all urban newcomers reported becoming more purposeful and deliberate since their move, while 73 percent of all rural newcomers reported becoming less deliberate. Over the period of a year, significantly more urban than rural newcomers reported some "strategy" for dealing with life in their new setting. For urbanites, this included increased vigilance, safety precautions, and repression of fear. In addition to these coping strategies, the theoretical perspectives of overload and overmanning would predict other coping responses. For example, based on overload and overmanning theories, it might be predicted that urbanites would attempt to exclude others from their experience. This should affect city dwellers' willingness to affiliate with strangers, and might also affect their willingness to help others who are in need.

Affiliative Behavior

On a number of dimensions, city life seems to be associated with a decreased desire for affiliation with strangers. This ties in well with several of our conceptual notions, but can also be explained in terms of reinforcement or past experience with city life (e.g., more experiences with crime). Newman and McCauley (1977) found that subjects' eye contact with strangers who looked them in the eye was relatively rare in center city Philadelphia, more common in a Philadelphia suburb, and very common in a rural Pennsylvania town (Table 8–2). In a study extending these findings, McCauley, Coleman, and De Fusco (1977) showed that commuters were less willing to meet a stranger's eye when they arrived at a downtown terminal than when they were in a suburban train station. How did urbanites and ruralites respond facially to attempts by strangers to take candid photos of them? When the pictures were given to other college students to rate, it was found that urbanites in the photos appeared to be less friendly, less easy going, and more tense than ruralites (Krupat, 1982). Finally, Milgram (1977) reported that when undergraduate students approached strangers on the street and extended their hands in a friendly manner (as if to initiate a handshake), only 38.5 percent of city dwellers reciprocated, compared with 66 percent of small town dwellers. (For some evidence that urbanites sometimes display affiliative behavior with "strangers", see the box on page 247.)

While this pattern of effects suggests that city dwellers are apt to avoid contact with strangers, it is important to assess whether this behavior extends to friends and acquaintances. In an experi-

Table 8–2. PERCENTAGE OF PASSERSBY MAKING EYE CONTACT WITH MALE AND FEMALE EXPERIMENTERS AT POST OFFICE AND STORE IN PARKESBURG, BRYN MAWR, AND PHILADELPHIA*

Sex of Experimenter	Parkesburg		Bryn Mawr		Philadelphia	
	Post Office	Store	Post Office	Store	Post Office	Store
Female	80	82	45	50	15	18
Male	75	73	40	45	12	10

*Reprinted from Joseph Newman and Clark McCauley, "Eye Contact with Strangers in City, Suburb, and Small Town," *Environment and Behavior*, Vol. 9, No. 4 (December, 1977) pp. 547–558.

THE FAMILIAR STRANGER

One thing our discussion has suggested is that urbanites are less likely to acknowledge strangers (e.g., by shaking hands and making eye contact) than rural dwellers. Some extremely interesting research by Milgram (1977) indicates that while city dwellers fail to display such amenities in everyday situations, they may show their feelings in other ways.

Milgram and his students found that many city residents have a number of people in their lives who may be called "familiar strangers." What is a familiar stranger? It's someone they observe repeatedly for a long period of time but never interact with, probably because of overload. Milgram found that commuters to New York City had an average of four individuals whom they recognized but never spoke to at their train station, and that 89.5 percent of the commuters had at least one "familiar stranger." How did the researchers find this out? They took pictures of groups waiting for a train at the station and had subjects tell them how many of those present met the definition of a "familiar stranger."

What is the difference in urbanites' behavior toward "familiar strangers" and other strangers? First, many passengers told the researchers they often think about their "familiar strangers" and try to figure out what kinds of lives they lead. There is evidence that urbanites are more likely to help a familiar stranger in need than an ordinary stranger. Finally, Milgram found that under some circumstances, familiar strangers do interact with each other, although it is never in the place where they usually meet. He suggests that the farther they are away from the scene of their routine encounter (a foreign country, for instance), the more likely they are to interact.

ment designed to test this hypothesis, McCauley and Taylor (1976) did a survey in which they asked small town and large city residents about yesterday's telephone conversations with friends and acquaintances. Phone conversations in the city were as often with close friends and as intimate in subject matter as conversations in small towns. This pattern is corroborated by additional research (see Korte, 1980). Many other studies (e.g., Glenn & Hill, 1977; Key, 1968) show no urban-rural differences in contact with relatives. This urban pattern of coldness to strangers and cursory acquaintances but not to friends and relatives was also observed in a study in which newcomers to a city and a small town were interviewed (Franck *et al.,* 1974). Initially, individuals moving to the city rated themselves as having fewer friends, as finding it harder to make friends, and as experiencing the city as a more difficult place to form close relationships than people moving to a small town. However, after a few months (when they were no longer strangers), all of these self-reported differences disappeared.

Prosocial Behavior

Does the urbanite's lack of desire to affiliate with strangers extend to a disregard for strangers who are in need? One group of studies assessing urban-rural differences in willingness to help consistently suggests this (cf. Korte, 1980). When a child claiming to be lost asked for aid in New York City and in several small towns, he or she was more likely to receive a helping hand in the smaller towns (Milgram, 1977). In a similar vein, Milgram found that willingness to allow a needy individual into one's house to use the telephone was higher in a small town than in a large city. Also, 75 percent of all city respondents answered the person in need by shouting through the closed door, while 75 percent of all rural respondents opened the door, reinforcing our earlier conclusion about urbanite avoidance of affiliation with strangers. Additional studies (Gelfand *et al.,* 1973; Korte & Kerr, 1975; Milgram, 1970) have also found that urbanites are less helpful than rural dwellers.

There are several possible explanations for the

lower helpfulness of urbanites. This response could be explained by overload theory. As that model would predict, the high levels of stimulation characteristic of the city make passersby less attentive to novel stimuli, such as someone needing help (Korte, 1980). Overmanning theory (detailed earlier) could offer a second explanation, and diffusion of responsibility (cf. Latané & Darley, 1971) a third. Work on diffusion of responsibility suggests that when there are many people around who *could* help (as would occur more in cities than in small towns), perceived responsibility to help lessens, which affects the likelihood of giving aid.

Although much research suggests less prosocial behavior in cities, a second group of studies failed to reflect this pattern (Forbes & Gromoll, 1971; Korte, Ypma, & Toppen, 1975; Weiner, 1976). These experiments indicate some limitations to the assertion that it is more difficult to receive help in the city than in the country. Korte and his colleagues suggested that urban and rural settings will lead to differences in helping only insofar as environmental input level (i.e., amount of incoming stimuli) is higher in cities. Their findings led them to conclude that input level may be the critical determinant of helping, rather than the urban-rural distinction per se. Similarly, others (e.g., Kammann, Thompson, & Irwin, 1979) suggest that pedestrian density in the area where help is to be given, rather than city size, is the major factor in whether or not aid will be given. And House and Wolf (1978) report intriguing evidence of lower urban helping only where crime rates make involvement inadvisable, suggesting that this may account for lack of prosocial action. Weiner (1976) and Forbes and Gromoll (1971) actually found greater helping by individuals raised in cities than by those raised in small towns. In interpreting her findings, Weiner posited that different patterns of social-perceptual learning in the city and the country may cause urbanites to be more socially effective in certain circumstances. In effect, she suggests that the experience of growing up in the city allows one to learn skills that may be particularly adaptive in certain dependency situations. Also, it seems that

deviants are *more* apt to receive aid in cities than in small towns (Hannson & Slade, 1977), and that the pattern of less helping in cities extends only to strangers and not to friends (Korte, 1980). Given the above qualifications, it is safe to conclude that nonwillingness to help is not necessarily an urban phenomenon, and that additional variables may be operating.

Performance

While there are very few, if any, "urban versus rural" studies that compare performance, a large number of "single variable" studies suggest that the types of stressors prevalent in urban areas take a toll. For example, in an experiment by Cohen, Glass, and Singer (1973) reviewed in Chapter 4, we noted that noise in a city apartment building from a nearby highway adversely affected reading scores in children. In the same vein, city children whose classrooms are parallel to train tracks read more poorly than children on a quieter side of the building (Bronzaft & McCarthy, 1975). And Cohen *et al.* (1980) reported that children from schools with high noise levels near Los Angeles airport were more likely to fail on a cognitive task, and more apt to "give up" before time had elapsed, than children from quieter control schools. Adverse effects also result from pollution. The air pollution index in Los Angeles is correlated with the number of automobile accidents, an effect that is attributed by investigators to decreased mental effectiveness and vigilance (Ury, Perkins, & Goldsmith, 1972). The oxidant level in Los Angeles smog has also been related to poor athletic performance (Wayne, Wehrle, & Carroll, 1967), and high pollution levels are associated with complete avoidance of outdoor and certain indoor activities (Chapko & Solomon, 1976; Peterson, 1975).

Levels of crowding, heat, and "extra demand and inconvenience" present in cities also affect performance adversely. Some studies have related urban crowding to performance decrements. Saegert, MacIntosh, and West (1975) did an experiment with shoppers in a midtown Manhattan department store during periods of high and low social density. The participants' task was to remember several aspects of the setting accurately. While no differences were found in recall of the merchandise (the main task), memory of incidental details was impaired in high density conditions. Langer and Saegert (1977) found that city shoppers' efficiency was impaired by high density, and that this could be ameliorated by affording shoppers a means of control (i.e., informing subjects in advance that high density may be arousing). Although no studies have specifically related heat in cities to performance, research reviewed in Chapter 5 indicates that heat negatively affects performance in certain situations (cf. Bell, Provins, & Hiorns, 1964; Provins & Bell, 1970). Finally, Shaban and Welling (cited in Glass & Singer, 1973) found evidence that hassles with bureaucrats can have negative consequences for performance on subsequent tasks and can even lead to learned helplessness.

Crime

While crime seems to be increasing everywhere (Gallup Poll, April 4, 1981), there is evidence that it is significantly more prevalent in urban than rural areas (cf. Carlstam & Levy, 1971; Fischer, 1976). To bring this issue closer to home, consider the results of a 1981 Gallup Poll, in which people were asked if they had been victims of crime in the past 12 months. Residents of central cities were especially likely to respond that they had—at least 28 percent had been victimized at least once. And when asked to list the top 10 problems facing their neighborhoods, residents of cities listed crime as the number one problem (Gallup Opinion Poll, April 4, 1981). Of those city residents wanting to relocate, crime was the major reason cited (Gallup Poll, April 19, 1981). An amusing anecdote related by Zimbardo (1969) suggests the intensity of crime in many cities. While repairing a flat tire alongside a highway in Queens, New York, a motorist was startled when he observed that his car hood was being raised, and a stranger was removing his battery. "Take it easy, buddy," said the thief to his assumed car-stripping colleague, "you can have the tires—all I want is the battery!"

Why is there more crime in cities than in small towns? (See Table 8–3.) Although these findings

Table 8–3. CRIME RATES BY POPULATION GROUPS. (VIOLENT CRIME INCLUDES MURDER, FORCIBLE RAPE, ROBBERY, AND AGGRAVATED ASSAULT. PROPERTY CRIME IS BURGLARY, LARCENY-THEFT, AND MOTOR VEHICLE THEFT)*

Size of Area	Number of Violent Crimes/100,000 Inhabitants	Number of Property Crimes/100,000 Inhabitants
>1,000,000	1,433.7	6,498.2
500,000–999,000	1,104.0	7,585.1
250,000–499,999	1,082.5	7,923.0
100,000–249,999	701.5	7,125.2
50,000–99,999	525.5	6,135.4
25,000–49,999	420.1	5,543.2
10,000–24,999	315.3	4,674.4
<10,000	278.6	4,225.3
Suburban Areas	355.5	4,477.4
Rural Areas	194.0	2,076.1

*From *Uniform Crime Reports*, 1979.

can be interpreted in terms of overload, stress, behavioral constraint or overmanning notions, several other explanations have been offered. One is the theory of *deindividuation*. It was used by Zimbardo (1969) to explain why an "abandoned" car he left in New York City was stripped of all movable parts within 24 hours, while a similar car left in Palo Alto, California was untouched. According to this theory, when we feel we are an anonymous member of a crowd (i.e., deindividuated), our inhibitions against antisocial behavior are released. This is partly because we feel it

---

ENVIRONMENTAL AND INDIVIDUAL DIFFERENCE FACTORS AND FEAR OF CRIME

Imagine being afraid to go outside of your apartment to buy food or cash a check, or opening the door in terror when someone knocks, hoping he or she is not a criminal. Fear of crime and associated stress are major problems in urban areas, problems which are influenced to some extent by environmental factors. In the chapter on personal space and territoriality we discussed how territorial markers can moderate fear of victimization; here we will mention some other determinants of crime stress.

Various aspects of the urban environment seem to impact on fear of crime. It has been suggested that physical decay of the environment and signs of urban "incivilities" (e.g., vandalism, graffiti, litter) can imply to people that the social order has broken down, and elicit fear of victimization. Teenage loitering, which can be facilitated or inhibited by environmental features, can similarly affect crime stress (Lavrakas, 1982). And as we have noted elsewhere (Chapter 6), environmental design can help promote cohesion among residents. Having supportive neighbors acts to *quell* fear of being victimized.

Interestingly, while there is no evidence that street lighting affects actual levels of crime, it decreases fear of crime (Tien *et al.,* 1979). And while it had been hypothesized that in urban areas with more pedestrian activity there would be less fear of crime, the *reverse* has been found in research (Baumer & Hunter, 1978). Finally, *propinquity* (discussed in detail in Chapter 10), affects how afraid people are of being victimized. The closer we live to a known crime victim, the more we fear that we could suffer the same fate (cf. Lavrakas, 1982).

In urban areas certain types of people seem to fear crime more than others. Those who are most concerned are people with lower incomes, females, blacks, and the aged. There are many possible reasons for this, ranging from greater victimization of some groups to lesser ability of others (e.g., the aged, women) to defend themselves. These people all feel they must restrict their activities greatly to avoid being victimized (Lavrakas, 1982).

In the case of the elderly, environmental design may help lessen crime stress. As we have noted, having socially supportive relationships moderates fear of being victimized. For the aged, this seems to occur more often in socially homogeneous living situations (e.g., retirement communities) than in other settings. In a study which is only suggestive because residents assigned themselves to living situations which differed in *many* respects, elderly people living in a heterogeneous central city core reported fewer support systems and perceived themselves to be less safe than those in a socially homogeneous retirement community. Residents in a typical suburban community were in between "core" and "retirement" residents on both measures (Sundeen & Mathieu, 1976). This suggests that environmental design may facilitate social cohesion and lower fear of crime. Of course, we must ask ourselves whether all the implications of homogeneous housing for the elderly are as good as those we've noted above. It may be that there are other, more negative effects in some areas which could counteract the good ones mentioned here. (For a complete discussion of homogeneous housing for the elderly, see Chapter 10.)

is very unlikely that we'll be identified and punished. Under such conditions, criminal behavior is clearly less costly and is more likely to be engaged in. Another explanation, which is at least in part a cause, is that there are simply more people, more goods to steal, and more outlets for stolen goods in cities than elsewhere. This may cause criminals to actually migrate to the cities!

What are the effects of the stress associated with the greater probability of being a crime victim in a city? While there is a little empirical evidence about the effects of crime stress, Roberts (1977) found that it was associated with emotional reactions of worry, fear of injury, fear of material loss, and feelings of loss of control. Continued stress associated with crime (which is likely since the objective threat of crime doesn't dissipate) can have extremely negative effects (e.g., it may be associated with nervous disorders and learned helplessness). Finally, fear about victimization through crime can lead to tremendous reduction of people's activities. In fact, compared to suburbanites, city dwellers report that they restrict their activities much more of the time due to fear of crime (Lavrakas, 1982). Far worse, fear of crime has led some, especially the elderly, to refrain entirely from leaving home (Ginsberg, 1975) (see the box p. 250 "Environmental and Individual Difference Factors and Fear of Crime).

Long-Term Behavioral Effects

While there have been too few studies to permit a definitive statement, living in an urban area involves some changes that may be interpreted as long-term behavioral effects. Importantly, these changes have both positive and negative aspects. On the negative side, Franck and her associates (1974) reported that urban newcomers were far more likely than rural newcomers to report becoming more cynical, fatalistic, helpless, distrustful, and callous after a year in their new home. On the positive side, they were more likely than rural newcomers to report that they had become more adaptive in a variety of situations, broadened their perspective, and experienced personal growth (Figure 8–10). This is not surprising: cultural innovations (e.g., new ideas) are "born" in

Figure 8–10. Nowhere but in the city are such diverse opportunities available to people.

urban areas and may take years to "trickle down" to smaller towns. The speed with which they spread to a particular area is a function of its size. The same holds for material innovations (Fischer, 1978).

The positive effects of urban life have been described quite eloquently by Proshansky (1976c). In line with his conceptualization, it appears that the experiences characterizing urban existence (cultural opportunities, noise, crowds, crime) can lead to important benefits (see the box on page 242). These may make the urbanite a more versatile and adaptable individual than his or her rural counterpart. For example, Jain (1978) reports that urbanites have more tolerance for competition than ruralites. This can be viewed as an adaptive response to urban conditions. Urban life allows the individual to learn many roles (subway commuter, museum visitor, concert listener, urban motorist), to engage in many activities, and to shift roles and activities when settings demand. Further, the urbanite learns to make choices among diverse environmental alternatives (going to the theater, a lecture, or a sporting event) and to cope with the constant presence of many others. Future research should be directed toward testing Proshansky's assertions and to looking more at the positive side of urban life.

Health

Caution should be used in interpreting data relating health to urban and rural settings. First, specialized medical care is generally more available in cities. In 1970, there were about twice as many physicians per capita in urban than rural America. Specialists, such as cardiologists and surgeons, are in especially short supply outside of cities (Dillman & Tremblay, 1977). Hospital facilities in cities are also superior. Second, individuals who are ill often migrate from the country (where they became sick) to the city (Srole, 1972). Nevertheless, contrary to popular belief, data on urban-rural health differences are rather equivocal and depend on the particular disease. Hay and Wantman (1969) studied the rate of hypertension and heart disease (both associated with stress) and found that hypertension rates were only slightly higher in New York City than in the nation overall. Arthritis and rheumatism rates were also found to be lower in New York City than in the country as a whole (Srole, 1972). On the other hand, tuberculosis, emphysema, bronchitis, and other respiratory diseases (often associated with pollution) occur more frequently in urban areas (Weinstein, 1980), and the incidence of lung cancer in cities is double that in rural areas (National Academy of Science Study, reported in the *Los Angeles Times,* September 11, 1972). Some experts predict that 25 percent of the annual deaths in the US due to respiratory diseases could be avoided if urban air pollution were reduced by 50 percent (Weinstein, 1980). Overall, it may be said that the city is not inherently pathological and that the relationship between urban and rural environments and disease is somewhat complex.

Turning from physical to mental health, we begin by looking at urban-rural differences in self-reported life satisfaction. Analysis of survey data indicates that there are urban-rural differences in terms of happiness and optimism about the future, and these differences are becoming more intense (Gallup Opinion Poll, 102, 1973; Hynson, 1975). Relative to their rural counterparts, urbanites are becoming more and more unhappy with their situation. Urbanites also show much lower levels of interpersonal trust than ruralites (Fischer, 1973). How are these differences reflected in rates of mental illness? While it is clear that mental hospital admissions are higher in cities than in rural areas (Clinard, 1964; Mann, 1964), it is not certain that urbanites are actually less mentally healthy (Srole, 1972). For example, of 17 studies comparing paper-and-pencil measures of adjustment in areas of different size, three found more personality problems in larger cities, five found that such difficulties were more common in small communities, and nine found no differences (Fischer, 1976). Srole (1976) reports that inhabitants of large cities are less likely to show symptoms of imminent nervous breakdown than residents of small towns. On the other hand, Dohrenwend and Dohrenwend (1972) contend that some forms of mental illness (e.g., psychoses) are more prevalent in rural areas, while other forms (e.g., neuroses, personality disorders) predominate in urban areas.

While mental illness may not differ reliably in urban and rural areas, two afflictions that are symptomatic of such disorders may show urban-rural differences. First, in the US it had been found that alcoholism was more common in large cities than in small towns (Trice, 1966), though more recent data (Fischer, 1976; Ross *et al.,* 1979) suggest that this is not necessarily true. Second, drug addiction is much more common in urban than in rural areas (Department of Health, Education, and Welfare, 1969). Obviously, these differences can be accounted for in terms of the overload and stress notions we reviewed earlier. Some other explanations include: greater availability of drugs and liquor, better treatment of alcoholics and drug addicts and hence more reporting of these afflictions, and better recordkeeping in cities. Finally, and rather surprisingly, there is no consistent difference in the suicide rates between urban and rural areas (Gibbs, 1971).

Summary

Environmental stressors are more intensely present in urban settings. These include noise, pollu-

LOOKING FOR THE GOOD AS WELL AS THE BAD: THE BENEFITS OF A POSITIVE FOCUS

For reasons mentioned earlier, most studies comparing life in urban and rural areas have focused primarily on the intensity of aversive environmental conditions (such as stress) across the two settings. Such studies are interesting and important, but we should design future research that allows us to make comparisons on positive as well as negative dimensions. Haney and Knowles (1977) employed such an evenhanded approach in assessing the characteristics of neighborhoods described by inner-city residents, outer-city residents, and suburbanites. The results, depicted in Table 8–4, are consistent with earlier studies in suggesting that the inner city has more negative characteristics than the outer city or the suburbs. However, observe that it was also found that the number of positive characteristics mentioned by each group was approximately equal, although the particular characteristics varied with the setting. The "positive characteristics" dimension, which isn't tapped by most studies, can provide valuable information for researchers on cities.

A similar evenhanded approach was taken by Krupat, Guild, and Miller (1977), who created a composite list of positive and negative adjectives and had a group of students rate the extent to which each was characteristic of large cities and small towns. While the results are complex, the procedures yielded both positive and negative information not usually obtained in urban-rural comparison studies. For example, cities were characterized by such *positive* traits as "offers much entertainment," "allows choice of life style," and "is liberal," along with the common negative traits "crowded," "competitive," "makes one feel anonymous and isolated," and "impersonal and untrusting." Small towns were characterized by such *negative* traits as "people gossip a lot," "people don't like outsiders," and "people are prejudiced," in addition to such common positive traits as "peaceful," "safe," "healthful," "intimate," and "relaxed."

Table 8–4. PERCENTAGE OF RESIDENTS CITING POSITIVE AND NEGATIVE CHARACTERISTICS OF THEIR NEIGHBORHOODS*

Neighborhood Characteristic	Inner City	Outer City	Suburb
Positive Responses			
Nice neighborhood	62	58	75
Friendly people	38	58	64
Closeness to services, stores	62	32	31
Quiet	25	26	22
Negative Responses			
Traffic and noise	44	26	8
Undesirable residents	19	5	0
Malodorousness	12	11	0

*From W. G. Haney and E. S. Knowles, "Perception of neighborhoods by city and suburban residents," *Human Ecology*, 1978, *6*, 201–214.

tion, heat, crowding, "extra demand," and crime. Studies suggest that individually and collectively these stressors have at least mildly negative effects on various dimensions of urban existence. Urban stressors are associated with increased coping behavior, less desire for affiliation with strangers, performance decrements, crime, long-term behavioral effects, and differences in some health-related indices. These can be interpreted in terms of the urban stress model we have proposed. However, certain effects such as crime can also be explained, at least in part, by other urban–rural differences (e.g., deindividuation). While there are many urban problems, future research needs to focus more on the positive effects of city life. This type of research is described in the box on page 253.

ENVIRONMENTAL SOLUTIONS TO URBAN PROBLEMS

As is painfully obvious, the modern American city has a wide variety of problems. Not surprisingly, both people and businesses have attempted to find true happiness by escaping from the city. Those who remain behind are often individuals whose social or economic position make them incapable of departing. What effect has this had on the cities? It has left them with a deteriorating physical condition, a dwindling tax base, and a population heavily composed of minority groups with high levels of unemployment and attendant social problems, such as crime. How can this situation be ameliorated? Many very significant social, economic, and physical changes are needed. Since such disciplines as political science and economics are beyond the scope of this text, we will restrict ourselves to discussing physical-environmental attempts to solve urban problems. However, a unified attack on many fronts will be needed to change the situation, and when compared with the possible effects of potential social and economic programs, the impact of the physical interventions we are proposing may be relatively slight.

Several possibilities exist for environmental solutions to certain urban problems (e.g., the high crime rate and the destruction of property in cities). It has been proposed that with proper environmental modifications and appropriate designs for new settings, such urban problems could be attenuated. Simultaneously, the design process could precipitate improvements in urban social and psychological life, yielding among other things more cohesive neighborhoods, more "neighborly" behavior, less fear of crime, and greater perceived control for urbanites.

Defensible Space

Newman and his colleagues (Newman, 1972, 1975; Newman & Franck, 1979) have focused on how physical aspects of a setting affect resident-based control of the environment. Newman argued that creating *defensible spaces*—clearly bounded or semiprivate spaces that appear to belong to someone—will lead to feelings of "owning" the space, promote social cohesion between neighbors, and foster informal surveillance of the area. These should reduce crime and antisocial behavior, and lead to improved social relations among urbanites. Although Newman's ideas were intended primarily to curb the high crime and property destruction occurring in public housing, they can be applied more broadly to urban life (cf. Taylor, Gottfredson, & Brower, 1980).

Does the concept of defensible space have the predicted effects? There is some definite support for at least parts of the model. Newman (1972) compared two public housing projects in New York, one of which was high in defensible space, while the other was low. The latter project had more crime and higher maintenance costs, and this could not be explained by tenant characteristics. Also, a demonstration project in Hartford implemented both physical and social changes designed to increase defensible space (Fowler *et al.*, 1979). This led to fewer burglaries, and residents perceived themselves to be less at risk. They reported walking in the neighborhood more, and believed it was easier to recognize strangers. In making changes which will enhance defensible space, it is important for residents to participate in the decision process, and they must view modifications as positive, not punitive (Taylor, Gottfredson, & Brower, 1980).

Unfortunately, there has been criticism of the way the defensible space model was originally formulated (e.g., Taylor *et al.*, 1980) and of how some research on it has been carried out (e.g., Patterson, 1977). Also, not all research has found that defensible space works to lower crime, increase neighborhood cohesion, etc. (e.g., Mawby, 1977). And while studies suggest that factors associated with more defensible space *may* affect crime and other outcomes in a favorable way, there is little evidence that this occurs, as Newman believes, because defensible space creates feelings of ownership and affects the social fabric of a setting. Recent research (e.g., by Taylor and his associates, and Newman and his) has tried to clarify and extend the model, and to measure the links between cognitions and behavior.

In addition to architectural features affecting defensible space as suggested by Newman, Taylor and his associates (e.g., Taylor *et al.*, 1980) believe this type of research and application should draw more heavily on the concept of territoriality (see Chapter 6). They suggest that some critical environmental features for controlling crime are signs of defense, signs of appropriation, and signs of incivility (Hunter, 1978). Signs of defense are symbolic and real barriers directed toward strangers that keep unwanted outsiders away. Signs of appropriation are territorial markers suggesting that a space is used and cared for. Signs of incivility are physical and social cues (e.g., environmental deterioration) that indicate a decay in the social order. These territorial signs give information to other residents and to strangers which affects whether or not crime occurs. Taylor *et al.* indicate that the presence of such signs is a subcultural expression, and will vary for different people. Also, territorial signs will be more common in homogeneous neighborhoods, and where there are strong local social ties. As opposed to Newman's model, then, Taylor *et al.* suggest sociocultural variables and social conditions, in addition to design, determine territorial cognitions and behaviors and ultimately the level of crime in a neighborhood. While the model has not been tested extensively, it has received partial support (e.g., Taylor *et al.*, 1978, 1980; Gottfredson *et al.*, 1979).

Land Use

A second approach implies that *land use* in an area will affect the crime rate. Jacobs (1961) has suggested that diverse land use is an important factor in deterring urban decay. Neighborhoods should contain commercial, residential, institutional, *and* leisure-oriented areas. This would attract a continuous flow of people, and insure informal surveillance. In effect, planning and zoning for heterogeneous rather than "specialized" urban districts would lead to positive effects. Research implies that there may be problems with this approach. Greenberg *et al.* (1982) found that low crime neighborhoods had fewer people on the streets than those with high crime. The flow of people into low crime neighborhoods was limited by *homogeneous* land use, fewer maor arteries, and by the nature of residential boundary streets. And Dietrick (1977) reported that residential burglary occurred more near commercial areas. This suggests that maintaining the residential character of neighborhoods and limiting access to outsiders may inhibit crime. Overall, it does seem that land use affects crime, but whether or not heterogeneous land use yields the best *overall* results is an open question.

Additional research helps clarify how land use may affect crime. O'Donnell and Lydgate (1980) catalogued the types of "physical" resources (e.g., restaurants, financial services) in different police beats in metropolitan Honolulu. The criminal acts occurring in the area were then correlated with the physical resources. Increased burglary was correlated with the presence of permanent and transient residences, and facilities offering alcohol consumption and entertainment. Forgery occurred in police beats where there were physical resources allowing one to obtain goods, services, or cash through this means (e.g., stores, bars, and restaurants). Fraud, larceny, and robbery were related to a cluster of tourist facilities, such as retail stores, restaurants, bars, transient residences, and entertainment. Violent offenses were *most* highly correlated with the presence of sex-related activities. The authors view these findings as suggesting that certain physical resources in the environment provide "opportunities" for crime. By cataloguing these resources we can plan better for police protection, and perhaps through zoning we can control crime rates.

Social Factors

It has been suggested that in coping with urban problems, *social networks* could play a significant role. Social networks are people living nearby who care about and depend on each other. People with strong social networks enjoy better physical health and psychological well-being, and respond better to crisis events (e.g., Antonovsky, 1979; Holahan & Moos, 1981). Also, the presence of social networks helps regulate access to an area by strangers, leads to less reliance on police for dealing with disturbances, and can exert significant pressure to conform on social deviants living inside a neighborhood (e.g., Suttles, 1968; Wheeldon, 1969) (see Figure 8–11). When social cohesion is absent, urban decay can get a strong foothold. Viable social networks are most likely to occur under certain conditions. For example, "neighboring" in urban environments is greater when there is racial similarity, shared socioeconomic status, psychological "investment" in a neighborhood, satisfaction with conditions there, and a positive sense of well-being (Unger & Wandersman, in press). Social networks can also be fostered or inhibited through environmental means. We will see later that they are very often strong in so-called "slums," and weak in many

urban renewal housing projects. According to Newman (1972, 1975) defensible space should also work to facilitate social network formation.

One way in which social networks can function effectively for the good of an urban area is when local organizations (often called "block organizations") are formed. These work for improvements such as better lighting, police protection, street repairs, or other common goals, Residents' participation in block organizations may be predicted by several factors: how important the block environment is to the individual; whether a person believes he or she could perform the behaviors necessary to participate; the perceived existence of common needs among residents; and how much a person generally participates in activities with other residents (Wandersman & Florin, 1981).

Urban Renewal

A major physical-environmental means of improving urban life is through urban renewal programs, which in the United States have caused the relocation of over 100,000 people a year. The assumption behind urban renewal was that it would provide better housing, *and* solve other problems of the poor as well. A better physical environment was expected to lead to better health, a more stable family, less crime and delinquency, greater motivation, an improved self-concept, and greater satisfaction with life (e.g., Schussheim, 1974). In effect, urban renewal was to be a panacea for many urban problems: There was assumed to be a causal relationship between poor housing and a "grab bag" of social ills. In fact, aside from studies relating poor housing to problems with physical and mental health (e.g., Duvall & Booth, 1978), there is little evidence to support this assumption.

Urban renewal can be defined as an integrated series of steps taken to maintain and upgrade the environmental, economic, and social health of an urban area (Porteus, 1977). To accomplish this, massive physical changes are often made in the environmental setting, which may involve demolishing housing and relocating residents. There is

Figure 8–11. Social networks, such as those involved in Neighborhood Crime Watch organizations, can be effective in ameliorating crime. (Barbara While)

frequently a conflict of interest of sorts between planners and those living in the slums that are torn down to make way for renewal (see Figure 8–12). Planners hope to attract wealthy individuals and businesses back into the city, to destroy eyesores, and to keep the city sufficiently attractive that people will make use of its cultural resources (Porteus, 1977). They tend to replace slums with luxury apartments and office buildings, forcing residents to move elsewhere. Unfortunately, the people who are relocated often do not perceive their area as a slum at all but as a pleasant neighborhood (Fried & Gleicher, 1961). The "slum" residents are usually the losers in a conflict with planners. They are forced to leave and are often adversely affected by it.

What are the psychological consequences of demolishing neighborhoods and forcing people to relocate? Clearly, this depends on a large number of situational conditions, including attraction to the former neighborhood. Overall, however, while forced relocation may occasionally have a mildly positive effect on family relationships (cf. Wilner *et al.*, 1962), it often has negative conse-

quences. It must be kept in mind that destroying a neighborhood not only eliminates buildings, but destroys a functioning social system and a sense of identity for people. According to Gans (1967), slum areas provide not only cheap housing, but offer the types of social support people need to keep going in a crisis-ridden existence.

An intensive study was made of the effects of an urban renewal project built in Boston's West End, an Italian working-class area that residents identified with greatly and liked very much. What were the consequences of relocation? Loss of home, neighborhood, and daily interactions with well-known neighbors caused an extreme upheaval in people's lives and disrupted their routines, personal relationships, and expectations. This led to a grief reaction in many of those who were displaced, especially in people who had been most satisfied with the status quo. It can be explained, in part, in terms of the relationship between the strength of social networks and physical and psychological well-being, discussed earlier. Among women who reported liking their neighborhood very much, 73 percent displayed short-term reactions of extreme grief, including vomiting, intestinal disorders, crying spells, nausea, and depression. About 20 percent of the residents were depressed for as long as two years after moving. These types of reactions, and more severe health effects, may be most common in people who are already "vulnerable" (e.g., those with previous problems) (e.g., Freeman, 1978). Interestingly, in terms of our discussion of cognitive mapping, people's reactions were mediated by knowledge of their former neighborhoods. The greater the familiarity, the stronger the grief (Fried, 1963) (see the box on page 258).

In addition to the kinds of losses caused by the demolition of neighborhoods, there is the problem of where people go when forced to relocate. Forced relocation frequently results in one of two housing options. Although affected individuals are generally promised alternative housing, the promise is often unfulfilled, and they tend to drift into slums. When this occurs, the net result of urban renewal is to lower the population of one

Figure 8–12. Unfortunately, what urban designers consider to be "slums" are often not viewed as such by area residents. (Peter Oliver)

THE PERSONAL TOLL OF RELOCATION: A DESCRIPTIVE ACCOUNT

While most of the research we've presented has been quantitative, often a descriptive account may add greatly to our understanding of environmental phenomena. The following commentary (Jacobs, 1961) describes the local culture in a high density urban neighborhood, characteristic of many targeted for urban renewal. It will give you an idea of the type of loss experienced when such neighborhoods are torn down. Jacobs observes that in such high density urban areas, sidewalks teem with excitement. Children play with each other on front stoops, and individuals stroll down the street conversing with merchants and looking into shop windows. In fact, such interactions constitute an important part of neighborhood life. Typically, residents know the merchants as well as many of the passersby from years of interaction. Relations with neighbors are very important to them. Over time, an atmosphere of trust develops. As Jacobs puts it:

The trust of a city street is formed over time from many, many little public sidewalk contacts. It grows out of people stopping by at the bar for a beer, getting advice from the grocer and giving advice to the newsstand man, comparing opinions with other customers at the bakery and nodding hello to the two boys drinking pop on the stoop, eyeing the girls while waiting to be called for dinner, admonishing the children, hearing about a job from the hardware man and borrowing a dollar from the druggist, admiring the new babies, and sympathizing over the way a coat faded.*

The atmosphere described by Jacobs has many important consequences for people's lives. First, it leads to a social structure characterized by a large number of individuals with whom one may have social contact and feel secure and accepted. Further, parents feel safe allowing their children to play outside in such settings, since they know others care. For example, when the neighborhood tailor spots a child who is lost and then calls the child's parents, the parents and the child benefit directly, and the child also learns that even people who are not formally related should display social responsibility to each other. In addition to experiencing social benefits and a degree of security about their children's welfare, Jacobs suggests that adults gain other benefits from the neighborhood culture. Thus, it is common in such neighborhoods for residents to leave apartment keys with a friendly shopkeeper when they are expecting company before they arrive home. The merchant may also receive packages for residents who are at work or let children playing in the street use the shop's bathroom.

In effect, the long-standing history of contacts between individuals forms a cement for mutual aid between neighborhood residents and for dealing with problematical situations. This is jeopardized when neighborhoods are demolished and long-term residents are forced to relocate. In many other ways, too, slum living provides sources of satisfaction for residents that are not visible to people from outside their culture and value system. For example, kinship and extended family ties play an important role in the life of people living in "slums." Unfortunately, urban designers, planners, and others generally fail to recognize these sources of support. Because they have different values and backgrounds, these groups have often concluded that the inner city is not characterized by a meaningful social life since it does *not* correspond to that common in middle-class communities.

*From J. Jacobs, "The death and life of great American cities." New York: Random House, 1961.

slum neighborhood while increasing the population of another. Alternatively, people are relocated in public housing, which is low-rent housing built for those with a relatively low income. Public housing often provides physical settings that are objectively much better than the residents' original homes, but such projects are often doomed to failure. In fact, even the physical improvements reflected in new public housing are often temporary, since in many cases they are ultimately destroyed by residents. And fear of crime and anxiety about being physically harmed are very important concerns of housing project residents (Argrist, 1974).

A classic example is the Pruitt-Igoe project in St. Louis, which was built in the inner city in 1954. In this project, 12,000 persons were relocated into 43 buildings 11 stories high, containing 2,762 apartments, and covering 57 acres. The buildings contained narrow hallways with no semiprivate areas for people to congregate—a design that was praised in *Architectural Forum* (April, 1951) for having no "wasted space." The project was expensive to build but very institutional in nature, containing such "features" as institutional wall tile (from which graffiti was easily removed), unattractive (but indestructible) light fixtures, and vandal-resistant radiators and elevators.

In spite of the way Pruitt-Igoe was built, within a few years it was a shambles. Take a walk with us through the project several years after it opened. First, there is a display of broken glass, tin cans, and abandoned cars covering the playgrounds and parking lots. Some of the building windows are broken; others have been boarded up with plywood. Inside, you smell the stench of urine, trash, and garbage. The elevator is in disrepair, and the presence of feces indicates it has been used as a toilet. Next, you notice that plumbing and electrical fixtures have been pulled out of apartment and hallway walls. When you come upon a resident and ask her about Pruitt-Igoe, she says she has no friends there; there is "nobody to help you." She also tells you that gangs have formed and that rape, vandalism, and robbery are common. Since crime frequently takes place in elevators and stairwells, the upper floors have been abandoned.

These conditions destroyed Pruitt-Igoe, and by 1970, 27 of the 43 buildings were vacant; they have now been totally demolished (Figure 8–13). Why did Pruitt-Igoe fail so miserably? There are multiple reasons. One explanation was proposed by Yancey (1972), who centered his argument around the fact that space in the buildings was primarily sociofugal. Since there were few semi-private, sociopetal spaces or other facilities that could promote the formation of a social order, the informal social networks which can play an important role in lower class neighborhoods did not develop. Lower class families like to congregate

Figure 8–13. The demolition of part of Pruitt-Igoe in 1972. (United Press International).

in informal spaces, typically along the street outside their home. This is facilitated in "slums" by low rise tenements, narrow streets, and lots of doorways to businesses in which to stop and talk. The design of many urban renewal projects does not facilitate such interaction. This architectural failure results in a lack of cohesion among residents as well as in conflict and crime. Yancey also contended that the high rise architectural design of the project was greatly to blame. It put children beyond their parents' sight and control whenever they were outside their home and gave them many hidden areas, such as stairwells and elevators, in which to cause mischief. Such areas also provided sanctuaries for teenagers and adults to engage in illicit activities almost anonymously. As one resident said, "All you have to do is knock out the lights on the landings above and below you. Then when someone comes . . . they stumble around and you can hear them in time to get out" (Yancey, 1972, p. 133).

Other explanations have also been put forward for the demise of Pruitt-Igoe. One suggested by Rainwater (1966) is that such "features" as vandal-proof radiators and walls may convey a self-threatening message of inferiority to residents and may actually challenge them to destroy these objects. In another context, Sommer (1974) and Stainbrook (1966) proposed that the environment can convey negative information that may adversely affect behavior. In a sense, the stigma of poverty was highlighted by the design of Pruitt-Igoe. It, like many public housing developments, had a look that set if off from other types of housing, and it was easily identified as "housing for the poor." The lack of "defensible space" (see the box "How to Design Public Housing") has also been suggested as an important explanation (Newman, 1972). Finally, it should be mentioned that Pruitt-Igoe was plagued by a poorly administered housing authority and by its isolation from the surrounding community.

Pruitt-Igoe is unfortunately not unique in its effects on residents, which has prompted many other housing projects to be studied by social scientists. One study was conducted in Puerto Rico by Hollingshead and Rogler (1963). Their findings will give you a feeling for the obstacles a public housing project is up against, even if it incorporates the types of improvements we've suggested. The project in question was less crowded and had better facilities, lower rents, and a healthier atmosphere than the slums from which the residents had moved. However, while only 35 percent had disliked the slums, 86 percent of the men and 71 percent of the women disliked the project. When their reasons were examined, they reflected many complaints that could not easily be remedied by design changes. One problem was loneliness, since the designers had not made provisions for housing the extended family people had lived with in the slums. Residents also resented their unknown neighbors and felt bored because they had lost the companions and pastimes they were used to. Finally, some were unhappy because they could no longer engage in certain illegal activities they had practiced in the slums (e.g., selling stolen goods, prostitution) due to greater surveillance.

What factors are associated with *satisfaction* in residents of low-income housing? A study by Rent and Rent (1978) surveyed residents from many housing projects in South Carolina. Those who lived in single family or "duplex" dwellings liked their residences much more than others. This satisfaction probably occurred, in part, because these residences are more often owned, which is another predictor of satisfaction in low-income housing. For other reasons, too (e.g., greater privacy), such dwellings produce more satisfaction. Not surprisingly, then, 75 percent of those surveyed said they would prefer to live in a single family dwelling, and 83 percent wanted to own one. Another important predictor of housing satisfaction is having friends in the neighborhood (often these turn out to be neighbors). Generally, the more satisfied one was with his or her neighbors, the greater the attraction to the living situation. An interesting finding was that overall life satisfaction was associated with liking one's residence. The happier one was with his or her life, the more satisfied they were with living arrange-

HOW TO DESIGN PUBLIC HOUSING

Our discussion of Pruitt-Igoe has read like a "how-not-to" guide for designing public housing. We now turn to some general guidelines for designing public housing so as to avoid these errors. Although few of our assertions have been extensively tested, they appear to be reasonable means for improving the functioning of public housing projects.

Our plan involves several elements. First, semiprivate spaces should be "designed in" to facilitate social interaction between residents and thus encourage the development of a social order. These areas should exist both inside and outside the building and should be planned so as to make pleasant social interactions almost inevitable. Can you think of any design schemes used in your dormitory or in other places that have successfully attained such a result? This strategy does have the desired effect. It has been shown experimentally that greater liking for housing and more interaction occurs when appropriate designs are incorporated into public housing (Holahan, 1976b; Mullins & Robb, 1977). Semiprivate spaces also encourage neighborliness and mutual helping (Wilner *et al.*, 1962).

The second element in our plan is derived from Newman's concept of defensible space. Buildings should be designed so that all space appears to "belong" to some individual or group. Such areas are defended and promote surveillance, which tends to reduce crime. How can this be accomplished in a housing project? Newman suggested that projects be divided into "subprojects" to promote territoriality. The areas around the building (e.g., playgrounds, parking spaces) should appear to "belong" to the building, as an external extension of internal living space. Public areas, such as hallways and elevators, should be eliminated to the extent possible (e.g., through horizontal rather than high rise construction). When this is not possible, "open air" hallways outside the building, combined with porches, or hallways and elevators that are accessible only to small groups of residents, can serve as territorial markers. Alternatively, fitting traditional corridors with windows can promote surveillance.

Design should also allow for surveillance by the police. Often, public housing has tried to create a "park like" atmosphere. There is a large interior open space surrounded by housing units. Vehicles, passersby (and also police) are denied visual access to the interior. Patrol cars cannot reach the area (Reppetto, 1976). To deal with this problem, more direct access to the interior should be available to police (by building roads that go there) and the interior space should be visible to those in the street.

Several other guidelines should also be followed. Projects should be kept small (between 150 and 350 units), only a limited number of large families should be allowed in each project, and a good management firm should be chosen (*Chicago Tribune,* 1974).

The above suggestions should be taken into account when designing or renovating public housing. Degree of compliance with them could also be used to predict the probability of problems, and to plan for police protection.

ments. Overall, then, social as well as physical factors may be important determinants of housing satisfaction among low-income individuals.

Fortunately, some of the more recent trends in government housing assistance have more elements associated with residential satisfaction than earlier project housing. When government assistance is provided, the US government has more or less stopped building "high rise" projects for low-income families. Instead, people are placed more often in townhouses or small apartment buildings. There have also been increased government assistance with home ownership, direct housing subsidies for the poor, and attempts to renovate or preserve current housing instead of demolition. This serves the admirable function of "fixing the building and leaving the people." Another recent innovation is "urban homesteading" where abandoned urban property is given to individuals who agree to rehabilitate it to meet existing housing codes and occupy it for a prescribed period of time. It has sometimes been quite successful, but in other instances the practical problems of having low-income families with limited resources play the role of "general contractor" have been overwhelming. Unfortunately, there has been one "backlash" from earlier fiascoes with public housing such as Pruitt-Igoe: Some municipalities refuse altogether to have any form of it within their boundaries.

When people *must* be moved due to urban renewal, is there some more humane way of accomplishing this? One possibility would be to move people to a new setting in established social groups. This would maintain the social cohesion of the former neighborhood (Young & Willmott, 1957). It could also be maintained, to some extent, by moving people to redeveloped areas near their old neighborhoods. Another important factor is citizen participation in planning the move and the new setting in which they will live (e.g., Arnstein, 1969). Designers and planners should encourage this, and be especially sensitive to cultural or subcultural differences in housing preferences.

Summary

Urban renewal is an environmental means that has been used in an attempt to solve the problems of cities. Unfortunately, while it may have beneficial effects on the city as a whole, it has often been quite costly to those whom it displaces. These "costs" could be reduced if planners attended to the needs of resident populations more closely, but some costs of forced relocation are probably unavoidable. With this in mind, we briefly turn to an alternative to city life, which unfortunately is open only to the more affluent.

ESCAPING FROM THE CITY

The great American dream appears to be to leave the city. Evidence of the dislike most city dwell-

ers have for their environs is suggested by the finding that almost 4 in 10 would like to move out of the city, though 7 in 10 say they could be induced to stay if conditions would improve (Gallup Report, March, 1978, vol. 2). Only 15 percent of those living in communities with less than 50,000 residents express a desire to leave (Gallup Poll, April 19, 1981). People wanting most to leave the cities are the younger, better educated, more affluent residents. In addition to crime, urbanites cite overcrowding, pollution, housing, traffic congestion, and noise as major reasons for leaving. Where would people rather live? A 1977 survey asked a representative American sample, "If you could live wherever you wanted, would you prefer a city, a suburban area, a small town, or a farm?" The results were: city, 13 percent; suburbs, 29 percent; small town, 20 percent; rural area or farm, 28 percent (Public Opinion, 1980). However, it doesn't appear that the city is being totally rejected: Many of those expressing a preference for rural areas still wanted to be near a medium-size or large city.

This explains the massive move to suburbia that has occurred in recent years. What exactly are suburbs? They are areas within a metropolis that are relatively distant from the center of population (Fischer, 1976). Suburban living has increased dramatically, especially since World War II, and at present more Americans live in the suburbs than in the center city or nonmetropolitan areas (Fischer, 1977). Why is this happening? Quite simply, because suburban living offers an answer to a number of urban problems. As one moves farther from the city, he or she is subjected to fewer crowds and to less dirt, noise, and pollution. In addition, although suburban crime rates are increasing, they are still much lower than in the city. For example, FBI statistics indicated that suburbanites were less than half as likely as urbanites to be murdered or to have a car stolen (Kelley, 1974).

What are the consequences of the move to suburbia for those who make it? There is some evidence that the move has a positive effect. Suburbanites are generally happier with their housing, their communities, and their lives than city dwellers, even when socioeconomic status and other differences between urban and rural populations are statistically controlled (Fischer, 1973; Marans & Rodgers, 1975). Also, people who move to the suburbs are much less afraid of crime victimization, and restrict their behavior less due to fear of crime (Lavrakas, 1982; Skogan & Maxfield, 1981). However, not all is well in suburbia. The price of typical suburban houses is rising tremendously, and it appears that fewer and fewer people will be able to afford or maintain a suburban life in the future. Further, as more and more people escape the city for the suburbs, crowding, pollution, and other urban problems are becoming suburban problems. As noted earlier, crime in the suburbs is increasing, and the use of drugs in suburban schools is cause for great concern. All this leaves one wondering if the suburban areas of today will be characterized by a full complement of "urban" problems in the future. But perhaps the worst problem created by the move to suburbia has its roots back in the cities. Abandoning urban areas to move to suburbia has jeopardized all that the city has to offer. We must find a way to solve urban problems so that people will want to live in the cities again and take advantage of the many benefits.

CHAPTER SUMMARY

The city is a salient environmental element in everyone's life. In fact, 70 percent of the American population lives in cities or suburbs. Our perception and experience of cities can be studied by investigating our cognitive maps, or "cities of the mind." Cognitive mapping reflects the way spatial information is acquired, stored, decoded, and applied to comprehension of the everyday physical environment. What shows up on our cognitive maps is a reflection of ourselves and our environment; complete cognitive maps are beneficial.

How does the urban setting affect individuals who live in it? A number of conceptual formulations have been derived to understand and predict the effects of the city on individuals; these include overload, environmental stress, behavioral con-

straint, and overmanning notions. Although they are often presented as competing concepts, it is probably true that overload, stress, constrained behavior, and insufficient resources each explains some of the consequences of an urban existence. Further, the predictions of each one can be integrated into the general environment–behavior model presented in Chapter 3. While this model hasn't been tested explicitly in research on cities, many of its assertions have been supported.

What are the results of experiments on the effects of city life? Two methodological perspectives (the "single variable" approach and the "urban versus rural" approach) have been used in past research. Each has its strengths and weaknesses. Overall, such urban stressors as noise, pollution, heat, crowding, extra demand, and crime have at least moderately detrimental effects on city dwellers. Further, when cities and nonurban areas are compared, there are urban-rural differences in terms of affiliative behavior, prosocial behavior, crime, stress, coping behavior, long-term aftereffects, and health. On most of these dimensions, urbanites come out on the short end. However, on dimensions not often studied by researchers (e.g., ability to adapt to diverse situations), urbanites may come out ahead.

Finally, a number of solutions have been tried to alleviate urban problems. One major attempt has been urban renewal. Unfortunately, this has often involved a conflict of interest between slum dwellers and city planners, with the former being forced to relocate. Forced relocation into public housing sometimes has disastrous consequences, which might be ameliorated by proper design of public housing. The dream of most urbanites, however, is suburbia; yet this is attainable only for those whose socioeconomic level permits it. Research on suburban living shows that it offers a solution to some of the negative aspects of the city for those who can make the move.

Suggested Projects

1. One assumption we've made is that cities differ from small towns on a number of dimensions. To test this hypothesis, first buy

copies of a few newspapers from large cities and small towns. Compare the following sections: entertainment, sports, and reports of local crime. Next, locate some telephone directories from large cities and small towns. Compare listings for the following: medical specialists, tradespeople, specialized restaurants of diverse nationalities, museums, religious institutions, educational facilities, and theaters. What pattern of urban-rural differences emerges on these various dimensions?

2. Have some friends majoring in different subjects draw sketches of your campus. Evaluate the maps in terms of the buildings featured and those omitted. Do you find, like Saarinen, that students with different majors draw different cognitive maps? Next, draw a "composite" cognitive map of your campus from all of the individual maps that you've collected. What features of the campus seem to be conspicuously absent? Can you form any hypotheses as to why? Can you imagine any design changes that would make them more salient? Which features of the campus seem to lend themselves best to mapping and why?

3. Think of three cities you've visited, and attempt to rate them in terms of "atmosphere." Can you identify specific physical or social aspects that led you to make these judgments?

4. Now that you've been exposed to an empirically based discussion of the city, what are your views of urban life? Has our assessment led you to become more positive or more negative toward cities than before?

5. Do a mini-experiment similar to that done by Bronzaft and McCarthy (1975) on the effects of noise on performance. First, find a classroom building or dormitory in which some areas are noisier than others. Next, choose some representative performance dimensions (e.g., grades, test scores, attendance, illness), and see if noise leads to performance decrements. If this type of measure isn't available, construct one that is (e.g., favorability of nonverbal cues given off). Try to use a setting where people in the noisy and quiet areas are randomly assigned to their particular setting. If this isn't possible, be sure to allow for the limitations that nonrandom assignment places on your findings (for a description of this problem, see the Appendix).

6. Obtain from the library several urban newspapers that include the daily pollution index for their metropolitan areas. Plot the index for a week, along with the number of reported crimes in various categories, and reports of serious traffic accidents and deaths in the same geographic area. See if you find evidence of a relationship between pollution levels and accidents or crime.

7. Try to replicate the studies Newman and McCauley did on reciprocation of eye contact (which signals accessibility for interactions). In a small town, and then in a city, position yourself near a doorway. When people passing by are a few feet away, initiate eye contact. Record the number of reciprocal gestures you receive in both settings. Do your results replicate those of Newman and McCauley?

8. Write a paragraph or two stating your agreement or disagreement with the following: "The 'bright side' of urban life has been missed by researchers." Give as much evidence as possible to support your position.

9 Architecture, Design, and Behavior

INTRODUCTION

You are finally moving out of the dormitory and into the "real world." A local newspaper ad reads "immaculate two bedroom apartment close to campus, recently redecorated." You become excited, and rush over to take a look. From the outside, the building looks as if it were poured out of a cement mixer—not too different from the dorms you are trying to escape. You had hoped for a more unique and inviting exterior, but still proceed inside with high hopes. Once the manager opens the door, your hopes are dashed. You were looking for a relaxing place to study and to entertain. Instead, you are confronted with a sofa upholstered in simulated leopard skin, situated between two mirrored walls. The carpeting is the most intense orange hue imaginable, and as you reach for your sunglasses the landlord remarks about how well the draperies match the carpeting. He turns on the lights (the cold fluorescent variety) so that you can better see the set of purple lounge chairs. Your headache intensifies.

Before you flee, you contemplate what it would be like to live there. The intensity of the apartment is totally inconsistent with your needs for a relaxing haven away from the everyday routine of school life. Would the apartment be a good place to study? There is no desk and the lighting is wrong, but besides that the room would be distracting to you when trying to concentrate. In fact, you are not even sure you could eat a snack there—the mirrors would make you too self-conscious of your weight. Could you entertain? One look at the way the furniture is arranged—hardly a conversational grouping with each piece along a different wall—convinces you that you'd be the host or hostess of the dullest parties on campus.

As should be clear from the above example, the architectural environment can play a significant role in our lives. People create it, and it in turn has a great deal of impact on their behavior. Our homes, classrooms, shops, work places—the settings where we spend a great deal of time—are all part of the built environment. The behavioral effects of the built environment (Fitch, 1972), interposed between people and the natural, untamed world, are extremely important. Not all settings are equally significant or central in terms of behavioral impact, but *primary* environments, those in which we spend most of our time, are very important factors in our psychological well-being and our actions (Stokols, 1978). *Secondary* environments, such as the restaurant or cafeteria you may have eaten in today, are ones in which we spend less time and which have fewer behavioral consequences. As we will see, however, these can also affect us. In this chapter we will consider the ways in which certain architectural and design features present in both primary and secondary environments (e.g., lights, color, furnishings) can influence our behavior.

In what ways can design affect behavior? The potential effects are too numerous even to contemplate, and we can only summarize a few here. In terms of the theories we discussed in Chapter 3, design elements may be viewed as affecting our level of arousal or stimulation, as well as the level of information we receive from the environment and how much a setting constrains our behavior. To the extent that each of these is affected, the various conceptual formulations (e.g., environmental load, behavior constraint) can be used to predict a host of behavioral consequences such as our affective state, whether we'll help others or aggress, and our performance at simple and complex tasks. Design can affect behavior in many other ways as well. For example, in Chapter 8 we found that "hardened" targets are less apt to sustain vandalism damage, and in Chapter 10 we will discuss how designs that foster interpersonal interaction by placing people in close proximity to each other can promote friendship.

Our general environmental stressor model can also be used to predict how we'll react to design elements which are nonoptimal. One way of coping with these is to *adjust* them so they become more compatible with our desires and needs. This could involve the use of design alternatives (other possible designs which have different effects). We could install incandescent lighting to replace fluorescent lighting if we find the latter to be objectionable. Alternatively, we can *adapt,* or "learn to live with" the existing environmental conditions, changing our behavior or desires to bring them more in line with the prevailing environment. Many of the behavioral effects of design elements could be viewed as adaptation. We have summarized just a few of the ways in which design can affect our behavior, and will discuss many more examples in this and the following two chapters.

Before proceeding, we should note that the relationships between architectural environments and our mood and behavior are complex, and that the temptation to oversimplify them must be resisted. In order to facilitate our understanding of this complexity, we will first examine some mechanisms through which built environments are thought to influence behavior, such as *architectural determinism* and *environmental probabilism.* Next, we will explore the effects of some specific design elements, such as light, color, and furnishings, on behavior. We will conclude this chapter with a look at the design process— the way in which design ideas are implemented. In the following two chapters, we will see how some of the above concepts apply to a number of specific environments (e.g., hospitals, office settings).

EXTENT OF ARCHITECTURAL INFLUENCE

An Historical Overview

Until recently, the behavioral effects of architecture and design were often underestimated. Though generally planned, the cities and buildings of history were rarely conceived of in terms of how they might influence behavior or the quality of life. Instead, aesthetic considerations were paramount in the eyes of designers. More behaviorally-oriented perspectives are only now being integrated systematically into the design process. There is now an increased awareness on the part of planners that design does affect behavior. However, researchers as well as designers have had difficulty in agreeing on the extent of archi-

tectural influence. At present, there are a variety of different views on this.

Architectural Determinism

One of the early conceptualizations of architectural influence on behavior was *architectural determinism*. Briefly, architectural determinism holds that the built environment shapes the behavior of the people within it. In its most extreme form, architecture and design are seen as the only causes of behavior. It has become clear, however, that such a view is too simplistic to adequately account for the effects of design. First, it ignores the fact that people engage in transactions with the environment—they influence and change the environment as it influences and changes them. Second, architectural determinism does not allow for the complex interactions which occur among physical, social, and psychological factors. Architectural design influences privacy, group formation, and the like, but our needs, ongoing activities, and relationships modify these effects. For example, whether one moves to a crowded dormitory floor on which several friends live or to an identical one where no friends live can determine whether he or she will experience crowding stress (Baum, Harpin, & Valins, 1975).

Environmental Possibilism

Other perspectives on behavior in the built environment have evolved as reactions to architectural determinism. One, called *environmental possibilism* (Porteus, 1977), views the environment as presenting us with opportunities as well as setting potential limits on behavior. The choices we make determine the degree to which any of these opportunities are realized, or the barriers are surmounted. Rather than assuming that the environment completely determines behavior (as does determinism), environmental possibilism views the environment as a context in which behavior occurs. According to this conceptualization, our outcomes are jointly determined by the environment and the choices *we* make.

Environmental Probabilism

Somewhere in between the determinist and the possibilist positions on architecture and behavior lies another orientation, *environmental probabilism* (Porteus, 1977). While determinism assumes that the environment determines behavior absolutely and possibilism ascribes such a large role to individual choice that it is hard to make predictions regarding environmental influence on behavior, probabilism is a compromise. It assumes that while an organism may choose a variety of responses in any environmental situation, there are *probabilities* associated with specific instances of design and behavior. These probabilities reflect the influence of nonarchitectural factors as well as design variables on behavior. Thus, one can say that, given all we know about people and the par-

ticular environment they are in, some behaviors are more likely to occur than others.

A simple example will serve to illustrate environmental probabilism. Let us assume that you have a class with a small number of others in a very large room. Under these conditions, discussion is minimal. After studying everything you can find about classrooms, you decide to change the arrangement of the desks. You have learned that, in most cases, if you arrange seating in a circle, people will talk more. Thus the chances are good that if you rearrange your classroom in this way, you will help to create more discussion. However, if the class was scheduled late in the day, or if the instructor has "turned students off," you may not succeed. There are no "sure bets," according to probabilism.

Regardless of your orientation, you will no doubt agree that social and psychological phenomena are to some extent influenced by architecture and design. We will now turn to a consideration of some specific, individual *interior* design elements which have been found to affect our behavior across a wide variety of settings. (For a consideration of the effects of some exterior design elements, see the box on p. 268.) In contrast to our focus here on individual design elements— the pieces which make up the whole—Chapters 10 and 11 will consider the behavioral effects of design in entire behavior settings.

BEHAVIOR AND ELEMENTS OF ARCHITECTURAL DESIGN

Lighting

How does interior lighting affect our behavior? Many of its behavioral effects are performance-related. Lighting can affect how well we perform in many contexts, ranging from an examination, to an experimental task in a laboratory, to a job on an automobile assembly line. At a very basic level, lighting affects performance by making it harder or easier to see what we are doing. At one extreme, the absence of light makes it impossible to take an exam because we cannot read the ques-

OUTSIDE AS WELL AS INSIDE:
THE EFFECTS OF EXTERIOR DESIGN ELEMENTS

Most research in environmental psychology has been concerned with interior architecture—the effects of design elements in *interior* spaces. The design elements we speak of in this chapter are also applicable to the exterior of a building. Lighting has behavioral effects outdoors as well as indoors, and the placement of windows on an exterior can help to evoke a desired image or feeling just as it does indoors. Here we will deal with a few issues involved in the design of exteriors—both buildings and exterior spaces.

(N.Y. Convention & Visitor's Bureau.)

Figure 9–1 A and B. The design of buildings or monuments can come to symbolize cities.

Distinctive exteriors of buildings lend their image to a city, so that we may think of New York City as the Empire State Building and the Statue of Liberty, of Washington, D.C. as the Capitol and Washington Monument, or of St. Louis as the Gateway Arch. Thus, striking or unusual architectural design of the outside of buildings or structures can provide material for our cognitive images of cities, as we mentioned in Chapter 8 (see Figure 9–1 A and B). Sometimes these images may be misleading—for instance, San Antonio is no longer accurately imaged as the Alamo. And images can be remade with new buildings of unusual merit or design. Baltimore has changed its image of a dreary industrial and port city by remaking its harbor areas.

Exterior design elements can also affect our mood. By building a bright new showcase area around the Inner Harbor and adding striking buildings to it, Baltimore has created a festive mood in a once dreary place (Figure 9–2 A and B). Also, recall the awe of a great gothic cathedral, or the excitement or happiness that can be derived from the design of an amusement park. To a

Figure 9–2 A and B. Redesign of exterior spaces can affect a city's image. (Kevin Blanc)

large extent, architecture has been deliberately concerned with the emotions that are evoked by design elements, and this more artistic concern has dominated architecture for a long time. Consider one example. A goal of design might be to evoke feelings of respect and reverence. This is particularly true in building memorials and monuments. The hushed dignity of the Lincoln Memorial in Washington is a case in point (see Figure 9–3). Or one can design for a different emotion or feeling, as is derived from the "skyline" of Las Vegas (see Figure 9–4).

Many of the ways in which exterior space affects people are also discussed in Chapters 8, 10, and 11, so we will not belabor the point here. The arrangement of space in parks, urban neighborhoods, playgrounds, and a number of other exterior spaces affects us just as arrangement of interior space does. For example, recall the research discussed in Chapter 7 about crowding in dormitories (see box on p. 206). Baum and Valins (1977) found that when design of interior dormitory space resulted in residents more frequently meeting people they did not know, crowding was experienced. Subsequent research also showed that exterior design features had the same

Figure 9–3.
The Lincoln
Memorial.
Some designs
can inspire
great awe,
reverence,
and respect.
(Kevin Blanc)

Figure 9–4.
"The Strip" in
Las Vegas.
(From Ittelson,
W. H. (Ed.),
*Environment
and Cognition.*
New York:
Seminar
Press, 1973,
p. 101.
Courtesy of
Venturi, Raush
and Scott
Brown.)

effects in urban neighborhoods (Baum, Davis, & Aiello, 1978). When stores or other attractive or heavily used facilities were dispersed on street corners in residential neighborhoods and resulted in many people walking to them along streets, crowding was more likely. Apparently, the arrangement of stores and houses caused people living along a street with a store on it to frequently encounter strangers outside their homes.

The effects of exterior design are not limited to the images and emotions that they evoke. Arrangement of space and its appearance can affect behavior as well. However, we presently have few systematic studies of these effects to go on. Further investigation of these effects is a very important area for future research.

tions. On the other hand, we may not be able to see the questions on the exam if there is too much light. Generally, the data indicate that as lighting increases up to a critical level, visual abilities and performance also improve (Boyce, 1975). Data also suggest that if at some point the level of lighting becomes too great, our visual abilities may actually decrease (e.g., Logan & Berger, 1961). Thus, the effects of lighting will follow the familiar "inverted U," with performance improving with lighting up to a point, while further increases in lighting detract from performance.

In addition to the amount of light, *glare* is also related to performance. What is glare? It refers to the introduction of bright light into a setting that is less intensely lit. This may reduce our ability to see things, and may adversely affect how well we perform various tasks (e.g., Boyce, 1975).

Different lighting conditions can also affect our mood, and may impact on our social behavior. These effects probably depend on the environmental context we are in. For example, dark spaces in the inner city may be depressing or frightening, while in other settings they can be quite romantic, facilitating intimacy. A dark room is certainly more conducive to making love than one that is brightly lit. In this vein, Gergen, Gergen, and Barton (1973) found that when college students who were strangers to each other were placed in a dark room for several hours, considerable verbal and physical intimacy occurred between them. Darkness and anonymity had apparently removed some customary barriers to intimacy.

On the more negative side, glare seems to elicit discomfort across environmental contexts (Boyce, 1975), and under some circumstances fluorescent lighting may have different effects than incandescent lighting. One study found that hyperactive behavior was reduced by changing from fluorescent to traditional lighting (Mayron *et al.*, 1977). Children were apparently calmed by the full-spectrum light as opposed to the harsher, "white" fluorescent light. Others have reported evidence of this as well, and it has been suggested that learning-disabled children are sensitive to the quality of lighting, particularly when fluorescent systems are in use (Wandersman *et al.*, in press).

Windows

Windows figure prominently in the general ambience, as well as the illumination, of a setting. Studies have considered the behavioral effects of windowless factories. Prichard (1964) has argued that this does not reduce worker efficiency, but research on underground factories in Sweden has suggested that workers in windowless environments tend to suffer more fatigue and somatic distress (e.g., headaches), and to express more negative feelings about the setting (Hollister, 1978). To some extent, lack of windows can be compensated for by providing high levels of lighting and air conditioning, but the general conclusion to be drawn is that workers do not like windowless settings (Collins, 1975).

In office environments, the presence of windows also appears to be important. Research has indicated that regardless of whether occupants are satisfied with most aspects of their offices, not having windows leads to dissatisfaction (Ruys, 1970). The desire for windows in an office environment appears to be sufficiently strong that Ruys (1970) concluded that the problems created by windowless offices could not be corrected without installing windows. Sommer (1974) did find worker attempts to compensate for a lack of windows by hanging travel posters, landscape pictures, and other decorations, but these did not appear to remove the problems.

Other evidence of the importance of windows comes from studies of windowless schools. Originally designed to reduce distraction in the classroom, as well as to lower heating costs and vandalism, these school buildings typically contain few if any windows. Research has suggested that the absence of windows in classrooms has no consistent effect on learning (some students improve; others show poorer performance), but that it does have a *negative* impact on mood (Architectural Research Library, 1965; Karmel, 1965).

Windows are clearly important in residential settings, classrooms, and offices. By providing a source of natural lighting and a view of the outdoors, they can make a room more attractive and pleasant. Since distraction is less relevant in the home than in other settings, it is difficult to argue against windows in this environment, though energy considerations can provide a case.

Color

Color, like lighting, may influence us directly as well as impact on the overall ambience of a setting. Lighting and color are difficult to separate because they heavily influence one another. The way in which we perceive a color will depend on the lighting; color may also determine how well illuminated a room appears to us. For example, it takes more illumination to achieve the same effective level of lighting in a black than in a yellow room. There is also some evidence suggesting that certain visual abilities may be affected by color (Eastman, 1968). It seems that we may be better able to discriminate colors in rooms of certain hues than in others.

Color also has independent effects on mood (e.g., Mehrabian & Russell, 1974); in fact, different colors may sometimes elicit different moods. We may feel that one color is soothing while another is more arousing, or that a third makes us feel secure and peaceful. Wilson (1966) has reported that red hues actually generate greater physiological arousal than do green hues, and Baum and Davis (1976) found that different intensities of the same color affected subjects' response to model rooms. Light green rooms appeared larger and less crowded than identical rooms painted a darker green. The latter study suggests that color can affect the ways in which we perceive settings. In similar research, Acking and Kuller (1972) had subjects rate a series of slides depicting rooms which varied in color. Results indicated that lighter rooms were seen as more open and spacious. However, ratings of the "pleasantness" of a room did not vary with its color.

Other studies have also considered the judged "pleasantness" of different colors, with somewhat different results. Helson and Lansford (1970) found that the most pleasant background colors were white, light shades of red, yellow,

green, and blue, as well as dark green and black. Overall, then, while judged "pleasantness" does not always vary with color, it does in some cases. Before concluding, we should note that individual differences in color preference are so great that you should not be surprised if your favorites were not those identified by Helson and Lansford. Also, colors that would be pleasant in one context (e.g., a recreation room) may be very unpleasant in another (e.g., a bedroom).

Aesthetics

One of the primary goals of a design is to evoke a particular response from people viewing the finished setting. Its aesthetic qualities play an important role in this regard. Some environments evoke awe while others may suggest informality and comfort. The design of churches may seek to dwarf humans, and therefore suggest the proper relationship between people and their deity. Thus, many churches are large, built seemingly for giants, and are sometimes awe-inspiring. A family restaurant, however, may be built to suggest a very different image, seeking to welcome people by implying a "homey" environment.

Architecture and design are forms of art. The aesthetic quality of the built environment can be as influential as natural beauty. The problem is that aesthetic considerations in design often operate contrary to behavioral ones. Some of the most beautiful structures we have created are also among the most impractical. However, one cannot simply dismiss aesthetic quality as less relevant than the behavioral effects of design. There is evidence that aesthetics as well may be important in determining behavior (e.g., Steinitz, 1968). (For a thorough discussion of general aesthetic principles, see Chapter 2.)

Reseach has underscored the behavioral consequences associated with the aesthetic quality of the environment. Studies of images of urban areas suggest that aesthetic qualities influence people's ability to find their way through a cityscape (Lynch, 1960). There is also evidence to suggest that aesthetic qualities can reduce the monotony of the city and maintain gratifying levels of stimulation (e.g., Berlyne, 1960; Lynch, 1960). Aesthetics are important in people's evaluations of environments—they may, for example, influence where someone chooses to live (Michelson, 1970). This appears particularly true for people who move from the city to the suburbs. (For a more thorough discussion of these issues, see Chapter 8.)

Research has also indicated that the aesthetic quality of a room—the extent to which it is pleasant or attractive—may affect the sorts of evaluations we make while in that setting. Maslow and Mintz (1956) compared subjects' ratings of a series of photographs in a "beautiful" room (well-decorated, well-lit, etc.), an average room (a professor's office), and an "ugly" room (resembling a janitor's closet). Their results showed that subjects rated the photos most positively if they had been in the beautiful room, and most negatively if they had been in the ugly room.

Attractive environments also make people feel better. Research has shown that decorated spaces make people feel more comfortable than ones which have not been decorated (Campbell, 1979). Also, the good moods which are associated with pleasant environments seem to increase people's willingness to help each other (Sherrod *et al.*, 1977). How does aesthetic quality affect one's work output? We can guess that for some kinds of work in certain settings the positive feelings associated with pleasant spaces may improve work efficiency and accuracy, while in other contexts an aesthetically pleasant environment may be disruptive. People feel more like talking to one another in pleasant settings (Russell & Mehrabian, 1978) and to the extent that socializing in the office detracts from efficient performance, aesthetic quality can be a problem. Research has also suggested that decorations may be distracting (e.g., Baum & Davis, 1976), but whether this is necessarily a problem appears to depend on other factors (Worchel & Teddlie, 1976).

Furnishings

Furniture, its arrangement, and other aspects of the interior environment are also important deter-

minants of behavior. In classroom settings, for example, it appears that the use of nontraditional seating patterns can influence student performance—horseshoe arrangements, circular patterns, or other less formal departures from the standard "rows of desks facing the teacher" seem to generate more student interest and participation (Sommer, 1969). There is also some evidence that within traditional classroom arrangements there are differences in performance according to where people sit. These findings are discussed in Chapter 6.

The arrangement of furnishings in a room can also affect the way in which the room is perceived. Some studies have served simply to confirm what most of us have always known or suspected. For example, Imamoglu (1973) found that empty rooms were perceived to be larger than furnished rooms, which were seen as larger than "overfurnished" rooms. This verifies the common experience reported by college students looking for off-campus housing—furnished apartments look smaller than unfurnished ones, and unfurnished apartments seem smaller once students have moved in.

Many studies of furniture arrangement have been conducted in institutional settings. Reusch and Kees (1956) have noted that the way in which patients arrange their furniture expresses their feelings regarding interaction in their space. Some arrangements (called *sociopetal*) are open and welcome interaction, while others (called *sociofugal*) are closed and discourage social contact. Sommer and Ross (1958) described the relation between furniture arrangement and behavior in a geriatric hospital. When chairs were arranged in rows along the walls, patients did not interact very much. This arrangement was simply not conducive to talking; it did not suggest that interaction was appropriate. When Sommer and Ross changed the arrangement, clustering the chairs in small groups, people began to talk to each other. The new juxtaposition facilitated conversation while the old one seemed to inhibit it. Holahan (1972) found the same kind of effect in a psychiatric hospital—patients seated around a table talked to each other more than patients seated in rows against the walls. (For a thorough discussion of design in selected institutional environments, see Chapter 10).

Furniture arrangement can also communicate status, as well as a desire for distance from others. For example, studies considering the effects of furniture placement in offices have found that the use of a desk as a "barrier" between the office occupant and a visitor can communicate a desire for physical and psychological distance, as well as status differences. It can also have implications for the pleasantness of the interaction and the visitor's level of comfort (Campbell, 1981). Consider the arrangements of office space in a college psychology department. Some professors arrange their offices so that visitors sit across a desk from them. Others arrange their offices to suggest less distance, placing no barriers between them and their students. Each arrangement can evoke different reactions (for additional discussion of office design, see Chapter 11).

Furniture arrangements can be used to help structure the preexisting architectural layout of a setting. In most environmental contexts, the walls, the location of the doors, and so on are *fixed*—they are rather difficult to move. To some extent, these elements do structure the space inside a building. However, the placement of furniture often provides additional structure. For example, if you have a large living room, you may arrange the furniture to suggest two rooms. Or, you may arrange it to unify the room. Examples of this are shown in Figures 9–5A and B. In Figure 9–5A, the furniture has been arranged to suggest two rooms. The first "room," including a dining table and television, has a busy "family room" feel to it, while the second "room" is more intimate. Separated from the first by the wall suggested by the bookcases, the second "room" gathers people around the fireplace, and evokes a more peaceful feeling.

Figure 9–5B depicts the same space and furniture as in Figure 9–5A, but the structure is very different. Here we have a single room—no attempt is made to break it into two. All of the furniture, except the chairs, is placed against the walls. This suggests distance—conversation is not facilitated in this arrangement. It actually looks more like a waiting room than a living room.

Arrangement is not the only aspect of furnishings that can affect mood and behavior. The quality of the furnishings is also important. Earlier, we discussed studies on the effects of "pretty" and "ugly" rooms and found that being in a pretty room could sometimes have beneficial psychological effects. Unfortunately, studies varying the quality of single pieces or sets of furniture have not been done systematically. However, there is research on the effects of large-scale improvements in furnishings. Holahan and Saegert (1973) reported on a large-scale refurbishing of a psychiatric hospital admissions ward, comparing it to another ward that was not redone. The refurbishing included bringing in new furniture, repainting, and creating different types of space. These improvements in the quality of the environment led to increases in social activity on the ward. Similar findings have been reported by Whitehead *et al.* (in press), who studied analogous changes in a psychiatric unit in a hospital setting. Both studies suggest that the quality of an environment can influence mood and behavior. However, because the improvements were so extensive, it is difficult to know what was primarily responsible for the observed results.

Ultimately, any decision about furnishings will be based on several criteria, including cost, aesthetics, and the function of the setting. This latter criterion is often the most difficult to evaluate. Sometimes a given space is expected to facilitate communication between employees working near each other, to serve as a meeting room on occasion, and to impress clients who come for consultations. Some of these functions are at odds with each other, and the choice and arrangement of furnishings must be accomplished with these complex issues in mind.

Privacy

One of the most important aspects of the design of interior space is the amount of privacy it provides. (For a definition of the concept of "privacy," see the box on page 276.) All of us some-

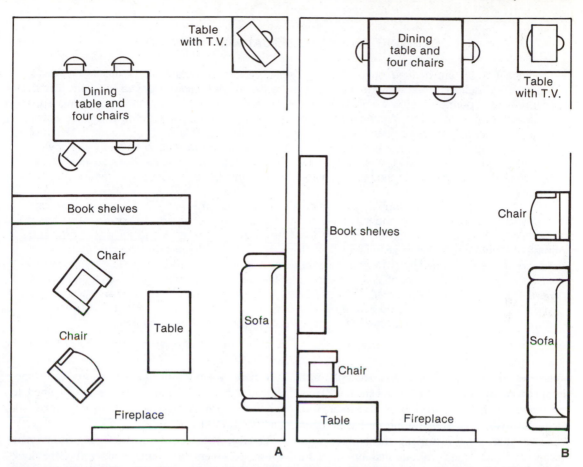

Figure 9–5A and B. Furniture arrangement can change the effect of a room dramatically. These rooms contain the same furniture but look very different. Which would be more pleasant for sitting with friends?

times need to be able to "get away from it all." Architectural design can increase or decrease the ease with which people can do so. In some settings we may find it very difficult to "be alone" while in others, getting away may be easier. For example, dormitories that house students one instead of two to a bedroom promote greater privacy. Likewise, the use of barriers around one's work area may increase the sense of privacy there. Often, then, privacy adjustment is centered around the structures that partition interior space. Some designs make privacy easy to achieve, while others make it more difficult.

One way in which an environment can directly affect feelings of privacy is by increasing or de-

creasing the possibility of seeing and being seen by other people. This refers to *visual intrusion*— that sense of privacy that is more difficult to achieve when people can still be seen. If you lived in a glass house and could see people outside and vice versa, your sense of privacy would be less than if you could block them out. Consistent with this, research has indicated that barriers that block views of other people decrease the impact of these people while barriers that do not obscure the view (e.g., clear panels) do not reduce their impact (e.g., Baum, Reiss, & O'Hara, 1974; Desor, 1972).

When an environment does not provide enough privacy for those using it, problems develop.

DEFINING AND CONCEPTUALIZING PRIVACY

Altman (1975) has defined privacy as the "selective control of access to the self or one's group." This definition has two important parts. The first is the notion of privacy as an *ability to withdraw or separate ourselves from other people*. In effect, this refers to the need or desire for seclusion. At the same time, Altman recognizes a second important aspect of privacy—*the ability to control information about ourselves*. Similarly, Ittelson *et al.* (1974) define privacy in terms of freedom to regulate the type or amount of self-information made available to others. Thus, privacy also refers to regulating what other people find out about us. We all keep some aspects of our personalities or some of our thoughts to ourselves, and this need is part of our requirement for privacy.

Privacy means different things to different people. Marshall (1972) has studied students' notions of privacy and compared them to their parents' definitions. Marshall reported evidence of six basic definitions, three of which loosely conform to Altman's description of "need for seclusion," and three of which parallel information regulation. The first three were the *desire to be able to be alone; having space that is away from where other people congregate;* and *having the ability to govern intimacy and maintain interpersonal distance*. More related to availability of personal information were the *abilities to keep secrets; limit self-disclosure;* and *regulate when and with whom one might interact*. Designs which optimize privacy have to consider both elements of Altman's definition, as well as the fact that privacy means different things to different people.

Vinsel *et al*. (1980) found that students who dropped out of college for "nonacademic" reasons were less likely to have been able to achieve adequate privacy in their dormitories than those who stayed in school. Among the problems the "dropouts" mentioned were an inability to find a quiet place to be alone and a reluctance to invite people to their rooms. Studies have also shown that apartment building designs that do not promote privacy between apartment units are associated with resident dissatisfaction (Zeisel & Griffin, 1975).

Design features which do not allow sufficient privacy may be associated with other difficulties as well. In 1972, the news media carried disturbing stories of fighting between crew members of the US aircraft carrier Kitty Hawk. According to reports, some 46 crewmen were injured in one brawl, and three crewmen were hurt seriously enough to be flown to an onshore hospital (Heffron, 1972). Naval ships are supposed to be the epitome of well-disciplined institutions, and shipboard disturbances constitute serious problems. Although the violence reported on the Kitty Hawk was interracial, tensions may have been aggravated by environmental conditions, most specifically that crew quarters were not planned to allow for sufficient privacy and to meet other social needs (Heffron, 1972).

Finally, the lack of privacy in prisons may cause prisoners to learn antisocial behaviors. Glaser (1964) has suggested that young prisoners may learn criminal behavior from older ones as a function of being housed in more open, less private dormitory units. Private quarters are often used as a reward and a younger prisoner may have to wait some time to earn the privilege of a private cell. During this period, the youthful prisoner must cope with the demands of older inmates. These demands may be in the form of physical attacks and homosexual advances. Glaser recommended greater privacy for young prisoners to help them resist the demands of older ones. Instead of waiting for private cells, younger prisoners should be housed in them at the start until they have developed coping skills for dealing with a prison environment. (Related to privacy in some ways is the level of environmental stimulation in a setting. For a discussion of this, see the box on p. 277.)

DESIGNING TO LESSEN OVERLOAD

We have discussed overload in several places in this book. It is an important perspective and a common problem in studying environment and behavior. (For a review of overload theory, refer to Chapter 3.) Too much stimulation, whether caused by social or nonsocial events, is a negative state than can be avoided through better design. Its converse, underload or monotony, can also be corrected. In effect, it *is* possible to design an environment in such a way as to achieve a reasonable level of stimulation.

There are many kinds of design innovations that can be used to regulate stimulation levels. Materials which prevent visual access, and which "deaden" sound, lower stimulation. Combinations of light and color contribute to how stimulating a setting may be. Complex or large numbers of furnishings increase stimulation, as do decorations of various kinds. In a study of crowding, for example, wall posters added to overall levels of stimulation under certain conditions (Baum & Davis, 1976).

Interior space arrangement can also affect levels of stimulation. Zimring (1980) found that lowering stimulation and increasing patients' sense of control by enclosing their living area reduced negative social experiences. Paulus and his colleagues (e.g., McCain, Cox, & Paulus, 1980a) found the same kind of result in prison environments. Social overload and negative outcomes associated with large prison dormitories were reduced by enclosing each prisoner's living space. Also, Baum and Davis (1980) intervened in a dormitory setting characterized by social overload by dividing the interior space into two smaller units (Figure 9–6). This reduced overload and eliminated most of the negative outcomes that had been observed before the intervention. It is clear that by manipulating the sorts of design elements reviewed in this chapter—color, lighting, and interior space arrangement—problems with overload can be ameliorated.

Figure 9–6. By dividing a long corridor dormitory (A) into two smaller units (B), and reducing group size, an architectural intervention was successful in reducing social overload and crowding stress (Baum & Davis, 1980, photos by Sherry Fisher).

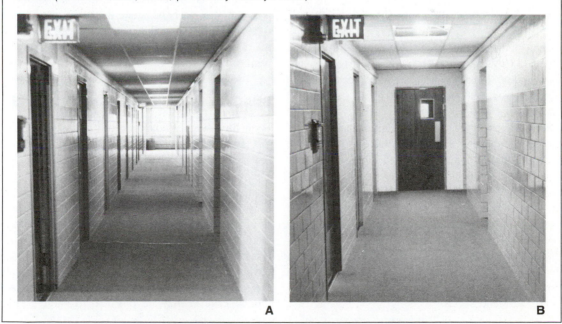

A   B

THE DESIGN PROCESS

At the beginning of this chapter, we considered different views of the extent to which architectural design can influence behavior. Next, we discussed some of the behavioral effects of specific design elements (e.g., light, color, degree of privacy). From a broader perspective, understanding what effects the different elements of design have is only part of a larger issue—that of putting this knowledge into practice in the *design process*. Actually, what we refer to as the design process is not a process, but a general description of how architectural designs are planned and implemented.

In discussing how designs are planned and implemented, we need to consider several basic concepts. Here we will discuss two: *congruence* and *design alternatives*.

Congruence

Congruence is a major goal of the design process. This construct refers to the degree of ''fit'' between user needs and preferences, and the design features of a given setting. The emphasis here is on the match between form and function. If they match well, the design ''supports'' the behaviors necessary for the function of the space, and positive outcomes typically occur (Studer, 1970). Designs that support or facilitate the desires and needs of the people using them are said to be congruent. However, arrangements of space inevitably restrict behavioral options (we cannot walk through a wall unless a door is there), and to the extent that these restrictions inhibit preferred ways of behaving, users will be dissatisfied and negative reactions will be manifested. One way to achieve greater congruence is to ''design in'' flexibility, thereby insuring that the space can support a variety of behaviors (Zeisel, 1975). Congruence is often referred to as *habitability*, particularly in residential settings. Habitability also refers to how well a particular environment fits the needs of its inhabitants (Nelson, 1976), which can range from basic survival (such as seeking shelter from the weather), to improvement of a setting that is already safe and secure.

Design Alternatives

Another important concept is that of design alternatives. Our adaptation or adjustment to the physical environment is determined in part by the number of potential design alternatives (or different ways we can think of to design or redesign a setting) (see the box on p. 279). If there are few design alternatives available, we will probably have to adapt to current conditons, which may be quite costly in some cases. When there are many design alternatives, we are apt to adjust environmental conditions through one means or another. Each different possible adjustment of our environment, then, can be called a design alternative. In effect, the various combinations or isolated uses of the design elements we have already discussed (e.g., different colors, lighting schemes, furnishings, or arrangements of space) all reflect design alternatives. In a given setting there may be an extremely large number of these, but as different criteria are brought to bear, more and more alternatives will be ruled out. For example, some alternatives may be too expensive, and others may be inappropriate due to their behavioral effects. The process of determining the proper design alternatives and weighing the importance of various criteria forms the heart of the *design process*. It is a complex process, since there are many interrelationships among design alternatives as well as many different social, economic, artistic, and cultural pressures that affect it.

STAGES IN THE DESIGN PROCESS

Each time we employ a design alternative to adjust our environment to make it more congruent (or habitable), we use the design process. (See Figure 9–7 for an outline of the various stages involved in the design process.) It begins with an *awareness* both of needs that have to be met, and of potential design alternatives (environmental adjustments). Once a need and a possible design alternative have been specified, it is necessary to develop *criteria* for determining how effectively the proposed alternatives resolve the need. Although criteria may be physical in nature, as in

DESIGN ALTERNATIVES WHICH REDUCE ILLNESS IN THE WORKPLACE

We all know that working can make people sick, but research on *mass psychogenic illness* has given new meaning to the notion. Improper design (e.g., when elements of a design elicit stress) can cause mass psychogenic illness (MPI), which is best defined as a spontaneously occurring and rapidly spreading set of illness symptoms, such as nausea and faintness, that springs up in work settings. Initially called "hysterical contagion" or "assembly line hysteria," these psychologically mediated "epidemics" are apparently caused when environmental stressors "overload" in the work setting.

A typical outbreak of MPI occurs in a setting in which a combination of environmental stressors are present. A design that does not absorb or prevent noise is a particularly common precipitating factor (Colligan, 1978; Stahl & Lebedun, 1974), but not the only one. Designs that foster air pollution within a factory (Shepard & Kroes, 1975), noxious odors (Colligan, 1978; Kerckhoff & Back, 1968), poor lighting (Colligan & Stockton, 1978), and other environmental factors are also associated with MPI. These stressors seem to create tension and emotional problems in workers and may engender physiological arousal as well (Frankenhaeuser & Gardell, 1976).

Against a backdrop of environmental stress, MPI usually develops in settings where people are also overloaded by task demands, production goals, and so on. Workers typically find that an accurate identification of the specific sources of their stress is difficult. Thus, those experiencing stress because of assembly-line noise may not be able to identify the noise as the source of their distress. As a result, they may begin to experience illness symptoms that they cannot understand. Another common condition associated with MPI is the feeling of isolation from other workers, or low group cohesion.

Although this helps to explain why some work settings make people feel sick, it does not explain sudden outbreaks of MPI. If the above conditions associated with MPI occur, people should feel sick all the time. If they have learned to cope with their symptoms, they should feel well. This may be true, but MPI is *triggered* by a sequence of events that both focuses concern on the symptoms that are experienced, and helps to explain why they are experienced. Typically, a change in the environment, such as a strange odor or a "new" noise, causes a worker to experience a relatively severe case of illness symptoms. He or she may suddenly feel faint, or may actually be ill because of some non-job-related factor. However, as other workers learn of this episode, they may decide that they've been feeling badly too, and that it must be the same illness that was reported by the first worker. As a result, the labeling of symptoms as "illness" spreads, and more and more people report feeling sick.

Although not common, MPI is costly. It results in greater absenteeism, reduced productivity, and some degree of disruption. Design alternatives that remove or reduce environmental stressors in the work place can help to prevent these outbreaks. There may also be design alternatives for settings where MPI is experienced, which are particularly likely to reduce its occurrence. For example, overload may be reduced by visually screening sections of a factory or workplace so that workers only see those they work with or some small group of other employees. These screens may also reduce noise, and increase the opportunity for social contact among workers within a particular station. Lighting may also be adjusted to reduce the intensity of stimulation, and the use of different color schemes may promote feelings of membership in a smaller group of workers. Since MPI appears to be caused by combinations of stress, overload, restricted social contact, and the like, these types of design alternatives might reduce MPI.

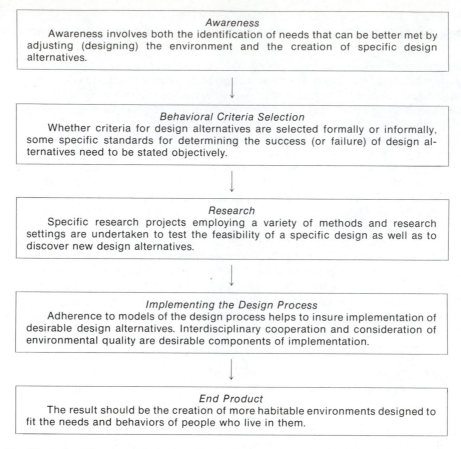

Awareness
Awareness involves both the identification of needs that can be better met by adjusting (designing) the environment and the creation of specific design alternatives.

Behavioral Criteria Selection
Whether criteria for design alternatives are selected formally or informally, some specific standards for determining the success (or failure) of design alternatives need to be stated objectively.

Research
Specific research projects employing a variety of methods and research settings are undertaken to test the feasibility of a specific design as well as to discover new design alternatives.

Implementing the Design Process
Adherence to models of the design process helps to insure implementation of desirable design alternatives. Interdisciplinary cooperation and consideration of environmental quality are desirable components of implementation.

End Product
The result should be the creation of more habitable environments designed to fit the needs and behaviors of people who live in them.

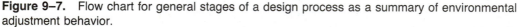

Figure 9–7. Flow chart for general stages of a design process as a summary of environmental adjustment behavior.

the quality specifications of building materials, our discussion of the design process will focus on behavioral criteria, such as ease of movement. Frequently, some kind of *research* or *evaluation* must be performed in order to know whether specific design alternatives measure up to the criteria established for them. When such evaluation indicates the desirability of a particular alternative, additional steps must be taken to *implement* the design. Models of the design process that stress interdisciplinary cooperation among different professions, consideration of environmental quality, and posthabitation evaluation by users can be effective tools in going beyond this step and arriving at the *end product* of a habitable environment.

We should note that the design process described in Figure 9–7 is a very general one. In fact, the actual procedures followed are somewhat different for each application. In the present context, we will use Figure 9–7 to structure the following discussion of the design process.

Awareness of Design Alternatives

The first step in the design process involves becoming aware of design alternatives which meet certain needs. This "awareness" derives from several sources. We learn about them indirectly from our daily contacts with new buildings or settings, and through travel and the media we encounter alternate ways of designing the built world. Environmental psychologists who have sought to study how we become aware of design alternatives (e.g., Sommer, 1972) have identified several additional factors which influence our awareness: social resistance to design change, group involvement in the design process, and the degree of attention given to users' needs.

Social Resistance to Design Alternatives.

In some cases, social resistance to possible design alternatives prevents us from becoming aware of different potential designs. It can also prevent new design alternatives from even being developed. How can social resistance constitute such a roadblock? Perhaps some specific examples will clarify the problem.

Kira (1976) observed that strong social traditions of privacy may discourage our becoming aware of, thinking about, and developing new and different bathroom designs. He pointed out that a strong preoccupation with bathroom privacy (at least in American culture) is evident even in the euphemisms we use, such as lounge, rest room, and powder room. Bathroom architecture reflects this quest for privacy, exemplified by the fact that the public rest room located high in the Eiffel Tower has windows of frosted glass (Kira, 1976). After all, rest room windows should not allow people to look in, even if the windows are hundreds of feet in the air! Even when the design process is highly structured and institutionalized, taboos about bathroom functions can make it difficult to propose design alternatives. For example, Kira noted that after astronauts complained about gravity-free toilet designs aboard spacecraft, there was a long delay before the National Aeronautics and Space Administration scheduled a formal planning conference specifically to discuss design alternatives for spacecraft toilets.

The bathroom is not the only setting for which people are reluctant to consider new design alternatives. Parsons (1972) found a similar hesitancy to talk about the bedroom as a setting for sexual encounters. Even though our culture considers the bedroom to be the most appropriate place for sex-

ual activity, there has been resistance to researching alternative designs intended to improve the bedroom as a setting for sexual behavior.

Design Awareness and Group Participation in the Design Process.

Any project to design or adjust the environment takes place in some social atmosphere or setting. The number and quality of the design alternatives that are generated and considered depend on the social context which evolves. As a case in point, modern design projects involve an increasingly complex relationship between members of design teams. They necessitate teamwork between these people, who are generally professionals with different backgrounds. Awareness of new design alternatives within these groups will depend in part on the ability of such interdisciplinary groups to work together to generate new ideas.

Awareness also depends on the relationship between the creators and the users of design alternatives. Often this is characterized by a gap between those who design environments and those who live in them (Mitchell, 1974). Clearly, this leads to a lack of awareness of possible design alternatives by both parties. Sometimes the gap is referred to as the difference between the *professionals,* who know the technical aspects of design, and the *clients* or *users,* who will use the settings created by the professionals. Mitchell noted that architectural clients frequently expressed a desire to participate more directly in the design process. Apparently, architects and designers are under growing social pressure to incorporate client or user inputs into their work.

Even so, when design planning takes place in a large social system, extensive gaps between those who create and those who use the products of the design process are likely. In many cases, the user group may not even be identified until the design process is complete. One result of this gap is a sense of helplessness (or simply passive acceptance) about the way buildings are designed. In effect, people who use the environments designed by others confine their design alternatives to those things they can do *after* they move into a setting.

Students who live in a state-planned dormitory alter their rooms (to the extent that rules allow) after they become residents. If privacy is insufficient in the rooms planned by the state committees, students may install makeshift walls with bookshelves made out of bricks and boards, macrame partitions, and even custom-designed lofts.

One way to close the gap between the planners and the users of environments is to include a *designer advocate* (Sommer, 1972) in the group of design professionals. The designer advocate could present user needs and ideas to the professionals and communicate possible design alternatives to groups of users. This is a direct intervention into the social system that currently removes design planning from design users. In a similar vein, Fowler (1972) suggested that a human-factors psychologist would make a good *ombudsman* mediating between the designer and client or user. Typically, human-factors psychologists study the fit of machines and environments to human abilities and characteristics. An ombudsman investigates citizen complaints about some issue. Perhaps a human-factors ombudsman could test how well design alternatives fit user needs long before complaints are registered. The feedback from this process could be given to designers.

The above discussion is not meant to suggest that every project is unsuccessful if designed by a group of people who are not the users of the end products. To the contrary, many products developed by professional design groups do work well and are liked by those who use them (Jones, 1970a). While such groups can and often do take user needs into consideration, using a designer advocate or an ombudsman could prove helpful in eliciting additional design alternatives.

Sensitivity to User Needs. At some level, then, sensitivity to user needs clearly plays an important role in making planners aware of design alternatives. Moreover, considering the needs and preferences of the people who will use a setting is crucial to good design. Employing *user-oriented design criteria* (design goals which are

linked to user needs) not only makes such needs an important consideration, but also emphasizes the active role of users in the design process. For example, one could create a *user-generated* design, in which the experiences and judgments of consumers are used in defining design criteria or goals (Sommer, 1972). One of the functions of the designer advocate would be to learn about user needs and satisfactions relative to existing versions of a particular design or setting. Ideally, a user-oriented designer would try to base plans on user inputs instead of simply creating the design he or she thinks is best.

One strategy for incorporating user input into the design process has been termed the "Volkswagen model" (Sommer, 1972). Patterned on the concept of the famous German automobile, this model advocates holding a basic design constant but instituting small incremental changes that improve its quality. Design alternatives are determined by user experience with the basic design, and major remodeling for the sake of marketing strategies or styling is avoided.

In incorporating user needs into the design process, a distinction should be made between *user needs* and *user wants* (Zeisel, 1975). User needs are related to the basic functions involved in any environment. For instance, what design requirements are necessary to make a physical structure a home? A home must provide food, shelter, child care, and other primary needs. A family living in a physical setting that provides the minimal space and amenities for meeting these needs can be considered to have a home. Studying how such a setting affects people is the domain of the environmental psychologist. However, a family may *want* a home with carpeting, a self-cleaning oven, and a swimming pool—amenities that go beyond the requirements of a basic living environment. The study of user wants is more in the domain of consumer psychology or marketing research than within the realm of environmental psychology.

Although user input is an important part of the design process, there is still a need for professional knowledge. Alexander (1969a) noted that in order to successfully relate professional knowledge to user needs, two things must occur. First, the parties concerned must realize that the built environment can and does influence behavior. Even though it is not always possible to prove that a setting directly affects behavior (Gutman, 1966), enough evidence has been found to conclude that these effects are real. Second, user needs and behaviors must be specified in concrete terms in order to be appreciated by design professionals. Observers have noted that it is often difficult for users of a setting to specify problems or possible causes of problems (e.g., Alexander, 1969a; Baum & Valins, 1977). When asked to describe problems or settings, behavioral information is often expressed vaguely, making it difficult for designers to incorporate behavioral criteria.

Selection of Behavioral Criteria

One result of increased awareness of both design alternatives and user needs is a greater interest in *behaviorally determined criteria* for designs. Recall that the specification of behavioral criteria is important for effective communication between behavioral scientists and designers or architects. Such criteria make it easier to establish standards of quality and also help guide research on the value of various design alternatives. If we are to adjust the environment to facilitate a particular behavior, we must be able to specify behavioral goals before generating design alternatives. Obviously, it is highly desirable to have explicit behavioral criteria in mind before a new building or setting is constructed. Such criteria are often scaled along dimensions or in clusters that can be identified and integrated into the planning of a project. One example of such a set of *user benefit criteria* has been proposed by Murtha (1976). Note that the term ''user benefit criteria'' emphasizes end goals: the maximization of gains or advantages that people will realize from the use of planned environments.

Murtha's criteria are classified along four dimensions of user benefits: behavior facilitation, physiological maintenance, perceptual maintenance, and social facilitation (see Table 9–1).

Behavior facilitation criteria measure how well a setting helps people accomplish important tasks, such as transactions at a bank teller's booth or crowd flow in a shopping mall. *Physiological maintenance* criteria involve the comfort and safety of the physical environment, particularly temperature and noise levels. *Perceptual maintenance* criteria deal with whether the range of environmental stimulation is appropriate to the behaviors performed in a given setting. For example, environmental stimulation might be minimized in a work setting requiring concentration but maximized in a recreational setting. Finally, *social facilitation* criteria (as defined by Murtha) involve the adequacy of environments to meet various social needs, such as personal space and control over crowding. The importance of each of these dimensions may vary from one setting to another. Physiological maintenance, for example, is far more important in a hospital than in a factory.

Once design criteria are established, they can be made part of *performance requirements* or standards. Performance requirements help establish desirable levels of operation for the various components of a building, including such things as structural soundness, plumbing pressure and capacity, and number of exits, as well as behavioral criteria. Such performance requirements can often be found in government publications, such as one issued by the National Bureau of Standards (Foster, 1972) that reviews building performance requirements, ranging from plumbing systems to windows, and also discusses behavioral performance requirements. Future performance requirements may place as much emphasis on behavior as on structural soundness and safety standards.

Behaviorally Based Research

One of the exciting consequences of increased awareness of environmental design is a rapidly growing body of research on how design is related to behavior. This research can be approached from a testing perspective, as in how existing design alternatives meet selected behavioral criteria (*criterion-oriented* research; cf. Alt-

Table 9–1.   EXAMPLES OF SPECIFIC USER BENEFIT DESIGN CRITERIA*

Behavioral Facilitation

Functional Conformance. Does the environment have the necessary components present to make a particular function possible? (*Example:* Offices should be set up with the appropriate furniture, lighting, bookshelves, and telephones.)

Spatial Conformance. Is there adequate spatial organization to benefit users? (*Example:* Hallways should be planned wide enough to permit crowd flow, and components of a setting should be placed close enough to minimize unnecessary movement.)

Physiological Maintenance

Climate Conformance. Is the climate of a setting adequate (in terms of temperature and humidity) for sustaining biological comfort? (*Example:* Building ventilation systems should be planned for comfort level and health.)

Hazard Regulation. Is the environment free of hazards or threats to user well-being? (*Example:* Electrical hazards such as exposed electrical wiring should be eliminated.)

Perceptual Maintenance

Sensory Initiation. Is the environment designed to accommodate various sensory functions? (*Example:* Lighting in work areas should meet the demands of the kind of visual tasks required.)

Sensory Conformance. Does the perceptual environment have an optimal level of stimulus patterning? (*Example:* Settings can be designed to increase or decrease the level of perceptual complexity.)

Social Facilitation

Social Initiation. Does the environment provide opportunity for desired levels of social behavior? (*Example:* Areas should be designated that individuals can claim as their own territory.)

Social Isolation. Can one regulate the amount of social isolation so that desired levels of privacy can be maintained? (*Example:* Room barriers or furniture groupings can be used to provide privacy.)

*Adapted from Murtha, D. M. *Dimensions of User Benefit.* Washington, D.C.: American Institute of Architects, 1976. Used with permission of the American Institute of Architects.

man, 1975); or, it may be seen as establishing guidelines for future design alternatives. The merits of such research are that it helps establish new behavioral criteria for design activity, and it helps integrate user needs into the design process. In Chapters 10 and 11 we will examine a small fraction of behaviorally-based research as it relates to selected behavior settings, ranging from the places where we work and learn to the places where we live and relax. For each of these selected environments we will relate the behavior in the setting to one or more aspects of the design of that setting.

Implementing the Design Process: Models for the Future

We have seen how design awareness and careful selection of behavioral criteria lead to research on the behavioral effects of design alternatives. Given this body of research, how can we implement the environmental design process to insure an *end product* such that future built environments are more habitable? Design professionals, such as architects, must keep many factors in mind—building site problems, projected costs, availability of materials, and performance standards for construction materials, to name a few.

What can we do to make sure that habitability is included in these considerations? In this section, we will examine three models that have been proposed with this end in mind. We should note that other equally useful models, which we do not have the space to describe, also exist. (Interested readers might wish to consult Broadbent, 1973; Kaplan, 1977; Jones, 1970b; Manheim, 1970; and Lang & Burnette, 1974.)

A Model for Establishing Environmental Quality Indicators. In Chapter 2, we discussed a procedure for determining perceived environmental quality, the PEQI, or Perceived Environmental Quality Index. Craik and Zube (1976) propose a model for establishing and implementing the PEQI which could result in increased habitability. This model, presented in Figure 9–8, emphasizes the importance of government and other organizations in the process of establishing and changing standards of environmental quality.

The Craik and Zube PEQI implementation model begins with social system inputs which, according to the conceptualization presented earlier in this chapter, would include increasing awareness of design alternatives that have implications for environmental quality. Also included in these inputs is social pressure stemming from technological changes or increased environmental education, which initiates the demand for more rigorous policies and specific standards.

In response to this social pressure, government agencies are brought in to implement environmental impact statements and to determine environmental quality criteria. PEQI systems would, of course, be used in this process, and these systems would emphasize user or public input in appraising environmental quality. The next steps in the model involve research to establish how PEQIs can best be developed and used along with demonstration projects for PEQI evaluation. Next, administrative units use these research and evaluation data to determine which PEQIs are employed directly by industry, various government bodies, and the public. After being cycled through the social system, the PEQI is now back in the hands of the public to await new pressures for environmental change. The PEQI model is one means of

Figure 9–8. Suggested model for implementation of Perceived Environmental Quality Indicators into an operational system that would ensure improved standards of environmental quality. (From Craik, K. H., & Zube, E. H., *Perceiving environmental quality*. New York: Plenum Press, 1976. Used by permission.)

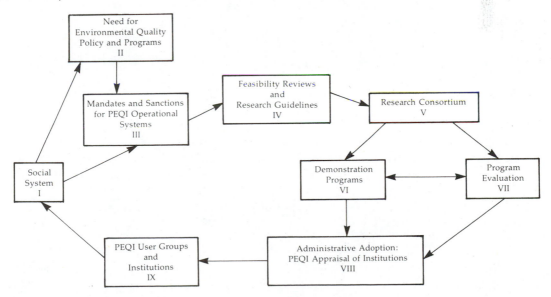

keeping us constantly aware of the quality of various environments. It is assumed that improved environmental design will follow this awareness.

A Model of the Design Cycle. How can we be even more certain that improved design will follow awareness of environmental quality and environmental design alternatives? Ideally, a continuous cycle of design planning and evaluation should occur for every building project (Zeisel, 1975). Such a design cycle would permit information gained from an existing project to be applied immediately to the next project, which in turn would be evaluated for the planning phase of still another project. Zeisel's model of this process includes five distinct steps that would be repeated for every new design project (Figure 9–9).

This model begins with a programming step intended to identify design criteria, then moves into a stage at which the criteria are synthesized into

Figure 9–9. Summary of Zeisel's model of a design cycle. (From Zeisel, J., The design cycle. *Sociology and Architectural Design.* Social Science Frontiers, No. 6. New York: Russell Sage Foundation, 1975. © 1975 Russell Sage Foundation. Used by permission.)

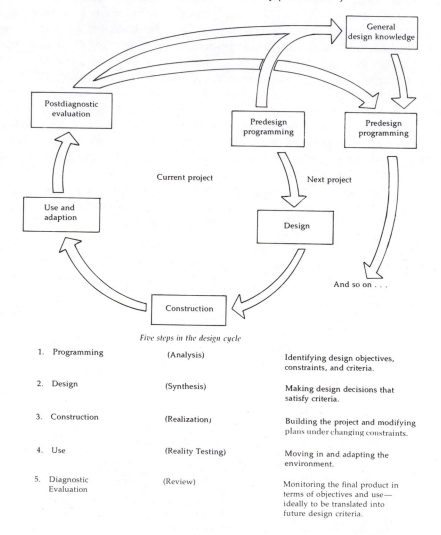

Five steps in the design cycle

1.	Programming	(Analysis)	Identifying design objectives, constraints, and criteria.
2.	Design	(Synthesis)	Making design decisions that satisfy criteria.
3.	Construction	(Realization)	Building the project and modifying plans under changing constraints.
4.	Use	(Reality Testing)	Moving in and adapting the environment.
5.	Diagnostic Evaluation	(Review)	Monitoring the final product in terms of objectives and use—ideally to be translated into future design criteria.

design features. In the third stage of the model, design modifications are made as construction conditions demand. In the fourth stage, the newly constructed environment is tested in actual use for habitability and other performance standards. The final, or diagnostic, step is to make follow-up evaluations of how well the finished project measures up to the behavioral design criteria developed during the planning stage. Such diagnostic data can then be used in the planning stage of the next project.

An Interdisciplinary Process Model. Altman (1973, 1975) proposes a somewhat more elaborate model that incorporates the basic elements of Zeisel's design cycle as one dimension (Figure 9–10). This model includes a second dimension to allow for different design emphases for different types of environments. The design of a bedroom, for example, would probably emphasize different factors than the design of a community. A third dimension in Altman's model allows for different behavioral emphases (or for more than

one behavioral criterion) in any given project. Privacy needs and personal space requirements might be evaluated differently for a hospital than for a neighborhood, and the planning and evaluation stages in the design cycle might approach these behaviors somewhat differently.

In proposing his model, Altman emphasizes that the design process must reflect the different approaches of the various people involved in environmental design. In particular, he feels that practitioners, such as architects, are inclined to attend primarily to design criteria and to particular places or settings. Researchers, on the other hand, are more likely to stress ongoing behavioral processes, such as privacy, territoriality, or personal space. Consequently, the practitioner may think of privacy more in terms of a setting, such as the home, or in terms of a design decision, such as locating bedrooms away from living areas to insure privacy. The social science researcher tends to think of privacy more as a continual coping behavior to control the level of social interaction in one's environment. Moreover, practitioners are

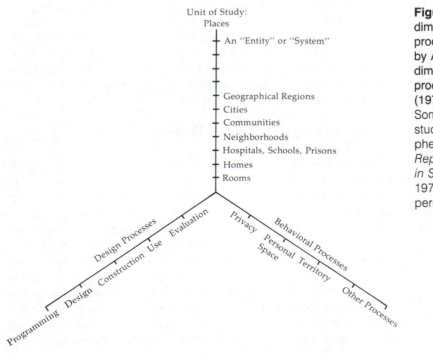

Unit of Study:
Places

An "Entity" or "System"

Geographical Regions
Cities
Communities
Neighborhoods
Hospitals, Schools, Prisons
Homes
Rooms

Design Processes
Programming Design Construction Use Evaluation

Privacy Personal Space Territory Behavioral Processes Other Processes

Figure 9–10. Three-dimensional design process model proposed by Altman. Note that one dimension is the design process cycle of Zeisel, (1975). (From Altman, I., Some perspectives on the study of man-environment phenomena, *Representative Research in Social Psychology,* 1973, *4,* 111. Used by permission.)

apt to want information that can be used immediately to solve a given problem, whereas researchers are often more interested in long-range projects that will reveal new discoveries. By including three dimensions in his model, each of which contains considerable breadth, Altman hopes to include the point of view of numerous practitioners and researchers.

In concluding this chapter, we would like to repeat Altman's emphasis on the necessity of interdisciplinary teamwork in the environmental design process. Perhaps more than any other factor, interdisciplinary cooperation offers the means of implementing behaviorally-oriented environmental design. One hopeful sign that this goal is closer to being attained than we might think is the occurrence of interdisciplinary design conferences. A case in point is the Coolfont Conference of Social Scientists and Architects, sponsored by the American Institute of Architects (Conway, 1973). Among other things, this conference concluded that social scientists could provide valuable inputs at most stages of environmental design work. For example, they could help define the psychological needs of a project even before the planning stage is formalized. In addition, they could conduct research that would help practitioners clarify the kinds of user needs the project should fulfill. The conference also affirmed that social science research evaluating the habitability of existing environments could be incorporated into the design planning stage of future projects. Social and behavioral scientists could also help with training programs on the use of a completed building, analysis of safety needs, bid negotiations, and follow-up evaluations on user satisfaction with design alternatives. Indeed, the interdisciplinary approach is indispensable for an effective environmental design process.

CHAPTER SUMMARY

As we noted at the start of this chapter, we spend much of our lives within the built environment. We wake up in our homes, learn in school, work in offices or libraries, shop in stores, go to theatres, and so on. In many ways, the architectural world represents an environment built by human hands that is interposed between people and the natural environment. What are the effects of this world? There are many intended and unintended behavioral effects of the environments we create.

In this chapter we considered the behavioral effects of several different individual features of built settings, such as lighting, color, ambience, furnishings, and so on. Each is capable of influencing mood and behavior by itself, but most work together. Thus, while the color of a room can influence your mood, the combination of lighting and color are more likely to affect you than is either one alone.

We have also considered the notion of arrangement of space. Architectural designs have many functions, but the most basic is to structure space. Designs shape the space within buildings as well as outside, and arrangements of furnishings can further structure space. This, too, can have a strong effect on mood and behavior.

Finally, we considered the design process. For any given building there are several important criteria: cost, durability, aesthetic quality, and the like. Among these are behavioral considerations, such as the congruence of fit between design and user needs. These criteria are used to decide between different design alternatives in a rather complex process.

Suggested Projects

1. Think about two different buildings. Pick two different kinds, for example a dormitory and a hospital. Now draw their designs and list the positive and negative effects that you think the designs might have. How may they affect privacy or where and how often people walk? Will being near a bathroom or nurse's station be better (convenience) or worse (all the noise, commotion, or people passing by) than being far from it? Now try moving walls and doors around to eliminate possible problems and enhance

virtues. Can you do better than the designers did?

2. The design process is complicated and sometimes resistant to behavioral input. Say that your college is building a new student union. How would you approach the possibility of providing information for the process? What design alternatives can you come up with?

3. Take a walk on your college campus. Make a list of all the buildings you see on your walk and record your feelings when you see them. The library may make you feel studious and quiet, the president's house may seem elaborate and give the impression of wealth. Try to list emotional responses, too. Now go back and list the prominent design features of each building. How big is each (how big is the scale)? How many stories? Are there columns? When you are done, check to see if there are any consistencies of features across different buildings—do the same features create the same feelings?

10 Design in Selected Environments

INTRODUCTION

Your first breaths are taken in a sterile room with very institutional surroundings. Your parents take you "home," and place you in a strange container with bars on two sides (called a crib), and when you look around, you see stuffed toys, a changing table, and a rocking chair. When you get a bit older you begin to explore your house, and continue to be affected greatly by its environment. Soon it's time for you to attend school. On your first day you are amazed by the large number of desks, their arrangement, and the whole educational environment. In some ways the classroom setting is stimulating, but in other ways it constricts your behavior, as compared to being at home. More time passes and you go to work. The work environment bears some similarity to the school setting, but in many ways it is different. You work in a large "open" office and, while you like the fact that you have easy access to your coworkers, you also feel you have insufficient privacy. You value your annual vacation, and enjoy spending time in recreational environments, away from the work setting. As you move up the organizational ladder, you experience other work environments, and note their positive and negative effects on yourself and your coworkers. After you retire, you live in a large retirement community. Although you appreciate having other retired people as well as medical facilities nearby, you miss aspects of the more heterogeneous environment you lived in before. But, in general, you have positive feelings about your living situation.

In previous chapters we have examined how specific aspects of the environment interact with our behavior. In Chapter 9 we saw how we can use knowledge of these environment–behavior relationships to design environments that will facilitate the behavior we want to occur. In this and the next chapter we will see how these principles can be brought together in specific environments. That is, we will select settings important to environmental psychologists and show how those particular environments influence behavior, and how the design of those environments can be modified to achieve desired effects. This chapter will examine environmental psychological research on residential settings, learning environments, pedestrian environments, hospitals, and facilities for the elderly. The next chapter will continue the same theme by examining work environments, leisure settings, and environments of the future.

THE RESIDENTIAL SETTING

We have talked about residential environments in earlier chapters and will consider them in detail in this one. It is no surprise that they have been mentioned so often—residential settings are so familiar and important to most of us that there has been a great deal of research interest in residential design and improvement.

As you know, there are a number of different kinds of residential settings. The most common, at least historically, is the single detached house that many of us grew up in. In urban settings, row houses or 2–3 story apartment buildings may be the rule, while in modern suburbia townhouses are becoming a predominant form. Also, of course, there are high-rise apartment buildings. Each of these kinds of environments is associated with a different style of living, and research has begun to address the similarities and differences among them.

DESIGNING FOR ENERGY CONSERVATION

With the advent of the energy crisis in the 1970s and recent price increases in the cost of home heating, some designers have turned to an energy-wise alternative for home building. Reversing our high-rise trend, more and more underground homes are appearing. Properly called earth-sheltered homes, they are built several feet into the ground.

The temperature of the ground just three or four feet below the surface is remarkably constant at about 50°F. By building a home into the earth at or below this level, it can cost as much as 75 percent less to heat it in the winter and to cool it during the summer. On a 0° morning, a good deal more energy is required to warm your home to 65° if it is above ground than if nestled in the 50° earth.

Earth-covered houses have very little surface area exposed. This also helps to keep energy use low, but is associated with perhaps the largest problem they have—the psychological effects of living underground. Although storms may pass harmlessly overhead, the common image of dark, humid caves can be a problem. Earth-covered homes must be built to avoid this dungeon-like quality. There can be no windows, of course, and as a result designing for psychological well-being can be a challenge.

Several solutions have evolved. The most common is to build the home into the side of a hill so that one side is open to the world. This results in some loss of energy efficiency, but the design still yields great savings. Another alternative is to build atria into the home—large vertical shafts or rooms that reach to the surface and are either roofed with glass or contain skylights. This brings light into the deepest of homes and helps to minimize the negative aspects of living underground.

Color use can also change the appearance of underground buildings. Bright colors that suggest an open, well-lighted room will do more to change the feeling of being underground than will the use of darker colors. Furnishings might also help. For example, landscape paintings in strategic wall space can be used to suggest windows.

Arrangement of space in underground structures can help reduce the negative aspects of such a design. If a central atrium is included, walls between this naturally lighted area and adjacent rooms should be minimal. In this way, more of the spaces in the building receive some natural light. Frequently used rooms should also be those nearest the atrium.

Life underground is not the same as life above ground. Despite the attractiveness and efficiency of building underground homes and offices, savings are not sufficient to overcome the problems associated with this kind of environment. If these environments are to remain feasible, intelligent use of design variables to counter potential problems will be necessary.

Preferences

With all of these different forms of housing, it has become important to examine the preferences that people have for residences. Research seems to suggest that people in North America and the British Commonwealth tend to describe the detached, single-family house as the "ideal" home (Cooper, 1972; Jandlin, 1972). This tendency does not appear to be a matter of socioeconomic class—people seem to reject apartment settings and prefer suburban homes regardless of ethnic or social background or the kind of housing environment they occupy (Dennis, 1966; Hinshaw & Allott, 1972; Ladd, 1972; Michelson, 1968).

Although you may have suspected that most people want a "nice little house in the suburbs," the reasons for this preference are not as clear. The most compelling explanation is the way these settings structure space. Michelson (1970), for example, has argued that the ways in which space is distributed in areas dominated by single-family homes allows residents to avoid intense interaction with neighbors. As you will recall, urban areas are often characterized by close neighborhood ties, extended families, and extensive social interaction. The single-family house appears to permit residents to avoid or control these social factors to a greater degree. Michelson also reports some evidence that single-family housing is generally regarded as family-oriented. Thus, people seem to want the family privacy afforded by these settings.

Choice of type of housing may be restricted by economic factors. It has become increasingly difficult for young families to purchase single-family houses and many have opted for townhouse or condominium settings. There are also factors that appear to determine the location that one lives in—where the house, townhouse, or the like is situated. Again, economic factors are important, since some areas of a city or its suburbs may be more expensive than others. Choices are often made between locations and types of housing. A family may be able to afford a single-family house in suburb A, but only a townhouse in suburb B. A number of things are ordinarily considered before making choices between locations and housing type.

Given the basic preference for the detached house, why might a family opt for a townhouse in a different suburb? Status may be an issue, if one of the two suburbs is very high or very low in prestige. Security and crime rates may be another—the detached home in suburb A may also be closer to high crime areas. Commuting time, closeness to and quality of schools, and availability of shopping and services may also be important. Clearly, preferences for and actual choice of housing is complex, with factors about the residential environment and its surrounding area being considered in each instance.

Use of Space in the Home

Despite differences in the ways in which people arrange their homes, consistent space-use patterns emerge. Black (1968), for example, found that leisure reading was most common in the living room and least common in the kitchen and dining room. The kitchen is often the center of family activity (Mehrabian, 1976). Bedrooms are the most frequently occupied areas of the home (Parsons, 1972), and may become personalized or private areas for individual family members.

The intended function of a room has important implications for its design and how it is used. Bedrooms are, for one thing, intended to be private space, and thus are likely to be set off from less private areas. They may be located down a hallway from the living and kitchen areas, or on a different floor altogether. Bedrooms are also supposed to be for sleeping and therefore must be quiet. However, as Parsons (1972) notes, some sleepers prefer noisier settings. Individual preferences are a problem for designers who wish to generalize designs across large numbers of residences (see the box on p. 293).

The bathroom is an especially interesting design problem. As can be seen in Table 10–1, there are many functions or purposes of a bathroom, especially when we consider everything we do there. To the physical hygienic functions that we are all familiar with, we can also add some

PREFERENCES FOR MESSY AND NEAT ROOMS: THE ODD COUPLE

Residential satisfaction applies not only to entire neighborhoods but also to single rooms. Recall the movie and television series about the "odd couple" who had to cope with each other's preference for a neat or messy apartment. A definite preference for a neat or messy room may be more than just a scriptwriter's whim. Personality and cultural background may influence whether a person will find satisfaction or annoyance with a room that is kept tidy or disorderly. Samuelson and Lindauer (1976) asked college students to describe rooms that were experimentally changed to look either messy or neat. The messy room had papers and pencils scattered about, an overflowing wastebasket, and a general look of disorder. In the neat room, objects were arranged in an orderly manner.

Students described the rooms differently and also showed different levels of preference for each room. Students who indicated they preferred more exciting or varied experiences were more satisfied with the messy room. Students less inclined toward experience-seeking (as measured by test scores) were more satisfied with the neat room. Just as each member of the odd couple found the apartment most satisfying when arranged his way, students differ in their preference for order or disorder in a setting. Those with adaptation levels closer to the "orderly" end of a "disorderly–orderly" dimension seem to find it easier to adapt to (and are more satisfied with) a neat room, whereas those whose adaptation levels lie closer to the "disorderly" end tend to be more comfortable in a messy room.

social functions. Many people use the bathroom as a "sanctum" for privacy. Social conventions frown on people interrupting one another while in the bathroom and, as a result, one can often escape there for a moment of peace and quiet. Thus, even though the bathroom can take on attributes of shared space, it can also serve as a place where privacy can be achieved on a tran-

Table 10–1. SOME TYPICAL FUNCTIONS OF A HOME BATHROOM*

Oral Hygiene	Miscellaneous Hygiene	Medical Hygiene
Brushing teeth	Vomiting	Washing wounds
Rinsing mouth	Using sanitary supplies	Soaking limbs or other body
Gargling	Treating skin blemishes	parts
Expectorating	Cleaning nose	Applying bandages
Cleaning and soaking	Cleaning ears	Applying medications
dentures	Applying cosmetics	Taking medicine internally
Massaging gums	Cleansing skin and	Inhaling steam
Using Water Pik or	applying treatments	Applying contraceptive devices
dental floss	Shaving	Taking enema
	Defecating	Douching
	Urinating	Cleaning and inserting contact
	Bathing	lenses

*Each of the functions normally carried out in the home bathroom could serve as the basis for a bathroom design criterion. (Adapted from Kira, 1976.)

sient basis. Of course, this is not the case with large bathrooms, such as those in a college dormitory. There, the small stalls within the bathroom may serve the same privacy function as the entire home bathroom.

Kira (1976) has examined the relationship between the design of bathrooms and their functions. Many of his suggestions are intended to increase convenience, including changes in sink and vanity design (see Figure 10–1) and placement of

Figure 10–1. This bathroom vanity has been designed to make a number of bath functions easy to perform, as well as providing other amenities. (From *The Bathroom* by Alexander Kira. Copyright © 1966, 1976 by Alexander Kira. By permission of Bantam Books, Inc. All rights reserved.)

shower control knobs, electrical outlets, and so on. Other suggestions are more adventurous, and one goes completely against the notion of privacy in the bathroom. Kira (1976) proposes the creation of a living room bath, which could be used for entertaining guests. He views such an unusual situation as a logical response to economic pressures. As residential settings become smaller because of energy and land costs, designers often include multipurpose spaces in homes. Because bathrooms are not used all of the time, they are prime candidates for new functions, and Kira argues that they can be used as living rooms as well as bath areas.

Satisfaction with the Home Environment

As we become accustomed to a specific residential setting, we develop more and more satisfaction with our ability to perform basic tasks in it. The more easily and conveniently these functions can be performed, the more satisfied we usually become. Steidl (1972) found that the size and floor plan of rooms were often mentioned as problems that affected the performance of tasks. Not having enough room to work, having too many rooms to clean, and being too close to noisy areas of the house were among these problems. A more recent study, however, suggests that some people are less likely to be satisfied with their residences regardless of their characteristics (Galster & Hesser, 1981). Younger people, female heads of households, blacks, married couples, and couples with many children appear to be somewhat dissatisfied with their housing on the average. Galster and Hesser also found that certain physical or environmental factors were associated with dissatisfaction. Poor plumbing, heating, or kitchen facilities were strongly related to dissatisfaction, as were neighborhood characteristics such as racial makeup, high density, or condition of the structures in the area.

Social ties also appear to be important in determining residential satisfaction. Fried and Gleicher (1961) found this to be more the case for residents of urban slums than for suburbanites. In urban areas, social ties appear to contribute to a sense of neighborhood and to the sharing of outdoor space by residents. Greenbaum and Greenbaum (1981), found that group identity in a neighborhood is related to territorial personalization and social interaction. When people were able to establish social bonds with those around them, they took more care in decorating the exteriors of their residences and the neighborhood took on the aura of group-owned territory.

Other social factors can be significant sources of satisfaction or dissatisfaction for many people. As you will recall from Chapter 9, privacy regulation is an important consideration in the design of environments. How a residence is designed can affect the ease with which we achieve privacy. Individuals differ, however, in the amount of privacy they want. Privacy in the single-family home, as reported by the male members of the household, could take two forms (Altman, Nelson, & Lett, 1972). One type of family controls privacy without using physical features of the environment as a means of control. In these families, bedroom doors are rarely closed and few areas of the home are considered the domain of one family member. A second family type is more likely to use environmental controls over privacy. These families help to insure privacy by designating rooms as specific territories for individual use. Clearly one cannot use a single residential design and expect both types of family to be satisfied. Variety of interior design of homes helps to ensure that individual family styles can be accommodated (see the box on p. 296).

Before concluding, we should note that it is impossible to cover all aspects of residential design in this discussion. Included in the concept of the home are survival-oriented needs for shelter, culturally bound preferences, expressions, and guidelines, and a highly personal conception of hearth and home. We know that people use the space in their homes in many different ways and that this use often reflects an individual's cultural background or preferred lifestyle (Weisner & Weibel, 1981). Despite some common uses (e.g., most of us prepare food in the kitchen), the wide variety of other uses of different forms of residential space makes designing it more difficult. The

HOMES AND THE PRIVACY GRADIENT

Understanding people's social values and practices is extremely important for developing a home design that will provide desirable levels of privacy. In our culture, a number of modern designs are based on open architecture that includes the kitchen as part of the area for entertaining guests. In Peru, however, a privacy gradient exists that restricts certain areas in terms of entertaining (Zeisel, 1975). Formal friends and acquaintances are permitted only in the room intended for social activities. As guests become better known, they may be invited into other areas, but only those closest to the homeowner are ever permitted into the kitchen. Alexander (1969b) suggested that a Peruvian house should be designed along a privacy gradient that places the *sala* (room for entertaining) at the front and the kitchen at the rear.

more flexible spaces are, the better they should suit a range of activities, as long as the basic function of a room can be carried out.

Propinquity: The Effect of Occupying Nearby Territories

Thus far we have considered several variables associated with residences. Another factor important in residential design is propinquity, or "nearness" between places people occupy. How close you are to other residents in a housing development, an apartment building, or even a dormitory or an office building will affect your social outcomes with them.

Two types of propinquity have been found to lead to favorable social outcomes. First, it has been observed that the closer the *objective physical distance* between two individuals, the more likely the individuals are to be friends. The classic study was conducted by Festinger, Schachter, and Back (1950), who investigated friendship patterns of apartment dwellers in Westgate West. When residents (who were randomly assigned to apartments) were asked "Which three people do you see most often socially?" it was found that people were friendliest with those who lived near them. In fact, residents were more likely to be friendly with a neighbor one door away than with a neighbor two doors away, and so on. Furthermore, this finding was replicated in a study by Ebbesen, Kjos, and Konecni (1976). Another study (Segal, 1974) provided corroborative evidence for the data on objective distance-friendship choice. In this experiment, Segal noted the friendship choices among trainees at the Maryland Police Academy, where trainees were assigned to rooms and to seats in classrooms on the basis of the alphabetical order of their last names. In effect, alphabetical order served as a manipulation of propinquity, and it was found that individuals were most likely to become friendly with others whose last initials were close to theirs in the alphabet.

Objective physical distance is not the only predictor of attraction, however. It has been found that *functional* distance, defined as the likelihood of two individuals coming into contact, also predicts whether people will become friends or like each other (Ebbesen *et al.*, 1976; Festinger *et al.*, 1950). Functional distance becomes a more accurate predictor of friendship than objective physical distance when architectural features of a building constrain individuals whose apartments or offices are physically distant from frequent interaction. For example, the concept of functional distance would best predict attraction between two individuals who live five floors apart in an apartment building (distant in an objective sense), but who have adjacent mailboxes in the lobby.

Why does propinquity lead to friendship? Freedman, Carlsmith, and Sears (1974) offer some fairly convincing explanations. First, it is impossible to find grounds for friendship with someone we have never met, and those who are close to us in terms of physical or functional distance are clearly more readily accessible to us and to each other than individuals who are more distant. Second, since we have to continue to interact in the future with others who live in close proximity to us, perhaps we try a bit harder to "see the good side" of them and exert ourselves a bit harder to "make it work." Third, continued interaction with individuals obviously leads to feelings of predictability and to a sense of security, which may make friendship more likely. Fourth, familiarity in and of itself may lead to attraction, as shown in studies conducted by Zajonc (1968). However, it should be noted that propinquity is more likely to lead to attraction under cooperative conditions where there is equity between individuals than under competitive conditions where there is inequity. In addition, conditions of equality and cooperation promote enhanced attraction more effectively if prior attitudes toward another individual are neutral or mildly positive than if they are highly negative.

One important attempt to promote propinquity, which many had hoped would lead to liking, has involved the integration of blacks and whites in American residential neighborhoods, schools, and workplaces. Unfortunately, in many cases where propinquity occurs between racially dissimilar others, the optimal conditions for positive relations are not met. In fact, conditions more closely parallel those which elicit negative responses. For example, when school desegregation occurs, there is generally not equality between whites and blacks, who have had inferior educational opportunities. The climate is often somewhat competitive, and the attitudes expressed by parents and others may be far from neutral. Thus, it isn't surprising that reviews of the school integration literature suggest some negative outcomes. While the studies that the results are based on are nonexperimental and there are many uncontrolled variables, the findings have been rather consistent (Stephan, 1978).

Research has also focused on the effects of interracial propinquity in residential areas. This has involved studies on the sudden integration of pub-

lic housing, and the effects of desegregating the "suburbs." Public housing projects built by the government feature low rent, and are "reserved" for those with low incomes. (We discussed public housing in more detail in Chapter 8.) Until the early 1950s, many public housing projects were segregated. When many were suddenly desegregated, research was done to compare racial attitudes of whites toward blacks for those living in integrated and segregated units. Results generally showed that propinquity led to less antiblack prejudice (e.g., Deutsch & Collins, 1951; Ford, 1973). There still may be a bit of prejudice remaining, however. It has been found that while most friendships between dissimilar others (e.g., blacks and whites) occur for those who live in very close proximity to one another, a greater proportion of friendships between similar others occurs for those who live farther away. In effect, propinquity may be the major factor in friendships between dissimilar others, while friendships between similar others can occur without it (Nahemow & Lawton, 1975).

Integration of suburban neighborhoods came much later, and many of our suburbs are still segregated. Also, there are several differences between public housing and suburban life which could suggest a different response to propinquity (e.g., people have a large financial investment in their homes; the socioeconomic status of residents differs). What happens when a black family buys a house down the street in a white neighborhood? Residents of the area report feeling that there is a significant "change in the nature of the neighborhood," discuss the event with a disapproving tone, and try to gather as much information as possible about the newcomers. They are also very concerned about property values. Over time, however, some positive changes often occur (see Table 10–2). From three months to a year after the newcomers move in, discussions about them become less negative and eventually quite positive. The apprehension about property values subsides, and it has even been found that there is eventually a decrease in *racism* scores (i.e., people in integrated neighborhoods hold less racist at-

Table 10–2. DISCUSSIONS AMONG RESIDENTS ABOUT THE NEW BLACK FAMILY* (PERCENTAGES)

Content of Discussions	Before Moved In	Time of Interview		
		After		
		One month	Three months	One year
None	54	50	32	33
Negative	27	25	29	8
Neutral	—	12	18	8
Positive	—	—	21	42

*Adapted from Hamilton & Bishop (1976).

titudes than those in segregated ones) (Hamilton & Bishop, 1976). Thus, residential propinquity can have favorable effects, at least in the long run.

LEARNING ENVIRONMENTS

Education is a central component of the socialization of youngsters and provides them with the

Figure 10–2. This is a study area in a college dormitory. How good a place would it be for studying? (Sherry Fisher)

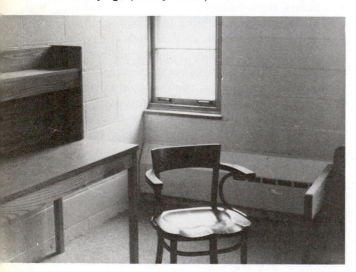

tools for life. Accordingly, the effects of the design of learning environments on the activities within them has been of great interest to researchers. These environments may range from small dormitory study areas such as the one depicted in Figure 10–2, to large formal library settings. If design features are causing problems, they must be remedied in order to allow educational goals to be attained. If a design change can increase the effectiveness of education, so much the better. Let us now look at several design factors in a variety of educational settings.

Classroom Environments

Changes in classroom environments have been made more or less continuously since we abandoned the one-room schoolhouse. However, as we shall see, we are no longer bound to traditional designs for physical reasons, and research has indicated that changes in classroom design can result in more positive student attitudes and greater participation in class (Sommer & Olsen, 1980). Let us consider some of these innovations.

Windowless Classrooms. One innovation, the building of windowless classrooms, has not proven overwhelmingly successful. Originally designed to reduce distraction in the classroom, as well as to reduce heating costs, these new school buildings typically contain few if any windows. Research has suggested that the absence of windows in classrooms has no consistent effect on learning (some students improve, others show worse performance), but that it does reduce the pleasantness of students' moods (Architectural Research Library, 1965; Karmel, 1965).

The Open Classroom Concept. The traditional design of classrooms, rectangularly shaped with straight rows of desks, dates back to medieval times, when the only source of light was natural light that came in through windows. Modern buildings, of course, do not rely solely on sunlight so that new design alternatives are possible. Open classrooms, like open offices, are designed to free students from traditional barriers, such as restrictive seating. In such settings, students should have more opportunity to explore the learning environment.

Research evaluating these designs is confounded by the fact that the environment is typically not the only difference between open and traditional schools. That is, an "open education" philosophy implies freedom for students to move around and less structure in class activities. However, these *could* occur in a traditionally designed classroom and don't necessarily occur in open classrooms. Interestingly, Rivlin and Rothenberg (1976) found that behavior and performance in

open-plan settings was not always consistent with the general philosophy of open education. In many open classrooms, students behave much as they do in traditional classrooms, and teachers often do not use all of the space provided. As is the case in traditional settings, students spend a great deal of time engaged in solitary tasks such as reading and writing (Rivlin & Rothenberg, 1976), as can be seen in Table 10–3. However, Gump (1974) observed that students in open classrooms spend less time in directed activity than students in traditional settings, and that groups in open classrooms show greater variability in size. Such heightened flexibility in open-plan rooms is often accompanied by greater activity than in the traditional classroom.

Two serious problems with open-plan designs are that they provide inadequate privacy and foster too much noise (e.g., Brunetti, 1972; Rivlin & Rothenberg, 1976). The flexibility provided by the open space can cause coordination problems, and frequently teachers do not know how to arrange furnishings so as to get the most use out of the space provided. It is conceivable that by combining aspects of traditional and open-design classrooms, better environments may be created. At present, however, reviews of this kind of physical design are mixed. As we will see in the next chapter, open plans in offices are also mixed blessings.

Table 10–3. EXAMPLES OF ACTIVITIES FROM BEHAVIOR MAPPING IN AN OPEN CLASSROOM*

Type of Study Activity Observed	Percent of Total Activities Observed
Writing	26.0
Arts and crafts	11.8
Talking	11.3
Reading	6.3
Working at projects	5.7
Teaching	4.3

*Observers record the type and location of student activity. (Adapted from Rothenberg & Rivlin, 1975.)

Environmental Complexity and Enrichment.
What is the proper amount of environmental complexity in an educational setting? As we have seen elsewhere in this book, studies have indicated that the complexity of an environment can affect arousal and performance in that setting (e.g., Evans, 1978). Too many stimuli may distract students, create overload, or increase fatigue. However, extremely simple settings may be boring and equally detrimental to performance.

Some researchers believe that classrooms should tend more toward the complex rather than the simple (Rosenzweig, 1966; Thompson & Heron, 1954). Having more stimuli and opportunities for environmental exploration present provides an enriched environment that facilitates learning. Others disagree, arguing that complex learning environments are distracting and make it difficult for the student to concentrate on school work (Vernon & McGill, 1957; Wohlwill, 1966). Comparative research is scant, but one study has examined the effects of variations in complexity of learning environments (Porteus, 1972). This study showed greater learning in less complex settings, supporting the position that overload and distraction are important problems in complex classrooms.

Libraries

Library designers have a number of unique problems with which they must deal. One familiar problem at university libraries is that patterns of use for study and reading areas move through periods of over- and underuse (e.g., Cziffra *et al.*, 1975). Because underuse wastes space that could be used for books, a proposed design alternative for a university library would reserve the library for the storage and dispensation of materials. Reading and study areas would be eliminated from this setting and dispersed to other areas on the campus (Figure 10–3). For many students, such a separation of library and study functions would mean a major change in work style and would sometimes prove inconvenient. After all, the campus library often is the one place where students know they can get school work done!

Figure 10–3. Books or people? Libraries have traditionally provided space both for books and reading or study. However, many libraries are caught in a conflict between space needs for a never-ending stream of new books and study space that is used only part of the time.

In another library use study, Lipetz (1970) observed how a sample of over 2,000 patrons used a library card catalog. Since a large proportion of users go to the catalog upon entering the building, the catalog is usually located near the entrance. It may come as little surprise that Lipetz found that students used the catalog system far more than the faculty did. Furthermore, the rate of library use varied across periods of the academic year, with some of the heaviest use occurring after vacations and semester breaks. After using the card catalog, people often have a difficult time locating the right stacks in a library, so Lipetz recommends better orientation aids than are typically available (see box, p. 301).

Museum Environments

Museums are, in a sense, learning environments, but they are quite different from classrooms. Since we use museums less regularly than class-

LOCATING A BOOK AT THE LIBRARY: A PROBLEM IN ORIENTATION

Finding a book in a library is partly a problem of orienting ourselves to a large setting. Where do we start? Where do we go for help? Do we ask for information or try to find our way by reading signs? Pollet (1976) is one librarian who is interested in helping libraries improve their orientation aids. One of the most important observations she makes is that library patrons must cope with information overload. Adding signs to help people find their way around contributes even more information to the environment. In particular, Pollet notes that clustering many signs together makes orientation information ineffective. People who are already receiving too much information are not apt to stop and look at a cluster of signs.

Libraries are learning to reduce the number of signs used and to experiment with critical locations of signs throughout the building. People need information at the point of making a decision about where to go next. One helpful technique is to use a specific color for orientation information. No matter where people are, they can look for that color and become oriented. However, Pollet concludes that using too many colors for different areas simply adds more information to be processed, and can cause disorientation.

As found in similar museum studies, many patrons will not ask for help in libraries. Pollet advocates a good sign system that will give patrons a sense of control over the environment instead of relying on attendants to answer questions. She also comments that it is hard to find attendants who can put up with answering the same questions all day. While library patrons may be experiencing stimulus overload, information attendants may experience understimulation, which can leave them bored and irritable.

rooms, the museum environment is somewhat more novel to us. Museums are also larger and do not provide a home base, such as a desk does in a classroom. In addition, the primary mode of activity in museums is exploration, as we make our way through halls and rooms, past endless cases of exhibits.

The ability to find things in museums is related to wayfinding in any setting. Museums that are confusing or hard to explore may result in less satisfaction with the visit (Winkel *et al.*, 1976). If you miss the exhibits you came to see because you could not find them, or if you find yourself constantly backtracking and going in circles, you probably have less fun than if everything were simpler. However, the complexity of museum environments is an almost inherent feature of their purpose—to display as many exhibits as possible.

One way of overcoming this inherent complexity is to provide aids for finding one's way through the museum. Winkel *et al.* (1976) sug-gest that people prefer to consult signs and maps and are uncomfortable if they have to ask museum employees for help. Maps that clearly depict a setting and *identify the viewer's location on the map* in relation to the setting seem to be particularly helpful. Such "you are here" maps show the position of the viewer and how to get from "here" to other parts of the setting (Levine, 1982). Not surprisingly, orientation aids such as maps and suggestions for what to see appear to increase satisfaction with the environment (Borun, 1977).

Overload notions may help explain why orientation aids are so valuable in museums. It has been found that the most popular museum exhibits are those that are of moderate complexity (Lakota, 1975; Melton, 1972; O'Hare, 1974; Robinson, 1928). Fatigue in a museum is not only a simple matter of walking around, but is also affected by the stimulation provided by the exhibits (Robinson, 1928). It may be, then, that museums can create overload if they are too complex or if it is difficult to get around inside (see Figure 10–4 A and B).

Research has also addressed the ways in which people explore museums. For example, people appear to have a right-handed bias; upon entering a gallery in a museum, they typically turn right and move around the room in that direction (Melton, 1933, 1936; Robinson, 1928). Once inside a museum, people usually stop at the first few exhibits and then become more selective, stopping

Figure 10–4A and B.   Modern museums have recognized the problem of environmental complexity and fatigue by creating exhibits that pace the amount of complexity so as to reduce fatigue and orient the visitor. (From A. Neal, *Help! For the Small Museum.* Boulder, Col.: Pruett Publishing, 1969.)

at fewer the longer they explore (Melton, 1933). The higher the *attraction gradient* of an exhibit, the more likely visitors are to explore it. Exits to other exhibit rooms are also important because people tend to use the first exit they see. Museum researchers refer to this ''pull'' of exits are the *exit gradient*. Due in part to attraction gradients and exit gradients, most people see only a part of each exhibit room rather than seeing everything before moving on (Parsons & Loomis, 1973). These patterns are depicted in Figure 10–5.

Fatigue in Museum Exploration. Predictable though it is, the pattern of physical movement within a museum shows some signs of being maladaptive. Walking in a museum should facilitate exploration of the environment. Yet, as we have seen, visitors frequently move past much of the exhibit without stopping or looking, thereby missing many of the rewards to be gained from a museum visit. Why is exploratory movement not more complete? One explanation is that fatigue

interferes with completing more thorough patterns of visual exploratory behavior.

Robinson (1928) first studied fatigue in museums many years ago. In spite of his work being old, many of his observations on exploratory fatigue are still important. He concluded that fatigue was not due just to physical exertion but also to the visitor growing tired of maintaining a high level of attention. Robinson coined the term ''museum fatigue'' to describe the phenomenon.

In a clever laboratory study, Robinson was able to demonstrate that museum fatigue was more than just physical exertion. He had persons seated at a table look at a series of copies of paintings from a gallery, presented in the same order as they hung in the gallery. Attention time for each painting was recorded and compared with the attention time observed in the gallery itself. It turned out that subjects seated at the table and looking through the stack of pictures began to show a drop in attention at about the same point in the sequence as visitors walking through the

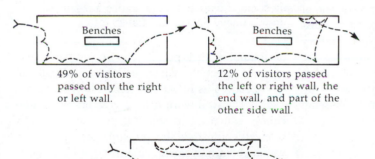

49% of visitors passed only the right or left wall.

12% of visitors passed the left or right wall, the end wall, and part of the other side wall.

Figure 10–5. Typical movement patterns found in one study of visitors to an art museum. (Adapted from A. W. Melton, Studies of Installations at the Pennsylvania Museum of Art. *Museum News*, 1933, *10*. Used with permission.)

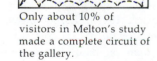

Only about 10% of visitors in Melton's study made a complete circuit of the gallery.

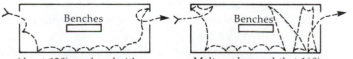

About 12% explored either the right or left wall and also one end wall.

Melton observed that 16% used an ambiguous, disorganized pattern of exploration.

museum. Robinson concluded that museum fatigue was due to psychological satiation or boredom as well as to fatigue from physical activity. He did not mean that visitors were bored by the exhibits. Rather, he noted that after visitors concentrated on several stimulating exhibits for a very long period, they became so satiated with the museum's environment that additional exhibits were relatively unstimulating. Recall from our discussion of information overload in Chapter 3 that when we receive the massively complex stimulation typical of many museum environments, we tend to ignore less important cues in order to attend to more important ones. This is the sort of phenomenon that occurs with museum fatigue: We become so satiated with complex information that we spend less and less time looking at the details of various exhibits.

Museum fatigue can be alleviated somewhat by building what Robinson called *discontinuity* into the design of an exhibit. Discontinuity refers to a change of pace in the stimuli presented. For example, a series of paintings might be broken up with a piece of sculpture or an arrangement of furniture. The number of paintings or objects displayed can also be reduced, since a single gallery may contain a collection large enough to tax the attention span of the most ardent art lover. Alleviating museum fatigue helps visitors gain more satisfaction from their exploration of the museum environment.

PEDESTRIAN ENVIRONMENTS: SHOPPING MALLS, PLAZAS, AND CROSSWALKS

Nearly every environment has characteristic patterns of pedestrian movement through it. People select paths and avoid obstacles in regular fashion (Figure 10–6). By understanding the development of these patterns, we can obtain important information about the design of several kinds of settings.

Research has revealed a number of principles of pedestrian movement patterns. One basic rule

Figure 10–6. People walking in an open plaza, as in the campus scene shown here, appear to be moving in a totally random manner. However, systematic observation of pedestrian movement has revealed that there is a predictable pattern to most movement. Some pathways, such as the most direct diagonal route across a plaza, will draw a heavy flow of foot traffic.

of thumb is that people choose simple, direct routes whether formalized as landscaped paths or freely chosen as in walking across lawns (Preiser, 1972). The well-worn paths across lawns on most college campuses, despite the presence of nearby sidewalks, illustrate this principle. Another observation about movement patterns regards the speed with which people walk. Generally, people conform their speed to that of people around them (Preiser, 1973). Larger crowds appear to move more slowly, and people walk slower on carpeting than on bare floors. Moreover, pedestrians match their speed somewhat to the pace of background music. These and other basic movement patterns apply in several different settings (e.g., Bovy, 1975).

We mentioned that movement patterns must also consider the effects of obstacles, such as automobile traffic. Frequently, people must negotiate traffic while walking somewhere. They may have to cross a street in order to get to a class-room building; or pass through a crowded parking lot en route to a shopping mall. People walk slower in such situations and often experience uncertainty in deciding whether to cross the traffic or wait (Henderson & Jenkins, 1974). In addition to traffic, large crowds can inhibit our movement and change patterns. The presence of people in one's way leads to frequent changes in speed and deviations from the most direct route one can take. For example, people will walk around a small group of people who are standing and talking rather than following a direct route between or through the group (Cheyne & Efran, 1972; Knowles *et al.*, 1976). Preiser (1973) has incor-

porated all of these influences on pedestrian movement into a *friction-conformity model*. That is, "frictions" such as those mentioned above impede pedestrian flow, and conformity pressures (e.g., the speed of others) exert additional influence on movement.

Knowles and Bassett (1976) have considered social cues that people use in deciding whether to stop or move in crowded settings. Their perception of whether the group is an interacting entity or a casual gathering of strangers appears to be important in determining behavior. When pedestrians encountered a group of people talking to one another they moved on. When they encountered a casual group of people who were simply standing and looking up in the air, they were

DESIGN RESEARCH FOR PEDESTRIAN WIND DISCOMFORT

No matter how efficient public transportation becomes, some pedestrian movement will be needed to get people to their final destination. Modern cities usually have high concentrations of pedestrian movement around business areas that consist of numerous high-rise buildings or skyscrapers. These buildings make it possible to locate many activities, such as work, shopping, entertainment, and living quarters, in a relatively small geographical area. However, there is increasing evidence that concentrated areas of high-rise buildings can alter ground level climate and pollution conditions because of the effects of building design on wind patterns (Hunt, 1975).

Engineers are now able to test the wind effects of proposed building designs in elaborate simulations that make use of wind tunnels (Peterka & Cermak, 1975). Such tests involve fitting models of proposed and existing buildings with pressure-sensitive recording devices. When the models are subjected to simulated wind levels typical of that city, researchers can examine structural stress effects as well as possible wind problems for pedestrians. Two common problems are if a smokestack on a tall building is too short, or if a tall building is located too close upwind from a short one. Resulting wind patterns can force pollutants toward the ground and trap them there, causing a variety of discomforts for pedestrians. Another problem arises when high-speed winds 30 or more feet off the ground strike a tall building. Typically, these winds are forced straight down. If the building has an open passageway at ground level, the winds rush through it, causing a "wind tunnel" effect. Pedestrians, especially those carrying opened umbrellas, may be literally sucked through the passageway. Design alternatives that include wind deflectors are one means of solving this problem.

Such wind tunnel simulations enable researchers to test potential wind effects on entire city blocks (Peterka & Cermak, 1977). Design solutions to anticipated problems can also be tested. In one case, tests revealed that high winds in a plaza could be avoided by erecting partial walls at the entrance (Peterka & Cermak, 1973). The beauty of this type of research is that design alternatives can be tested before construction commitments are made.

more likely to stop and join in (Knowles & Bassett, 1976).

Sometimes we like to watch others pass by us. "People watching" occurs when people seek out benches or seats where they can watch others (Preiser, 1972). Snyder and Ostrander (1972) observed this phenomenon among residents of retirement homes who often locate themselves in areas where they can watch staff and other residents. Similarly, Zeisel and Griffin (1975) reported that elderly residents of an apartment complex preferred to sit along sidewalk areas so that they could watch other people go by. People watching is certainly not restricted to the elderly. For example, teenagers who use an area shopping mall as a "hangout" may sit for hours watching people pass, looking for friends and visiting with those they find.

Understanding pedestrian patterns is useful in several ways. Knowing how people move through shopping areas, for instance, may help in designing malls and arranging shops so that they are optimally patronized. In other settings, obstacles can be minimized and short, direct routes between places can be provided. By doing these things we can facilitate comfortable movement through a number of settings.

HOSPITAL SETTINGS

Much of what we know about design in hospital settings is derived from research on acute care and psychiatric hospital environments (Reizenstein, 1982). Most data-based investigations have considered psychiatric patients, perhaps because of greater ease and accessibility in using these subjects. Whatever the reason, this fact necessarily limits what we can conclude about design in hospital settings, since there is no guarantee that hospital patients respond comparably regardless of their reasons for being patients.

In addition, the literature on hospital environments is limited by methodology—much of it is based on descriptive or noninvestigative approaches. In other words, a lot of what we know about these settings is based on observation and opinion rather than on careful study of behavior in them, although there are some notable exceptions (e.g., Canter, 1972; Noble & Dixon, 1972; Wolfe, 1975).

One aspect of hospital settings that has received attention is the low control or "low choice" forced upon patients and visitors (Olsen, 1978; Taylor, 1979). Hospitals typically have a great number of rules and allow patients only minimal control over the small spaces that they use. Olsen has pointed out that hospital designs can communicate this message—that people are "sick and dependent and should behave in an accordingly passive manner . . ." (Olsen, 1978, p. 7). Provision of greater spatial complexity or providing more options or variations in design can improve the situation and lead to more positive emotional responses (Olsen, 1978).

Ronco (1972) observed that hospital settings are usually designed for staff rather than patient needs. For example, it is conceivable that a ward design which facilitates staff functioning might also cause a patient to sense an overwhelming loss of personal control and privacy. Such feelings in turn may contribute to the patient's becoming overdependent on the hospital and withdrawing from normal activities. These and other considerations have led researchers to look for design alternatives which alleviate the negative effects of hospitalization and stimulate the healing process, as well as facilitate staff needs.

Do some designs and locations of nurses' stations promote more efficient patient care (i.e., behavioral facilitation), as some suggest (cf. Lippert, 1971)? In order to answer this question, Trites *et al.* (1970) investigated nurse efficiency and staff satisfaction with three different hospital ward designs (Figure 10–7). In general, a radial ward design was found to be the most desirable (relative to single and double corridor designs), both in terms of saving unneccessary ward travel and of increasing time with patients. Moreover, members of the nursing staff indicated a preference for assignment to the radial ward. The fact that nursing staff in the radial unit had more free time was interpreted as an indication that more

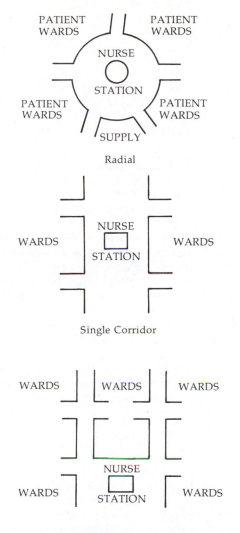

Figure 10–7. These designs represent three types of hospital wards. The radial unit appeared to be the most desirable in terms of staff satisfaction and amount of time spent with patients. (Adapted from Trites *et al.* Copyright 1970, Sage Publications, Inc.)

patients could be housed on the ward. In another ward study, however, Lippert (1971) found no one ward design particularly superior to any other, using efficiency in patient care stops as the behavioral criterion. Nevertheless, it is clear that

hospital design can have significant impact on and well-being of both patients and staff.

Another issue that has received attention is the degree to which different designs affect social interaction among patients. Beckman (1974) suggests that an appropriate design is one which encourages patients to leave their rooms and seek out others, and which supports social interaction. This design goal reflects an understanding and concern for the same kinds of issues raised in studies of residential environments—the recognition that the arrangement of space can affect the frequency and quality of social contact (Baum & Valins, 1977).

We noted in the previous chapter that some types of furniture arrangements (i.e., sociopetal vs. sociofugal) facilitate patient interaction more than others. In addition, keeping down the number of beds on a ward promotes social interaction and reduces withdrawal (Ittelson *et al.*, 1970). Social interaction concerns extend to other relationships as well. Pill (1967), for example, discusses how designs that place nursing staff in close proximity to patients do not allow nurses to satisfy their privacy needs. Another important form of interaction, disclosure between patient and physician, is facilitated by pleasantly designed institutional settings (Reizenstein, 1976). Other studies have shown that windowless intensive care units have a higher incidence of postoperative problems, ranging from negative psychological outcomes to physiological complications (Wilson, 1972), and that uncontrollable noise increases experienced pain and is associated with greater use of pain killers by surgery patients (Minckley, 1968).

A series of studies by Wolfe and Rivlin (Rivlin & Wolfe, 1972; Wolfe, 1975) has examined a number of design variables and their effects on behavior in a children's psychiatric hospital. One important variable turned out to be bedroom size and occupancy. Ittelson *et al.* (1970), for example, found that the more patients in a room, the fewer types of behavior were observed. Wolfe (1975) similarly reported that design elements which increased the number of children assigned

PRISON DESIGN AND BEHAVIOR

Even during the economically difficult period of the 1980s, one thing society seems to be building is more prisons. Given that prisoners are confined for long periods of time, it would seem that prison design could have important consequences. Research by Paulus and his colleagues has led to some important conclusions regarding the behavioral effects of prison design. Among other things, they found that different architectural layouts of residence space in prisons affected behavior and health. Grouping prisoners together in large numbers was less healthy than grouping them together in smaller numbers (Cox *et al.,* 1982). Single or double occupancy cells were better (i.e., judged as less crowded) than were cells grouping small numbers of prisoners. Small groupings, in turn, seemed better than large groupings. Further, if large groups were "broken up" by partitions or segmentation of space (so that the large group became several smaller ones), psychological and physical health was improved.

These findings provide strong evidence that the design of prisons influences mood and behavior of prisoners. At one level, this is not surprising. Prisons are usually designed along functional criteria and are not built for aesthetic reasons. Space is designed to facilitate order and regimentation. Bars and walls are deliberate attempts to constrain behavior, and economy is usually an important factor in determining the use of space. However, it is also clear that prison designs can have unintended, demoralizing effects, and new prisons have been increasingly designed to avoid some of these consequences (Luxenberg, 1977). This has occurred in spite of objections based on differing penal philosophies and increased costs.

The ethic that guided traditional prison design evolved from 19th century concepts of correctional activity. Treatment was seen as being best accomplished by isolation from society, both physically and symbolically. To some extent, prisons' clear separation from society may be traced to this ethic. At another level are the economic considerations that we have already mentioned. Most people see prisoners as nonproductive elements of society, so we place a special emphasis on economy. As a result of these pressures, prisons are usually large, located in remote areas, and surrounded by high exterior walls that deny inmates usual access to the outside world.

"New" prison designs usually seek to do several things. First, they attempt to provide more "humane" environments, replacing gun towers with natural barriers, adding color and lighting to otherwise drab settings, and increasing opportunities for privacy by providing more single-occupancy cells (Figure 10–8A and B). There has also been an attempt to build more cells into exterior walls so that inmates can have a view of the outside world. Control over the environment has also been heightened in some prisons, with inmates gaining control over heating, lighting, and so on, in their own cells. These improvements have been made in conjunction with changing philosophies in dealing with people who break the law. Their usefulness remains to be tested.

Figure 10–8A and B. The top picture displays a traditional prison gun tower and security wall. The bottom picture is an architect's rendering of a proposed prison at Stillwater, Minnesota. Note the absence of gun towers. Security is provided by the natural terrain of the land which forms an impenetrable wall around the setting. Observe also the spread-out appearance which causes the prison to look more like an industrial or educational campus. (Bottom print courtesy of the Winsor/Faricy Architects, St. Paul, Minn.: Gruzen & Partners, Consultants.)

IS A PSYCHOTHERAPIST'S OFFICE PART OF THE THERAPY?

Psychotherapists have long been aware that factors not directly related to therapy can sometimes influence a client's progress. There has been recent interest in whether one of these factors is the kind of office environment a therapist maintains. In an experimental study, Bloom, Weigel, and Trautt (1977) manipulated the kind of office in which clients received therapy. One office was set up in a standard "medical" arrangement, with formal furniture in a room and impressive diplomas on the wall. A second office (one that the researchers called a "humanistic" setting) was furnished informally and had wall posters instead of diplomas. Clients were asked to characterize male and female therapists solely on the basis of their offices. In general, clients viewed therapists in the "medical" office as more qualified professionally, but further results revealed an interesting relationship between sex of therapist and type of office. Clients felt that female therapists who had "humanistic" offices were less credible than female therapists who had "medical" offices. Just the opposite was true for male therapists, who were considered more credible in humanistic offices. The researchers concluded that because of these differences in judgments about therapists, office design factors might well influence the therapy process.

---

to a hospital room decreased its use and had inhibiting effects on patients' behavior. (For a discussion of the effects of the design of a psychotherapist's office, see the box above.)

Design of play space in psychiatric facilities for children has also received attention (Rivlin, Wolfe, & Beyda, 1973). In general, little consideration is given to age level differences in planning play space in these facilities. Younger children, especially, seem to have difficulty in adapting to highly controlled hospital ward space. Rivlin and her colleagues suggested that the behaviors younger children display in handling their disorientation to ward space may be interpreted by staff members as part of their disorder. In reality, the younger child may be reacting as any child might to restrictions on play caused by inadequate space. Consequently, special care facilities should be designed not only for treating illness but also for encouraging the normal activities of a particular age group.

RESIDENTIAL CARE FACILITIES FOR THE AGED

As a greater proportion of our population becomes aged, providing specialized short- and long-term residential care facilities for these people becomes important. Certain characteristics of the aged population should be kept in mind when designing such environments. Most importantly, the elderly are a heterogeneous lot. Too often designers have assumed that aged people are a homogeneous group, when actually they have only age and certain health problems in common. In fact, there is probably no other segment of the population with such a broad diversity of individual problems and needs. Some elderly citizens have trouble hearing, others have difficulty with vision, and still others have problems with locomotion. Many have no physical disabilities at all. Some elderly people suffer from psychological difficulties (e.g., withdrawal, distorted thought processes) while others do not. Another source of diversity in aged populations is the fact that individuals have established long-term behavior patterns, and these differ greatly among people. All of these considerations argue for "designing in" flexibility in residential care facilities for the aged.

How should designers approach the task of planning residential care facilities for this population? They should attempt to compensate as much as possible for the physical and psychological difficulties which some aged individuals have, without unduly constraining the lives of people who have no particular problems. A variety of environmental options should be provided, so that people can continue to engage in the same activities as they did prior to institutionalization. Also, it is important for designers to attempt to view things from the perspective of aged residents, which may differ from the needs and ideas of the staff of the facility or the designer him- or herself. Too often facilities for the aged are designed in accord with an architect's vision (which may not be sufficiently informed about the elderly), or are planned so that they make life easy for the nursing, cleaning, or maintenance staff of the institution (e.g., Fontaine, 1982).

A number of design features would seem to be useful to incorporate in a short- or long-term residential care facility for the aged. First, it is important for the environment to provide for *safety and convenience*. To promote safety, a facility should permit sufficient staff surveillance to prevent accidents or to detect them when they do occur, while not eliciting the feeling that there is no privacy. In addition, specific design features should be included to prevent accidents (e.g., handrails in halls, "nonslip" surfaces), and aspects of the design certainly should not cause accidents. Also, elements should be included that permit clients to notify the staff if they have a problem in a private area (e.g., call buttons in bathrooms). The design should promote convenience by providing orientation aids (e.g., color-coded floors, cues to differentiate halls), as well as by affording comfort (e.g., the main entrance should be sheltered from sun and rain). Convenience is also fostered to the extent that the setting is "barrier free," and allows a large proportion of the population to move about independently. Finally, important facilities (e.g., bathrooms, communal areas) should be within easy access of rooms. In many ways, facilities conforming to the above criteria will promote feelings of personal control, prevent helplessness, and elicit positive effects in residents. (For a review on the concepts of control and helplessness, see Chapter 3.)

The design of a residential care facility for the aged should also foster *choice* (and in doing so,

feelings of control). The location of the facility should be sufficiently close to a community to allow residents to choose among a variety of available services (e.g., grocery stores, movie theaters). Choice is also facilitated when the design contains various types of spaces which can be used for special purposes (e.g., recreation, privacy, dyadic as opposed to large group communication). Recreation areas should be designed to elicit communication (i.e., should be sociopetal), but some areas should afford privacy (i.e., should be sociofugal). It is very important that there be a range of social and recreational choices available to each resident (Lawton, 1979). Also, each resident should have access to both a bathtub and a shower, and it is preferable for each room to have individual heating controls. Without adequate degrees of choice being promoted by physical design, the environment can promote loss of perceived control and helplessness.

In addition to providing choices, objective *physical conditions* of the facility should be adequate and appropriate. Rooms should be of sufficient size, there should be enough recreational space for the resident population, and the construction should be of reasonable quality. Objective physical conditions affect patient behavior in many ways. When large sitting areas are occupied by relatively few residents, there seems to be a low level of interaction. Designs including long corridors appear to discourage resident mobility. When physical arrangements cause residents to be grouped in areas closely accessible to staff, some positive outcomes occur (e.g., the staff has more surveillance over accidents and danger). However, some negative outcomes also occur under these circumstances (e.g., the staff may behave in ways that encourage patient dependency) (Harris, Lipman, & Slater, 1977). It is also important for patients to have their own kitchen facility, or else residents tend to depend on staff members even to get a cup of coffee (Lipman & Slater, 1979). This situation encourages helplessness.

In addition to the physical environment, the social environment is extremely important to the well-being of the institutionalized elderly. A great deal of recent research has found that when the social environment fosters perceived choice and personal control, the well-being of elderly populations is enhanced. Unfortunately, both the social conditions under which many people arrive at institutions and institutional life itself typically promote a loss of control. The new resident is often stripped of his or her accustomed relationships and satisfactions, and must give up personal property which has served as a means of self-identification. Also, people frequently come to a residential care facility after having problems with illness, financial setbacks, and family difficulties, all of which foster a loss of control. Often the family decides that the person cannot remain at home any longer and to which institution the person will go (Fontaine, 1982). The very character of institutional life (e.g., one must submit to rules and regulations, to authority, to "standardized" schedules and procedures) adds to one's loss of control (Wack & Rodin, 1978).

One's response to being relocated and entering a long-term residential care facility is more positive if he or she is afforded a degree of control over the process. Reactions are more favorable when the person has chosen to be institutionalized, has picked the particular facility that he or she will live in, and when the difference in control between the pre- and post-relocation environments is not great (Ferrari, 1960; Schulz & Brenner, 1977). In addition to providing control, one way to increase predictability (and hence resident well-being) is to give people preparatory information about their forthcoming move, which actually decreases mortality rates after relocation (Pastalan, 1976; Zweig & Csank, 1975).

One problem for residents is that with subsequent declines (or improvements) in health, further relocation may be necessary. In order to minimize the negative effects of this movement, multilevel facilities—those that offer *many* levels of care and supervision in one place—are becoming popular. These are beneficial because they minimize the effects of relocation by making the move from one part of the facility to another, rather than from one facility to another. People can still have access to their friends and can be moved easily if their condition again improves or deteriorates. While there are benefits to this type of design, there are criticisms as well. Some say that the presence of people in deteriorated states of health can undermine the morale and create dependency (and even illness) in relatively more healthy residents (Gutman, 1978). The verdict still is not in on multilevel designs, and further research is necessary. (Figure 10–9A and B).

Once one has relocated and is living in an institution for the aged, aspects of the institutional environment (both physical and social), can foster a sense of loss of control. For example, a great deal more is done for residents of old age institutions than was the case in their former environments. What can we do to reverse this loss of control, which can eventually result in helplessness? One important element in solving the problem is for residents to be encouraged to do more things for themselves. In Chapter 3 we noted a study by Langer and Rodin (1976) in which one group of institutionalized elderly was treated in a way designed to increase feelings of control. In the group where control was fostered, residents were happier, their conditions had improved somewhat after several months, and they showed more activity (e.g., were more apt to attend a movie, and to participate in a contest) than in the condition where control was not encouraged.

Similar results were reported by Mercer and Kane (1979) and, in general, it seems that increasing control consistently leads to important positive physical and psychosocial effects (box, p. 314). Not only does it improve individual functioning, but it improves the overall atmosphere of the institution (Fontaine, 1982). Do the effects of control-increasing interventions persist? Here, the evidence is mixed: Some studies (e.g., Rodin & Langer, 1977) show long-term effects, while others (e.g., Schulz & Hanusa, 1978) do not.

Noninstitutional Residences for the Aged

While it become necessary at some point for many elderly to enter an institution, this is not uniformly the case. In many ways, it is probably

Figure 10–9A and B. Providing several levels of care in a facility for the aged can minimize difficulties associated with relocation, but can also reduce the morale of healthier patients.

AN IDEAL RESIDENTIAL CARE FACILITY FOR THE AGED: INCREASING ENVIRONMENTAL AND SOCIAL CONTROL

We have suggested that aspects of the physical and social environments which afford control will have favorable effects on aged residents of institutional care facilities. While some attempt has been made to increase control in such institutions, there are many more steps that can be taken. One impediment is that in the short-run, giving control to residents may be perceived by staff as causing more work for them, or taking away their authority. But as we have seen, in the long-run it could lead to better functioning residents who are much more able to care for themselves, rather than depending on staff members.

What would an ideal residential care facility for the aged be like? In an interesting speculative essay based on past research on the effects of control in institutional settings for the aged, Fontaine (1982) suggests several important elements. The ideal facility would be relatively small, which would afford residents more control in dealing with staff, the environment, and other residents. People would be given a choice of large single or double rooms. All rooms would contain movable, rearrangeable furniture so people could control their immediate environment, and each room would have a private bathroom. Residents would be encouraged to bring their own furniture, pictures, and certain other possessions with them. This is important for maintaining one's self-image, and a sense of continuity in life. Double rooms would have partitions which residents could arrange to suit their needs. It would be the job of residents, where possible, to maintain and to clean their rooms, again affording control over the immediate environment. There would be a shop on the premises where residents could buy their own personal effects and disposable items, thus promoting control and reducing dependency on staff and family members.

Complementing the institutional kitchen would be a kitchen for people who do not want to eat what everyone else is eating on a particular day, or who want to prepare food for guests or friends. (Each patient would have a food storage closet and refrigerator space.) An ideal facility would also permit residents a great deal of choice in the planning of institutional meals, and there could be choices of what dishes they would be served at a particular meal.

Choice would also be heavily incorporated into recreational offerings. Television sets would be available for use in rooms by request, as well as in one of the day rooms. All sorts of recreational areas would be available, some fostering large-group, and others promoting individual and small-group, activity. Outside there would be a large courtyard where residents could plant flowers (which they could give as gifts or use to decorate their rooms), and vegetables (which they could eat). (The role of gardening as a recreational activity is highlighted in the box on page 328.)

Choice would also be incorporated into the everyday routine. Within reason, residents would be allowed to get out of bed and get washed whenever they wished. They would help choose daily activities, which would insure that they had interesting things to do. Any complaints would be handled in a democratic way, giving residents some control over the way the facility is run.

While the above means of establishing environmental control for residents sound good, there are some caveats. Fontaine notes that the amount of control one can handle depends on one's physical and psychological condition. Having more control than one can exercise could be bad, rather than good, for people. However, almost anyone can exercise some degree of control (e.g., which side to lie on in bed, what they would like to eat). And even those who cannot exercise much control can benefit from information about what will be occurring in the institution, which affords a feeling that events are predictable, if not entirely controllable.

better if one can stay at home or in a relatively "homelike" setting without having to endure certain almost inevitable problems associated with institutional environments. Accordingly, special residential housing facilities for the elderly have been planned and built. Also, many services (e.g., "Meals on Wheels," home nursing care) are now made available to elderly citizens who are living "at home."

What type of residential housing for the aged seems to be best? Various elements (e.g., high and rising rents for people on fixed incomes, long-term residences being turned into condominiums) can make it difficult for the elderly to find a decent place to live at a reasonable price. Overall, studies suggest that providing planned housing specifically for the aged is superior to leaving them to find a residence on the "open market" (e.g., Carp, 1966; Lawton & Cohen, 1974). Is it best for aged people to live in "age-segregated" or in heterogeneous environments? While arguments could be made citing costs and benefits of each environmental arrangement, the confluence of evidence suggests that the elderly prefer age-segregated housing. Living with others one's own age is associated with housing satisfaction, neighborhood mobility, and positive morale (Grant, 1970). Why is this the case? Perhaps it is because more similar others are in close proximity when the neighborhood is "age-segregated," and both similarity and propinquity elicit attraction (Byrne, 1971). In addition, age segregation probably results in more activities that are appropriate to an elderly population. There are other possibilities as well, such as the provision of more medical and other services needed by the elderly in age-segregated settings.

What other factors should be taken into consideration when planning noninstitutional residences for the elderly? One important element in residential living for the aged population is adequate transportation. Too often, transportation is not sufficiently accessible for the elderly in the community. Planners should be certain there are bus routes running through areas with many aged citizens, and these should include stops at places where these people must go (e.g., medical complexes, shopping areas). Buses should also be accessible to elderly citizens (and others) with handicaps. In addition to making transportation systems physically available to the elderly, designers must explore means of making other aspects of the community accessible as well. Many elements in the environment (e.g., exterior stairways, nonautomatic doors) may be discouraging and dangerous to an aged population.

CHAPTER SUMMARY

In American culture, strong preferences exist for single-family detached homes, apparently because such housing provides high control over social interaction. Economic and other factors, however, often lead to choices of other types of housing.

The more easily we can perform given tasks in a setting, the more satisfied we are with it. Other factors affecting residential satisfaction include noise, ease of cleaning, and adequate plumbing, heating, and kitchen facilities. For inner-city residents, satisfaction with a neighborhood is closely tied to social bonds.

Privacy is a significant mediator of activities in residences but is not a simple process. Whereas some families have a very open structure, others use design within the home to structure privacy for all family members. Another important issue is functional criteria in residential design. One current consideration is to combine several functions in one room, such as using a sunken bathtub as a conversation pit in a living room.

Propinquity involves both objective physical distance and functional distance, or the likelihood that two individuals will come into contact. Both types of propinquity facilitate the formation of friendships. Designing for optimal conditions can use propinquity to promote racial harmony and other favorable social relationships.

Research on classroom design has shown that windowless classrooms have no consistent effects on academic performance, but that presence of windows promotes pleasant moods. Open-plan classrooms also show mixed restults, with some research showing an increase in activity associated with open classrooms, as well as increases in noise and decreases in privacy. Apparently, an optimal level of complexity in the classroom environment promotes learning.

Libraries have a problem of periodic overuse and underuse of facilities. One proposal would separate the "normal" library functions from the study function it often serves. In addition, evidence indicates additional orientation aids would help many libraries. Orientation is also a problem in museums, with some evidence suggesting improved orientation enhances satisfaction. Exploration of a museum tends to be systematic and is heavily influenced by the attraction gradient of exhibits. Museum fatigue may be caused by overstimulation, and can be alleviated by designing discontinuity into exhibits.

Pedestrian movement also tends to be systematic, with people preferring the shortest route. Crowds slow down pedestrian movement, as does carpeting. People tend to match their walking speed to the flow of the crowd and to background music. A friction-conformity model has been proposed to explain these relationships.

Hospitals are often oriented toward a high-control, low-choice atmosphere to facilitate staff functioning. This tendency, however, reduces perceived control on the part of the patient, as well as privacy. Designs that restore control and foster social interaction can help in this regard, and can also facilitate patient recovery. A radial design of wards around a nursing station can improve staff efficiency and increase the amount of time staff spend with patients.

Care facilities for the aged need to consider the fact that characteristics and needs of the elderly vary widely, so designs should allow for flexibility. Safety and convenience, choice and control, and physical conditions are important considerations. Large sitting areas may discourage social interaction. Long corridors may discourage mobility. Whereas proximity of residents to staff facilitates surveillance, it may also encourage dependence. Although providing several levels of care in one facility minimizes negative effects of relocation, morale of healthier residents can suffer from too much interaction with those in deteriorated states of health. Clearly, providing perceived control is one of the most effective intervention strategies for the institutionalized elderly. For those outside of institutions, planned housing in age-segregated areas seems to enhance satisfaction and morale, and adequate transportation and shopping are also important.

Suggested Projects

1. Try to visit open classrooms and conventional classrooms in your area. Which seems to have the most activity? Which seems to be more noisy?
2. Visit your local museum and note exploration patterns of visitors. Can you identify attraction gradients and discontinuities? Do visitors tend to use the same route through displays?
3. Visit a nursing home or retirement home and note the location of lounge areas. Look for lounge areas that have a lot of interaction, and those with little interaction. What factors account for the differences?

11 Environments for Work, Leisure, and the Future

INTRODUCTION

Harry and Sue were looking forward to the weekend. Harry's job at the factory was getting more and more unpleasant. The machines were so loud the company doctor had informed him last week he was losing his hearing in the sound frequencies most necessary for conversation. What was worse, relationships among his coworkers were deteriorating. Management was pressing for increased productivity, and the only way for him to produce more was to make faster trips between the supply room and his work station. Other workers were doing the same thing, though, and they were all getting in each other's way. If his work station could be closer to the supply room, at least one problem would be solved.

Sue was equally hassled. Her firm had just moved into a new office without interior walls. It was supposed to reduce maintenance costs and increase ease of communication to have everyone in one large room. She couldn't stand it, though. She had had to reprimand a secretary yesterday and there was no place to do it except at her desk where everyone else could hear the conversation. To make matters worse, her doctor had called today with unfavorable news on some lab tests, and it seemed as if everyone in the office heard at least her end of the conversation. Noise was a problem for her, too. She worked hard on a marketing report due today, but it took much longer than necessary because of all the distraction from phones ringing and everybody else talking. The chatter of the computer printer 10 feet from her desk didn't help much either.

To get away from these headaches, Harry and Sue decided to go camping in the state park in the next county. After all, the convenience of the park was one reason they had chosen Rockport as a home. Arriving at the park entrance, the ranger informed them they were just in time to get one of the last two campsites available. They felt fortunate, though when they pulled into the campground it was discouraging to see that one of the remaining campsites was too muddy to pitch a tent on and the other was next to a motorcycle gang having a loud party. This was getting away from it all?

Have you had experiences similar to those described above? Unfortunately, they occur more often than we would like. Environmental psychologists and others concerned about these kinds of situations have asked whether or not environmental design can make a difference. Are there ways of designing the factory, the office, and the leisure setting so that undesired effects are minimized and desired results are maximized? In this chapter we will see some of the answers uncovered so far by researchers, and we will also take a look at some design considerations for specialized environments of the future, such as space colonies and undersea habitats. As with the previous chapter, we are concerned with organizing our discussion around the setting itself, and seeing how design principles influence the activity within the setting.

WORK ENVIRONMENTS

In previous chapters we have discussed the effects of noise, temperature, and territorial identification on behavior, and in Chapter 9 we saw how such factors as lighting, color, and furnishings need to be considered in environmental design. In the present section we will examine how these and other components of the environment can be incorporated into the process of designing the work environment, which is sometimes called the *workspace*. For those who wish to study the design of the work environment more thoroughly, detailed reviews of previous research exist elsewhere (Becker, 1981; Sundstrom & Sundstrom, 1983; Wineman, 1982). For our purposes, we will highlight some of the important findings of this research. We should note that research in the area continues, and the knowledge available for designing the workspace continues to grow.

Why Study the Design of the Work Environment?

Before the Industrial Revolution, nonfarm work was typically done in small spaces, often in the craftsperson's or businessperson's home. With the advent of machinery and mass production, the factory and office building became more efficient places of doing work. The design of these places of work was dependent on technology (e.g., Sundstrom & Sundstrom, 1983). Factories, for example, were rather narrow, long buildings situated near sources of water power. A water wheel outside the factory turned a long shaft that extended into the factory. Off this shaft ran a series of belts that powered the factory's machinery. Thus, the technology of the power source dictated a long narrow building, and the same technology plus construction with stone and wood dictated a low-rise building. Lighting by natural sunlight, as well as the mechanics of the water wheel power

shaft, meant that the building had to be narrow in order for each worker to have adequate window lighting. The office building was similarly restricted by technology. Stone construction and the absence of elevators meant that buildings could not be more than six to ten stories high, and the need for adequate lighting through windows dictated a fairly narrow building. Two developments in technology changed both the factory and the office. First, iron and later structural steel, combined with concrete, made it possible to span larger spaces as well as to build higher and higher. (With stone construction walls had to be so thick at the base for support of upper floors as to make tall buildings impractical.) Second, commercially available electricity allowed for more extensive indoor lighting and elevators in tall buildings, as well as the ability to separate manufacturing machines from a central power shaft. It then became technologically possible to set up a factory or office in an almost infinite number of ways. With these developments, design of workspace could escape the bounds of technological feasibility and focus on safety and health, productivity, and job satisfaction. Especially in this century, then, designers, owners and managers of plants, and labor organizations all became concerned with whether a well-designed, safe work environment (i.e., the quality of the work environment) would lead to better productivity and greater job satisfaction (see also Davis & Szigeti, 1982; Moleski & Lang, 1982; Wineman, 1982).

Productivity and the Work Environment. Can the design of an office or factory be used to increase productivity? If so, managers and others would want to take advantage of design principles for this purpose. In general, two principles seem to dominate current thinking along these lines. First, the principle of *workflow* (originally called straight-line flow of work) indicates that the lay-out of a factory or office should provide for the shortest possible distance between work stations along which the work moves (e.g., Hicks, 1977). For example, an assembly line should be arranged so that workers do not have to spend long amounts of time walking from the point where they finish their assignment on a product back to the point where they start the assignment on the next item. Also, space for supplies should be provided as close to the assembly line as possible so that workers do not have to spend excessive time moving from the supply area to the assembly area. Similarly, an office should be arranged so that related departments are close to each other. If paperwork moves from office A to office B to office C to office D, in that order, the offices should not be arranged with A on the tenth floor, C next to it, B on the fifth floor, and D on the sixth floor. Rather, the offices should be located in the order that the paperwork actually flows. Careful attention to the design of the work environment can certainly facilitate the movement of work in this regard.

A second consideration for productivity in designing work environments involves physical comfort and safety. In general, this consideration means providing the appropriate amount of lighting, noise reduction, ventilation, and other physical considerations as necessary. Prior to the twentieth century, choking fumes and deafening noise, for example, were considered part of the normal manufacturing process. Concern for the safety and health of workers, along with studies showing that productivity and accident rates could be influenced by physical working conditions, has led to standards of lighting, ventilation, noise reduction, and so on which not only provide for greater safety, but also avoid conditions that reduce productivity.

The effects of these various physical conditions on job performance are conceptualized within the framework of the environment–behavior theories discussed in Chapter 3. For example, noise or poor ventilation can increase arousal, narrow attention, or elevate stress to such an extent that performance is impaired. Consideration of these psychological mediators, then, is important in designing the work environment.

Job Satisfaction and the Work Environment. In addition to productivity, managers and others have become concerned that design of the work environment can influence job satisfaction. It is usually believed that the more satisfied the worker, the better an employee he or she makes in terms of such factors as loyalty, absenteeism, productivity, cooperation, and other important qualities. In general, employees do indeed list physical conditions as important for job satisfaction, though the physical environment is not as important in this regard as such factors as job security, pay, and friendly coworkers (e.g., Herzberg *et al.,* 1957). One theory suggests that an adequate work environment does not substantially enhance job satisfaction, but a substandard environment definitely leads to dissatisfaction (Herzberg *et al.,* 1957; Herzberg, Mausner, & Snyderman, 1959; McCormick & Tiffen, 1974). Whatever the case, it is clear that appropriate working conditions are important considerations in the design process.

Designing the Office Landscape

We have mentioned that the use of structural steel in buildings has allowed architects to design larger and larger open spaces. With previous construction methods, the need for support walls required a building to be separated into smaller rooms. Accordingly, a relatively small number of workers shared an office. Typically, a manager or executive would have a totally private office, and several clerical workers would share an adjoining space. Such office designs are still common today, but there is also an alternative permitted by a large open space. To facilitate work flow, for example, work stations for 100 or more clerks could be put in the same large room, with supervisor's offices along the sides of the large room. With the growth of the human relations movement in the 1950s, more open communication between workers and managers was encouraged, employees were allowed and even encouraged to participate in decision making, and barriers of status and authority became less prominent. These developments encouraged what is now known as the *open plan office,* or *open office,* for short (Figure 11–1A and B). This concept originated in Germany with work by the Schnelle brothers and their Quickborner Team consulting firm (Sundstrom & Sundstrom, 1983). Basically, the idea involves arranging desks, filing cabinets, and other office furniture in such a manner as to make maximum use of the large open space but still provide for efficient work flow. This *office landscape* design typically places a supervisor very near workers and arranges work areas close together or far apart so that work flow and communication between related areas is unimpeded by myriad enclosed offices. In some schemes, portable screens are used to set areas off from others, or shelving and filing cabinets may accomplish the same purpose. As you might expect, such an office design has a number of advantages, but also carries with it a number of disadvantages (cf., Sundstrom & Sundstrom, 1983). Let us examine some of these separately.

Advantages of the Open Plan Office. We have already mentioned one advantage of the open office: It provides for a more efficient flow of work and communication. In addition, it often costs less because there are no internal walls to construct, and lighting can be shared by several workspaces. Maintenance costs may also be reduced due to less painting and faster cleaning of work areas, and more people can be accommodated in the same interior space without walls. Moreover, it is easier to make changes in the design of the office when new jobs are added or eliminated or the number of people working on a project changes, because there are no fixed walls to move or add to change spatial arrangements. Finally, the open office permits easier supervision of workers. That is, a supervisor can see all workers from his or her desk without having to walk through several offices.

Disadvantages of the Open Office Plan. Typically, changes in any environment cannot be made without trade-offs, and open offices are no exception. For all the advantages of the open office, it carries disadvantages that fall into two major categories: increased noise and distraction,

Figure 11–1 A and B. Examples of the traditional office plan (left) and open office plan (right). (Photos courtesy of John L. Rundell, Jr.)

and lack of adequate privacy. When offices are separated by walls, the noise from typewriters, phones, and duplicating machines in one area does not carry over that much into the next office. With the open office plan, however, the noises may be very distracting to those in neighboring work stations. Similarly, conversation travels, and as we saw in Chapter 4, noise that is interpretable as conversation is quite distracting. Movement of people as they walk about doing assigned tasks is also more noticeable in the open office plan, and adds still another source of distraction. Solutions to the problem of noise and distraction include office machinery designed to be quieter, and the use of portable barriers (partitions, shelving, cabinets) to help screen out the distraction.

Loss of privacy is also very noticeable in open offices. Personal conversations are easily overheard and communication between supervisors and workers becomes more difficult to keep confidential. Just as open offices facilitate supervision, so they also reduce privacy. Every move a worker makes is open for public view. Phone calls with family members are overheard. Errors and embarrassing behavior are there for all to see. As with noise and distraction, use of portable barriers may help solve the privacy problem in the open office, but these barriers cannot provide the privacy of an enclosed, individual office (e.g., Hundert & Greenfield, 1969; Pile, 1978; Sundstrom & Sundstrom, 1983).

In sum, open office plans provide both advantages and disadvantages. The increased opportunity for communication may facilitate some flow of work, but also increases distraction and reduces privacy. Depending on the functions to be accomplished in a given office, the advantages may outweigh the disadvantages, or the disadvantages may be substantial enough to suggest the need for an alternative office plan (see also Goodrich, 1982; Marans & Spreckelmeyer, 1982; Sundstrom, Herbert, & Brown, 1982).

Personalization

There are a number of reasons for people's desires to personalize and decorate spaces in which they work. It is one's way of making the space his or her "own." By placing objects or decorating walls in certain ways we can identify spaces as being ours and project some of our feelings, goals, and values. In addition, decoration of spaces makes them more pleasant. Research has indicated that pleasant or attractive rooms make people feel better than do stark or ugly rooms (Maslow & Mintz, 1956). Another factor which may affect people's moods at work is the provision of music (see the box below).

MUSIC TO WORK BY

Although the noise from office machines and conversations is usually found to be intrusive in the work environment, there is some belief that music may actually improve the work setting, though the evidence is mixed. Sundstrom and Sundstrom (1983) review the evidence on music in the workplace and report that although much of the research is the private, inaccessible property of firms that sell music systems to businesses, published research may or may not support the idea that music enhances the work environment. At one time it was actually thought that singing and/or listening to music with a steady, somewhat upbeat rhythm improved productivity. Later it was felt that pleasant music made employees cheerful and the environment enjoyable. Research indicates that in factories, music may or may not slightly improve productivity, but employees like it anyway. In offices, music may facilitate vigilance tasks (e.g., where an employee must monitor a screen), though it can be distracting for some. Employees often report that music helps provide a pleasant atmosphere, and the mere belief that it does so probably ensures that it will always be found in some work settings.

This positive effect on mood makes pleasantness an interesting issue for the design of workspace. It is reasonable to assume that if attractive work areas make people feel better, they will help to increase efficiency or accuracy in work. Research has shown that decorated spaces make people feel more comfortable than do undecorated spaces (Campbell, 1981) and that good moods associated with pleasant environments seem to increase people's willingness to help each other (Sherrod *et al.*, 1977). Yet we can also guess that for some kinds of work, the positive feelings associated with decorated spaces may also be disruptive. People feel more like talking to one another in pleasant settings (Russell & Mehrabian, 1978) and to the extent that socializing in the office detracts from effective or efficient working, pleasantness can be a problem. Research has also suggested that room decorations may be distracting (e.g., Baum & Davis, 1976), but whether this is a problem depends on how a setting is perceived (Worchel & Teddlie, 1976).

Territoriality and Status in the Work Environment

We discussed territoriality in Chapter 6 as it relates to many of our relationships with the environment. Some researchers also believe that territories are important in work environments. Often the concept relates to assignment of a specific area or machine to a worker, and is termed *assigned workspace* (Sundstrom & Sundstrom, 1983). It is often believed, for example, that if a large machine in a factory is assigned to one worker, that worker will take better care of it than if all workers roam from machine to machine. The same concept may also be important in offices (e.g., Davis & Altman, 1976), where the concept is often called the *fixed workspace*. Sundstrom and Sundstrom (1983) suggest that the right to treat a workspace as a territory might lead to more personal attachment to it, more perceived control over it, and thus more of a sense of responsibility for it and more signs of personalization of the workspace. Whether workers in fact prefer territories and whether territories improve

job satisfaction or productivity is up to question. Most likely, territories become more important to workers the higher the rank they have in the organization. At higher ranks, territories may become symbols of status (Sundstrom & Sundstrom, 1983).

Status symbols in the office or factory may be important in several ways. For example, they communicate status and power to others, they compensate employees as a nonmonetary benefit, and they serve as props or tools (such as larger desks, filing cabinets, computer terminals), which the worker is privileged to use on the job (Sundstrom & Sundstrom, 1983). In addition to furnishings, such as desks and size and comfort of chairs, typical status symbols include amount of floorspace, the capacity to regulate privacy and accessibility (e.g., through an enclosed office), and the right to personalize the workspace. One large firm, for example, provides carpeting, a bottled water dispenser, and plants as one moves up the corporate ladder into fancier and fancier offices. Apparently, the more one can attach status to the office space, the more satisfied one is with the job (Konar *et al.*, 1982).

Summary of Design in the Work Environment

Technological developments permit great flexibility in designing work environments. Central to workspace design are the issues of: (1) productivity, especially as it relates to work flow, safety, and health; and (2) job satisfaction. In general, work environments can be designed to maximize productivity through facilitating work flow and providing safe and healthy working conditions. Job satisfaction is related to quality of the work environment, though other factors are usually more important. Open offices may save on construction and maintenance costs, facilitate communication and work flow, increase flexibility of floorspace, and enhance supervision. On the other hand, open offices increase noise and other distractions and reduce privacy. Finally, the ability to treat a workspace as a territory and to personalize it serves as a form of status and may increase job satisfaction, though the issue is likely more relevant at higher ranks in the organization.

LEISURE AND RECREATION ENVIRONMENTS

Before beginning our discussion of recreation environments, perhaps we should define the term *recreation*. All of us have an intuitive idea of what it is, but more formally, we'll consider recreation to be "an experience which is derived from the user's voluntarily participating in recreational activities during nonobligated time" (Driver & Tocher, 1974). The recreation experience is the sum of the participant's mental, physical, spiritual, or other responses to a recreation engagement (Driver & Tocher, 1974).

The range of recreation environments is almost

Figure 11–2. Children need recreation environments close to home. Backyards are good examples. (Sherry Fisher)

endless. Some of us recreate in bars, some on golf courses, some in senior centers, and others in wilderness areas or parks. Many of us spend our leisure time in shopping malls walking around, people watching, window shopping, and stopping for an occasional slice of pizza, a chocolate chip cookie, or a drink. All of us value our leisure time and spend a great deal of it in recreation environments. Some have even moved to "planned recreational communities," which offer tennis courts, swimming pools, golf courses, and even boating and skiing in certain cases. If present trends continue, most of us will have more time for recreation in the future than we do today (US Department of Health, Education and Welfare, 1979), so developing an understanding of how we use recreation environments and how they affect us becomes important.

What sorts of recreational activities do we engage in? Murphy *et al.* (1973) suggest that there are eight types of recreational involvement: *socializing behaviors* (e.g., dancing, dating, meeting others); *associative behavior* (e.g., grouping together of people with common interests—such as a photography club); *competitive behaviors* (e.g., sports or games, competition in the performing arts); *risk-taking behaviors* (e.g., in which the stakes may be money, or even physical injury); *exploratory behavior* (e.g., travel, scuba diving); *vicarious experience* (e.g., reading, watching television or movies, watching sporting events); *sensory stimulation* (e.g., sexual activity, drug use, drinking, rock concerts); and *physical expression* (e.g., running, swimming, yoga).

Clearly, our needs for recreational involvement differ at different points in our lives, so that the types of recreation environments we require change over time as well. (We probably engage to some extent in each type of recreational involvement at each point in the life cycle, though for certain periods some needs become more "primary.") Children need recreation areas in or close to home in which they can play and socialize with other kids (Figure 11–2). Playgrounds (which we will discuss later) play a role in this regard, as do backyards and play areas in an apartment or home. For young adults it is essential to have a place to meet others, to form social groups, and to engage in courtship behaviors. Since more of us are waiting longer to marry and since more are divorced than was the case in earlier years, such recreation environments have become more and more important. But many of us do marry and have families—in fact, the statistical norm is still to be married and to raise a family. Families center most of their recreational activities around their community, and kids join little league, cub scouts, etc. Mothers and fathers join local clubs and fitness programs, and use neighborhood pools and tennis courts, along with children. In the "middle years" (for parents), children become relatively independent, and parents often need more recreational activities during this period, since they have more leisure time. Finally, during retirement, needs for specialized recreational facilities (e.g., senior centers, golden age clubs) become evident.

Given the various types of recreational involvement at different points in the life cycle, and the fact that personality (e.g., Driver & Knopf, 1977) and socioeconomic status also affect one's type of recreational involvement (Marans, 1972), a very wide variety of environmental settings must be designed and made available to allow satisfaction of our needs. In addition to aspects of individuals (e.g., age, personality) affecting their use of recreation environments, the availability of recreational facilities in an area determines to some extent how we recreate (Marans, 1972). The presence of community swimming, tennis, and boating facilities increases the frequency of these recreational activities (Marans, 1972), and more people will probably spend their time skiing if there are ski slopes nearby. For some activities (e.g., water for swimming), an environmental setting is a necessary and sufficient condition to afford a particular recreational goal. For other recreational activities, the environmental setting may vary (e.g., we can listen to music at home, in a car, in a concert hall, or at an outdoor amphitheater). In an overall sense, variation in recreational behavior may be viewed as an interaction between individual differences in people (e.g., their recreational wants and needs) and available recreation environments. Recreational behavior is also affected to some extent by the times (e.g., "hot tubs" in the 1980s)—it reflects to some extent the current perception of the "good life." Unfortunately, however, at present there is no encompassing theory or model of recreation behavior or a model which can accurately explain or predict the types of recreational facilities people want.

In this section, we will discuss several recreation environments, and some of the issues environmental psychologists have explored for each. Of the broad range of recreation environments, we have selected a few for more intensive consideration. The study of recreation environments by environmental psychologists is a recent event, and much work remains to be done.

Wilderness and Camping Areas

One recreational setting that has received a relatively large amount of research attention is wilderness and camping areas. A factor underlying this interest is the fact that many of our national parks and other similar facilities are overcrowded, and environmental planners need to know how to deal with the demand. Clearly, more and more of us are trying to "get away from it all"—to spend some of our time in the wilderness. Sometimes we go to user-oriented areas (outdoor recreation areas close to where we live, designed for short-term use), sometimes to intermediate use areas (within an hour's drive, designed for day-long use), and occasionally to resource-based areas (especially nice or significant areas far from home, reserved for vacation use). When we visit any of these, we are involved in a direct transaction with the physical environment which may strongly affect our behavior.

One major environmental psychological issue is how to add additional capacity to national parks and wilderness areas to accommodate more visitors without changing the characteristics of the natural setting that attracts people to it. Also, how do current and projected levels of crowding affect user satisfaction? Answering these questions and others requires an understanding of the motivations of users, their demographic characteristics, what they do in the recreation area, and the aspects of the setting which produce user satisfaction. This is extremely important since often the perceptions of resource planners (who make the important decisions) differ from those of users (Driver & Knopf, 1977).

Who uses national parks and wilderness areas? Interestingly, some evidence suggests that while all types of people use them, users tend to be disproportionately higher income individuals, people with professional and technical occupations, those who live in urban areas, and people who have done college and postgraduate work (US Department of the Interior, 1979). Although some research fails to report such differences between users and nonusers (Lindsay & Ogle, 1972), the above findings are fairly consistent.

Why do people spend time in the "wilderness"? One answer may be derived from the environment–behavior models reviewed in Chapter 3. We may visit national parks to escape the *overload, overarousal,* or *stress* associated with daily life. This may partially explain why urbanites visit them more than ruralites. The *behavior constraint* approach would suggest that visits to the wilderness allow us to engage in many behaviors we are constrained from in everyday life although, due to their primitive nature, wilderness settings probably also constrain our behavior in some ways. Overall, one way of viewing the wilderness experience is as a way of coping with stressful aspects of everyday life (e.g., Driver, 1972). In fact, all recreation behavior may be viewed as behavior engaged in to solve problems (or to reach preferred states), that can be enacted better in recreational than in everyday settings (Driver, 1975). Unfortunately, however, overcrowding, littering, and other problems currently associated with the wilderness experience are probably making it less of an optimal experience than it once was.

Other motivations for spending time in the wilderness may include the need to: develop, main-

tain, or project a particular type of self-image; retain or develop a new social identity; affiliate with certain other people; enhance our self-esteem; develop or display certain skills; exercise power; engage in self-fulfillment; or achieve mastery (Driver, 1972). In addition, one could add the aesthetic delight associated with many wilderness areas (e.g., breath-taking views) and the emotional experience such visits can generate. Having considered why we *do* spend time in wilderness settings, you might like to consider reasons why some of us *do not* frequent outdoor parks and recreation areas. These are summarized in Figure 11–3.

What characteristics do we prefer in wilderness areas, and what do we find distasteful? The answers to these questions have important implications for resource planners. Haas (1975) reported that *solitude* is an extremely important element of a positive wilderness experience. This probably refers to solitude from unknown others, since very few of those studied were traveling alone. Overall, people in wilderness areas prefer to interact and to develop relationships with those in their own party, but not to meet others along the trail. Even worse than trail encounters for destroying the experience of solitude is having others infringe on one's campground. Interestingly, the nature of the infringement (e.g., by a motorized vehicle vs. a person on foot) affects the perception of lost solitude. The more mechanized the source of privacy violation, the more disturbing (Lucas, 1964), and violations by large groups of people are more aversive than violations by small groups. Finally, evidence of previous use of an area (e.g., due to littering or environmental deterioration) probably also detracts from the experience of solitude.

In addition to solitude, people definitely prefer wilderness areas that are especially aesthetically pleasing. In fact, one study suggests that positive aesthetic experiences comprise a very important predictor of enjoyment of wilderness visits. What determines the quality of our aesthetic experience? People do seem to prefer varied over repetitious scenery (Shafer & Mietz, 1972). However,

Deterrents to the Use of Parks and Recreation Areas

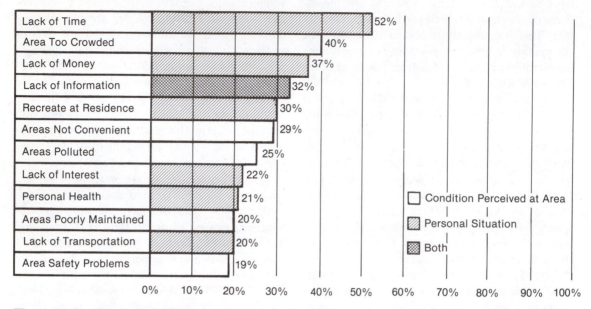

Percentage of General Population Survey Respondents Citing Reasons for
Not Visiting Parks and Recreation Areas

Figure 11–3. Reasons given by people for not using parks and recreation areas. (From the *Third Nationwide Outdoor Recreation Plan, Appendix I.* Washington, D.C.: US Department of the Interior, Heritage Conservation and Recreation Service, 1979.)

a part of the variation should not be human made: Human elements may detract from aesthetic pleasure in wilderness environments. Also, as we noted when discussing solitude, signs of use by others—such as littering or environmental deterioration—detract from the aesthetic quality of the wilderness environment. Unfortunately, relatively little is known about what aspects of a natural environment are related to aesthetic preference. (For a review of what we do know and the methods used to gain such knowledge, refer to Chapter 2.)

It should be noted that there are strong *individual differences* in people's preferences in natural settings (e.g., how much solitude they desire, and which aesthetic features they prefer) (Lucas, 1964). For example, while wilderness campers prefer solitude, others who could be called "general campers" (e.g., families who go camping) actually desire to meet and interact with people

outside their immediate group. Part of what makes camping attractive to them is the expectation of meeting new people (Haas, 1975). Also, more educated people, urbanites, males, and older people insist on an extremely pristine environment for their wilderness experience more than those with less educaton, ruralites, females, and younger people (Cicchetti, 1972). One's expectations for a setting also importantly affect his or her reactions to it. If we do not expect to meet other people and we do, this will be more disturbing than if we do expect to meet others and encounter them. Moreover, campers who expect good facilities and a particular level of comfort will be more disturbed if these conveniences are not present than will those with lower expectations. In the same vein, whether or not we meet our objective in visiting a recreation area can affect our reactions to it (Driver & Knopf, 1976).

Different recreational facilities carry with them different objectives. If we go fishing and don't catch fish, we'll be more dissatisfied than if we just came for the view.

What are the effects one actually experiences from spending time in wilderness settings? Many positive outcomes have been suggested (e.g., improved physical and mental health, realization of human potential, social benefits), but few have been documented through actual research. It is probably true that the outcomes one experiences from recreating in wilderness environments (and in other outdoor settings as well) depend jointly on physical elements (e.g., the scenery), facilities or equipment (e.g., having a good or a bad tent), characteristics of the user (e.g., the state of one's health), and on managerial decisions (e.g., whether or not what we want to do is "allowed") (Driver, 1975). What sorts of outcomes has research shown to be associated with spending time in wilderness settings? A number of studies suggest the potential for positive changes in self-con-

cept or personality following a wilderness experience (e.g., Risk, 1976; Stogner, 1978). For a group of psychiatric day-care patients, a five-day back-packing trip in the Sierras led to improvement in many areas (e.g., less obsessive thought patterns, fewer dependency needs, lower feelings of helplessness) (Slotsky, 1973). Finally, participating in outdoor recreation activities may lead to greater family cohesiveness (West & Merriam, 1970).

Before concluding, we should note that people enjoy the outdoors in ways other than going hiking or camping (see the box, p. 328). For many urban residents, human-made parks contain many of the elements of more isolated wilderness settings (e.g., lakes, trees, grass), and afford swimming, skiing, golfing, tennis, and other activities (Figure 11–4). For others of us taking a drive in the country provides an extremely inviting recreational activity. Clearly, a car ride in the right setting can constitute a significant interaction with the environment. In fact, many highways are

Figure 11–4. Human-made parks and playgrounds can be very important in areas where wilderness is not available. (Sherry Fisher)

PEOPLE-PLANT INTERACTION: THE GARDEN AS A RECREATIONAL ENVIRONMENT

One outdoor environment used by many for recreational purposes is as nearby as the closest plot of land or windowbox. Gardening is a common form of recreation, and one which may have important environmental and psychological benefits. Lewis (1973) has researched the effects of providing recreational gardening environments for residents of run-down urban areas in New York City. The New York City Housing Authority sponsored recreational gardening opportunities, in which any group of tenants wanting to garden could apply to the Authority, which gave them a garden site close to their project, turned over the ground for them, and also provided $25.00 for seeds and plants, along with a gardening manual.

Providing a garden setting for residents had many beneficial effects. It added social cohesion in the community by providing a meeting place, and a chance for people to work together toward a common end. Gardens were even used for other purposes (e.g., for taking wedding and graduation pictures). When describing the effects of the New York City program, one woman said:

. . . everyone gets to know each other, everyone smiles and discusses our garden. They worry about too much rain, they're all so pleased that the children are interested in caring, not destroying. From early morning till late at night you can see neighbors leaning over their garden fence. It has become the center spot of our court where everyone is a friend.

In addition to its effect on community social life, Lewis (1973) reports that recreational gardening by inner-city residents led to deeper pride of accomplishment, to increased self-esteem, and to reduced vandalism outside as well as inside the buildings. It is as if the pride residents feel for the gardens generalizes to other aspects of the environment. Gardening may also increase the proprietary sense of territoriality, and thus make nearby space more apt to be defended and defensible (see Chapter 8). Working in the garden and competing in a contest for the best garden also provided a constructive activity for many gang members, who became heavily immersed in the project. The positive effects of recreational gardening on nearby vandalism have been documented elsewhere as well (Beatty, 1974).

Why is recreational gardening beneficial? There are many possible reasons. In addition to their natural beauty and potential as a food source, Lewis (1973) suggests that "plants are nonthreatening in a world that is constantly judgmental. Plants respond to the care, not the race, color, intellect, or physical capacity of the gardener. Individuals with all their real and imagined handicaps can find in plants a first step to confidence, a friend who doesn't talk back." Gardening allows people to display mastery over the environment, to gain a sense of control, and provides a rest from other worries and cares. Urban gardening may also be a surrogate for the need to escape into nature for those without the means to do so. Of course it also beautifies the urban setting.

designed with the aesthetic tastes of drivers in mind (Figure 11–5).

Recreation Environments Affording Exercise

In addition to going camping or spending time on a trail, we can take advantage of many other in-door and outdoor recreation environments which afford exercise. A 1978 Gallup poll reported that 47 percent of all Americans engaged in some type of exercise—twice as many as in 1961 (*US News and World Report,* 1978). There are at least 10 million Americans who jog regularly (*Runner's World,* 1977), 15 million who swim regularly, 29

Figure 11–5. Driving and looking at the scenery is one popular form of outdoor recreation.

million who play tennis regularly, 46 million who walk to stay fit, 19 million who bicycle, 22 million who bowl, and 22 million who play golf (US Department of Health, Education and Welfare, 1977). Many other sports are also thriving. For example, the number of racquetball players increased seven-fold within only three years, from 1974 to 1977 (US Racquetball Association, 1978). The recent popularity of clubs offering universal gym and Nautilus equipment is another case in point.

These data have several implications for environmental psychologists. Clearly, people are spending much more time than ever before in indoor and outdoor recreational environments that offer the potential for exercise (Figure 11–6). Planners have responded with some unique settings, such as physical fitness "trails" with "stations" that afford different types of exercise, and use of public or private sector multipurpose facilities for midday exercise programs. Often, however, environments for physical exercise are overcrowded and even unavailable, and in many cases the settings that must be used are not optimally designed. There have been too many accidents at-

Figure 11–6. Recreation involving exercise can be good for the mind and the body. (Kevin Blanc)

tributed to poor design of athletic facilities. To date, relatively little research has been done on human–environment interaction in athletic settings, and on design alternatives which could have beneficial effects.

The fact that accidents occur from poor human-environment fit in settings where we exercise should not detract from the very positive overall health-related effects of spending time in such environments. Data clearly support the relationship between physical fitness and health. For example, regular physical exercise offers a degree of protection against heart disease, high blood pressure, high levels of cholesterol, and obesity (Kraus, 1978). Which types of regular exercise contribute the most to overall fitness? Of the 14 sports rated, jogging, bicycling, swimming, and skating contributed most to overall fitness; golf, softball, and bowling the least (Conrad, 1976). However, even moderate forms of exercise like dancing and walking have positive impact. *How* does spending time in environments where one can exercise impact on physical health? Obviously, exercise can have direct physiological benefits which affect health (e.g., making our heart work more efficiently). However, exercise also functions to control psychological stress, which has negative consequences for health (Kraus, 1978). In this way as well, exercise can be beneficial.

Physical fitness has similarly been related to good mental health and overall performance. In fact, studies suggest that physical fitness is associated with mental exactness, high motivation, persistence, social acceptance, self-confidence, and learning achievement (Vitalo, 1978). In one study, the physical education department of Phillips Academy introduced an experimental morning physical activity program. Students in the morning gym class even performed significantly better *academically* than those in a control group (Levin, 1965).

While most of the data on the effects of spending time in recreational environments concerns the benefits of environments affording physical exercise, the few studies that have been done suggest that other recreation environments can also be beneficial. A study by Heywood (1978) reported that placing subjects in a recreational setting (e.g., allowing them to listen to music) after a stressful work experience resulted in physiological changes indicative of lessened stress. Menninger (1948) has stated that "mentally healthy people participate in some form of volitional activity to supplement their required daily work . . . There is considerable evidence that the healthy personality is one who not only plays, but takes his play seriously. Furthermore, there is also evidence that the inability or unwillingness to play reveals an insecure or disordered aspect of personality." Further, studies show that recreational participation is linked to maintaining emotional stability among college students (Richardson, 1962).

Recreation also affects an individual's life satisfaction and work adjustment (see Tinsley, Barrett, & Kass, 1977). Among the young, recreational participation leads to the development of cognitive skills, to creative learning, and to better self-expression (Kraus, 1978). When recreational activities (e.g., camping, visits to museums) involve the entire family, they can serve the goals of stimulating family togetherness and creating greater cohesion. It has even been found that adding recreational settings to hospital environments helps to lessen the isolation of patients, to minimize introspection and anxiety, and to provide the patient with familiar social roles which promote constructive interaction with others (Kraus, 1978). Recreational participation may actually shorten the stay of hospital patients and reduce the need for medication (Wolfe, 1975).

Recreational Environments for Children

Having focused on recreational environments for the "older set," we now turn our attention to settings used by children. Children spend their recreational hours in all types of environmental contexts, including playgrounds, recreation rooms, museums, vacant lots, alleyways, street corners, and driveways. Very little research has been done on these diverse recreational environments, or their effects on children. Nevertheless, play activity has great significance for children, and serves as an important vehicle for learning about the world. The various types of recreational environments available or unavailable to a child (e.g., because they do not exist, or are considered dangerous or unsafe) could have a significant impact on the child's development (box below). Also, the way in which available play spaces are designed can impact greatly on what children realize from their interaction with them.

How are children's play spaces designed? A number of researchers believe that environmental designers do not take the preferences or concerns of children or parents enough into consideration (e.g., Bishop & Peterson, 1971; Moore, 1973). Designers tend to treat children as objects, and to assume that play only occurs in playgrounds (Moore, 1973). Also, the reasoning that goes into play space design often involves untested assumptions about children (Hayward *et al.*, 1976). Con-sequently, we should ask how well the resultant play spaces actually meet the needs of the user population. Due to design-related problems and an overall inadequate number of good play spaces in many areas, children may spend too many of their recreational hours in inappropriate (and sometimes dangerous) environments.

Of the research which has been done on children's play environments, most has focused on playgrounds. Again, this may reflect the mistaken assumption that children play *only* in playgrounds. Hayward *et al.* (1976) have compared children's activities and outcomes in three types of playground environments: *adventure, contemporary,* and *traditional* playgrounds. What is an "adventure" playground? (To get a preliminary idea, it might help to know they are also referred to as "junk" playgrounds.) Adventure playgrounds began in Europe, and are often located in

---

THE TWO SIDES OF RECREATION

While it is clear that spending time in settings that afford recreation has mostly favorable effects, this isn't always the case. Some types of recreation can have negative effects, as can spending time in recreational environments (e.g., video arcades) when one is supposed to be in school.

What are some of the negative effects of certain types of recreation? Research has demonstrated that live or televised viewing of violent physical aggression in hockey, wrestling, football, basketball, soccer, roller derby, etc. can stimulate aggressive antisocial acts in the viewer (e.g., Alderman, 1974; Harrison, 1974; Taylor, 1971). Other types of television content (e.g., westerns, detective shows) can also lead to aggression, especially when programs contain aggressive content. It has been estimated that before reaching adulthood, the average child vicariously participates in 18,000 murders through television (*Newsweek,* February 21, 1977). Direct participation in certain recreational activities can also involve human costs. Orlick (1975a, 1975b, 1975c) has found that many children drop out of competitive sports because of the physical and emotional strains inherent in coaches' and parents' "win at all costs" attitude. Ogilvie and Tutko (1971) suggest that sometimes such "zero sum" recreational activities can be harmful to long-term personality development and mental health. Perhaps society should promote recreational activities involving art, music, skiing, swimming, pleasure skating, etc., which do not necessarily involve competition and its related costs.

Finally, another set of negative outcomes from recreation involves the environment. We must explore the biological, ecological, and environmental consequences of recreational activities. For example, noise from snowmobiles can cause hearing loss. In the name of recreation we have sometimes wasted precious natural resources, contaminated the air we breathe, and deformed our natural environment. We must start to evaluate the environmental impact of our leisure-time activities.

vacant lots or other available spaces. Instead of traditional play equipment, other materials (e.g., wood, hammers, and nails) are supplied. Children are encouraged to institute changes—building structures, taking them down, and building new ones—as time goes on and interests evolve. Some believe the adventure playground can expand the range of play opportunities available to children (Cooper, 1970; Nicholson, 1970), while others (often members of the community) complain about their unplanned nature and unattractive appearance. Adventure playgrounds differ a great deal from traditional and contemporary playgrounds, which are more similar to each other. Traditional playgrounds contain the standard apparatus (e.g., swings, monkey bars, etc.), while contemporary playgrounds include essentially the same elements, but with a contemporary flair (e.g., the slide may extend from a wooden structure built to look like a ship, rather than a traditional ladder-type arrangement). Also, in contemporary as opposed to traditional playgrounds, a given apparatus often serves multiple rather than single play functions.

When studying the three types of playgrounds, Hayward *et al.* (1976) found that each attracted a somewhat different clientele. This finding is probably due to the characteristics of each of these recreation environments. Practically no preschool children attended the adventure playground, while about one-third of the users in the other two settings fell into this age group. In contrast, about twice as many school-age children were found in the adventure playground as in the other two playgrounds (Hayward *et al.*, 1976). Finally, fewer adults were present in the adventure playground than in the contemporary or traditional playgrounds. This latter finding is in all likelihood due to fewer young children being present, but it nevertheless has implications for the level of supervision in the three settings. The presence of adults may be one reason why fewer school-age children attended the traditional or contemporary playgrounds than the adventure playgrounds, since school-age children desire a degree of independence.

The activities engaged in at the three play-

grounds differed as well, and the data clearly imply that environmental features had a strong effect on behavior. In the traditional playground, swinging was the most common activity; but at the contemporary playground, children engaged in a continuous mode of activity which included playing on varied equipment. This result is probably due in part to the equipment at the contemporary playground being less discrete than that at the traditional playground (e.g., there was much more "multipurpose" equipment). At the adventure playground the most popular activity was playing in the "clubhouse," an option which did not exist in the other two settings. The essence of the differences in activity at the three playgrounds is probably most apparent from the transcripts of the experimenters (see Figure 11–7).

The degree of novelty of an apparatus also seemed to affect its use: There were traditional slides at the traditional playground, but at the contemporary playground a slide was built on a cobblestone "mountain" with tunnels running through it. Whereas the novel slide was extremely popular, the traditional one was used relatively infrequently. Overall, for the three playgrounds, it may be seen that the opportunities and constraints provided by the environment predict the predominant activities engaged in by children. Such opportunities and constraints also affect *how* the children play (e.g., alone or in groups) and the focus of their interaction (e.g., on the "here and now" vs. fantasy). For example, fantasy play was least common in the traditional playground.

Summary of Leisure and Recreation Environments

There are a variety of different types of recreation and leisure. One classification scheme lists socializing behaviors, associative behaviors, competitive behaviors, risk-taking behaviors, exploratory behaviors, vicarious experience, sensory stimulation, and physical expression as types of recreation or leisure experience. Our interest in specific modes of recreation varies with age, personality, socioeconomic status, and availability of facilities. Wilderness hiking or camping may be viewed as ways of coping with stressful aspects

Excerpt from traditional playground

The older girl (Adrienne, age 10) is pumping, she's swinging, she's very capable. Both girls are now yelling "I'm going higher." Adrienne just said "I want to do something fun," and she stopped swinging. She's speaking to the grandmother. Now she's off the swing and she's turning it completely around. And Adrienne is saying "This is going to be so much fun, and I'm going to go so high." Now she put the swing on her stomach, and she's just going 'round. And the swing was too low. She's trying to lift her feet but she keeps knocking them on the ground. Adrienne's swinging. She's going back and forth. She said she wants to stay here a while. She's still going back and forth. She's still just swinging back and forth. Everytime she pumps she says "Oooh, oooh," as if it's a lot of effort.

List of activities:	swinging	15 min.[a]
	monkey bars	6 min.
	sitting	3 min.
	monkey bars	5 min.
Entered with:	grandmother and 8-year-old sister	

Excerpt from contemporary playground

The boy I'm watching is about nine. He came in with a day camp. The day camp had around 20 people in it. He's on the slide. The boy next to him said "Let's slide down together" and they did. They waited until they were both on the thing and they both slid down. Now he's climbing on the monkey bars. He jumped off. He just yelled, "This is fun," and is going back up the pyramid (slide is attached). The other boy went down and he was laughing. He doesn't just sit down. He carefully spreads his hands out. It's like a long process. Now the girl came down and she said, "Let's hold hands." And so the girl and boy are holding hands and a younger boy sat next to them and so the three of them are holding hands and they all slid down and they were all screaming "Aaah."

List of activities:	multiple equipment	9 min.[a]
	pretend play	9 min.
	sprinkler	2 min.
	buying ices	3 min.
	multiple equipment	20 min.
Entered with:	day camp	

Excerpt from adventure playground

(Jane, 10, was actively involved in assembling tires and boards, began building a structure.) It is now 5 minutes til 4, and Jane still hasn't completed her house. She's still looking for some more wood. Now the rain is coming down much heavier than it did before. Jane went back and picked up another tire; she's placing it to make another row for the wall. She's going back to area 8 for another one. Now she picked up a board. The rain is coming down pretty heavily now, but Jane is still continuously building her wall. Now she got a little help from the play leader Matt. Now Matt just left. The rain is coming down much heavier now. The little girl seems not to care about the rain. She's running back to get another piece of wood to make a roof on her house. The time is now 2 minutes til 4 and she is leaving the playground.

List of activities:	building	30 min.[a]
Entered with:	self	

[a]Activity from which excerpt was taken.

Figure 11–7. Excerpts of Typical Transcripts From the Behavior Settings' Records (From Hayward, D. G., Rothenberg, M., & Beasley, R. R. Children's play and urban playground environments. A comparison of traditional, contemporary, and adventure playground types. In H. M. Proshansky, W. H. Ittelson, & L. Rivlin, *Environmental psychology,* 2d ed. New York: Holt, Rinehart and Winston, 1976.)

of everyday life, though crowding, littering, and other problems associated with camping may work against the coping function, and desire for personal growth may be equally important in our wilderness experiences. Solitude and aesthetics are two major expectations of wilderness campers, and if the experience meets these expectations, the outing can have positive psychological and health benefits for us. Exercise in a recreational context can also have significant positive impact on health, psychological outlook, and social relationships, though poor design of exercise facilities can lead to accidents. Play activities also have significant consequences for children and the design of a playground affects the behavior in it. In one study, for example, play behavior in a contemporary playground was more continuous than play in a traditional one. In an adventure playground, however, children were much more creative. Clearly, recreation and leisure opportunities are important for people of all ages, and design considerations are paramount in determining what opportunities are available in given recreation and leisure environments.

FUTURE ENVIRONMENTS

Today's future is tomorrow's reality. Throughout history, what once seemed almost surrealistic and extraordinary became somewhat more mundane when it finally came to pass. So it is for environments. Movies of the 1920s and 1930s depicted life as the moviemakers thought it would be many years in the future, often to the amusement of today's audiences. However, some visions do come to pass. Garden cities, discussed at the turn of the century (Howard, 1898), were seen as self-sufficient towns of 30,000 people designed to minimize pollution and congestion while maximizing feelings of openness and opportunities for play. To varying degrees, these garden cities are present today in the "new towns" and planned communities in the United States, Britain, Israel, Scandinavia, and parts of Africa and Asia (Porteus, 1977).

One of the most well-known "future" planners is Soleri (1969) whose enormous project, Arcosanti, is presently being built in the American Southwest. Soleri has planned a future utopia—a large, enclosed city where all residents will be housed in similar, high-rise buildings called arcologies. Each of these buildings will house a million inhabitants. Others have proposed plans that may also seem unbelievable to us. For example, Fuller (1967) has described large communities of up to a million people floating on the oceans. As strange as such designs may seem, we should study them carefully and attempt to make them withstand behavioral as well as economic scrutiny.

One aspect of future environments is our seemingly unlimited ability to design for and adapt to unfamiliar conditions that threaten our survival. With adequate protection from the elements, humans can adapt to a number of harsh settings including South Pole habitats, spacelabs, submarines, underwater environments, and even the moon's surface. What is amazing is that people not only survive in these habitats, but actually adapt so well that the unique environment takes on the familiarity of an everyday one. Future living quarters in space or under the sea will have to be designed with our adaptive capabilities in mind. We conclude our discussion of environmental design by examining some future environments. Specifically, we will review some research on how people may live in space and how aquanauts have coped with living underwater in very limiting quarters. Finally, we will see how experts envision the design of entire space colonies and undersea communities.

Living in Space

The human foray into space has been a successful and growing venture. We have put men in orbit and on the moon, have launched deep space probes that have photographed distant worlds, and have launched and manned orbiting space stations. We have not yet reached the level of space habitation in *Star Wars* or *Star Trek,* but the space shuttle is a recent, dramatic step in that direction. Ultimately, we expect, large colonies will live in extraterrestrial settings, space stations, huge orbiting habitats, or other planets or moons.

This scenario is not as far-fetched as it may seem. For instance, the National Aeronautics and Space Administration (NASA) published a report entitled "Space Settlements: A Design Study" that considers fundamental design needs for a system of colonizing space. The study indicates that "permanent communities can be built off the Earth . . . space colonization appears to be technically feasible (and) the obstacles to further expansion of human frontiers in this way are principally philosophical, political, and social rather than technological'' (p. 1).

The colony habitat considered in the study is one that could house and employ 10,000 people (see Figure 11–8). The structure is round with spokes extending from a central area, and it is expected to orbit the earth like a second moon. Housing for residents is to be in the outer ring, actually a large, hollow tube. The central area is to be an area for spacecraft docking, loading, and

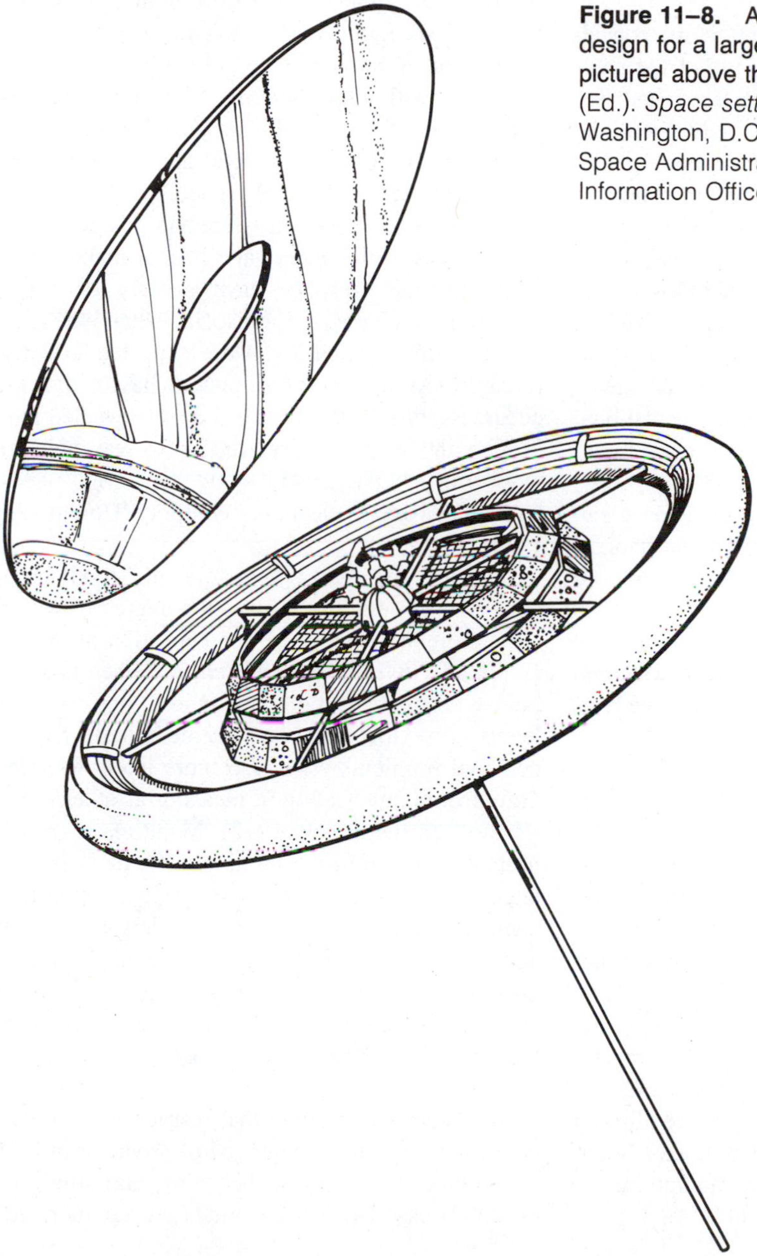

Figure 11–8. A drawing of the exterior of a design for a large space colony. A large mirror is pictured above the colony. (From Johnson, R. D. (Ed.). *Space settlements: A design study.* Washington, D.C.: National Aeronautics and Space Administration, Scientific and Technical Information Office, 1977.)

unloading. The spokes provide access to living and agricultural areas in the ring.

Illumination is to be by natural sunshine, deflected by a large mirror onto smaller ones that would reflect it into the colony. Agricultural enterprise in the ring is expected to produce enough food to support the inhabitants on only 153 acres of growing area.

Of particular interest in the study is the consideration of human needs in the design of the habitat. The effects of weightlessness, size, and isolation are taken into account. Diversity and variability of the appearance of the habitat are designed to avoid monotony and boredom. Many of the finishing details of the outer ring are to be left to the colonists so that they can personalize the habitat, and vegetation is to be included to approximate earth settlements. Several different kinds of space are to be part of the habitat, ranging from residential zones to commercial areas, public and semiprivate spaces, open recreational areas, service industry zones, and agricultural areas (see Figure 11–9).

Clearly, we are not ready to launch a space colony tomorrow. It is not even certain that habitats like the one we have described will exist in your lifetime. The likelihood that people will live in outer space, however, appears to be high. We have much to learn about designing extraterrestrial environments, but there is much that we have already learned.

Experimental Undersea Environments

In order to learn more about the depths of the oceans, the United States government has sponsored deep-sea laboratories, Sealab II and Tektite 2, in which aquanauts have lived for extended periods of time. These underwater habitats make it possible to explore for long periods of time because they allow divers to remain underwater once they have adapted to deep levels: Rapid surfacing is dangerous because time must be allowed for decompression. This constraint makes aquanauts as dependent on underwater laboratories as astronauts are on their space capsules.

Tektite 2 consists of four rooms organized around two circular towers connected by a tunnel (Figure 11–10). Living quarters for five aquanauts are contained in one tower, while research space is built into the other tower. Despite the fact that space is so limited that expedition members cannot stretch out in bed if others are present in the living area, aquanauts have lived in this setting for a full six months (Helmreich, 1974).

Data have been collected by observing crew members with closed-circuit television, and recording use of space in logs. Special attention has been paid to movement around and occupation of laboratory areas, leisure space, and working space. Because the small space and design of living quarters of the underwater habitat make it difficult for the crew to have privacy or avoid crowding, incidents of antisocial behavior, such as quarreling or fighting, were expected in early research. As it turned out, such behavior did not occur. Results of the Tektite 2 study revealed that despite the high density, the crew was able to work out social, spatial, and territorial needs without a great deal of conflict (Helmreich, 1974).

One of the best predictors of good crew performance and morale was the degree to which crew members engaged in conversation at meals. In a study involving a different undersea habitat, Sealab II's crew members whose performance levels were low and who seemed to be having personal problems were also more likely to withdraw from conversation at meals or at other times (Radloff & Helmreich, 1972). Mealtime is an important break from the monotony frequent in isolated environments, and the social interaction that centers around meals can provide leisure activity and tension release. It may also provide an informal opportunity to resolve problems by talking about them, and may add to an unusual situation the structure that is reminiscent of normal life at home.

In Chapter 7 we noted that restriction of movement, loss of control, and lack of privacy can lead to withdrawal, antisocial behavior, and stress-induced illness. Undersea habitats are far more re-

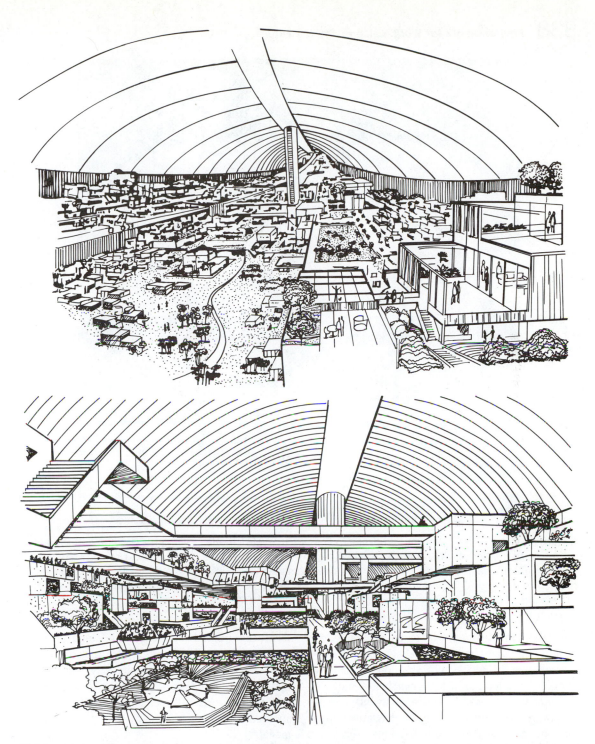

Figure 11–9. The interior of the space habitat would look much like earth communities with vegetation, walkways, and buildings. (From Johnson, R.D. (Ed.). *Space settlements: A design study.* Washington, D.C.: National Aeronautics and Space Administration, Scientific and Technical Information Office, 1977.)

Figure 11–10. Artist's drawing of *Tektite 2.* The upper level in the left cylinder is a command (bridge) area with the major off-duty room located below. The major work area is in the lower room of the left cylinder. (From Helmreich, R. Evaluations of Environments: Behavioral observations in an undersea habitat. In J. Lang, C. Burnette, W. Moleski, & D. Vachon (Eds.), *Designing for human behavior.* Stroudsburg, Pa.: Dowden, Hutchinson, & Ross, Copyright 1974, Reprinted by permission of the publisher.)

strictive than prisons or other environments discussed in the previous chapter. Why do maladaptive behaviors not develop in undersea habitats? We have noted the benefits of social involvement at meals. In addition, undersea crews are aware that they are going to be confined to the lab for a limited amount of time. They are screened and trained to prepare them for duty, and their confinement is voluntary. Helmreich (1974) makes note of the special rewards of

sealab environments. Despite the high costs of danger and isolation, they provide rewards of personal accomplishment, special pay, and social recognition. Undersea laboratory experiments suggest that carefully selected, well-trained persons can tolerate and adapt to unique environments.

A Permanent Undersea Habitat. Human beings have long speculated about living under the sea. Since the ocean occupies 70 percent of the earth's surface, efforts to build habitable underwater environments could have important long-range implications for the world's population. Kilmer (1972), a designer who believes that we should develop the ocean as a place to live, suggests that people will live in underwater "sub-burbs" with land surfaces reserved for work and recreational activities. Our experience with sealab and other experimental underwater environments makes this notion at least plausible, but building permanent underwater cities is quite another task.

Kilmer's ideas are based on a strong structure of interconnected spheres (see Figure 11–11). Underwater environments have to withstand extreme physical conditions. One solution to this problem is Kilmer's addition of adjustable ballast tanks to

Figure 11–11. Kilmer's design for a permanent underwater habitat links a series of spherical chambers together. (From Kilmer, W., *Undersea habitat,* 1972. Used by permission.)

compensate for changing buoyancy conditions. The ballast stored in the bottom of each sphere could also be desalinated and used for domestic purposes.

Kilmer's plan also makes the environment rewarding for the men and women who would live there. In Figure 11–12 we can see that there are private quarters for members and even a lounge area. Kilmer believes that these extensive living spaces are important for morale. Clearly, if large-scale underwater living areas are ever built, it will be necessary to anticipate the kinds of environmental satisfactions that should be included in such a habitat.

CHAPTER SUMMARY

Work environments have developed flexibility because of technological innovations allowing removal of equipment from rigid power sources and construction of expansive and high-rise spaces. The principle of work flow states that work stations should be arranged in the order that provides immediate flow of work from one point in the work cycle to the next necessary point. Attention to the principle of work flow enhances productivity; attention to design factors that promote safe and healthy working conditions also facilitates productivity. The quality of the work environment also affects job satisfaction, though job security, working relationships, and other factors are usually found to have more impact on job satisfaction than does quality of the environment.

A major innovation in office design is the open office plan, or office landscape. The advantages of the open office include reduced maintenance costs, easier communication, better workflow, and easier supervision. Disadvantages of open offices, which may in some circumstances outweigh advantages, include increased noise and other distractions, as well as reduced privacy. Portable partitions may help overcome some of these disadvantages, however.

The ability to treat one's workspace as a territory, as well as the right to personalize it, may serve as a form of status in the organization. Especially at high ranks in a firm, such territorial treatment and personalization may correlate with job satisfaction.

Recreation and leisure opportunities are important for people of all ages, and design alternatives help determine which opportunities exist in a given recreation or leisure environment. The type of recreation and leisure opportunity we most prefer varies with age, personality, and socioeconomic status. Wilderness and camping experiences permit opportunities for personal growth and can help with everyday stresses. However, crowded camping areas and other problems can defeat the stress-reducing aspects of camping. Among the most important expectations of wilderness campers are solitude and aesthetic appreciation. Benefits of solitude, aesthetic experiences, and other encounters during camping can improve our psychological outlook and benefit our health. Similarly, recreational exercise benefits our health and psychological outlook and can improve family and other social relationships. Poorly designed exercise facilities, however, often result in accidents that are clearly not beneficial to our health. For children, opportunities for play have a significant socializing impact. Adventure playgrounds, for example, result in more creative interactions among children.

Studies of undersea habitats provide us with useful information on human adaptation to unusual environmental designs. Indeed, humans in cramped quarters can learn to accommodate one another's personal space needs, and can learn to work effectively in crowded settings. Perhaps adaptation to these unusual designs is facilitated by careful selection and training, by prior knowledge of the confinement, and by high rewards for volunteering to undergo such experiences.

Suggested Projects

1. Take a tour of one or more local factories or large offices and look for ways in which the principle of workflow is incorporated into the factory design. How would you

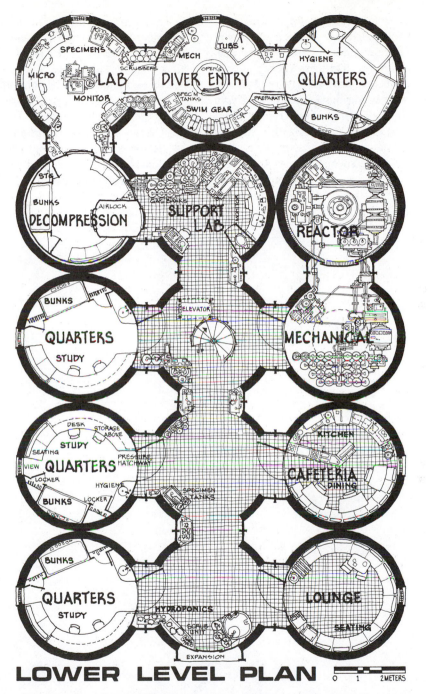

LOWER LEVEL PLAN 0 1 2 METERS

Figure 11–12. The system of linked chambers would permit much more room than is currently found in underwater habitats. Lounge and cafeteria rooms are important factors in increasing crew satisfaction. (From Kilmer, W. *Undersea habitat, 1972.* Used by permission.)

redesign the factory to facilitate workflow? On your tour, also note the location of windows, the ventilation system, and the adequacy of lighting. Do these seem appropriate for the tasks performed?

2. Take a tour of various offices around your campus, and note the various types of personalization. Does personalization seem to vary with status, sex of occupant, type of job, or academic specialization? Are offices where the public is often present personalized differently from offices to which the public rarely has access?

3. Explore several types of recreation environments and note the concentration of ages in them, as well as the types of benefits people seem to be getting from them. Are there systematic differences? What design changes would be necessary to provide other recreation opportunities?

4. Design your own future environment, such as one on the lunar surface. What design considerations are important? How do work areas, recreation areas, and residential areas differ?

12 Changing Behavior to Save the Environment

INTRODUCTION

Imagine that you are a shepherd and that you share a pasture known as "the commons" with the other shepherds of your village. Further assume that the commons cannot be enlarged—it constitutes all the land you and the others have on which to graze your animals. Although you share the pasture land, the economic benefits you gain from your herd are yours, and from time to time you are confronted with the decision of whether to purchase another sheep for your flock. The commons is becoming depleted, but you feel that you'd enjoy the economic advantage of owning another animal. You reason that the cost (to you) of one additional sheep grazing on the commons is quite low, and you conclude that you are acting rationally by deciding to make the purchase. However, force yourself to consider what would happen if all the shepherds added one extra animal. The eventual result would be complete depletion of the commons, and all would suffer. After you have ruminated on this for a while, you become disturbed and uncertain about what to do.

This story is taken from Hardin's "The Tragedy of the Commons" (1968). As you have probably realized, it offers an excellent analogy with many aspects of contemporary life. Many resources are being consumed at too high a rate, which is endangering the future availability of the resource. At a personal level we often find ourselves faced with resource-related decisions that are modern-day equivalents of whether or not to add another sheep to our herd. In a sense, our needs are pitted against those of the larger community. We are faced with a choice between satisfying our immediate needs with the prospect of negative future consequences to society, and restricting our present consumption for the future good of the community. The way we resolve such dilemmas obviously has important implications. Hardin argues that if we want the commons to survive, each of us must give up some of our freedom. While the individual shepherd will benefit by adding to his or her flock, one must refrain for the greater good. But as logical as this seems, your experience may suggest to you that it will require more than reasoning to make people refrain from behaviors that are environmentally destructive, although personally satisfying. Unfortunately, people frequently fail to respond to reason alone.

John Platt (1973) considered situations like the commons dilemma, in which short-term *personal* gains conflict with long-term *societal* needs, to be types of "social traps." In general, Platt feels that social traps are hard to break out of but claims it is essential for researchers to design strategies enabling us to do just that. Various methods have been suggested to help us break out of the commons dilemma (cf. Edney, 1980; Platt, 1973). For example, researchers have tried to increase short-term costs of environmentally destructive behaviors so that they become less attractive behavioral alternatives, and attempted to decrease the costs of environmentally constructive acts. Environmental psychologists have also tried to educate people (e.g., by conducting environmental seminars) to make them realize their interdependence and to make the long-term societal costs of squandering resources more salient, and added reinforcers to encourage behaviors incompatible with those that waste precious resources. Some have also supplied people with feedback about the extent to which they are depleting the commons, and assessed the effects on resource overconsumption of dividing up available resources (e.g., through rationing) (see the box below).

SIMULATING THE COMMONS DILEMMA: HOW IT'S DONE AND WHAT IS FOUND

To test different techniques for helping us break out of the "commons dilemma," a number of simulations have been developed which incorporate the central elements that people face in such contexts. (For a complete discussion of simulation techniques, see the Methodology Appendix.) In these simulations, various *interventions* are attempted to determine those which would cause us to behave in a more constructive way. Thus far, the simulations have included computer analogs (e.g., Brechner, 1977; Cass & Edney, 1978), as well as noncomputerized methods involving portable (e.g., Edney, 1979) and nonportable apparatus (e.g., Edney & Harper, 1978). In addition to being useful for exploring strategies for helping us to break out of the commons dilemma, simulations can be used as teaching devices to aid us in understanding the dynamics of our environmentally destructive behaviors.

To give you a feel for these simulation techniques, we will discuss Edney's (1979) "nuts game" simulation in some detail. Recall that commons dilemmas include: (1) a limited resource that may regenerate itself somewhat, but which can be endangered through overconsumption; and (2) people who have the choice between restricting current individual consumption for the good of society (and the future of the resource pool), and exploiting the resource for their own immediate good. A successful simulation would have to include these elements.

How can this be done? Edney's "nuts game" accomplishes it quite nicely. A small number of subjects enter the lab and sit around an open bowl that originally contains 10 hexagonal nuts, made of hardwood. The bowl symbolizes the pool of resources, and the nuts symbolize the individual resources themselves. Participants are told that their goal is to obtain as many nuts as possible. (This simulates the fact that typically we try to maximize our outcomes in life.) Players can take as many nuts as they want at any time after a trial begins. The experimenter also states that the number of nuts remaining in the bowl after every 10-second interval will be doubled by him or her. This replenishment cycle simulates natural resource regeneration rates. The above events continue until the time limit for the game is exceeded, or until the players empty the bowl.

How do subjects behave during the "nuts game"? We would hope that they would take at most a few nuts out of the pool per 10-second period, which would allow the game to continue and maximize the long-term outcomes. However, in his research, Edney (1979) found that 65 percent of the groups depleted the pool completely before the first replenishment stage. They took out all 10 nuts (i.e., depleted the resource pool completely) during the first few seconds of the game. As in the "real world," people exploit the commons, with unfortunate results.

The next question involves what conditions can be introduced into commons dilemma simula-

ENVIRONMENTAL PSYCHOLOGY AND SAVING THE ENVIRONMENT

In this concluding chapter we will discuss a broad range of techniques that have been used by environmental psychologists in an attempt to change an array of human behaviors that are not in our best interests environmentally. Some environmentally destructive behaviors are easily amenable to conceptualization in terms of the "commons dilemma" and "social trap" analyses we have described, while others require a different type of conceptualization. Therefore, the approaches we will discuss for dealing with environmentally destructive behavior include the sorts of techniques mentioned as useful for attacking "commons dilemma" type problems, as well as other methods.

tions to cause people to behave in a more constructive way. In past research, using Edney's simulation and others, it has been found that cooperation among players is essential for proecological outcomes; consequently there must be trust between participants (Edney, 1979). Also, if groups are allowed time to study the game and to communicate, they derive their own strategies, which frequently are proecological. Other research shows that giving groups immediate and detailed resource feedback about the effects of their behavior (Seligman & Darley, 1977; Stern, 1976), or the ability to communicate about the commons (Brechner, 1977; Edney & Harper, 1978; Dawes, McTavish, & Shaklee, 1977) leads to maintaining the commons for a longer period of time. Groups who are afforded both feedback and communication are especially successful at maintaining the commons (Jorgenson & Papciak, 1981).

Additional interventions have also been attempted. When one's individual behavior in commons dilemma situations is subject to the scrutiny of others, he or she is less apt to overexploit the commons (Jerdee & Rosen, 1974). Other studies have explored the effects of knowing one is interdependent with others for a resource, rather than having his or her own supply. Generally, individually owned resources are handled more efficiently than common or "pooled" resources. In fact, obtaining knowledge of resource interdependence seems to increase the intensity of behaviors aimed at "getting as much as possible for oneself," which ends up depleting the commons (Brechner, 1977; Cass & Edney, 1978). This suggests that rationing resources could be a useful strategy.

Experiments have studied whether educating people about the optimal strategy for using resources in commons dilemma situations leads to proecological actions. As we will see later when we discuss environmental education, often it is quite ineffective (Edney & Harper, 1978). On the other hand, when subjects arrive at an optimizing strategy *themselves* through communication, it can have the desired effect (Edney & Harper, 1978). Also, different leadership and decision-making rules have been related to commons dilemma outcomes. A study by Shippee (1978) found that personal participation in choosing a group's leadership, and in implementing decisions to limit resource use led to quite successful conservation results. This, coupled with the earlier findings on being involved in choosing an optimizing strategy, highlights the importance of individual participation.

What does all of the above mean? Clearly, commons dilemma analogues can give us some good hypotheses regarding how to deal with "real-life" situations. They might eventually provide some important partial solutions to pressing contemporary problems. However, we must keep in mind that the external validity of these procedures has not been proven, and it is still an open question whether or not the sorts of interventions which are successful in simulations would work in the "real world."

Clearly, changing human behavior to save the environment is an extremely important topic. However, past research in environmental psychology has focused more on the effects of environmental variables (e.g., crowding, deteriorated environments) than on how to modify our behavior to *save* the environment. Environmental psychologists have documented that certain environments affect us adversely, but have done less research on how to change our behaviors so they don't have adverse effects on the environment. There is a big difference between knowing that people react negatively to filthy urban areas or to gas lines, and getting them to do something about solving these problems. We need to devote more research attention to studying how we can have a positive effect on the environment, as opposed to focusing on how it affects us.

What unique contribution can environmental psychology make to help deal with the many environmental problems we face (e.g., insufficient and expensive fuels, air and water pollution, a generally deteriorating environment)? The approaches other disciplines have taken have emphasized *physical technology*. For example, a great deal of attention has been focused on developing nuclear and solar energy, and antipollution techniques. Many seem to think that solving our environmental problems only requires the right technologies. In contrast, relatively less attention has focused on strategies for preserving the environment which involve changes in people's *behavior*. Where these techniques have been used they are often regarded as "stopgap" measures—until technology bails us out of our current problems. We will argue that although physical technology certainly has a role, behavior change—sometimes involving substantial modifications in how we act on an "everyday" basis—will have to make a significant contribution if things are to improve. In fact, sometimes behavior change will be more important than physical technology in effecting solutions.

Why do we (and many other environmental psychologists) feel this way? First, in some cases physical technologies have gotten us into this mess. Modern transportation has solved problems in locomoting, but caused pollution, an energy shortage, unsightly commercial "strips," etc. Modern packaging allows us to preserve all types of food, but has created a tremendous litter problem. Most technologies have unfortunate "side effects," and in this chapter we will see that psychological techniques for behavior change could help eliminate them. Second, in some cases (e.g., dealing with littering) there is no efficient physical technology, so changing behavior is our best means of coping. Even when there is an efficient technology for dealing with environmental problems (e.g., building smaller, more efficient homes; retrofitting existing ones), particular behaviors are often necessary to ensure that people use available technology. For example, motorists have disconnected catalytic converters in automobiles in order to increase gas mileage and eliminate attendant smells. By doing so, they subvert pollution control technology. More generally, we could say that the impact of any technology depends on people's behavior—how they *use* the technology. Finally, behavior does have strong effects on the environment: We would not be exaggerating if we asserted that almost everything anyone of us does has either a positive or a negative impact on our environment.

Two questions remain: Will changing our behavior to save the environment require a lower "quality of life," and "can it be done"? Generally, the answer to the first is "no." If we changed our behavior so fewer of us drove cars and more used public transportation, there would be less pollution, we would have significantly more money to spend, we could walk or ride bicycles anywhere, there would be a lower rate of inflation due to dependence on foreign oil, etc. So, in many ways, the quality of life would actually improve. Do the behavior change techniques that we'll be describing in this chapter work? We'll leave that for you to decide after reading our presentation of the evidence in the coming pages. We will, however, suggest that there is lots of room for environmental psychologists to improve our environment-relevant behaviors. For example, energy consumption often varies by a factor of two or three for similar people living in identical homes (Socolow, 1978; Winnett *et al.*, 1979). Different behaviors certainly do impact on energy use!

If we could influence environmentally relevant behaviors to improve the environment, what would we focus on? We'd probably want to promote *environmentally protective* behaviors (e.g., picking up litter, recycling things), and discourage *environmentally destructive* ones (e.g., throwing litter on the ground, driving cars that are "gas hogs") (Cone & Hayes, 1980). It should be noted that both types of behaviors impact on the same problems. Encouraging environmentally protective acts (e.g., by rewarding people for picking up litter) and discouraging environmentally destructive behavior (e.g., through high fines for littering) will improve the litter situation. Unfortunately, programs that encourage protective behaviors don't necessarily inhibit destructive behaviors, and vice-versa (Cone & Hayes, 1980). Also, not all environmentally protective and destructive behaviors have the same impact on the environment. A program that stops people from littering is sure to have direct environmental impact; one that encourages people to vote for conservation-oriented legislators will probably have a more diffuse impact. Finally, we should stress that the effects of any environmentally protective or destructive behavior are complex. Suppose we could get people to recycle *all* newspapers. This would save trees, but might cause water pollution from the ink removal process. It would save energy since we wouldn't need to process virgin wood, but the recycling process itself uses a great deal of energy. Sometimes it is hard to figure out when we are really "ahead."

What is the range of environmental problems that we would like to improve if we could? These may be categorized as: problems of *environmental aesthetics* (e.g., prevention and control of litter, protection of natural resources, preventing urban deterioration); *health-related problems* (e.g., pollution, radiation, high levels of noise); and *resource problems* (e.g., overconsumption of non-renewable resources, such as oil) (Cone & Hayes, 1980). These categories are neither exhaustive nor mutually exclusive. Often, environmental problems, such as overdependence on the automobile, impact on all three categories. While we will not be able to deal with all of the environmental problems needing solutions, later in this chapter we will discuss specific approaches for coping with several of them in detail.

At this point, let's consider a range of general techniques used by environmental psychologists which can be applied to almost any sort of environmental problem. These methods are *environmental education,* appropriate environmental *prompts and cues,* various *reinforcement strategies,* and techniques that combine several of the approaches. Some of these methods may hold great promise for solving the critical problems that now confront us.

ENVIRONMENTAL EDUCATION: TEACHING US WHAT IS WRONG AND HOW TO RESPOND TO IT

Essentially, environmental education involves making people aware of the scope and nature of environmental problems and of behavioral alternatives that might alleviate them. This approach has been used to promote energy conservation, to lower the levels of pollution and littering, and to encourage other proecological attitudes and behavior. The guiding assumption of most such programs is that education will lead to environmental awareness and attitude change, which in turn will affect behavior advantageously (Bruvold, 1973; O'Riordan, 1976; Winston, 1974).

Environmental educators employ all manner of techniques to attain these goals. One strategy makes use of the mass media to reach large segments of the population. Such techniques are employed by the Environmental Protection Agency (EPA), by public utilities, and by private industry (especially major oil companies). Another method involves formal course work at the elementary, secondary, or college level. In this context, special texts, workbooks, comic books, and simulations have been developed to help "get the point across" (see Figure 12–1). Diagnostic tests have been designed to pinpoint deficiencies in student knowledge and to provide an index of learning. Less formally, environmental workshops and displays are set up locally at shopping malls and regionally at state fairs and museums. Finally, although this does not complete the list of sources of environmental education, organizations such as the Sierra Club regularly disseminate educational information.

How effective are environmental education programs? Research suggests that there is sometimes a significant lack of environmental knowledge (Ditton & Goodale, 1974; Towler & Swan, 1972), and that educational programs may be helpful in enhancing awareness as well as in changing attitudes for the better (Allen, 1972; Cohen, 1973). However, the link between envi-

ronmental education and behavior appears to be weak (Cone & Hayes, 1980; Heberlein, 1976). For example, it was reported that of all the persons who attended one of the first environmental "teach-ins" in 1970, only a few decided to make substantial alterations in their behavior. Specifically, 60 percent of the participants didn't plan any changes on the basis of what they had learned; the 40 percent who planned to take action mostly chose very moderate measures (e.g., writing congresspersons). Of the latter group, only 13 percent indicated a desire to significantly modify their life style (Lingwood, 1971). These findings are striking for two reasons. First, individuals had voluntarily attended the workshop for the express purpose of finding out what behavioral alternatives were available. Second, the dependent measures were of behavioral intentions rather than of actual behavior. If actual behavior had been mea-

Figure 12–1. Sample of environmental education. (From "Fun with the environment," US Environmental Protection Agency, Washington, D.C.)

sured, possibly even less commitment to change would have been seen.

Are the rather weak results reported by Lingwood typical of other environmental education programs? Unfortunately, there is evidence that many other programs also have been ineffective in changing environmentally destructive behavior. In one study, Howell and Warmbrod (1974) reported no difference in attitude between students whose classes used a manual oriented to environmental problems and solutions and those whose classes did not. If environmental education is not effective even in changing attitudes, it is unlikely to bring about behavioral change. Similarly, Winston (1974) found no relationship between a measure of environmental awareness and an index of positiveness of environmentally-oriented behavior, a finding that casts serious doubts on the worth of environmental education efforts.

In spite of these discouraging data, you should not conclude prematurely that all environmental education will fail to yield positive effects. A two-year study by Asch and Shore (1975) found that compared to a control group, school classes that had been taken on field trips to a nature area (a form of environmental education) displayed greater respect for wildlife, plant life, soil, and water. Thus, it could be that environmental education is most successful with young children who do not have well-established habits. Some researchers believe that the effectiveness of environmental education would be improved if it focused more on presenting solutions to problems than on increasing awareness of them (Rankin, 1969). More and more people seem to recognize the existence of an ''environmental crisis,'' but many have little or no knowledge of specific ways to deal with it. Finally, it seems likely that the effectiveness of environmental education would be especially high under certain circumstances. This may be the case when we are unaware that a problem exists, when we have little or no information about how to deal with it, and when the information provided suggests a specific, relatively low-cost solution.

Although they are sometimes successful, why do environmental education programs so often fail to have a positive effect on behavior? What do *you* think interferes with the effectiveness of environmental education? Many reasons have been proposed, most centering around the lack of correspondence that social psychologists often find between attitudes and behavior.

As we mentioned earlier, proponents of environmental education programs (cf. Leff, 1974) assume that information will lead to awareness, to attitude change, and finally to behavior change. Unfortunately, in view of social psychological work and work in environmental psychology indicating that attitudes frequently fail to predict behavior (see Chapter 3), these assumptions are not very sound (Wicker, 1969). An example should bring home our point about attitude-behavior discrepancies. Bickman (1972) planted trash on a path and watched students' *behavior*—they walked right past it. Although 98.6 percent did not pick up the litter, 94 percent endorsed the *attitude* statement, ''It should be everyone's responsibility to pick up litter when they see it'' (p. 324).

O'Riordan (1976) has listed several attitude-behavior assumptions that environmental education may mistakenly rest on:

1. The assumption that human beings are rational and consistent creatures who will modify their motivations on the basis of new information from, say, self-interest to altruism.
2. The assumption that by concentrating upon one set of cognitions, we can change other relevant cognitions.
3. The assumption that attitude shifts will be sufficiently strong and long-lasting to influence behavior.

It is also the case that attitudes are only one possible determinant of behavior. The behavior of lowering one's thermostat may depend less on one's attitudes toward conservation than on one's feelings of comfort, the reaction of one's family, etc. (Pallack *et al.*, 1980). And we should keep in mind that sometimes attitudes may follow from behavior (Bem, 1972) rather than precede it, as environmental educators typically assume.

These criticisms undermine the bedrock on which environmental education stands. Indeed, some argue that we have generally turned to environmental education after realizing that physical technology has been unable to provide a solution to environmental problems, only to find that it, too, is ineffective (Cone & Hayes, 1980). But there are those who disagree with such a dismal appraisal: They feel it is far too soon to display such pessimism about environmental education.

Some researchers point out that studies do show reasonable relations between *specific* environmental attitudes (which *could* be affected through environmental education) and behavior. The specific attitude that conserving energy by lowering the thermostat could adversely effect health and comfort is associated with nonconservation, and believing the energy crisis will have direct effects on oneself is positively associated with conservation behavior (Olsen, 1981; Seligman *et al.*, 1979). Advocates of environmental education also point out that the methodological problems inherent in assessing the relationship between attitudes and behavior cast doubt on the conclusion that educational strategies to change attitudes won't lead to behavior change (Schuman & Johnson, 1976; Weigel & Newman, 1976). Overall, we might tentatively conclude that while research has not strongly supported the effectiveness of environmental education, future studies may reveal programs that have value, and methodological refinements may allow us to better assess the effects of these. Even if environmental education programs do not *change* behavior, they may serve a useful function in *reinforcing* proecological behavior and attitudes in people already committed to proecological action.

PROMPTS: REMINDERS OF WHAT TO DO AND OF WHAT NOT TO DO

In addition to environmental education, appropriate prompts (cues that convey a message) are commonly used to encourage environmentally constructive behavior and to discourage environmentally destructive acts. Signs, such as those represented in Figure 12–2A, B, and C, are examples of typical prompts. However, these examples should not give you the idea that prompts are restricted to such mundane causes—they have been used for all types of proecological purposes. Prompts are *antecedent* behavioral change techniques. They occur before the target behavior and are designed to increase the likelihood of favorable acts (approach prompts) and decrease the probability of unfavorable ones (avoidance prompts).

Some prompts are general in nature (e.g., "Help keep our community clean") while others are specific (e.g., "Drive 55 mph to save energy"). Some prompts signify incentives or disincentives for certain behaviors (e.g., "$100 fine for littering"; "5 cents for each bottle returned"), and others (e.g., the presence of police cars) may remind us of disincentives (e.g., speeding tickets if we exceed speed limits). Frequently, *approach prompts* specify an incentive for engaging in some behavior; *avoidance prompts* a disincentive for enacting it (Geller, Winnett, & Everett, 1982). While prompts are generally administered in written or spoken form, the actions of social models (i.e., other people) and the condition of the environment may also function as prompts. How do the various types of prompts affect the way we act? It is assumed that they moderate environmentally destructive behavior by making certain social norms (e.g., the norm that we shouldn't litter) either more or less salient in a given situation.

Clearly, the most common type of prompt consists of simple written and verbal messages. These have the advantage of being relatively inexpensive, and are effective in a number of contexts. For example, in an attempt to decelerate environmentally destructive lawn-walking behavior in a new "mini-park," Hayes and Cone (1977a) erected signs that read "University Mini-Park— Please Don't Trample the Grass." This accounted for a significant reduction in the rate of lawn-walking behavior. As we will see later in this

Figure 12–2 A, B, and C. Signs such as these exemplify typical prompts. (Sherry Fisher & Marjory Fisher)

chapter, simple written prompts can also encourage energy conservation and decrease littering. In Beaver Stadium (capacity 60,000) at Pennsylvania State University (Baltes & Hayward, 1974), a written prompt accounted for a 45 percent reduction in littering at a football game!

While written and verbal prompts *may* be effective, under certain conditions they are not. Pirages and Ehrlich (1974) reported that despite an appeal from the San Francisco Bay Area Pollution

Control District for people to avoid using their cars during a serious smog episode, there was no demonstrable reduction in traffic flow. Generally, when the cost of obeying a prompt is too high, or when the prompt deals with a very essential behavior, it may go unheeded. Prompts accompanied by *contingencies* (e.g., offering a reward for the correct behavior or a penalty for the incorrect one) make it more likely that inconvenient pro-ecological behaviors will be adopted (Geller *et al.*, 1982). Prompts *without* such contingencies are most effective when they suggest responses that are easy to emit or avoid, are specific (say exactly which behavior should or should not be enacted), and are given in close proximity to an opportunity to perform the act. If contingencies do not accompany a prompt, it is unlikely to be effective in modifying behavior requiring more effort than adjusting a thermostat, turning off a light, or purchasing drinks in a recyclable container (Geller *et al.*, 1982).

Another determinant of the effectiveness of

prompts is the specific wording of the message. Under some conditions, psychological reactance (described in Chapter 3) may be aroused. While antilitter prompts of the "Please don't litter" variety can be effective, overly forceful prompts ("Don't you *dare* litter," or "You *must* not litter") are quite ineffective (Reich & Robertson, 1979) because they may elicit reactance. Such prompts can actually cause people to do exactly what it is hoped they will avoid (Reich & Robertson, 1979). The size and the salience of prompts would also be expected to impact on effectiveness, though the relationship is somewhat complex. Obviously, a prompt must be sufficiently large and salient to be seen in order to have an effect, but when it is too large or salient, it may be perceived as overly forceful and elicit reactance (e.g., Luyben, 1980).

In addition to prompts that employ verbal or written messages, the state of the environment and the behavior of models can also function as prompts that affect behavior. A clean or dirty environment may convey information about how one is expected to behave, and thus make the antilittering norm more or less salient. In this way, it may serve as an anti- or prolitter prompt (e.g., Krauss *et al.*, 1978; Reiter & Samuel, 1980). Similarly, a human model who litters or doesn't litter may undermine or bolster the antilittering norms with which we are socialized, and thus serve as a prompt. Models can consist of other live individuals or people portrayed in the media. As well as demonstrating a specific behavior, models often provide information for us about the positive or negative consequences of an act.

A final type of prompt is the physical presence of an environmentally constructive alternative. This is usually an object which, if used, could prevent an environmentally destructive act. For example, a nearby sidewalk might serve as a prompt not to walk on newly planted grass, or a nearby garbage can might function as a cue not to litter (Figure 12–3). Of course, such objects don't serve as prompts in a strict sense, since they provide a behavioral alternative to environmentally destructive behavior. Be that as it may, many re-

Figure 12–3. Sometimes the physical presence of an object, which if used, could prevent environmentally destructive behavior, can be considered a prompt. In the case of this trash can, the prompt appears to have been quite effective! (Sherry Fisher)

searchers (especially those doing work on littering) consider such objects to be a type of prompt and have measured how they affect environmentally destructive acts.

REINFORCEMENT TECHNIQUES: WHAT YOU DO DETERMINES WHAT YOU GET

In addition to environmental education and the use of prompts, reinforcement techniques have been employed to modify environmentally destructive behavior. In contrast to prompts, which are *antecedent* strategies (i.e., occur before an event), reinforcers are *consequence* strategies (come after it). Some of the most successful efforts to date have involved reinforcement methods.

One such strategy is termed *positive reinforcement*. In this technique, individuals are given positively valued stimuli for performing environmentally constructive acts (e.g., they may be offered money for turning in paper at a recycling center). The purpose of positive reinforcement is to increase the probability that a desirable response will occur in the future. In contrast to positive reinforcement, *negative reinforcement* increases desirable behavior because we are motivated to avoid an aversive stimulus (e.g., a fine) or escape some ongoing noxious stimulus (e.g., high electric bills). A third technique is called *punishment*. It usually entails administering a noxious or painful stimulus to those who engage in environmentally destructive behavior (e.g, a reprimand or fine to someone who litters). Behaviors are decreased in frequency when followed by punishment, at least in the short run. The final reinforcement-related technique may be termed *feedback*. This method provides information about whether one is attaining or failing to attain an environmental goal (e.g., reducing fuel consumption). As such, feedback may constitute positive reinforcement or punishment, depending on whether the recipient is succeeding or failing. It is important to note that the same reinforcer can often be perceived as a positive or a negative reinforcer or as punishment, depending on the context and the observer's perspective. For a program to be successful, it is essential that the target population perceive things in the same way as the program director or designer (Geller *et al.*, 1982).

We turn now to a general discussion of the efficacy of using positive reinforcement, negative reinforcement, punishment, and feedback. While reinforcement strategies are often effective, like prompts they can backfire (e.g., when they elicit reactance). Consequence techniques may affect one's perception of control, and when we believe we have lost our freedom and are being "manipulated," we may work against the goals of the program and refuse to emit the target behavior.

Skinner (1971) suggested that positive reinforcement is less apt to cause reactance than negative reinforcement or punishment.

Positive Reinforcement: Encouraging Good Behavior

Positive reinforcers have been used in the vast majority of studies employing reinforcement techniques. These have ranged from financial rewards (either small or large) to nonmonetary benefits (e.g., decals stating "I conserve energy"). Positive reinforcers are the most socially acceptable of all the reinforcement strategies, the easiest to administer, and probably the most cost-effective in the long run (Geller *et al.*, 1982). Interestingly, government programs have favored the use of negative reinforcers or punishment (e.g., laws and ordinances for littering) to positive reinforcers (e.g., the bottle bill). Because they require an elaborate enforcement apparatus, negative reinforcers and punishment are often relatively more expensive to administer than positive reinforcers.

In some cases, positive reinforcers are administered continuously, while in others they are given less frequently. Sometimes positive reinforcement is given contingent on performing a particular *response;* in other instances it is given when a particular *outcome* is achieved. Examples of response-contingent positive reinforcement are: raffle tickets for bringing paper to a recycling center (e.g., Ingram & Geller, 1975), and a merchandise token for using public transportation (Deslauriers & Everett, 1977). Examples of outcome-contingent reinforcement are: giving someone money for cleaning up a yard to criterion (Chapman & Risley, 1974), and payment for maintaining a 10 percent reduction in home heating energy (Winnett & Nietzel, 1975). Since response-contingent reinforcers provide us with information about what specific behaviors are appropriate, while outcome-contingent reinforcers often do not, the latter may ultimately be less effective in encouraging proecological behavior (Geller *et al.*, 1982).

Studies using positive reinforcement strategies can be divided into two groups. One has used these techniques to improve environments that are already disturbed (e.g., littered, noisy); the second has used them to prevent negative consequences from occurring in the first place. In studies employing positive reinforcements to restore disturbed environments, strong changes in behavior have occurred, at least for the period in which the reinforcement contingency remains in effect.

An especially interesting set of such studies has dealt with eliminating excessive noise in elementary and secondary schools. In one project, Schmidt and Ulrich (1969) monitored noise levels in a second- and a fourth-grade classroom and found an average of 52 dB. When students were told they could earn extra minutes of gym for each 10-minute period in which sound levels didn't exceed 42 dB, dramatic and stable reductions resulted. Similarly, Wilson and Hopkins (1973) used automated equipment to record the percentage of time that sound in seventh- and eighth-grade home economics classes exceeded 70 dB. When the sound level dropped below the 70 dB threshold, the students' favorite radio station was played. Although the noise before treatment exceeded 70 dB for 30 percent of the time, during the treatment it exceeded the threshold for only 5 percent of the time. Clearly, the appropriate use of positive reinforcers may be an important technique in improving disturbed environmental conditions.

Up until now we've discussed positive reinforcement techniques in terms of their capacity to restore disturbed environments. However, as we noted earlier, a second group of studies has used these methods to prevent negative environment-related effects from occurring in the first place. Studies in this area involve anticipatory attempts to forestall negative effects by reinforcing people when they engage in appropriate behaviors. In this research, both monetary and nonmonetary reinforcers (such as faster commuting times) have been used to promote energy conservation. For example, in Miami, faster passage (a nonmonetary reinforcer) is offered to cars with three or more passengers by allowing them to travel in special lanes with less traffic. Similar nonmonetary benefits are provided by special buses, operated by many cities, which take commuters from suburban parking areas to the city center. These buses make it unnecessary to search for parking space (a considerable benefit) and reduce the tension associated with driving in city traffic. Unfortunately, the effectiveness of such programs is not well researched.

In contrast to programs using nonmonetary positive reinforcers to prevent negative effects on the environment, research has measured the effects of monetary reinforcers. These studies show that offering money can increase behaviors that forestall environmental damage. Encouraging results were found in a study that employed monetary reinforcers to increase student ridership of a campus bus system (Everett, Hayward, & Meyers, 1974). Increased ridership means less pollution, less gasoline consumption, etc. As we will see later in this chapter, studies also suggest that monetary reinforcers can be employed to increase energy conservation in the home (Hayes & Cone, 1977b; Kohlenberg, Phillips, & Proctor, 1976; Winett & Nietzel, 1975).

In general, the use of various types of positive reinforcers is an effective technique both for restoring disturbed environmental conditions and for preventing environmentally destructive behaviors. However, while we have painted a rather glowing picture thus far, we should mention a few negative aspects that are associated with such techniques. First, they are often quite expensive. For example, in several studies on energy conservation, the costs of the program exceeded the value of the energy saved. Second, in a number of instances it has been found that target behaviors that improved during the reinforcement period returned to baseline levels soon after reinforcement contingencies were removed (Everett *et al.*, 1974). This is a rather disconcerting finding, and it is sometimes a problem in other reinforcement-related methods as well. Since people are responding to externally imposed contingencies, they may find little motivation to retain desirable behaviors once reinforcements are removed.

Negative Reinforcement and Punishment: Alternatives to Positive Reinforcement

We've devoted considerable attention to positive reinforcement as a moderator of environmentally directed behavior, but what of the effects of negative reinforcement and punishment? In general, negative reinforcement as conceptualized here involves avoiding unpleasant aspects of a situation, and punishment consists of adding aversive elements to it. Not surprisingly, researchers have used these methods much less than positive reinforcement to control environmentally directed behavior. We discuss some suggestions for employing negative reinforcement and punishment, but it should be noted that few such programs currently exist.

Many possible applications of negative reinforcers to combat unfavorable environmental conditions are in the planning stages. For example, Cone and Hayes (1980) suggest that we might prohibit aircraft that exceed certain noise standards from landing at convenient airports, so that airline companies and aircraft manufacturers might reduce noise levels in order to avoid the prohibitions. Another use of negative reinforcement would be to threaten to cut off important corporate tax benefits for companies polluting our water and air. While all these options may be promising, most have not yet been implemented, and those that are in operation have not yet been subjected to scientific study.

How might punishment be used to discourage behaviors that are not in our environmental best interests? Some uses of punishment are rather common, e.g., fines for companies that pollute, and for people who drop trash along the roadside. Platt (1973) has suggested that we could reduce the use of large, gas-guzzling automobiles by taxing them heavily. Another suggestion, which would lower traffic in urban centers and on nearby freeways, is to change parking and toll rates to make it much more expensive for those who travel by private automobile during peak hours. While this has been done with respect to parking rates in some parts of England, it has not yet been tried much in the United States. Unfortunately, since programs employing them have not yet been implemented or studied in many cases, we will have to reserve judgment on the use of negative reinforcement and punishment to regulate environmentally destructive behavior. They may hold great hope, but only the future can tell.

Feedback: Letting Us Know How We're Doing

The final reinforcement-related strategy is termed "feedback." Feedback may be viewed as a form of response-contingent reinforcement. As we noted earlier, it may be either positive or negative, depending on whether the performance it refers to is successful or unsuccessful. In this way, it may constitute either positive reinforcement or punishment, although it may actually be intended only to inform, not to reward or punish. How has feedback been used to improve environment-related behavior? Examples of its use include feedback on energy use given monthly or weekly (e.g., Kohlenberg *et al.,* 1976), and placing estimates of community litter on the front page of the local newspaper (Schnelle *et al.,* 1980). In general, feedback has been employed alone or in combination with other strategies (e.g., environmental education, prompts), as well as with certain reinforcers, such as money. While it is often difficult to separate the effects of the feedback component of the treatment from the other elements, studies we will review later in this chapter suggest that feedback can be a very effective technique.

INTEGRATING AND EVALUATING THE VARIOUS APPROACHES TO ELIMINATING ENVIRONMENTALLY DESTRUCTIVE BEHAVIOR

We have considered environmental education, use of prompts, and reinforcement-related techniques as separate strategies for improving the quality of the environment. While it is true that these methods have often been employed separately by researchers, and that such a presentation makes the material easier for the reader to digest, it is also true that many studies have used several methods simultaneously. Often, a combined strategy enables the researcher to tailor his or her attack to the specific qualities of the problem and yields the strongest possible program. While we could never hope to survey the many combined strategies that have been used to combat environmentally destructive behavior, we would like to offer an example that will be relevant to many of our readers.

As you undoubtedly know if you've ever resided in a college dormitory, noise can become a tremendous problem. Further, you have probably observed that the coping strategies of dormitory residents are many and varied. In an attempt to combat the "noise nemesis," Meyers, Artz, and Craighead (1976) structured a program that included elements of both reinforcement-related techniques and environmental education. The treatment package consisted of: (a) an *educational* component, in which residents were given information about noise and how to deal with it; (b) a *feedback* component, which included a doorbell set to ring when a serious noise transgression occurred; and (c) a *reinforcement* component, which took several forms, including monetary reward. What were the effects of this combined approach? It accounted for a striking decrease in noise transgressions from 345 per day during a baseline period to 148 per day during treatment. Thus, the combination of a reinforcement approach with environmental education and feedback may have yielded unique benefits otherwise unavailable. It should be noted that combined programs have also been successful in other contexts.

While it is apparent that combined strategies may often be quite effective, you may be wondering at this point how various individual methods (environmental education, prompts, and reinforcements) measure up relative to each other. In general, reinforcement strategies are strongest, prompts are moderately effective, and environmental education is weakest (Cone & Hayes, 1980). One study that allows us to draw these

conclusions involved an ingenious attempt to measure the effectiveness of several antilittering strategies in theaters (Clark, Hendee, & Burgess, 1972). It evaluated the following approaches: (1) showing a Walt Disney antilittering cartoon (environmental education); (2) adding extra trash cans, distributing litter bags, or distributing both litter bags and instructions (all of which are prompts); and (3) providing money and movie tickets as incentives for full litter bags (reinforcements). To evaluate the effectiveness of the various strategies, in each condition the proportion of the total litter that was deposited appropriately was measured. As can be seen in Figure 12–4, environmental education had little effect. The use of prompts proved quite variable, with some strategies having a mildly positive effect and others not. However, when reinforcements in the form of money or free tickets were added, the positive effects were truly formidable.

How representative is this pattern of results? It can be stated that it generally reflects other studies designed to allow a comparison of all three approaches, as well as studies designed to compare the relative effectiveness of only two of the strategies (Geller, Chafee, & Ingram, 1975; Hayes & Cone, 1977b; Kohlenberg et al., 1976; Luyben & Bailey, 1975). But relative effectiveness is not all that should be taken into account in designing a program to counter environmentally destructive behavior. As noted throughout this chapter, each of the techniques we've mentioned has *unique* costs and benefits, which should be assessed completely before deciding on a strategy. For example, reinforcements appear to have strong effects but often are relatively expensive to administer. In contrast, prompts are somewhat less effective but are relatively inexpensive. Thus, the dictates of the situation should determine which combination of costs and benefits is most appropriate. Included in any program should be elements that increase desirable behaviors along with elements that decrease undesirable ones (e.g., fines for dumping toxic wastes, along with tax benefits for proper disposal). To insure this, a mixture of strategies is frequently necessary. Further, it

Percentage of Litter Returned by Audience

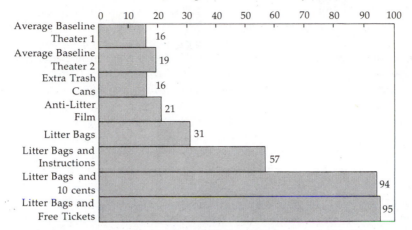

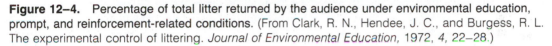

Figure 12–4. Percentage of total litter returned by the audience under environmental education, prompt, and reinforcement-related conditions. (From Clark, R. N., Hendee, J. C., and Burgess, R. L. The experimental control of littering. *Journal of Environmental Education,* 1972, *4,* 22–28.)

should always be ascertained that the selected treatments do not have unintended negative side effects. In the end, the choice is quite complex and can best be made by individuals who are familiar with the situation, and who weigh all the relevant factors carefully before reaching a conclusion.

APPROACHES TO SPECIFIC ENVIRONMENTAL PROBLEMS

Armed with an understanding of some useful general techniques for curbing environmentally destructive behavior, we will consider some *specific* approaches that have been applied to cope with several major environmental problems—littering, energy overconsumption both at home and in transportation settings, and finally, vandalism.

Littering

In the United States, about 145 million tons of trash are "created" each year, and too much of this ends up as litter. For example, 4 billion tons of litter collect annually alongside our highways (Ward, 1975). It costs more than $1 billion to clean up this mess in public areas (e.g., high-

ways, parks) and in private ones (e.g., business and industrial property) (Keep American Beautiful, 1970). In addition to being profoundly ugly, litter represents a hazard to our health and safety and may cause damage to animal life. Who helps to create these unseemly conditions? Young people litter more than older ones, males more than females, and people who are alone litter more than those in groups (Osborne & Powers, 1980).

The whole range of strategies we've discussed (e.g., prompts, reinforcers) has been used in an attempt to prevent people from littering, and to motivate them to clean up litter left by careless individuals. We will discuss the various techniques, and find that some methods have been more effective than others. (For more detailed reviews, see Brasted, Mann, & Geller, 1979; Cone & Hayes, 1978; Geller, 1980; Osborne & Powers, 1980). In addition, bottle bill legislation (requiring a deposit on all bottles and cans) has been effective in reducing by 75 percent this type of litter at the roadside and in saving energy through recycling (Osborne & Powers, 1980).

Many studies have employed prompts and cues as antecedent strategies to prevent littering. For example, handbills with an antilitter prompt are less apt to be littered than those without a prompt (Geller *et al.,* 1982) (see Figure 12–5). Generally, prompts that state the specific antilitter response desired (e.g., ''Place this paper in a trashcan'') are more effective than general ones. Antilitter prompts are also more effective when given in close temporal proximity to an opportunity to dispose of litter, when proper litter disposal is relatively convenient, and when the prompt is phrased in polite, nondemanding language (Geller *et al.,* 1982). Even under optimal circumstances, the absolute magnitude of change effected by these sorts of prompts is often relatively small (though statistically significant), and to have a meaningful effect they may have to be experienced by many people over a long time frame.

Other antecedent factors that may serve as prompts include the amount of litter already in a setting, the behavior of models, and the presence of trash receptacles. Generally, ''litter begets litter''—the more littered an environment the more littered it becomes. In fact, studies have shown up to a five-fold increase in littering in ''littered''

as opposed to ''clean'' settings (e.g., Finnie, 1973; Geller, Witmer, & Tuso, 1977; Krauss, Freedman, & Whitcup, 1978). Extrapolating from these findings, we could expect vandalism to beget more vandalism and graffiti to prompt more of the same (Sharpe, 1976). In addition to the pattern noted in the box on page 359, an exception to the ''litter begets litter'' finding has been reported in some natural settings where people are less apt to litter and more apt to pick up other people's trash when their picnic areas are littered than clean. This may be because in such settings environmental cleanliness plays an especially important role for people, since they are there to appreciate natural beauty (cf. Geller *et al.,* 1982).

Like the state of the environment, directly observing the behavior of models can serve as a prompt that reduces or produces environmentally destructive behavior. Cialdini (1977) exposed subjects to a model who littered or did not litter in a clean or dirty environment. After seeing the model fail to litter in the clean setting subjects littered the least; after seeing him litter in the dirty setting they littered the most. And Jason, Zolik,

---

SPECIALS of the WEEK

Martin's Ice Cream_ _ _ _ _ _ _ _ _$1.29 (1/2 gal)

Cannon Peanut Butter_ _ _ _ _ _ _ _ 69¢(18 oz)

Boston Lettuce, large head _ _ _ 2/49¢

Wolfe Canned Hams _ _ _ _ _ _ $4.79 (3 lb)

Knox toothpaste _ _ _ _ _ _ _ _ _ 79¢ (7 oz)

Sunset Soda Gallon Pack _ _ _ _ _ 79¢ plus bottle
                                           deposit

Landis Pork and Beans _ _ _ _ _ _ _ 39¢ (28 oz)

Please don't litter.
Please dispose of properly

Figure 12–5. Type of prompt used in a number of littering studies. (Adapted from the work of E. Scott Geller.)

IS A LITTLE LITTER A MORE EFFECTIVE PROMPT THAN NONE AT ALL?

We suggested that more environmentally destructive behavior typically occurs when there is evidence of previous misdeeds (litter on the ground) than when there is not. While this is usually true, work by Cialdini (1977) brought out an interesting caveat. While he found (like previous investigators) that a perfectly clean environment produces less littering than a dirty environment, he also observed that the *least* littering occurs in a setting that is clean except for one piece of litter. The studies were run as follows: Subjects were handed a public service-related circular as they walked down a path. Beforehand, the experimenter had positioned 0, 1, 2, 4, 8, or 16 pieces of litter in front of them. As indicated in Figure 12–6, 18 percent of the subjects littered in the "no litter" condition, but only 10 percent littered in the "one piece of litter" condition. Beyond that, littering by subjects increased in proportion to the amount of litter positioned by the experimenter.

Why did Cialdini observe such a "check mark" pattern for the relationship between the amount of litter in the environment and subsequent littering? He reasoned that while a perfectly clean environment makes the "no littering" norm salient, an environment clean except for one violation makes it even more salient. With increasing violations, however, the norm becomes undermined, and littering is facilitated. These findings are provocative, and if replicated in other contexts they could have practical implications for environmental education as well as for environmental design. For example, do you think you'd be more likely to return your shopping cart at the supermarket if all but one of the remaining carts were neatly stacked, or if there were no violations of the "return your cart" norm?

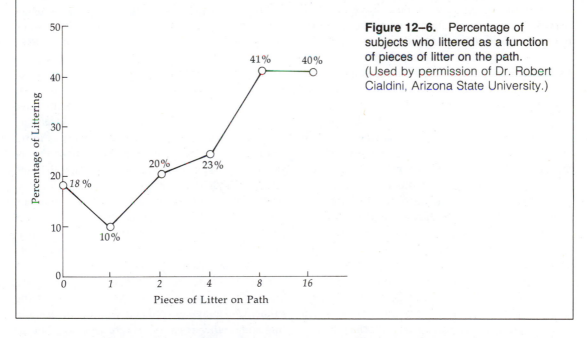

Figure 12–6. Percentage of subjects who littered as a function of pieces of litter on the path. (Used by permission of Dr. Robert Cialdini, Arizona State University.)

and Matese (1979) found that observing a proecological model who showed people how to pick up dog droppings with a "pooper scooper" led to a target area more free of feces. Unfortunately, other studies are less optimistic about the potential of models to prevent environmentally destructive behavior (cf. Geller *et al.,* 1982). From social psychological research we can predict that modeling will be most effective when the model is liked and respected by the target person, and is reinforced for his or her proecological actions (Bandura, 1969; Bandura & Walters, 1967).

A final antecedent strategy to prevent littering is the presence of waste receptacles. Finnie (1973) reported that compared to a condition in which no trash cans were in sight, their presence reduced littering by about 15 percent along city streets and by nearly 30 percent on highways. When a greater number of trash cans were present, littering decreased still more. (Imagine a world with trash cans placed every two feet in an attempt to efficiently control littering!) The value of trash cans or similar objects as antilitter prompts may depend on their attractiveness or distinctiveness. Finnie (1973) observed that colorful garbage cans reduced littering by 14.9 percent over baseline levels, while ordinary cans led to a reduction of only 3.15 percent. Similarly, Miller *et al.* (1976) reported that brightly colored cans resembling birds were much more effective than plain cans in eliciting appropriate disposal. Finally, an ingenious garbage can in the shape of a hat worn by students to Clemson University football games greatly reduced trash in the area of the college football stadium (Miller *et al.*, 1976; O'Neill *et al.*, 1980)! Such cans serve both as prompts to prevent litter from being disposed of inappropriately and to motivate people to pick it up, since it can be reinforcing to deposit litter in them. The Clemson hat dispenses a mechanical "Thank You" to anyone who deposits litter in it.

We turn now to consequence strategies for litter control (i.e., methods to encourage people to pick up existing litter), which have generally been more effective than antecedent techniques (Cone & Hayes, 1980). Prompts have been used as a consequence technique, in addition to being employed as an antecedent strategy. Unfortunately, picking up someone else's litter and putting it in a receptacle is often a more costly behavior than depositing one's own litter, and it seems to be relatively unresponsive to prompts. For example, 10 experiments by Geller and associates (Geller, 1976; Geller, Mann, & Brasted, 1977) found that

prompts have minimal effects on people's likelihood of removing litter and disposing of it. The only exception may be in natural areas, like campgrounds, where prompts may elicit litter removal (cf. Crump *et al.*, 1977). The ineffectiveness of prompts is especially unfortunate, since much money is spent on them by state litter control authorities and organizations like Keep America Beautiful (see the box on page 361).

Reinforcement-based techniques are more successful than prompts in motivating people to clean up littered environments. In fact, when prompts are coupled with reinforcements for obeying them, they can be rather effective. Kohlenberg and Phillips (1973) positioned a prompt which said "Depositing Litter May Be Rewarded," and then proceeded to reward litter depositors on different reinforcement schedules. This technique precipitated a rather dramatic clean up. Another study involved a combination of prompts, environmental education, and reinforcers (in this case feedback). Investigators organized local newspaper coverage about the littering problem (which served as a prompt and a form of education), along with daily feedback on littering in certain target areas. These methods accounted for a decrease in litter compared to baseline conditions (Schnelle *et al.*, 1980). Other experiments have similarly coupled reinforcers with educational techniques and prompts. In these studies, the rewards generally account for much more of the resultant improvement in the litter situation than the other methods (Cone & Hayes, 1980). However, while reinforcement methods are useful, they sometimes require costly supervision to monitor behavior and dispense reinforcers. What alternatives are there for reinforcing litter depositors without supervision?

One group of studies has used novelty trash cans, which reinforce litter depositors by talking to them, displaying a "thank you" sign, or emitting some other response. There is short-, but little long-term research suggesting that these may be effective in motivating people to pick up litter (Geller *et al.*, 1982). Reinforcements can also be administered on the "honor system." A sign in a

KEEP AMERICA BEAUTIFUL: THE CLEAN COMMUNITY SYSTEM

A national organization called Keep America Beautiful has developed the Clean Community System (CCS), a hybrid set of strategies which has had widespread impact on litter control. The CCS has been implemented in 207 US communities and six other countries, and is an excellent model for community action aimed at solving environmental problems.

How does CCS work? A community must apply for CCS certification by showing its commitment to an antilitter program. To join, the city's mayor must endorse CCS, the public works director must submit an evaluation of the litter and solid waste situation in the community, and a committee must be formed representing the commercial, government, and consumer sectors. There are other requirements as well. When a community is accepted for membership, CCS gives a workshop for the local "project team," provides program modules, and many other types of useful support.

What is the philosophy of CCS? It includes elements of both environmental education as well as the behavioral techniques we've discussed (e.g., prompts). CCS assumes that unacceptable norms and attitudes cause littering, and that these can be changed by using behavioral principles. It is believed that when negative attitudes change, littering will decrease. What types of tactics does the CCS program include? Prompts and cues may be placed appropriately, as well as increased trash receptacles. Also, educational programs are developed and presented, media are used to focus attention on people who engage in commendable antilitter activities, incentive programs are developed to reward appropriate waste disposal, punishment contingencies are clarified so they can be enforced effectively, and new antilittering laws may be added (e.g., those who litter may be required to pick up litter along the highway). Finally, a major part of CCS is an evaluation component, to check up on how well the procedures are working and to suggest modifications to enhance effectiveness.

How do environmental psychologists evaluate the CCS system? Geller *et al.* (1982) commend it as a model for community participation in dealing with environmental problems, but pinpoint a number of interesting conceptual and methodological issues. First, they disagree with the assumption that changing attitudes about litter is a necessary prerequisite for dealing with the litter problem. In fact, some environmental psychologists argue that CCS works not due to its attitude change component, but because of other elements. (We noted earlier in this chapter that antilittering attitudes won't guarantee nonlittering *behavior*, due to the persistent discrepancy between attitudes and behavior.) Second, Geller *et al.* (1982) suggest that the procedures could be even more effective if they held more closely to behavioral principles. Third, they point out a number of methodological problems in the way the effectiveness of CCS is evaluated.

US forest area offered people either 25 cents (sent to them by mail) or a chance to win a larger reward if they filled a plastic trash bag with garbage and completed an "information card" stating their name and address. Compared to a prompt only condition (which asked people to fill up a bag but offered no reward), the "honor system" reinforcement condition was much more successful (Powers *et al.*, 1973).

A clever and effective use of positive reinforcement that motivates people to pick up litter is the "litter lottery." A litter lottery offers people an opportunity to win valuable prizes just for depositing litter appropriately. In one version of the technique (Bacon-Prue *et al.*, 1980; Hayes, Johnson, & Cone, 1975), experimenters distribute specially marked items on the ground amidst the litter that is habitually present (Figures 12–7 and 12–8). People are told some litter is marked in an undetectable fashion, and if an experimenter verifies that they have collected a marked item, they will be awarded a substantial prize. In another

Figure 12–7. Paying for the collection of litter from highways, parks, and other public places costs Americans over one billion in tax dollars per year. It is important to find ways to motivate people to pick it up. (Sherry Fisher)

Figure 12–8. Perhaps if a litter lottery were in effect, trash would not be piled up right next to a garbage can! (Sherry Fisher)

version (Kohlenberg & Phillips, 1973), the experimenter merely observes litter deposits and rewards ecologically minded people intermittently. Both techniques have achieved dramatic results toward cleaning up the environment, but both require costly human intervention. The "marked item" strategy can, however, be "automated" and introduced widely. Imagine the following scenario for improving litter control throughout the United States. Litter marked with radioactive isotopes (or in some other way) would be distributed at random, as would special trash cans (indistinguishable from ordinary ones) that would deliver valuable reinforcers automatically if a "marked item" were deposited. Whenever you had some spare time, you might find yourself absentmindedly picking up garbage, throwing it in a trash can, and fantasizing about future wealth!

In conceiving of any technique for improving environmental conditions, one should be careful to think about ways in which it could be "subverted." One problem with the litter lottery is that it may not prevent people from throwing litter on the ground—the piece they throw away can't possibly be "marked." Children participating in a litter lottery still disposed of litter inappropriately (LaHart & Bailey, 1975). On the other hand, the more garbage litter lottery participants deposit inappropriately, the more difficult it should be to find "marked" items. Adults may be aware of this contingency, and it may keep them from littering. When reinforcements are given per bag of litter collected (as in Powers *et al.*, 1973), this too may be problematic because it encourages people to pick up large but not small pieces of litter. They may not pick up litter from the target area at all, but may bring it from home. And when rewards are based on some criterion (e.g., a clean campsite), this may encourage some people to clean the area by throwing trash somewhere else.

To summarize, several strategies have been used to prevent littering, and to encourage people to pick up extant litter. Prompts and cues (e.g., signs, verbal appeals, a clean environment, availability of trash cans) may be somewhat effective antecedent techniques. They are especially effective when depositing litter is convenient, the request is specific, and certain other conditions are met. However, antecedent prompt techniques rarely improve the litter situation by more than about 20 percent. Prompts without accompanying reinforcements are *not* effective in motivating people to pick up extant litter. Reinforcements coupled with prompts or reinforcements used along with other techniques are often quite effective in facilitating a cleanup of a littered environment. In fact, their use can often effect a speedy cleanup of an environmental setting, and cleanups that account for as much as 95 percent of the litter are not uncommon. However, some such programs may be costly due to supervision and the cost of reinforcers. Also, without careful planning, reinforcement programs may be subverted.

Saving Energy at Home: Residential Energy Conservation

Another environmental issue which has received research attention is energy conservation in the home. About 20 percent of all the energy used in the United States is consumed in private residences, and much of this is wasteful (Cone & Hayes, 1980). In fact, the energy used in the "typical" American home could be reduced by 50 percent (Socolow, 1978) by making some simple physical and behavioral changes. A way to accomplish this is suggested in the box on page 364. But how can we motivate people to make these sorts of changes?

One approach to residential energy conservation has been through environmental education. Various brochures and pamphlets (see Figure 12–9) have been prepared by local utilities and by national organizations like the Federal Energy Administration. Even though people are frequently misinformed about energy use and its consequences (e.g., they believe turning down thermostats in winter will lead to ill health, or to increased energy use when "turned up" in the

THERMAL ADAPTATION AND ADJUSTMENT AT HOME

Could you "get used" to a mean winter temperature of 62°F in your home and feel as comfortable as you did at the previous setting? If you could it would certainly save money since studies show up to a 3.7 percent savings in electricity for each degree a thermostat is lowered (Socolow, 1978). A group of researchers at Virginia Tech attempted to answer that question (Winett, Neale, & Grier, 1979; Winett *et al.*, 1979). Subjects were people living in all electric homes, who were provided with a schedule for *gradually* turning down their thermostats. The schedule employed day and night setbacks, and was designed to produce the greatest conservation with the least discomfort (Beckey & Nelson, 1981). In addition to the temperature reduction "schedules," participants were shown videotapes of models enacting conservation behaviors, feedback on their electric usage, and a listing of the insulation value of different articles of clothing (see Table 12–1).

Table 12–1. SAMPLES OF CLOTHING AND ASSOCIATED CLO VALUES*

Samples of Women's Clothing			
Description	Fabric Construction	Typical Fiber Content	CLO
Underwear			
Bra		Cotton	0.02
Panties		Acetate	0.02
Long Underwear			
Tops	Knit		0.25
Bottoms	Knit		0.25
Socks and Hosiery			
Panty Hose		Nylon	0.01
Tights	Knit		0.25
Shoes			
Low Shoes			0.03
Knee High Boots, Leather			
Lined			0.30
Blouses			
Short Sleeve Blouse	Plain Weave	Rayon	0.17
Heavy Long Sleeve Shirt	Plain Weave	Wool	0.37
Pants			
Light Pants	Knit	Polyester	0.26
Jeans	Twill Weave	Cotton	0.26
Dresses and Skirts			
Heavy Skirt	Twill Weave	Wool	0.22
Sweaters			
Long Sleeve Sweater	Knit	Wool	0.37
Blazers and Vests			
Light Vest	Weave		0.20
Heavy Blazer	Weave	Wool	0.43

Warmer clothing was suggested as one way of dealing with the cooler indoor temperature, and models were shown wearing it.

The results showed that you *could* "get used" to a mean winter temperature of 62°F! Subjects who got daily feedback on conservation and/or were exposed to models successfully reduced their thermostats to an average of 62°F by the end of the study, and saved 26 percent of the energy used for heating, and 15 percent of overall electric consumption. They also expressed no change in perceived comfort from before the study, perhaps because they increased the CLO (insulation) value of their clothing by 10 percent (see Table 12–1). In contrast, subjects in a control group experienced no changes in energy use. The researchers at Virginia Tech have also shown that similar procedures could reduce electric usage in summer by up to 20 percent.

Samples of Men's Clothing			
Description	Fabric Construction	Typical Fiber Content	CLO
Underwear			
Briefs	Knit	Cotton	0.05
Sleeveless Undershirt	Knit	Cotton	0.08
Long Underwear			
Tops	Knit		0.25
Bottoms	Knit		0.25
Socks			
Light Socks	Knit		0.03
Heavy Knee High Socks	Knit		0.08
Shoes			
High Shoes			0.15
Shirts			
Short Sleeve Light Knit	Knit	Cotton	0.22
Long Sleeve Woven	Plain Weave	Polyester and Cotton Blend	0.29
Pants			
Heavy Trousers	Twill Weave	Wool	0.32
Sweaters			
Sleeveless Sweater	Knit	Orlon	0.17
Sports Coats and Vests			
Heavy Vest	Weave		0.30
Heavy Sport Coat	Twill Weave	Wool	0.49

*From Geller, E. S., Winett, R. A., and Everett, P. B. *Preserving the environment: New strategies for behavior change.* New York: Pergamon Press, 1982. Reprinted by permission.

When the heat is on . . .

- Lower your thermostat to 65 degrees during the day and 55 degrees at night. You can save about 3 percent on your fuel costs for every degree you reduce the *average temperature* in your home. In addition, you can save about 1 percent on your heating bills for every degree you dial down *only at night.*

- Keep windows near your thermostat tightly closed, otherwise it will keep your furnace working after the rest of the room has reached a comfortable temperature.

- Have your oil furnace serviced at least once a year, preferably each summer to take advantage of off-season rates. This simple precaution could save you 10 percent in fuel consumption.

- Clean or replace the filter in your forced-air heating system each month.

- Check the duct work for air leaks about once a year if you have a forced-air heating system. To do this, feel around the duct joints for escaping air when the fan is on.

- Relatively small leaks can be repaired simply by covering holes or cracks with duct tape. More stubborn problems may require caulking as well as taping. You could save almost 9 percent in heating fuel costs this way.

- If you have oil heat, check to see if the firing rate is correct. Chances are it isn't. A recent survey found that 97 percent of the furnaces checked were overfired.

- If your oil furnace doesn't run almost constantly on a very cold day, call a service man.

- Don't let cold air seep into your home through the attic access door. Check the door to make sure it is well insulated and weatherstripped, otherwise you'll be wasting fuel to heat that cool air.

- Dust or vacuum radiator surfaces frequently. Dust and grime impede the flow of heat. And if the radiators need painting, use flat paint, preferably black. It radiates heat better than glossy.

- Keep draperies and shades open in sunny windows; close them at night.

- For comfort in cooler indoor temperatures, use the best insulation of all—warm clothing.

- The human body gives off heat, about 390 BTU per hour for a man, 330 for a woman. Dressing wisely can help you retain natural heat.

- Wear closely woven fabrics. They add at least a half a degree in warmth.

- *For women.* Slacks are at least a degree warmer than skirts.

- *For men and women.* A light longsleeved sweater equals almost 2 degrees in added warmth; a heavy long-sleeved sweater adds about 3.7 degrees; and two lightweight sweaters add about 5 degrees in warmth because the air between them serves to keep in more body heat.

morning), studies have suggested that educating them is ineffective in changing energy-relevant behaviors (e.g., Heberlein, 1975; Palmer, Lloyd, & Lloyd, 1978; Winett *et al.,* 1978). For example, Heberlein (1975) gave people either a typical booklet of energy saving tips prepared by the electric company, an informational letter educating them in the personal and social costs of not conserving energy, or an informational pamphlet urging people to use *more* energy! (Actually, such appeals by profit-minded utilities are still being given today.) What were the effects of the educational strategies? None of them had any appre-

ciable effect on behavior. In a similar vein, Geller (1981) gave educational workshops on energy use and found they were very effective in changing attitudes and intentions regarding it, but follow-up audits of participants' homes revealed that changes suggested in the workshops had not been implemented. Correct information should thus be conceptualized as a necessary element in any intervention, and as something which may well affect attitudes, but it is not sufficient to promote behavior change.

Under what conditions do educational programs on home energy conservation have the greatest

If every household in the United States lowered its average heating temperatures 6 degrees over a 24-hour period, we would save more than 570,000 barrels of oil per day or more than 3.5 percent of our current oil imports.

Cooling Energy Savers

Overcooling is expensive and wastes energy. Don't use or buy more cooling equipment capacity than you actually need.

Regarding air-conditioning equipment . . .

- If you need central air-conditioning, select the smallest and least powerful system that will cool your home adequately. A larger unit than you need not only costs more to run but probably won't remove enough moisture from the air.

- Ask your dealer to help you determine how much cooling power you need for the space you have to cool and for the climate in which you live. (For further information, see page 19, Energy Efficiency Ratios.)

- Make sure the ducts in your air-conditioning system are properly insulated, especially those that pass through the attic or other uncooled spaces. This could save you almost 9 percent in cooling costs.

- If you don't need central air-conditioning, consider using individual window or through-the-wall units in rooms that need cooling from time to time. Select the smallest and least powerful units for the rooms you need to cool. As a rule, these will cost less to buy and less to operate.

- Install a whole-house ventilating fan in your attic or in an upstairs window to cool the house when it's cool outside, even if you have central air-conditioning.

- It will pay to use the fan rather than air-conditioning when the outside temperature is below 82 degrees. When windows in the house are open, the fan pulls cool air through the house and exhausts warm air through the attic.

When you use air-conditioning . . .

- Set your thermostat at 78 degrees, a reasonably comfortable and energy-efficient indoor temperature.

- The higher the setting and the less difference between indoor and outdoor temperature, the less outdoor hot air will flow into the building.

- If the 78°F setting raises your home temperature 6 degrees (from 72°F to 78°F, for example), you should save between 12 and 47 percent in cooling costs, depending on where you live.

Figure 12–9. A typical page from an information brochure. "Tips for Energy Savers," Federal Energy Administration. (Reprinted from Geller, E. S., Winett, R. A. & Everett, P. *Preserving the environment: New strategies for behavior change.* New York: Pergamon, 1982).

potential for success? An educational program for high school students, which included an energy audit and teaching students how to monitor home consumptions, positively affected student behaviors and those of parents (Stevens *et al.,* 1979). This program may have been productive because it taught *specific* conservation behaviors, not general ones. An energy audit (especially a "type A" audit in which an auditor comes to the home, makes specific suggestions and discusses them with the owner or occupant) also shows special promise, though more evaluation is needed (Geller *et al.,* 1982). And fairly often, educa-

tional strategies have positive effects when they are coupled with incentives that make it easier to engage in the practices they suggest (Stern & Gardner, 1981).

In addition to environmental education, prompts and cues have been applied to residential energy overconsumption. Winett *et al.* (1981) produced a series of videotaped programs on how to adapt to cooler temperatures at home (e.g., change thermostats gradually, wear warmer clothing, use extra blankets). Models who enacted these behaviors were rewarded (i.e., the vignette ended with them being happy with each other);

those who approached the situation inappropriately were punished (i.e., the vignette ended with them being angry with each other). To enhance modeling effects (cf. Bandura, 1977), models in the tapes were similar to the target population of viewers in age, dress, etc. Did the modeling intervention work? The answers is *yes:* Overall electricity use was down 14 percent and energy used for heating decreased 26 percent.

More typical sorts of prompts have also been applied to the problem. Television announcers may prompt us to use energy wisely, or signs in university dormitories may remind us that "Empty rooms love darkness." These procedures are certainly cheaper than some other strategies we'll discuss, but do they work? As we noted earlier in this chapter, they're more apt to if they are specific, well timed, well placed, and the behavior they request is easily enacted (Geller *et al.,* 1982). The "Empty rooms love darkness" prompt would work best if placed on the back of the door you open to leave, and if it also said "Turn off the lights when going out!" An effective use of prompts to curtail unnecessary use of air conditioners was devised by Becker and Seligman (1978). They strategically placed a light that would turn on in the kitchens of homes when air conditioning was on and outside temperatures were below 68 degrees F. The prompt indicated that air conditioning was unnecessary, and the light went off only when the air conditioner was turned off. This achieved an energy savings of 15 percent.

The energy conservation technique that has perhaps been used most successfully is an array of reinforcement-based strategies (e.g., financial payments). One set of studies using reinforcers has been done in master-metered apartments where people do not get information about their energy use and frequently don't pay for it; the other has been done in individually metered residences. An energy conservation method used in master-metered apartments is rebating all or some part of the money saved by energy-conscious residents to them. If $10,000 is saved through energy conservation in an apartment building, half

might be divided among residents, the other half kept by management. This procedure becomes more effective conservationwise as the proportion of savings given to residents increases, and when there is greater cohesion among residents (Slaven *et al.,* 1981). Walker (1979) tried another reinforcement strategy with people living in master-metered apartments. It was publicized that people with thermostats set above 74° F. in summer who had their windows closed when air conditioning was on would receive a $5.00 payment. Apartments were selected randomly for inspection, and those meeting the criteria were reinforced. This technique led to a 4–8 percent savings in energy use throughout the apartment complex.

More research has been done in individually metered residences (e.g., private homes or apartments with separate meters). Here, too, researchers have used financial incentives to motivate people to save energy. Some studies have used such reinforcers to change the *pattern* of our energy use.* To decrease peak demand in some places, financial incentives are provided (i.e., rates are lowered for consumers during nonpeak hours, and raised during peak demand). These price incentives and disincentives may be effective in switching some discretionary energy-consuming activities (e.g., washing and drying clothes) from peak to nonpeak periods, with benefits to both the utility and the consumer.

Other studies have employed reinforcers to decrease the overall amount of energy we use rather than to affect our pattern of use. Rate structures that favor low utilization by increasing the cost per kilowatt hour as consumption increases have been suggested and are employed in some states. (At present, rates *decrease* with increasing use in most areas.) Another approach to conservation has simply been to let costs rise, as is exemplified in deregulating oil and natural gas pricing in the

---

*Utilities save money when they can rely on their least expensive sources of power, which is typically the case during hours of "nonpeak" demand. When demand "peaks" they must augment their supply with more expensive sources of power. Therefore, it is advantageous to utilities to shift the pattern of energy use from "peak" to "nonpeak" periods.

United States. This approach does not seem to be very effective in reducing consumption. Doubling the price of energy leads to only a 10 percent decrease in use (Stern & Gardner, 1981). Unfortunately, little study has been done on the effects of most energy ''rate structures.'' In addition to adjusting utility rates, some studies have simply paid residents of individually metered residences to lower their energy utilization. These techniques have proven quite effective alone, and when combined with feedback (Cone & Hayes, 1980). Paying people for lowering residential energy use seems to have quite a bit of potential, yet it may be difficult to implement in a way that is cost effective. Finally, financial incentives in the form of tax credits have been offered for home retrofitting, but at current levels they are not sufficient to encourage a high level of this behavior (Stobaugh & Yergin, 1979).

In individually metered residences, the most extensively studied method of improving energy conservation has been feedback. Relatively immediate feedback may be effective in reducing energy use for several reasons (Figure 12–10). It can familiarize users with the units electricity is measured in, and strengthen the relation between patterns of use and energy-related outcomes. Feedback can tell people when they are wasting energy, and it can also reinforce (and thereby bolster) energy conserving behaviors. Often energy use feedback compares our consumption this year with the same period last year. Good feedback should correct for differences between current weather and weather during the correspond-

Figure 12–10. In institutional settings, "energy waste reminders" may function as a form of feedback.

ENERGY WASTE

REMINDER

Energy   Office

A Physical Plant staff person has found the following energy waste in your area:

1. Lights were left on.
2. Radiators and/or vents are blocked.
3. Windows were open.
4. Drapes/shades/blinds were open.
5. _____

Date: 1/25/80   Time: 6:00 A.M.   By: _____

Please help us conserve energy by turning off energy consuming equipment when not in use and by following the energy tips on the back of this card. Thank you. If you have any questions, comments, or energy saving ideas, please contact the Energy Office at X-3116.

University of Connecticut
Physical Plant Division

ing period last year, so that doing better or worse isn't an artifact of warmer or cooler temperatures. It should also focus on an individual's *own* outcomes, rather than a group's conservation outcomes. However, combining both types of feedback—our own outcomes and those of others—can be very effective (Winett *et al.*, 1979). Studies have typically given energy consumption feedback in written form—a paper with appropriate data is supplied to consumers at agreed upon intervals—though in other experiments more sophisticated feedback devices (e.g., energy meters) have been used. At present, we don't know which mode is most effective, or whether feedback on energy use is most effective if represented as a percentage change in use (compared to the previous year), the amount of money saved, absolute differences in kilowatt hours consumed, etc. (Cone & Hayes, 1980).

The more frequent the energy consumption feedback, the more conservation occurs (Seligman & Darley, 1977), though relatively infrequent feedback can sometimes be surprisingly effective (Hayes & Cone, 1981). Feedback is more effective at decreasing energy use when the cost of energy relative to peoples' income is high (Winkler & Winett, 1982). Some studies suggest that feedback is especially effective during periods of high energy use (e.g., hot humid days of summer; the coldest days of winter) (Cone & Hayes, 1980), and giving customers energy reduction goals along with feedback enhances its effects (Becker, 1978). Conservation efforts due to feedback may be retained for as long as 12 weeks after the feedback program ends (Winett *et al.*, 1981).

While feedback is often effective in reducing energy use, giving it in some forms is not cost-effective. Having someone read the meter and supply written feedback, at least on a frequent basis, can be quite expensive (Geller *et al.*, 1982). Sometimes recording and/or signaling devices (cf. Becker & Seligman, 1978) may be more cost-effective, at least in the long run. But the least expensive form of feedback is self-monitoring—teaching people how to read their own power meters and encouraging them to do it regularly. Although much prompting may be necessary to get people to do this consistently, studies show it is possible and that such procedures result in conservation (Winett, Neale, & Grier, 1979).

Overall, research suggests that feedback may be the single most effective technique for promoting residential energy conservation. Ellis and Gashell (1978) posit that to conserve energy in the home, people must be *motivated* to conserve and must *learn* how the home energy system works (i.e., what behaviors have what consequences for energy use). Thus, information and prompts do not motivate people, incentives motivate them but don't teach them the necessary relationships, and only feedback can (under ideal circumstances) provide both the motivational and informational elements necessary.

What other methods have been used to promote home energy conservation? Some residential energy conservation can be legislated. For example, Davis, California is an extremely energy-efficient town, in part due to housing codes. Building specifications require heavily insulated homes, and actually give priority in construction permits to builders with the most energy-efficient plans. They also limit the number and size of windows, specify that most must face north and south, and indicate that some windows must be shaded. If a homeowner wants more windows, he or she must "compensate" by putting in more insulation, adding water filled columns to retain heat or cold, or use concrete slab construction (*The Hartford Courant*, November 25, 1979). For an interesting additional means of conserving energy, see the box on page 371.

A final and theoretically different approach to energy savings in the home relies on the finding in social psychology that the greater one's degree of commitment to an issue (e.g., energy conservation), the more likely it is that his or her future behavior will follow. In a series of studies, Pallak *et al.* (1980) manipulated the degree of commitment homeowners had to energy conservation and measured subsequent energy use. Homeowners all agreed to participate in a study to see if home

---

THE MARKETPLACE AS A SOURCE OF ENERGY EFFICIENCY

Another way of achieving home energy savings, quite different from those we've discussed so far, involves psychological strategies to encourage people to purchase the most energy-efficient equipment that exists whenever they buy any energy-consuming device (e.g., air conditioner, water heater, automobile). If we can understand the dynamics of the purchase situation sufficiently well and structure it so people make energy-efficient purchasing choices, we'll go a long way toward solving the energy problem. Stern and Gardner (1981) have suggested that this strategy, rather than the types of techniques we've discussed, represents the best way to save energy. For example, purchasing the most energy-efficient automobile on the market today would achieve a 20 percent savings over the average car on the road, buying the most efficient heating equipment an 8 percent savings, the most efficient refrigerator about a 2 percent savings, etc.

In comparison to the savings from buying the most efficient equipment, Stern and Gardner suggest that the types of behavioral techniques focused on most by researchers often save *less* energy. For example, replacing six major equipment items with the most efficient alternatives yields an energy savings of 33.2 percent, compared to 12.5 percent from using existing devices in the most energy-efficient way. This argument is clearly interesting, and there are valuable insights to be gained from it. However, Geller (1982) suggests that the Stern and Gardner estimates of savings from efficient use may be underestimates, and that they have not considered all the energy waste involved in replacing old equipment with new (e.g., costs of disposal, energy used in the manufacturing process). Regardless of these points of contention, there is much to be said for developing psychological techniques for encouraging consumers to purchase the most energy-efficient equipment available.

---

energy could be saved. One group (high commitment) was told that the list of people in the energy conservation study would be publicized along with the experiment's results; another group (low commitment) was assured of anonymity. Subjects in the high commitment condition used less energy than those in the low commitment or control conditions, and these effects persisted for as much as six months after the study had terminated. Thus, the more committed we can make people to conserving energy, the more likely they will be to enact energy-saving behaviors.

Energy Conservation and Transportation

About 30 to 40 percent of all the fuel we use is for transportation (Everett, 1977). Unfortunately, our choices among the available forms of transport are often inefficient and lead to overuse of fuel, to problems with air and noise pollution (Chapter 4 and 5), and to other difficulties (e.g.,

ugly "strip" areas in urban and suburban neighborhoods). What means have been employed to improve energy efficiency in our use of transportation? One group of studies has focused on the inefficiency in our use of private "family" automobiles. Strategies have been directed toward reducing the overall number of miles we drive, and toward increasing the number of miles we get per gallon. Another set of studies has tried to encourage us to use more efficient forms of transportation (e.g., vanpools, instead of cars).

Let us turn first to our overreliance on the private family car, which wastes a great deal of energy compared to mass transit and ridesharing arrangements. Our general use of private automobiles corresponds in many ways to the social trap analysis we described earlier. The short-term benefits of the passenger car (e.g., privacy, prestige, speed, and convenience) accrue to the driver, while its negative consequences (e.g., pollution, furthering our energy problems) are long-range, and shared by the driver and others. Later we'll discuss how we can wean ourselves away from this energy hog and use more efficient forms of transportation. But first let us consider environmental psychologists' attempts to reduce the number of miles we travel in our cars, and to increase the number of miles we get per gallon.

If each car in the United States were driven 10 miles less per week, 5 percent of the annual demand for gasoline would be saved (Federal Energy Administration, 1977). Foxx and Hake (1977) offered subjects various rewards (e.g., cash, tours) to reduce the number of miles they drove. The rewards led to a 20 percent reduction in miles driven, compared to a control group where mileage increased by about 5 percent. In an extension of the initial study, Hake and Foxx (1978) replicated their original findings, and documented that when a leader of one type or another (e.g., a teacher, a supervisor) was in a particular experimental group, the energy savings in that group were greatly enhanced. This may prove to be a potent added force in favor of conservation for programs based in educational or business settings, for example. Other studies have found that competition between teams enhances mileage reductions, and that giving lottery tickets (instead of cash payments) can be an effective motivator to drive less (Reichel & Geller, 1980).

We could also compel people to drive fewer miles through some sort of fuel rationing. Studies of the commons dilemma suggest that rationing may lead to conservation of resources (e.g., Cass & Edney, 1978). When we divide the "commons" up, people may use their portion more carefully. There are some experiments, however, that find no effect of rationing on conservation (Stern, 1976), and whether rationing would work when applied on a broad scale is an open question. Also, from a political standpoint, rationing could be very difficult to implement.

Another approach to saving transportation energy involves increasing mileage per gallon. Laws have accomplished this by forcing automakers to market more fuel-efficient fleets, but proper driving habits (e.g., driving 55 mph, not accelerating

rapidly from a stop) can make any vehicle yield better gasoline mileage. While few studies have been done in this area, people can be motivated to improve their m.p.g. Lauridsen (1977) did a small pilot study involving feedback and a lottery. Drivers received either continuous miles per gallon feedback or the same feedback after each hour they drove. For each tenth of a gallon improvement in m.p.g. they received a ticket to a lottery, so the more they conserved, the better the chance of winning. Results were encouraging, but do not allow us to determine whether they were due to the feedback or the lottery, or to some combination of the two.

A larger scale study was run by Runnion *et al.* (1978), and involved 195 intermill and long-distance drivers for a textile company. Drivers were given instructions on how to save fuel, as well as certificates commending them when they reduced consumption. Public feedback was provided by charting fleet and individual m.p.g. each day, and peer competition was fostered by a weekly lottery in which chances to win were based on improvements in m.p.g. The program had impressive results: Mileage improved up to 9 percent, and the company saved enough money over two years to run its entire truck fleet for a month!

Although it is obviously useful for us to drive less and more efficiently, we also need to abandon our love affair with the car for more efficient ways of "getting around." These include car- and vanpools, mass transit, walking, and riding bikes. Most of the research has focused on encouraging people to join some type of "pool," or to use mass transit.

Ridesharing (i.e., either car- or vanpooling) is very efficient compared to driving to work by private auto. An average eight-passenger vanpool can save 5,000 gallons of gasoline in just one year (Pratsch, 1977)! How can we encourage people to ride together in carpools and vanpools? One way is to offer them some sort of benefit. As we mentioned earlier, this has sometimes involved providing special lanes of highways for cars with more than a particular number of passengers. Using these lanes makes for a faster, less congested commute. Most of the situations where this has been implemented have not been evaluated, but in one case, a priority lane seems to have increased carpooling (Rose & Hinds, 1976). Unfortunately, priority lanes for carpoolers are difficult to enforce: People pick up unknown others at bus stops to "qualify," and some have even bought inflatable dummies to place in the car! In addition to priority lanes, other incentives to promote carpooling have involved giving people preferred parking spaces (e.g., closer to the place they work), or offering them free or reduced-rate tolls or parking. These can have the desired effects (Hirst, 1976). Note that some of these techniques not only reward carpoolers, but make solo driving more difficult.

A major problem in starting carpools is finding others in similar locations with compatible work schedules. Many programs have tried to match people via computer matching procedures. Employees are given lists of potential carpools, and must then organize a working carpool. It is consistently found that the mere distribution of lists of names without other employer-initiated incentives does little to increase carpooling. Although employees typically express positive attitudes toward ridesharing, they rarely do it when provided with lists of convenient partners. When employers do provide incentives along with listing partners, programs can be effective (Jacobs *et al.*, 1982). However, it seems that the incentives are the major factor in this success (Geller *et al.*, 1982).

Why would you avoid joining a carpool or other ridesharing plan? The chances are that in addition to inconvenience factors (e.g., it takes longer to get to work), social factors may play a role. Carpooling is actually a social arrangement, so social aspects of the situation may be important. Barkow (1974) reported that a major impediment to carpooling is our hesitancy to deal with strangers. He found that we'd prefer to carpool with an acquaintance rather than a stranger, and if one has to carpool with a stranger, both sexes would prefer that their "poolmate" be female. Other major social impediments to ridesharing center on constraints to freedom (e.g., the neces-

sity of being "on time," and being civil to strangers on a repeated basis). To be successful, carpooling seems to require mature individuals who are flexible and willing to accommodate each other. What did carpoolers view as the major benefits? They appreciated the monetary savings, and avoiding the tension and responsibility of driving. Based on this study, one could suggest that appeals to promote carpooling could focus on lowering our fear of interacting with strangers (e.g., by allowing members to meet each other beforehand), and highlight financial savings and the relaxation of "not being in the driver's seat."

Vanpools accomplish the same conservation goals as carpools, but they are even more fuel efficient. Like carpools they necessitate fewer parking spaces at the work site and relieve traffic congestion, but unlike carpools the van often belongs to one's employer or sponsoring agency. With vanpools, income from the operation (e.g., charging customers 7 cents/mile) often pays for the program. Usually there is a van coordinator who drives the van, maintains it, bills participants, and who may make a small profit from the operation. Reactions to vanpooling have often been quite positive (Owens & Sever, 1977), and more vanpools are being "born" each year. However, before vanpools will become truly pervasive, they will have to overcome many of the social and other objections associated with carpools.

If we can't interest you in a car- or vanpool, how about riding the bus or another form of mass transit? Some studies have tried to increase mass transit ridership by adding positive elements (e.g., cost savings, offering merchandise coupons as rewards). Others have removed unpleasant aspects typically associated with mass transit (e.g., it is perceived as slow, uncomfortable, high in crime, noisy, unreliable).

Attempts to provide rewards for use of mass transit have been successful. Giving passengers hamburger coupons for buying a monthly bus pass increased sales by 86 percent in Syracuse, N.Y. (American Public Transit Association, 1975). Others have increased bus ridership by giving money to people as they entered the vehicle (Everett, 1973). Deslauriers and Everett (1977) increased ridership on a campus bus system by giving riders tokens that could be redeemed at local establishments. The tokens were passed out either to all of the bus riders, or to a preset proportion of them. Both reinforcement schedules increased ridership as compared to controls, and the lower, "proportionate" payoff schedule did not occasion lower ridership than continuous reinforcement. This suggests that less costly reinforcement schedules may often be just as effective. The trick is to find the optimal "payoff ratio."

In addition to adding reinforcers, bus ridership should increase when the punishments many of us associate with it (e.g., paying fares, crowding, a slower ride) are removed. It has been found that removing bus fares (i.e., giving people a free ride), leads to increased ridership (Everett *et al.*, 1978). Making commuting time shorter by adding bus lanes also improves ridership (Rose & Hinds, 1976). Hopefully, in the future it will be possible to remove other negative aspects from the public transit system so that more of us will participate in it.

Vandalism

While vandalism shares some characteristics with the environmental problems we've discussed thus far, there are often differences in the motivations behind it, and in the means of solving the problem. Vandalism can be defined as the "willful or malicious destruction, injury, disfigurement, or disfacement of any public or private property" (Uniform Crime Reporting Handbook, 1978, p. 90). There are several types of vandalism: *acquisitive vandalism* (looting, petty theft); *tactical/ideological vandalism* (to draw attention to oneself or to an issue of concern); *vindictive vandalism* (aimed at revenge); *play vandalism* (to combat boredom); and *malicious vandalism* (due to diffuse frustration and rage, often occurring in public settings).

How big a problem is vandalism? Its cost in American schools, parks, recreation areas, public housing and transit systems is estimated at from $1 to 4 billion per year, and the costs are increasing rapidly (Einolander, 1976) (Figure 12–11). This is more than the entire fiscal year budget of a state such as Connecticut, and doesn't even take into account the costs of physical and psychological injuries from vandalism, the inability to use facilities, the cost of alternative arrangements, etc.

Surprisingly, relatively little research has been done on vandalism. It has been found that certain *physical* and *social* conditions promote it. As discussed in Chapter 8, when the design of a setting allows residents little territorial control, vandalism becomes more common (Ley & Cybriwsky, 1974; Newman, 1972). Thus, preventative strategies could focus on increasing territorial control (e.g., designing areas to promote defensible space). Aesthetic factors associated with an object's appearance (e.g., physical beauty) also seem to affect the level of vandalism. There is some evidence that vandalism is lower when aesthetic properties of a setting are high (Pablant & Baxter, 1975). And just as aesthetic variables affect how much we enjoy socially acceptable interactions with an object, they affect the pleasure we experience from vandalizing it. Objects which

Figure 12–11. Vandalism causes extensive damage in almost every sector of society. (Peter Oliver)

break in aesthetically interesting or pleasing ways may be more apt to be vandalized than those which break in dull, uninteresting ways (Allen & Greenberger, 1980; Greenberger & Allen, 1980). Designing objects (e.g., street lights) that won't break in a satisfying manner may be another road to decreasing vandalism.

Other factors have been implicated as causes of vandalism. Allen and Greenberger (1980) suggest that low perceived control (which can have many causes) will, under certain conditions, elicit vandalism as a means of reestablishing control (for a discussion of perceived control, see Chapter 3). When we come to believe we cannot control our outcomes (e.g., college students may not feel that they have enough control over policies in the dormitories), we sometimes resort to vandalism as a way of showing ourselves and others that we can control at least certain things. This would suggest that the greater people's overall control of a setting, the less vandalism. Also, it has been suggested that vandalism results when there is a "lack of fit" between the person and the environment (e.g., school vandalism may be due to poor congruence between personal characteristics of students and the social or physical environment of

the school). According to this conceptualization, increasing the goodness of the fit through social and/or environmental means could help lower vandalism. And work by Richards (1979) has identified peer relationships (i.e., associations with antisocial peers) and adult-child conflict as major causes of vandalism by middle-class adolescents (Figure 12–12A and B). Vandalism may also occur due to financial need, in the pursuit of social causes, due to nonmalicious play, or due to poor achievement (cf. Cohen, 1973; Sabatino *et al.*, 1978).

A new, rather complete model of vandalism has been proposed by Fisher and Baron (1982). Under the concept of perceived inequity, this model encompasses many of the reasons suggested above for why vandalism occurs. What is perceived inequity? Equity theories in social psychology imply that we are socialized to believe we should treat others fairly (or equitably), and be treated equitably by others. When this does not occur (e.g., when we perceive we are being inequitably or unfairly treated), we become upset and try to restore equity. This can be done in several ways, but it typically involves our attempting to get more out of the relationship for what we put

Figure 12–12 A and B. In an attempt to inhibit vandalism, signs such as these have been placed in public settings. (Sherry Fisher)

ENCOURAGING RECYCLING VIA THE "FOOT IN THE DOOR" TECHNIQUE

In an attempt to provide detailed discussions of ways of dealing with some environmental problems, we have had to neglect others. One of those is recycling behavior. An interesting approach to encouraging recycling involves the "foot in the door" technique which has been used in some classic studies in social psychology on gaining compliance. Like the salesperson who stands a better chance of making the sale if he can only get his "foot in the door," environmental psychologists may be more apt to get people to recycle (or engage in other proecological behavior) after eliciting a small commitment from them.

The standard "foot in the door" paradigm goes like this. The experimenter first makes a small request of the subject, which very few are likely to refuse (e.g., sign a petition for a highly respectable proenvironmental cause). This is followed by progressively larger requests (e.g., recycle your soft drink containers). Because people who comply with the small, initial request come to view themselves as interested in preserving the environment, they are more apt to agree to the second, larger request than subjects who were never presented with the initial request.

Arbuthnot *et al.,* (1976–1977) used this strategy to increase recycling behavior. Their initial smaller requests were to answer survey items favoring environmental protection, to save aluminum cans for a week, and to send in a postcard urging officials to expand a local recycling program. Did being confronted with these initial requests affect long-term use of a recycling center? The answer is yes: As long as 18 months after the initial request, subjects were more apt to use the center than those not exposed to the "foot in the door" strategy.

The above findings have some interesting implications. We might view responding to prompts to turn off lights, etc. as analogous to initial requests in the foot in the door technique. This would suggest that responding to the multiple "small requests" being made of us to improve the environment these days may in some way "prime" us to comply with the larger, more important environmental demands we will face in the years ahead.

The study also suggests some potential problems with the reinforcement techniques for encouraging proecological behavior, which we've discussed in this chapter. Self-perception theory in social psychology implies that often we infer our attitudes from observing our behavior and the circumstances under which it occurs (Bem, 1972). Arbuthnot proposed that people in his study agreed to the larger requests because, after complying with the initial request, they inferred from their behavior that they had proenvironmental attitudes. Since they had no incentives for their initial compliance, they must really care about the environment. This proecological self-perception may have been why long-term changes in recycling occurred in the foot in the door study. On the other hand, what would people infer about themselves from their behavior after recycling because they were offered a sizeable financial reward or reinforcement? Bem would say that instead of inferring that they care about the environment—a conclusion that could be associated with continued recycling—they might conclude they merely did it for the money. Such a self-perception could lead them to stop recycling as soon as the rewards for it were removed.

into it, or trying to insure that the other gets less out of the relationship for what he or she puts in.

Fisher and Baron's model implies that vandalism may be one way of restoring equity in settings characterized by perceived inequity (or unfairness) between the parties. Vandalism can therefore be viewed as a way to restore equity by responding to one type of perceived rule breaking—unfairness in interpersonal relations—with another type (i.e., disregard for another's property rights). In effect, some types of vandalism say, "If I don't get any respect, I won't give you any either." What types of inequity are apt to promote vandalism? Inequity that may elicit vandalism may occur as a product of *ordinary economic exchange* (e.g., between a shopkeeper and a customer); from *discriminatory practices and inequitable rules and regulations* (e.g., between employer and employee, housing authority and resident); and from *aspects of the physical environment in and of itself* (e.g., defective machines or facilities that cause an inequitable input/output ratio). Inflexible environmental settings (e.g., windows that won't open, thermostats we can't adjust, dormitory furniture that won't move), may also make it difficult for us to receive a fair level of outcomes relative to our inputs, and may promote vandalism.

Will every instance of inequity result in vandalism? Obviously not. Fisher and Baron suggest that inequity will result in vandalism only when the person who feels inequitably treated has low perceived control—or little likelihood of influencing how equity will be restored. When we have high perceived control, we restore equity within the system (e.g., complain to the authorities), and when we have very low perceived control we become helpless and simply accept our fate. But when we have moderate to low control, we are likely to opt for a way of restoring equity—like vandalism—which is an immediate, low effort, and certain means of paying society back.

CURBING ENVIRONMENTALLY DESTRUCTIVE ACTS: AN ASSESSMENT OF THE PRESENT AND THE FUTURE

How can we sum up the state of the art that deals with applying environmental psychology to moderate environmentally destructive behavior? It is probably fair to say that the techniques discussed in this chapter give us a good start toward improving many adverse environmental conditions, but we still have a long way to go. Each of the methods we've presented has important strengths and weaknesses, and each needs to be refined and improved by researchers in the future (see box, p. 376). It is unfortunate that at present there is no overriding theory to help us conceptualize environmentally destructive behavior. Such a formulation would greatly enhance our efforts and could lead to a more focused attack by both researchers and practitioners. Finally, we should remember that the problems we face are multifaceted and complex and will certainly defy a simple solution. Therefore, we should not expect one.

Taking a broader scope, how would we evaluate the progress that environmental psychology as a field has made so far? While our current position vis-à-vis the environment is far from our ideal goal, it is in some ways quite encouraging. In just a few years, environmental psychologists have been able to identify many of the positive and negative effects of the environment on behavior and to design some important conceptual frameworks for understanding them. They have also made some efforts to develop strategies for changing our destructive environmentally related behaviors and for facilitating those that have positive effects. This, added to the facts that we are becoming more acutely aware of our environment every day and that technology is more advanced than ever before, should give great hope. But, in the end, all of us, individually and collectively, will decide our environmental future (Figure 12–13).

CHAPTER SUMMARY

Much environmentally destructive behavior can be conceptualized in terms of social traps. These are situations in which personal interests with a short-term focus conflict with societal needs with a long-term focus. For example, driving large gas-guzzling cars, littering, and purchasing nonreturnable bottles are all forms of social traps. How can we escape from such traps? In this chapter, environmental education, use of environmentally relevant prompts, reinforcement-related techniques, and other methods are considered as potential means of altering environmentally destructive behavior.

Each of these techniques has unique costs and

Figure 12–13. If we preserve our environment, it will undoubtedly be a source of great pleasure to us. (Sherry Fisher)

when the reinforcement contingency is withdrawn.

After reviewing the major techniques for dealing with environmentally destructive behavior, we considered specific strategies used to cope with littering, energy overconsumption, and vandalism. Some of these offer promise of significantly improving aspects of our environment.

Suggested Projects

1. Design an environmental education program that you feel would have an optimal chance of effectively changing behavior in an environmentally constructive direction. Use whatever media you like, focus on whatever population you desire, and choose a target behavior that corresponds to your area of major interest in environmental psychology.

2. Select an environmentally destructive target behavior on your university campus, and design a prompt that would help alleviate the problem. If you can get the necessary permission from authorities, attempt to test the effectiveness of your technique.

3. Test Cialdini's hypothesis that a setting with a single violation of a norm serves as a more effective prompt than one with no evidence of norm violation. Some possible subjects for your investigation are shopping carts at a local supermarket, graffiti in a rest room, or vandalism in a university building.

4. If you have lived in a college dormitory, design a program (using the techniques described in this chapter) to help alleviate noise. You may use the study we reported by Meyers and his colleagues as a jumping-off point, but try to use your own experience as a dormitory resident to form hypotheses and to structure your program.

benefits. Environmental education seems to be a relatively ineffective method at this time. However, future research may reveal situations in which it may lead to positive results. The use of environmentally related prompts is somewhat effective and relatively inexpensive. Finally, reinforcement techniques (positive reinforcement, negative reinforcement, punishment, and feedback) appear to be most effective, although they have several drawbacks. For example, reinforcement techniques may be quite expensive, and there is evidence that the effects often disappear

Appendix

Methodological Approaches to Environmental Psychology

David R. Mandel

INTRODUCTION

Much of the information in this book is derived from systematic investigations performed by environmental researchers. These investigations use both general research methods common to the social sciences (which you may have studied in previous courses), and methods unique to environmental psychology. Chapter 1 briefly outlines the many methodological perspectives from which environmental research can be initiated, and subsequent chapters deal with the results of various studies and their interpretations. The purpose of this Appendix is to describe in more detail the variety of research methods and techniques that have been utilized in the study of environmental psychological problems. This is not intended to be a "how-to" manual, but a discussion of the various research strategies and measurement techniques available to the environmental researcher. A thorough reading of this Appendix should provide you with a basic understanding of the variety of ways that environmental psychologists study phenomena. If you desire additional information on environmental methodology, supplementary readings are included at the end of the Appendix.

Research in environmental psychology is somewhat different from research in other areas of psychology. One important distinction is that the physical environment is of central concern to investigators. Physical environmental variations are systematically examined as part of the research instead of being eliminated or controlled, as they are in other areas of psychology. For example, research on crowding frequently varies the size of the room as its central experimental manipulation (see Chapter 7). Similarly, environmental psychologists might study how high and low levels of environmental stimulation affect different personality types. In contrast, social psychologists studying attitude change would take pains to ensure that room size and environmental stimulation were constant under all experimental conditions.

Another special characteristic of environmental psychology is the way in which research methods are chosen. In some research endeavors, methods tend to be selected primarily because they have been used by earlier investigators. In environmental psychology, many of the issues of interest to the researcher have not been previously investigated, so the choice of methods used may not be dictated by previous research. This allows for a greater variety and novelty in the strategies chosen. One hallmark of such an approach is the frequent use of multiple-method research strategies. This is because a single method often cannot fully answer the question the experimenter is studying. For example, Baum and Valins (1977) investigated the effects of architectural variations in dormitories on interpersonal behavior by using three quite different methodologies (field, laboratory, and simulation techniques). Each allows a different view of the problem, as we will see when we review these techniques later.

Environmental researchers also tend to use a range of outcome measures, instead of only a single measure when investigating the effects of experimental conditions (Altman, 1978). It is probably fair to state that environmental psychologists, more than other psychologists, adopt this strategy. For example, Aiello, Epstein, and Karlin (1975a) measured the effects of high density dormitory living on four different dimensions (perceptual, observational, physiological, and medically related measures). Researchers in environmental psychology are also more concerned with the longitudinal effects of phenomena (that is, with studying reactions over time) than are researchers in some other fields (Altman, 1978). Thus, it is not uncommon for them to assess the long-term effects of environmental conditions at various intervals, rather than to rely on single measurements taken at a particular time. Finally, the methods used in environmental psychology tend to be more interdisciplinary than those employed in other areas of psychology (Altman, 1978; Proshansky, 1972). This approach probably developed because environmental psychology transcends many traditional disciplinary boundaries and has involved researchers from other fields (sociology, geography, anthropology), who come armed with their own techniques.

This Appendix is divided into four major sections. First, we will consider several criteria for evaluating the adequacy of any research design. These criteria should be considered whenever we plan research or assess the value of studies we may be reading. Next, we will discuss the various types of research methods that are available to the environmental psychologist. Our coverage will include methods in which the experimenter creates the conditions that will be studied (experimental research), methods that assess relationships between naturally occurring environmental variations and various response dimensions (correlational research), and methods that report reactions that occur in a particular environmental context (descriptive research). Third, we will focus on some of the measurement techniques and instruments that have been employed by researchers. Finally, we will discuss ethical concerns confronting anyone who engages in environmental research.

EVALUATING THE ADEQUACY OF ENVIRONMENTAL RESEARCH

There are a number of important criteria that should be considered in planning and evaluating research in environmental psychology as well as in other areas of psychology. These criteria may be conceptualized as validity issues. Broadly viewed, validity is an index of the extent to which the research was able to measure what it was intended to measure. Because the concept of validity is really more intricate than this, we can best understand it by dividing it into smaller components. We will discuss four types of validity: internal validity, external validity, construct validity, and experiential realism. Each deals with an important element of the overall validity of envi-

ronmental research (Cook & Campbell, 1979). It should be remembered that the four validity criteria apply to *all* of the design methodologies that will be covered in this Appendix.

Internal Validity

Internal validity is concerned with whether an observed relationship between two or more variables represents a "real" finding, or whether it was caused by spurious variables not taken into account by the investigator. Simply stated, internal validity determines whether or not research findings permit a clear causal inference. For example, suppose a researcher finds that people stand closer to liked than to disliked others (see Chapter 6) and assumes that attraction leads to close interpersonal positioning. If the experiment is properly designed, this is probably the case. However, other conditions not accounted for by the study might be causing the differences. What if the researcher measured the distance between people who liked each other in a bar (where people are spatially constrained) and measured the distance between people who disliked each other in a park (where people are not constrained)? Such a study would have low internal validity, since it is likely that the relationship observed was caused by the differences in the settings and not by being liked or disliked.

Some common threats to internal validity are differences in the experimental procedures from one group to the next (as occurred in our example), bias in the selection of subjects for the groups being compared, and use of inaccurate measurement techniques. In an experimental design, random assignment of subjects into experimental groups (those receiving some planned change or manipulation) and control groups (those not receiving the planned effect) helps alleviate certain threats by ensuring that all subjects have an equal likelihood of assignment to each condition. In field studies, in which random assignment is not always possible, the researcher must be more aware of possible alternative causes for the effects observed.

Construct Validity

A second criterion is construct validity, which is important when attempting to use the results of a study to draw conclusions about a theory or model. In such research, investigators often assume that the variables being studied are representative of particular aspects of the theory. However, sometimes the variables, as manipulated, do not adequately represent these elements. To the extent this is true, construct validity, or the ability of the study to adequately test the theory, is said to be low. Perhaps an example will give you a better grasp of this notion.

Assume that a researcher wishes to test a theory that "high social density" produces decrements in performance for those in the setting. The inves-

tigator decides that high social density will be represented by six people in a 7 ft. x 6 ft. room, and assumes that the performance of people in this condition will constitute a test of the theory. However, the leap from experimental results to conclusions about theory is questionable, because there is no direct means to confirm that six people in a 7 ft. x 6 ft. room actually constitutes an adequate representation of the *construct* of "high social density." One way to bolster construct validity is to test alternative arrangements which should create different intensities of social density and see if performance is affected based on the severity of the various conditions.

External Validity

A third dimension on which research is assessed is external validity, or the extent to which the results of an experiment can be generalized from the context in which the study was done to other contexts (i.e., to other populations, settings, and times). Note that although construct validity is concerned with generalizability of the data to theoretical issues, external validity is concerned with generalizability of the data to other settings. This type of validity tends to be low when the population, setting, and time in which a study was performed are not representative of other populations, settings, and times. High external validity is of particular importance in the area of environmental psychology because the results of research potentially have direct design and behavioral applications. External validity tends to be a problem in environmental research done in laboratory settings because such research generally lacks the realism of the natural environment. It can also be a problem in field research, if subject populations are not representative of the larger population.

Experiential Realism

A final validity consideration may be termed experiential realism (Patterson, 1977). Experiential realism is a joint function of the extent to which the experimental manipulation, as operationalized, has impact on the subject and is representative of events that occur in the real world. Imagine yourself participating in an experiment studying community planning, in which your job is to cut out buildings from cardboard, tape them together, and place them appropriately on an artificial-looking map of a community. How valid do you think your responses would be? According to Patterson, when subjects are asked to respond to highly artificial variables or operations within settings that have no correspondence to their everyday life, the experiential realism of the situation suffers and the validity of people's responses are suspect. (For a discussion of the relationships between the various types of validity, see the box on this page.)

RESEARCH DESIGN METHODOLOGIES

Having explored validity criteria for evaluating environmental research methods, we now turn to a discussion of the methods themselves. Note, however, that validity concerns will be discussed further in the context of the material presented in this section. Our discussion will begin with a brief overview of each of the three primary research methods used by environmental psychologists: (1) experimental methods; (2) correlational methods; and (3) descriptive techniques. Follow-

ing this overview, we will describe in some detail the various individual methods subsumed under each category.

Briefly, *experimental methods* employ a fairly standard and rigorous set of procedures. First the investigator manipulates, or varies, the independent variable, which is the condition whose effects are being studied. For example, to study the effects of spatial density on perceptions of crowding, the independent variable might be two different size rooms with an equal number of people in each. This variation in density is assessed by a dependent variable, which is the reaction of interest (such as, whether people say they are more crowded in one room than the other). In addition to the independent and dependent variables, experimental procedures generally involve random assignment of subjects, appropriate control groups and other components of this method (Cook & Campbell, 1979; Kerlinger, 1973). These characteristics of experimental methods, while safeguarding internal validity and allowing for a clearer interpretation of cause and effect from the results, typically create an artificial atmosphere which leads to low external validity and low experiential realism.

The second category, *correlational methods*,

INTERRELATIONSHIPS AND "TRADE-OFFS" BETWEEN THE FOUR TYPES OF VALIDITY

While the distinctions we've drawn among the four types of validity may make them appear to be independent of each other, in actuality they are closely intertwined. Consequently, maximizing one type of validity may reduce another (Cook & Campbell, 1979). For example, to increase internal validity, one is apt to choose a highly controlled laboratory experiment, in order to minimize the extraneous variables that can interfere with causal inferences. Unfortunately, this approach reduces the degree of external validity in the study. Such "trade-offs" suggest that, depending on the purpose of the study, the experimenter must place a value on one type of validity relative to another. If theory testing is of primary importance, internal validity should receive first priority, followed by construct validity and external validity. A highly controlled laboratory or field experiment would be appropriate in this case. On the other hand, perhaps a researcher wants to investigate whether an effect will generalize to a variety of settings and has little interest in isolating its cause. In this case, external validity has a higher priority than internal validity, and less rigorous field research methods may be in order.

capitalizes on naturally occurring variations, and typically involves research in "real world" settings, where experimental rigor may not be possible. For example, a researcher might study reactions to naturally occurring variations in density at a train station. In this context, the experimenter does not manipulate the independent variable, cannot randomly assign subjects to conditions, and may not be able to exercise complete control over measurement of the dependent variable. Such research tends to be low in internal validity (and low in ability to make causal inferences), since experimental rigor has not been maintained.

However, the researcher is generally able to gain a degree of knowledge about the causal relationship between the variables. Some relatively sophisticated statistical approaches to correlational data, such as path analysis and linear structural modeling (see Jöreskog & Sörbom, 1978; Kenny, 1981), may even allow for the estimation of causal results and interpretation. In general, correlational research in environmental psychology can be designed to be both high in external validity and experiential realism since it tends to involve real world contexts.

The third category, *descriptive research*, is generally conducted in real world settings, but it provides information neither about causal relationships among variables nor about correlations among them. Instead, it describes reactions that occur within the environmental context. Since descriptive research is not constrained by a need to infer causality or association, it can be quite flexible methodologically. Typically, it involves having subjects describe their reactions to an environment via questionnaires or interviews, or observing people's behavior in a particular setting. Descriptive research is frequently employed to gain initial insight into an area being investigated before more formal data are collected, or it is used after the formal research has been conducted to better understand the results. It is also used when it is not possible to implement other methods, yet the researcher believes that the situation justifies some systematic investigation.

Experimental Research: When the Researcher Creates the Conditions

Laboratory Experiments. Research that applies traditional experimental methodologies to investigate environmental problems has generally been conducted in laboratory settings. This research has been able to study closely the effects of many environmental variables. For example, research by Glass and Singer (1972) clearly demonstrated the effects of *control* on reactions to unpredictable noise (see Chapter 4). In these studies, subjects in a laboratory room were exposed to noise and had an opportunity to control this stimulation by using a response button. As you may recall, it was shown that the negative consequences of exposure to unpredictable noise can be attenuated if an appropriate means of control is afforded. Owing to the nature of the phenomenon and the need to systematically isolate individual causes, it is probable that only laboratory experimentation could have provided such a clear interpretation.

Although laboratory experiments have contributed to the development of environmental psychology, these methods have also shown significant limitations. As we mentioned earlier, they are often characterized by low external validity and low experiential realism. Thus, it may be naive to expect to understand complex environmental phenomena by looking at the effects of a somewhat artificial representation of reality on simple dependent measures. A good example of the limitations of laboratory research comes from examining research on high density. Laboratory studies of this phenomenon often show no effects or an absence of significant findings, while field studies demonstrate stronger effects. This is not surprising, since subjects in a laboratory are exposed only briefly to high density and know that they will soon be able to leave the setting. Even when effects are observed under such "short-term" conditions, it is questionable whether subjects are actually experiencing crowding stress or just reporting feeling crowded based on the size of the room or group (Epstein & Baum, 1978). In one innovative experiment, Epstein, Woolfolk, and Lehrer (1981) were able to repeatedly expose subjects to high density laboratory settings over a three-week period, thus allowing for more extended density experiences and the ability to test for habituation to high density conditions. Even so, the dependent measures used in such experiments are typically designed for that setting, rather than being representative of everyday life (Altman, 1978). These restrictions limit generalizability of findings to real world situations.

Field Experiments. As a partial answer to some of the problems inherent in laboratory experimentation techniques, such as lack of realism, researchers have suggested conducting experiments in field settings. This procedure retains randomization of subjects and manipulation of the independent variables (and thus the ability to make causal inferences), while affording the experimenter a realistic look at how people respond to a variety of environmental conditions. Although relatively few field experiments have been run by environmental psychologists due to the difficulty of experimenters being able to manipulate independent variables or randomly assign people to conditions in a "real life" setting, those that have been conducted demonstrate how causal interpretation of the data can be accomplished within natural environments. However, it should be noted that the demands of experimental design typically produce some artificiality in the field. Hence, field experiments are sometimes not as externally or experientially valid as field studies that capitalize on naturally occurring variations.

An example of the value of field experimentation is provided by a study of territoriality conducted by Edney (1975). In general, research on territoriality has been difficult to carry out in the laboratory, because it requires the experimenter to induce feelings of ownership in subjects. Since territoriality already exists in one's home environment, Edney decided to run a field experiment using students' dormitory rooms as the laboratory. He randomly assigned half the subjects to their own room (the "resident" condition) and half to

the rooms of other students as "visitors." Subjects performed a variety of tasks within this context. The results, reviewed in more detail in Chapter 6, showed that people experience more control when on their home ground than when visiting the territory of another, and perceive their own territory as more pleasant and private. More important for our present purposes is that Edney successfully used a naturalistic setting to observe an environmental phenomenon and to study its effects in a systematic causal manner. Because subjects were randomly assigned (i.e., to resident and visitor conditions), a degree of control was established over extraneous variables. Experiential realism and external validity were enhanced by the field setting, so this study represents the best of both experimental and field research.

Simulations. For a variety of reasons, researchers intent on increasing external validity and experiential realism over traditional laboratory research are often unable to do research in the field. One common reason is the inability to locate an appropriate field setting. This may be due to excessive cost, time restrictions, geographical constraints, or other elements that enter into the feasibility of performing research in the "real world." Another problem is that it is seldom possible to attain the degree of experimental control achieved by Edney when using actual settings. Some researchers have responded to these problems by using simulation methods, either by creating a "near real" setting or by introducing components of a real environment into an artificial setting. By simulating the essential elements of a naturalistic setting in the laboratory, experiential realism and external validity are increased, and experimental rigor is generally retained. In the paragraphs to follow, we will review only a few of the many simulation techniques used by environmental psychologists. It should be remembered that simulations can be constructed to test the effects of almost any environmental variable.

An interesting example of a simulation technique is an experiment performed by Baum and Greenberg (1975), who studied the effects of crowding using two confederates and a subject. The experimenters created a situation in which the subject believed that either a small or a large number of others would be participating in the experiment. This deception was accomplished by a manipulation of the number of instructional sheets, pencils, and clipboards, and by a speech that caused the subject to believe that others would be arriving shortly. Because it is difficult to find crowded situations in the real world that allow the experimenter a degree of control, simulation is especially valuable in this area. Baum and Greenberg's procedures produced results similar to those of the more traditional crowding studies, and their simulation had the economic benefits of using fewer people and taking less time.

Another form of simulation that has been employed in crowding research involves the use of *model rooms*. Basically, the researcher constructs a scale model of a room. He or she then manipulates characteristics of this setting (e.g., by moving partitions) and asks subjects to place "people" (represented by clothespins with tacks on the bottom) in the room until they perceive it to be uncomfortably crowded (e.g., Bell & Barnard, 1977). The rationale for this type of simulation is the assumption that to the extent that settings make people feel crowded, subjects will place fewer figures in them. In an early study using this technique, Desor (1972) varied the shape of the room (rectangular versus square), the location of the doors and windows, and the size of the partitions. The variations in the model rooms did yield differential crowding responses by subjects (the specific details of her findings are reviewed in Chapter 7). It should be noted, however, that model rooms have been only partially successful in replicating the results of studies conducted in real environments (see Epstein & Baum, 1978). Some problems stem from subjects' inability to accurately experience the setting they are judging because of its small size and the absence of tactile and olfactory stimulation. Subjects also may be unable to become involved with the situation presented in the model room or to identify with the behaviors and spatial needs of each setting. Note

that some of the same problems have arisen when simulations are used in research on personal space (see the discussion in Chapter 6).

Obviously, simulation techniques are useful for studying aspects of human–environment behavior other than crowding. One area of environmental psychology, discussed in Chapter 2, is concerned with how people perceive their environment and what factors affect their preference for various settings. Clearly, it would be impractical to study these phenomena by driving subjects around to a variety of places and having them make ratings; yet, at the Berkeley Environmental Simulation Laboratory, people can be "driven through" suburban neighborhoods or urban blocks by means of a large-scale environmental simulator (McKechnie, 1977). One of the elements in the lab consists of a scale replica of the environment placed on a large platform. Suspended overhead is a gantry on which the camera can move in any direction and give the viewer an "eye-level" perspective while moving around the model. With the increased sophistication of computers and computer-aided design systems, sophisticated simulations using computer graphic representations of various environments for research purposes should not be far in the future.

A more conventional means to experimentally view the natural environment is by showing subjects photographic slides of a wide range of settings. In such a simulation, researchers might vary the complexity of urban and rural slides (Kaplan, 1974; Wohlwill, 1976) that subjects are asked to rate. This would provide information about how complexity affects preference in urban and rural contexts. Overall, slides offer several advantages as a simulation of the real environment: They are easy to present to a small or large group, they are inexpensive to produce and obtain, and they allow a wide variety of scenes to be shown at one time.

An underlying assumption in this form of simulation is that slides constitute accurate reproductions of the human-made and natural environments and can therefore be used in their place. Some interesting research provides support for this contention. A study conducted by Seaton and Collins (1972) had subjects rate color slides, black and white film, videotape, and actual settings on several dimensions. It was found that the ratings agreed fairly closely across modalities, which was taken to mean that using simulation techniques is as good as using the real environment. However, a series of studies by Danford and associates (Danford & Willems, 1976; Danford, Starr, & Willems, 1980) cast a shadow on these findings and other confirmatory results. The authors concluded that the measures used to assess variations among modes of presentation were not sufficiently sensitive to pick up differences that may have existed. Other problems with pictorial simulations include the following: Slides present only a small angle of what would be seen if one were physically present; people do not "scan" slides as they do the actual environment; and simulations arbitrarily determine what is to be viewed.

Correlational Studies: Capitalizing on Naturalistic "Manipulations"

Some of the most interesting research in environmental psychology has resulted from assessing the effects of natural variations in environmental conditions. Unlike field experiments, this type of research does not manipulate environmental occurrences or prescribe who should be involved as subjects. In addition, events occurring prior to the involvement of the researcher and concurrent actions of other factors in the setting may interfere with the conclusions that are drawn. Thus, studies that are initiated using naturally occurring variations may be open to questions of internal validity and often do not encourage strong causal inferences. Overall, the degree of realism and the quality of information that can be obtained in the real world challenge the investigator to subject naturally occurring phenomena to research methods that are as systematic as possible. In this section, we will discuss correlational strategies that may be used to investigate naturally occurring events.

Field Studies.   Field studies differ from field experiments in that the researcher cannot randomly assign subjects to conditions and has no power to manipulate the independent variables. As in field experiments, the researcher attempts to discover the effects of variations in environmental conditions (naturally occurring ones in this case) through the use of various measuring instruments. However, it is important to note that since experimental rigor is absent, the internal validity problems discussed earlier generally make it impossible to infer causality. Thus, field studies usually should be considered as yielding valuable information but not definitive causal evidence.

An example of a field study is an investigation by Sundstrom *et al.* (in press) on whether office workers' privacy differed by job functions and by the types of work space they had. Privacy measures, collected through questionnaires completed by the workers, and work space type, observed by the investigation team, indicated that the best single predictor of privacy was the number of partitions surrounding the workers' space. Clearly, the study lacked strict experimental standards, and alternative explanations could be made. However, the demand of true experimentation in this case (i.e., randomly assigning workers for extended periods of time to a variety of work space types) is typically out of the question, so that while this research must be interpreted cautiously, it offers good evidence on the issue.

As we have stressed, we can seldom make causal inferences when we are not able to manipulate experimental conditions or randomly assign subjects. However, field study designs that limit such threats to internal validity are available. These are called "quasi-experimental designs" (Cook & Campbell, 1979; Christensen, 1977). The "quasi" in quasi-experimentation refers to the attempts made to create controls that are as close as possible to those used in true experimentation, thereby retaining the ability to approximate causal inferences from the results. Thus, while noncausal field research is certainly respectable if nothing better is available, the astute field researcher or scientist involved in evaluation research is always on the lookout for a quasi-experimental design that is applicable to the experimental context (see the box on page 388 for more details on quasi-experiments). It should be noted, however, that while quasi-experimentation is superior to field studies, it is not nearly as desirable as true experimentation.

Descriptive Research: Telling It Like It Is

In addition to experimental research and correlational research, another method for assessing the effects of environmental conditions is through descriptive studies. As noted earlier, descriptive research typically allows neither causal inferences nor measures of relationships (correlations). It does not lend itself to traditional statistical analysis, yet it is valuable in its own right as a means of evaluating reactions to particular sets of environmental conditions. Its use is prompted to a great extent by the phenomena being studied. As Proshansky (1972, p. 455) stated, the environmental psychologist "must be [concerned at this point] with searching out the dimensions and more specific properties of phenomena involving human behavior in relation to physical settings." Thus, for now we must often answer such basic questions as, "What are the patterns of space utilization?" before using more sophisticated methodologies to test for underlying causes.

An example of such an exploratory investigation is Barker's observational study comparing the behavior settings in two towns, "Yoredale" and "Midwest," as discussed in the box on page 14. The experimenter obviously did not manipulate any aspects of the towns being compared and certainly couldn't randomly assign towns to conditions. Thus, any findings that accrue from such a comparison must be considered descriptive; it may not be said that any particular aspects of the towns caused the differential types and numbers of behavior settings that were observed. Nevertheless, the findings of the study are interesting and important in their own right.

Another descriptive study investigated whether people's life styles were reflected in the physical design of their homes (Weisner & Weibel, 1981). Through interviews with various family members and systematic observations of the home, researchers were able to derive a discrete number of dimensions that characterized the home environment. These were later used to compare various homes and life styles, and the results indicated that life style *was* related to the physical design of one's residence.

Up to now, we have discussed experimental, correlational, and descriptive research. Before moving on to cover the measurement techniques used with these, refer to the box on page 390 which discusses one type of research—evaluation research—which can employ experimental, correlational, or descriptive methods, and another—social impact assessment—which is generally descriptive.

THE MEASUREMENT TECHNIQUES

We have presented a wide range of research designs and methods for gathering information about behavior in the physical environment. In this section, we will discuss various *measurement techniques* that may be used with almost any of these methods. These techniques range from some that are common in all areas of psychology to others that are specific to environmental psychology. To help you keep track of the various methods to be discussed, refer to Table A–1 throughout this section. As can be seen, the methods are listed within subcategories along the left side of the table. A representative author who used the technique and some aspects of its use are listed in the vertical columns. These studies are meant to illustrate the use of the techniques and are not necessarily exemplary. Since the scope of this Appendix permits us only to describe each technique briefly and to cite some relevant examples, additional references are cited at the end of the chapter.

Self-Report Measures

A method frequently used for collecting information about individuals involves self-report or sur-

SOME EXAMPLES OF QUASI-EXPERIMENTAL DESIGNS

To give you an idea of what a quasi-experimental design entails, we will briefly describe several examples. A more complete discussion and additional examples may be found in Cook and Campbell (1979), and Christensen (1977). The symbols used to describe each design in the examples are relatively simple. *Y* signifies the dependent measure, and *X* signifies the experimental treatment. Subscripts represent the number of times the measure has been given, if it has been repeated.

Design 1 is frequently used in research when random assignment of subjects into experimental or control groups is not possible, as when comparing redesigned institutional facilities in one town with a nontreated control institution in another town. The design is the same as a true experimental design, with the important difference that subjects in the experimental and control groups are probably dissimilar in some ways. A nonequivalent control group is clearly better than none, since it potentially eliminates a variety of alternative explanations for experimental results. For example, changes in national policy that dictate small design adjustments in institutions would affect both the experimental and the control groups equally and thus be eliminated as an alternative explanation for experimental findings. However, a nonequivalent control group is never as good as an equivalent control group. Because of the nonequivalence of the experimental and control groups, we might expect them to respond differently at times, even in the absence of an experimental treatment.

In Design 2 (time series), the researcher takes a number of premeasures over time before the occurrence or administration of treatment and then takes several measures, again over time, after the treatment. The results are examined for any discontinuities in the measures from the pre- to the post-series. This method eliminates many threats to internal validity, except for history (events that intervene between observations). Unfortunately, however, statistical tests with time series designs are relatively difficult to perform.

An interesting example of the use of a time series analysis is a study on the impact of water conservation measures in a California town (Maki, Hoffman, & Berk, 1978). Owing to an increase in population during the 1960s, the water supply had become inadequate. A moratorium was placed on new water hookups, water use was restricted, and an educational program on water conservation was implemented. A time series analysis was used to look at changes before and after the implementation, to see if a modification of usage had occurred. The analysis made use of monthly data on water consumption for the seven years preceding the moratorium and for three years after. As can be seen in Figure A–1, a discontinuity was observed in the level of consumption at the point of the moratorium. This accounted for an average reduction of 15 percent over the three years, even though it appears that the trend was being reversed by 1976.

vey procedures—techniques in which people offer information about their behaviors, attitudes, or feelings to the investigator. These procedures include questionnaires, interviews, rating scales, and projective techniques (e.g., cognitive mapping). Self-report measures can be contrasted with another form of data collection, "non-self-report," in which information is collected without

1. NONEQUIVALENT BEFORE–AFTER DESIGN

	Pretest Measure	*Treatment*	*Posttest Measure*
Experimental group	Y_1	X	Y_2
Control group (nonequivalent to experimental group)	Y_1		Y_2

2. TIME SERIES DESIGN

Pretest Measures				*Treatment*	*Posttest Measures*			
Y_1	Y_2	Y_3	Y_4	X	Y_5	Y_6	Y_7	Y_8

Figure A–1. Time series graph showing the relationship of water consumption over a period of 10 years. (This figure is reprinted from Judith E. Maki, Donnie M. Hoffman, and Richard A. Berk, "A Time Series Analysis of the Impact of a Water Conservation Campaign," *Evaluation Quarterly*, Vol. 2, No. 1, February 1978, with permission of Sage Publications, Inc.)

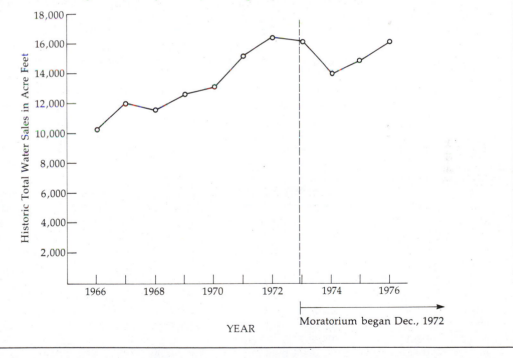

depending on the subject's own interpretation. Such data generally come from behavioral and physiological measures that entail some form of observation and recording by the investigator.

Self-report measures are frequently prepared by the investigator to meet the needs of a specific study. Alternatively, the researcher can use self-report measures that are standardized instruments

STUDIES WITH POLICY IMPLICATIONS: EVALUATION RESEARCH AND SOCIAL IMPACT ASSESSMENT

Many changes that are made in the environment (e.g., urban redevelopment) have important policy implications, and research that assesses these holds important information for policy makers. If it is to have impact on future policy, environmental psychology must direct research to such issues and must present its findings in a form that is comprehensible to those in policy-making positions. Two research methods that are attempting to supply such policy-relevant data are *evaluation research* and *social impact assessment*. We will describe each of these techniques below. In terms of the categories of research in this Appendix, it should be noted that evaluation research may be correlational, experimental, or descriptive, while social impact assessment tends to be only descriptive.

Evaluation research in environmental psychology is concerned with assessing the effects of ongoing environmentally relevant programs or events, on the social and physical welfare of participants. In effect, the researcher attempts to find out whether or not the project being implemented is attaining its goals. An example is a study by Knight, Weitzer, and Zimring (1978) that assessed the consequences of a significant change in a large state institution for the mentally retarded. The project investigated the effects on both patients and staff of converting open-ward dormitory buildings into private and semiprivate rooms. Important questions addressed by the reseachers included whether the severely mentally retarded would use the now more private areas, if other aspects of patient behavior would change, and what effects, if any, the staff would experience. Using a longitudinal design (i.e., a design that permits plotting behavior change over time), residents and staff were observed during five periods over a year and a half. Initial results indicated that the new environment did produce mildly positive effects on the behavior and attitude of the residents and on their relationships with the staff.

In contrast to evaluation research, which concerns itself with ongoing programs, social impact assessment in environmental psychology is the prediction and evaluation of the social effects of projects while they are still in the planning stage (Wolf, 1975). It is an anticipatory form of research that attempts to answer questions about the future impact of environmental innovations on the population. This type of investigation is becoming increasingly popular and is frequently a necessary part of projects sponsored by the federal government. The process of impact assessment is presented in the following example.

Before plans to construct the John F. Kennedy Library in Cambridge, Massachusetts were implemented, an impact assessment was conducted (Francis, 1975). A first step was to identify those groups of people who might be affected by the library complex. They were categorized as those who currently used the environment for living, shopping, and working, and those who would be future users (researchers, visitors, and staff). Each group was seen as having distinct needs and differing degrees of involvement with the project. Thus, the impact of the library complex would vary for each group. Some major effects that had to be predicted were number of visitors, level of traffic, land values, and aesthetic and ecological problems. Data were collected from a great variety of sources and included economic and environmental information gathered by experts in their respective areas. Although the report concluded that the project would have no detrimental effects on the community, for a variety of reasons it generated a major controversy in Cambridge. This example points up a peril in both environmental impact assessment and evaluation research—the tremendous affective involvement of particular population subgroups. Thus, the investigator must be content with performing the research in as technically correct a manner as possible, realizing that it is impossible for the conclusions to please everyone.

Table A–1. A TAXONOMY OF MEASUREMENT TECHNIQUES*

Measurement Technique	Author	Human–Environment Interrelations and Dimensions Tapped	Measurement Device Used
Self-Report			
Questionnaires			
Standardized	Moos and Gerst	Social climate of dormitories	University Resident Environment Scale
Nonstandardized	Onibokun	Attitude, preference	Questionnaires
Interviews			
Structured	Lynch	Perception of urban setting	Interviewer and tape recording
Unstructured	Cooper	Attitudes toward housing	Questionnaire for interviewer
Rating scales			
Check list	Epstein *et al.*	Mood, affect	Mood adjective check list
Bipolar adjective	Fisher	Environmental quality	Questionnaire
Semantic differential	Mehrabian and Russell	Perception, attitudes	Questionnaire
Other methods			
Model rooms	Desor	Perception of classroom	Scale models with furnishings
Cognitive mapping	Saarinen	Perception and attitudes	Questionnaire and blank paper for drawing
Non-Self-Report			
Observational			
Behavior setting	Bechtel	Environmental activity	Observation system
Behavior specimen	Bechtel	Daily activity	Trained observers
Behavior mapping	Ittelson *et al.*	Location of activity	Coding forms for observation
Instrumentation			
Still photographs	Hansen and Altman	Amount of wall decoration	35 mm camera
Time lapse	Davis and Ayers	Movement patterns	Time lapse super-8 camera
Video taping	Preiser	Movement patterns	Video tape recorder
Electrodermal tests	Aiello *et al.*(a)	Physiological arousal	Skin conductance level
Biochemical tests	Aiello *et al.*(b)	Physiological arousal	Urine samples
Hodometer	Bechtel	Behavioral movement	Electrical microswitches
Task Performance	Sherrod	Success on cognitive tasks	Test instrument
Indirect Measures			
Erosion	Webb *et al.*	Wearing of physical features	Observation and measurement
Accretion	Geller *et al.*	Anti-litter instructions	Counting and observation
Running records	Newman	Crime and architecture	Existing records
Episodic records	McCain *et al.*	Illness and density	Existing records

*From Lozar, C. C. *Methods & measures in man-environment interactions: Evaluations and applications*, Part II. D. Carson, Ed. Copyright © 1974, by Dowden, Hutchinson & Ross, Inc. Stroudsburg, Pa. Adapted by permission of the publisher.

(i.e., surveys designed and tested on samples of similar populations under similar circumstances), or may adapt sections of existing instruments to better suit the needs of the study. Because most researchers have specific questions to ask, they generally design their own self-report measures. For a variety of reasons, such measures can present problems. For example, the researcher may not be able to properly pilot-test the items to see if they are understood as they are intended. Under these circumstances, the way in which concepts are understood may elicit misleading answers to questions that the researcher thinks are clear. Research by Mandel, Baron, and Fisher (1980) found that when given a choice between two definitions of crowding, one dealing with too many people in a setting and the other stressing limited space, men chose both about evenly, while women chose the former definition more often than the latter one. The importance of this finding is that subjects responding to self-report measures may have different ideas than the experimenter about what these terms mean, and subjects may even differ from each other in interpretations. One way to overcome this problem, at least in part, is for experimenters using self-reports to define for subjects what they mean by such words as *territory, personal space, privacy,* and *crowding*.

Other problems also arise when self-report measures are designed to meet the needs of a specific study. For example, not all researchers in a given content area (e.g., crowding) have used the same self-report items, which makes it difficult to compare their research. Often, this may be the cause of discrepancies in the results of studies, rather than conceptual differences in the manipulations themselves. Further, a problem common to all types of self-report methods (standardized and nonstandardized), except for the open-ended interview, is that in giving subjects a choice of responses, we may lead them to label their reactions along these dimensions rather than along those they feel are truly appropriate. In effect, asking subjects how crowded they feel offers them a label on which to peg an emotion, but it does not necessarily tell the researcher that they truly feel crowded. Having considered some general properties of self-report measures, we now turn to a discussion of some specific self-report techniques that have been used by environmental researchers.

A UNIQUE SELF-REPORT METHOD: THE TIME BUDGET

How can we collect accurate data on how people spend their time in various settings? When subjects are given a standard questionnaire or interview and are asked to describe their activities over a period of time, their memory is typically rather inexact. Since accurate data are of great concern to researchers interested in how people use the time they spend in different settings, a technique called the time budget or activity log has been developed. This is essentially a diary kept either for periods of time specified by the experimenter or for all the subject's waking hours. The instrument should be so constructed as to be simple to fill out, while yielding information correctly and accurately.

Figure A–2 is an example of a page from a time budget (Michelson & Reed, 1975). This form is fairly open-ended, allowing the user to record times after each activity listed. It affords greater accuracy than the standard interview and is much less expensive than another alternative—sending in an observer to record a subject's behavior 24 hours a day. Try to use the time budget in Figure A–2 to record your activities in a common environmental setting. When you review the observations, you may be able to use the "data" to reassess some of your activity patterns for greater efficiency and enjoyment!

Figure A–2. A time budget recording sheet. (From Michelson, W. and Reed, P. In W. Michelson (Ed.), *Behavioral Research Methods in Environmental Design.* Stroudsburg, Pa.: Dowden, Hutchinson, & Ross, 1975.)

Questionnaires. Questionnaires represent a wide range of self-report paper-and-pencil techniques used to obtain direct information from subjects. Not surprisingly, questionnaire items are generally formulated as queries into various areas. Items may call for factual responses (e.g., demographics, recall of activities), as well as emotive responses (e.g., attitudes, values, and beliefs). There are several "pluses" in using questionnaires for data collection. They are easy and relatively inexpensive to produce and distribute, they require little skill to administer, they can be given to a large number of subjects at a time, and they afford anonymity. As with all self-report measures, there are both standardized and nonstandardized questionnaires.

An example of the *standardized* questionnaire is a set of measures designed to assess "social climate" (Moos & Gerst, 1974). These questionnaires have been pretested to ensure that they are answered reliably over time and in similar situations, and that they are valid (i.e., measure what they profess to measure). Specifically, the social climate scales assume that social institutions have "personalities" representative of the type of activities and interactions that occur in the setting. Thus, they contain measures to index social climates in industrial, academic, residential, military, and treatment settings, each containing between 90 and 100 items and measuring 7 to 10 dimensions. An example is the URES, The University Residence Environment Scale, which is summarized in Table A–2.

With *nonstandardized* questionnaires, on the other hand, the researcher generally decides on the dimensions for which information is needed and constructs questionnaires to elicit the necessary data. As noted earlier, there are a number of problems inherent in the use of nonstandardized measures. However, they are often necessary, since the stock of standardized questionnaires for environmental researchers to draw on is quite small.

How would you, as a researcher, go about constructing questionnaire items? There are a wide variety of ways in which to ask questions of sub-

jects. If the investigator is using the questionnaire as an exploratory device to seek "possible" answers, then *open-ended* questions may offer a range of useful information. Open-ended questions allow subjects to supply additional information that is important to them or that would give depth to their initial response. There are, however, several problems in using this format as an exclusive way of gaining information. Often, subjects may not wish to take the time or effort to reply to open-ended questions, especially if they include a large number of items. Also, they may not be able to express themselves accurately on the dimensions on which they are asked to respond. It is also frequently difficult for the investigator to categorize and code open-ended responses, especially if there is a wide range of answers. Content analysis procedures are available—some even computerized—that may be of assistance in organizing open-ended data responses (Kerlinger, 1973).

One way to circumvent some of these problems is to use open-ended responses in pilot studies which are then used to create *directed* or *closed* questions in which the experimenter offers a range of possible answers to the subjects. The use of multiple-choice or matching responses from a specified list of alternatives offers the investigator a more concise list to code and interpret. What some researchers do in order to allow a partially open-ended response to a question is to offer an "other" category, which the subjects may fill in if none of the response choices fit. Unfortunately, this type of category is often subject to the same problems as open-ended questions. Thus, it is best to do sufficient pilot work to ensure that the response options provided by the questionnaire are as complete as possible.

Interview Techniques. The interview technique is often overlooked by environmental researchers who wish to use self-report measures. Like questionnaires, interviews may be standardized or nonstandardized and may contain open-ended or directed questions. They may also be divided into structured and unstructured methods.

Table A–2. SUMMARY OF SUBSCALE CONTENTS FOR THE UNIVERSITY RESIDENCE ENVIRONMENT SCALE*

Subscale	Relationship Dimensions
Involvement	Degree of commitment to the house and residents; amount of interaction and feeling of friendship in the house.
Emotional Support	Extent of manifest concern for others in the house; efforts to aid one another with academic and personal problems; emphasis on open and honest communication.

	Personal Growth or Development Dimensions
Independence	Diversity of residents' behaviors allowed without social sanctions, versus socially proper and conformist behavior.
Traditional Social Orientation	Stress on dating, going to parties, and other "traditional" heterosexual interactions.
Competition	The degree to which a wide variety of activities, such as dating and grades, are cast into a competitive framework.
Academic Achievement	Extent to which classroom and academic accomplishments and concerns are prominent in the house.
Intellectuality	Emphasis on cultural, artistic, and other scholarly intellectual activities in the house, as distinguished from classroom achievements.

	System Maintenance and System Change Dimensions
Order and Organization	Amount of formal structure or organization (e.g., rules, schedules, established procedures) in the house; neatness.
Student Influence	Extent to which student residents (not staff or administration) perceive they control the running of the house, formulate and enforce the rules, control use of the money and selection of staff, food, roommates, and policies.
Innovation	Organizational and individual spontaneity of behaviors and ideas; number and variety of activities; new activities.

*Reproduced by special permission of the publisher, Consulting Psychologist Press, Inc., From the University Residence Environment Scale Manual, by Rudolf Moos and Marvin Gerst, Copyright 1974. Further reproduction is reprinted.

An unstructured interview is perceived as somewhat informal, with a few lead-in questions but little in the way of specific probes. The subject is allowed to speak as he or she wishes, with the interviewer intervening only for clarification or redirection. An example of this type of technique is Lynch's (1960) work on how people perceive the image of the city (see the box on page 231 of Chapter 8 for more details). On the other hand, a structured interview (or interview schedule) has specific objectives on which the questions are based. Cooper (1971) performed an extensive

case study of a low-income housing project. As a way of gaining background information and in order to develop a comprehensive questionnaire, she asked specific questions about the needs and values of the residents. Even though the questions were open-ended, the structure (asking similar items of each respondent) enabled her to amass a great deal of data that could be compared across individuals.

Interviews offer several advantages over questionnaires. First, a subject can explain any inconsistencies in responses, if the interviewer feels the initial answers are too vague or are uninterpretable. Suppose the investigator is using the measure to explore possible explanations for a behavior, or to expand the range of possibilities of which he or she is aware. People may be more likely to speak their opinions than to write them down. The interviewer also has an opportunity to establish rapport with individuals who may be averse to filling out forms. On the negative side, interviews may be much more costly to implement than questionnaires, especially if a large number of subjects are involved. If time is a problem, they may be worth doing only if a large staff is available. Further, interviewers may sometimes unwittingly transmit nonverbal cues, which subjects might interpret as approval or disapproval of what they have said. This may affect subsequent responses. Finally, subjects may perceive that they have less anonymity in interviews than in questionnaires, which may lead to more ''socially desirable'' responses.

Rating Scales. A specialized self-report instrument often used by itself as well as in questionnaires and in interviews, is the rating scale. In this technique, scaling procedures are used to record subjects' impressions of objects or of other people on a number of dimensions that are relevant to the research. Like closed-ended questionnaires, the dimensions for which ratings are being made are always fully specified. The most common procedure is to assess what is being rated (e.g., a dormitory) on a scale with a continuum that can be numerically coded. Often, a series of such scales is linked together in order to get a composite view of the target of the ratings (i.e., in order to rate the target on an array of related dimensions). Like questionnaires, rating scales may be standardized or nonstandardized.

Examples of standardized rating scales that have been used to assess affective states in environmental research include the Subjective Stress Scale (see Emiley, 1975), and Nowlis Mood Adjective Check List (see Epstein *et al.*, 1981). Some other standardized rating scales are intended to measure people's preferred level of environmental stimulation (see Zuckerman, 1971) and to obtain their description of architectural forms, as shown in Table A–3 (Hershberger & Cass, 1974; Kasmar, 1970).

The most common form of rating scale is the *bipolar adjective scale,* an example of which is presented in Figure 1–10, page 15. Bipolar adjective scales can be designed to suit the researcher's

Table A–3. SEMANTIC SCALES USED TO MEASURE DESIGNED ENVIRONMENTS*

Factors	Primary Scales	Alternative Scales
General evaluation	Good–bad	Pleasing–annoying
Utility evaluation	Useful–useless	Friendly–hostile
Aesthetic evaluation	Unique–common	Interesting–boring
Activity	Active–passive	Complex–simple
Space	Cozy–roomy	Private–public
Potency	Rugged–delicate	Rough–smooth
Tidiness	Clean–dirty	Tidy–messy
Organization	Ordered–chaotic	Formal–casual
Temperature	Warm–cool	Hot–cold
Lighting	Light–dark	Bright–dull

*From Hershberger, R. G. and R. C. Cass. Predicting User Responses to Buildings, in *Man-environment interactions: Evaluations and applications,* Part II, D. Carson, Ed., Table A. Copyright © 1974 by Dowden, Hutchinson & Ross, Inc., Stroudsburg, Pa. Reprinted by permission of the publisher.

particular needs and are a relatively common means of obtaining a subject's impressions of a variety of aspects of an environment. In this procedure, subjects are instructed to check an appropriate point along a line on a number of categories, ranging from one extreme of an attribute to the other. You have probably filled out one or more bipolar adjective scales if you've ever participated in a social psychology experiment.

One specialized form of the bipolar adjective scale is the *semantic differential rating technique*. This procedure is intended to derive the *connotative meaning* of what is being rated (Osgood, Suci, & Tannenbaum, 1957) by having subjects check off a point on a bipolar adjective continuum, based on how well it describes the setting they are rating. Osgood and his associates found that when a large number of adjectives are used, three conceptual components are represented by the scale. Some items describe evaluative aspects of what is being measured (e.g., good–bad), some measure potency (e.g., strong–weak), and some measure activity (e.g., active–passive). Other researchers have created their own semantic differential scales, such as the scale by Mehrabian and Russell (1974) designed to assess emotional states. This scale is shown in Figure A–3.

Some criticisms have been made of the use of rating scale methods in environmental research (Bechtel, 1976). One problem centers around the differential information afforded by those scale items that are "denotative" and those that are "connotative." Denotative refers to objective descriptions of the setting or activity. Connotative adjectives describe secondary qualities of the setting (e.g., "arousing–dull") and represent an affective or expressive dimension of the subjects' perceptions. While connotative adjectives may describe one's feeling about a particular setting, they tell the researcher little in terms of the specific properties that cause these responses. Since one objective of environmental research is to locate and identify the properties of the environment that cause such feelings, connotative items tell only half the story. The researcher must then infer the relationship between the affective terms and the actual setting. Finally, the connotative–denotative problem is exacerbated by items that

Figure A–3. Semantic differential scales for measuring emotional state. (From Mehrabian, A. and Russell, J. A., *An approach to environmental psychology*. Cambridge, Ma.: M.I.T. Press, 1974).

Pleasure

Happy	----:----:----:----:----:----:----:----	Unhappy
Pleased	----:----:----:----:----:----:----:----	Annoyed
Satisfied	----:----:----:----:----:----:----:----	Unsatisfied
Contented	----:----:----:----:----:----:----:----	Melancholic
Hopeful	----:----:----:----:----:----:----:----	Despairing
Relaxed	----:----:----:----:----:----:----:----	Bored

Arousal

Stimulated	----:----:----:----:----:----:----:----	Relaxed
Excited	----:----:----:----:----:----:----:----	Calm
Frenzied	----:----:----:----:----:----:----:----	Sluggish
Jittery	----:----:----:----:----:----:----:----	Dull
Wide awake	----:----:----:----:----:----:----:----	Sleepy
Aroused	----:----:----:----:----:----:----:----	Unaroused

Dominance

Controlling	----:----:----:----:----:----:----:----	Controlled
Influential	----:----:----:----:----:----:----:----	Influenced
In control	----:----:----:----:----:----:----:----	Cared for
Important	----:----:----:----:----:----:----:----	Awed
Dominant	----:----:----:----:----:----:----:----	Submissive
Autonomous	----:----:----:----:----:----:----:----	Guided

have a double meaning, being at times connotative and at other times denotative. For example, "hot–cold" may refer to a feeling one has about a setting based upon the color and the use of materials in a room, but it also may refer to the actual thermal comfort of a setting.

Other Self-Report Measures. In addition to questionnaires, interviews, and rating scales, other techniques constitute "self-report" measures that can be used to gain information about responses to the environment. For example, simulations (which were discussed previously in the context of experimental methods) can also be used solely for having subjects report their impressions of the environment. The same types of model rooms used to evaluate the effect of environmental modifications on crowding can also be used to have subjects construct scale models of the environment as they perceive it. For example, third-grade students were trained by a teacher and an architect regarding what the characteristics of an "ideal" classroom should be (van Wagenberg, Krasner, & Krasner, 1981). The students then created a series of models of their ideal settings, first on paper, then with blocks and cans, and finally in cardboard. These measures are of value because they are a way for subjects to express nonverbally how they feel, how they perceive the environment, and even how they would like to alter it.

Another form of self-report measure is cognitive mapping, which is used to create "maps of the mind" (see Chapter 8). Through a variety of procedures, described in the box on page 398 such images are transposed to paper. Cognitive maps are extremely valuable to researchers as a means of understanding how people code spatial information about their everyday environment. In addition to examining the mapping of city environments, studies have looked at how college campuses, local neighborhoods, and even nations are perceived. Through the use of these techniques, perceptions of various demographic groups can be measured and compared, and factors that afford qualitatively different perceptions

can be identified. While these data-gathering methods can be extremely valuable, some criticisms have been leveled at cognitive mapping. These also are presented in the box on page 231.

Pros and Cons of Self-Report Measures. Like any instrument, self-report measures are better for some forms of data-gathering than others (see Margulis, 1981 for a more detailed discussion). Self-report measures allow investigators to analyze a large number of interrelated issues, such as the many factors that relate to people's attitudes toward their residences. They are also one of the best means of obtaining people's opinions at various points over a period of time. Self-report measures can be highly valid and reliable indices if the questions being asked are salient to the respondents and if the issues covered are not too complex or abstract. Finally, self-report procedures can obtain information from a large number of people in a relatively brief period of time.

Self-report techniques also have a number of drawbacks, as discussed by Marans (1975). First, one is not able to directly observe, measure, or analyze ongoing processes. Collecting survey data is a static process of measuring what a person thinks and feels at a particular time and location, and such opinions may or may not reflect long-term beliefs. Second, the technique relies on the individual's memory, which may be far from accurate in the recall of specific components of settings or events. Third, surveys are not very useful in providing information about unknown users of an environment. For example, if one is involved in the planning of an innovative design for a building, it may be difficult to predict its effectiveness and acceptance without experiencing it for a time. A fourth problem concerns whether attitudes (the "output" of much survey research) are good predictors of behavior. This has been the source of an active debate within psychology (data on this issue are summarized in Chapter 2). A final concern is the "reactive" nature of surveys. People may not wish to answer certain questions honestly or may feel that specific types of responses are being demanded from them. One obvious means of circumventing these problems is to augment survey data with information acquired by other means (i.e., to take a multi-method approach).

Non-Self-Report Measures

Non-self-report measures hold an important place in environmental psychology. Since much of the field's research is directed toward investigating individuals and groups in natural surroundings under ordinary conditions, the obtrusiveness (use of overt methods) of self-reports may bias or cover up the effect the researcher wishes to investigate. While self-report measures are mainly attitudinal or perceptual (i.e., reflecting the overt concerns of the people studied), non-self-report measures are observations of behavior or behavioral outcomes—of how individuals actually perform, rather than how they would like to perform, or how they think they performed. Non-self-report measures may be either obtrusive or unobtrusive, depending upon how the experimenter structures the data collection.

Observational Techniques. A major measurement technique in environmental psychology, probably second in use only to questionnaires, is direct observation. In this method, people view others and record their behavior and interactions in a given setting. This technique can take many forms, ranging from informal observation of an environment, to a recorded narrative of what is seen, to structured observation in which areas of the setting are preselected, and particular behaviors are recorded on special coding forms (see Lofland, 1973). Note that earlier in this Appendix we discussed observation as a means of performing descriptive research. We refer to it here as a non-self-report measure that can be employed in experimental, correlational, *or* descriptive studies.

The advantage of observational methods over other techniques is the opportunity to gain first-hand knowledge of the way people behave in natural settings (see box, below). Unlike self-report measures, which assume subjects are able to express themselves, observational methods measure actions people may not even be aware they are

---

BEHAVIOR MAPPING: OBSERVING PEOPLE IN PLACES

Few techniques are available to observe and record information about a large number of people in a given area. From such a mass of activity, an interpretable measure of behavior must be constructed. One specialized means of accomplishing this task is *behavior mapping,* which is concerned with accurately recording people's actions in a particular space. In this technique, observers record the behaviors occurring in one or more settings with the use of a preconstructed coding form developed through a series of steps (Ittelson, Rivlin, & Proshansky, 1976). First, the area to be investigated is defined. It may be a large hospital ward, a series of classrooms, or even a single room. The observers initially make narrative observations of the behavior occurring in the setting, either by taking notes or by tape-recording their impressions. From this information, categories of behavior and interactions are organized and listed on a coding form. Using such forms, the observers code actions that occur in each area of the setting during the period of research.

Behavior mapping can serve a variety of purposes (Ittelson *et al.*, 1976). It may be used to describe behaviors in the setting. In this context, schemes can be developed to code interactions among specified individuals and also to index the type of interaction and where it is taking place. Mapping may also be used to compare behaviors occurring in different situations and settings or behaviors in the same setting at different times of day. It is also a means of learning about the utilization of equipment and facilities (e.g., whether areas are used as intended). Finally, behavior mapping can be employed to predict the use of new facilities.

performing. They can also be used with those who are unable to communicate their thoughts, such as young children and the severely mentally retarded. Since they may be used without the subject's knowledge, they minimize those responses that are reactions to being watched.

Although they offer many benefits, observational methods have a number of disadvantages that are worthy of mention. One is that human error may be made in coding behavior. For example, misidentifying one behavior for another, or being unable to code all the activity because it is occurring too quickly, can damage a study. Observational methods are also time-dependent, which means that the investigator must be present when the behavior under study is taking place. This can often be inconvenient and time-consuming, especially for behaviors that are infrequent. Some of these problems can be alleviated through the use of instrumentation (e.g., photographic equipment), which will be discussed in the next section. Finally, as with any measure, observations may be misused. For example, if the categories used to code behaviors and interactions are too broad or abstract, the observer is forced to make inferences about what is being observed, which can increase error in the recording.

Probably the most famous of the observational techniques used by environmental researchers are the *behavior setting methods* developed by Roger Barker (1968), which are described in Chapter 3. Barker employs 64 observational scales, which are coded by a team of trained observers over a period of 12 months. Observational sessions usually last for 30 to 45 minutes, and samples are taken during various times of the day over a period of a year. The technique involves observers who comment on the type of activities and social interactions that are occurring. What is recorded is left up to the observers, though guidelines are set, and the observers have been trained in the process. The relatively unstructured format allows the observer to list unusual or curious events that may later prove helpful in describing the workings of the behavior setting or any problems within it.

Another technique developed by Barker (Barker & Wright, 1955) is the *Behavior Specimen Recording Method*. This is one of the more taxing observational methods, for it entails continuously observing an individual over a period of time (an entire day, for example) and keeping a complete record of that person's activities, conversations, and behaviors, as well as any comments the observer may have. The data are later dissected into behavior episodes, distinct social units that can be coded in terms of who is interacting with whom, during what activity, and for how long. These episodes can then be analyzed along with other aspects of the behavior setting, such as the number of rooms in a home, how they are used, and the occupant's attitudes toward his or her environment. Such an analysis may permit investigators to determine if the setting can be better organized for the uses that are made of it.

Barker's techniques are still being used by environmental researchers to aid in the design of new facilities and for evaluations of existing settings. Bechtel (1977) not only discusses some current uses for these techniques, but has also published the various measures and instructions for their use.

Concerning more structured forms of observation, researchers have used techniques both in the laboratory and in the field to record nonverbal behavior related to comfort, stress, emotion, movement, and choice. Hutt and Vaizey (1966) observed brain-damaged, autistic, and normal children in high, medium, and low spatial and social density settings. The behaviors the experimenters were interested in included aggressive actions, such as fighting and snatching or breaking toys, movements to different locations in the room (e.g., to the boundaries or the center), and the number of social encounters. One finding suggested that both brain-damaged and normal children became more aggressive when in large groups. Another example of structured observation is a study by Fisher and Byrne (1975). In this research project, experimenters observed where males and females placed books and personal effects in a library, considering this to reflect the space each sex preferred to "block off" against intruders. As indicated in Chapter 6, men positioned their books and personal effects predominantly in front of themselves, while women placed such objects at their sides.

Instrumentation. There are times when human observation is not the most productive, economical, or feasible way to collect data. For example, Lozar (1974) pointed out that behavioral events may be sporadic, taxing the attention of the observer and wasting time in long waits with little opportunity to collect data. Also, some studies need sophisticated on-line feedback to computers or physiological equipment. Instrumentation is required in these cases, since it can be directly attached to the subjects in order to measure biological functions. Finally, the area being observed may be too large for one or even several individuals to cover. In this case, the researcher must either create a device that will do the job or choose from available instruments.

One type of instrumentation that functions quite well as a surrogate observer is photographic equipment. With the increasing availability of photographic supplies at reasonable cost, photographs, movies, and even videotapes are being widely used by researchers. Photographs and slides were discussed earlier as part of simulation research, but they are even more versatile as observational instruments and collectors of data. These media preserve records of the environment and events in it for future reference. They may be viewed repeatedly, even for different purposes and different studies.

Davis and Ayers (1975) listed a number of uses for photographs. First, they may be used to inventory the physical environment. For example, Hansen and Altman (1976) employed photographic records of dormitory room walls to code the types of posters and (using a superimposed grid) to estimate the extent to which the walls were covered. Second, photographic techniques offer the investigator a means of counting the number of occurrences of a behavior or the number of people in a given setting. In one study, Preiser (1973) video-

taped a large suburban shopping center and later coded the tape to determine the number of persons in particular areas. Third, photography can be used to identify and investigate selected details of activity. For example, a study by Baxter and Deanovich (1970) employed the camera to record personal space between subjects. Fourth, sequential experience recording can be performed accurately with movie film, which has a constant rate of frames per second. In one study, Davis and Ayers (1975) investigated pedestrian flow on an airport escalator. They were able to sequentially record visual searching by those coming off the escalator, progression into the movement system, and other multiple behavior sequences. Finally, photographic techniques offer supplementary information to be used in reporting a study. Baron *et al.* (1976), in conducting their investigation of high density living in dormitories, documented a typical example of a high density room (see Figure A–4, which speaks for itself).

Another case in which instrumentation functions as a surrogate observer is with physiological measures. Direct physiological measurement is often used to record arousal or stress in subjects

Figure A–4 Crowded dormitory room at a major university. (Fred Malven)

as a function of environmental conditions. One well-known measure, galvanic skin response, records changes in the skin conductance levels. Aiello, Epstein, and Karlin (1975a) used this technique to demonstrate that high density in a laboratory situation causes increased physiological arousal. One problem, however, is that electrodes must be attached to the subject, which is hardly unobtrusive. Also, subjects need to have a base rate against which the test results are compared, and this may be difficult to obtain. A second physiological technique that offers evidence of long-term stress is biochemical analysis of urine samples. Aiello, Epstein, and Karlin (1975b), in a field study of the effects of high density living, took two samples over time from a group of subjects and observed a change in stress as a result of crowding. Other physiological indices that have been used include the Palmar Sweat Test, which measures arousal as indicated by the opening and closing of pores on finger tips; the electrocardiograph, which measures heart rate; and other devices which measure heart functions through the pulse. In the future, radiotransmitted tracking will make it possible to monitor the physiological functions of people as they move about. At present, though, such tracking equipment is expensive and only good for short ranges.

A very interesting type of instrumentation that was created for a specialized purpose (mapping the standing and movement patterns of museum visitors) is the hodometer. Invented by Robert Bechtel (1970), the device consists of pressure-sensitive pads covering the entire floor of the room. Counters are attached by cable to each of the pads, so that every time someone walks on a pad, the counter increases by one. Figure A–5 shows a grid of a hodometer with the frequency of steps in each box. The darker shade indicates greater use.

Finally, engineers, architects, and designers have developed techniques to measure the full range of ambient conditions, such as the amount of light, noise, temperature, humidity, and air motion (see Rubin & Elder, 1980 for a description of these measures). Some of the methods are

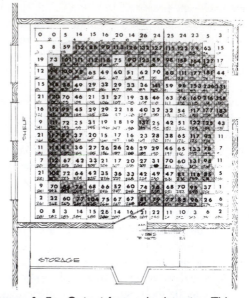

Figure A–5. Output from a hodometer. This device measures locomotion through areas by using pressure-sensitive foot pads attached to recording devices. (From Srivastava, R. and Peel, T. Human movement as a function of color stimulation, Environmental Research and Development Foundation, 1968. Figure 4, p. 25.)

inexpensive and easy to learn to use. Since environmental psychologists study the physical setting as well as the behavior occurring within it, ambient conditions are critical measures in studies that must either control for these factors, or systematically manipulate them. As an example, Weinstein (1980) measured noise levels on the street of a heavily trafficked urban neighborhood as a means of selecting subjects who lived close enough to the noise to be affected by it.

Task Performance. Besides the variety of non-self-report measures we've discussed thus far, there are circumstances in which researchers want to know if the environment is having an effect on subjects' specific abilities to perform. For example, it is important to know if conditions such as high-volume intermittent noise, confinement in isolation, high levels of density, and thermal extremes cause people to perform at a less than optimal level. Tasks used to assess environmental effects on performance may deal with manual dexterity and eye–hand coordination, with performance on cognitive tasks, or with virtually any other aspect of performance. One important thing to keep in mind is that if we wish to posit an underlying cause, such as stress, for poor performance scores, we should have specific background data indicating that the task is stress-sensitive. We will discuss only a few tasks used in environmental research, although a brief search through the literature would reveal many others.

One task used to test environmental consequences on performance is the Stroop Color–Word Test. Subjects are given a sheet of paper on which the names of colors are printed in the same color of ink as the color name as well as in a contrasting color of ink. Subjects are then asked to read aloud the ink color of each word. The competing response between the word color names and the ink color names makes the task more complex than one would think. Time spent on the test and number of errors are then tabulated and are assumed to constitute a measure of how environmental conditions affect performance. A greater number of errors is considered to be indicative of increased stress.

Another performance measure involves testing the persistence subjects have in a given task before becoming frustrated (see Chapter 4). This has often been done by using a frustration tolerance task developed by Feather (1961). In this measure, which is also discussed in relation to Glass and Singer's (1972) noise research in Chapter 4 (see also Figure 4-9, page 108), four line drawings are presented on separate pieces of paper. Subjects are given each type of drawing and are told to trace each line without going over any line twice and without lifting the pencil from the sheet. If they make an error, they are to start on a new form. Subjects are also told that if they complete a particular form or give up on it, they should go on to the others. Unknown to them, however, two of the puzzles are insoluble, and constitute the measure for frustration tolerance. All the experimenter has to do to measure persistence is count the number of discarded forms.

In addition to cognitive performance tasks, motor tasks have also been used in environmental research. In testing the effects of chemical pollutants in drinking water, Rotton, Tikofsky, and Feldman (1982) gave subjects small samples of water with chemicals typically found in municipal water supplies and then had them perform two simultaneous tasks: tracking a target on an oscilloscope by moving a lever back and forth, and monitoring a series of blinking lights. Results indicated that those people receiving "polluted" water were less attentive at their tasks.

Indirect Measures. A final set of non-self-report measures is classified as "indirect," because these data are usually collected after the behavior in question has occurred and the subject is no longer in the setting. Some of these measures may be deemed historical. For example, old records may be investigated to produce evidence for a hypothesis of historical importance. But such data may also be only a few days or even a few hours old. Indirect measures are clearly unobtrusive (which makes the data nonreactive), since the subject does not know that he or she is producing data for research purposes. However, because the investigator lacks control not only over subject selection and randomization but also over environmental factors and record keeping methods, these findings must be examined with caution and are best used to support or verify data collected by other means.

Webb and his colleagues (1966, 1981) sorted indirect measures into two classifications, the first of which is *physical traces*. Physical traces are evidence that can be interpreted as clues to specific actions (e.g., cigarette butts in an ashtray or a half-filled water glass are standard detective novel clues that someone has been using a room). They can be subdivided into two categories: erosion and accretion. *Erosion* of areas in a physical setting is apparent from age and use. Webb *et al.* reported the popularity of a chick-hatching exhibit at a science museum, as evidenced by the increased wear of the floor tiles only in that part of the building. Wear patterns in the lawns of your university campus may show where sidewalks *should* have been constructed.

Accretion measures are the opposite of erosion; they signify the deposit of materials in the physical environment. For example, littering may be seen as an indication of the perceived quality of a setting and of the perceived degree of personal responsibility for it. A study by Geller, Witmer, and Orebough (1976) varied the antilitter message on the bottom of handbills that were given to shoppers in a grocery. By counting the number of handbills deposited in the proper receptacles (a measure of accretion), they were able to show that when shoppers were given the location of trash cans, they were more apt to dispose of the paper properly. Patterson (1978), while studying the issue of fear of crime in the elderly, counted the number of visible markers (signs such as "No Trespassing," barriers such as fences, viewing devices in the doors, and personalized items such as welcome mats) as indications of territoriality. His findings indicated that greater territoriality was related to less expressed fear of crime.

In addition to the physical traces of erosion and accretion, a second category of indirect measures is *archival records*. Archival records are documents that may never have been intended to be studied. Such data may be rich in information not obtainable by the researcher in any other way; yet there are questions of whether the recording is accurate and unbiased. Archival evidence may be divided into two groups: running and episodic records.

Running records are archival data collected over time. They may be grouped into four sources: actuarial, political-judicial, other government-related (e.g., traffic citations), and mass media (e.g., advertisements). These records, some of which are well documented, have been used in various contexts in environmental psychology. For example, Newman (1972) used the records of the Public Housing Bureau and the New York City Police Department to relate architectural variations to crime. This research is described in detail in Chapter 8. Other examples are sociological–correlational studies, which look at variations in density in urban centers and relate them to various social pathologies (see Chapter 7).

The second type of archival measure is the *episodic record*. This is usually private or restricted documentation kept for specific purposes. It may be a diary or a financial record of an individual, sales records of a shop, or school records of faculty or students. One study of the effects of long-term high density living used episodic records as a major dependent variable. McCain, Cox, and Paulus (1976) looked at the effects of living in dormitory-type prison cells versus individual cells. They found, by checking the records of the prison infirmary, that convicts in dormitory facilities had a greater number of illnesses than those in single cells.

ETHICAL CONSIDERATIONS IN ENVIRONMENTAL RESEARCH

Before concluding this Appendix, we should suggest some of the ethical problems and considerations that arise in all environmental research. As you may have noticed, many design and measurement techniques require that the subject be unaware that an investigation is taking place. Clearly, this frequently improves the validity of research in a number of important ways, which we discussed earlier. Unfortunately, however, it also raises a number of serious ethical problems.

In 1953, the American Psychological Association (APA) issued a statement on ethics in research, which has been revised since then. Many general texts on social research have devoted entire chapters to ethics (Carlsmith, Ellsworth, & Aronson, 1976; Christensen, 1977; Selltiz *et al.*, 1976), and environmental psychology is also beginning to address this concern. In addition, the United States Department of Health and Human Services has issued directives concerning protection of human subjects when environmental research is being performed under a government grant or contract. Many colleges and universities have peer review boards to advise the investigator on difficult ethical issues in research design.

Many ethical considerations appear relevant to environmental research. Two that are especially important are lack of full and informed consent by the subject and invasion of privacy. We will limit our discussion to these topics, but the interested reader is encouraged to seek out other sources. As we progress with our discussion of ethics, try to get a feeling for your own position on the various issues.

Informed Consent

One of the APA ethical principles states that whenever possible, subjects should be informed of all aspects of a research project, so they can decide whether or not they wish to participate. The assumption is that a lack of such notification restricts freedom of choice. However, careful consideration suggests that informed consent is not always possible or desirable. For example, the researcher working with the mentally retarded may find it impossible to fully explain a highly technical study. Further, many field studies must be performed unobtrusively, or subjects' knowledge would bias the results to the extent that they are misleading. In considering these problems, Patterson (1974) writes that before unobtrusive field research is undertaken, an assessment has to be made concerning the extent to which human welfare and dignity are in jeopardy, and these concerns must be weighed against the value of the experiment. In effect, the researcher should assure himself or herself that the major issues to be illuminated by the study justify the slight discomfort to subjects who are not offered an opportunity to give consent.

Another issue related to informed consent concerns whether subjects who participate in experiments without their knowledge should be debriefed. Is it better to leave subjects unaware, so that they will not be upset by the realization of having been in an experiment? Or is it the right of all subjects to receive a full explanation of the purpose and intent of the study? Informing subjects after the experiment has taken place may oversensitize them to the possibility of future research or observation taking place in everyday settings.

For some people, the fear of being unwitting participants in research at other times might be quite distressing. On the other hand, there are strong ethical concerns (e.g., the subject's right to know) which the researcher must weigh before withholding such information.

Invasion of Privacy

What is the rationale for assuming it is permissible under some conditions to observe people without their knowledge? Obviously, an invasion of privacy is involved in such situations. Since people in public settings realize they are under informal observation by others, most researchers believe formal observation should be no more threatening. However, Davis and Ayres (1975) suggest that if experimental subjects in a public setting become aware of being observed and choose not to participate, the experimenter should provide them with an alternative route or area that is not being monitored. While potentially this leads to selection bias in subjects involved in the study, it may importantly protect people's right to privacy.

The assumption that under some conditions researchers have the "right" to observe people requires us to judge when behavior falls in the public domain and when it should be considered private. A comment by Koocher (1977) concerning a study reviewed in Chapter 6, in which people's personal space was invaded in a restroom, highlights this issue. You may recall that Middlemist and his coworkers (1976) assessed the physiological effects of personal space invasion in a men's lavatory by measuring duration and persistence of urination. This was accomplished by stationing an observer with a periscope and a stopwatch out of the sight of restroom users. Among other things, Koocher commented that the experiment invaded the subjects' privacy, even though it was in a public place, because of the nature of the observation. He also felt there was potential harm for subjects who might have discovered accidentally that they were being observed. In response, Middlemist et al. (1977) stated that the information obtained was available to anyone, and that the subjects were involved in an everyday public occurrence. Further, they mentioned that in a pilot study, half of the subjects were later informed that they had been watched and had no objection to the procedure. Obviously, both Koocher and Middlemist *et al.* may have valid points, and we should realize that sometimes there cannot be absolute ethical guidelines. It is the responsibility of every researcher to consider ethical questions as well as experimental design in conducting behavioral studies.

This concludes our discussion of methodological approaches to environmental psychology. As you read this text, you will frequently encounter studies using the various methods, and the familiarity you gained with these techniques by reading this Appendix should be of value to you. If you desire additional information concerning methodological issues, we recommend that you refer to the references listed here.

SUPPLEMENTARY READINGS

Bechtel, Robert E. *Enclosing Behavior*. Stroudsburg, Pa.: Dowden, Hutchinson, & Ross, 1977.

Cook, Thomas D., and Campbell, Donald T. *Quasi-Experimental Design and Analysis for Field Settings*. New York: Rand McNally, 1979.

Michelson, W. (Ed.). *Behavioral Research Methods in Environmental Design*. Stroudsburg, Pa.: Dowden, Hutchinson, & Ross, 1975.

Webb, Eugene J., Campbell, Donald T., Schwartz, Richard D., Sechrest, Lee, and Grove, Janet Belew. *Nonreactive Measures in Social Sciences*, 2d ed. Boston: Houghton Mifflin, 1981.

Zeisel, John. *Inquiry by Design: Tools for Environment–Behavior Research*. Monterey, Calif.: Brooks/Cole, 1981.

References

Abey-Wickrama, I., A'Brook, M.F., Gattoni, F.E.G., & Herridge, C.F. Mental hospital admissions and aircraft noise. *Lancet,* 1969, *2,* 1275–1277.

Abramson, L.Y., Seligman, M.E.P., & Teasdale, J.D. Learned helplessness in humans: Critique and reformulation. *Journal of Abnormal Psychology,* 1978, *87,* 49–74.

Acking, D.A., & Kuller, R. The perception of an interior as a function of its color. *Ergonomics,* 1972, *15,* 645–654.

Acton, W.I. Speech intelligibility in a background noise and noise-induced hearing loss. *Ergonomics,* 1970, *13,* 546–554.

Adam, J.M. Military problems of air transport and tropical service. In C.N. Davies, P.R. Davis, & F.H. Tyrer (Eds.), *The effects of abnormal physical conditions at work.* London: E. & S. Livingstone, 1967.

Adams, J.R. Review of *Defensible space. Man–Environment Systems,* 1973, 267–268.

Aiello, J.R. A further look at equilibrium theory: Visual interaction as a function of interpersonal distance. *Environmental Psychology and Nonverbal Behavior,* 1977, *1,* 122–140.

Aiello, J.R., & Aiello, T.D. Development of personal space: Proxemic behavior of children six to sixteen. *Human Ecology,* 1974, *2,* 177–189.

Aiello, J.R., Baum, A., & Gormley, F. Social determinants of residential crowding stress. *Personality and Social Psychology Bulletin,* 1981, *7,* 643–644.

Aiello, J.R., & Cooper, R.E. *Personal space and social affect: A developmental study.* Paper presented at the meeting of the Society for Research in Child Development, San Francisco, 1979.

Aiello, J.R., DeRisi, D., Epstein, Y., & Karlin, R. Crowding and the role of interpersonal distance preference. *Sociometry,* 1977, *40,* 271–282.

Aiello, J.R., Epstein, Y.M., & Karlin, R.A. Effects of crowding on electrodermal activity. *Sociological Symposium,* 1975, *14,* 43–57. (a)

Aiello, J.R., Epstein, Y.M., & Karlin, R.A. *Field experimental research in human crowding.* Paper presented at the meeting of the Eastern Psychological Association, 1975. (b)

Aiello, J.R., & Jones, S.E. Field study of the proxemic behavior of young school children in three subcultural groups. *Journal of Personality and Social Psychology,* 1971, *19,* 351–356.

Aiello, J.R., Nicosia, G., & Thompson, D. Physiological, social, and behavioral consequences of crowding on children and adolescents. *Child Development,* 1979, *50,* 195–202.

Aiello, J.R., & Thompson, D.E. When compensation fails: Mediating effects of sex and locus of control at extended interaction distances. *Basic and Applied Social Psychology,* 1980, *1,* 65–82. (a)

Aiello, J.R., & Thompson, D.E. Personal space, crowding, and spatial behavior in a cultural context. In I. Altman, J.F. Wohlwill, & A. Rapoport (Eds.), *Human behavior and environment.* (Vol. 4). New York: Plenum, 1980. (b)

Albert, S., & Dabbs, J.M., Jr. Physical distance and persuasion. *Journal of Personality and Social Psychology,* 1970, *15,* 265–270.

Alderman, R.B. *Psychological behavior in sports.* Philadelphia: Saunders, 1974.

Alexander, C. Major changes in environmental form required by social and psychological demands. *Ekistics,* 1969, *28,* 78–85.

Alland, A. *The human imperative.* New York: Columbia University, 1972.

Allen, G.H. How deep is environmental awareness? *Journal of Environmental Education,* 1972, *3,* 1–3.

Allen, V.L., & Greenberger, D.B. Destruction and perceived control. In A. Baum & J.E. Singer (Eds.), *Advances in environmental psychology* (Vol. 2). Hillsdale, N.J.: Erlbaum, 1980.

Allgeier, A.R., & Byrne, D. Attraction toward the opposite sex as a determinant of physical proximity. *Journal of Social Psychology,* 1973, *90,* 213–219.

Allport, F.H. *Theories of perception and the concept of structure.* New York: Wiley, 1955.

Allport, G., & Pettigrew, T. Cultural influence on the perception of movement: The trapezoidal illusion among the Zulus. *Journal of Abnormal and Social Psychology,* 1957, *55,* 104–113.

Altman, I. Some perspectives on the study of man–environment phenomena. *Representative Research in Social Psychology,* 1973, *4,* 109–126.

Altman, I. *The environment and social behavior.* Monterey, Calif.: Brooks/Cole, 1975.

Altman, I. Environmental psychology and social psychology. *Personality and Social Psychology Bulletin,* 1976, *2,* 96–113. (a)

Altman, I. A response to Epstein, Proshansky, and Stokols. *Personality and Social Psychology Bulletin,* 1976, *2,* 364–370. (b)

Altman, I. Crowding: Historical and contemporary trends in crowding research. In A. Baum & Y.M. Epstein (Eds.), *Human response to crowding.* Hillsdale, N.J.: Erlbaum, 1978.

Altman, I., & Chemers, M. *Culture and environment.* Monterey, Calif.: Brooks/Cole, 1980.

Altman, I., Nelson, P.A., & Lett, E.E. The ecology of home environments. *Catalog of Selected Documents in Psychology.* Washington, D.C.: American Psychological Association, 1972.

Altman, I., & Vinsel, A.M. Personal space: An analysis of E.T. Hall's proxemics framework. In I. Altman & J.F. Wohlwill (Eds.), *Human behavior and environment: Advances in theory and research* (Vol. 1). New York: Plenum, 1977.

American Public Transit Association. State funds flowing to R-GRTA. *Passenger Transport,* May 16, 1975, *33,* 20(9).

Amir, Y. Contact hypothesis in ethnic relations. *Psychological Bulletin, 1969, 71,* 319–342.

Anderson, B., Erwin, N., Flynn, D., Lewis, L., & Erwin, J. Effects of short-term crowding on aggression in captive groups of pigtail monkeys. *Aggressive Behavior,* 1977, *3,* 33–46.

Anderson, T.W., Zube, E.H., & MacConnell, W.P. Predicting scenic resource values. In E.H. Zube (Ed.), *Studies in landscape perception.* Publication No. R-76-1. Amherst: Institute for Man and Environment, University of Massachusetts, 1976.

Ando Y., & Hattori, H. Statistical studies in the effects of intense noise during human fetal life. *Journal of Sound and Vibration,* 1973, *27,* 101–110.

Antonovsky, A. *Health, stress, and coping.* San Francisco: Jossey-Bass, 1979.

Appleyard, D. Why buildings are known. *Environment and Behavior,* 1969, *1,* 131–156.

Appleyard, D. Styles and methods of structuring a city. *Environment and Behavior,* 1970, *2,* 100–118.

Appleyard, D. *Planning a pluralistic city.* Cambridge, Mass.: M.I.T. Press, 1976.

Appleyard, D., & Lintell, M. The environmental quality of city streets: The residents' viewpoint. *Journal of the American Institute of Planners,* 1972, *38,* 84–101.

Arbuthnot, J., Tedeschi, R., Wayner, M., Turner, J., Kressel, S., & Rush, R. The induction of sustained recycling behavior through the foot-in-the-door technique. *Journal of Environmental Systems,* 1976–1977, *6,* 355–358.

Ardrey, R. *The territorial imperative.* New York: Atheneum, 1966.

Argrist, S.S. Dimensions of well-being in public housing families. *Environment and Behavior,* 1974, *6,* 495–517.

Argyle, M., & Dean, J. Eye-contact, distance and affiliation. *Sociometry,* 1965, *28,* 289–304.

Arkkelin, D. *Effects of density, sex, and acquaintance level on reported pleasure, arousal, and dominance.* Doctoral dissertation, Bowling Green State University, 1978.

Arnstein, S.R. A ladder of citizen participation. *Journal of American Institute of Planners,* 1969, *35,* 217.

Aronow, W.S., Harris, C.N., Isbell, M.W., Rokaw, M.D., & Imparato, B. Effect of freeway travel on angina pectoris. *Annals of Internal Medicine,* 1972, *77,* 669–676.

Aronson, E., & Osherow, N. Cooperation, prosocial behavior, and academic performance. In L. Bickman (Ed.), *Applied social psychology annual.* Beverly Hills: Sage, 1980.

Asch, J., & Shore, B.M. Conservation behavior as the outcome to environmental education. *Journal of Environmental Education,* 1975, *6,* 25–33.

Assael, M., Pfeifer, Y., & Sulman, F.G. Influence of artificial air ionization on the human electroencephalogram. *International Journal of Biometeorology,* 1974, *18,* 306–312.

Auble, D., & Britton, N. Anxiety as a factor influencing routine performance under auditory stimuli. *Journal of General Psychology,* 1958, *58,* 111–114.

Auliciems, A. Some observed relationships between the atmospheric environment and mental work. *Environmental Research,* 1972, *5,* 217–240.

Averill, J. Personal control over aversive stimuli and its relationship to stress. *Psychological Bulletin,* 1973, *80,* 286–303.

Bacon-Prue, A., Blount, R., Pickering, D., & Drabman, R. An evaluation of three litter control procedures—Trash receptacles, paid workers, and the marked item technique. *Journal of Applied Behavior Analysis,* 1980, *13,* 165–170.

Baird, L.L. Big school, small school: A critical examination of the hypothesis. *Journal of Educational Psychology,* 1969, *60,* 253–260.

Baker, G.W., & Chapman, D.W. (Eds.). *Man and society in disaster.* New York: Basic Books, 1962.

Baltes, M.M., & Hayward, S.C. Application and evaluation of strategies to reduce pollution: Behavioral control of littering in a football stadium. *Journal of Applied Psychology,* 1976, *61,* 501–506.

Bandura, A. *Principles of behavior modification.* New York: Holt, Rinehart and Winston, 1969.

Bandura, A. *Aggression: A social learning analysis.* Englewood Cliffs, N.J.: Prentice-Hall, 1973.

Bandura, A. Analysis of modeling processes. In A. Bandura (Ed.), *Modeling: Conflicting theories.* New York: Lieber-Atherton, 1974.

Bandura, A. *Social learning theory.* Englewood Cliffs, N.J.: Prentice-Hall, 1977.

Bandura, A., & Walters, R.H. *Social learning and personality development.* New York: Holt, Rinehart and Winston, 1967.

Banzinger, G., & Owens, K. Geophysical variables and behavior: II. Weather factors as predictors of local social indicators of maladaptation in two non-urban areas. *Psychological Reports,* 1978, *43,* 427–434.

Barash, D.P. Human ethology: Personal space reiterated. *Environment and Behavior,* 1973, *5,* 67–73.

Barefoot, J.C., Hoople, H., & McClay, D. Avoidance of an act which would violate personal space. *Psychonomic Science,* 1972, *28,* 205–206.

Barefoot, J., & Kleck, R. *The effects of race and physical proximity of a co-actor on the social facilitation of dominant responses.* Unpublished manuscript, Carleton University, 1970.

Barker, M.L. Planning for environmental indices: Observer appraisals of air quality. In K.H. Craik & E. H. Zube (Eds.), *Perceiving environmental quality: Research applications.* New York: Plenum, 1976.

Barker, R.G. Ecology and motivation. In M.R. Jones (Ed.), *Nebraska Symposium on Motivation* (Vol. 8). Lincoln: University of Nebraska Press, 1960.

Barker, R.G. *Ecological psychology: Concepts and methods for studying the environment of human behavior.* Stanford, Calif.: Stanford University Press, 1968.

Barker, R.G. Settings of a professional lifetime. *Journal of Personality and Social Psychology,* 1979, *37,* 2137–2157.

Barker, R.G., & Gump, P.V. *Big school, small school.* Stanford, Calif.: Stanford University Press, 1964.

Barker, R.G., & Schoggen, P. *Qualities of community life.* San Francisco: Jossey-Bass, 1973.

Barker, R.G., & Wright, H. *Midwest and its children.* New York: Row, Peterson, 1955.

Barkow, B. *The psychology of car pooling.* Ontario, Canada: Ministry of Transportation and Communication, 1974.

Baron, R.A. Aggression as a function of ambient temperature and prior anger arousal. *Journal of Personality and Social Psychology,* 1972, *21,* 183–189.

Baron, R.A. The reduction of human aggression: A field study of the influence of incompatible reactions. *Journal of Applied Social Psychology,* 1976, *6,* 260–274.

Baron, R.A. *Human aggression.* New York: Plenum, 1977.

Baron, R.A. Aggression and heat: The "long hot summer" revisited. In A. Baum, J.E. Singer, & S. Valins (Eds.), *Advances in environmental psychology* (Vol. I). Hillsdale, N.J.: Erlbaum, 1978.

Baron, R.A., & Bell, P.A. Aggression and heat: Mediating effects of prior provocation and exposure to an aggressive model. *Journal of Personality and Social Psychology,* 1975, *31,* 825–832.

Baron, R.A., & Bell, P.A. Aggression and heat: The influence of ambient temperature, negative affect, and a cooling drink on physical aggression. *Journal of Personality and Social Psychology,* 1976, *33,* 245–255. (a)

Baron, R.A., & Bell, P.A. Physical distance and helping: Some unexpected benefits of "crowding in" on others. *Journal of Applied Social Psychology,* 1976, *6,* 95–104. (b)

Baron, R.A., & Lawton, S.F. Environmental influences on aggression: The facilitation of modeling effects by high ambient temperatures. *Psychonomic Science,* 1972, *26,* 80–83.

Baron, R.A., & Ransberger, V.M. Ambient temperature and the occurrence of collective violence: The "long hot summer" revisited. *Journal of Personality and Social Psychology,* 1978, *36,* 351–360.

Baron, R.M., Mandel, D.R., Adams, C.A., & Griffen, L.M. Effects of social density in university residential environments. *Journal of Personality and Social Psychology,* 1976, *34,* 434–446.

Baron, R.M., & Rodin, J. Personal control as a mediator of crowding. In A. Baum, J.E. Singer, & S. Valins (Eds.), *Advances in environmental psychology* (Vol. 1). Hillsdale, N.J.: Erlbaum, 1978.

Barrios, B.A., Corbitt, L.C., Estes, J.P., & Topping, J.S. Effect of social stigma on interpersonal distance. *The Psychological Record,* 1976, *26,* 343–348.

Bartley, S.H. *Principles of perception.* New York: Harper, 1958.

Barton, R. The patient's personal territory. *Hospital and Community Psychiatry,* 1966, *17,* 336.

Bass, B.M., & Weinstein, M.S. Early development in interpersonal distance in children. *Canadian Journal of Behavioral Science,* 1971, *3,* 368–376.

Baum, A., Aiello, J., & Calesnick, L.E. Crowding and personal control: Social density and the development of learned helplessness. *Journal of Personality and Social Psychology,* 1978, *36,* 1000–1011.

Baum, A., Calesnick, L.E., Davis, G.E., & Gatchel, R.J. Individual differences in coping with crowding: Stimulus screening and social overload. *Journal of Personality and Social Psychology,* 1982, *43,* 821–830.

Baum, A., & Davis, G.E. Spatial and social aspects of crowding perception. *Environment and Behavior,* 1976, *8,* 527–545.

Baum, A., & Davis, G.E. Reducing the stress of high-density living: An architectural intervention. *Journal of Personality and Social Psychology,* 1980, *38,* 471–481.

Baum, A., Davis, G.E., & Aiello, J.R. Crowding and neighborhood mediation of urban density. *Journal of Population,* 1978, *1*(3), 266–279.

Baum, A., Deckel, A.W., & Gatchel, R.J. Environmental stress and health: Is there a relationship? In G.S. Sanders & J. Suls (Eds.), *Social psychology of health and illness*. Hillsdale, N.J.: Erlbaum, 1982.

Baum, A., & Fisher, J.D. *Situation-related information as a mediator of responses to crowding*. Unpublished manuscript, Trinity College, 1977.

Baum, A., Fisher, J.D., & Singer, J.E. *Basic and applied social psychology*. New York: Random House, in press.

Baum, A., Fisher, J.D., & Solomon, S. Type of information, familiarity, and the reduction of crowding stress. *Journal of Personality and Social Psychology*, 1981, *40*, 11–23.

Baum, A., Fleming, R., & Davidson, L.M. Natural disaster and technological catastrophe. *Environment and Behavior*, 1983, *15*, 333–354.

Baum, A., Fleming, R., & Singer, J.E. Stress at Three Mile Island: Applying psychological impact analysis. In L. Bickman (Ed.), *Applied social psychology annual*. Beverly Hills: Sage, 1982.

Baum, A., & Gatchel, R.J. Cognitive determinants of response to uncontrollable events: Development of reactance and learned helplessness. *Journal of Personality and Social Psychology*, 1981, *40*, 1078–1089.

Baum, A., Gatchel, R.J., & Schaeffer, M.A. Emotional, behavioral and physiological effects of chronic stress at Three Mile Island. *Journal of Consulting and Clinical Psychology*, in press.

Baum, A., Gatchel, R., Streufert, S., Baum, C.S., Fleming, R., & Singer, J.E. *Psychological stress for alternatives of decontamination of TMI-2 reactor building atmosphere*. U.S. Nuclear Regulatory Commission (NUREG/CR-1584), 1980.

Baum, A., & Greenberg, C.I. Waiting for a crowd: The behavioral and perceptual effects of anticipated crowding. *Journal of Personality and Social Psychology*, 1975, *32*, 667–671.

Baum, A., Harpin, R.E., & Valins, S. The role of group phenomena in the experience of crowding. *Environment and Behavior*, 1975, *7*, 185–197.

Baum, A., & Koman, S. Differential response to anticipated crowding: Psychological effects of social and spatial density. *Journal of Personality and Social Psychology*, 1976, *34*, 526–536.

Baum, A., Reiss, M., & O'Hara, J. Architectural variants of reaction to spatial invasion. *Environment and Behavior*, 1974, *6*, 91–100.

Baum, A., Shapiro, A., Murray, D., & Wideman, M. Mediation of perceived crowding and control in residential dyads and triads. *Journal of Applied Social Psychology*, 1979, *9*, 491–507.

Baum, A., Singer, J.E., & Baum, C.S. Stress and the environment. *Journal of Social Issues*, 1981, *37*, 4–35.

Baum, A., & Valins, S. *Architecture and social behavior: Psychological studies of social density*. Hillsdale, N.J.: Erlbaum, 1977.

Baum, A., & Valins, S. Architectural mediation of residential density and control: Crowding and the regulation of social contact. In L. Berkowitz (Ed.), *Advances in experimental social psychology*, (Vol. 12). New York: Academic Press, 1979.

Baumer, T.L., & Hunter, A. *Street traffic, social integration, and fear of crime*. Evanston, Ill.: Center for Urban Affairs, Northwestern University, 1978.

Baxter, J.C., & Deanovich, B.S. Anxiety-arousing effects of inappropriate crowding. *Journal of Consulting and Clinical Psychology*, 1970, *35*, 174–178.

Beal, J.B. Electrostatic fields, electromagnetic fields and ions—Mind/body/environment interrelationships. In J.G. Llaurado, A. Sances, & J.H. Battocletti (Eds.), *Biologic and clinical effects of low-frequency magnetic and electric fields*. Springfield, Ill.: Charles C Thomas, 1974.

Beard, R. & Grandstaff, N. Carbon monoxide exposure and cerebral function. *Annals of New York Academy of Sciences*, 1970, *174*, 385–395.

Beard, R.R., & Wertheim, G.A. Behavioral impairment associated with small doses of carbon monoxide. *American Journal of Public Health*, 1967, *57*, 2012–2022.

Beatty, V.L. Highrise horticulture. *American Horticulturist*, 1974, *58*, 44–46.

Bechtel, R.B. Human movement and architecture. In H.M. Proshansky, W.H. Ittelson, & L.G. Rivlin (Eds.), *Environmental psychology: Man and his physical setting*. New York: Holt, Rinehart and Winston, 1970.

Bechtel, R.B. Perception of environmental quality: Some new wineskins for old wine. In K.H. Craik & E.H. Zube (Eds.), *Perceiving environmental quality: Research applications*. New York: Plenum, 1976.

Bechtel, R.B. *Enclosing behavior*. Stroudsburg, Pa.: Dowden, Hutchinson, & Ross, 1977.

Becker, F.D. Study of spatial markers. *Journal of Personality and Social Psychology*, 1973, *26*, 439–445.

Becker, F.D. *Workspace: Creating environments in organizations*. New York: Praeger, 1981.

Becker, F.D., & Mayo, C. Delineating personal space and territoriality. *Environment and Behavior*, 1971, *3*, 375–381.

Becker, F.D., Sommer, R., Bee, J., & Oxley, B. College classroom ecology. *Sociometry*, 1973, *36*, 514–525.

Becker, L., & Seligman, C. Reducing air-conditioning waste by signalling it is cool outside. *Personality and Social Psychology Bulletin*, 1978, *4*, 412–415.

Becker, L.J. The joint effect of feedback and goal setting on performance: A field study of residential energy conservation. *Journal of Applied Psychology*, 1978, *63*, 228–233.

Beckey, T., & Nelson, L.W. Field test of energy savings with thermostat setback. *ASHRAE Journal*, January 1981, 67–70.

Beckman, R. Getting up and getting out: Progressive patient care. *Progressive Architecture*, November 1974, 64.

Beighton, P. Fluid balance in the Sahara. *Nature*, 1971, *233*, 275–277.

Bell, C.R., Provins, K.A., & Hiorns, R.F. Visual and auditory vigilance during exposure to hot and humid conditions. *Ergonomics,* 1964, *7,* 279–288.

Bell, P.A. Effects of noise and heat stress on primary and subsidiary task performance. *Human Factors,* 1978, *20,* 749–752.

Bell, P.A. Effects of heat, noise, and provocation on retaliatory evaluative behavior. *Journal of Social Psychology,* 1980, *40,* 97–100.

Bell, P.A. Physiological, comfort, performance, and social effects of heat stress. *Journal of Social Issues,* 1981, *37,* 71–94.

Bell, P.A. *Theoretical interpretations of heat stress.* Paper presented at the American Psychological Association meeting, Washington, D.C., August 1982.

Bell, P.A., & Barnard, S.W. *Sex differences in the effects of heat and noise stress on personal space permeability.* Paper presented at the meeting of the Rocky Mountain Psychological Association, Albuquerque, May 1977.

Bell, P.A., & Baron, R.A. Environmental influences on attraction: Effects of heat, attitude similarity, and personal evaluations. *Bulletin of the Psychonomic Society* 1974, *4,* 479–481.

Bell, P.A., & Baron, R.A. Aggression and heat: The mediating role of negative affect. *Journal of Applied Social Psychology,* 1976, *6,* 18–30.

Bell, P.A., & Baron, R.A. Aggression and ambient temperature: The facilitating and inhibiting effects of hot and cold environments. *Bulletin of the Psychonomic Society,* 1977, *9,* 443–445.

Bell, P.A., & Baron, R.A. Ambient temperature and human violence. In P.F. Brain & D. Benton (Eds.), *A multidisciplinary approach to aggression research.* Amsterdam: Elsevier/North-Holland Biomedical Press, 1981.

Bell, P.A., & Byrne, D. Repression-sensitization. In H. London & J. Exner (Eds.), *Dimensions of personality.* New York: Wiley, 1978.

Bell, P.A., & Doyle, D.P. Effects of heat and noise on helping behavior. *Psychological Reports,* 1983, *53,* 955-959.

Bell, P.A., Garnand, D.G., Heath, D. Effects of ambient temperature and seating arrangement on personal and environmental evaluations. *Journal of General Psychology,* in press.

Bell, P.A., & Greene, T.C. Thermal stress: Physiological, comfort, performance, and social effects of hot and cold environments. In G.W. Evans (Ed.), *Environmental stress.* London: Cambridge University Press, 1982.

Bell, P.A., Loomis, R.J., & Cervone, J.C. Effects of heat, social facilitation, sex differences, and task difficulty on reaction time. *Human Factors,* 1982, *24,* 19–24.

Bell, R.W., Miller, C.E., Ordy, J.M., & Rolsten, C. Effects of population density and living space upon neuroanatomy, neurochemistry and behavior in the C57B1/10 mouse. *Journal of Comparative and Physiological Psychology,* 1971, *75,* 258–263.

Bellet, S., Roman, L., & Kastis, J. The effects of automobile driving on catecholamine and adrenocortical excretion. *The American Journal of Cardiology,* 1969, *24,* 365–368.

Bem, D. *Beliefs, attitudes, and human affairs.* Belmont, Calif.: Brooks/Cole, 1971.

Bem, D.J. Self-perception theory. In L. Berkowitz (Ed.), *Advances in experimental social psychology* (Vol. 6). New York: Academic Press, 1972.

Benedak, T. *Psychosexual functions of women: Studies in psychosomatic medicine.* New York: Ronald Press, 1952.

Bennet, R., Rafferty, J.M., Canivez, G.L., & Smith, J.M. *The effects of cold temperature on altruism and aggression.* Paper presented at the Midwestern Psychological Association meeting, Chicago, May 1983.

Bennett, C. *Spaces for people: Human factors in design.* Englewood Cliffs, N.J.: Prentice-Hall, 1977.

Benson, G.P., & Zieman, G.L. *The relationship of weather to children's behavior problems.* Unpublished manuscript, Colorado State University, 1981.

Beranek, L.L. Criteria for office quieting based on questionnaire rating studies. *Journal of the Acoustical Society of America,* 1956, *28,* 833–850.

Beranek, L.L. Revised criteria for noise in buildings. *Noise Control,* 1957, *3,* 19–26.

Berglund, B., Berglund, U., & Lindvall, T. Psychological processing of odor mixtures. *Psychological Review,* 1976, *83,* 432–441.

Bergman, B.A. *The effects of group size, personal space and success–failure on physiological arousal, test performance, and questionnaire responses.* Doctoral dissertation, Temple University, 1971.

Berkowitz, L. The contagion of violence. In W.J. Arnold & M.M. Page (Eds.), *Nebraska Symposium on Motivation* (Vol. 18). Lincoln: University of Nebraska Press, 1970.

Berlyne, D.E. *Conflict, arousal and curiosity.* New York: McGraw-Hill, 1960. (a)

Berlyne, D.E. Conflict and information-theory variables as determinants of human perceptual curiosity. *Journal of Experimental Psychology,* 1960, *53,* 399–404. (b)

Berlyne, D.E. *Aesthetics and psychobiology.* New York: Appleton, 1972.

Berlyne, D.E. (Ed.). *Studies in the new experimental aesthetics: Steps toward an objective psychology of aesthetic appreciation.* New York: Halsted Press, 1974.

Bickman, L. Environmental attitudes and actions. *Journal of Social Psychology,* 1972, *87,* 323–324.

Bickman, L., Teger, A., Gabriele, T., McLaughlin, C., Berger, M., & Sunaday, E. Dormitory density and helping behavior. *Environment and Behavior,* 1973, *5,* 465–490.

Bishop, R.L., & Peterson, G.L. *A synthesis of environmental design recommendations from the visual preferences of children.* Northwestern University Department of Civil Engineering, 1971.

Black, J.C. *Uses made of spaces in owner-occupied houses*. Unpublished doctoral dissertation, University of Utah, 1968.

Blackman, S., & Catalina, D. The moon and the emergency room. *Perceptual and Motor Skills*, 1973, *37*, 624–626.

Blaut, J., & Stea, D. Studies of geographical learning. *Annals of the Association of American Geographers*, 1971, *61*, 387–393.

Bleda, P.R., & Bleda, S.E. *Sex differences in personal space invasion at a shopping mall*. Paper presented at the meeting of the American Psychological Association, Washington, D.C., September 1976.

Bleda, P., & Bleda, S. Effects of sex and smoking on reactions to spatial invasion at a shopping mall. *Journal of Social Psychology*, 1978, *104*, 311–312.

Bleda, P.R., & Sandman, P.H. In smoke's way: Socioemotional reactions to another's smoking. *Journal of Applied Psychology*, 1977, *62*, 452–458.

Bloom, L., Weigel, R., & Trautt, G. Therapeugenic factors in psychotherapy: Office orientation, sex of therapist, and sex of subject and their effects on therapist credibility. *Journal of Consulting and Clinical Psychology*, 1977, *45*, 867–873.

Bolt, Beranek, & Newman, Inc. Occupational noise: The subtle pollutant. In J. Ralof, *Science News*, 1982, *121*(21), 347–350.

Boman, B. Behavioral observation on the Granville train disaster and significance of stress for psychiatry. *Social Science and Medicine*, 1979, *13*, 463–471.

Bonio, S., Fonzi, A., & Saglione, G. Personal space and variations in the behaviour of ten-year-olds. *Italian Journal of Psychology*, 1978, *10*, 15–25.

Bornstein, M.H. The pace of life revisited. *International Journal of Psychology*, 1979, *14*, 83–90.

Bornstein, M.H., & Bornstein, H.G. The pace of city life. *Nature*, 1976, *259*, 551–559.

Borsky, P.N. Effects of noise on community behavior. In W.D. Ward & J.E. Fricke (Eds.), *Noise as a public health hazard*. Washington, D.C.: The American Speech and Hearing Association, 1969.

Borun, M. *Measuring the unmeasurable*. Washington, D.C.: Association for Science Technology Centers, 1977.

Bossard, J.H. Residential propinquity as a factor in marriage selection. *American Journal of Sociology*, 1931, *38*, 219–224.

Boucher, M.L. Effect of seating distance on interpersonal attraction in an interview situation. *Journal of Consulting and Clinical Psychology*, 1972, *38*, 15–19.

Bouska, M.L., & Beatty, P.A. Clothing as a symbol of status: Its effect on control of interaction territory. *Bulletin of the Psychonomic Society*, 1978, *4*, 235–238.

Bovy, P. *Pedestrian planning and design: A bibliography* (No. 918). Council of Planning Librarians Exchange Bibliography, 1975.

Boyanowsky, E.O., Calvert, J., Young, J., & Brideau, L. Toward a thermoregulatory model of violence. *Journal of Environmental Systems*, 1981–82, *11*, 81–87.

Boyce, P.R. The luminous-environment. In D. Canter & P. Stringer (Eds.), *Environmental interactions: Psychological approaches to our physical surroundings*. New York: International Universities Press, 1975.

Brasted, W., Mann, M., & Geller, E.S. Behavioral interventions for litter control: A critical review. *Cornell Journal of Social Relations*, Summer 1979, *14*, 75–90.

Brechner, K.C. An experimental analysis of social traps. *Journal of Experimental Social Psychology*, 1977, *13*, 552–564.

Brehm, J.W. *A theory of psychological reactance*. New York: Academic Press, 1966.

Brehm, J.W. *Responses to loss of freedom: A theory of psychological reactance*. Morristown, N.J.: General Learning Press, 1972.

Brehm, S.S., & Brehm, J.W. *Psychological reactance: A theory of freedom and control*. New York: Academic Press, 1981.

Breisacher, P. Neuropsychological effects of air pollution. *American Behavioral Scientist*, 1971, *14*, 837–864.

Broadbent, D.E. Some effects of noise on visual performance. *Quarterly Journal of Experimental Psychology*, 1954, *6*, 1–5.

Broadbent, D.E. *Perception and communication*. Oxford: Pergamon, 1958.

Broadbent, D.E. Differences and interactions between stresses. *Quarterly Journal of Experimental Psychology*, 1963, *15*, 205–211.

Broadbent, D.E. *Decision and stress*. New York: Academic Press, 1971.

Broadbent, D.E., & Little, E. Effects of noise reduction in a work situation. *Occupational Psychology*, 1960, *34*, 133–140.

Broadbent, G.B. *Design in architecture*. New York: Wiley, 1973.

Brokemann, N.C., & Moller, A.T. Preferred seating position and distance in various situations. *Journal of Counseling Psychology*, 1973, *20*, 504–508.

Bromet, E. *Preliminary report on the mental health of Three Mile Island residents*. Pittsburgh, Pa.: Western Psychiatric Institute, University of Pittsburgh, 1980.

Bronzaft, A.L., Dobrow, S.B., & O'Hanlon, T.J. Spatial orientation in a subway system. *Environment and Behavior*, 1976, *8*, 575–594.

Bronzaft, A.L., & McCarthy, D.P. The effects of elevated train noise on reading ability. *Environment and Behavior*, 1975, *7*, 517–527.

Brown, B.B. *Territoriality and residential burglary*. Paper presented at the meeting of the American Psychological Association, New York, August 1979.

Brown, G.I. The relationship between barometric pressure and relative humidity and classroom behavior. *Journal of Educational Research, 1964, 57*, 368–370.

Brown, I.D., & Poulton, E.C. Measuring the spare ''mental capacity'' of car drivers by a subsidiary task. *Ergonomics*, 1961, *4*, 35–40.

Brunetti, F. *Open space schools project bulletin*. Stanford, Calif.: School Planning Laboratory, School of Education, Stanford University, March 1970.

Brunswik, E. *Perception and the representative design of psychological experiments*. Berkeley: University of California Press, 1956.

Brunswik, E. The conceptual framework of psychology. In O. Neurath, R. Carnap, & C. Morris (Eds.), *Foundation of the unity of science: Toward an international encyclopedia of unified science*. Chicago: University of Chicago Press, 1969.

Bruvold, W.H. Belief and behavior as determinants of environmental attitudes. *Environment and Behavior*, 1973, *5*, 202–218.

Bryan, M.E., & Tempest, W. Are our noise laws adequate? *Applied Acoustics*, 1973, *6*, 219–232.

Buchwald, A. *Son of the great society*. New York: Putnam, 1966.

Budd, G.M. Australian physiological research in the Antarctic and the Subarctic, with special reference to thermal stress and acclimatization. In O.G. Edholm & E.K.E. Gunderson (Eds.), *Polar human biology*. London: Heineman, 1973.

Bull, A.J., Burbage, S.E., Crandall, J.E., Fletcher, C.I., Lloyd, J.T., Ravenberg, R.L., & Rockett, S.L. Effects of noise and intolerance of ambiguity upon attraction for similar and dissimilar others. *Journal of Social Psychology*, 1972, *88*, 151–152.

Bulman, R.J., & Wortman, C.B. Attribution of blame and coping in the "real world": Severe accident victims react to their lot. *Journal of Personality and Social Psychology*, 1977, *35*, 351–363.

Burrows, A.A., & Zamarin, D.M. Aircraft noise and the community: Some recent survey findings. *Aerospace Medicine*, 1972, *43*, 27–33.

Bursill, A.E. The restriction of peripheral vision during exposure to hot and humid conditions. *Quarterly Journal of Experimental Psychology*, 1958, *10*, 113–129.

Burton, I., & Kates, R.W. Perception of hazards in resource management. *Natural Resources Journal*, 1964, *3*, 412–441.

Burton, I., Kates, R.W., & White, G.F. The human ecology of extreme geophysical events. *Natural Hazard Research Working Paper* No. 1, University of Toronto, 1968.

Byrne, D. Repression-sensitization as a dimension of personality. In B. Mayer (Ed.), *Progress in experimental personality research* (Vol. 1). New York: Academic Press, 1964.

Byrne, D. *The attraction paradigm*. New York: Academic Press, 1971.

Byrne, D., Baskett, G.D., & Hodges, L. Behavioral indicators of interpersonal attraction. *Journal of Applied Social Psychology*, 1971, *1*, 137–149.

Byrne, D., & Clore, G.L. A reinforcement model of evaluative responses. *Personality: An International Journal*, 1970, *1*, 103–128.

Byrne, D., Ervin, C.R., & Lamberth, J. Continuity between the experimental study of attraction and real life computer dating. *Journal of Personality and Social Psychology*, 1970, *16*, 157–165.

Byrne, R. Memory for urban geography. *Quarterly Journal of Experimental Psychology*, 1979, *31*, 147–154.

Cahoon, R.L. Simple decision making at high altitude. *Ergonomics*, 1972, *15*, 157–163.

Calhoun, J.B. Population density and social pathology. *Scientific American*, 1962, *206*, 139–148.

Calhoun, J.B. The social use of space. In W. Mayer & R. Van Gelder (Eds.), *Physiological mammalogy*. New York: Academic Press, 1964.

Calhoun, J.B. Ecological factors in the development of behavior anomalies. In J. Zubin & H.F. Hunt (Eds.), *Comparative psychopathology*. New York: Grune & Stratton, 1967.

Calhoun, J.B. Space and the strategy of life. *Ekistics*, 1970, *29*, 425–437.

Calhoun, J.B. Space and the strategy of life. In A.H. Esser (Ed.), *Behavior and environment: The use of space by animals and men*. Bloomington: University of Indiana Press, 1971.

Cameron, P., Robertson, D., & Zaks, J. Sound pollution, noise pollution, and health: Community parameters. *Journal of Applied Psychology*, 1972, *56*, 67–74.

Campbell, D.E. Interior office design and visitor response. *Journal of Applied Psychology*, 1979, *64*, 648–653.

Campbell, D.E. Lunar-lunacy research: When enough is enough. *Environment and Behavior*, 1982, *14*, 418–424.

Campbell, D.E., & Beets, J.L. Meteorological variables and behavior: An annotated bibliography. *JSAS Catalog of Selected Documents in Psychology*, 1977, *7*, 1 (Ms. No. 1403).

Campbell, D.E., & Beets, J.L. Lunacy and the moon. *Psychological Bulletin*, 1978, *85*, 1123–1129.

Campbell, D.E., & Beets, J.L. *Human response to naturally occurring weather phenomena: Effects of wind speed and direction*. Unpublished manuscript, Humboldt State University, 1981.

Campbell, D.T., Kruskal, W.H., & Wallace, W.P. Seating aggregation as an index of attitude. *Sociometry*, 1966, *29*, 1–15.

Cannon, W.B. *Bodily changes in pain, hunger, fear, and rage*. Boston: Branford, 1929.

Cannon, W.B. Studies on the conditions of activity in the endocrine organs, XXVII. Evidence that the medulliadrenal secretion is not continuous. *American Journal of Physiology*, 1931, *98*, 447–452.

Canter, D.V., & Craik, K.H. Environmental psychology. *Journal of Environmental Psychology*, 1981, *1*, 1–11.

Cantor, D. Royal hospital for sick children: A psychological analysis. *Architects Journal*, 1972, *6*, 525–564.

Carlsmith, J.M., & Anderson, C.A. Ambient temperature and the occurrence of collective violence: A new analysis. *Journal of Personality and Social Psychology*, 1979, *37*, 337–344.

Carlsmith, J.M., Ellsworth, P.C., & Aronson, E. *Methods of research in social psychology*. Reading, Mass.: Addison-Wesley, 1976.

Carlstam, G., & Levi, L. *Urban conglomerates as psychosocial human stressors*. Report to Swedish Preparatory Committee for the United Nations Conference on the Human Environment, Stockholm, October 1971.

Carlton-Foss, J.A., & Rohles, F.H. Personality factors in thermal acceptability and comfort. *ASHRAE Transactions*, 1982, *88*, Pt. 2.

Carp, F.M. Housing and living environments of older people. In R.H. Binstock & E. Shanas (Eds.), *Handbook of aging and the social sciences*. New York: Van Nostrand, 1976.

Carp, F.M., Appleyard, D., Shokrkon, H., & Zawadski, R.T. *Residential quality prior to the opening of BART. BART Impact Studies, BART-II, Part II, Volume III*. Berkeley: Institute of Urban and Regional Development, University of California, 1973.

Carpenter, C.R. Territoriality: A review of concepts and problems. In A. Roe and G.G. Simpson (Eds.), *Behavior and evolution*. New Haven, Conn.: Yale University Press, 1958.

Cass, R., & Edney, J.J. The commons dilemma: A simulation testing the effects of resource visibility and territorial division. *Human Ecology*, 1978, *6*, 371–386.

Cervone, J.C. *An environmental-social approach to an arousal-behavior relationship*. Unpublished master's thesis, Colorado State University, 1977.

Chapko, M.K., & Solomon, M. Air pollution and recreation behavior. *Journal of Social Psychology*, 1976, *100*, 149–150.

Chaplin, J.P., & Krawiec, T.S. *Systems and theories of psychology*. New York: Holt, Rinehart and Winston, 1960.

Chapman, C., & Risley, T.R. Anti-litter procedures in an urban high-density area. *Journal of Applied Behavior Analysis*, 1974, *7*, 317–384.

Chapman, R., Masterpasqua, F., & Lore, R. The effects of crowding during pregnancy on offspring emotional and sexual behavior in rats. *Bulletin of the Psychonomic Society*, 1976, *7*, 475–477.

Charry, J.M., & Hawkinshire, F.B.W. Effects of atmospheric electricity on some substrates of disordered social behavior. *Journal of Personality and Social Psychology*, 1981, *41*, 185–197.

Cheyne, J.A., & Efran, N.G. The effect of spatial and interpersonal variables on the invasion of group-controlled territories. *Sociometry*, 1972, *35*, 477–489.

Chicago Tribune. Is it shameful to be poor? *Urban Problems Background Report*, 1974.

Chowns, R.H. Mental hospital admissions and aircraft noise. *Lancet*, 1970, *1* (7644), 467.

Christensen, L.D. *Experimental methodology*. Boston: Allyn & Bacon, 1977.

Christian, J.J. Effects of population size on the adrenal glands and reproductive organs of male mice in populations of fixed size. *The American Journal of Physiology*, 1955, *182*, 292–300.

Christian, J.J. Pathology of overpopulation. *Military Medicine*, 1963, *128*, 571–603.

Cialdini, R. *Littering as a function of extant litter*. Unpublished manuscript, Arizona State University, 1977.

Cialdini, R.B., & Kenrick, D.T. Altruism as hedonism: A social development perspective on the relationship of negative mood state and helping. *Journal of Personality and Social Psychology*, 1976, *54*, 907–914.

Cicchetti, C. A review of the empirical analyses that have been based upon the national survey. *Journal of Leisure Research*, 1972, *4*, 90–107.

Clark, R.E., & Flaherty, C.F. Contralateral effects of thermal stimuli on manual performance capability. *Journal of Applied Psychology*, 1963, *18*, 769–771.

Clark, R.N., Hendee, J.C., & Burgess, R.L. The experimental control of littering. *Journal of Environmental Education*, 1972, *4*, 22–28.

Clinard, M.B. Deviant behavior: Urban–rural contrasts. In L.E. Elias, Jr., J. Gillies, & S. Reimer (Eds.), *Metropolis: Values in conflict*. Belmont, Calif.: Wadsworth, 1964.

Cobb, S. Social support as a moderator of life stress. *Psychosomatic Medicine*, 1976, *38*, 300–314.

Coffin, D., & Stokinger, H. Biological effects of air pollutants. In A. C. Stern (Ed.), *Air pollution* (3rd ed., Vol. 3). New York: Academic Press, 1977.

Cohen, H., Moss, S., & Zube, E. Pedestrians and wind in the urban environment. In A.D. Seidel & S. Danford (Eds.), *Environmental design: Research, theory, and application*. Washington, D.C.: Environmental Design Research Association, 1979.

Cohen, J.L., Sladen, B., & Bennett, B. The effects of situational variables on judgments of crowding. *Sociometry*, 1975, *38*, 273–281.

Cohen, M.R. Environmental information vs. environmental attitudes. *Journal of Environmental Education*, 1973, *5*, 5–8.

Cohen, S. Environmental load and the allocation of attention. In A. Baum, J.E. Singer, & S. Valins (Eds.), *Advances in environmental psychology* (Vol. 1). Hillsdale, N.J.: Erlbaum, 1978.

Cohen, S. Aftereffects of stress on human performance and social behavior: A review of research and theory. *Psychological Bulletin*, 1980, *87*, 578–604.

Cohen, S., Evans, G.W., Krantz, D.S., & Stokols, D. Physiological, motivational, and cognitive effects of aircraft noise on children: Moving from the laboratory to the field. *American Psychologist*, 1980, *35*, 231–243.

Cohen, S., Evans, G.W., Krantz, D.S., Stokols, D., & Kelly, S. Aircraft noise and children: Longitudinal and cross-sectional evidence on adaptation to noise and the effectiveness of noise abatement. *Journal of Personality and Social Psychology*, 1981, *40*, 331–345.

Cohen, S., Glass, D.C., & Phillips, S. Environment and health. In H.E. Freeman, S. Levine, & L.G. Reeder (Eds.), *Handbook of medical sociology*. Englewood Cliffs, N.J.: Prentice-Hall, 1977.

Cohen, S., Glass, D.C., & Singer, J.E. Apartment noise, auditory discrimination, and reading ability in children. *Journal of Experimental Social Psychology,* 1973, *9,* 407–422.

Cohen, S., & Lezak, A. Noise and inattentiveness to social cues. *Environment and Behavior,* 1977, *9,* 559–572.

Collett, P. Training Englishmen in the non-verbal behavior of Arabs: An experiment of intercultural communication. *International Journal of Psychology,* 1971, *6,* 209–215.

Colligan, M.J. *An investigation of apparent mass psychogenic illness in a furniture assembly plant.* Unpublished report prepared for the National Institute for Occupational Safety and Health, Cincinnati, Ohio, 1978.

Colligan, M.J., & Murphy, L.R. A review of mass psychogenic illness in work settings. In M.J. Colligan, J.W. Pennebaker, & L.R. Murphy (Eds.), *Mass psychogenic illness.* Hillsdale, N.J.: Erlbaum, 1982.

Colligan, M.J., & Stockton, W. The mystery of assembly line hysteria. *Psychology Today,* June 1978, 93–116.

Collins, B.L. Windows and people: A literature survey. Psychological reaction to environments with and without windows. *NBS Building Science Series,* June 1975, *70,* 88.

Collins, D.L., Baum, A., & Singer, J.E. Coping with chronic stress at Three Mile Island: Psychological and biochemical evidence. *Health Psychology,* 1983, *2,* 149–166.

Commoner, B. *Science and survival.* New York: Viking, 1963.

Cone, J.D., & Hayes, S.C. Applied behavior analysis and the solutions of environmental problems. In J.F. Wohlwill & I. Altman (Eds.), *Human behavior and environment: Advances in theory and research* (Vol. 2). New York: Plenum 1978.

Cone, J.D., & Hayes, S.C. *Environmental problems/behavioral solutions.* Monterey, Calif.: Brooks/Cole, 1980.

Conrad, C. How different sports rate in promoting physical fitness. *Medical Times,* 1976.

Conroy, J., III, & Sundstrom, E. Territorial dominance in a dyadic conversation as a function of similarity of opinion. *Journal of Personality and Social Psychology,* 1977, *35,* 570–576.

Conway, D. *Social science and design: A process model for architect and social scientist collaboration.* Washington, D.C.: American Institute of Architects, 1973.

Cook, M. Experiments on orientation and proxemics. *Human Relations,* 1970, *23,* 61–76.

Cook, S. Motives in a conceptual analysis of attitude-related charm. In W. Arnold & D. Levine (Eds.), *Nebraska Symposium on Motivation* (Vol. 17). Lincoln: University of Nebraska Press, 1969.

Cook, T.D., and Campbell, D.T. *Quasi-experimental design and analysis for field settings.* New York: Rand-McNally, 1979.

Cooper, C. Adventure playground. *Landscape Architecture,* 1970, *61,* 18–29; 88–91.

Cooper, C. St. Francis Square: Attitudes of its residents. *A.I.A. Journal,* December 1971, 22.

Cooper, C. The house as symbol. *Design and Environment,* 1972, *3,* 30–37.

Corcoran, D.W.J. Noise and loss of sleep. *Quarterly Journal of Experimental Psychology,* 1962, *14,* 178–182.

Cotton, J.L. *Temperature, humidity, and violent crime.* Paper presented at the American Psychological Association meeting, Washington, D.C., August 1982.

Coughlin, R.E., & Goldstein, K.A. *The extent of agreement among observers on environmental attractiveness.* Regional Science Research Institute Paper No. 37. Philadelphia: Regional Science Research Institute, 1970.

Cox, V.C., Paulus, P.B., McCain, G., & Karlovac, M. The relationship between crowding and health. In A. Baum & J.E. Singer (Eds.), *Advances in environmental psychology* (Vol. 4). Hillsdale, N.J.: Erlbaum, 1982.

Craik, K.H. *A system of landscape dimensions: Appraisal of its objectivity and illustration of its scientific application.* Report to Resources for the Future, Inc. Berkeley, Calif.: Institute of Personality Assessment and Research, University of California, 1970. (a)

Craik, K.H. The environmental dispositions of environmental decision-makers. *Annals,* 1970, *389,* 80–94. (b)

Craik, K.H., & Appleyard, D. Streets of San Francisco: Brunswik's lens model applied to urban inference and assessment. *Journal of Social Issues,* 1980, *36,* 72–85.

Craik, K.H., & Zube, E.H. *Perceiving environmental quality.* New York: Plenum, 1976.

Crawshaw, R. Reactions to a disaster. *Archives of General Psychiatry,* 1963, *9,* 157–162.

Crew, F.A., & Mirskowa, L. Effects of density on adult mouse populations. *Biologia Generalis,* 1931, *7,* 239–250.

Crockford, G.W. Heat problems and protective clothing in iron and steel works. In C.N. Davies, P.R. Davis, & F.H. Tyrer (Eds.), *The effects of abnormal physical conditions at work.* London: E. & S. Livingstone, 1967.

Crook, M.A., & Langdon, F.J. The effects of aircraft noise on schools in the vicinity of the London Airport. *Journal of Sound and Vibration,* 1974, *34,* 241–248.

Crowe, M.J.. Toward a "definitional model" of public perceptions of air pollution. *Journal of the Air Pollution Control Association,* 1968, *18,* 154–157.

Crump, S.L., Nunes, D.L., & Crossman, E.K. The effects of litter on littering behavior in a forest environment. *Environment and Behavior,* 1977, *9,* 137–146.

Cunningham, M.R. Weather, mood, and helping behavior: Quasi experiments with the sunshine samaritan. *Journal of Personality and Social Psychology,* 1979, *37,* 1947–1956.

Cunningham, M.R., Steinberg, J., & Grev, R. Wanting to and having to help: Separate motivations for positive mood and guilt-induced helping. *Journal of Personality and Social Psychology,* 1980, *38,* 181–192.

Cziffra, P., Graydon, E., Klath, N., & Wiggens, T. *Science and technology libraries space report.* Princeton, N.J.: Princeton University Library, 1975.

Dabbs, J.M. Physical closeness and negative feelings. *Psychonomic Science,* 1971, *23,* 141–143.

Dabbs, J., Fuller, P., & Carr, S. *Personal space when cornered: College students and prison inmates.* Paper presented at the meeting of the American Psychological Association, Montreal, Canada, 1973.

Dabbs, J.M., Jr., & Stokes, N.A. Beauty is power: The use of space on the sidewalk. *Sociometry, 1975, 38,* 551–557.

Dahlof, L., Hard, E., & Larsson, K. Influence of maternal stress on offspring sexual behavior. *Animal Behavior, 1977, 25,* 958–963.

Damon, A. The residential environment, health, and behavior: Simple research opportunities, strategies, and some findings in the Solomon Islands and Boston, Massachusetts. In L.E. Hinckle, Jr., & W.C. Loring (Eds.), *The effect of the man-made environment on health and behavior.* Atlanta: Center for Disease Control, Public Health Service, 1977.

Danford, S., Starr, N., & Willems, E.P. The case against subjective, cognitive report in environmental design and research: A critical test. In *Environmental design: Research, theory and application. Proceedings of the tenth annual conference of the Environmental Design Research Association.* Buffalo: Environmental Design Research Association, 1980.

Danford, S., & Willems, E.P. Subjective responses to architectural displays: A question of validity. *Environment and Behavior, 1976, 8,* 486–516.

Daniel, T.C., & Boster, R.S. *Measuring landscape esthetics: The Scenic Beauty Estimation method* (Paper RM-167). USDA Forest Service, 1976.

D'Atri, D. Psychophysiological responses to crowding. *Environment and Behavior, 1975, 7,* 237–251.

D'Atri, D., & Ostfeld, A. Crowding: Its effects on the elevation of blood pressure in a prison setting. *Preventive Medicine, 1975, 4,* 550–566.

Daves, W.F., & Swaffer, P.W. Effect of room size on critical interpersonal distance. *Perceptual and Motor Skills, 1971, 33,* 926.

Davidson, L.M., Baum, A., & Collins, D.L. Stress and control-related problems at Three Mile Island. *Journal of Applied Social Psychology, 1982, 12,* 349–359.

Davis, G., & Altman, I. Territories at the work-place: Theory into design guidelines. *Man–Environment Systems, 1976, 6,* 46–53.

Davis, G., & Ayers, V. Photographic recording of environmental behavior. In W. Michelson (Ed.), *Behavioral research methods in environmental design.* Stroudsburg, Pa.: Dowden, Hutchinson & Ross, 1975.

Davis, G., & Szigeti, F. Programming, space planning, and office design. *Environment and Behavior, 1982, 14,* 299–317.

Davis, G.E. *Crowding and helping: An empirical test of the social overload hypothesis.* Doctoral dissertation, State University of New York—Stony Brook, 1977.

Davis, K.A. *World urbanization 1950–1970* (Vol. 2). Berkeley: Institute of International Studies, 1972.

Davis, K.A. Introduction. In K. Davis (Ed.), *Cities.* San Francisco: Freeman, 1973.

Dawes, R., McTavish, J., & Shaklee, H. Behavior, communication, and assumptions about other people's behavior in a commons dilemma situation. *Journal of Personality and Social Psychology, 1977, 35,* 1–11.

Dean, L., Pugh, W., & Gunderson, E. Spatial and perceptual components of crowding: Effects on health and satisfaction. *Environment and Behavior, 1975, 7,* 225–236.

Dean, L., Pugh, W., & Gunderson, E. The behavioral effects of crowding. *Environment and Behavior, 1978, 10,* 419–431.

Dean, L.M., Willis, F.N., & Hewitt, J. Initial interaction distance among individuals equal and unequal in military rank. *Journal of Personality and Social Psychology, 1975, 32,* 294–299.

DeGroot, I. Trends in public attitudes toward air pollution. *Journal of the Air Pollution Control Association, 1967, 17,* 679–681.

De Jonge, D. Images of urban areas. *Journal of American Institute of Planners, 1962, 28,* 266–276.

DeLong, A.J. Kinesic signals at utterance boundaries in preschool children. *Dissertation Abstracts, 1973, 33.*

Denison, D.M., Ledwith, F., & Poulton, E.C. Complex reaction times at simulated cabin altitudes of 5,000 ft. and 8,000 ft. *Aerospace Medicine, 1966, 37,* 1010.

Dennis, W. *Group values through children's drawings.* New York: McGraw-Hill, 1966.

DeSanctis, M., Halcomb, C.G., & Fedoravicius, A.S. *Meteorological determinants of human behavior: A holistic environmental perspective with special reference to air ionization and electrical field effects.* Unpublished manuscript, Texas Tech University, 1981.

Deslauriers, B.C., & Everett, P.B. Effects of intermittent and continuous token reinforcement on bus ridership. *Journal of Applied Psychology, 1977, 62,* 360–375.

Desor, J.A. Toward a psychological theory of crowding. *Journal of Personality and Social Psychology, 1972, 21,* 79–83.

Deutsch, M., & Collins, M.E. *Interracial housing: A psychological evaluation of a social experiment.* Minneapolis: University of Minnesota Press, 1951.

Dexter, E. School deportment and the weather. *Educational Review, 1904, 19,* 160–168.

Dietrick, B. *The environment and burglary victimization in a metropolitan suburb.* Paper presented at the annual meeting of the American Society of Criminology, Atlanta, Georgia, November 16–20, 1977.

Digon, E., & Block, H. Suicides and climatology. *Archives of Environmental Health, 1966, 12,* 279–286.

Dillman, D., & Tremblay, K., Jr. The quality of life in rural America. *Annals of the American Academy of Political and Social Sciences, 1977, 429,* 115–129.

Ditton, R.B., & Goodale, T.L. Water quality perceptions and attitudes. *Journal of Environmental Education, 1974, 6,* 21.

Dohrenwend, B.P., Dohrenwend, B.S., Kasl, S.V., & Warheit, G.J. *Report of the Task Group on Behavioral Effects to the President's Commission on the Accident at Three Mile Island.* Washington, D.C., October 1974.

Dohrenwend, B.S., & Dohrenwend, B.P. Psychiatric disorder in urban settings. In G. Caplan (Ed.), *American handbook of psychiatry,* (Vol. 3). rev. ed. Warheit, New York: Basic Books, 1972.

Donnerstein, E., & Wilson, D.W. Effects of noise and perceived control on ongoing and subsequent aggressive behavior. *Journal of Personality and Social Psychology,* 1976, *34,* 774–781.

Doob, L.W. The behavior of attitudes. *Psychological Review,* 1947, *54,* 135–156.

Dooley, B.B. *Crowding stress: The effects of social density on men with ''close'' or ''far'' personal space.* Unpublished doctoral dissertation, University of California at Los Angeles, 1974.

Doring, H.J., Hauf, G., & Seiberling, M. Effects of high intensity sound on the contractile function of the isolated ileum of guinea pigs and rabbits. In *Noise as a public health problem, Proceedings of the Third International Congress.* ASHA Reports, No. 10, 1980.

Dosey, M., & Meisels, M. Personal space and self-protection. *Journal of Personality and Social Psychology,* 1969, *11,* 93–97.

Downs, R.M., & Stea, D. Cognitive maps and spatial behavior: Process and products. In R.M. Downs & D. Stea (Eds.), *Image and environment: Cognitive mapping and spatial behavior.* Chicago: Aldine, 1973.

Downs, R.M., & Stea, D. *Maps in minds: Reflections on cognitive mapping.* New York: Harper & Row, 1977.

Drabek, T., & Quarantelli, E. Scapegoats, villains, and disasters. *Trans-Action,* 1967, *4,* 12–17.

Driver, B.L. Potential contributions of psychology to recreation resource management. In J. Wohlwill & D.H. Carson (Eds.), *Environment and the social sciences: Perspectives and applications.* Washington, D.C.: American Psychological Association, 1972.

Driver, B.L. Quantification of outdoor recreationists' preferences. In *Research camping and environmental education* (Pennsylvania State Series II). University Park: Pennsylvania State University, 1975.

Driver, B.L., & Knopf, R.C. Temporary escape: One product of sport fisheries management. *Fisheries,* 1976, *1,* 21–29.

Driver, B.L., & Knopf, R.C. Personality, outdoor recreation, and expected consequences. *Environment and Behavior,* 1977, *9,* 169–193.

Driver, B.L., & Tocher, S.R. Toward a behavioral interpretation of recreation, with implications for planning. In B.L. Driver (Ed.), *Elements of outdoor recreation planning.* Ann Arbor: University of Michigan Press, 1974.

Dubos, R. *Man adapting.* New Haven, Conn.: Yale University Press, 1965.

Duke, M.P., & Nowicki, S. A new measure and social learning model for interpersonal distance. *Journal of Experimental Research in Personality,* 1972, *6,* 119–132.

Duke, M.P., & Wilson, J. The measurement of interpersonal distance in pre-school children. *Journal of Genetic Psychology,* 1973, *123,* 361–362.

Durkheim, E. *Suicide: A study in sociology.* New York: Free Press, 1897/1951.

Duvall, D., & Booth, A. The housing environment and women's health. *Journal of Health and Social Behavior,* 1978, *19,* 410–417.

Easterbrook, J.A. The effects of emotion on cue-utilization and the organization of behavior. *Psychological Review,* 1959, *66,* 183–201.

Eastman, W.F. First intercourse. *Sexual Behavior,* 1972, *2,* 22–27.

Eastmann, A.A. Color contrast versus luminescence contrast. *Illuminating Engineering,* 1968, *63,* 613–620.

Ebbesen, E.B., Kjos, G.L., & Konecni, V.J. Spatial ecology: Its effects on the choice of friends and enemies. *Journal of Experimental Social Psychology,* 1976, *12,* 505–518.

Eberts, E.H., & Lepper, M.R. Individual consistency in the proxemic behavior of pre-school children. *Journal of Personality and Social Psychology,* 1975, *32,* 481–489.

Edney, J.J. Property, possession and permanence: A field study in human territoriality. *Journal of Applied Social Psychology,* 1972, *2,* 275–282.

Edney, J.J. Human territoriality. *Psychological Bulletin,* 1974, *81,* 959–975.

Edney, J.J. Territoriality and control: A field experiment. *Journal of Personality and Social Psychology,* 1975, *31,* 1108–1115.

Edney, J.J. Human territories: Comment on functional properties. *Environment and Behavior,* 1976, *8,* 31–48.

Edney, J.J. The nuts game: A concise commons dilemma analogue. *Environmental Psychology and Nonverbal Behavior,* 1979, *3,* 252–254.

Edney, J.J. The commons problem: Alternative perspectives. *American Psychologist,* 1980, *35,* 131–150.

Edney, J.J., & Harper, C.S. The effects of information in a resource management problem: A social trap analog. *Human Ecology,* 1978, *6,* 387–395.

Edney, J.J., & Uhlig, S.R. Individual and small group territories. *Small Group Behavior,* 1977, *8,* 457–468.

Edwards, D.J.A. Approaching the unfamiliar: A study of human interaction distances. *Journal of Behavioral Sciences,* 1972, *1,* 249–250.

Edwards, D.J.A. A cross-cultural study of social orientation and distance schemata by the method of doll placement. *Journal of Social Psychology,* 1973, *89,* 165–173.

Efran, M.G., & Cheyne, J.A. Shared space: The cooperative control of spatial areas by two interacting individuals. *Canadian Journal of Behavioural Science,* 1973, *5,* 201–210.

Efran, M.G., & Cheyne, J.A. Affective concomitants of the invasion of shared space: Behavioral, physiological, and verbal indicators. *Journal of Personality and Social Psychology,* 1974, *29,* 219–226.

Ehrlich, P. *The population boom.* New York: Ballantine, 1968.

Eibl-Eibesfeldt, I. *Ethology: The biology of behavior,* New York: Holt, Rinehart and Winston, 1970.

Einolander, J.C. Vandalism at Red Rock. In S. Alfano & A. Magill (Eds.), *Vandalism and outdoor recreation: Symposium proceedings.* USDA Forest Service Technical Report, PSW-17/1976.

Ellis, P., & Gashell, G. *A review of social research on the individual energy consumer.* Unpublished manuscript, 1978.

Emiley, S.F. The effects of crowding and interpersonal attraction on affective responses, task performance, and verbal behavior. *Journal of Social Psychology,* 1975, *97,* 267–271.

Environmental Protection Agency (EPA). *Report to the President and Congress on noise.* Washington, D.C.: U.S. Government Printing Office, 1972.

Eoyang, C.K. Effects of group size and privacy in residential crowding. *Journal of Personality and Social Psychology,* 1974, *30,* 389–392.

Epstein, Y.M., & Baum, A. Crowding: Methods of study. In A. Baum & Y. Epstein (Eds.), *Human response to crowding.* Hillsdale, N.J.: Erlbaum, 1978.

Epstein, Y.M., & Karlin, R.A. Effects of acute experimental crowding. *Journal of Applied Social Psychology,* 1975, *5,* 34–53.

Epstein, Y.M., Woolfolk, R.L., & Lehrer, P.M. Physiological, cognitive, and nonverbal responses to repeated experiences of crowding. *Journal of Applied Social Psychology,* 1981, *11,* 1–13.

Erikson, K.T. Loss of communality at Buffalo Creek. *American Journal of Psychiatry,* 1976, *133,* 302–305.

Ernsting, J. The ideal relationship between inspired oxygen concentration and cabin altitude. *Aerospace Medicine,* 1963, *34,* 991–997.

Ernsting, J. Physiological hazards of low pressure. In C.N. Davies, P.R. Davis, & F.H. Tyrer (Eds.), *The effects of abnormal physical conditions at work.* London: E. & S. Livingstone, 1967.

Esser, A.H. Interactional hierarchy and power structure on a psychiatric ward. In S.J. Hutt & C. Hutt (Eds.), *Behavior studies in psychiatry.* New York: Oxford University Press, 1970.

Esser, A.H. Cottage fourteen: Dominance and territoriality in a group of institutionalized boys. *Small Group Behavior,* 1973, *4,* 131–146.

Esser, A.H. Discussion of papers presented in the symposium "Theoretical and empirical issues with regard to privacy, territoriality, personal space, and crowding." *Environment and Behavior,* 1976, *8,* 117–125.

Esser, A.H. Chamberlain, A.S., Chapple, E.P., & Kline, N.S. Territoriality of patients on a research ward. In J. Wortis (Ed.), *Recent advances in biological psychiatry.* New York: Plenum, 1965.

Evans, G.W. An examination of the information overload mechanism of personal space. *Man–Environment Systems,* 1974, *4,* 61.

Evans, G.W. *Behavioral and physiological consequences of crowding in humans.* Unpublished doctoral dissertation, University of Massachusetts, 1975.

Evans, G.W. Crowding and the developmental process. In A. Baum & Y. Epstein (Eds.), *Human response to crowding.* Hillsdale, N.J.: Erlbaum, 1978. (a)

Evans, G.W. Human spatial behavior: The arousal model. In A. Baum & Y. Epstein (Eds.), *Human response to crowding.* Hillsdale, N.J.: Erlbaum, 1978. (b)

Evans, G.W. Behavioral and physiological consequences of crowding in humans. *Journal of Applied Social Psychology,* 1979, *9,* 27–46. (a)

Evans, G.W. Design implications of spatial research. In J. Aiello & A. Baum (Eds.), *Residential crowding and design.* New York: Plenum, 1979. (b)

Evans, G.W. Environmental cognition. *Psychological Bulletin,* 1980, *88,* 259–287.

Evans, G.W., & Howard, H.R.B. A methodological investigation of personal space. In W.J. Mitchell (Ed.), *Environmental design: Research and practice, Proceedings of EDRA3/AR8 Conference.* Los Angeles: University of California, 1972.

Evans, G.W., & Howard, R.B. Personal space. *Psychological Bulletin,* 1973, *80,* 334–344.

Evans, G.W., & Jacobs, S.V. Air pollution and human behavior. *Journal of Social Issues,* 1981, *37,* 95–125.

Evans, G.W., Jacobs, S., & Frager, N. *Human adaptation to photochemical smog.* Paper presented at the American Psychological Association meeting, New York, 1979.

Evans, G.W., Jacobs, S.V., & Frager, N.B. Behavioral responses to air pollution. In A. Baum & J. Singer (Eds.), *Advances in environmental psychology.* Hillsdale, N.J.: Erlbaum, 1982.

Evans, G.W., & Pezdek, K. Cognitive mapping: Knowledge of real-world distance and location information. *Journal of Experimental Psychology: Human Learning and Memory,* 1980, *6,* 13–24.

Everett, P.B. The use of the reinforcement procedure to increase bus ridership. *Proceedings of the Eighty-First Annual Convention of the American Psychological Association,* 1973, *8,* 891–892.

Everett, P.B. *A behavior science approach to transportation systems management.* Unpublished manuscript, 1977.

Everett, P.B., Deslauriers, B.C., Newson, T., & Anderson, V.B. The differential effects of two free ride dissemination procedures on bus ridership. *Transportation Research,* 1978, *12,* 1–6.

Everett, P.B., Hayward, S.C., & Meyers, A.W. The effects of a token reinforcement procedure on bus ridership. *Journal of Applied Behavior Analysis,* 1974, *7,* 1–9.

Feather, N.T. The relationship of persistence at a task to expectation of success and achievement related motives. *Journal of Abnormal and Social Psychology,* 1961, *63,* 552–561.

Federal Bureau of Investigation. *Uniform crime reporting handbook*. Washington, D.C.: U.S. Government Printing Office, 1978.

Federal Energy Administration. *Tips for energy savers*. Washington, D.C.: U.S. Government Printing Office, 1977.

Felipe, N.J., & Sommer, R. Invasions of personal space. *Social Problems*, 1966, *14*, 206–214.

Ferrari, N.A. *Institutionalization and attitude change in aged population: A field study in dissonance theory*. Doctoral dissertation, Western Reserve University, June 1960.

Festinger, L.A. A theory of social comparison processes. *Human Relations*, 1954, *7*, 117–140.

Festinger, L.A. *A theory of cognitive dissonance*. Stanford, Calif.: Stanford University Press, 1957.

Festinger, L.A., Schachter, S., & Back, K. *Social pressures in informal groups*. New York: Harper & Row, 1950.

Finckle, A.L., & Poppen, J.R. Clinical effects of noise and mechanical vibrations of a turbo-jet engine on man. *Journal of Applied Physiology*, 1948, *1*, 183–204.

Fines, K.D. *Landscape evaluation: A research project in East Sussex*. Elmsford, N.Y.: Pergamon, 1968.

Finkleman, J.M. Effects of noise on human performance. *Sound and Vibration*, 1975, *36*, 26–28.

Finkleman, J.M., & Glass, D.C. Reappraisal of the relationship between noise and human performance by means of a subsidiary task measure. *Journal of Applied Psychology*, 1970, *54*, 211–213.

Finnie, W.C. Field experiments in litter control. *Environment and Behavior*, 1973, *5*, 123–144.

Firestone, I.J. Reconciling verbal and nonverbal models of dyadic communication. *Environmental Psychology and Nonverbal Behavior*, 1977, *2* 30–44.

Fischer, C.S. Urban malaise. *Social Forces*, 1973, *52*, 221–235.

Fischer, C.S. *The urban experience*. New York: Harcourt Brace Jovanovich, 1976.

Fischer, C.S. Urban to rural diffusion of opinions in contemporary America. *American Journal of Sociology*, 1978, *84*, 151–159.

Fishbein, M. Attitude and the prediction of behavior. In M. Fishbein (Ed.), *Readings in attitude theory and measurement*. New York: Wiley, 1967.

Fishbein, M., & Azjen, I. *Belief, attitude, intention, and behavior: An introduction to theory and research*. Reading, Mass.: Addison-Wesley, 1975.

Fisher, J.D. Situation-specific variables as determinants of perceived environmental aesthetic quality and perceived crowdedness. *Journal of Research in Personality*, 1974, *8*, 177–188.

Fisher, J.D., & Baron, R.M. An equity-based model of vandalism. *Population and Environment*, 1982, *5*(3), 182–200.

Fisher, J.D., & Baum, A. Situational and arousal-based messages and the reduction of crowding stress. *Journal of Applied Social Psychology*, 1980, *10*, 191–201.

Fisher, J.D., & Byrne, D. Too close for comfort: Sex differences in response to invasions of personal space. *Journal of Personality and Social Psychology*, 1975, *32*, 15–21.

Fisher, R.L. Social schema of normal and disturbed school children. *Journal of Educational Psychology*, 1967, *58*, 88–92.

Fisher, W.A., Fisher, J.D., & Byrne, D. Consumer reactions to contraceptive purchasing. *Personality and Social Psychology Bulletin*, 1977, *3*, 293–297.

Fitch, J. *American building: The environmental forces that shape it*. Boston: Houghton Mifflin, 1972.

Fleming, R., Baum, A., Gisriel, M.M., & Gatchel, R.J. Mediation of stress at Three Mile Island by social support. *Journal of Human Stress*, 1982, *8*(3), 14–22.

Flynn, C.B. Three Mile Island telephone survey. U.S. Nuclear Regulatory Commission (NUREG/CR-1093), 1979.

Folk, G.E., Jr. *Textbook of environmental physiology*. Philadelphia: Lea & Febiger, 1974.

Fontaine, A. *Loss of control in the institutionalized elderly*. Unpublished manuscript, University of Connecticut, 1982.

Forbes, G., & Gromoll, H. The lost letter technique as a measure of social variables: Some exploratory findings. *Social Forces*, 1971, *50*, 113–115.

Ford, J.G., & Graves, J.R. Differences between Mexican-American and White children in interpersonal distance and social touching. *Perceptual and Motor Skills*, 1977, *45*, 779–785.

Ford, W.S. Interracial public housing in a border city: Another look at the contact hypothesis. *American Journal of Sociology*, 1973, *78*, 1426–1447.

Fortenberry, J.H., Maclean, J., Morris, P., & O'Connell, M. Mode of dress as a perceptual cue to deference. *Journal of Social Psychology*, 1978, *104*, 139–140.

Foster, B.E. (Ed.). Performance concept in buildings (Special publication No. 361, Vol. A). Washington, D.C.: National Bureau of Standards, 1972.

Fowler, F.D. A consumer ombudsman: The human factors engineer. *Human Factors*, 1972, *11*, 7–12.

Fowler, F.J., McCall, M.E., & Mangione, T.W. *Reducing residential crime and fear: The Hartford neighborhood crime prevention program*. Washington, D.C.: U.S. Government Printing Office, 1979.

Fox, W.F. Human performance in the cold. *Human Factors*, 1967, *9*, 203–220.

Foxx, R.M., & Hake, D.F. Gasoline conservation: A procedure for measuring and reducing the driving of college students. *Journal of Applied Behavior Analysis*, 1977, *10*, 61–74.

Francescato, D., & Mebane, W. How citizens view two great cities: Milan and Rome. In R.M. Downs & D. Stea (Eds.), *Image and environment: Cognitive mapping and spatial behavior*. Chicago: Aldine, 1973.

Francis, M. Urban impact assessment and community involvement: The case of the John Fitzgerald Kennedy Library. *Environment and Behavior*, 1975, *7*, 373–404.

Franck, K.D., Unseld, C.T., & Wentworth, W.E. *Adaptation of the newcomer: A process of construction.* Unpublished manuscript, City University of New York, 1974.

Frank, F. The causality of microtine cycles in Germany. *Journal of Wildlife Management,* 1957, *21,* 113–121.

Frankel, A.S., & Barrett, J. Variations in personal space as a function of authoritarianism, self-esteem, and racial characteristics of a stimulus situation. *Journal of Consulting and Clinical Psychology,* 1971, *37,* 95–98.

Frankenhaeuser, M. Behavior and circulating catecholamines. *Brain Research,* 1971, *31,* 241–262.

Frankenhaeuser, M. *Coping with job stress: A psychobiological approach.* Reports from the Department of Psychology, University of Stockholm, 1978, 532.

Frankenhaeuser, M., & Gardell, B. Underload and overload in working life: Outline of a multidisciplinary approach. *Journal of Human Stress,* 1976, *2,* 35–46.

Frankenhaeuser, M., Jarpe, G., & Mattel, G. Effects of intravenous infusions of adrenaline and noradrenaline on certain psychological and physiological functions. *Acta Physiologica Scandinavia,* 1961, *51,* 175–186.

Frankenhaeuser, M., & Lundberg, U. The influence of cognitive set on performance and arousal under different noise loads. *Motivation and Emotion,* 1977, *1,* 139–149.

Frankenhaeuser, M., Nordheden, B., Myrsten, A.L., & Post, B. Psychophysiological reactions to understimulation and overstimulation. *Acta Psychologia,* 1971, *35,* 298–308.

Freedman, J.L. *Crowding and behavior.* San Francisco: Freeman, 1975.

Freedman, J.L., Birsky, J., & Cavoukian, A. Environmental determinants of behavioral contagion: Density and number. *Basic and Applied Social Psychology,* 1980, *1,* 155–161.

Freedman, J.L., Carlsmith, J.M., & Sears, D.O. *Social psychology,* (2nd ed). Englewood Cliffs, N.J.: Prentice-Hall, 1974.

Freedman, J.L., Heshka, S., & Levy, A. Population density and pathology in metropolitan areas. In J.L. Freedman (Ed.), *Crowding and behavior.* San Francisco: Freeman, 1975.

Freedman, J.L., Klevansky, S., & Ehrlich, P.I., The effect of crowding on human task performance. *Journal of Applied Social Psychology,* 1971, *1,* 7–26.

Freedman, J.L., Levy, A.S., Buchanan, R.W., & Price, J. Crowding and human aggressiveness. *Journal of Experimental Social Psychology,* 1972, *8,* 528–548.

Freedman, J.L., & Perlick, D. Crowding, contagion, and laughter. *Journal of Experimental Social Psychology,* 1979, *15,* 295–303.

Freeman, H. Mental health and the environment. *British Journal of Psychiatry,* 1978, *132,* 113–124.

Frejka, T. The prospects for a stationary world population. *Scientific American,* 1973, *228,* 15–23.

Frey, J., Rotton, J., & Barry, T. The effects of the full moon on human behavior: Yet another failure to replicate. *Journal of Psychology,* 1979, *103,* 159–162.

Fried, M. Grieving for a lost home. In L.J. Dohl (Ed.), *The urban condition.* New York: Basic Books, 1963.

Fried, M., & Gleicher, P. Some sources of residential satisfaction in an urban slum. *Journal of the American Institute of Planners,* 1961, *27,* 305–315.

Frisancho, A.R. *Human adaptation.* St. Louis: Mosby, 1979.

Fry, A.M., & Willis, F.N. Invasion of personal space as a function of the age of the invader. *Psychological Record,* 1971, *2,* 385–389.

Fuller, B. Man with a chronofile. *Saturday Review,* April 1967, 14–18.

Galle, O.R., Gove, W.R., & McPherson, J.M. Population density and pathology: What are the relationships for man? *Science,* 1972, *176,* 23–30.

Galloway, W. *et al.* 1974. In J. Ralof (Ed.), Occupational noise—the subtle pollutant. *Science News,* 1982, *121*(21), 347–350.

Gallup Opinion Index. Princeton, N.J.: American Institute of Public Opinion, 1973, No. 102.

Gallup Poll, March 1978, 2.

Gallup Poll, April 4, 1981.

Gallup Poll, April 19, 1981.

Galster, G., & Hesser, G. Residential satisfaction: Compositional and contextual correlates. *Environment and Behavior,* 1981, *13,* 735–759.

Gans, H.J. *The Levittowners.* New York: Pantheon, 1970.

Garber, J., & Seligman, M.E.P. (Eds.). *Human helplessness: Theory and applications.* New York: Academic Press, 1981.

Gardner, E. *Fundamentals of neurology.* Philadelphia: Saunders, 1975.

Gardner, G.T. Effects of federal human subjects regulations on data obtained in environmental stressor research. *Journal of Personality and Social Psychology,* 1978, *36,* 628–634.

Garfinkel, H. Studies of the routine grounds of everyday activities. *Social Problems,* 1964, *11,* 225–250.

Garland, H., & Pearce, J. Neurological complications of carbon monoxide poisoning. *Quarterly Journal of Medicine,* 1967, *36,* 445–455.

Garzino, S.J. Lunar effects on mental behavior: A defense of the empirical research. *Environment and Behavior,* 1982, *4,* 395–417.

Gaydos, H.F. Effect on complex manual performance of cooling the body while maintaining the hands at normal temperatures. *Journal of Applied Physiology,* 1958, *12,* 373–376.

Gaydos, H.F., & Dusek, E.R. Effects of localized hand cooling versus total body cooling on manual performance. *Journal of Applied Physiology*, 1958, *12*, 377–380.

Geen, R.G., & O'Neal, E.C. Activation of cue-elicited aggression by general arousal. *Journal of Personality and Social Psychology*, 1969, *11*, 289–292.

Geen, R.G., & O'Neal, E.C. (Eds.). *Perspectives on aggression*. New York: Academic Press, 1976.

Gelfand, D.M., Hartman, D.P., Walder, P., & Page, B. Who reports shoplifters? A field-experimental study. *Journal of Personality and Social Psychology*, 1973, *25*, 276–285.

Geller, D.M. Response to urban stimulation: A balanced approach. *Journal of Social Issues*, 1980, *36*, 86–100.

Geller, E.S. *Behavioral approaches to environmental problem solving: Littering and recycling*. Symposium presentation at the Association for the Advancement of Behavior Therapy meeting, New York, 1976.

Geller, E.S. Applications of behavioral analysis for litter control. In D. Glenwik & L. Jason (Eds.), *Behavioral community psychology: Progress and prospects*. New York: Praeger, 1980.

Geller, E.S. Evaluating energy conservation programs: Is verbal report enough? *Journal of Consumer Research*, 1981, *8*, 331–335.

Geller, E.S., Chaffee, J.L., & Ingram, R.E. Promoting paper recycling on a university campus. *Journal of Environmental Systems*, 1975, *5*, 39–57.

Geller, E.S., Mann, M., & Brasted, W. *Trash can design: A determinant of litter-related behavior*. Paper presented at the American Psychological Association meeting, San Francisco, 1977.

Geller, E.S., Winnett, R.A., & Everett, P.B. *Preserving the environment: New strategies for behavior change*. New York: Pergamon, 1982.

Geller, E.S., Witmer, J.F., & Orebaugh, A.L. Instructions as a determinant of paper disposal behaviors. *Environment and Behavior*, 1976, *8*, 417–441.

Geller, E.S., Witmer, J.F., & Tuso, M.E. Environmental interventions for litter control. *Journal of Applied Psychology*, 1977, *62*, 344–351.

Gergen, K.J., Gergen, M.K., & Barton, W.H. Deviance in the dark. *Psychology Today*, 1973, *7*, 129–130.

Gibbs, J.P. Suicide. In R.K. Merton & R.A. Nisbet (Eds.), *Contemporary social problems*, (3rd ed). New York: Harcourt Brace Jovanovich, 1971.

Gibson, J.J. *The perception of the visual world*. Boston: Houghton Mifflin, 1950.

Gibson, J.J. *The senses considered as perceptual systems*. Boston: Houghton Mifflin, 1966.

Gibson, J.J. *An ecological approach to visual perception*. Boston: Houghton Mifflin, 1979.

Giel, R., & Ormel, J. Crowding and subjective health in the Netherlands. *Social Psychiatry*, 1977, *12*, 37–42.

Gifford, R., & Peacock, J. Crowding: More fearsome than crime-provoking? *Psychologia*, 1979, *22*, 79–83.

Gillis, A.R. Coping with crowding: Television, patterns of activity, and adaptation to high density environments. *Sociological Quarterly*, 1979, *20*, 267–277.

Ginsberg, Y. *Jews in a changing neighborhood*. New York: Free Press, 1975.

Ginsburg, H., Pollman, V., Wauson, M., & Hope, M. Variation of aggressive interaction among male elementary school children as a function of changes in social density. *Environmental Psychology and Nonverbal Behavior*, 1977, *2*, 67–75.

Glaser, D. *The effectiveness of a prison and parole system*. Indianapolis: Bobbs-Merrill, 1964.

Glass, D.C. *Behavior patterns, stress, and coronary disease*. Hillsdale, N.J.: Erlbaum, 1976.

Glass, D.C., & Singer, J.E. *Urban stress*. New York: Academic Press, 1972.

Glass, D.C., Singer, J.E., & Friedman, L.W. Psychic cost of adaptation to an environmental stressor. *Journal of Personality and Social Psychology*, 1969, *12*, 200–210.

Glass, D.C., Singer, J.E., Leonard, H.S., Krantz, D., Cohen, S., & Cummings, H. Perceived control of aversive stimulation and the reduction of stress responses. *Journal of Personality*, 1973, *41*, 577–595.

Glenn, N., & Hill, L. Rural–urban differences in attitudes and behavior in the United States. *The Annals of the American Academy of Political and Social Science*, 1977, *429*, 36–50.

Gleser, G., Green, B., & Winget, C. Quantifying interview data on psychic impairment of disaster survivors. *Journal of Nervous and Mental Disease*, 1978, *166*, 209–216.

Gleser, G., Green, B., & Winget, C. *Prolonged psychosocial effects of disaster: A study of Buffalo Creek*. New York: Academic Press, 1981.

Gliner, J., Raven, P., Horvath, S., Drinkwater, B., & Sutton, J. Man's physiological response to long-term work during thermal and pollutant stress. *Journal of Applied Physiology*, 1975, *39*, 628–632.

Gloug, A. Nonauditory effects of noise exposure. *Sounds and Vibration*, 1971, *5*, 28–29.

Goeckner, D., Greenough, W., & Maier, S. Escape learning deficit after overcrowded rearing in rats: Test of a helplessness hypothesis. *Bulletin of the Psychonomic Society*, 1974, *3*, 54–57.

Goldring, P. Role of distance and posture in the evaluation of interactions. *Proceedings of the 75th Annual Convention of the American Psychological Association*, 1967, *2*, 243–244.

Goldsmith, J.R. Effects of air pollution on human health. In A.C. Stern (Ed.), *Air pollution*, (2nd ed) New York: Academic Press, 1968.

Goldsmith, J., & Friberg, L. Effects of air pollution on human health. In A.C. Stern (Ed.), *Air pollution* (3rd ed., Vol. 3). New York: Academic Press, 1977.

Goodchild, B. Class differences in environmental perception. *Urban Studies,* 1974, *11,* 59–79.

Goodrich, R. Seven office evaluations: A review. *Environment and Behavior,* 1982, *14,* 353–378.

Goranson, R.E., & King. D. *Rioting and daily temperature: Analysis of the U.S. riots in 1967.* Unpublished manuscript, York University, 1970.

Gottfredson, S.D., Brower, S., & Taylor, R.B. *Design, social networks, and human territoriality: Predicting crime-related and social control outcomes.* Paper presented at the annual meeting of the American Psychological Association, New York, September 1979.

Gottman, J. The growing city as a social and political process. *Transactions of the Bartlett Society,* 1966, *5,* 9–46.

Grandjean, E., Graf, P., Lauber, A., Meier, H.P., & Muller, R. A survey on aircraft noise in Switzerland. In W.D. Ward (Ed.), *Proceedings of the International Congress on Noise as a Public Health Problem.* Washington, D.C.: U.S. Government Printing Office, 1973.

Grant, D.P. Architect discovers the aged. *Gerontologist,* 1970, *10,* 275–281.

Greenbaum, P.E., & Greenbaum, S.D. Territorial personalization: Group identity and social interaction in a Slavic-American neighborhood. *Environment and Behavior,* 1981, *13*(5), 574–589.

Greenberg, C.I. Toward an integration of ecological psychology and industrial psychology: Undermanning theory, organization size, and job enrichment. *Environmental Psychology and Nonverbal Behavior,* 1979, *3,* 228–242.

Greenberg, C.I., & Baum, A. Compensatory response to anticipated densities. *Journal of Applied Social Psychology,* 1979, *9,* 1–12.

Greenberg, C., & Firestone, I. Compensatory responses to crowding: Effects of personal space intrusion and privacy reduction. *Journal of Personality and Social Psychology,* 1977, *35,* 637–644.

Greenberg, S.W., Williams, J.R., & Rohe, W.M. Safety in urban neighborhood: A comparison of physical characteristics and informal territorial control in high and low crime neighborhoods. *Population and Environment,* 1982, *5,* 141–165.

Greenberger, D.B., & Allen, V.C. Destruction and complexity; An application of aesthetic theory. *Personality and Social Psychology Bulletin,* 1980, *6,* 479–483.

Greene, L.R. Effects of verbal evaluation feedback and interpersonal distance on behavioral compliance. *Journal of Consulting Psychology,* 1977, *24,* 10–14.

Greene, T.C. *Land-use, instructional set, and policies for landscape evaluation.* Unpublished doctoral dissertation, Colorado State University, 1983.

Greene, T.C., & Bell, P.A. Additional considerations concerning the effects of "warm" and "cool" wall colours on energy conservation. *Ergonomics,* 1980, *23,* 949–954.

Greene, W.A. The psychosocial setting of development of leukemia and hyphomia. *Annals of New York Academy of Science,* 1966, *125,* 794–801.

Gregory, R.L. *Eye and brain.* London: Weidenfeld & Nicolson, 1966.

Griffiths, I.D. The thermal environment. In D.C. Canter (Ed.), *Environmental interaction: Psychological approaches to our physical surroundings.* New York: International Universities Press, 1975.

Griffiths, I.D., & Boyce, P.R. Performance and thermal comfort. *Ergonomics,* 1971, *14,* 457–468.

Griffitt, W. Environmental effects on interpersonal affective behavior: Ambient effective temperature and attraction. *Journal of Personality and Social Psychology,* 1970, *15,* 240–244.

Guenther, R. Ways are found to minimize pollutants in airtight houses. *Wall Street Journal,* August 4, 1982, p. 25.

Gump, P.V. Operating environments in schools of open and traditional design. *School Review,* August 1974, 575–593.

Gump, P.V., & Adelberg, B. Urbanism from the perspective of ecological psychologists. *Environment and Behavior,* 1978, *10,* 171–191.

Gunderson, E.K.E. Mental health problems in Antarctica. *Archives of Environmental Health,* 1968, *17,* 558–564.

Gutman, G.M. Issues and findings relating to multilevel accommodation for seniors. *Journal of Gerontology,* 1978, *33,* 592–600.

Gutman, R. Site planning and social behavior. *Journal of Social Issues,* 1966, *22,* 103–105.

Haas, G. *Relationships among campers in Shenandoah National Park as related to social interaction, activity patterns, camping style, and descriptive characteristics.* Unpublished master's thesis, Pennsylvania State University, 1975.

Haase, R.S., & Pepper, D.T. Nonverbal components of empathic communication. *Journal of Counseling Psychology,* 1972, *19,* 417–424.

Haber, G.M. *The organization of space in the college classroom.* Doctoral dissertation, New York University, 1976.

Hackett, T.P., & Weisman, A.D. Reactions to the imminence of death. In G.H. Grosser, H. Weschler, & M. Greenblatt (Eds.), *The threat of impending disaster.* Cambridge, Mass.: M.I.T. Press, 1964.

Hackney, J., Linn, W., Karuza, S., Buckley, R., Law, D., Bates, D., Hazucha, M., Pengelly, L., & Silverman, F. Effects of ozone exposure in Canadians and Southern Californians. *Archives of Environmental Health,* 1977, *32,* 110–116.

Hake, D.F., & Foxx, R.M. Promoting gasoline conservation: The effects of reinforcement schedules, a leader and self-recording. *Behavior Modification,* 1978, *2,* 339–369.

Hall, E.T. *The silent language.* New York: Doubleday, 1959.

Hall, E.T. A system for the notation of proxemic behavior. *American Anthropologist,* 1963, *65,* 1003–1026.

Hall, E.T. *The hidden dimension*. New York: Doubleday, 1966.

Hall, E.T. Proxemics. *Current Anthropology*, 1968, *9*, 83–107.

Hamilton, D.L., & Bishop, G.D. Attitudinal and behavioral effects of initial integration of white suburban neighborhoods. *Journal of Social Issues*, 1976, *32*, 47–68.

Hamilton, P., & Copeman, A. The effect of alcohol and noise on components of a tracking and monitoring task. *British Journal of Psychology*, 1970, *61*, 149–156.

Hammel, H.T., Elsner, R.W., Andersen, K.L., Scholander, P.F., Coon, C.S., Medina, A., Strozzie, L., Milan, F.A., & Hock, R.J. Technical Report No. 60-633, Wright Air Development Division, 1960 (cited in LeBlanc, 1975).

Handlin, D. The detached house in the age of the object and beyond. In W. Mitchell (Ed.), *Environmental design: Research and practice*. Los Angeles: University of California/EDRA 3.

Haney, W.G., & Knowles, E.S. *Perception of neighborhoods by city and suburban residents*. Unpublished manuscript, University of Wisconsin-Green Bay, 1977.

Hannson, R.O., & Slade, K.M. Altruism toward a deviant in city and small town. *Journal of Applied Social Psychology*, 1977, *7*, 272–279.

Hansen, W.B., & Altman, I. Decorating personal places: A descriptive analysis. *Environment and Behavior*, 1976, *8*, 491–505.

Hanson, S., Vitek, J.D., & Hanson, P.O. Natural disaster: Long-range impact on human response to future disaster threats. *Environment and Behavior*, 1979, *11*, 268–284.

Hanusa, B.H., & Schulz, R. Attributional mediators of learned helplessness. *Journal of Personality and Social Psychology*, 1977, *35*, 602–611.

Harburg, E., Erfrut, J.C., Chape, C., Hauenstein, L.S., Schull, W.J., & Schork, M.A. Socioecological stressor areas and black–white blood pressure. *Journal of Chronic Diseases*, 1973, *26*, 595–611.

Hardin, G. The tragedy of the commons. *Science*, 1968, *162*, 1243–1248.

Hargreaves, A.G. Coping with disaster. *American Journal of Nursing*, April 1980, p. 683.

Harris, H., Lipman, A., & Slater, R. Architectural design: The spatial location and interactions of old people. *Gerontology*, 1977, *23*, 390–400.

Harris, V.A., & Jellison, J.M. Fear-arousing communications, false physiological feedback, and the acceptance of recommendations. *Journal of Experimental Social Psychology*, 1971, *7*, 269–279.

Harrison, P. Soccer's tribal wars. *New Society*, 1974, *29*, 602–604.

Hart, R.A., & Moore, G.T. The development of spatial cognition: A review. In R.M. Downs & D. Stea (Eds.), *Image and environment: Cognitive mapping and spatial behavior*. Chicago: Aldine, 1973.

Hart, R.H. The concept of APS: Air Pollution Syndrome(s). *Journal of the South Carolina Medical Association*, 1970, *66*, 71–73.

The Hartford Courant. Town pointing way in saving energy, November 25, 1979, p. 18.

Hartnett, J.J., Bailey, F., & Gibson, W. Personal space as influenced by sex and type of movement. *Journal of Psychology*, 1970, *76*, 139–144.

Hawkins, L.H., & Barker, T. Air ions and human performance. *Ergonomics*, 1978, *21*, 273–278.

Hay, D.G., & Wantman, M.J. Selected chronic diseases: Estimates of prevalence and of physician's service. New York: Center for Social Research, Graduate Center, City University of New York, 1969.

Hayduk, L.A. Personal space: An evaluative and orienting overview. *Psychological Bulletin*, 1978, *85*, 117–134.

Hayduk, L.A. The permeability of personal space. *Canadian Journal of Behavioral Science*, 1981, *13*, 274–287.

Hayduk, L.A., & Mainprize, S.A. Personal space of the blind. *Social Psychology Quarterly*, 1980, *43*, 216–223.

Hayes, S.C., & Cone, J.D. Decelerating environmentally destructive lawn-walking behavior. *Environment and Behavior*, 1977, *9*, 511–534. (a)

Hayes, S.C., & Cone, J.D. Reducing residential electrical energy use: Payments, information and feedback. *Journal of Applied Behavior Analysis*, 1977, *10*, 425–435. (b)

Hayes, S.C., & Cone, J.D. Reduction of residential consumption of electricity through simple monthly feedback. *Journal of Applied Behavior Analysis*, 1981, *14*, 81–88.

Hayes, S.C., Johnson, V.S., & Cone, J.D. The marked item technique: A practical procedure for litter control. *Journal of Applied Behavior Analysis*, 1975, *8*, 381–386.

Hayward, D.G., Rothenberg, M., & Beasley, R.R. Children's play and urban playground environments: A comparison of traditional, contemporary and adventure playground types. In H.M Proshansky, W.H. Ittelson, & L. Rivlin (Eds.), *Environmental psychology*, (2nd ed). New York: Holt, Rinehart and Winston, 1976.

Heath, D., & Williams, D.R. *Man at high altitude: The patho-physiology of acclimatization and adaptation*. Edinburgh: Churchill Livingstone, 1977.

Hebb, D.O. *Textbook of psychology* (3rd ed). Philadelphia: Saunders, 1972.

Heberlein, T.A. The land ethic realized: Some social psychological explanations for changing environmental atttitudes. *Journal of Social Issues*, 1972, *28*, 79–87.

Heberlein, T.A. Conservation information: The energy crisis and electricity consumption in an apartment complex. *Energy Systems and Policy*, 1975, *1*, 105–117.

Heberlein, T.A. Some observations on alternative mechanisms for public involvement: The hearing, the public opinion poll, and the quasi-experiment. *Natural Resources Journal,* 1976, 16, 197–212.

Heberlein, T.A., & Black, J.S. Attitudinal specificity and the prediction of behavior in a field setting. *Journal of Personality and Social Psychology,* 1976, *33,* 474–479.

Heberlein, T.A., & Black, J.S. Cognitive consistency and environmental action. *Environment and Behavior,* 1981, *13,* 717–734.

Hediger, H. *Wild animals in captivity.* London: Butterworth, 1950.

Heffron, M.H. The naval ship as an urban design problem. *Naval Engineers Journal,* 1972, *12,* 49–64.

Heft, H. The role of environmental features in route-learning: Two exploratory studies of wayfinding. *Environmental Psychology and Nonverbal Behavior,* 1979, *3,* 172–185. (a)

Heft, H. Background and focal environmental conditions of the home and attention in young children. *Journal of Applied Social Psychology,* 1979, *9,* 47–69. (b)

Heft, H. An examination of constructivist and Gibsonian approaches to environmental psychology. *Population and Environment,* 1981, *4,* 227–245.

Heimstra, N.W., & McFarling, L.H. *Environmental psychology* (2nd ed). Monterey, Calif.: Brooks/Cole, 1978.

Heller, J., Groff, B., & Solomon, S. Toward an understanding of crowding: The role of physical interaction. *Journal of Personality and Social Psychology,* 1977, *35,* 183–190.

Helmreich, R. The evaluation of environments: Behavioral observations in an undersea habitat. In J. Lang, C. Burnette, W. Moleski, & D. Vachon (Eds.), *Designing for human behavior.* Stroudsburg, Pa.: Dowden, Hutchinson & Ross, 1974.

Helson, H. *Adaptation level theory.* New York: Harper & Row, 1964.

Helson, H., & Lansford, T.G. The role of spectral energy of source and background color in the pleasantness of object odors. *Applied Optics,* 1970, *9,* 1513–1562.

Henderson, L.F., & Jenkins, D.M. Response of pedestrians to traffic challenge. *Transportation Research,* 1974, *8,* 71–74.

Herridge, C.F. Aircraft noise and mental health. *Journal of Psychosomatic Research,* 1974, *18,* 239–243.

Herridge, C.F., & Low-Beer, L. Observations of the effects of aircraft noise near Heathrow Airport on mental health. In W.D. Ward (Ed.), *Proceedings of the International Congress on Noise as a Public Health Problem.* Washington, D.C.: U.S. Government Printing Office, 1973.

Hershberger, R.G., & Cass, R.C. Predicting user responses to buildings. In D. Carson (Ed.), *Man–environment interactions: Evaluations and applications* (Part 2). Stroudsburg, Pa.: Dowden, Hutchinson & Ross, 1974.

Herzberg, F., Mausner, B., Peterson, R.O., & Capwell, D.F. *Job attitudes: Review of research and opinion.* Pittsburgh: Psychological Service of Pittsburgh, 1957.

Herzberg, F., Mausner, B., & Snyderman, B. *The motivation to work.* New York: Wiley, 1959.

Heshka, S., & Nelson, Y. Interpersonal speaking distance as a function of age, sex, and relationship. *Sociometry,* 1972, *35,* 491–498.

Heshka, S., & Pylypuk, A. *Human crowding and adrenocortical activity.* Paper presented at the meeting of the Canadian Psychological Association, Quebec, June 1975.

Heywood, L.A. Perceived recreative experience and the relief of tension. *Journal of Leisure Research,* 1978, *10,* 86–97.

Hicks, P.E. *Introduction to industrial engineering and management science.* New York: McGraw-Hill, 1977.

Higbee, K.L. Fifteen years of fear arousal: Research on threat appeals. *Psychological Bulletin,* 1969, *72,* 426–444.

Hildum, D.C, & Brown, R.W. Verbal reinforcement of interviewer bias. *Journal of Abnormal and Social Psychology,* 1956, *53,* 108–111.

Hill, J.W. Applied problems of hot work in the glass industry. In C.N. Davies, P.R. Davis, & F.H. Tyrer (Eds.), *The effects of abnormal physical conditions at work.* London: E. & S. Livingstone, 1967.

Hinshaw, M., & Allott, K. Environmental preferences of future housing consumers. *Journal of the American Institute of Planners,* 1972, *38,* 102–107.

Hiroto, D.S. Locus of control and learned helplessness. *Journal of Experimental Psychology,* 1974, *102,* 187–193.

Hirst, E. Transportation energy conservation policies. *Science,* 1976, *192,* 15–20.

Hoch, I. Urban scale and environmental quality. In P. Ridker (Ed.), *Population resources and the environment* (Vol. 3). Washington, D.C.: U.S. Government Printing Office, 1972.

Hockey, G.R.F. Effect of loud noise on attentional selectivity. *Quarterly Journal of Experimental Psychology,* 1970, *22,* 28–36.

Holahan, C.J. Seating patterns and patient behavior in an experimental dayroom. *Journal of Abnormal Psychology,* 1972, *80,* 115–124.

Holahan, C.J. Environmental change in a psychiatric setting: A social systems analysis. *Human Relations,* 1976, *29,* 153–166. (a)

Holahan, C.J. Environmental effects on outdoor social behavior in a low income urban neighborhood: A naturalistic investigation. *Journal of Applied Social Psychology,* 1976, *6,* 48–63. (b)

Holahan, C.J. *Environment and behavior.* New York: Plenum, 1978.

Holahan, C.J., & Moos, R.H. Social support and psychological distress: A longitudinal analysis. *Journal of Abnormal Psychology,* 1981, *49,* 365–370.

Holahan, C.J., & Saegert, S. Behavioral and attitudinal effects of large-scale variation in the physical environment of psychiatric wards. *Journal of Abnormal Psychology,* 1973, *83,* 454–462.

Holland, G.J., Benson, D., Bush, A., Rich, G., & Holland, R. Air pollution simulation and human performance. *American Journal of Public Health,* 1968, *58,* 1684–1690.

Hollander, J., & Yeostros, S. The effect of simultaneous variations of humidity and barometric pressure on arthritis. *Bulletin of the American Meteorological Society,* 1963, *44,* 489–494.

Hollingshead, A.B., & Rogler, L.H. Attitudes toward slums and public housing in Puerto Rico. In L.J. Duhl (Ed.), *The urban condition.* New York: Simon & Schuster, 1963.

Hoover, J.E. Crime in the United States, In *Uniform Crime Reports,* Washington, D.C.: U.S. Department of Justice, August 1966.

Hore, T., & Gibson, D. Ozone exposure and intelligence tests. *Archives of Environmental Health,* 1968, *17,* 77–91.

Horowitz, M.J., Duff, D.F., & Stratton, L.O. Body-buffer zone. *Archives of General Psychiatry,* 1964, *11,* 651–656.

Horvath, S.M., Dahms, T.E., & O'Hanlon, J.F. Carbon monoxide and human vigilance: A deleterious effect of present urban concentrations. *Archives of Environmental Health,* 1971, *23,* 343–347.

House, J.S., & Wolf, S. Effects of urban residence on interpersonal trust and helping behavior. *Journal of Personality and Social Psychology,* 1978, *36,* 1029–1043.

Houts, P.S., Miller, R.W., Tokuhata, G.K., & Ham, K.S. *Health-related behavioral impact of the Three Mile Island nuclear incident.* Report submitted to the TMI Advisory Panel on Health Research Studies of the Pennsylvania Department of Health, Part I, April 8, 1980.

Howard, E. *Tomorrow: A peaceful path to reform.* London: Sonnenschein, 1898.

Howell, D.L., & Warmbrod, J.R. Developing student attitudes toward environmental protection. *Journal of Environmental Education,* 1974, *5,* 29–30.

Hughes, J., & Goldman, M. Eye contact, facial expression, sex, and the violation of personal space. *Perceptual and Motor Skills,* 1978, *46,* 579–584.

Hummel, C.F. *Effects of induced cognitive sets in viewing air pollution scenes.* Unpublished doctoral dissertation, Colorado State University, 1977.

Hummel, C.F., Levitt, L., & Loomis, R.J. *Research strategies for measuring attitudes toward pollution.* Unpublished manuscript, Colorado State University, 1973.

Hummel, C.F., Levitt, L., & Loomis, R.J. Perceptions of the energy crisis: Who is blamed and how do citizens react to environment-lifestyle trade-offs? *Environment and Behavior,* 1978, *10,* 37–88.

Hummel, C.F., Loomis, R.J., & Hebert, J.A. *Effects of city labels and cue utilization on air pollution judgments (Working Papers in Environmental-Social Psychology,* No. 1). Unpublished manuscript, Colorado State University, 1975.

Hundert, A.J., & Greenfield, N. Physical space and organizational behavior: A study of an office landscape. *Proceedings of the 77th Annual Convention of the American Psychological Association,* 1969, *4,* 601–602.

Hunt, J. Fundamental studies of wind flow near buildings: Models and systems in architecture and building. *LUBFS Conference Proceedings* (2). Lancaster, England: Construction Press, 1975.

Hunt, T.J., & May, P.I. *A preliminary investigation into a psychological assessment of driving stress.* London: Metropolitan Police Accident Research Unit, 1968.

Hunter, A. Persistence of local sentiments in mass society. In D. Street (Ed.), *Handbook of contemporary urban life.* San Francisco: Jossey-Bass, 1978.

Huntington, E. *Civilization and climate.* New Haven: Yale University Press, 1915.

Huntington, E. *Mainsprings of civilization.* New York: Wiley, 1945.

Hurt, H. The hottest place in the whole U.S.A. *Texas Monthly,* 1975, *3,* 50ff.

Hutt, C., & Vaizey, M.S. Differential effects of group density on social behavior. *Nature,* 1966, *209,* 1371–1372.

Hynson, L.M. Rural–urban difference in satisfaction among the elderly. *Rural Sociology,* 1975, *46,* 64–66.

Ickes, W., Patterson, M.L., Rajecki, D.W., & Tanford, S. Behavioral and cognitive consequences of reciprocal versus compensatory responses to pre-interaction expectancies. *Social Cognition,* in press.

Imamoglu, V. The effect of furniture density on the subjective evaluation of spaciousness and estimation of size of rooms. In R. Kuller (Ed.), *Architectural psychology: Proceedings of the Lund Conference.* Stroudsburg, Pa.: Dowden, Hutchinson & Ross, 1973.

Ingram, R.E., & Geller, E.S. A community integrated behavior modification approach to facilitating paper recycling. *JSAS Catalog of Selected Documents in Psychology,* 1975, *5,* 327 (Ms. No. 1097).

Insko, C.A. Verbal reinforcement of attitude. *Journal of Personality and Social Psychology,* 1965, *2,* 621–623.

Isen, A.M. Success, failure, attention, and reaction to others: The warm glow of success. *Journal of Personality and Social Psychology,* 1970, *15,* 294–301.

Ising, H., & Melchert, H.U. Endocrine and cardiovascular effects of noise. In *Noise as a public health problem, Proceedings of the Third International Congress.* ASHA Reports No. 10, 1980.

Ittelson, W.H. *Environmental psychology and architectural planning.* Paper presented at the American Hospital Association Conference on Hospital Planning, New York, 1964.

Ittelson, W.H. Perception of the large-scale environment. *Transactions of the New York Academy of Sciences,* 1970, *32,* 807–815.

Ittelson, W.H. (Ed.). *Environment and cognition.* New York: Seminar Press, 1973.

Ittelson, W.H. Some issues facing a theory of environment and behavior. In H.M. Proshansky, W.H. Ittelson, & L.G. Rivlin

(Eds.), *Environmental psychology: People and their physical settings.* New York: Holt, Rinehart and Winston, 1976.

Ittelson, W.H. Environmental perception and urban experience. *Environment and Behavior,* 1978, *10,* 193–213.

Ittelson, W.H., Proshansky, H., & Rivlin, L. Bedroom size and social interaction of the psychiatric ward. *Environment and Behavior,* 1970, *2,* 255.

Ittelson, W.H., Proshansky, H.M., & Rivlin, L.G. Bedroom size and social interaction of the psychiatric ward. In J. Wohlwill & D. Carson (Eds.), *Environment and the social sciences.* Washington, D.C.: American Psychological Association, 1972. (Reports based on the same data appeared in: Ittelson, W.H., Proshansky, H.M., & Rivlin, L.G. A study of bedroom use on two psychiatric wards. *Hospital and Community Psychology,* 1970, *21*(6), 25–28; and Ittelson, W.H., Proshansky, H.M., & Rivlin, L.G. The environmental psychology of the psychiatric ward. In H.M. Proshansky, W.H. Ittelson, & L.G. Rivlin (Eds.), *Environmental psychology.* New York: Holt, Rinehart and Winston, 1970.)

Ittelson, W.H., Proshansky, H.M., Rivlin, L.G., & Winkel, G.H. *An introduction to environmental psychology.* New York: Holt, Rinehart, and Winston, 1974.

Ittelson, W.H., Rivlin, L.G., & Proshansky, H.M. The use of behavioral maps in environmental psychology. In H.M. Proshansky, W.H. Ittelson, & L.G. Rivlin (Eds.), *Environmental psychology: People and their physical settings.* New York: Holt, Rinehart and Winston, 1976.

Iwata, O. Selected personality traits as determinants of the perception of crowding. *Japanese Psychological Research,* 1979, *21,* 1–9.

Izmerov, N. Establishment of air quality standards. *Archives of Environmental Health,* 1971, *22,* 711–719.

Jackson, E.L. Responses to earthquake hazard: The west coast of America. *Environment and Behavior,* 1981, *13,* 387–416.

Jackson, J.B. The historic American landscape. In E.H. Zube, R.O. Brush, & J.G. Fabos (Eds.), *Landscape assessment: Values, perceptions, and resources.* Stroudsburg, Pa.: Dowden, Hutchinson & Ross, 1975.

Jacobs, H., Fairbanks, D., Doche, C., & Bailey, J.S. Behavioral community psychology: Multiple incentives in encouraging carpool formation on a university campus. *Journal of Applied Behavior Analysis,* 1982, *15,* 141–149.

Jacobs, J. *The death and life of great American cities.* New York: Random House, 1961.

Jain, U. Competition tolerance in high- and low-density urban and rural areas. *Journal of Social Psychology,* 1978, *105,* 297–298.

Janis, I.L. *Psychological stress: Psychoanalytic and behavioral studies of surgical patients.* New York: Wiley, 1958.

Jansen, G. Non-auditory effects of noise—Physiological and psychological reactions in man. *Proceedings of the International Congress on Noise as a Public Health Problem.* Dubrovnik, Yugoslavia, May 13–18, 1973. Washington, D.C.: U.S. Environmental Protection Agency.

Jason, L.A., Zolik, E.S., & Matese, F. Prompting dog owners to pick up dog droppings. *American Journal of Community Psychology,* 1979, *7,* 339–351.

Jerdee, T.H., & Rosen, B. Effects of opportunity to communicate and visibility of individual decisions on behavior in the common interest. *Journal of Applied Psychology,* 1974, *59,* 712–716.

Johnson, J.E. Effects of accurate expectations about sensations on the sensory and distress components of pain. *Journal of Personality and Social Psychology,* 1973, *27,* 261–275.

Johnson, J.E., & Leventhal, H. Effects of accurate expectations and behavioral instructions on reactions during a noxious medical examination. *Journal of Personality and Social Psychology,* 1974, *29,* 710–718.

Jones, J.C. *Design methods: Seeds of human futures.* New York: Wiley, 1970. (a)

Jones, J.C. An experiment for planning and design. In G.T. Moore (Ed.), *Emerging methods in environmental design and planning.* Cambridge, Mass.: M.I.T. Press, 1970. (b)

Jones, J.W. Adverse emotional reactions of nonsmokers to secondary cigarette smoke. *Environmental Psychology and Nonverbal Behavior,* 1978, *3,* 125–127.

Jones, J.W., & Bogat, G.A. Air pollution and human aggression. *Psychological Reports,* 1978, *43,* 721–722.

Jones, S.E., & Aiello, J.R. A test of the validity of projective and quasi-projective measures of interpersonal distance. *The Western Journal of Speech Communication,* 1979, *43,* 143–152.

Jöreskag, K.G., & Sörbom, D. *LISREL IV: Analysis of lineal structural relationships by the method of maximum likelihood.* Chicago: National Educational Resources, 1978.

Jorgenson, D.O. Locus of control and the perceived causal influence of the lunar cycle. *Perceptual and Motor Skills,* 1981, *52,* 864.

Jorgenson, D.O., & Dukes, F.O. Deindividuation as a function of density and group membership. *Journal of Personality and Social Psychology,* 1976, *34,* 24–39.

Jorgenson, D.O., & Papciak, A.S. The effects of communication, resource feedback, and identifiability on behavior in a simulated commons. *Journal of Experimental Social Psychology,* 1981, *17,* 373–385.

Jourard, S.M., & Rubin, J.E. Self-disclosure and touching: A study of two modes of interpersonal encounter and their interrelation. *Journal of Humanistic Psychology,* 1968, *8,* 39–48.

Joy, V.D., & Lehmann, N. *The cost of crowding: Responses and adaptations.* Unpublished manuscript, New York State Department of Mental Hygiene, 1975.

Kahn, R., & French, J.R.P. Status and conflict: Two themes in the study of stress. In J.E. McGrath (Ed.), *Social and psychological factors in stress.* New York: Holt, Rinehart and Winston, 1970.

Kahneman, D. *Attention and effort.* Englewood Cliffs, N.J.: Prentice-Hall, 1973.

Kain, J.F., Fauth, G.R., & Zax, J. *Forecasting auto ownership and mode choice for U.S. metropolitan areas.* Cambridge, Mass.: Harvard University Department of City and Regional Planning, 1977.

Kammann, R., Thompson, R., & Irwin, R. Unhelpful behavior in the street: City size or immediate pedestrian density? *Environment and Behavior,* 1979, *11,* 245–250.

Kane, J.N., & Alexander, G.C. *Nicknames of cities and states in the United States.* New York: Scarecrow Press, 1965.

Kaplan, R. Some methods and strategies in the prediction of preference. In E.H. Zube, J.G. Fabos, & R.O. Brush (Eds.), *Landscape assessment: Values, perceptions, and resources.* Stroudsburg, Pa.: Dowden, Hutchinson & Ross, 1974.

Kaplan, R. Patterns of environmental preference. *Environment and Behavior,* 1977, *9,* 195–216.

Kaplan, S. Cognitive maps in perception and thought. In R.M. Downs & D. Stea (Eds.), *Image and environment: Cognitive mapping and spatial behavior.* Chicago: Aldine, 1973.

Kaplan, S. An informal model for the prediction of preference. In E.H. Zube, J.G. Fabos, & R.O. Brush (Eds.), *Landscape assessment: Values, perceptions, and resources.* Stroudsburg, Pa.: Dowden, Hutchinson, & Ross, 1975.

Kaplan, S. Participation in design process: A cognitive approach. In D. Stokols (Ed.), *Perspectives on environment and behavior: Theory, research, and applications.* New York: Plenum, 1977.

Kaplan, S. Concerning the power of content-identifying methodologies. In T.C. Daniel, E.H. Zube & B.L. Driver (Technical Coordinators), *Assessing amenity resource values* (USDA Forest Service General Technical Report RM-68). Fort Collins, Colo.: Rocky Mountain Forest and Range Experiment Station, 1979. (a)

Kaplan, S. Perception and landscape: Conceptions and misconceptions. In G. Elsner & R. Smardon (Technical Coordinators), *Proceedings of our national landscape: A conference on applied techniques for the analysis and management of the visual resource.* (USDA Forest Service General Technical Report PSW-35). Berkeley, Calif.: Pacific Southwest Forest and Range Experiment Station, 1979. (b)

Kaplan, S., & Kaplan, R. *Humanscape: Environments for people.* North Scituate, Mass.: Duxbury, 1978.

Kaplan, S., & Kaplan, R. *Cognition and environment.* New York: Praeger, 1982.

Kaplan, S., Kaplan, R., & Wendt, J.S. Rated preference and complexity for natural and urban visual material. *Perception and Psychophysics,* 1972, *12,* 354–356.

Karabenick, S.A., & Meisels, M. Effects of performance evaluation on interpersonal distance. *Journal of Personality,* 1972, *40,* 275–286.

Karlin, R.A., Epstein, Y., & Aiello, J. Strategies for the investigation of crowding. In A. Esser & B. Greenbie (Eds.), *Design for communality and privacy.* New York: Plenum, 1978.

Karlin, R.A., Katz, S., Epstein, Y., & Woolfolk, R. The use of therapeutic interventions to reduce crowding-related arousal: A preliminary investigation. *Environmental Psychology and Nonverbal Behavior,* 1979, *3,* 219–227.

Karlin, R.A., McFarland, D., Aiello, J.R., & Epstein, Y.M. Normative mediation of reactions to crowding. *Environmental Psychology and Nonverbal Behavior,* 1976, *1*(1), 30–40.

Karlin, R.A., Rosen, L., & Epstein, Y. Three into two doesn't go: A follow-up of the effects of overcrowded dormitory rooms. *Personality and Social Psychology Bulletin,* 1979, *5,* 391–395.

Karmel, L.J. Effects of windowless classroom environment on high school students. *Perceptual and Motor Skills,* 1965, *20*(1), 277–278.

Kasl, S.V., & Cobb, S. Blood pressure changes in men undergoing job loss: A preliminary report. *Psychosomatic Medicine,* 1970, *32,* 19–38.

Kasmer, J. The development of a useful lexicon of environmental descriptors. *Environment and Behavior,* 1970, *2,* 135–169.

Kates, R.W. Experiencing the environment as hazard. In H.M. Proshansky, W.H. Ittelson, & L.G. Rivlin (Eds.), *Environmental psychology: People and their physical settings* (2nd ed.) New York: Holt, Rinehart and Winston, 1976.

Katz, P. *Animals and men.* New York: Longmans, Green, 1937.

Keating, J., & Snowball, H. Effects of crowding and depersonalization on perception of group atmosphere. *Perceptual and Motor Skills,* 1977, *44,* 431–435.

Keep America Beautiful, Inc. *Fact sheet: Litter is a national disgrace.* New York, 1970.

Kelley, C.M. *Crime in the United States, 1973.* Washington, D.C.: Federal Bureau of Investigation, U.S. Government Printing Office, 1974.

Kelley, H., & Arrowood, A. Coalitions in the triad: Critique and experiment. *Sociometry,* 1960, *23,* 231–244.

Kenny, D.A. *Correlation and causality.* New York: Wiley, 1981.

Kenrick, D.T., & Johnson, G.A. Interpersonal attraction in aversive environments. A problem for the classical conditioning paradigm. *Journal of Personality and Social Psychology,* 1979, *37,* 572–579.

Kerchoff, A.C., & Back, K.W. *The June bug: A study of hysterical contagion.* New York: Appleton-Century-Crofts, 1968.

Kerlinger, F.N. *Foundations of behavioral research* (2nd ed.). New York: Holt, Rinehart and Winston, 1973.

Key, W. Rural–urban social participation. In S. Fava, (Ed.), *Urbanism in world perspective.* New York: Crowell, 1968.

Keyfitz, N. Population density and the style of social life. *Bioscience.* 1966, *16,* 868–873.

Kilmer, W. *Undersea habitat.* Personal publication, 1972.

Kinarthy, E.L. *The effect of seating position on performance and personality in a college classroom.* Doctoral dissertation, University of Southern California, 1975.

Kinzel, A.S. Body buffer zone in violent prisoners. *American Journal of Psychiatry,* 1970, *127,* 59–64.

Kira, A. *The bathroom.* New York: Viking, 1976.

Kleck, R.E., Buck, P.L., Goller, W.C., London, R.S., Pfeiffer, J.R., & Vukcevic, D.P. Effect of stigmatizing conditions on the use of personal space. *Psychological Reports*, 1968, *23*, 111–118.

Klein, K., & Harris, B. Disruptive effects of disconfirmed expectancies about crowding. *Journal of Personality and Social Psychology*, 1979, *37*, 769–777.

Klopfer, P.H. From Ardrey to altruism: A discourse on the biological basis of human behavior. *Behavioral Science*, 1968, *13*, 399–401.

Knight, R., Weitzer, W.H., & Zimring, C.M. *Opportunity for control and the built environment: The ELEMR project*. Amherst: University of Massachusetts, 1978.

Knowles, E.S. Boundaries around social space: Dyadic responses to an invader. *Environment and Behavior*, 1972, *4*, 437–447.

Knowles, E.S. Boundaries around group interaction: The effect of group and member status on boundary permeability. *Journal of Personality and Social Psychology*, 1973, *26*, 327–331.

Knowles, E.S. The gravity of crowding: Application of social physics to the effects of others. In A. Baum & Y. Epstein (Eds.), *Human response to crowding*. Hillsdale, N.J.: Erlbaum, 1978.

Knowles, E.S. Convergent validity of personal space measures: Consistent results with low intercorrelations. *Journal of Nonverbal Behavior*, 1980, *4*, 240–248.

Knowles, E.S., & Bassett, R.I. Groups and crowds as social entities: Effects of activity, size and member similarity on non-members. *Journal of Personality and Social Psychology*, 1976, *34*, 837–845.

Knowles, E.S., & Brickner, M.A. Social cohesion effects on spatial cohesion. *Personality and Social Psychology Bulletin*, 1981, *7*, 309–313.

Knowles, E.S., & Johnsen, P.K. Intrapersonal consistency and interpersonal distance. *JSAS Catalog of Selected Documents in Psychology*, 1974, *4*, 124.

Knowles, E.S., Kreuser, B., Haas, S., Hyde, M., & Schuchart, G.E. Group size and the extension of social space boundaries. *Journal of Personality and Social Psychology*, 1976, *33*, 647–654.

Kohlenberg, R., & Phillips, T. Reinforcement and rate of litter depositing. *Journal of Applied Behavior Analysis*, 1973, *6*, 391–396.

Kohlenberg, R., Phillips, T., & Proctor, W. A behavioral analysis of peaking in residential electrical energy consumers. *Journal of Applied Behavior Analysis*, 1976, *9*, 13–18.

Konar, E., Sundstrom, E., Brady, C., Mandel, D., & Rice, R.W. Status demarcation in the office. *Environment and Behavior*, 1982, *14*, 561–580.

Konecni, V.J., Libuser, L., Morton, H., & Ebbesen, E.B. Effects of a violation of personal space on escape and helping responses. *Journal of Experimental Social Psychology*, 1975, *11*, 288–299.

Koneya, M. Location and interaction in row-and-column seating arrangements. *Environment and Behavior*, 1976, *8*, 265–283.

Konzett, H. Jahre osterreichischle Pharmakologie. *Wien Med Wochenscher*, 1975, *125* (1–2 suppl): 1–6.

Konzett, H., Hortnagel, H., Hortnagel, L., & Winkler, H. On the urinary output of vasopressin, epinephrine and norepinephrine during different stress situations. *Psychopharmacologia*, 1971, *21*, 247–256.

Koocher, G.P. Bathroom behavior and human dignity. *Journal of Personality and Social Psychology*, 1977, *35*, 120–121.

Korte, C. Urban–nonurban differences in social behavior and social psychological models of urban impact. *Journal of Social Issues*, 1980, *36*, 29–51.

Korte, C., & Kerr, N. Responses to altruistic opportunities under urban and rural conditions. *Journal of Social Psychology*, 1975, *95*, 183–184.

Korte, C., Ypma, I., & Toppen, A. Helpfulness in Dutch society as a function of urbanization and environmental input level. *Journal of Personality and Social Psychology*, 1975, *32*, 996–1003.

Kosslyn, S.M. Information representation in visual images. *Cognitive Psychology*, 1975, *7*, 341–370.

Kosslyn, S.M., Ball, T.M., & Reiser, B.J. Visual images preserve metric spatial information: Evidence from studies of image scanning. *Journal of Experimental Psychology: Human Perception and Performance*, 1978, *4*, 47–60.

Kosslyn, S.M., & Pomerantz, J.P. Imagery, propositions, and the form of internal representations. *Cognitive Psychology*, 1977, *9*, 52–76.

Kramer, B.M. *Residential contact as a determinant of attitudes toward Negroes*. Unpublished doctoral dissertation, Harvard University, 1950.

Kraus, R. *Recreation and leisure in modern society*. Santa Monica, Calif.: Goodyear, 1978.

Krauss, R.M., Freedman, J.L., & Whitcup, M. Field and laboratory studies of littering. *Journal of Experimental Social Psychology*, 1978, *14*, 109–122.

Krebs, C.J. *Ecology: The experimental distribution and abundance*. New York: Harper & Row, 1972.

Krupat, E. *People in cities*. Unpublished manuscript, Massachusetts College of Pharmacy and Allied Health Sciences, 1982.

Krupat, E., Guild, W., & Miller, M. *Characteristics of large and medium sized cities, and small towns*. Unpublished manuscript, Boston College, 1977.

Kryter, K.D. *The effects of noise on man*. New York: Academic Press, 1970.

Kuipers, B. The map in the head metaphor. *Environment and Behavior*, 1982, *14*, 202–220.

Lacey, J.I. Somatic response patterning and stress: Some revisions of activation theory. In W.H. Appley & R. Trumball (Eds.), *Psychological stress*. New York: Appleton-Century-Crofts, 1967.

Ladd, F.C. Black youths view their environment: Neighborhood maps. *Environment and Behavior*, 1970, *2*, 74–99.

Ladd, F.C. Black youths view their environments. *Journal of the American Institute of Planners, 1972, 38,* 108–115.

Lagerwerff, J. Prolonged ozone inhalation and its effects on visual parameters. *Aerospace Medicine, 1963, 34,* 471–481.

La Hart, D., & Bailey, J.S. Reducing children's littering on a nature trail. *Journal of Environmental Education, 1975, 7,* 37–45.

Lakota, R.A. *The National Museum of Natural History as a behavioral environment. Part I: An environmental analysis of behavioral performance.* Washington, D.C.: Office of Museum Programs, The Smithsonian Institution, 1975.

Landsberg, H.E. *Weather and health.* New York: Doubleday, 1969.

Lang, J. Theories of perception and "formal" design. In J. Lang, C. Burnette, W. Moleski, & D. Vachon (Eds.), *Designing for human behavior: Architecture and the behavioral sciences.* Stroudsburg, Pa.: Halsted Press, 1974.

Lang, J., & Burnette, C. A model of the designing process. In J. Lang, C. Burnette, W. Moleski, & D. Vachon (Eds.), *Designing for human behavior.* Stroudsburg, Pa.: Dowden, Hutchinson & Ross, 1974.

Langer, E.J., & Rodin, J. The effects of choice and enhanced personal responsibility for the aged: A field experiment in an institutional setting. *Journal of Personality and Social Psychology, 1976, 34,* 191–198.

Langer, E., & Saegert, S. Crowding and cognitive control. *Journal of Personality and Social Psychology, 1977, 35,* 175–182.

Lassen, C.L. Effects of proximity on anxiety and communication in the initial psychiatric interview. *Journal of Abnormal Psychology, 1973, 81,* 226–232.

Latané, B., & Darley, J.M. *The unresponsive bystander: Why doesn't he help?* New York: Prentice-Hall, 1970.

Latta, R.M. Relation of status incongruence to personal space. *Personality and Social Psychology Bulletin, 1978, 4,* 143–146.

Lauridsen, P.K. *Decreasing gasoline consumption in fleet-owned automobiles through feedback, and feedback plus lottery.* Unpublished master's thesis, Drake University, 1977.

Lave, L.B., & Seskin, E.P. *Air pollution and human health.* Baltimore: Johns Hopkins Press, 1973.

LaVerne, A.A. Nonspecific Air Pollution Syndrome (NAPS): Preliminary report. *Behavioral Neuropsychiatry, 1970, 2,* 19–21.

Lavrakas, P.J. Fear of crime and behavior restriction in urban and suburban neighborhoods. *Population and Environment, 1982, 5,* 242–264.

Lawson, B.R., & Walters, D. The effects of a new motorway on an established residential area. In D. Canter & T. Lee (Eds.), *Psychology and the built environment.* New York: Wiley, 1974.

Lawton, M.P. Therapeutic environments for the aged. In D. Canter & S. Canter (Eds.), *Designing for therapeutic environments: A review of research.* Chichester, England: Wiley, 1979.

Lawton, M.P., & Cohen, J. Environment and the well-being of elderly inner-city residents. *Environment and Behavior, 1974, 6,* 194–211.

Lazarus, R. *Psychological stress and the coping process.* New York: McGraw-Hill, 1966.

Lazarus, R.S., & Cohen, J.B. Environmental stress. In I. Altman & J.F. Wohlwill (Eds.), *Human behavior and the environment: Current theory and research* (Vol. 2). New York: Plenum, 1977.

Lazarus, R.S., & Launier, R. Stress-related transactions between person and environment. In L.A. Pervin & M. Lewis (Eds.), *Perspectives in interactional psychology.* New York: Plenum, 1978.

Leary, R.W., & Moroney, R.J. The effects of home-cage environments in monkeys. *Journal of Comparative and Physiological Psychology, 1962, 55,* 256–259.

LeBlanc, J.S. Impairment of manual dexterity in the cold. *Journal of Applied Physiology, 1956, 9,* 62–64.

LeBlanc, J.S. Local adaptation to cold of Gaspě fishermen. *Journal of Applied Physiology, 1962, 17,* 950–952.

LeBlanc, J. *Man in the cold.* Springfield, Ill.: Charles C Thomas, 1975.

Lebo, C.P., & Oliphant, K.P. Music as a source of acoustical trauma. *Laryngoscope, 1968, 78,* 1211–1218.

Lee, D.H.K. Terrestrial animals in dry heat: Man in the desert. In D.B. Dill, E.G. Adolph, & C.G. Wilber (Eds.), *Handbook of physiology.* Washington, D.C.: The American Physiological Society, 1964.

Lee, T.R. Perceived distance as a function of direction in the city. *Environment and Behavior, 1970, 2,* 39–51.

Leff, H.L. *Experience, environment, and human potentials.* New York: Oxford University Press, 1974.

Leithead, C.S., & Lind, A.R. *Heat stress and heat disorders.* London: Cassell, 1964.

Lerner, R.N., Iwawaki, S., & Chihara, T. Development of personal space schemata among Japanese children. *Developmental Psychology, 1976, 12,* 466–467.

Lester, D. Temporal variation in suicide and homicide. *American Journal of Epidemiology, 1979, 109,* 517–520.

Lester, D., Brockopp, G.W., & Priebe, K. Association between a full moon and completed suicide. *Psychological Reports, 1969, 25,* 598.

Leventhal, H. Findings and theory in the study of fear communications. In L. Berkowitz (Ed.), *Advances in experimental social psychology* (Vol. 5). New York: Academic Press, 1970.

Levin, P.L. Putting muscles into marks. *New York Times Magazine,* November 28, 1965, p. 118.

Levine, M. You-are-here maps: Psychological considerations. *Environment and Behavior, 1982, 14,* 221–237.

Levy, L., & Herzog, A.N. Effects of population density and crowding on health and social adaptation in the Netherlands. *Journal of Health and Social Behavior, 1974, 15,* 228–240.

Lewin, K. Formalization and progress in psychology. In D. Cartwright (Ed.), *Field theory in social science.* New York: Harper, 1951.

Lewis, C.A. People–plant interaction: A new horticultural perspective. *American Horticulturist, 1973, 52,* 18–25.

Lewis, J., Baddeley, A.D., Bonham, K.G., & Lovett, D. Traffic pollution and mental efficiency. *Nature, 1970, 225,* 95–97.

Ley, D., & Cybriwsky, R. The spatial ecology of stripped cars. *Environment and Behavior,* 1974, *6,* 53–68. (a)

Ley, D., & Cybriwsky, R. Urban graffiti as territorial markers. *Annals of the Association of American Geographers,* 1974, *64,* 491–505. (b)

Lieber, A.L., & Sherin, C.R. Homicides and the lunar cycle: Toward a theory of lunar influence on human emotional disturbance. *American Journal of Psychiatry,* 1972, *129,* 101–106.

Lifton, R.J., & Olson, E. The human meaning of total disaster: The Buffalo Creek experience. *Psychiatry,* 1976, *39,* 1–18.

Lindsay, J.J., & Ogle, R.A. Socioeconomic patterns of outdoor recreation use near urban areas. *Journal of Leisure Research,* 1972, *4,* 19–24.

Lingwood, D.A. Environmental education through information-seeking: The case of an environmental teach-in. *Environment and Behavior,* 1971, *3,* 220–262.

Link, J.M., & Pepler, R.D. Associated fluctuations in daily temperature, productivity and absenteeism. *ASHRAE Transactions,* 1970, *76* (Pt. 2), 326–337.

Linton, D.L. The assessment of scenery as a natural resource. *Scottish Geographical Magazine,* 1968, *84,* 219–238.

Lipetz, B. *User requirements in identifying desired works in a large library.* New Haven, Conn.: Yale University Library, 1970.

Lipman, A. Chairs as territory. *New Society,* 1967, *20,* 564–566.

Lipman, A., & Slater, R. Homes for old people: Toward a positive environment. In D. Canter & S. Canter (Eds.), *Designing for therapeutic environments: A review of research.* Chichester, England: Wiley, 1979.

Lippert, S. Travel in nursing units. *Human Factors,* 1971, *13,* 269–282.

Lipsey, M.W. Attitudes toward the environment and pollution. In S. Oskamp (Ed.), *Attitudes and opinions.* Englewood Cliffs, N.J.: Prentice-Hall, 1977.

Little, K.B. Personal space. *Journal of Experimental Social Psychology,* 1965, *1,* 237–247

Little, K.B. Cultural variations in social schemata. *Journal of Personality and Social Psychology,* 1968, *10,* 1–7.

Littler, W.A., Honour, A.J., & Sleight, P. Direct arterial pressure and electrocardiogram during motor car driving. *British Medical Journal,* 1973, *2,* 273–277.

Litton, R.B., Jr. *Forest landscape description and inventories—a basis for land planning and design.* (USDA Forest Service Research Paper PSW-49). Berkeley, Calif.: Pacific Southwest Forest and Range Experiment Station, 1968.

Lockhard, J.S., McVittie, R.I., & Isaac, L.M. Functional significance of the affiliative smile. *Bulletin of the Psychonomic Society,* 1977, *9,* 367–370.

Lofland, J. *Analyzing social settings.* New York: Belmont Books, 1973.

Logan, H.J., & Berger, E. Measurement of visual information cues. *Illuminating Engineering,* 1961, *56,* 393–403.

Logue, J.N., Hansen, F., & Struening, E. Emotional and physical distress following Hurricane Agnes in the Wyoming Valley of Pennsylvania. *Public Health Reports,* 1979, *94,* 495–502.

Lomranz, J., Shapira, A., Choresh, N., & Gilat, Y. Children's personal space as a function of age and sex. *Developmental Psychology,* 1975, *11,* 541–545.

Loo, C. The effects of spatial density on the social behavior of children. *Journal of Applied Social Psychology,* 1972, *4,* 372–381.

Loo, C. Important issues in researching the effects of crowding on humans. *Representative Research in Social Psychology,* 1973, *4,* 219–226.

Loo, C. Density, crowding, and preschool children. In A. Baum & Y. Epstein (Eds.), *Human response to crowding.* Hillsdale, N.J.: Erlbaum, 1978.

Loo, C. A factor-analytic approach to the study of spatial density effects on preschoolers. *Population,* 1979, *2,* 47–68.

Loo, C., & Kennelly, D. Social density: Its effects on behaviors and perceptions of preschoolers. *Environmental Psychology and Nonverbal Behavior,* 1979, *3,* 131–146.

Loo, C., & Smetana, J. The effects of crowding on the behavior and perception of 10-year-old boys. *Environmental Psychology and Nonverbal Behavior,* 1978, *2,* 226–249.

Lorenz, K. *On aggression.* New York: Harcourt Brace Jovanovich, 1966.

Lott, A.J., & Lott, B.E. A learning theory approach to interpersonal attitudes. In A.G. Greenwald, T.C. Brock, & T.M. Ostrom (Eds.), *Psychological foundations of attitudes.* New York: Academic Press, 1968.

Lott, B.S., & Sommer, R. Seating arrangements and status. *Journal of Personality and Social Psychology,* 1967, *7,* 90–95.

Love, K.D., & Aiello, J.R. Using projective techniques to measure interaction distance: A methodological note. *Personality and Social Psychology Bulletin,* 1980, *6,* 102–104.

Lowenthal, D., & Riel, M. *Publications in environmental perception.* New York: American Geographical Society, 1972.

Lozar, G.C. Methods and measures. In D. Carson, (Ed.), *Man–environment interactions: Evaluations and applications* (Part 2). Stroudsburg, Pa.: Dowden, Hutchinson & Ross, 1974.

Lucas, R.C. The recreational capacity of the Quetico-Superior area. (Research paper 5–15). Washington, D.C.: Lake State Forest Experiment Station, Forest Service, USDA, 1964.

Lundberg, U. Urban commuting: Crowdedness and catecholamine excretion. *Journal of Human Stress,* 1976, *2,* 26–32.

Luquette, A.J., Landiss, C.W., & Merki, D.J. Some immediate effects of a smoking environment on children of elementary school age. *Journal of School Health,* 1970, *40,* 533–536.

Luxenberg, S. Crime pays: A prison boom. *The New York Times,* July 17, 1977, pp. 1–5.

Luyben, P.D. Effects of informational prompts on energy conservation in college classrooms. *Journal of Applied Behavior Analysis,* 1980, *13,* 611–617.

Luyben, P.D., & Bailey, J.S. *Newspaper recycling behaviors: The effects of reinforcement versus proximity of containers.* Paper presented at the meeting of the Midwestern Association for Behavior Analysis, Chicago, March 1975.

Lynch, K. *The image of the city.* Cambridge, Mass.: M.I.T. Press, 1960.

Maccoby, E. (Ed.). The *development of sex differences.* Stanford, Calif.: Stanford University Press, 1966.

Mack, R. Ecological patterns in an industrial shop. *Social Forces,* 1954, *32,* 118–138.

MacKenzie, B.K. The importance of contact in determining attitudes toward Negroes. *Journal of Abnormal Psychology,* 1948, *43,* 417–441.

MacKenzie, S.T. *Noise and office work: Employee and employer concerns.* Ithaca: New York State School of Industrial and Labor Relations, Cornell University, 1975.

Magaña, J.R. An empirical and interdisciplinary test of a theory of urban perception. (Doctoral dissertation, University of California, Irvine, 1978.) *Dissertation Abstracts International,* 1978, *39,* 1460B. (University Microfilms, No. 78-15, 840.)

Malm, W., Kelley, K., Molenar, J., & Daniel, T. *Human perception of visual air quality (layered haze).* Unpublished manuscript, National Park Service, 1982.

Maloney, M.P., Ward, M.O., & Braucht, C.N. A revised scale for the measurement of ecological attitudes and knowledge. *American Psychologist,* 1975, *30,* 787–790.

Mandel, D.R., Baron, R.M., & Fisher, J.D. Room utilization and dimensions of density. *Environment and Behavior,* 1980, *12,* 308–319.

Manheim, M.L. A design process model: Theory and applications to transportation planning. In G.T. Moore (Ed.), *Emerging methods in environmental design and planning.* Cambridge, Mass.: M.I.T. Press, 1970.

Mann, P.H. *An approach to urban sociology.* London: Routledge & Kegan Paul, 1964.

Marans, R.W. Outdoor recreation behavior in residential environments. In J.F. Wohlwill & D.H. Carson (Eds.), *Environment and the social sciences: Perspectives and applications.* Washington, D.C.: American Psychological Association, 1972.

Marans, R.W. Survey research. In W. Michelson (Ed.), *Behavioral research methods in environmental design.* Stroudsburg, Pa.: Dowden, Hutchinson, & Ross, 1975.

Marans, R.W., & Rodgers, W. Toward an understanding of community satisfaction. In A. Hawley & V. Rock (Eds.), *Metropolitan America in contemporary perspective.* New York: Halsted Press, 1975.

Marans, R.W., & Spreckelmeyer, K.F. Evaluating open and conventional office design. *Environment and Behavior,* 1982, *14,* 333–351.

Margulis, J. *A methodology for evaluation of housing in use: A case study approach.* Springfield, Va.: National Technical Information Services, 1981.

Marine, G. I've got nothing against the colored, understand. *Ramparts,* 1966, *5,* 13–18.

Mark, L.S. Modeling through toy play: A methodology for eliciting topological representations in children. In W.J. Mitchell (Ed.), *Environmental design: Research and practice.* Los Angeles: University of California, EDRA 3, 1972.

Markham, S. *Climate and the energy of nations.* New York: Oxford University Press, 1947.

Marsden, H.M. Crowding and animal behavior. In J.F. Wohlwill & D.H. Carson (Eds.), *Environment and the social sciences: Perspectives and applications.* Washington, D.C.: American Psychological Association, 1972.

Marsella, A.J., Escudero, M., & Gordon, P. The effects of dwelling density on mental disorders in Filipino men. *Journal of Health and Social Behavior,* 1970, *11,* 288–294.

Marshall, M. Privacy and environment. *Human Ecology,* 1972, *1,* 93–110.

Martindale, D.A. Territorial dominance behavior in dyadic verbal interactions. *Proceedings of the Annual Convention of the American Psychological Association,* 1971, *6,* 305–306.

Maslow, A.H., & Mintz, N.C. Effects of esthetic surrounding: I. Initial effects of three esthetic conditions upon perceiving "energy" and "well-being" in faces. *Journal of Psychology,* 1956, *41,* 247–254.

Mathews, K.E., & Canon, L.K. Environmental noise level as a determinant of helping behavior. *Journal of Personality and Social Psychology,* 1975, *32,* 571–577.

Mathews, K.E., Canon, L.K., & Alexander, K. The influence of level of empathy and ambient noise on the body buffer zone. *Proceedings of the American Psychological Association Division of Personality and Social Psychology,* 1974, *1,* 367–370.

Maurer, R., & Baxter, J.C. Image of the neighborhood and city among Black, Anglo, and Mexican-American children. *Environment and Behavior,* 1972, *4,* 351–388.

Mawby, R.I. Defensible space: A theoretical and empirical appraisal. *Urban Studies,* 1977, *14,* 169–179.

Mayron, L.W., Ott, J., Nations, R., Mayron, E. Light, radiation and academic behavior: Initial studies on the effects of full-spectrum lighting and radiation shielding on behavior and academic performance on school children. *Academic Therapy,* 1974, *10,* 33–47.

McBride, G., King, M.G., & James, J.W. Social proximity effects on galvanic skin responses in human adults. *Journal of Psychology,* 1965, *61,* 153–157.

McBurney, D.H., Levine, J.M., & Cavanaugh, P.H. Psychophysical and social ratings of human body odor. *Personality and Social Psychology Bulletin,* 1977, *3,* 135–138.

McCain, G., Cox, V.C., & Paulus, P.B. The relationship between illness complaints and degree of crowding in a prison environment. *Environment and Behavior,* 1976, *8,* 283–290.

McCain, G., Cox, V.C., & Paulus, P.B. The relationship between crowding and manifestations of illness in prison settings. In D.J. Osborne, M.M. Gruneberg, & J.R. Eiser (Eds.), *Research in psychology and medicine* (Vol. 2). London: Academic Press, 1980.

McCallum, R., Rusbult, C., Hong, G., Walden, T., & Schopler, J. Effect of resource availability and importance of behavior on the experience of crowding. *Journal of Personality and Social Psychology,* 1979, *37,* 1304–1313.

McCauley, C., Coleman, G., & DeFusco, P. Commuters' eye contact with strangers in city and suburban train stations: Evidence of short-term adaptation to interpersonal overload in the city. *Environmental Psychology and Nonverbal Behavior,* 1977, *2,* 215–225.

McCauley, C., & Taylor, J. Is there overload of acquaintances in the city? *Environmental Psychology and Nonverbal Behavior,* 1976, *1,* 41–55.

McCaull, J. Discriminatory air pollution. If poor, don't breathe. *Environment,* 1977, *18,* 26–31.

McClelland, L.A. *Crowding and social stress.* Unpublished doctoral dissertation, University of Michigan, 1974.

McCormick, E.J. *Human factors in engineering and design.* New York: McGraw-Hill, 1976.

McCormick, E.J., & Tiffin, J. *Industrial psychology,* (6th ed). Englewood Cliffs, N.J.: Prentice-Hall, 1974.

McFarland, R.A. Psychophysiological implications of life at high altitude and including the role of oxygen in the process of aging. In M.K. Yousef, S.M. Horvath, & R.W. Bullard (Eds.), *Physiological adaptations: Desert and mountain.* New York: Academic Press, 1972.

McGrath, J.E. *Social and psychological factors in stress.* New York: Holt, Rinehart and Winston, 1970.

McGuire, W.J. Resistance to persuasion confirmed by active and passive prior refutation of the same and alternative counter-arguments. *Journal of Abnormal and Social Psychology,* 1961, *63,* 326–332.

McKechnie, G.E. *Manual for the Environmental Response Inventory.* Palo Alto, Calif.: Consulting Psychologists Press, 1974.

McKechnie, G.E. Simulation techniques in environmental psychology. In D. Stokols (Ed.), *Perspectives on environment and behavior.* New York: Plenum, 1977.

McLean, E.K., & Tarnopolsky, A. Noise, distress, and mental health. *Psychological Medicine,* 1977, *7,* 19–62.

McMillan, R. *Analysis of multiple events in a ghetto household.* Doctoral dissertation, Columbia University Teachers College, 1974.

Mechanic, D. *Students under stress.* New York: Free Press, 1962.

Medalia, N.Z. Air pollution as a socio-environmental health problem: A survey report. *Journal of Health and Human Behavior,* 1964, *5,* 154–165.

Megargee, E. The association of population density, reduced space, and uncomfortable temperatures with misconduct in a prison community. *American Journal of Community Psychology,* 1977, *5,* 289–298.

Mehrabian, A. Relationships of attitude to seated posture, orientation, and distance. *Journal of Personality and Social Psychology,* 1968, *10,* 26–30.

Mehrabian, A. A questionnaire measure of individual differences in stimulus screening and associated differences in arousability. *Environmental Psychology and Nonverbal Behavior,* 1976–1977, *1*(2), 89–103.

Mehrabian, A., & Diamond, S.G. Effects of furniture arrangement, props, and personality on social interaction. *Journal of Personality and Social Psychology,* 1971, *20,* 18–30.

Mehrabian, A., & Russell, J.A. *An approach to environmental psychology.* Cambridge, Mass.: M.I.T. Press, 1974.

Meisels, M., & Dosey, M.A. Personal space, anger arousal, and psychological defense. *Journal of Personality,* 1971, *39,* 333–334.

Meisels, M., & Guardo, C.J. Development of personal space schemata. *Child Development,* 1969, *49,* 1167–1178.

Melton, A.W. Studies of installation at the Pennsylvania Museum of Art. *Museum News,* 1933, *10*(15), 5–8.

Melton, A.W. Visitor behavior in museums: Some early research in environmental design. *Human Factors,* 1972, *14,* 393–403.

Mendelsohn, R., & Orcutt, G. An empirical analysis of air pollution dose–response curves. *Journal of Environmental Economics and Management,* 1979, *6,* 85–106.

Menne, J.M.C., & Sinnett, E.R. Proximity and social interaction in residence halls. *Journal of College Student Personnel,* 1971, *12,* 26–31.

Menninger, W. Recreation and mental health. *Recreation,* November 1948, 23–24.

Mercer, S., & Kane, R.A. Helplessness and hopelessness among the institutionalized aged: An experiment. *Health and Social Work, 1979, 4,* 90–116.

Meyers, A.W., Artz, L.M., & Craighead, W.E. The effects of instructions, incentives and feedback on a community problem: Dormitory noise. *Journal of Applied Behavior Analysis,* 1976, *9,* 445–457.

Michaels, K.M. The effect of expressway design on driver tension responses. *Public Roads,* 1962, *32,* 107–112.

Michelini, R.L., Passalacqua, R., & Cusimano, J. Effects of seating arrangement on group participation. *The Journal of Social Psychology,* 1976, *99,* 179–186.

Michelson, W. Most people don't want what architects want. *Trans-Action,* 1968, *5,* 37–43.

Michelson, W. *Man and his urban environment: A sociological approach.* Reading, Mass.: Addison-Wesley, 1970.

Middlemist, R.D., Knowles, E.S., & Matter, C.F. Personal space invasions in the lavatory: Suggestive evidence for arousal.

Journal of Personality and Social Psychology, 1976, *33,* 541–546.

Miles, S. Medical hazards of diving. In C.N. Davies, P.R., Davis, & F.H. Tyrer (Eds.), *The effects of abnormal physical conditions at work.* London: E. & S. Livingstone, 1967.

Milgram, S. The experience of living in cities. *Science,* 1970, *167,* 1461–1468.

Milgram, S. *The individual in a social world.* Reading, Mass.: Addison-Wesley, 1977.

Milgram, S., Greenwald, J., Kessler, S., McKenna, W., & Waters, J. A psychological map of New York City. *American Scientist,* 1972, *60,* 194–200.

Miller, I.W., III., & Norman, W.H. Learned helplessness in humans: A review and attribution-theory model. *Psychological Bulletin,* 1979, *86,* 93–118.

Miller, J.D. Effects of noise on people. *Journal of the Acoustical Society of America,* 1974, *56,* 729–764.

Miller, J.F. *The effects of four proxemic zones on the performance of selected sixth-, seventh-, and eighth-grade students.* Doctoral dissertation, East Tennessee State University, 1978.

Miller, M. Cited in J. Raloff, Occupational noise—the subtle pollutant. *Science News,* 1982, *121,* 347–350.

Miller, M., Albert, M., Bostick, D., & Geller, E.S. *Can the design of a trash can influence litter-related behavior?* Paper presented at Southeastern Psychological Association meeting, New Orleans, 1976.

Mills, C. *Living with the weather.* Cincinnati: Caxton Press, 1934.

Milne, G. Cyclone Tracey: 1. Some consequences of the evacuation for adult victims. *Australian Psychologist,* 1977, *12,* 39–54.

Minckley, B. A study of noise and its relationship to patient discomfort in the recovery room. *Nursing Research,* 1968, *17,* 247–250.

Miransky, J., & Langer, E.J. Burglary (non)prevention: An instance of relinquishing control. *Personality and Social Psychology Bulletin,* 1978, *4,* 399–405.

Mitchell, H.E. Professional and client: An emerging collaborative relationship. In J. Lang, C. Burnette, W. Moleski, & D. Vachon (Eds.), *Designing for human behavior: "Architecture and the behavioral sciences."* Stroudsburg, Pa.: Dowden, Hutchinson & Ross, 1974.

Moleski, W.H., & Lang, J.T. Organizational needs and human values in office planning. *Environment and Behavior,* 1982, *14,* 319–332.

Montagu, A. *Touching: The human significance of the skin.* New York: Columbia University Press, 1971.

Moore, G.T. Developmental variations between and within individuals in the cognitive representation of large-scale spatial environments. *Man–Environment Systems,* 1974, *4,* 55–57.

Moore, H.E. Some emotional concomitants of disaster. *Mental Hygiene,* 1958, *42,* 45–50.

Moore, R.C. Childhood city. In W.F.E. Preiser (Ed.), *Environmental design research, Vol. 2: Symposia and workshops.* Stroudsburg, Pa.: Dowden, Hutchinson & Ross, 1973.

Moos, R.H. *The human context: Environmental determinants of behavior.* New York: Wiley, 1976.

Moos, R.H. *The environmental quality of residential care settings.* Paper presented at annual conference of Environmental Design Resarch Association, Charleston, S.C., 1980.

Moos, R.H., & Gerst, M.S. *University Residence Environment Scale.* Palo Alto, Calif.: Consulting Psychologists Press, 1974.

Moos, W.S. The effects of "Foehn" weather on accident rates in the city of Zurich (Switzerland). *Aerospace Medicine,* 1964, *35,* 643–645.

Morasch, B., Groner, N., & Keating, J. Type of activity and failure as mediators of perceived crowding. *Personality and Social Psychology Bulletin,* 1979, *5,* 223–226.

Muecher, H., & Ungeheuer, H. Meteorological influence on reaction time, flicker fusion frequency, job accidents and use of medical treatment. *Perceptual and Motor Skills,* 1961, *12,* 163–168.

Mullins, P., & Robb, J. Residents' assessment of a New Zealand public-housing scheme. *Environment and Behavior,* 1977, *9,* 573–625.

Murphy, J.F., Williams, J.G., Niepoth, E.W., & Brown, P.B. *Leisure service delivery system: A modern perspective.* Philadelphia: Lea & Febiger, 1973.

Murphy-Berman, V., & Berman, J. Importance of choice and sex invasions of personal space. *Personality and Social Psychology Bulletin,* 1978, *4,* 424–428.

Murray, J.R., Minor, M.J., Bradburn, N.M., Cotterman, R.F., Frankel, M., & Pisarski, A.E. Evolution of public response to the energy crisis. *Science,* 1974, *184,* 257–264.

Murtha, D.M. *Dimensions of user benefit.* Washington, D.C.: American Institute of Architects, 1976.

Myers, K., Hale, C.S., Mykytowycs, R., & Hughes, R.L. Density, space, sociality and health. In A.H. Esser (Ed.), *Behavior and environment.* New York: Plenum, 1971.

Nahemow, L., & Lawton, M.P. Similarity and propinquity in friendship formation. *Journal of Personality and Social Psychology,* 1975, *32,* 205–213.

Nash, R. *Wilderness and the American mind* (rev. ed.) New Haven, Conn.: Yale University Press, 1974.

National Academy of Sciences. *Medical and biological effects of environmental pollutants.* Washington, D.C.: National Academy of Sciences, 1977.

National Academy of Sciences. *The effect on human health from long-term exposure to noise* (Report of Working Group 81). Washington, D.C.: National Academy Press, 1981.

Neilson, W. An empirical analysis of urban environmental preferences. *Journal of the American Institute of Planners,* 1976, *32,* 325–330.

Neisser, V. *Cognitive psychology.* New York: Appleton-Century-Crofts, 1967.

Nelson, P.D. *Psychologists in habitability research.* Paper presented at the meeting of the American Psychological Association, Washington, D.C., September 1976.

Nemecek, J., & Grandjean, E. Results of an ergometric investigation of large space offices. *Human Factors,* 1973, *15,* 111–124.

Newcomb, T.M. *The acquaintance process.* New York: Holt, Rinehart and Winston, 1961.

Newman, C.J. Children of disaster: Clinical observations at Buffalo Creek. *American Journal of Psychiatry,* 1976, *133,* 306–309.

Newman, J., & McCauley, C. Eye contact with strangers in city, suburb, and small town. *Environment and Behavior,* 1977, *9,* 547–558.

Newman, O. *Defensible space.* New York: Macmillan, 1972.

Newman, O. Reactions to the defensible space study and some further findings. *International Journal of Mental Health,* 1975, *4,* 48–70.

Newman, O., & Franck, K. *Factors influencing crime and instability in urban housing developments. Draft Executive Summary.* New York: Institute for Community Analysis, 1979.

Newsweek. A.C. Nielsen Survey, February 21, 1977, p. 63.

Ng, L.K.Y., Marsden, H.M., Colburn, R.W., & Thoa, N.B. Population density and social pathology in mice. Differences in catecholamine metabolism associated with differences in behavior. *Brain Research,* 1973, *59,* 323–330.

Nicholson, M. *The environmental revolution.* London: Hodder & Stoughton, 1970.

Niit, T. General trends in the development of theories about the interrelationship of man and his surroundings. In H. Mikkin, J. Orn, & E.M. Vernik (Eds.), *Man–environment interaction.* Tallinn U.S.S.R.: Tallinn Pedagogic Institute, 1980.

Noble, A., & Dixon, R. *Ward evaluation: St. Thomas Hospital.* London: Medical Architecture Research Unit, The Polytechnic of North London, 1977.

Novaco, R.W., Stokols, D., Campbell, J., & Stokols, J. Transportation stress and community psychology. *American Journal of Community Psychology,* 1979, *4,* 361–380.

O'Donnel, R., Mikulka, P., Heinig, P., & Theodore, J. Low level carbon monoxide exposure and human psychomotor performance. *Journal of Applied Toxicology and Pharmacology,* 1971, *18,* 593–602.

O'Donnell, C.R., & Lydgate, T. The relationship of crimes to physical resources. *Environment and Behavior,* 1980, *12,* 207–230.

Ogilvie, B.C., & Tutko, T.A. Sport: If you want to build character, try something else. *Psychology Today,* October 1971, 61–63.

O'Hare, M. The public's use of art: Visitor behavior in an art museum. *Curator,* 1974, *17,* 309–320.

Oldham, G.R., & Brass, D.J. Employee reactions to an open-plan office: A naturally occurring quasi-experiment. *Administrative Science Quarterly,* 1979, *24,* 267–284.

Olsen, M.E. Consumers' attitudes toward energy conservation. *Journal of Social Issues,* 1981, *37,* 108–131.

Olsen, R. *The effect of the hospital environment.* Doctoral dissertation, City University of New York, 1978.

Olszewski, D.A., Rotton, J., & Soler, E.A. *Conversation, conglomerate noise, and behavioral after-effects.* Paper presented at the meeting of the Midwestern Psychological Association, Chicago, May 1976.

O'Neal, E.C., Brunault, M.A., Carifio, M.S., Troutwine, R., & Epstein, J. Effects of insult upon personal space preferences. *Journal of Nonverbal Behavior,* 1980, *5,* 56–62.

O'Neal, E.C., Brunault, M.A., Marquis, J.F., & Carifio, M. Anger and the body-buffer zone. *The Journal of Social Psychology,* 1979, *108,* 135–136.

O'Neal, E.C., Caldwell, C., & Gallup, G. *Territorial invasion and aggression in young children.* Unpublished manuscript, Tulane Universiy, 1975.

O'Neal, E.C., & McDonald, P.J. The environmental psychology of aggression. In R.G. Geen & E.C. O'Neal (Eds.), *Perspectives on aggression.* New York: Academic Press, 1976.

O'Neill, G.W., Blanck, L.S., & Joyner, M.A. The use of stimulus control over littering in a natural setting. *Journal of Applied Behavior Analysis,* 1980, *13,* 379–381.

O'Neill, S.M., & Paluck, B.J. Altering territoriality through reinforcement. *Proceedings of the 81st Annual Convention of the American Psychological Association,* Montreal, Canada, 1973, *8,* 901–902.

O'Riordan, T. Attitudes, behavior, and environmental policy issues. In I. Altman & J.F. Wohlwill (Eds.), *Human behavior and environment: Advances in theory and research* (Vol. 1). New York: Plenum, 1976.

Orleans, P. Differential cognition of urban residents: Effects of social scale on mapping. In R.M. Downs & D. Stea (Eds.), *Image and environment: Cognitive mapping and spatial behavior.* Chicago: Aldine, 1973.

Orleans, P., & Schmidt, S. Mapping the city: Environmental cognition of urban residents. In W. Mitchell (Ed.), *EDRA 3.* Los Angeles, University of California, 1972.

Orlick, T.D. *Games of acceptance and psycho-social adjustment.* Paper presented at the Conference on Mental Health and Aspects of Sports, Exercise and Recreation, Atlantic City, N.J., June 1975. (a)

Orlick, T.D. The sports environment: A capacity to enhance, a capacity to destroy. In B.S. Rushall (Ed.), *The status of psycho-*

motor learning and sport psychology research. Dartmouth, Nova Scotia: Sport Science Associates, 1975. (b)

Orlick, T.D. *Every kid can win.* Chicago: Nelson-Hall, 1975. (c)

Osborne, J.G., & Powers, R.B. Controlling the litter problem. In G.L. Martin & J.G. Osborne (Eds.), *Helping the community: Behavioral applications.* New York: Plenum, 1980.

Osgood, C., Suci, G., & Tannenbaum, P. *The measurement of meaning.* Urbana: University of Illinois Press, 1957.

Osmond, H. Function as the basis of psychiatric ward design. *Mental Hospitals* (Architectural Supplement), 1957, *8*, 23–29.

Owens, R.D., & Sever, H.L. *The 3M commute-a-van program (progress report).* St. Paul, Minn.: 3M Company, 1977.

Pablant, P., & Baxter, J.C. Environmental correlates of school vandalism. *Journal of the American Institute of Planners,* July 1975, 270–279.

Page, R.A. Noise and helping behavior. *Environment and Behavior,* 1977, *9*, 559–572.

Page, R.A. *Environmental influences on prosocial behavior: The effect of temperature.* Paper presented at the Midwestern Psychological Association meeting, Chicago, May 1978.

Palamarek, D.L., & Rule, B.G. The effects of temperature and insult on the motivation to retaliate or escape. *Motivation and Emotion, 1979, 3,* 83–92.

Pallack, M.S., Cook, D.A., & Sullivan, J.J. Commitment and energy conservation. In L. Bickman (Ed.), *Applied Social Psychology Annual, 1980, 1,* 235–253.

Palmer, J.F., & Zube, E.H. Numerical and perceptual landscape classification. In E.H. Zube (Ed.), *Studies in landscape perception.* (Publication No. R-76-1) Amherst: Institute for Man and Environment, University of Massachusetts, 1976.

Palmer, M.H., Lloyd, M.E., & Lloyd, K.D. An experimental analysis of electricity conservation procedures. *Journal of Applied Behavior Analysis,* 1978, *10,* 665–672.

Parker, G. Psychological disturbance in Darwin evacuees following Cyclone Tracey. *Medical Journal of Australia,* 1975, *1,* 650–652.

Parkes, C.M. *Bereavement: Studies of grief in adult life.* New York: International Universities Press, 1972.

Parr, A.E. Psychological aspects of urbanology. *Journal of Social Issues,* 1966, *22,* 39–45.

Parsons, H.M. The bedroom. *Human Factors,* 1972, *14,* 421–450.

Parsons, P., & Loomis, R.J. *Patterns of museum visitor exploration: Then and now.* Washington, D.C.: The Smithsonian Institution, 1973.

Pastalan, L. *Report on Pennsylvania nursing home relocation program: Interim research findings.* Ann Arbor: Institute of Gerontology,University of Michigan, 1976.

Patterson, A.H. Methodological developments in environment–behavioral research. In D. Stokols (Ed.), *Perspectives on environment and behavior.* New York: Plenum, 1977.

Patterson, A.H. Territorial behavior and fear of crime in the elderly. *Human Ecology,* in press.

Patterson, M.L. *Factors affecting interpersonal spatial proximity.* Paper presented at the annual meeting of the American Psychological Association, New Orleans, September 1974.

Patterson, M.L. Personal space: Time to burst the bubble? *Man-Environment Systems,* 1975, *5,* 67.

Patterson, M.L. An arousal model of interpersonal intimacy. *Psychological Review,* 1976, *83,* 235–245.

Patterson, M.L. Interpersonal distance, affect, and equilibrium theory. *Journal of Social Psychology,* 1977, *101,* 205–214.

Patterson, M.L. Arousal change and the cognitive labeling: Pursuing the mediators of intimacy exchange. *Environmental Psychology and Nonverbal Behavior,* 1978, *3,* 17–22.

Patterson, M.L., & Holmes, D.S. Social interaction correlates of MMPI extraversion–introversion scale. *American Psychologist,* 1966, *21,* 724–725.

Patterson, M.L., Kelly, C.E., Kondracki, B.A., & Wulf, L.J. Effects of seating arrangement on small-group behavior. *Social Psychology Quarterly,* 1979, *42,* 180–185.

Patterson, M.L., Mullens, S., & Romano, J. Compensatory reactions to spatial intrusion. *Sociometry,* 1971, *34,* 114–121.

Patterson, M.L., & Sechrest, L.B. Interpersonal distance and impression formation. *Journal of Personality,* 1970, *38,* 161–166.

Paulus, P.B. *Crowding in the laboratory and its relation to social facilitation.* Paper presented at the meeting of the Midwestern Psychological Association, Chicago, 1977.

Paulus, P.B., Annis, A.B., Seta, J.J., Schkode, J.K., & Matthews, R.W. Crowding does affect task performance. *Journal of Personality and Social Psychology,* 1976, *34,* 248–253.

Paulus, P., Cox, V., McCain, G., & Chandler, J. Some effects of crowding in a prison environment. *Journal of Applied Social Psychology,* 1975, *5,* 86–91.

Paulus, P., & Matthews, R. Crowding, attribution, and task performance. *Basic and Applied Social Psychology,* 1980, *1,* 3–13.

Paulus, P., McCain, G., & Cox, V. Death rates, psychiatric commitments, blood pressure and perceived crowding as a function of institutional crowding. *Environmental Psychology and Nonverbal Behavior,* 1978, *3,* 107–116.

Pawson, I.G., & Corneille, J. The high-altitude areas of the world and their cultures. In P.T. Baker (Ed.), *The biology of high altitude peoples.* New York: Cambridge University Press, 1978.

Payne, R.J., & Pigram, J.J. Changing evaluations of floodplain hazard: The Hunter Valley, Australia. *Environment and Behavior,* 1981, *13,* 461–480.

Pearson, O.P. The prey of carnivores during one cycle of mouse abundance. *Journal of Animal Ecology,* 1966, *35,* 217–233.

Pearson, O.P. Additional measurements of the impact of carnivores on California voles *(Microtus californicus)*. *Journal of Mammalogy*, 1971, *52*, 41–49.

Pederson, D.M. Developmental trends in personal space. *Journal of Psychology*, 1973, *83*, 3–9.

Pederson, D.M., & Shears, L.M. A review of personal space research in the framework of general systems theory. *Psychological Bulletin*, 1973, *80*, 367–388.

Pellegrini, R.J., & Empey, J. Interpersonal spatial orientation in dyads. *Journal of Psychology*, 1970, *76*, 67–70.

Pempus, E., Sawaya, C., & Cooper, R.E. *"Don't fence me in": Personal space depends on architectural enclosure*. Paper presented at the meeting of the American Psychological Association, Chicago, 1975.

Penick, E.C., Powell, B.J., & Sieck, W.A. Mental health problems and natural disaster: Tornado victims. *Journal of Community Psychology*, 1976, *4*, 64–67.

Pennebaker, J.W., & Newtson, D. Observation of a unique event: The psychological impact of the Mount Saint Helens volcano. In H.T. Reiss (Ed.), *Naturalistic approaches to studying social interaction. New directions for methodology of social and behavioral science* (No. 15). San Francisco: Jossey-Bass, 1983.

Penwarden, A.D. Acceptable wind speeds in towns. *Building Science*, 1973, *8*, 259–267.

Pepler, R.D. Performance and well-being in heat. In C.M. Herzfeld (Ed.), *Temperature: Its measurement and control in science and industry* (Vol. 3, Pt. 3). New York: Reinhold, 1963.

Pepler, R.D. The thermal comfort of students in climate controlled and non-climate controlled schools. *ASHRAE Transactions*, 1972, *78*, 97–109.

Persinger, M.A., Ludwig, H.W., & Ossenkopf, K.P. Psychophysiological effects of extremely low frequency electromagnetic fields: A review. *Perceptual and Motor Skills*, 1973, *26*, 1131–1159.

Peterka, J.A., & Cermak, J.E. *Wind engineering study of Mountain Bell Denver Service Center* (Tech. Rep. CER73-74JAP-JEC14). Fort Collins: Colorado State University Fluid Mechanics Program, October 1973.

Peterka, J.A., & Cermak, J.E. *Wind engineering study of Merchant's Plaza, Indianapolis, Indiana* (Tech Rep. CER74–75JAP-JEC47). Fort Collins: Colorado State University Fluid Mechanics Program, July 1975.

Peterka, J.A., & Cermak, J.E. *Wind tunnel study of phase I building, Block 141, Denver* (Tech. Rep. CER76-77JAP-JEC36). Fort Collins: Colorado State University Fluid Mechanics Program, January 1977.

Peters, G., & Kennedy, C. Close friendships in the college community. *Journal of College Student Personnel*, 1970, *11*, 449–456.

Peterson, R.L. *Air pollution and attendance in recreation behavior settings in the Los Angeles basin*. Paper presented at the American Psychological Association meeting, Chicago, 1975.

Pile, J.F. *Open office planning*. New York: Whitney Library of Design, 1978.

Pill, R. Space and social structure in two children's wards. *Sociological Review*, 1967, *15*, 179–192.

Pirages, D.C., & Ehrlich, P.R. *Ark II: Social response to environmental imperatives*. San Francisco: Freeman, 1974.

Pitelka, F.A. Some aspects of population structure in the short-term cycle of the brown lemming in northern Alaska. *Cold Spring Harbor Symposia on Quantitative Biology*, 1957, *22*, 237–251.

Pitt, D.G. Physical dimensions of scenic quality in streams. In E.H. Zube (Ed.), *Studies in landscape perception*. (Publication No. R-76-1). Amherst: Institute for Man and Environment, University of Massachusetts, 1976.

Pitt, D.G., & Zube, E.H. The Q-sort method: Use in landscape assessment research and landscape planning. In *Proceedings of our national landscape: A conference on applied techniques for analysis and management of the visual resource* (USDA Forest Service General Technical Report PSW-35). Berkeley, Calif., Pacific Southwest Forest and Range Experiment Station, 1979.

Platt, J. Social traps. *American Psychologist*, 1973, *28*, 641–651.

Pokorny, A., Davis, F., & Harberson, W. Suicide, suicide attempts, and weather. *American Journal of Psychiatry*, 1963, *120*, 377–381.

Pollack, L.M., & Patterson, A.H. Territoriality and fear of crime in elderly and nonelderly homeowners. *The Journal of Social Psychology*, 1980, *111*,119–129.

Pollet, D. You can get there from here. *Wilson Library Bulletin*, 1976, 456–462.

Population and the American future: The report of the Commission of Population Growth and the American Future. New York: American Library, 1972.

Porteous, C.W. *Learning as a function of molar environmental complexity*. Unpublished master's thesis, University of Victoria, British Columbia, 1972.

Porteus, J. *Environment and behavior*. Reading, Mass.: Addison-Wesley, 1977.

Poulton, E.C. *Environment and human efficiency*. Springfield, Ill.: Charles C Thomas, 1970.

Poulton, E.C. Arousing environmental stress can improve performance, whatever people say. *Aviation Space and Environmental Medicine*, 1976, *47*, 1193–1204.

Poulton, E.C., Hunt, J.C.R., Mumford, J.C., & Poulton, J. Mechanical disturbance produced by steady and gusty winds of moderate strength: Skilled performance and semantic assessments. *Ergonomics*, 1975, *18*, 651–673.

Poulton, E.C., & Kerslake, M.McK. Initial stimulating effect of warmth upon perceptual efficiency. *Aerospace Medicine*, 1965, *36*, 29–32.

Powers, R.B., Osborne, J.G., & Anderson, E.G. Positive reinforcement of litter removal in the natural environment. *Journal of Applied Behavior Analysis*, 1973, *6*, 579–586.

Pratsch, L. *Vanpooling discussion paper*. Washington, D.C.: Federal Highway Administration, unpublished manuscript, April 1977.

Preiser, W.F.E. Application of unobtrusive observation techniques in building performance appraisal. In B.E. Foster (Ed.), *Performance concept in buildings* (Special publication No. 361, Vol. 1). Washington, D.C.: National Bureau of Standards, 1972.

Preiser, W.F.E. An analysis of unobtrusive observations of pedestrian movement and stationary behavior in a shopping mall. In R. Kuller (Ed.), *Architectural psychology*. Stroudsburg, Pa.: Dowden, Hutchinson & Ross, 1973.

Price, G.H., & Dabbs, J.M. *Sex, setting, and personal space: Changes as children grow older*. Paper presented at the meeting of the American Psychological Association, New Orleans, August 1974.

Price, J.L. *The effects of crowding on the social behavior of children*. Unpublished doctoral dissertation, Columbia University, 1971.

Pritchard, D. Industrial lighting in windowless factories. *Light and Lighting*, 1964, *57*, 265.

Proshansky, H.M. Methodology in environmental psychology: Problems and issues. *Human Factors*, 1972, *14*, 451–460.

Proshansky, H.M. Theoretical issues in ''environmental psychology.'' *Representative Research in Social Psychology*, 1973, *4*, 93–107.

Proshansky, H.M. Comment on environmental and social psychology. *Personality and Social Psychology Bulletin*, 1976, *2*, 359–363. (a)

Proshansky, H.M. Environmental psychology and the real world. *American Psychologist*, 1976, *31*, 303–310. (b)

Proshansky, H.M. City and self-identity. Paper presented at the annual meeting of the American Psychological Association, Washington, D.C., September 1976. (c)

Proshansky, H., & Altman, I. Overview of the field. In W.P. White (Ed.), *Resources in environment and behavior*. Washington, D.C.: American Psychological Association, 1979.

Proshansky, H.M., Ittelson, W.H., & Rivlin, L.G. (Eds.). *Environmental psychology: Man and his physical setting*. New York: Holt, Rinehart and Winston, 1970.

Provins, K.A. Environmental conditions and driving efficiency: A review. *Ergonomics*. 1958, *2*, 63–88.

Provins, K.A. Environmental heat, body temperature, and behavior. *Australian Journal of Psychology*, 1966, *18*, 118–129.

Provins, K.A., & Bell, C.R. Effects of heat stress on the performance of two tasks running concurrently. *Journal of Experimental Psychology*, 1970, *85*, 40–44.

Provins, K.A., & Clarke, R.S.J. The effect of cold on manual performance. *Journal of Occupational Medicine*, 1960, *2*, 169–176.

Putz, J. The effects of carbon monoxide on dual-task performance. *Human Factors*, 1979, *21*, 13–24.

Pylyshyn, Z.W. What the mind's eye tells the mind's brain: A critique of mental imagery. *Psychological Bulletin*, 1973, *80*, 1–24.

Quarantelli, E.L. (Ed.). *Disasters: Theory and research*. Beverly Hills, Calif.: Sage, 1978.

Quarantelli, E.L., & Dynes, R.R. When disaster strikes. *Psychology Today*, 1972, *5*(9), 66–70.

Quick, A.D., & Crano, W.D. *Effects of sex, distance, and conversation in the invasion of personal space*. Paper presented at the Midwestern Psychological Association convention, 1973.

Radloff, R., & Helmreich, R. *Groups under stress: Psychological research in Sealab 2*. New York: Appleton-Century-Crofts, 1968.

Rainwater, L. Fear and the house as haven in the lower class. *Journal of the American Institute of Planners*, 1966, *32*, 23–31.

Raloff, J. Occupational noise—The subtle pollutant. *Science News*, 1982, *121*(21), 347–350.

Ramsey, J. Oxygen reduction and reaction time in hypoxic and normal drivers. *Archives of Environmental Health*, 1970, *20*, 597–601.

Rangell, L. Discussion of the Buffalo Creek disaster: The course of psychic trauma. *American Journal of Psychiatry*, 1976, *133*, 313–316.

Rankin, R.E. Air pollution control and public apathy. *Journal of the Air Pollution Control Association*, 1969, *19*, 565–569.

Rapoport, A. Toward a redefinition of density. *Environment and Behavior*, 1975, *7*, 133–158.

Rawls, J.R., Trego, R.E., McGaffey, C.N., & Rawls, D.J. Personal space as a predictor of performance under close working conditions. *The Journal of Social Psychology*, 1972, *86*, 261–267.

Reddy, D.M., Baum, A., Fleming, R., & Aiello, J.R. Mediation of social density by coalition formation. *Journal of Applied Social Psychology*, 1981, *11*, 529–537.

Reich, J.W., & Robertson, J.L. Reactance and normal appeal in antilittering messages. *Journal of Applied Social Psychology*, 1979, *9*, 91–101.

Reichel, D.A., & Geller, E.S. *Group versus individual contingencies to conserve transportation energy*. Paper presented at the Southeastern Psychological Association meeting, Washington, D.C., 1980.

Reichner, R. Differential responses to being ignored: The effects of architectural design and social density on interpersonal behavior. *Journal of Applied Social Psychology*, 1979, *9*, 13–26.

Reiter, S.M., & Samuel, W. Littering as a function of prior litter and the presence or absence of prohibitive signs. *Journal of Applied Social Psychology*, 1980, *10*, 45–55.

Reizenstein, J. E. *Social research and design: Cambridge hospital social service offices*. Springfield, Va.: National Technical Information Service, 1976.

Reizenstein, J.E. Hospital design and human behavior: A review of the recent literature. In A. Baum & J.E. Singer (Eds.), *Advances in environmental psychology* (Vol. 4). Hillsdale, N.J.: Erlbaum, 1982.

Rent, G.S., & Rent, C.S. Low income housing factors related to residential satisfaction. *Environment and Behavior,* 1978, *10,* 459–488.

Reppetto, T.A. Crime prevention through environmental policy. *American Behavioral Scientist,* 1976, *20,* 275–288.

Reusch, J., & Kees, W. *Nonverbal communication: Notes on the visual perception of human relations.* Berkeley: University of California Press, 1956.

Richards, P. Middle class vandalism and the age-status conflict. *Social Problems,* 1979, *26,* 482–497.

Richardson, L.H. Relationship of the use of leisure time in high school to effectiveness in college. *School Activities,* May 1962, 262–264.

Rim, Y. Psychological test performance during climatic heat stress from desert winds. *International Journal of Biometeorology,* 1975, *19,* 37–40.

Risk, P.H. *Effects of an experimental wilderness survival experience on self-concept, personality and values.* Unpublished doctoral dissertation, Michigan State University, 1976.

Rivlin, L.G., & Rothenberg, M. The use of space in open classrooms. In H.M. Proshansky, W.H. Ittelson, & L.G. Rivlin (Eds.), *Environmental psychology: People and their physical settings.* New York: Holt, Rinehart and Winston, 1976.

Rivlin, L.G., & Wolfe, M. The early history of a psychiatric hospital for children: Expectations and reality. *Environment and Behavior,* 1972, *4,* 33–72.

Rivlin, L.G., Wolfe, M., & Beyda, M. Age-related differences in the use of space. In W.F.E. Preiser (Ed.), Environmental design research. Stroudsburg, Pa.: Dowden, Hutchinson & Ross, 1973.

Roberts, C. Stressful experiences in urban places: Some implications for design. *EDRA 8 Conference Proceedings,* 1977.

Robinson, E.S. *The behavior of the museum visitor (No. 5 in Publications of the American Association of Museums New Series).* Washington, D.C.: American Association of Museums, 1928.

Rodin, J. Crowding, perceived choice and response to controllable and uncontrollable outcomes. *Journal of Experimental Social Psychology,* 1976, *12,* 564–578.

Rodin, J., & Baum, A. Crowding and helplessness: Potential consequences of density and loss of control. In A. Baum & Y. Epstein (Eds.), *Human response to crowding.* Hillsdale, N.J.: Erlbaum, 1978.

Rodin, J., & Langer, E. Long-term effects of control-relevant interventions with the institutionalized aged. *Journal of Personality and Social Psychology,* 1977, *35,* 897–902.

Rodin, J., Solomon, S., & Metcalf, J. Role of control in mediating perceptions of density. *Journal of Personality and Social Psychology,* 1978, *36,* 989–999.

Roger, D.B., & Schalekamp, E.E. Body-buffer zone and violence: A cross-cultural study. *The Journal of Social Psychology,* 1976, *98,* 153–158.

Rohe, W., & Patterson, A.H. *The effects of varied levels of resources and density on behavior in a day care center.* Paper presented to Environmental Design Research Association, Milwaukee, 1974.

Rohles, F.H., Jr. The modal comfort envelope and its use in current standards. *Human Factors,* 1974, *16,* 314–322.

Ronco, P. Human factors applied to hospital patient care. *Human Factors,* 1972, *14,* 461–470.

Rose, E.F., & Rose, M. Carbon monoxide: A challenge to the physician. *Clinical Medicine,* 1971, *78,* 12–18.

Rose, H.S., & Hinds, D.H. South Dixie Highway contraflow bus and car pool lane demonstration project. *Transportation Research Record,* 1976, *606,* 18–22.

Rosen, S., Bergman, M., Plestor, D., El-Mofty, A., & Satti, M. Presbycosis study of a relatively noise-free population in the Sudan. *Annals of Otology, Rhinology, and Laryngology,* 1962, *71,* 727–743.

Rosenfeld, H.M. Effect of an approval-seeking induction on interpersonal proximity. *Psychological Reports,* 1965, *17,* 120–122.

Ross, M., Layton, B., Erickson, B., & Schopler, J. Affect, facial regard, and reactions to crowding. *Journal of Personality and Social Psychology,* 1973, *28,* 69–76.

Ross, P., Bluestone, H., & Hines, F. *Indicators of social well-being in U.S. counties.* Washington, D.C.: U.S. Department of Agriculture, 1979.

Rothbaum, F., Weisz, J.R., & Synder, S.S. Changing the world and changing the self: A two-process model of perceived control. *Journal of Personality and Social Psychology,* 1982, *42,* 5–37.

Rotter, J. Generalized expectancies for internal vs. external control of reinforcement. *Psychological Monographs,* 1966, *80* (Whole No. 609).

Rotton, J. *Air pollution is no choke.* Unpublished manuscript, University of Dayton, 1978.

Rotton, J. Affective and cognitive consequences of malodorous pollution. *Basic and Applied Social Psychology,* 1983, in press.

Rotton, J., Barry, T., Frey, J., & Soler, E. Air pollution and interpersonal attraction. *Journal of Applied Social Psychology,* 1978, *8,* 57–71.

Rotton, J., & Frey, J. *Weather, air pollution, and social pathology: First approximations.* Unpublished manuscript, Florida International University, May 1981.

Rotton, J., & Frey, J. *Air pollution, weather, and psychiatric emergencies: A constructive replication.* Unpublished manuscript, Florida International University, 1982.

Rotton, J., Frey, J., Barry, T., Milligan, M., & Fitzpatrick, M. The air pollution experience and interpersonal aggression.

Journal of Applied Social Psychology, 1979, *9,* 397–412.

Rotton, J., Oszewski, D., Charleton, M., & Soler, E. Loud speech, conglomerate noise, and behavior after-effects. *Journal of Applied Psychology,* 1978, *63,* 360–365.

Rotton, J., Tikofsky, R., & Feldman, H. Behavioral effects of chemicals in drinking water. *Journal of Applied Psychology,* 1982, *67,* 230–238.

Rotton, J., Yoshikawa, J., Francis, J., & Hoyler, R. *Urban atmosphere: Evaluative effects of malodorous air pollution.* Paper presented at the Southeastern Psychological Association meeting, Atlanta, 1978.

Rotton, J., Yoshikawa, J., & Kaplan, F. *Perceived control, malodorous pollution, and behavioral aftereffects.* Paper presented at the Southeastern Psychological Association meeting, New Orleans, 1979.

Rubin, A.I., & Elder, J. *Building for people.* Washington, D.C.: U. S. Government Printing Office Special Publication #474, 1980.

Rummo, N., & Sarlanis, K. The effect of carbon monoxide on several measures of vigilance in a simulated driving task. *Journal of Safety Research,* 1974, *6,* 126–130.

Runner's World. From the publisher, November 1977, pp. 3–4.

Runnion, A., Watson, J.D., & McWhorter, J. Energy savings in interstate transportation through feedback and reinforcement. *Journal of Organizational Behavior Management,* 1978, *1,* 180–191.

Russel, M.B., & Bernal, M.E. Temporal and climatic variables in naturalistic observation. *Journal of Applied Behavior Analysis,* 1977, *10,* 399–405.

Russell, J.A., & Mehrabian, A. Environmental task, and temperamental effects on work performance. *Humanitas,* 1978, *14,* 75–95.

Russell, M., Cole, P., & Brown, E. Absorption by non-smokers of carbon monoxide from room air polluted by tobacco smoke. *Lancet,* 1973, *1,* 576–579.

Ruys, T. Windowless offices. *Man–Environment Systems,* 1970, *1,* 49.

Saarinen, T.F. *Image of the Chicago Loop.* Unpublished manuscript, 1964.

Saarinen, T.F. *Image of the University of Arizona Campus.* Unpublished manuscript, 1967.

Saarinen, T.F. *Perception of environment* (Resource Paper No. 5). Washington, D.C.: Association of American Geographers, Commission on College Geography, 1969.

Sabatino, D.A., Meald, J.E., Rothman, S.G., & Miller, T.L. Destructive norm-violating social behavior among adolescents. A review of protective efforts. *Adolescence,* 1978, *13,* 675–680.

Sadalla, E.K., & Magel, S.G. The perception of traversed distance. *Environment and Behavior,* 1980, *12,* 65–79.

Sadalla, E.K., & Staplin, L.J. An information storage model for distance cognition. *Environment and Behavior,* 1980, *12,* 183–193. (a)

Sadalla, E.K., & Staplin, L.J. The perception of traversed distance: Interactions. *Environment and Behavior,* 1980, *12,* 167–182. (b)

Sadalla, E.K., & Stea, D. Approaches to a psychology of urban life. *Environment and Behavior,* 1978, *10,* 139–146.

Saegert, S. *Effects of spatial and social density on arousal, mood, and social orientation.* Unpublished doctoral dissertation, University of Michigan, 1974.

Saegert, S. High density environments: Their personal and social consequences. In A. Baum & Y.M. Epstein (Eds.), *Human response to crowding.* Hillsdale, N.J.: Erlbaum, 1978.

Saegert, S., MacIntosh, E., & West, S. Two studies of crowding in urban public spaces. *Environment and Behavior,* 1975, *1,* 159–184.

Samuelson, D.J., & Lindauer, M.S. Perception, evaluation, and performance in a neat and messy room by high and low sensation seekers. *Environment and Behavior,* 1976, 8(2), 291–306.

Sanborn, D.E., Casey, T.M., & Niswander, G.D. Suicide: Seasonal patterns and related variables. *Diseases of the Nervous System,* 1970, *31,* 702–704.

Sanders, J.L. Relation of personal space to the human menstrual cycle. *The Journal of Psychology,* 1978, *100,* 275–278.

Savinar, J. The effect of ceiling height on personal space. *Man–Environment Systems,* 1975, *5,* 321–324.

Schachter, S. *The psychology of affiliation.* Stanford, Calif.: Stanford University Press, 1959.

Schachter, S., & Singer, J.E. Cognitive, social, and physiological determinants of emotional states. *Psychological Review,* 1962, *69,* 379–399.

Schaeffer, M., & Baum, A. *Consistency of stress response at Three Mile Island.* Paper presented at the annual meeting of the American Psychological Association, August 1982.

Schavio, S. *Factors mediating responses of invasions of personal space.* Paper presented at the annual meeting of the Rocky Mountain Psychological Association, 1975.

Scheier, M.F., Carver, C.S., & Gibbons, F.X. Self-directed attention, awareness of bodily states, and suggestibility. *Journal of Personality and Social Psychology,* 1979, *37,* 1576–1588.

Scherer, S.E. Proxemic behavior of primary school children as a function of their socioeconomic class and subculture. *Journal of Personality and Social Psychology,* 1974, *29,* 800–805.

Schettino, A.P., & Borden, R.J. Group size versus group density: Where is the affect? *Personality and Social Psychology Bulletin,* 1976, *2,* 67–70.

Schiffenbauer, A., & Schiavo, R.S. *Physical distance and attraction: An intensification effect.* Unpublished manuscript, Virginia

Polytechnic Institute and State University, 1975.

Schkade, J. *The effects of expectancy set and crowding on task performance*. Doctoral dissertation, University of Texas at Arlington, 1977.

Schmidt, C.W., & Ulrich, R.E. Effects of group contingent events upon classroom noise. *Journal of Applied Behavior Analysis*, 1969, *2*, 171–179.

Schmidt, D.E., & Keating, J.P. Human crowding and personal control: An integration of the research. *Psychological Bulletin*, 1979, *86*, 680–700.

Schmidt, J.R. *Territorial invasion and aggression*. Doctoral dissertation, Louisiana State University and Agricultural and Mechanical College, 1976.

Schmitt, R.C. Density, health, and social disorganization. *American Institute of Planners Journal*, 1966, *32*, 38–40.

Schneider, F.W., Lesko, W.A., & Garrett, W.A. Helping behavior in hot, comfortable, and cold temperatures. *Environment and Behavior*, 1980, *12*, 231–240.

Schneiderman, N. Animal behavior models of coronary heart disease. In D.S. Krantz, A. Baum, & J.E. Singer (Eds.), *Handbook of psychology and health* (Vol. 3). Hillsdale, N.J.: Erlbaum, 1982.

Schnelle, J.F., Gendrich, J.G., Beegle, G.P., Thomas, M.M., & McNess, M.P. Mass media techniques for prompting behavior change in the community. *Environment and Behavior*, 1980, *12*, 157–166.

Schopler, J., McCallum, R., & Rusbult, C. *Behavioral interference and internality–externality as determinants of subject crowding*. Unpublished manuscript, University of North Carolina, 1978.

Schopler, J., & Stockdale, J. An interference analysis of crowding. *Environmental Psychology and Nonverbal Behavior*, 1977, *1*, 81–88.

Schopler, J., & Walton, M. *The effects of structure, expected enjoyment, and participant's internality–externality upon feelings of being crowded*. Unpublished manuscript, University of North Carolina, 1974.

Schulte, J.H. Effects of mild carbon monoxide intoxication. *Archives of Environmental Health*. 1963, *7*, 524–530.

Schultz, D.B. *Sensory restriction*. New York: Academic Press, 1965.

Schulz, R. The effects of control and predictability on the psychological and physical well-being of the institutional aged. *Journal of Personality and Social Psychology*, 1976, *33*, 563–573.

Schulz, R., & Brenner, G. Relocation of the aged: A review and theoretical analysis. *Journal of Gerontology*, 1977, *32*, 323–333.

Schulz, R., & Hanusa, B.H. Long-term effects of control and predictability enhancing interventions. Findings and ethical issues. *Journal of Personality and Social Psychology*, 1978, *36*, 1194–1201.

Schuman, H., & Johnson, M.P. Attitudes and behavior. *Annual Review of Sociology*, 1976, *2*, 161–207.

Schussheim, M.J. *A modest commitment to cities*. Lexington, Mass.: Lexington Books, 1974.

Schwartz, B., & Barsky, S.P. The home advantage. *Social Forces*, 1977, *55*, 641–661.

Schwartz, D.C. On the ecology of political violence: ''The long hot summer'' as a hypothesis. *American Behavioral Scientist*, July–August 1968, 24–28.

Schwarz, H., & Werbik, H. Eine experimentelle Untersuchung über den Einfluss der syntaktischen Information der Anordnung von Baukörpern entlang einer Strasse auf Stimmungen des Betrachters. *Zeitschrift fur experimentelle und angewandte Psychologie*, 1971, *18*, 499–511.

Schwebel, A.I., & Cherlin, D.L. Physical and social distancing in teacher–pupil relationships. *Journal of Educational Psychology*, 1972, *63*, 543–550.

Seaton, R., & Collins, J. Validity and reliability of simulated buildings. In W. Mitchell (Ed.), *Environmental design: Research and practice* (Vol. 1). Stroudsburg, Pa.: Dowden, Hutchinson & Ross, 1972.

Segal, M.W. Alphabet and attraction: An unobtrusive measure of the effect of propinquity in a field setting. *Journal of Personality and Social Psychology*, 1974, *30*, 655–657.

Segall, M.H., Campbell, D.T., & Herskovits, M.J. *The influence of culture on visual perception*. Indianapolis: Bobbs-Merrill, 1966.

Seligman, C., & Darley, J.M. Feedback as a means of decreasing residential energy consumption. *Journal of Applied Psychology*, 1977, *62*, 363–368.

Seligman, C., Kriss, M., Darley, J.M., Fazio, R.H., Becker, L.J., & Pryor, J.B. Predicting summer energy consumption from homeowners' attitudes. *Journal of Applied Social Psychology*, 1979, *9*, 70–90.

Seligman, M.E.P. *Helplessness*. San Francisco: Freeman, 1975.

Sell, R. *Cooperation and competition as a function of residential environment, consequences of game strategy choices, and perceived control*. Doctoral dissertation, State University of New York—Stony Brook, 1976.

Sells, S.B., & Will, D.P. *Accidents, police incidents, and weather: A further study of the city of Fort Worth, Texas, 1968* (Technical Report No. 15). Fort Worth: Group Psychology Branch, Office of Naval Research and Institute of Behavioral Research, Texas Christian University, 1971.

Selltiz, C., Wrightsman, L.S., & Cook, S.W. *Research methods in social relations* (3rd ed). New York: Holt, Rinehart and Winston, 1976.

Selye, H. *The stress of life*. New York: McGraw-Hill, 1956.

Seta, J.J., Paulus, P.B., & Schkade, J.K. Effects of group size and proximity under cooperative and competitive conditions. *Journal of Personality and Social Psychology*, 1976, *34*, 47–53.

Shaban, J., & Welling, G. Cited in D.C. Glass & J.E. Singer, *Urban stress*. New York: Academic Press, 1972.

Shafer, E.L., Hamilton, J.F., & Schmidt, E.A. Natural landscape preferences: A predictive model. *Journal of Leisure Research,* 1969, *1,* 1–19.

Shafer, E.L., & Mietz, J. Aesthetic and emotional experiences rate high with northeast wilderness hikers. In J.F. Wohlwill & D.H. Carson (Eds.), *Environment and the social sciences: Perspectives and applications*. Washington, D.C.: American Psychological Association, 1972.

Sharpe, G.W. *Interpreting the environment*. New York: Wiley, 1976.

Sheflen, A.E. *Human territories: How we behave in space-time*. Englewood Cliffs, N.J.: Prentice-Hall, 1976.

Shepard, R.D., & Kroes, W.H. *Report of an investigation at the James Plant*. Internal report prepared for the National Institute of Occupational Safety and Health, Cincinnati, Ohio, 1975.

Shepard, R.N. Form, formation, and transformation of internal representation. In R.L. Solso (Ed.), *Information processing and cognition: The Loyola Symposium*. Hillsdale, N.J.: Erlbaum, 1975.

Sherrod, D.R. Crowding, perceived control and behavioral aftereffects. *Journal of Applied Social Psychology,* 1974, *4,* 171–186.

Sherrod, D.R., Armstrong, D., Hewitt, J., Madonia, B., Speno, S., & Fenyd, D. Environmental attention, affect and altruism. *Journal of Applied Social Psychology,* 1977, *7,* 359–371.

Sherrod, D.R., & Cohen, S. Density, personal control, and design. In J. Aiello & A. Baum (Eds.), *Residential crowding and design*. New York: Plenum, 1979.

Sherrod, D.R., & Downs, R. Environmental determinants of altruism: The effects of stimulus overload and perceived control on helping. *Journal of Experimental Social Psychology,* 1974, *10,* 468–479.

Sherrod, D.R., Hage, J., Halpern, P.L., & Moore, B.S. Effects of personal causation and perceived control on responses to an aversive environment: The more control the better. *Journal of Experimental Social Psychology,* 1977, *13,* 14–27.

Shippee, G.E. *Leadership, group participation, and avoiding the tragedy of the commons*. Unpublished doctoral dissertation, Arizona State University, 1978.

Shippee, G.E., Burroughs, J., & Wakefield, S. Dissonance theory revisited: Perception of environmental hazards in residential areas. *Environment and Behavior,* 1980, *12,* 35–51.

Siegel, J.M., & Steele, C.M. Environmental distraction and interpersonal judgments. *British Journal of Social and Clinical Psychology,* 1980, *19,* 23–32.

Simpson-Housley, P., Moore, R.J., Larrain, P., & Blair, D. Repression-sensitization and flood hazard appraisal in Carman, Manitoba. *Psychological Reports,* 1982, *50,* 839–842.

Sims, J.H., & Baumann, D.D. The tornado threat: Coping styles of the North and the South. *Science,* 1972, *176,* 1386–1391.

Singer, J.E., Lundberg, U., & Frankenhaeuser, M. Stress on the train: A study of urban commuting. In A. Baum, J.E. Singer, & S. Valins (Eds.), *Advances in environmental psychology,* (Vol. 1). Hillsdale, N.J.: Erlbaum, 1978.

Skeen, D.R. Influence of interpersonal distance in serial learning. *Psychological Reports,* 1976, *39,* 579–582.

Skinner, B.F. *Beyond freedom and dignity*. New York: Knopf, 1971.

Skogan, W., & Maxfield, M. *Coping with crime*. Beverly Hills, Calif.: Sage, 1981.

Skotko, V.P., & Langmeyer, D. The effects of interaction distance and gender on self-disclosure in the dyad. *Sociometry,* 1977, *40,* 178–182.

Slaven, R.E., Wodarksi, J.S., & Blackburn, B.L. A group contingency for electricity conservation in master-metered apartments. *Journal of Applied Behavior Analysis,* 1981, *14,* 357–363.

Sloan, A.W. *Man in extreme environments*. Springfield, Ill.: Charles C Thomas, 1979.

Slote, L. An experimental evaluation of man's reaction to an ionized air environment. *Proceedings of the International Conference on Ionization of the Air,* 1961, *2,* 1–22.

Slotsky, R.J. *Wilderness experience; A therapeutic modality*. San Francisco: California School of Professional Psychology, 1973.

Smith, P., & Connolly, K. Social and aggressive behavior in preschool children as a function of crowding. *Social Science Information,* 1977, *16,* 601–620.

Smith, R.J., & Knowles, E.S. Attributional consequences of personal space invasions. *Personality and Social Psychology Bulletin,* 1978, *4,* 429–433.

Smith, R.J., & Knowles, E.S. Affective and cognitive mediators of reactions to spatial invasions. *Journal of Experimental Social Psychology,* 1979, *15,* 437–452.

Snyder, L.H., & Ostrander, E.R. *Spatial and physical considerations in the nursing home environment: An interim report of findings*. Paper presented at the Cornell University Conference on Nursing Homes, Ithaca, New York, June 1972.

Snyder, R.L. Fertility and reproductive performance of grouped male mice. In K. Benirschke (Ed.), *Symposium on comparative aspects of reproductive behavior*. Berlin: Springer Press, 1966.

Socolow, R.H. *Saving energy in the home*. Cambridge, Mass.: Ballinger Publishing Company, 1978.

Soleri, P. *Arcology: The city in the image of man*. Cambridge, Mass.: M.I.T. Press, 1969.

Sommer, R. Studies in personal space. *Sociometry,* 1959, *22,* 247–260.

Sommer, R. Further studies of small group ecology. *Sociometry,* 1965, *28,* 337–348.

Sommer, R. Man's proximate environment. *Journal of Social Issues,* 1966, *22,* 59–70.

Sommer, R. Classroom ecology. *Journal of Applied Behavioral Science,* 1967, *3,* 489–503.

Sommer, R. *Personal space*. Englewood Cliffs, N.J.: Prentice-Hall, 1969.

Sommer, R. *Design awareness*. San Francisco: Rinehart Press, 1972.

Sommer, R. *Tight spaces: Hard architecture and how to humanize it*. Englewood Cliffs, N.J.: Prentice-Hall, 1974.

Sommer, R., & Olsen, H. The soft classroom. *Environment and Behavior*, 1980, *12*, 3–16.

Sommer, R., & Osmond, H. Symptoms of institutional care. *Social Problems*, 1961, *8*, 254.

Sommer, R., & Ross, H. Social interaction on a geriatrics ward. *International Journal of Social Psychiatry*, 1958, *4*, 128–133.

Sommers, P., & Moos, R. The weather and human behavior. In R.H. Moos (Ed.), *The human context: Environmental determinants of behavior*. New York: Wiley, 1976.

Sonnenfeld, J. Variable values in space and landscape: An inquiry into the nature of environmental necessity. *Journal of Social Issues*, 1966, *22*, 71–82.

Southwick, C.H. The population dynamics of confined mice supplied with unlimited food. *Ecology*, 1955, *36*, 212–225.

Southwick, C.H. An experimental study of intragroup agnostic behavior in rhesus monkeys (Macaca mulatta). *Behavior*, 1967, *28*, 182–209.

Srivastava, R.K. Undermanning theory in the context of mental health care environments. In D.H. Carson (Ed.), *Man–environment interactions* (Part 11). Stroudsburg, Pa.: Dowden, Hutchinson & Ross, 1974.

Srole, L. Urbanization and mental health: Some reformulations. *American Scientist*, 1972, *60*, 576–583.

Srole, L. The city vs. the country: New evidence on an ancient bias. In L. Srole & A. Fischer (Eds.), *Mental health in the metropolis* (2nd ed.) New York: Harper & Row, 1976.

Staats, A.W. Social behaviorism and human motivation: Principles of the attitude-reinforcer-discriminative system. In A.G. Greenwald, T.C. Brock, & T.M. Ostrom (Eds.), *Psychological foundations of attitudes*. New York: Academic Press, 1968.

Staff, I. *Proximity, task and room size: The appropriateness of interpersonal distance*. Doctoral dissertation, Columbia University, 1976.

Stahl, S.M., & Lebedun, M. Mystery gas: An analysis of mass hysteria. *Journal of Health and Social Behavior*, 1974, *15*, 44–50.

Stainbrook, E. Architects not only design hospitals: They also design patient behavior. *Modern Hospital*, 1966, *106*, 100.

Stea, D. Architecture in the head: Cognitive mapping. In J. Lang, C. Burnette, W. Moleski, & D. Vachon (Eds.), *Designing for human behavior*. Stroudsburg, Pa.: Dowden, Hutchinson & Ross, 1974.

Steidl, R.E. Difficult factors in homemaking tasks: Implications for environmental design. *Human Factors*, 1972, *14*(5), 471–482.

Steinitz, C. Meaning and congruence of urban form and activity. *Journal of the American Institute of Planners*, 1968, *34*, 233–248.

Steinzor, B. The spatial factor in face-to-face discussion groups. *Journal of Abnormal and Social Psychology*, 1950, *45*, 552–555.

Stephan, W. School desegregation: An evaluation of predictions made in Brown vs. the Board of Education. *Psychological Bulletin*, 1978, *85*, 217–238.

Sterling, E. The impact of air pollution on residential design. In A.D. Seidel & S. Danford (Eds.), *Environmental design: Research, theory, and application*. Washington, D.C.: Environmental Design Research Association, 1979.

Stern, P.C. Effect of incentives and education on resource conservation decisions in a simulated commons dilemma. *Journal of Personality and Social Psychology*, 1976, *25*, 1285-1292.

Stern, P.C. Psychological research and steady state society. *Population and Environmental Psychology Newsletter*, 1977, *4*, 10–15.

Stern, P.C., & Gardner, G.T. Psychological research and energy policy. *American Psychologist*, 1981, *4*, 329–342.

Stevens, A., & Coupe, P. Distortions in judged spatial relations. *Cognitive Psychology*, 1978, *10*, 422–437.

Stevens, S.S. The measurement of loudness. *Journal of the Acoustical Society of America*, 1955, *27*, 815–829.

Stevens, W., Kushler, M., Jeppesen, J., & Leedom, N. *Youth energy education strategies: A statistical evaluation*. Lansing, Mich.: Energy Extension Service, Department of Commerce, 1979.

Stires, L. Classroom seating location, student grades, and attitudes: Environment or selection? *Environment and Behavior*, 1980, *12*, 241–254.

Stobaugh, R., & Yergin, D. *Energy future: Report of the energy project of the Harvard Business School*. New York: Random House, 1979.

Stogner, J.D. *The effects of a wilderness experience on self-concept and academic performance*. Unpublished Manuscript, Virginia Polytechnic Institute and State University, 1978.

Stokols, D. On the distinction between density and crowding: Some implications for future research. *Psychological Review*, 1972, *79*, 275–278.

Stokols, D. The experience of crowding in primary and secondary environments. *Environment and Behavior*, 1976, *8*, 49–86.

Stokols, D. A typology of crowding experiences. In A. Baum & Y. Epstein (Eds.), *Human response to crowding*. Hillsdale, N.J.: Erlbaum, 1978.

Stokols, D., & Novaco, R. Transportation and well-being: An ecological perspective. In I. Altman, J.F. Wohlwill, & P.B. Everett (Eds.), *Transportation and behavior*. New York: Plenum, 1981.

Stokols, D., Novaco, R. W., Stokols, J., & Campbell, J. *Traffic congestion, type A behavior, and stress*. Paper presented at the annual meeting of the American Psychological Association, San Francisco, August 1977.

Stokols, D., Novaco, R.W., Stokols, J., & Campbell, J. Traffic congestion, type A behavior, and stress. *Journal of Applied Psychology,* 1978, 63, 467–480.

Stokols, D., & Ohlig, W. *The experience of crowding under different social climates.* Paper presented at the meeting of the American Psychological Association, Chicago, 1975.

Stokols, D., Ohlig, W., & Resnick, S. Perception of residential crowding, classroom experiences, and student health. In J.R. Aiello & A. Baum (Eds.), *Residential crowding and design.* New York: Plenum Press, 1979.

Stokols, D., Rall, M., Pinner, B., & Schopler, J. Physical, social and personal determinants of the perception of crowding. *Environment and Behavior,* 1973, *5,* 87–117.

Stone, G.L., & Morden, C.J. Effect of distance on verbal productivity. *Journal of Counseling Psychology,* 1976, *23,* 486–488.

Stone, J., Breidenbach, S., & Heimstra, N. Annoyance response of nonsmokers to cigarette smoke. *Perceptual and Motor Skills,* 1979, *49,* 907–916.

Storms, M.D., & Thomas, G.C. Reactions to physical closeness. *Journal of Personality and Social Psychology,* 1977, *35,* 412–418.

Strahilevitz, N., Strahilevitz, A., & Miller, J.E. Air pollution and the admission rate of psychiatric patients. *American Journal of Psychiatry,* 1979, *136,* 206–207.

Strakhov, A.B. *Some questions of the mechanism of the action of noise on an organism* (Report N67-11646). Washington, D.C.: Joint Publication Research Service, 1966.

Strodtbeck, F., & Hook, H. The social dimensions of a 12-man jury table. *Sociometry,* 1961, *24,* 397–415.

Studer, R. The organization of spatial stimuli. In L. Pastalan & D. Carson (Eds.), *The spatial behavior of older people.* Ann Arbor: University of Michigan Press, 1970.

Suedfeld, P. The benefits of boredom: Sensory deprivation reconsidered. *American Scientist,* 1975, *63,* 60–69.

Sulman, F.G., Danon, A., Pfeifer, Y., Tal, E., & Weller, C.P. Urinalysis of patients suffering from climatic heat stress (Sharav). *International Journal of Biometeorology,* 1970, *14,* 45–53.

Sundeen, R.A., & Mathieu, J.T. Fear of crime and its consequences among elderly in three urban communities. *The Gerontologist,* 1976, *16,* 211–219.

Sundstrom, E. Interpersonal behavior and the physical environment. In L.S. Wrightsman (Ed.), *Social psychology* (2nd ed). Monterey, Calif.: Brooks/Cole, 1976.

Sundstrom, E. An experimental study of crowding: Effects of room size, intrusion, and goal-blocking on nonverbal behaviors, self-disclosure, and self-reported stress. *Journal of Personality and Social Psychology,* 1975, *32,* 645–654.

Sundstrom, E. Crowding as a sequential process: Review of research on the effects of population density on humans. In A. Baum & Y.M. Epstein (Eds.), *Human response to crowding,* Hillsdale, N.J.: Erlbaum, 1978.

Sundstrom, E., & Altman, I. Personal space and interpersonal relationships: Research review and theoretical model. *Human Ecology,* 1976, *4,* 47–67.

Sundstrom, E., Herbert, R.K., & Brown, D.W. Privacy and communication in an open-plan office: A case study. *Environment and Behavior,* 1982, *14,* 379–392.

Sundstrom, E., & Sundstrom, M.G. Personal space invasions: What happens when the invader asks permission? *Environmental Psychology and Nonverbal Behavior,* 1977, *2,* 76–82.

Sundstrom, E., & Sundstrom, M.G. *Work places: Psychology of the physical environment in offices and factories.* Monterey, Calif.: Brooks/Cole, 1983.

Sundstrom, E., Town, J., Brown, D., Forman, A., & McGee, C. Physical enclosure, type of job, and privacy in the office. *Environment and Behavior,* 1982, *14,* 543-560.

Suttles, G.D. *The social order of the slum: Ethnicity and territory in the inner city.* Chicago: University of Chicago Press, 1968.

Swan, J.A. Response to air pollution: A study of attitudes and coping strategies of high school youths. *Environment and Behavior,* 1970, *2,* 127–152.

Swanson, C.P. *The natural history of man.* Englewood Cliffs, N.J.: Prentice-Hall, 1973.

Taggart, P., Gibbons, D., & Sommerville, W. Some effects of motor-car driving on the normal and abnormal heart. *British Medical Journal,* 1969, *4,* 130–134.

Tasso, J., & Miller, E. The effects of the full moon on human behavior. *The Journal of Psychology,* 1976, *93,* 81–83.

Taylor, I.R. Soccer consciousness and soccer hooliganism. In S. Cohen (Ed.), *Images of deviance.* London: Penguin, 1971.

Taylor, L. *A theoretical and experimental investigation of the relationship between expectations and crowding.* Doctoral dissertation, Rutgers University, 1976.

Taylor, R.B. Human territoriality: A review and a model for future research. *Cornell Journal of Social Relations,* 1978, *13,* 125–151.

Taylor, R.B., & Brooks, D.K. Temporary territories: Responses to intrusions in a public setting. *Population and Environment,* 1980, *3,* 135–145.

Taylor, R.B., & Ferguson, G. *Solitude and intimacy: Privacy experiences and the role of territoriality.* Paper presented at the annual meeting of the American Psychological Association, Toronto, 1978.

Taylor, R.B., Gottfredson, S.D., & Brower, S. The defensibility of defensible space: A critical review and a synthetic framework for future research. In T. Hirshi & M. Gottfredson (Eds.), *Understanding crime.* Beverly Hills, Calif.: Sage, 1980.

Taylor, R.B., & Lanni, J.C. Territorial dominance: The influence of the resident advantage in triadic decision making. *Journal of Personality and Social Psychology*, 1981, *41*, 909–915.

Taylor, R.B., & Stough, R.R. Territorial cognition: Assessing Altman's typology. *Journal of Personality and Social Psychology*, 1978, *36*, 418–423.

Taylor, V., & Quarantelli, E. *Some needed cross-cultural studies of disaster behavior*. Columbus, Ohio: Disaster Research Center, 1976.

Teaff, J.D., Lawton, M.P., Nahemow, L., & Carlson, D. Impact of integration on the well-being of the elderly tenants in public housing. *Journal of Gerontology*, 1978, *33*, 126–133.

Tennen, H., & Eller, S.J. Attributional components of learned helplessness and facilitation. *Journal of Personality and Social Psychology*, 1977, *35*, 265–271.

Tennis, G.H., & Dabbs, J.M. Sex, setting and personal space: First grade through college. *Sociometry*, 1975, *38*, 385–394.

Terry, R.L., & Lower, M. Perceptual withdrawal from an invasion of personal space. *Personality and Social Psychology Bulletin*, 1979, *5*, 396–397.

Thalhofer, N.N. Violation of a spacing norm in high social density. *Journal of Applied Social Psychology*, 1980, *10*, 175–183.

Thompson, W.R., & Heron, W. The effects of restricting early experience on the problem-solving capacity of dogs. *Canadian Journal of Psychology*, 1954, *8*, 17–31.

Tien, J.M., O'Donnell, V.F., Barnett, A., & Mirchandini, P.B. *Street lighting projects*. Washington, D.C.: Department of Justice, 1979.

Tinsley, H.E.A. Barrett, T.C., & Kass, R.A. Leisure activities and need satisfaction. *Journal of Leisure Research*, 1977, *9*, 110–120.

Titchener, J., & Kapp, F.I. Family and character change at Buffalo Creek. *American Journal of Psychiatry*, 1976, *133*, 295–299.

Tolman, E.C. Cognitive maps in rats and men. *Psychological Review*, 1948, *55*, 189–208.

Towler, J., & Swan, J.E. What do people really know about pollution? *Journal of Environmental Education*, 1972, *4*, 54–57.

Trice, H.M. *Alcoholism in America*. New York: McGraw-Hill, 1966.

Trites, D., Galbraith, F.D., Sturdavent, M., & Leckwart, J.F. Influence of nursing unit design on the activities and subjective feelings of nursing personnel. *Environment and Behavior*, 1970, *2*, 203–234.

Truscott, J.C., Parmalee, P., & Werner, C. Plate touching in restaurants—Preliminary observations of a food-related marking behavior in humans. *Journal of Personality and Social Psychology*, 1977, *3*, 425–428.

Tuan, Y.F. *Topophilia*. Englewood Cliffs, N.J.: Prentice-Hall, 1974.

Tucker, L.R. The environmentally concerned citizen: Some correlates. *Environment and Behavior*, 1978, *10*, 389–418.

Turk, A., Johnston, J.W., & Moulton, D.G. (Eds.). *Human responses to environmental odors*. New York: Academic Press, 1974.

Turk, A., Turk, J., Wittes, J. T., & Wittes, R. *Environmental science*. Philadelphia: Saunders, 1974.

Turner, F.J. *The frontier in American history*. New York: Holt, Rinehart and Winston, 1920.

Tyler, T.R. Perceived control and behavioral reactions to crime. *Personality and Social Psychology Bulletin*, 1981, *7*, 212–217.

Unger, D., & Wandersman, A. Neighboring in an urban environment. *American Journal of Community Psychology*, in press.

United States Riot Commission. *Report of the National Advisory Commission on Civil Disorders*. New York: Bantam, 1968.

Ury, H. Photochemical air pollution and automobile accidents in Los Angeles: An investigation of oxidant and accidents, 1963 and 1965. *Archives of Environmental Health*, 1968, *17*, 334–342.

Ury, H.K., Perkins, N.M., & Goldsmith, J.R. Motor vehicle accidents and vehicular pollution in Los Angeles. *Archives of Environmental Health*, 1972, *25*, 314–322.

U.S. Department of Health Education and Welfare. *The mental health of urban America: The urban programs of the National Institute of Mental Health*. (Public Health Service Publication. No. 1906). Washington, D.C.: U.S. Government Printing Office, 1969.

U.S. Department of Health, Education and Welfare, President's Council on Physical Fitness and Sports. *Organization, objectives, programs, situation report*. Washington, D.C.: U.S. Government Printing Office, 1977.

U.S. Department of Health, Education and Welfare, Public Health Service, Alcohol, Drug Abuse and Mental Health Administration. *Stress*. Washington, D.C.: U.S. Government Printing Office, 1979.

U.S. Department of the Interior, Heritage Conservation and Recreational Service. *Federal Outdoor Recreation Fee Program—1977*. Washington, D.C.: U.S. Government Printing Office, 1979.

U.S. Department of the Interior, Heritage Conservation and Recreation Service. *The Third Nationwide Outdoor Recreation Plan*. Washington, D.C.: U.S. Government Printing Office, 1979.

U.S. Environmental Protection Agency. *The Glut: Fun with the environment. A fun-as-you-learn book for kids who care about the environment*. Washington, D.C.

U.S. News and World Report. The fitness mania. February 27, 1978.

U.S. Racquetball Association, Skokie, Ill. Unpublished estimates, 1978.

Van Wagenberg, D., Krasner, M.,& Krasner, L. Children planning an ideal classroom: Environmental design in an elementary school. *Environment and Behavior*, 1981, *13*, 349–359.

Vinsel, A., Brown, B., Altman, I., & Foss, C. Privacy regulation, territorial displays, and effectiveness of individual functioning. *Journal of Personality and Social Psychology, 1980, 39,* 1104–1115.

Vitalo, R.L. *Principles of psychiatric rehabilitation.* Amherst Mass.: Human Resources Development Press, 1978.

Von Euler, U.S. Twenty years of noradrenaline. *Pharmacological Review, 1966, 18,* 29.

Wack, J., & Rodin, J. Nursing homes for the aged: The human consequences of legislation-shaped environments. *Journal of Social Issues, 1978, 34,* 6–21.

Walder, D.N. Decompression sickness in tunnel workers. In C.N. Davies, P.R. Davis, & F.H. Tyrer (Eds.), *The effects of abnormal physical conditions at work.* London: E. & S. Livingstone, 1967.

Walker, J.M. Energy demand behavior in a master-meter apartment complex: An experimental analysis. *Journal of Applied Psychology, 1979, 64,* 190–196.

Wall, G. Public response to air pollution in South Yorkshire, England. *Environment and Behavior, 1973, 5,* 219–248.

Wallis, D.A. Aggression in social insects. In D. Carthy & H. Ebling (Eds.), *The natural history of aggression.* New York: Academic Press, 1964.

Wallston, B., Alagna, S., DeVellis, B., & DeVellis, R. *Social support and physical health.* Unpublished manuscript, Peabody College of Vanderbilt University, 1982.

Wandersman, A., Andrews, A., Riddle, C., & Fancett, C. Environmental psychology and prevention. In R. Felner, S. Farber, L. Jason, & J. Moritsugu (Eds.), *Preventive psychology: Theory, research and practice.* New York: Pergamon, in press.

Wandersman, A., & Florin, P. A cognitive social learning approach to the crossroads of cognitive social behavior and the environment. In J. Harvey (Ed.), *Cognitive social behavior and environment.* Hillsdale, N.J.: Erlbaum, 1981.

Ward, L.M., & Suedfeld, P. Human responses to highway noise. *Environmental Research, 1973, 6,* 306–326.

Ward, P. Deadly throwaways: Plastic six-pack binders and metal pull-tabs doom wildlife. *Defenders,* 1975.

Watson, O.M., & Graves, T.D. Quantitative research in proxemic behavior. *American Anthropologist, 1966, 68,* 971–985.

Wayne, W., Wehrle, P., & Carroll, R. Oxidant air pollution and athletic performance. *Journal of the American Medical Association, 1967, 199,* 901–904.

Webb, E.J., Campbell, D.T., Schwartz, R.D., & Sechrest, L. *Unobtrusive measures: Non-reactive research in the social sciences.* Chicago: Rand McNally, 1966.

Webb, E.J., Campbell, D.T., Schwartz, R.D., Sechrest, L., & Grove, J.B. *Nonreactive measures in social sciences* (2nd ed.). Dallas: Houghton Mifflin, 1981.

Weigel, J., & Weigel, R.H. Environmental concern: The development of a measure. *Environment and Behavior, 1978, 10,* 3–16.

Weigel, R.H., & Newman, L.S. Increasing attitude–behavior correspondence by broadening the scope of the behavioral measure. *Journal of Personality and Social Psychology, 1976, 33,* 793–802.

Weiner, F.H. Altruism, ambiance, and action: The effects of rural and urban rearing on helping behavior. *Journal of Personality and Social Psychology, 1976, 34,* 112–124.

Weinstein, L. Social schemata of emotionally disturbed boys. *Journal of Abnormal Psychology, 1965, 76,* 457–461.

Weinstein, M.S. *Health in the city: Environmental and behavioral influences.* New York: Pergamon, 1980.

Weinstein, N.D. The statistical prediction of environmental preferences. *Environment and Behavior, 1976, 8,* 611–626.

Weisman, J. Evaluating architectural eligibility: Way finding in the built environment. *Environment and Behavior, 1981, 13,* 189–204.

Weisner, T., & Weibel, J. Home environments and family lifestyles in California. *Environment and Behavior, 1981, 13,* 417–460.

Wellens, A.R., & Goldberg, M.L. The effects of interpersonal distance and orientation upon the perception of social relationships. *The Journal of Psychology, 1978, 99,* 39–47.

West, P.C., & Merriam, L.C., Jr. Outdoor recreation and family cohesiveness: A research approach. *Journal of Leisure Research, 1970, 2,* 251–259.

Weyant, J.M. Effects of mood states, costs, and benefits on helping. *Journal of Personality and Social Psychology, 1978, 36,* 1169–1176.

Wheeldon, P.D. The operation of voluntary associations and personal networks in the political processes of an interethnic community. In J.C. Mitchell (Ed.), *Social networks in urban situations.* Manchester N. H.: University of Manchester Press, 1969.

White, M. Interpersonal distance as affected by room size, status, and sex. *The Journal of Social Psychology, 1975, 95,* 241–249.

White, M., & White, L. *The intellectual versus the city.* Cambridge, Mass.: Harvard University Press and the M.I.T. Press, 1962.

Whitehead, C., Polsky, R.H., Crookshank, C., & Fik, E. *An ethological evaluation of psychoenvironmental design.* In press.

Wicker, A.W. Attitudes versus actions: The relationship of verbal and overt behavioral responses to attitude objects. *Journal of Social Issues, 1969, 24,* 41–78. (a)

Wicker, A.W. Size of church membership and members' support of church behavior settings. *Journal of Personality and Social Psychology, 1969, 13,* 278–288. (b)

Wicker, A.W. *An introduction to ecological psychology.* Monterey, Calif.: Brooks/Cole, 1979.

Wicker, A.W., & Kauma, C. Effects of a merger of a small and a large organization on members' behaviors and experiences.

Journal of Applied Psychology, 1974, *59,* 24–30.

Wicker, A.W., & Kirmeyer, S. From church to laboratory to national park: A program of research on excess and insufficient populations in behavior settings. In S. Wapner, S.B. Cohen, & B. Kaplan (Eds.), *Experiencing the environment.* New York: Plenum, 1976.

Wicker, A.W., Kirmeyer, S.L., Hanson, L., & Alexander, D. Effects of manning levels on subjective experiences, performance, and verbal interaction in groups. *Organizational Behavior and Human Performance,* 1976, *17,* 251–274.

Wicker, A.W., McGrath, J.E., & Armstrong, G.E. Organization size and behavior setting capacity as determinants of member participation. *Behavioral Science,* 1972, *17,* 499–513.

Wicker, A.W., & Mehler, A. Assimilation of new members in a large and a small church. *Journal of Applied Psychology,* 1971, *55,* 151–156.

Wilkinson, R.T. Individual differences in response to the environment. *Ergonomics,* 1974, *17,* 745–756.

Wilkinson, R.T., Fox, R.H., Goldsmith, R., Hampton, I.F., & Lewis, H.E. Psychological and physical responses to raised body temperature. *Journal of Applied Physiology,* 1964, *29,* 287–292.

Will, D.P., & Sells, S.B. *Prediction of police incidents and accidents by meteorological variables* (Technical Report No. 14). Fort Worth: Group Psychology Branch, Office of Naval Research and Institute of Behavioral Research, Texas Christian University, 1969.

Willis, F.N. Initial speaking distance as a function of the speakers' relationship. *Psychonomic Science,* 1966, *5,* 221–222.

Willis, F.N., Carlson, R., & Reeves, D. The development of personal space in primary school children. *Environmental Psychology and Nonverbal Behavior,* 1979, *3,* 195–204.

Wills, T.A. Downward comparison principles in social psychology. *Psychological Bulletin,* 1981, *90,* 245–271.

Wilner, D., Walkley, T., Pinderton, T., & Tayback, M. *The housing environment and family life.* Baltimore, Md.: Johns Hopkins Press, 1962.

Wilson, C.W., & Hopkins, B.L. The effects of contingent music on the intensity of noise in junior high home economics classes. *Journal of Applied Behavior Analysis,* 1973, *6,* 269–275.

Wilson E.O. *Sociobiology.* Cambridge, Mass.: Harvard University Press, 1975.

Wilson, G.D. Arousal properties of red versus green. *Perceptual and Motor Skills,* 1966, *23,* 947–949.

Wilson, S. Intensive care delirium. *Archives of Internal Medicine,* 1972, *130,* 225.

Wineman, J.D. Office design and evaluation: An overview. *Environment and Behavior,* 1982, *14,* 271–298.

Winkel, G., Olsen, R., Wheeler, F., Cohen, M. *The museum visitor and orientational media: An experimental comparison of different approaches in the Smithsonian Institution and National Museum of History and Technology.* New York: City University of New York Center for Environment and Behavior, 1976.

Winkler, R.C., & Winnett, R.A. Behavioral interventions in resource management. *American Psychologist,* 1982, *37,* 421–435.

Winnett, R.A., Hatcher, J., Leckliter, I., Ford, T.R., Fishback, J.F., Riley, A.W., & Love, S. *The effects of videotape modeling and feedback on residential comfort, the thermal environment and electricity consumption: Winter and summer studies.* Unpublished manuscript, Department of Psychology, Virginia Polytechnic Institute and State University, 1981.

Winnett, R.A., Kagel, J.H., Battalio, R.C., & Winkler, R.C. Effects of monetary rebates, feedback and information on residential energy conservation. *Journal of Applied Psychology,* 1978, *63,* 73–78.

Winnett, R.A., Neale, M.S., & Grier, H.C. The effects of self-monitoring and feedback on residential electricity consumption. *Journal of Applied Behavior Analysis,* 1979, *12,* 173–184.

Winnett, R.A., Neale, M.S., Williams, K.R., Yokley, J., & Kauder, H. The effects of individual and group feedback on residential electricity consumption: Three replications. *Journal of Environmental Systems,* 1979, *8,* 217–233.

Winnett, R.A., & Nietzel, M.T. Behavioral ecology: Contingency management of consumer energy use. *American Journal of Community Psychology,* 1975, *3,* 123–133.

Winsborough, H. The social consequences of high population density. *Law and Contemporary Problems,* 1965, *30,* 120–126.

Winston, B.J. The relationship of awareness to concern for environmental quality among selected high school students. *Dissertation Abstracts International,* 1974, *35A,* 3412.

Wofford, J.C. Negative ionization: An investigation of behavioral effects. *Journal of Experimental Psychology,* 1966, *71,* 608–611.

Wohlwill, J.F. The physical environment: A problem for a psychology of stimulation. *Journal of Social Issues,* 1966, *22,* 29–38.

Wohlwill, J.F. The emerging discipline of environmental psychology. *American Psychologist,* 1970, *25,* 303–312.

Wohlwill, J.F. Human response to levels of environmental stimulation. *Human Ecology,* 1974, *2,* 127–147.

Wohlwill, J.F. Environmental aesthetics: The environment as a source of affect. In I. Altman & J.F. Wohlwill (Eds.), *Human behavior and environment: Advances in theory and research* (Vol. 1). New York: Plenum, 1976.

Wohlwill, J., & Kohn, I. The environment as experienced by the migrant: An adaptation level view. *Representative Research in Social Psychology,* 1973, *4,* 135–164.

Wolfe C.P. Editorial preface. *Environment and Behavior,* 1975, *7,* 259–264.

Wolfe, M. Room size, group size, and density: Behavior patterns in a children's psychiatric facility. *Environment and Behavior,* 1975, *7,* 199.

Wolfe, R.I. About cottages and cottagers. *Landscape,* 1965, *15,* 6–8.

Woodhead, M.M. Visual searching in intermittent noise. *Journal of Sound Vibration,* 1964, *1,* 157–161.

Worchel, S. The experience of crowding: An attributional analysis. In A. Baum & Y. Epstein (Eds.), *Human response to crowding.* Hillsdale, N.J.: Erlbaum, 1978.

Worchel, S., & Teddlie, C. The experience of crowding: A two-factor theory. *Journal of Personality and Social Psychology,* 1976, *34,* 36–40.

Worchel, S., & Yohai, S. The role of attribution in the experience of crowding. *Journal of Experimental Social Psychology,* 1979, *15,* 91–104.

Wyndham, C. Adaptation to heat and cold. *Environmental Research,* 1969, *2,* 442–469.

Wyndham, C.H. Adaptation to heat and cold. In D.H.K. Lee & D. Minard (Eds.), *Physiology, environment, and man.* New York: Academic Press, 1970.

Wynne-Edwards, V.C. *Animal dispersion in relation to social behavior.* Edinburgh: Oliver & Boyd, 1962.

Yancey, W.L. Architecture, interaction, and social control: The case of a large scale housing project. In J.F. Wohlwill & D.H. Carson (Eds.), *Environment and the social sciences: Perspectives and applications.* Washington, D.C.: American Psychological Association, 1972.

Yinon, Y., & Bizman, A. Noise, success, and failure as determinants of helping behavior. *Personality and Social Psychology Bulletin,* 1980, *6,* 125–130.

Young, M., & Willmott, P. *Family and kinship in East London.* Baltimore: Penguin, 1957.

Zajonc, R.B. Attitudinal effects of mere exposure. *Journal of Personality and Social Psychology,* 1968, *8,* 1–29, Monograph.

Zarling, L.H., & Lloyd, K.E. *A behavioral analysis of feedback to electrical consumers.* Unpublished manuscript, 1978.

Zeisel, J. *Sociology and architectural design. Social science frontiers* (6). New York: Russell Sage Foundation, 1975.

Zeisel, J., & Griffin, M. *Charlesview housing: A diagnostic evaluation.* Cambridge, Mass.: Harvard University Graduate School of Design, 1975.

Zelnick, M., & Kanter, J.F. The resolution of teenage first pregnancies. *Family Planning Perspectives,* 1974, *6,* 74.

Zillmann, D. *Hostility and aggression.* Hillsdale, N.J.: Erlbaum, 1979.

Zillmann, D., Baron, R.A., & Tamborini, R. Social costs of smoking: Effects of tobacco smoke on hostile behavior. *Journal of Applied Social Psychology,* 1981, *11,* 548–561.

Zillmann, D., Katcher, A.H., & Milavsky, B. Excitation transfer from physical exercise to subsequent aggressive behavior. *Journal of Experimental Social Psychology,* 1972, *8,* 247–259.

Zimbardo, P.G. The human choices: Individuation, reason, and order versus deindividuation, impulse, and chaos. In W.J. Arnold & D. Levine (Eds.), *Nebraska Symposium on Motivation.* Lincoln: University of Nebraska Press, 1969.

Zimring, C.M. Stress and the designed environment. *Journal of Social Issues,* 1981, *37,* 145–171.

Zlutnick, S., & Altman, I. Crowding and human behavior. In J. Wohlwill & D. Carson (Eds.), *Environment and the social sciences: Perspectives and applications.* Washington, D.C.: American Psychological Association, 1972.

Zube, E.H. Scenery as a natural resource: Implications of public policy and problems of definition, description, and evaluation. *Landscape Architecture,* 1973, *63,* 126–132.

Zube, E.H., & Mills, L.V., Jr. Cross-cultural explorations in landscape perception In E.H. Zube (Ed.), *Studies in landscape perception* (Publication No. R-76-1). Amherst: Institute for Man and Environment, University of Massachusetts, 1976.

Zube, E.H., Pitt, D.G., & Anderson, T.W. Perception and measurements of scenic resources in the southern Connecticut River Valley. Amherst: Institute for Man and Environment, University of Massachusetts, 1974.

Zubek, J.P. (Ed.). *Sensory deprivation: Fifteen years of research.* New York: Appleton-Century-Crofts, 1969.

Zuckerman, M. Dimensions of sensation seeking. *Journal of Consulting and Clinical Psychology,* 1971, *36,* 45–52.

Zweig, J., & Csank, J. Effects of relocation on chronically ill geriatric patients of a medical unit: Mortality rates. *Journal of American Geriatrics Society,* 1975, *23,* 132–136.

Name Index

Abey-Wickrama, I., 106
Abramson, L. Y., 72
Acking, D. A., 272
Acton, W. I., 108
Adam, J. M., 126
Adams, J. R., 187
Adelberg, B., 240
Aiello, J. R., 150, 153, 154, 158, 159, 160, 167, 169, 202, 203, 208, 209, 210, 215, 219, 220, 221, 270, 380, 391, 402
Aiello, T. D., 159, 160
Ajzen, I., 56
Albert, S., 165
Alderman, R. B., 331
Alexander, C., 282, 283, 296
Alexander, G. C., 238
Alexander, K., 110
Alland, A., 176
Allen, G. H., 348
Allen, V. L., 375
Allgeier, A. R., 155
Allott, K., 292
Allport, F. H., 29
Allport, G., 29

Altman, I., 5, 10, 42, 69, 70, 150, 153, 158, 159, 161, 169, 176, 177, 179, 180, 181, 183, 184, 185, 215, 216, 219, 276, 283–284, 287–288, 295, 322, 380, 384, 391, 401
Anderson, C. A., 131
Anderson, T. W., 38, 50
Ando, Y., 105
Antonovsky, A., 256
Appleyard, D., 26, 31, 110, 230, 232, 233
Arbuthnot, J., 376
Ardrey, R., 176, 198
Argrist, S. S., 259
Argyle, M., 168
Arkkelin, D., 221
Armstrong, G. E., 76, 240
Arnstein, S. R., 262
Aronow, W. S., 116
Aronson, E., 404
Arrowood, A., 221
Artz, L. M., 356
Asch, J., 349

Auble, D., 107
Auliciems, S., 140
Averill, J., 71
Ayers, V., 391, 401, 405

Back, K., 279, 296
Bacon-Prue, A., 361
Bailey, F., 159
Bailey, J. S., 356, 363
Baird, L. L., 76
Baker, G. W., 86
Ball, T. M., 32
Baltes, M. M., 351
Bandura, A., 48, 110, 360, 368
Banzinger, G., 136
Barash, D. P., 174
Barefoot, J., 172, 174
Barker, M. L., 29, 142, 144
Barker, T., 141
Barkow, B., 373
Barnard, S. W., 110, 385
Baron, R. A., 88, 128, 129, 130, 131, 133, 173, 177
Baron, R. M., 204, 205, 214, 215, 221, 223, 375, 376,

377, 392, 401
Barrett, J., 160
Barrett, T. C., 330
Barrios, B. A., 156
Barry, T., 138
Bartley, S. H., 29
Barton, R., 187
Barton, W. H., 161, 271
Baskett, G. D., 161
Bassett, R., 305, 306
Baum, A., 70, 77, 78, 86,
    88, 89, 92, 95, 161, 201,
    202, 203, 206, 207, 209,
    212, 213, 214, 215, 216,
    219, 220, 221, 222, 223,
    267, 269, 270, 272, 273,
    275, 277, 283, 307, 322,
    380, 384, 385
Baum, C. S., 77
Baumann, D. D., 28, 86
Baumer, T. L., 250
Baxter, J. C., 31, 233, 374,
    401
Beal, J. B., 141
Beard, R. R., 145, 146
Beasley, R. R., 333
Beatty, P. A., 175
Beatty, V. L., 328
Bechtel, R. B., 49, 74, 391,
    397, 400, 402, 406
Becker, F. D., 163, 182, 184,
    318
Becker, L. S., 368, 370
Beckey, T., 364
Beckman, R., 307
Beets, J. L., 136, 138, 139,
    140
Beighton, P., 122
Bell, C. R., 125, 249
Bell, P. A., 28, 63, 110, 114,
    122, 126, 127, 128, 129,
    130, 131, 132, 133, 173,
    385
Bell, R. W., 197
Bem, D., 55, 350, 376
Benedak, T., 159

Bennet, K., 133
Bennett, B., 220
Benson, G. P., 126
Beranek, L. L., 108
Berger, E., 271
Berglund, B., 143
Berglund, V., 143
Bergman, B. A., 167, 210
Berk, R. A., 387, 388
Berkowitz, L., 64, 110
Berlyne, D. E., 41–44, 63,
    65, 273
Berman, J., 173
Bernal, M. E., 140
Beyda, M., 310
Bickman, L., 14, 208, 349
Birsky, J., 218
Bishop, G. D., 298
Bishop, R. L., 331
Bizman, A., 115
Black, J. C., 292
Black, J. S., 55
Blackman, S., 138
Blaut, J., 231
Bleda, P. R., 173
Bleda, S. E., 173
Block, H., 140
Bloom, L., 310
Boman, B., 91
Bonio, S., 170
Booth, A., 256
Borden, R. J., 209
Bornstein, M. H., 244
Borsky, P. N., 102
Borun, M., 301
Boster, R. S., 38
Boucher, M. L., 167
Bouska, M. L., 175
Bovy, P., 304
Boyanowsky, E. O., 131,
    133
Boyce, P. R., 125, 271
Brass, D. J., 74
Brasted, W., 357, 360
Braucht, C. N., 52–54
Brechner, K. C., 344, 345

Brehm, J. W., 51, 71
Brehm, S., 71
Breisacher, P., 146
Brenner, G., 312
Brickner, M. A., 174
Britton, N., 107
Broadbent, D. E., 63, 65, 66,
    107, 109, 285
Brockopp, G. W., 138
Brokemann, N. C., 163
Bromet, E., 94
Bronzaft, A. L., 104, 248
Brooks, D. K., 176, 181, 184
Brower, S., 254
Brown, B. B., 187, 188
Brown, D. W., 321
Brown, G. I., 140
Brown, I.D., 66
Brunetti, F., 299
Brunswick, E., 26
Bruvold, W. H., 56, 347
Bryan, M. E., 23
Budd, G. M., 123
Bull, A. J., 110
Burgess, R. L., 356, 357
Burnette, C., 285
Burroughs, J., 28
Burrows, A., 102
Bursill, A. E., 127
Burton, I., 26
Byrne, D., 28, 31, 46, 47,
    88, 127, 155, 156, 161,
    170–171, 181, 224, 400

Cahoon, R. L., 139
Caldwell, C., 184
Calesnick, L. E., 78, 215
Calhoun, J. B., 5, 89, 192,
    195–198
Cameron, P., 105
Campbell, D., 29, 156, 273,
    274, 380, 382, 386, 387,
    406
Campbell, D. E., 136, 138,
    139, 140, 322
Campbell, J., 116

Cannon, W. B., 89

Canon, L. K., 110, 113–114

Canter, D., 6, 7, 306

Carlsmith, J. M., 131, 296, 404

Carlson, R., 159

Carlton-Foss, J. A., 125

Carp, F. M., 50, 315

Carpenter, C. R., 176, 178, 183

Carr, S., 161, 222

Carroll, R. E., 146, 248

Carver, C. S., 64

Casey, T. M., 140

Cass, R., 344, 345, 372, 396

Catalina, D., 138

Cavanaugh, P. H., 142

Cavoukian, A., 218

Cermak, J. E., 305

Cervone, J. C., 65, 127

Chafee, J. L., 356

Chapko, M. K., 146, 248

Chaplin, J. P., 19

Chapman, C., 353

Chapman, D. W., 86

Chapman, R., 197

Charry, J. M., 141

Chemers, M., 150, 176, 177

Cherlin, D. L., 163

Cheyne, J. A., 175, 305

Chowns, R. H., 106

Christensen, L. B., 386, 387, 404

Christian, J. J., 192, 193, 194, 195, 198

Cialdini, R., 14, 132, 134, 358, 359

Cicchetti, C., 326

Clark, R. E., 133

Clark, R. H., 356, 357

Clarke, R. S. J., 133

Clinard, M. B., 252

Clore, G. L., 46, 47

Cobb, S., 86, 87

Coffin, D., 144

Cohen, H., 136

Cohen, J., 3.5

Cohen, J. B., 77

Cohen, J. L., 220

Cohen, M. R., 348, 375

Cohen, S., 66, 72, 80, 85, 87, 88, 89, 104, 105, 106, 113, 214, 248

Colburn, R. W., 192

Coleman, G., 246

Collett, P., 167

Colligan, M. J., 105, 279

Collins, B. L., 271

Collins, D. L., 88, 92, 95

Collins, J., 386

Collins, M. E., 297

Commoner, B., 193

Cone, J. D., 347, 348, 350, 354, 355, 356, 357, 360, 361, 363, 369, 370

Connolly, K., 208

Conrad, C., 330

Conroy, J., III, 185

Conway, D., 288

Cook, M., 160

Cook, S. W., 13

Cook, T., 380, 382, 386, 387, 406

Cooper, C., 292, 332, 391, 395

Cooper, R. E., 159, 161

Copeman, A., 107

Corcoran, D. W. J., 107

Corneille, J., 137

Cotton, J. L., 131

Coughlin, R. E., 39

Coupe, P., 31

Cox, V. C., 204, 277, 308, 404

Craighead, W. E., 356

Craik, K. H., 6, 7, 26, 39, 49, 50, 285

Crano, W. D., 174

Crawshaw, R., 91

Crew, F. A., 194

Crockford, G. W., 126

Crook, M. A., 104

Crowe, M. J., 143

Crump, S. L., 360

Cunningham, M. R., 132, 133, 134

Cusimano, J., 164

Cybriwsky, R., 180, 182, 183, 197, 374

Czank, J., 312

Cziffra, P., 300

Dabbs, J. M., 156, 159, 161, 165, 167, 222

Dahlof, L., 197

Dahms, T. E., 146

Damon, A., 104

Danford, S., 386

Daniel, T. C., 38

Darley, J. M., 181, 248, 345, 370

D'Atri, D. A., 204

Daves, W. F., 95

Davidson, L. M., 86, 92

Davis, F., 140

Davis, G., 207, 222, 223, 270, 272, 273, 277, 318, 322, 391, 401, 405

Davis, K. A., 228

Dawes, R., 345

Dean, J., 168

Dean, L., 204

Dean, L. M., 156

Deanovich, B. S., 401

De Fusco, P., 246

DeGroot, I., 144

De Jonge, D., 232

Delong, A. J., 181

Denison, D. M., 139

Dennis, W., 292

DeSanctis, M., 141

Deslauriers, B. C., 353, 374

Desor, J. A., 216, 222, 225, 385, 391

Deutsch, M., 297

Dexter, E., 136, 140

Diamond, S. G., 160, 164

Diffrient, N., 402

Digon, E., 140
Dillman, D., 243, 252
Dietrick, B., 255
Ditton, R. B., 348
Dixon, R., 306
Dohrenwend, B. P., 94, 252
Dohrenwend, B. S., 252
Doob, L. W., 46
Dooley, B. B., 207, 210, 211, 219
Doring, H. J., 105
Dosey, M., 156, 157
Downs, H., 71, 89, 115
Downs, R. M., 31
Doyle, D. P., 114, 132, 138
Drabek, T., 93
Driver, B., 323, 324, 325, 326, 327
Dubos, R., 145, 193
Duff, D. F., 160
Duke, M. P., 150, 154, 159, 160
Dukes, F. O., 208
Durkheim, E., 120
Dusek, E. R., 133
Duvall, D., 256
Dynes, R. R., 91

Easterbrook, J. A., 66, 102
Eastman, W. F., 224, 272
Ebbesen, E. B., 296
Eberts, E. H., 159
Edney, J. J., 178, 179, 181, 183, 184, 344–345, 372, 384
Edwards, D. J. A., 155, 158
Efran, M. G., 175, 305
Ehrlich, P., 205
Ehrlich, P. R., 55, 193, 351
Eibl-Eibesfeldt, I., 183
Einolander, J. C., 374
Elder, J., 402
Eller, S. J., 72
Ellis, P., 370
Ellsworth, P. C., 404
Emiley, S. F., 396

Empey, J., 159
Eoyang, C. K., 219
Epstein, Y. M., 202, 203, 205, 221, 380, 384, 385, 391, 396, 402
Erikson, K. T., 91, 93
Ernsting, J., 137
Ervin, C. R., 155
Escudero, M., 204
Esser, A. H., 177, 181
Evans, G. W., 23, 31, 32, 63, 71, 87, 89, 142, 143, 144, 145, 146, 150, 165, 171, 172, 201, 202, 210, 211, 231, 232, 234, 300
Everett, P. B., 350, 353, 354, 365, 371, 374

Feather, N. T., 403
Fedoravicius, A. S. 141
Feldman, H., 403
Felipe, N. J., 169
Ferguson, G., 176
Ferrari, N. A., 312
Festinger, L., 55, 64, 296
Fines, K. D., 39
Finkelman, J. M., 107
Finnie, W. C., 358, 360
Firestone, I., 168, 216
Fischer, C. S., 242, 243, 249, 251, 252, 262, 263
Fishbein, M., 56
Fisher, J. D., 15, 88, 168, 170–171, 181, 213, 220, 223, 224, 375, 376, 377, 391, 392, 400
Fisher, R. L., 160
Fisher, W. A., 224
Fitch, J., 265
Flaherty, C. F., 133
Fleming, R., 86, 95
Florin, P., 256
Flynn, C. B., 94
Folk, G. E., Jr., 124
Fontaine, A., 311, 312, 314
Fonzi, A., 170

Forbes, G., 208, 248
Ford, J. G., 158
Ford, W. S., 297
Fortenberry, J. H., 175
Foster, B. E., 283
Fowler, F. D., 254, 282
Fox, W. F., 133
Foxx, R. M., 372
Frager, N., 23, 144, 146
Francescato, D., 31
Francis, M., 390
Franck, K. D., 245, 246, 247, 251, 254
Frank, F., 199
Frankel, A. S., 160
Frankenhaeuser, M., 87, 89, 105, 203, 279
Freedman, J. L., 202, 204, 205, 209, 210, 218, 242, 296, 358
Freeman, H. 257
Frejka, T., 193
Frey, J., 131, 138, 145, 148
Friberg, L., 144
Fried, M., 257, 295
Friedman, L. N., 107
Frisancho, A. R., 122, 134, 137, 138, 139
Fry, A. M., 173
Fuller, B., 334
Fuller, P., 161, 222

Galle, O. R., 204, 209
Gallop, G., 184
Galloway, W., 102
Galster, G., 295
Gans, H., 257
Garber, J., 71
Gardell, B., 279
Gardner, E., 98, 121
Gardner, G. T., 72, 367, 369, 371
Garfinkel, H., 173
Garland, H., 144
Garnand, D. G., 128
Garrett, W. A., 132

Garzino. S. J., 138
Gashell, G., 370
Gatchel, R. J., 95, 215
Gaydos, H. F., 133
Geen, R. G., 64, 111, 112, 184
Gelfand, D. M., 208, 247
Geller, E. S., 242, 350, 351, 353, 356, 357, 358, 359, 360, 361, 365, 367, 368, 370, 371, 372, 373, 391, 404
Gergen, K. J., 161, 271
Gergen, M. K., 161, 271
Gerst, M. S., 391, 394, 395
Gibbons, D., 116
Gibbons, F. X., 64
Gibbs, J. P., 252
Gibson, D., 146
Gibson, J. J., 24, 25
Gibson, W., 159
Giel, R., 220
Gifford, R., 209
Gillis, A. R., 220
Ginsberg, Y., 251
Ginsburg, H., 208
Glaser, D. 276
Glass, D. C., 23, 71, 87, 88, 89, 101, 104, 105, 107, 108, 112, 214, 239, 244, 248, 249, 383, 403
Gleicher, P., 257, 295
Glenn, N., 247
Gleser, G., 93, 94
Glioner, J., 146
Glorig, A. 105
Goeckner, D. 197
Goldberg, M. L., 156
Goldman, M., 175
Goldsmith, J. R., 128, 144, 248
Goldstein, K. A., 39
Goodale, T. L., 348
Goodchild, B., 233
Goodrich, R., 321
Goranson, R. E., 128, 129

Gordon, P., 204
Gormley, F., 221
Gottfredson, S. D., 254, 255
Gottman, J., 228
Gove, W. R., 204, 209
Grandjean, E., 105, 108
Grandstaff, N., 146
Grant, D. P., 315
Graves, J. R., 158
Green, B., 93, 94
Greenbaum, P. E., 295
Greenbaum, S. D., 295
Greenberg, C. I., 77, 78, 202, 205, 206, 216, 255, 384, 385
Greenberger, D. B., 375
Greene, L. R., 164
Greene, T. C., 33, 37, 41, 45, 122, 127
Greene, W. A., 86
Greenfield, N., 321
Greenough, W., 197
Gregory, R. L., 29
Grev, R., 132
Grier, H. C., 364, 370
Griffin, M., 276, 306
Griffiths, I. D., 125, 126
Griffitt, W., 127, 129
Groff, B., 210, 211
Gromoll, H., 208, 248
Groner, N., 213
Grove, J. B., 406
Guardo, C. J., 159
Guenther, R., 142
Guild, W., 253
Gump, P. V., 74, 76, 240, 299
Gunderson, E., 132, 204
Gutman, R., 283, 312

Haas, G., 325, 326
Haase, R. S., 156
Haber, G. M., 180, 184
Hackett, T. P., 86
Hackney, J., 145
Hake, D. F., 372

Halcomb, C. G., 141
Hall, E. T., 5, 150, 153, 154, 158, 163, 165
Hamilton, D. L., 298
Hamilton, J. F., 37
Hamilton, P., 107
Hammel, H. T., 123
Haney, W. G., 253
Hannson, R. O., 248
Hansen, F., 91
Hansen, W. B., 179, 391, 401
Hanson, P. O., 28
Hanson, S., 28
Hanusa, B. H., 72, 312
Harberson, W., 140
Harburg, E., 87
Hard, E., 197
Hardin, G., 343
Hargreaves, A. G., 94
Harper, C. S., 344, 345
Harpin, R. E., 267
Harris, B., 210
Harris, H., 311
Harris, V. A., 51
Harrison, P., 331
Hart, R. A., 31
Hart, R. H., 145
Hartnett, J. J., 159
Hatton, H., 105
Hawkins, L. H., 141
Hawkinshire, F. B. W., 141
Hay, D. G., 252
Hayduk, L. A., 152, 154, 158, 160, 161, 167
Hayes, S. C., 345, 348, 350, 354, 355, 356, 357, 360, 361, 363, 369, 370
Hayward, D. G., 331, 332, 333
Hayward, S. C., 351, 354
Heath, D., 137
Hebb, D. O., 63, 65
Heberlein, T. A., 55, 348, 367
Hebert, J. A., 145

Hediger, H., 150
Heffron, M. H., 276
Heft, H., 24, 67
Heimstra, N. W., 7
Heller, J., 210, 211, 213
Helmreich, R., 336, 338
Helson, H., 68, 272
Hendee, J. C., 356, 357
Henderson, L. F., 305
Herbert, R. K., 321
Heron, W., 300
Herridge, C. F., 106
Hershberger, R. G., 396
Herskovits, M. J., 29
Herzberg, F., 319
Herzog, A. N., 204
Heshka, S., 155, 160, 203
Hesser, G., 295
Hewitt, J., 156
Heywood, L. A., 330
Hicks, P. E., 319
Higbee, K. L., 50
Hill, J. W., 126
Hill, L., 247
Hinds, D. H., 373, 374
Hinshaw, M., 292
Hiorns, R. F., 125, 249
Hiroto, D. S., 72
Hirst, E., 373
Hoch, I., 243
Hockey, G. R. J., 107
Hodges, L., 161
Hoffman, D., 387, 388
Holahan, C. J., 187, 237, 256, 261, 273, 274
Holland, G. J., 146
Hollander, J., 140
Hollingshead, A. B., 260
Holmes, D. S., 160
Honour, A. J., 116
Hook, H., 164
Hoople, H., 174
Hopkins, B. L., 354
Hore, T., 146
Horowitz, M. J., 160
Horvath, S. M., 146

House, J. S., 248
Houts, P. S., 78, 94
Howard, E., 334
Howard, R. B., 150, 165, 171, 172
Howell, D. L., 349
Hughes, J., 175
Hummel, C. F., 55, 56, 143
Hundert, A. J., 321
Hunt, J., 305
Hunter, A., 250, 255
Huntington, E., 120
Hurt, H., 121
Hutt, C., 206, 208, 400
Hynson, L. M., 252

Ickes, W., 168
Imamoglu, V., 273
Ingram, R. E., 353, 356
Irwin, R., 248
Isaac, L. M., 175
Isen, A. M., 113
Ittelson, W. H., 5, 6, 21, 22, 70, 206, 270, 276, 307, 391, 399
Iwata, O., 219
Izmerov, N., 146

Jackson, E. L., 28
Jackson, J. B., 33
Jacobs, H., 373
Jacobs, J., 255, 258
Jacobs, S. V., 23, 71, 87, 142, 143, 144, 145, 146
Jain, U., 251
James, J. W., 171
Janis, I. L., 88
Jarpe, G., 89
Jason, L. A., 358
Jellison, J. M., 51
Jenkins, D. M., 305
Jerdee, T. H., 345
Johnsen, P. K., 154
Johnson, G. A., 110
Johnson, J., 88
Johnson, J. E., 222

Johnson, M. P., 350
Johnson, R. D., 335, 337
Johnson, V. S., 361
Johnston, J. W., 143
Jones, J. C., 282, 285
Jones, S. E., 154, 158, 159, 169
Jöreskog, K. G., 383
Jorgenson, D. O., 138, 208, 345
Jourard, S. M., 155, 159
Joy, V. D., 207

Kahneman, D., 65
Kammann, R., 248
Kane, J. N., 238
Kane, R. A., 312
Kantor, J. F., 224
Kaplan, A., 285
Kaplan, F., 146
Kaplan, R., 37, 41, 42–44, 385
Kaplan, S., 31, 37, 39, 41, 42–44, 232
Kapp, F. I., 93, 94
Karabenick, S. A., 156, 160, 161
Karlin, R. A., 202, 203, 205, 221, 222, 380, 402
Karmel, L. J., 271, 299
Kasl, S. V., 86
Kass, R. A., 330
Katcher, A. H., 64
Kates, R. W., 26, 27
Katz, P., 150
Kauman, C., 76
Keating, J., 206, 213
Keating, J. P., 214
Kees, W., 273
Kelley, C. M., 262
Kelley, H., 221
Kennelly, D., 108
Kenny, D., 383
Kenrick, D. T., 110, 132, 134
Kerchoff, A. C., 279

Kerlinger, F. N., 382, 394
Kerr, N., 208, 247
Kerslake, M. McK., 125, 127
Key, W., 247
Keyfitz, N., 193
Kilmer, W., 339–340, 341
Kinarthy, E. L., 163
King, D., 128, 129
King, M. G., 171
Kinzel, A. S., 160
Kira, A., 281, 293, 294, 295
Kirmeyer, S., 74, 76
Kjos, G. L., 296
Kleck, R., 156, 172
Klein, K., 210
Klevansky, S., 205
Klopfer, P. H., 176
Knight, R. C., 390
Knopf, R. C., 324, 325, 326
Knowles, E. S., 152, 154,
    169, 171, 172, 173, 174,
    175, 253, 305, 306
Kohlenberg, R., 354, 355,
    356, 360, 363
Kohn, I., 219, 245
Koman, S., 89, 206, 209,
    213, 220, 223
Konar, E., 322
Konecni, V. J., 112, 169,
    170, 173, 296
Koneya, M., 163
Konzett, H., 89
Koocher, G. P., 405–406
Korte, C., 208, 243, 247, 248
Kosslyn, S. M., 32
Kovrigin, S. D., 109
Krasner, L., 398
Krasner, M., 398
Kraus, R., 330
Krauss, R. M., 352, 358
Krawiec, T. S., 19
Krebs, C. J., 199
Krupat, E., 228, 246, 253
Kruskal, W. H., 156
Kryter, K. D., 101, 106, 107,
    109
Kuller, R., 272

Lacey, J. I., 65
Ladd, F., 234, 292
Lagerwerff, J., 146
LaHart, D., 363
Lakota, R. A., 301
Lamberth, J., 155
Lang, J., 285
Lang, J. T., 318
Langdon, F. J., 104
Langer, E., 71, 88, 220, 222,
    223, 249, 312
Langmeyer, D., 163
Lanni, J. C., 185
Lansford, T. G., 272
Larsson, K., 197
Latanè, B., 181, 248
Latta, R. M., 156
Launier, R., 87
Lauridsen, P. K., 372
Lave, L. B., 144
LaVerne, A. A., 145
Lavrakas, P. J., 250, 251,
    263
Lawson, B. R., 102
Lawton, M. P., 297, 311,
    315
Lawton, S. F., 128
Lazarus, R., 77, 78, 79, 85,
    87
LeBlanc, J. S., 123
Lebo, C. P., 103
Ledwith, F., 139
Lee, D. H. K., 31, 122
Leff, H. L., 349
Lehmann, N., 207
Lehrer, P. M., 384
Leithead, C. S., 122
Lepper, M. R., 159
Lerner, R. N., 159
Lesko, W. A., 132
Lester, D., 138
Lett, E. D., 180
Lett, E. E., 295
Leventhal, H., 51, 88, 222
Levi, L., 249
Levin, P. L., 330
Levine, J. M., 142

Levitt, L., 56, 143
Levy, L., 204
Lewin, K., 5
Lewis, C. A., 328
Lewis, J., 146
Ley, D., 180, 182, 183, 187,
    371
Lezak, A., 113
Lieber, A. L., 138
Lifton, R. J., 91, 93, 94
Lind, A. R., 122
Lindauer, M. S., 293
Lindsay, J. J., 325
Lindvall, T., 143
Lingwood, D. A., 348, 349
Link, J. M., 126
Lintell, M., 110
Lipetz, B., 300
Lipman, A., 180, 311
Lippert, S., 306, 307
Lipsey, M. W., 144
Little, E. A. J., 109
Little, K. B., 154, 158, 161
Littler, W. A., 116
Litton, R. B., Jr., 33
Lloyd, K. D., 367
Lloyd, M. E., 367
Lockhard, J. S., 175
Lofland, J., 399
Logan, H. J., 271
Logue, J. N., 91
Lomránz, J., 159
Loo, C., 206, 208, 209, 216
Loomis, R. J., 56, 127, 143,
    303
Lorenz, K., 176, 183, 198
Lott, A. J., 46
Lott, B. E., 46
Lott, B. S., 156
Love, K. D., 154
Low-Beer, L., 106
Lowenthal, D., 238
Lower, M., 170
Lozar, C. C., 391, 401
Lucas, R. C., 325, 326
Ludwig, H. W., 141
Lundberg, U., 87, 105, 203

Luxenberg, S., 308
Luyben, P. D., 352, 356
Lydgage, T., 255
Lynch, K. A., 30, 31, 229, 231, 232, 272, 273, 391, 395

Maccoby, E., 155, 159, 172, 202
MacConnell, W. P., 38
MacIntosh, E., 202, 210, 248
Mack, R., 183
Mackenzie, S. T., 108, 109
Magaña, J. R., 231
Maier, S., 197
Mainprize, S. A., 160
Maki, J. E., 387, 388
Malm, W., 40
Maloney, M. P., 52–54
Mandel, D. R., 392
Manheim, M. L., 285
Mann, M., 357, 360
Mann, P. H., 252
Marans, R. W., 263, 321, 324, 398
Margulis, J., 398
Marine, G., 183
Mark, L. S., 231
Markham, S., 120
Marsden, H. M., 192
Marsella, A. J., 204
Marshall, M., 276
Martindale, D. A., 185
Maslow, A. H., 273, 321
Masterpasqua, F., 197
Matese, F., 359
Mathews, K., 110, 113–114
Mathieu, J. T., 250
Mattel, G., 89
Matter, C. F., 171, 172
Matthews, R. W., 223
Maurer, R., 31, 233
Mausner, B., 319
Mawby, R. I., 254
Maxfield, M., 263
Mayo, C., 182, 184
Mayron, L. W., 271

McBride, G., 171
McBurney, D. H., 142
McCain, G., 204, 277, 391, 404
McCallum, R., 213
McCarthy, D. P., 104, 248
McCauley, C., 246, 247
McCaull, J., 245
McClay, D., 174
McClelland, L. A., 210
McCormick, E. J., 319
McDonald, P. J., 183
McFarland, R. A., 139
McFarling, L. H., 7
McGill, T. E., 300
McGrath, J. E., 74, 76, 86, 240
McGuire, W. J., 54
McKechnie, G. E., 49, 385
McLean, E. K., 102
McMillan, R., 180
McPherson, J. M., 204, 209
McTavish, J., 345
McVittie, R. I., 175
Mebane, W., 31
Medalia, N. Z., 144
Mehler, A., 76
Mehrabian, A., 41, 49, 63, 88, 156, 160, 164, 272, 273, 292, 322, 391, 397
Meisels, M., 156, 157, 159, 160, 161
Melton, A. W., 301, 302, 303
Mendelsohn, R., 144
Menninger, W., 330
Mercer, S., 312
Merriam, L. C., Jr., 327
Metcalf, J., 214
Meyers, A. W., 334, 356
Michaels, K. M., 116
Michelini, R. L., 164
Michelson, W., 273, 292, 392, 393, 406
Middlemist, R. D., 171, 172, 405–406
Mietz, J., 325

Mikheyev, A. P., 109
Milavsky, B., 64
Miles, S., 137, 139
Milgram, S., 31, 66, 67, 208, 213, 231, 232, 237, 238, 246, 247
Miller, E., 138
Miller, I. W., III, 72
Miller, J. D., 106
Miller, J. E., 145
Miller, J. F., 162, 163
Miller, M., 86, 103, 253, 360
Mills, C., 120, 140
Mills, L. V., Jr., 38
Milne, G., 91
Mintz, N. C., 273, 321
Miransky, J., 71
Mirskowa, L., 194
Mitchell, H. E., 281
Moleski, W. H., 318
Moller, A. T., 163
Montagu, A., 151
Moore, G. T., 31
Moore, H. E., 86, 91
Moore, R. C., 331
Moos, R. H., 71, 136, 139, 140, 256, 391, 394, 395
Morasch, B., 213
Moss, S., 136
Moulton, D. G., 143
Muecher, H., 136, 140
Mullens, S., 169, 173
Mullins, P., 261
Murphy, J. F., 323
Murphy, L. R., 105
Murphy-Berman, V., 173
Murray, J. R., 55
Murtha, D. M., 283, 284
Myers, K., 194

Nahemow, L., 297
Nash, R., 33
Neal, A., 302
Neale, M. S., 364, 370
Neisser, U., 19
Nelson, L. W., 364

Nelson, P. A., 180, 295
Nelson, P. D., 278
Nelson, Y., 155, 160
Nemecek, J., 108
Newman, C. J., 91, 94
Newman, J., 246
Newman, L. S., 55, 350
Newman, O., 187, 254, 255, 256, 260, 261, 374, 391, 404
Newtson, D., 86
Ng, L. K. Y., 192
Nicholson, M., 332
Nietzel, M. T., 353, 354
Niit, T., 6
Niswander, G. D., 140
Noble, A., 306
Norman, W. H., 72
Novaco, R., 115, 116
Nowicki, S., 150, 154, 160

O'Donnel, R., 146
O'Donnell, C. R., 255
Ogilvie, B. C., 331
Ogle, R. A., 325
O'Hanlon, J. F., 146
O'Hara, J., 161
O'Hare, M., 301
Ohlig, W., 204, 220
Oldham, G. R., 74
Oliphant, K. P., 103
Olsen, H., 298
Olsen, M. E., 350
Olsen, R., 306
Olson, E., 91, 93, 94
Olszewski, D. A., 108
O'Neal, E. C., 64, 111, 112, 157, 183, 184
O'Neill, G. W., 360
O'Neill, S. M., 193
Orcutt, G., 144
Orebaugh, A. L., 404
O'Riordan, T., 55, 56, 347, 349
Orleans, P., 31, 234
Orlick, T. D., 331

Ormel, J., 220
Osborne, J. G., 357
Osgood, C., 397
Osmond, H., 5, 164
Ossenkopf, K. P., 141
Ostfeld, A., 204
Ostrander, W. B., 306
Owens, K., 136
Owens, R. D., 373

Pablant, P., 374
Page, R. A., 114, 132
Palamarek, D. L., 130
Pallack, M. S., 349, 370
Palmer, J. F., 38
Palmer, M. H., 367
Paluck, R. J., 183
Papciak, A. S., 345
Parkes, C. M., 86
Parmalee, P., 181
Parr, A. E., 67
Parsons, H. M., 281, 292
Parsons, P., 303
Passalacqua, R., 164
Patterson, A. H., 11, 161, 189, 208, 381, 404, 405
Paulus, P. B., 63, 204, 210, 219, 222, 223, 277, 404
Pawson, I. G., 137
Payne, R. J., 28
Peacock, J., 209
Pearce, J., 144
Pearson, O. P., 199
Pederson, D. M., 159
Pellegrini, R. J., 159
Pempus, E., 161
Penick, E. C., 91
Pennebaker, J. W., 86
Penwarden, A. D., 135, 136
Pepler, R., 125, 126, 127
Pepper, D. T., 156
Perkins, N. M., 128, 248
Perlick, D., 218
Persinger, M. A., 141
Peterka, J. A., 305
Peterson, G. L., 331

Peterson, R. L., 146
Pettigrew, T., 29
Pezdek, K., 32
Phillips, S., 105
Phillips, T., 354, 360, 363
Pigram, J. J., 28
Pile, J. F., 321
Pill, R., 307
Pirages, D. C., 55, 351
Pitt, D. G., 38, 39, 50
Platt, J., 343, 344, 355
Pokorny, A., 140
Pollack, L. M., 189
Pollet, D., 301
Pomerantz, J. P., 32
Porteous, C., 300
Porteus, J., 232, 238, 256, 257, 267, 334
Poulton, E. C., 66, 125, 126, 127, 133, 136, 139
Powell, B. J., 91
Powers, R. B., 357, 361, 363
Pratsch, L., 372
Preiser, W. F. E., 304, 305, 306, 391, 401
Price, G. H., 159
Price, J., 208
Priebe, K., 138
Pritchard, D., 271
Proctor, W., 354
Proshansky, H. M., 5, 6, 7, 10, 11, 13, 45, 63, 70, 206, 228, 242, 251–252, 380, 389, 399
Provins, K. A., 125, 127, 128, 133, 249
Pugh, W., 204
Putz, J., 146
Pylypuk, A., 203
Pylyshyn, Z. W., 32

Quarantelli, E., 86, 91, 93
Quick, A. D., 174

Radloff, R., 336
Rainwater, L., 260

Raloff, J., 102, 103
Ramsey, J., 146
Rankin, R. E., 144, 349
Rangell, L., 91, 93
Ransberger, V. M., 130
Rapoport, A., 216
Rawls, D. J., 210
Reddy, D. M., 221
Reed, P., 392, 393
Reeves, D., 159
Reich, J. W., 352
Reichel, D. A., 372
Reichner, R., 207
Reiser, B. J., 32
Reiss, M., 161, 222, 275
Reiter, S. M., 352
Reizenstein, J., 306, 307
Rent, C. S., 260
Rent, G. S., 260
Resnick, S., 220
Reusch, J., 273
Richards, P., 375
Richardson, L. H., 330
Riel, M., 238
Rim, Y., 136
Risk, P. H., 327
Risley, T. R., 353
Rivlin, C. G., 307, 310
Rivlin, L. G., 5, 6, 70, 206, 299, 399
Robb, J., 261
Roberts, C., 251
Robertson D., 105
Robertson, J. L., 352
Robinson, E. S., 301, 302, 303, 304
Rodgers, W., 263
Rodin, J., 70, 71, 88, 214, 215, 223, 312
Roger, D. B., 160
Rogler, L. H., 260
Rohe, W., 208
Rohles, F. H., 125
Romano, J., 169, 173
Ronco, P. G., 306
Rose, E. F., 144

Rose, H. S., 373, 374
Rosen, B., 345
Rosen, S., 103
Rosenfeld, H. M., 156
Rosenzweig, M. R., 300
Ross, H., 164, 273
Ross, M., 202, 203, 205, 220
Ross, P., 252
Rothbaum, F., 71
Rothenberg, M., 299, 333
Rotter, J., 28
Rotton, J., 48, 89, 108, 131, 138, 145, 146, 147, 148, 243, 403
Rubin, A. I., 402
Rubin, J. E., 155, 159
Rule, B. G., 130
Rummo, N., 146
Runnion, A., 372
Rusbult, C., 213
Russell, J. A., 41, 49, 63, 272, 273, 322, 391, 397
Russell, M. B., 140
Ruys, T., 271

Saarinen, T. F., 26, 234, 237, 391
Sabatino, D. A., 375
Sadalla, E. K., 32, 239
Saegert, S., 71, 88, 187, 202, 210, 213, 220, 222, 223, 248, 249, 274
Saglione, G., 170
Samuel, W., 352
Samuelson, D. J., 293
Sanborn, D. E., 140
Sanders, J. L., 159
Sarlanis, K., 146
Savinar, J., 161, 222
Sawaya, C., 161
Schachter, S., 64, 86, 89, 296
Schaeffer, M. A., 95
Schalekamp, E. E., 160
Schavio, S., 174
Scheier, M. F., 64

Scherer, S. E., 158
Schettino, A. P., 209
Schiavo, R. S., 218
Schiffenbauer, A., 218
Schkade, J. K., 63, 211
Schmidt, D. E., 214
Schmidt, E. A., 37
Schmidt, G. W., 354
Schmidt, J. R., 184
Schmidt, S., 234
Schmitt, R. C., 204
Schneider, F. W., 132, 133
Schneiderman, N., 89
Schnelli, J. F., 355, 360
Schoggen, P., 14, 74
Schopler, J., 212, 213, 219
Schulte, J. H., 144
Schultz, D. B., 67
Schulz, R., 71, 72, 312
Schuman, H., 350
Schussheim, M. J., 256
Schwartz, D. C., 130
Schwartz, R. D., 406
Schwarz, H., 42
Schwebel, A. I., 163
Sears, D. O., 296
Seaton, R., 386
Sechrest, L., 167, 406
Segal, M. W., 296
Segall, M. H., 29
Seligman, C., 345, 368, 370
Seligman, M. E. P., 71, 72, 215, 350
Sell, R., 207
Sells, S. B., 140
Selltiz, C., 13, 404
Selye, H., 77, 79, 88, 89, 194
Seskin, E. P., 144
Seta, J. J., 63
Sever, H. L., 373
Shaban, J., 249
Shafer, E. L., 37, 325
Shaklee, H., 345
Sharpe, G. W., 358
Sheflen, A. E., 180

Shepard, R. N., 32
Sherin, C. R., 138
Sherrod, D. R., 71, 72, 89, 107, 115, 211, 214, 220, 273, 322, 391
Shippee, G., 28, 345
Shore, B. M., 349
Sieck, W. A., 91
Siegel, J. M., 110
Simpson-Housley, P., 28
Sims, J. H., 28, 86
Singer, J. E., 23, 64, 71, 77, 87, 88, 89, 95, 101, 104, 107, 108, 112, 203, 214, 239, 244, 249, 383, 403
Skeen, D. R., 162
Skinner, B. F., 353
Skogan, W., 263
Skotko, V. P., 163
Slade, K. M., 248
Sladen, B., 220
Slater, R., 311
Slaven, R. E., 368
Sleight, P., 116
Sloan, A. W., 122
Slote, L., 141
Slotsky, R. J., 327
Smetana, J., 209
Smith, P., 208
Smith, R. J., 169, 173, 174
Snowball, H., 206
Snyder, L. H., 306
Snyder, R. L., 194, 195
Snyder, S. S., 71
Snyderman, B., 319
Socolow, R. H., 347, 363, 364
Soler, E. A., 108
Soleri, P., 334
Solomon, M., 146, 248
Solomon, S., 88, 210, 211, 214, 223
Sommer, R., 5, 23, 24, 26, 149, 150, 156, 158, 160, 162, 163, 164, 169, 176, 182, 260

Sommers, P., 136
Sommerville, W., 116
Sonnenfeld, J., 69
Sörbom, D., 383
Southwick, C. H., 195, 197
Spreckelmeyer, K. F., 321
Srivastava, R. K., 77
Srole, L., 252
Staats, A. W., 46
Staff, I., 219
Staplin, L. J., 32
Starr, N., 386
Stea, D., 31, 229, 231, 239
Steel, C. M., 110
Steidl, R. E., 295
Steinberg, J., 132
Steinitz, C., 232, 272
Stephan, W., 297
Sterling, E., 142
Stern, P. C., 345, 367, 369, 371, 372
Stevens, A., 31
Stevens, S. S., 101
Stevens, W., 367
Stires, L., 163
Stobaugh, R., 369
Stockdale, J., 212, 213
Stockton, W., 279
Stogner, J. D., 327
Stokes, N. A., 156
Stokinger, H., 144
Stokols, D., 70, 115, 116, 204, 205, 209, 210, 211, 213, 216, 220, 244, 265
Stokols, J., 116
Storms, M. D., 168
Stough, R. R., 176, 180, 184
Strahilevitz, A., 145
Strahilevitz, N., 145
Strakhov, A. B., 106
Stratton, L. O., 160
Strodtbeck, F., 164
Struening, E., 91
Studer, R., 278
Suci, G., 397
Suedfeld, P., 104, 106

Sulman, F. G., 141
Sundeen, R. A., 250
Sundstrom, E., 169, 174, 178, 181, 185, 202, 206, 213, 219, 220, 318, 320, 321, 322, 386
Sundstrom, M. G., 169, 174, 318, 320, 321, 322
Suttles, G. D., 180, 256
Swaffer, P. W., 161
Swan, J. A., 144
Swan, J. E., 348
Swanson, C. P., 201
Szigeti, F., 318

Taggart, P., 116
Tannenbaum, P., 397
Tarnopolsky, A., 102
Tasso, J., 138
Taylor, I. R., 331
Taylor, J., 247
Taylor, R. B., 176, 178, 180, 181, 182, 184, 185, 202, 254, 255
Taylor, S. E., 306
Taylor, V., 91
Teasdale, J. D., 72
Teddlie, C., 205, 218, 222, 273, 322
Tempest, W., 23
Tennen, H., 72
Tennis, G. H., 161
Terry, R. L., 170
Thalhofer, N. N., 174
Thoa, N. B., 192
Thomas, G. C., 168
Thompson, D. E., 150, 153, 154, 158, 167, 169
Thompson, R., 248
Thompson, W. R., 300
Tien, J. M., 250
Tiffen, J., 319
Tikofsky, R., 403
Tinsley, H. E. A., 330
Titchener, J., 93, 94
Tocher, S. R., 323

Tolman, E. C., 29
Toppen, A., 208, 248
Towler, J., 348
Trautt, G., 310
Tremblay, K., Jr., 243, 252
Trice, H. M., 252
Trites, D., 306, 307
Truscott, J. C., 181
Tuan, Y. F., 238
Tucker, L. R., 55
Turk, A., 100, 111, 142
Turk, J., 100, 111
Turner, F. J., 33
Tuso, M. E., 358
Tutko, T. A., 331
Tyler, T. R., 71

Uhlig, S. R., 181, 185
Ulrich, R. E., 354
Ungeheuer, H., 136, 140
Unger, D., 256
Unseld, C. T., 245
Ury, H. K., 128, 146, 248

Vaizey, M. J., 206, 208, 400
Valins, S., 88, 201, 206,
    207, 212, 213, 214, 215,
    222, 267, 269, 271, 273,
    281, 282, 283, 298, 307,
    380
Van Wagenberg, D., 398
Vernon, J., 300
Vinsel, A. M., 153, 158,
    161, 276
Vitalo, R. L., 330
Vitek, J. D., 28

Wack, J., 312
Wakefield, S., 28
Walder, D. N., 137, 139
Walker, J. M., 368
Wall, G., 224
Wallace, W. P., 156
Wallis, D. A., 183
Walters, D., 102

Walters, R. H., 360
Walton, M., 213, 219
Wandersman, A., 256, 271
Wantman, M. J., 252
Ward, L. M., 104, 106
Ward, M. O., 52–54
Ward, P., 357
Warmbrod, J. R., 349
Watson, O. M., 158
Wayne, W. S., 146
Webb, E. J., 15, 391, 403,
    406
Wehrle, P. F., 146, 248
Weibel, J., 295, 389
Weigel, J., 55
Weigel, R., 310
Weigel, R. H., 55, 350
Weiner, F. H., 208, 242, 248
Weinstein, L., 160
Weinstein, M. S., 252, 402
Weinstein, N. D., 39
Weisman, A. D., 86
Weisner, T., 295, 389
Weisz, J. R., 71
Weitzer, W. H., 390
Wellens, A. R., 156
Welling, G., 249
Wendt, J. S., 42
Wentworth, W. E., 245
Werbik, H., 42
Werner, C., 182
Wertheim, G. A., 146
West, P. C., 327
West, S., 202, 210, 248
Weyant, J. M., 132, 134
Wheeldon, P. D., 256
Whitcup, M., 358
White, G. F., 26
White, M., 161
Whitehead, C., 274
Wicker, A. W., 55, 74, 75,
    76, 213, 240, 349
Wilkinson, R. T., 125, 127
Will, D. P., 140
Willems, E. P., 386
Williams, D. R., 137

Willis, F. N., 156, 158, 159,
    173
Willmott, P., 262
Wills, T. A., 64
Wilner, D., 257
Wilson, D. W., 71, 172, 354
Wilson, E. O., 199
Wilson, G. D., 272
Wilson, J., 159
Wilson, S., 307
Wineman, J. D., 318
Winget, C., 93, 94
Winkel, G. H., 301
Winkler, R. C., 370
Winnett, R. A., 347, 350,
    353, 354, 364, 365, 367,
    370
Winsborough, H., 204
Winston, B. J., 347, 349
Witmer, J. F., 358, 404
Wittes, J. T., 100, 111
Wittes, R., 100, 111
Wofford, J. C., 141
Wohlwill, J. F., 41, 42, 43,
    44, 67, 68, 69, 144, 219,
    245, 300, 385
Wolf, S., 248
Wolfe, C. P., 306
Wolfe, M., 307, 310, 330
Woodhead, M. M., 107
Woolfolk, R. L. 384
Worchel, S., 205, 218, 222,
    273, 322
Wright, H., 74, 400
Wrightsman, L. S., 13
Wyndham, C., 126, 127
Wynne-Edwards, V. C., 198

Yancey, W. L., 259, 260
Yeostros, S., 140
Yergin, D., 369
Yinon, Y., 115
Yoshikawa, J., 146
Young, M., 262
Ypma, I., 208, 248

Zajonc, R. B., 297
Zaks, J., 105
Zamarin, D. M., 102
Zeisel, J., 276, 278, 282,
    286, 287, 296, 306, 406
Zelnick, M., 224

Zieman, G. L., 126
Zillmann, D., 64
Zimbardo, P. G., 249, 250
Zimring, C. M., 273, 390
Zlutnick, S., 70
Zolik, E. S., 358

Zube, E. H., 38, 49, 50, 136,
    285
Zubek, J., 67
Zuckerman, M., 396
Zweig, J., 312
Zwicker, E., 101

Subject Index

Accidents, temperature and, 128
climation, 122
Acclimatization, 122–123
  to high altitudes, 138–139
Accommodation, and perception of
    distance, 34
Accretion, in environment, as measure of
    behavior, 404
Adaptation
  city living and, 69, 246
  environmental perception and, 23
  hazard perception and, 27
  heat tolerance and, 127
  levels of, 45, 68–70
  to disasters, 27
  to high population density, 216
  to stress, 79, 86, 87, 88
  vs. adjustment, 69–70
Adaptation Level Theory, 68–70
Adequately manned behavior setting, 75
Adjective scale, bipolar, 396
Adjustment vs. adaptation, 69–70
Aerial perspective, 35
Aesthetics, environmental, 41–44, 272–273
Affect, effects of population density on,
    202

Affiliation, city living and, 246–247
Affordances, perception of, 24–25
Age, personal space and, 159–160
Aged, environmental design of residential
    care facilities for the, 310–315
Aggression
  crowding and, 197, 198, 208–209
  heat and, 128–131
  noise and, 110–113
  television watching and, 331
  territoriality and, 183–184, 198–199
Air conditioners, 121
Air pollution
  behavior and, 140–148
  effects of, 2
  health and, 144–145
  perception of, 29, 40, 142–144
  in national parks, 40
  performance and, 145–146
  primitive, 141, 142
  sources of, 141
Air Pollution Syndrome, 145
Air pressure, behavioral effects of, 137–140
Alarm reaction, 77, 78
Altitude, 137–140
Altruism

crowding and, 207–208
heat and, 131–132
noise and, 113–115
Ambient conditions, measurement of, 402
Ambient temperature, 121–125
American Psychological Association, 6
Amplitude, of sound waves, 97
Animals, effects of population density on, 192–199
Applicants, in behavior setting, 75
Appraisal
challenge, 87
of stressors, 87–88
threat, 86
Architectural design, see Design, architectural
Architectural determinism, 266–267
Architectural psychology, 5
Architecture, behavior and, 265–277
Archival records, in research, 404
Arousal
crowding and, 202–203
detection of, 63–65
Yerkes-Dodson Law of, 64
Arousal approach, environment–behavior relationships, 63–65
Arousal theory, of personal space, 150, 171
Assigned workspace, 322
Association for the Study of Man–Environment Relations, 5
Attitude(s)
changing, 50–56
drive reduction and, 50–51
fear appeals and, 50
"inoculation" and, 54
psychological reactance to, 51, 54
classical conditioning of, 45–48
formation of, 45–49
instrumental conditioning of, 48
social learning of, 48–49
toward environment, see Environment, attitudes toward
Attraction
crowding and, 204–206
heat and, 127–128, 129
interpersonal distance and, 154–156

noise and, 110
Automobiles, use of, 3

"Back to nature" philosophy, 33
Barometric pressure, 137–140
Bathrooms, design features of, 292–295
Beaufort wind scale, 135
Beauty, environment and, see Aesthetics, environmental
Bedrooms, design features of, 292
Behavior
adaptive, see Adaptation
architecture and, 265–277
attitudes and, 55–56
changing, to save the environment, 343–378
city living and, see City (cities)
cold and, 119, 122–123, 132–134
color and, 272
environmentally destructive, elimination of, 350–357
exploratory, in museums, 303–304
flight, in invasions of personal space, 169
furniture and furnishings and, 273–274
heat and, 119–132
lighting and, 267–271
moon phases and, 138
nonverbal, 150
population density and, see Population density
prosocial, see Prosocial behavior
standing patterns of, 73
temperature, atmospheric, and, 119–134
territorial, see Territoriality
weather and, 119–141, 148
windows and, 271–272
Behavior constraint theory, 70–73
and natural disasters, 91
of personal space, 150
of population density, 212, 214
of urban behavior, 239–240
Behavior mapping, 399
Behavior setting(s), 14, 73
applicants in, 75
capacity of, 75
maintenance minimum of, 74

nonperformers in, 75
performers in, 75
population regulation in, 76
Behavioral facilitation, in environmental design, 283, 284
Behavioral interference formulation, 212
Behavioral sink, 196, 197, 198
"Bends," 139
Binocular cues, in perception of distance, 34
Bipolar adjective scale, 396
Body odor, 142
Body temperature, deep, 121
"Bubble" concept, of personal space, 149, 150, 152
Buffalo Creek flood, 92–93, 94, 96
Byrne-Clore reinforcement–affect model, of evaluative responses, 47

Camping areas, 324–328
Campus, cognitive map of, 29, 30
Capacity, of behavior setting, 75
"Capsule images," of cities, 238
Carbon monoxide, effects of, on health, 144
Cataclysmic events, 85–86
Catastrophes, technological, *see* Technological catastrophes
Challenge appraisals, 86
Change, perception of, 23–26
Chill factor, 123–124, 125
City (cities), 227–263
    as overmanned environment, 240
    "capsule images" of, 238
    cognitive maps of, 30
    crime in, 249–251
    effects of, 238–254
        long-term, 251–252
        on affiliative behavior, 246–247
        on coping, 246
        on performance, 248–249
        on prosocial behavior, 247–248
        positive, 242, 253
        research methodologies applied to, 243–254
        stressful, 239, 243–245
        theories applied to, 238–242
    environmental solutions to problems of, 254–262
    "familiar strangers" in, 247
    "image" factor of, 232
    land use in, 255
    movement from, to suburbs, 262–263
    perception of, *see* Cognitive map(s)
    public housing in, 259–261
    social networks and, 255–256
    urban renewal and, 256–262
Classical conditioning, of attitudes, 45–48
Classrooms
    environmental design and, 298–300
    open, 299
    windowless, 298–299
Clean Air Act, 141
Climate, behavior and, 119–140
Closure, principle of, 20
Cognition, environmental, 29–33
Cognitive map(s), 29–33, 228–231, 232, 398
    components of, 30
    construction of
        by subway commuters, 234
        race and, 233–234
        relevant experience and, 234–238
        sex and, 234
        socioeconomic status and, 232
    errors in, 31
    functions of, 31
    memory and, 32
Cognitive processes, perception and, 19, 21
Coherence, 43
Cold, effects of, 119, 122–123, 132–134
    on performance, 133
    on social behavior, 133
    physiological disorders, 125
Color, behavior and, 272
"Commons dilemma," 343–345
Communication
    effects of noise on, 108
    personal space as, 150
Commuting, 115–117
Comparison, social, 64
Complexity, 41, 42, 43
Conditioning, attitudes and, 45–48
Congruence, design process and, 278

Consent, informed, in research, 405
Conservation, energy, designing for, 291
Constraint theory, *see* Behavior constraint theory
Construct validity, in research, 381
Construction, perceptual, principles of, 20
Continuity, principle of, 20
Contrast, 34, 35, 37
Controls, research and, 11
Convergence, 34, 35
Coping, *see* Adaptation
Coping strategies, 78
Core temperature, 121–122, 123, 127
Correlational research, 12–13, 386–387
Crime
    cities and, 249–251
    population density and, 60
    territoriality and fear of, 189
Crisis effect, 26
Crosswalks, environmental design and, 304–306
Crowding, *see* Population density
Culture, as determinant of personal space, 153–154

Data collection methods, 13–15
Decibels, 99
Defensible spaces, 254–255
Dehydration, 122
Density
    illness and, 204
    inside, 201
    outside, 201
    population, *see* Population density
    social, 194, 223
    spatial, 194, 223
"density-dependent controls," 199
Density–intensity model, 218
Dependent variable, experimental research and, 11
Depth, perception of, 34
Descriptive research, 13, 14, 193, 388–389
Design, architectural
    behavior and, 267–277
    exterior, 268–270
    overload theory and, 277

    privacy and, 274–276
Design, environmental, *see* Environmental design
Design alternatives, 278, 279
    awareness of, 280–281
    social resistance to, 281
Design cycle, 286–287
Design process, 278–288
    congruence and, 278
    design awareness and, 281
    group participation in, 281–282
    implementing the, 284–288
    selection of behavioral criteria, 283
    stages in the, 278
Designer advocate, 282
Destructive acts, curbing, 377
Determinism, 60
    architectural, 266–267
    climatic, 120
Disaster(s)
    natural, 86, 90–92
    perception of, 26–27
    rumors in, 93
    scapegoating in, 93
Distance, perception of, 34
Distance cue(s), 34–36
Diversity, 42, 68
Diversive exploration, 41
Dormitories, design of, 4
Drive reduction, and attitude change, 50–51
Driving, effects of temperature on, 128
Droughts, 27

Ear, 98–99
Echoes, as distance cues, 35
Ecological Attitude Survey, 52–54
Ecological perception, of environment, 24
Ecological psychology, 73–77
    applied to population density, 212
Education, environmental, 347–350
Educational settings, environmental design and, 298–304
Effective temperature, 123, 124
Empirical level of research, 60
Energy conservation

designing for, 291
residential, 363–371
transportation and, 371–374
Energy resources, pollution and, 8
Enframement, 34–35
Environment
aesthetics and, 41–44, 272–273
attitudes toward, 55–56
changing, 50–56
forming, 45–49
conditioning of, 45–48
measurement of, 49
social learning of, 48–49
perception of, *see* Environmental
perception
scenic, assessment of, 33–45
Environment and Behavior (journal), 6
Environmental aesthetics, 41–44, 272–273
Environmental cognitions, *see* Cognition,
environmental
Environmental Concern Scale, 55
Environmental design
alternatives in, 278, 279
behavioral facilitation in, 283, 284
end product in, 284
energy conservation and, 291
implementation of, 284–288
PEQI in, 285
in bathroom layout, 292–295
in bedroom layout, 292
in classrooms, 298–300
in educational settings, 298–304
in home settings, 291–298
in hospital settings, 306–307, 310
in leisure settings, 323–334
in library setting, 300, 301
in museum settings, 300–304
in pedestrian environments, 304–306
in prisons, 308–309
in public housing, 261
in recreation areas, 323–334
in residential care facilities for the aged,
310–315
in residential settings, 291–298
in shopping malls, 304–306
in undersea habitats, 336–340
in work settings, 318–323
performance requirements in, 283
physiological maintenance in, 283, 284
social facilitation in, 283, 284
wind and, 305
Environmental Design Research
Association, 6
Environmental education, 347–350
Environmental load theory, 65–67
See also Overload theory
Environmental perception, 18–45
characteristics of, 21–22
cultural influences on, 28–29
social influences on, 28–29
Environmental possibilism, 267
Environmental preference, 43–44
Environmental probabilism, 267
Environmental Protection Agency, 48
hearing loss surveys, 103, 105
Environmental psychology
characteristics of, 6–10
content areas of, 15–16
data collection, 13–15
definitions of, 5–6, 7
historical perspective, 5–6
holistic approach to, 7, 22
rationale for, 1, 5
relation to other disciplines, 9–10
research and, *see* Research
study of, reasons for, 1, 5
systems approach in, 7
theory (theories) and, 59–62
Environmental stress theory, 77–80, 84–89
Episodic records, in research, 404
Erosion, in environment, as measure of
behavior, 403
Ethics, in environmental research, 72, 404–
406
Ethological models, of personal space, 150
Evaluation, research, 380–382, 390
Exercise, recreation areas and, 328–330
Exhaustion stage, of reaction to stress, 78,
79
Experience, relevant, cognitive mapping
and, 234–238
Experiential realism, 381–382

Experimental research, 11–12, 199, 383–386

Exploration, 41
   in library environment, 301
   in museum environment, 303–304

External validity, in research, 381

"Familiar strangers," in cities, 247

Fatigue, in museum exploration, 303–304

Fear appeals, and attitude change, 50

Feedback, 355
   to improve environmentally related behavior, 355

Field experiments, 201

Field research, 201

Field studies, 201, 385–387

Fixed workspace, 322

Floods, 27, 28

Frequency, of sound waves, 97

Frostbite, 125, 132

Functionalism, 19
   probabilistic, 26

Furniture and furnishings, behavior and, 273–274

Future environments, 334–340

Galvanic skin response, 402

Gardening, recreational, 328

Gender, cognitive mapping and, 234

General adaptation syndrome, 77–79

Gestalt principles, 20

Group behavior, territorial aspects of, 180–181

Group space, response to invasion of, 174

Habituation, and environmental perception, 23

Harm–loss, 78

Harm or loss assessments, 87

Hassles, daily, 86–87

Hazards, preception of, 26–28

Health
   air pollution and, 144–145
   cold temperatures and, 132
   effect of noise on, 103–106
   hot temperatures and, 124
   population density and, 204

Hearing
   in detection of distance, 35
   loss of, noise and, 103, 105

Heart attack, heat-induced, 124

Heat
   behavior and, 119–132
   effects of, 119–132
      on aggression, 128–131
      on attraction, 127–128, 129
      on helping behavior, 131–132
      on performance, 125–127
      on social behavior, 127–131

Heat asthenia, 124

Heat exhaustion, 124

Heat stress, 124

Heat stroke, 124

Hedonic tone, 41

Height, in visual field, 35, 36

Helping, see Altruism

Helplessness, learned, 71, 72–73
   population density and, 215

Hodometer, 402

Homes, design features of, 291–298

Hospitals, design features of, 306–307, 310

Housing
   design, psychology and, 1, 4
   environmental design and, 291–298

Hypothalamus, 122, 131

Hypothermia, 125, 132

Hypothesis, 60

Hypoxia, 137, 139

Illness
   crowding and, 204
   mass psychogenic, 279

"Image" factor, of city environments, 232

Impedance, commuting and, 116–117

Incongruity, 41, 42

Independent variable, 11

Individual differences, personal space and, 151, 153, 158–161

Information overload, 66

Informed consent, 405

"Inoculation," and attitude change, 54

Inside density, 201

Instrumental conditioning, of attitudes, 48

Instrumentation, research and, 401–402

Integration, 297–298
Intensity of environmental stimulation, 68
Interdisciplinary environmental design, 287–288
Interdisciplinary perspective, 8
Internal validity, 380–381
Interrelationships, 8
Intervening constructs, 61
Interviews, 394–396
Invariant functional properties, 24

Job satisfaction, work environment and, 319

Kaplan model of environmental preference, 42–44

Laboratory experimentation, 199, 383–384
Land use, cities and, 255
Learned helplessness, 71, 72–73
  population density and, 215
Learning
  crowding and, 197
  environment and, 298–304
  noise and, 104
Legibility, 43
Leisure
  environmental design and, 323–334
  impact on crowding, 220
Levee effect, 27
Libraries
  design features of, 300, 301
  orientation to, 301
Life styles, impact on crowding, 220
Lighting, behavior and, 267–271
Linear perspective, 34, 36
Littering, 357–363, 404
"Long, hot summer effect," 119, 128
Loudness
  as distance cue, 35
  measurement of, 97
  perception of, 97, 99
Love Canal, 85, 92, 96

Maintenance minimum, of behavior setting 74
Manning, 74–77, 91, 96

Mapping
  behavior, 399
  cognitive, *see* Cognitive map(s)
Mass psychogenic illness, 279
Mediating variables, 61
Mental illness, noise and, 105–106
Memory, cognitive maps and, 32
Monocular cues, in perception of distance, 34, 36
Moon, phases of, and behavior, 138
"Mouse universe," 192, 196
Movement, perception of, 22
Movement perspective, 35
Müller-Lyer illusion, 29
Museum(s)
  design features of, 300–304
  fatigue in, 303–304
Music, work environment and, 321
Mystery, 43

National Park Service, 49
National parks, air pollution in, 40
Natural disasters, 86, 90–92
  characteristics of, 90
  effects of, 91–92
Naturalistic observation, 193, 194
Noise, 97–115
  definition of, 97
  effects of
    on aggression, 110–113
    on altruism, 113–115
    on attraction, 110
    on concentration, 9
    on hearing, 103, 105
    on learning, 104
    on mental health, 105–106
    on performance, 9, 107–110
    on physical health, 105
    on social behavior, 110–115
    physiological, 103–106
  measurement of, 96, 402
  occupational, 103
  perception of, *see* Loudness; Sound
  sources of, 102–103
  transportation and, 102–103
  variables associated with, 101–102
  white, 97

Nonperformers, in behavior setting, 75
Non-self-report measures, of behavior, 389, 394–404
Nonverbal behavior, 150
Novelty, 41, 42
Nowlis Mood Adjective Check List, 396

Observational methods, of research, 193, 194, 399–401
Occupational noise, 103
Occupational Safety and Health Administration, 103
Office work, environmental design applied to, 319–321
Olfaction
    and detection of air pollution, 142–143
    in detection of distance, 35
Olfactory membrane, 142–143
Open classrooms, design features of, 299
Open office plan, 320-321
Operant conditioning, of attitudes, 48
Optimal group size, 198
Outer space, living in, 334–336
Outside density, 201
Overlap, 35
Overload theory
    environmental design and, 277
    of personal space, 150
    of population density, 212
    of urban behavior, 238–239
Overmanning theory, 75

Palmar Sweat Test, 402
Panic, 91
Patterning, of environmental stimulation, 68
Pavlovian conditioning, see Classical conditioning
Pedestrian environments, environmental design and, 304–306
Pedestrian movement, 304–306
    friction–conformity model of, 305
    obstacles to, 304–305
    pathway selection in, 304
Perceived Environmental Quality Index (PEQI), 49, 50

in environmental design, 285
Perceived Visual Air Quality (PVAQ), 40
Perception
    cognitive processes and, 19, 21
    conventional, 19
    conventional approaches to, 19, 24
    constructivist viewpoint of, 19
    ecological approach to, 24
    environmental, see Environmental perception
    functionalism perspective, 19
    Gibsonian approach to, 24
    of affordances, 24–25
    of air pollution, 29, 40, 142–144
    of change, 23–26
    of depth, 34
    of distance, 34
    of hazards, 26–28
    of movement, 22
    of sound, 97
    probabilistic model of, 26
Perceptual construction, principles of, 20
Perceptual maintenance, in environmental design, 284
Performance
    air pollution and, 145–146
    city living and, 248–249
    cold and, 133
    crowding and, 197, 210–211
    heat and, 125–127
    measurement of, in behavioral research, 402–403
    noise and, 9, 107–110
Performance requirements, in environmental design, 283
Performers, in behavior setting, 75
Personal space, 149–175
    age and, 159–160
    arousal theory, 150, 165
    attraction and, 154–156
    behavior constraint approach, 150, 165
    "bubble" concept of, 149, 150, 152
    communicative functions of, 150
    cross-cultural variations, 158
    culture and, 153–154, 167
    defined, 149

ethological models of, 150
functions of, 150–154
goal fulfillment and, 162–164
inappropriate, consequences of, 164–169
individual differences and, 151, 153, 158–161
invasions of, 169–175
flight from, 169
groups and, 174
overload theory, 150
personality and, 160–161
physical determinants of, 161
sex and, 159, 170–171
situational conditions and, 153, 154–158
stress theory, 150
studying, methods for, 154
subcultural differences, 158
Personality, hazard perception and, 28
Personality determinants, of spatial behavior, 160–161
Personalization, work environment and, 321–322
Pesticides, 49, 51
Phons, 101
Photography, in behavioral research, 401
Physical traces, 403
Physiological consequences, of high density for animals, 194
Physiological maintenance, in environmental design, 283, 284
Physiological measurement, 401–402
Piloerection, 122
Pollution
energy resources, 8
psychology and problem of, 1
See also Air pollution; Urban pollution
Population density, 192–225
adaptation to, 216
as crowding, 216
crime and, 60
effects of, 3, 5, 192–225
on affect, 202
on aggression, 197, 198, 208–209
on altruism, 207–208
on animals, 192–199
on arousal, 202–203
on attraction, 204–206
on health, 204
on humans, 199–225
on learned helplessness, 215
on learning, 197
on performance, 192, 210–211
on social behavior, 195–197, 204–210
on withdrawal, 197, 206–207
physiological, 194
illness and, 204
leisure and, 220
optimal group size and, 198
reduction of, 218–223
territoriality and, 198–199
theories of, 211–218
Possibilism, environmental, 267
Preference, environmental, 43–44
Kaplan model of, 42–44
Prison(s), design features of, 308–309
Privacy
home environment and, 292–296
invasion of, 405–406
optimal levels of, 69
Probabilism, environmental, 267
Productivity, work environment and, 318–319
Prompts, to preserve environment, 350–352
Propinquity, 296–298
Prosocial behavior
city living and, 247–248
population density and, 207–208
Proxemics, 5
Proximity, principle of, 20
Pruitt-Igoe housing project, 259–260
Psychological reactance, 51, 54, 71
Psychological stress, 77
Psychology
architectural, 5
environmental, *see* Environmental psychology
Public housing
design features of, 261
Pruitt-Igoe projects as, 259–260

Quasi-experimentation, 201, 387
Questionnaires, 394

Race, cognitive mapping and, 233–234
Rating scales, 396–398
  bipolar adjective, 396
  Nowlis, 396
  semantic differential, 397
Reactance, psychological, 51, 54, 71
Realism, experiential, 381–382
Recreation, defined, 323
Recreation environments, 323–334
Refractory periods, 89
Reinforcement
  negative, 355
    to discourage environmental
    destruction, 355
  positive, 353
    to encourage environmental
    preservation, 353–354
Reinforcement–affect model of evaluative
    responses, 47
Religion, 60
Research, 379–406
  applied, 8
  behaviorally based, 283–284
  correlational, 12–13, 386–387
  criterion-oriented, 283
  data collection methods, 13–15
  descriptive, 13, 14, 193, 388–389
    observations in, 193
  empirical level of, 60
  environmental psychology and, 8–9, 10–
    15
  ethical considerations in, 72, 404–406
  evaluation, 380–382, 390
  experimental, 11–12, 199, 383–386
    in field setting, 384
    laboratory, 193, 194, 383–384
    simulations in, 384–386
  informed consent and, 405
  instrumentation in, 401–402
  interviews and, 394–396
  measurement techniques in, 403–404
    indirect, 403–404
    self-report, 389–399
  observation in, 193, 194, 399–401
  questionnaires in, 394
  rating scales, 396–398

sociological–correlational, 201–202
  task performance in, 402–403
  theoretical, 8
  time budget and, 392, 393
  validity in, 380–382
    construct, 381
    external, 381
    experiential realism and, 381–382
    internal, 380–381
Residential care facilities for the aged,
    environmental design and, 310–315
Residential settings, environmental design
    and, 291–298
Resistance, social, to design alternatives,
    281
Resistance stage, of response to
    environmental stress, 77, 78
Respondent conditioning, *see* Classical
    conditioning
Reticular formation, 63
Retinal disparity, 34
Rumors, disasters and, 93
Running records, research and, 404

Scapegoating, in response to disaster, 93
Scenic environment, assessment of, 33–45
Scenic value
  descriptive approach to, 33–37
  physical–perceptual approaches to, 37–39
  psychological approach to, 39–45
Schools, design features of, 298–300
Scientific method, 59
Self-report measures, 389–399
Semantic differential rating scale, 397
Sensation, 19
  auditory, 97
Sex
  cognitive mapping and, 234
  personal space and, 159, 170–171
Shadowing, 35
Shopping malls, environmental design and,
    304–306
Similarity, principle of, 20
Simulations, research and, 154, 384–386,
    398
Situation, as determinant of personal space,
    153, 154–158

Size, perception of, 34, 36
Skinnerian conditioning, *see* Instrumental conditioning
Smell, detection of air pollution through, 142–143
Social behavior
  air pollution and, 146–147
  cold and, 133
  heat and, 127–131
  noise and, 110–115
  population density and, 195–197, 204–210
Social comparison, 64
Social density, 194, 223
  social facilitation, in environmental design, 283, 284
Social learning, of attitudes, 48–49
Social networks, 255–256
Social psychology, relationship to environmental psychology, 9, 10
Social traps, 343
Socioeconomic status, cognitive mapping and, 232–233
Sociofugal space, 164
Sociological–correlational research, 201–202
Sociopetal spacing, 164
Sones, 101
Sonic booms, 111
Sound
  detection of, threshold of, 98
  loudness of, 35
  measurement of, 97
  perception of, 35, 97, 98
  See also Noise
Sound waves
  amplitude of, 97
  frequency of, 97
Space
  living in, 334–336
  personal, *see* Personal space
Spatial density, 184, 223
Specific exploration, 41
Status, work environment and, 322
Stimulation
  categories of, 68
  dimensions of, 68

optimizing, 69
Stimulus (stimuli), 19
Stimulus generalization, 48
Stress
  adaptation and, 79, 86, 87, 88
  city living and, 239, 243–245
  cold, 122–123, 125
  commuting, 115–117
  environmental, 77, 84–118
    adaptation to, 79, 86
    alarm reaction to, 77, 78
    coping responses to, 78
    exhaustion from, 78, 79
    resistance to, 77, 78
  heat, 124
  psychological, 77
  systemic, 77
Stress response, 85
  characteristics of, 88–89
Stress theory, of personal space, 150
Stressors
  appraisal of, 87–88
  background, 86–87, 97
  characteristics of, 85–87
  defined, 85
  personal, 86
Strip zoning, 25
Structuralism, 19
Suburbia, 262–263
Sunlight, impact on humans, 134
Supersonic transport, noise problems of, 111
Surprisingness, 41, 42
Surveys, 398
Sweating, 122
Systemic stress, 77
Systems approach, 7

Task performance, *see* Performance
Technological catastrophes, 92–96
Television, aggression and, 331
Temperature
  ambient, 121–125
  atmospheric, behavior and, 119–134
  body, deep, 121
  core, 121–122, 123, 127
  effective, 123, 124

effects of, *see* Cold; Heat
  perception of, 121
    as distance cue, 35
  physiological reaction to, 121–125
Territoriality, 149, 175–190
  aggression and, 183–184
  fear of crime and, 189
  functions of, 178–179
  indications of, 404
  population density and, 198–199
  research on, 179–187, 404
  signals of, 181–183
  work environment and, 322
Texture, 34, 36
Theories
  components of, 61
  defined, 61
  environment–behavior relationships, 58–83
  functions of, 61
  uses of, 61
Thermoreceptors, 121
Threat appraisals, 86
Three Mile Island accident, 2, 78, 86, 92, 94–96
Threshold, of detectable sound, 98
Timbre, 97
Time budget, 392, 393
Tonal quality, 97
Transportation, 4
  energy conservation and, 371–374
  noise and, 102–103
  See also Mass transit
Type I conditioning, *see* Classical conditioning
Type II conditioning, *see* Instrumental conditioning

Uncertainty, 59, 92
Uncertainty–arousal, 41
Undermanning, 75, 76, 91
Undersea environments, 336–340
Understimulation theory, 67–68
Unwanted interaction, 212, 214
Urban habitat, *see* City (cities)
Urban pollution, 25
Urban renewal, 256–262

Validity, in research, 380–382
  construct, 381
  experiential realism and, 381–382
  external, 381
  internal, 380–381
Vandalism, 374–377
Variable(s)
  dependent, 11
  independent, 11
  mediating, 61
Vision, in detection of air pollution, 143
Visual cues
  binocular, 34
  monocular, 34, 36
Visual field, height in, 35, 36

Weather, behavior and, 119–141, 148
Weber-Fechner Law, 23–24, 26
White noise, 97
Wilderness areas, 324–328
Wind
  Beaufort scale for, 135
  behavior and, 134–137
  building design and, 305
  perception of, 135–136
Wind-chill index, 123–124, 125
Windows, behavior and, 271
Withdrawal, effects of population density on, 197, 206–207
Work environment
  environmental design applied to, 318–323
  job satisfaction and, 319
  music and, 321
  personalization and, 321–322
  productivity and, 318–319
  status and, 322
Workplace, design alternatives which reduce illness in the, 279
Workspace
  assigned, 322
  fixed, 322

Yerkes-Dodson Law, 64, 107, 127, 171

Zoning, 255